Government & the Media in Conflict /1970-74

Government & the Media in Conflict/1970-74

Editor: Edward W. Knappman

Contributing Editors: Mary Elizabeth Clifford, Evan Drossman, Joseph Fickes, Stephen Orlofsky, Gerald Satterwhite

FACTS ON FILE · 119 WEST 57TH STREET · NEW YORK, NEW YORK

**Government & the Media
in Conflict/1970-74**

Copyright, 1974, by Facts On File, Inc.

Library of Congress Catalog Card No. 74-78636
ISBN 0-87196-356-6
9 8 7 6 5 4 3 2

PRINTED IN THE UNITED STATES OF AMERICA

Contents

Preface

Nearly 200 years ago, Thomas Jefferson wrote: "... Were it left to me to decide whether we should have a government without newspapers, or newspapers without a government, I should not hesitate a moment to prefer the latter." Fortunately, Americans have never had to choose between such stark alternatives. A free press has been preserved without the sacrifice of effective government.

But conflict has been the natural—and perhaps the most fitting—relationship between government and the news media during most of our history. Almost every American president, including Jefferson, has been sufficiently piqued by critical reporting to attack the press for abusing its prerogatives. Animosity between an administration and the news media, however, never before reached the level of intensity and bitterness that has prevailed during the Nixon Administration.

The chapters of this book trace the major aspects of the present conflict between government and the media from late 1969 through early 1974. Each consists of a detailed narrative covering the relevant events and a balanced cross-section of full-text editorials. Selected from over 100 American newspapers, they represent a full spectrum of interpretations and viewpoints on the present conflict and on the rights and responsibilities of a free press in a free society.

Edward W. Knappman
April 12, 1974

Politics
& the Media

Throughout his political career Richard Nixon's relationship with the working press had been chilly at best. His presidential campaign in 1968 won the editorial support of the vast majority of American newspapers, reflecting the traditional Republican allegiance of most newspaper publishers. But his supporters among the journalists who covered the campaign were in a distinct minority.

President Nixon's distrust of reporters percolated down from the White House to administration spokesmen in daily contact with reporters. The estrangement grew rancorous in 1970 as Vice President Spiro T. Agnew repeatedly lashed out at the media in speeches during the midterm election campaign. Given this context, many reporters and broadcast executives interpreted governmental intervention of any sort in the industry as an infringement on the freedoms guaranteed to the press by the First Amendment. This chapter reviews some of the general developments in the conflict between government and the media. Subsequent chapters cover such specific issues as the Pentagon Papers case, the Watergate Affair and the right of journalists to protect confidential sources.

Agnew assails TV news coverage. Vice President Spiro T. Agnew assailed the three national TV networks Nov. 13, 1969 for their news coverage. He suggested a self-examination and public pressure for "responsible news presentations." Agnew charged that the network commentators were hostile to President Nixon's Nov. 3 speech on Vietnam; that TV's immense power over public opinion was in the hands of "a small and unelected elite" of network producers, commentators and newsmen; that these men were often biased and, "to a man," reflected the "geographical and intellectual confines of Washington, D.C. or New York City." He also said "the views of the majority of this fraternity do not—and I repeat not—represent the views of America."

Agnew's attack was delivered before the Midwest Regional Republican Committee at Des Moines, Iowa. It was carried live by all three networks, whose presidents defended their networks in

statements the same day. Julian Goodman of the National Broadcasting Co. (NBC) said Agnew's "attack on television news is an appeal to prejudice" and use of high office "to criticize the way a government-licensed news medium covers the activities of government itself. . . . Evidently he would prefer a different kind of television reporting—one that would be subservient to whatever political group was in authority at the time."

Dr. Frank Stanton of Columbia Broadcasting System (CBS) called it an "unprecedented attempt by the vice president of the United States to intimidate a news medium which depends for its existence upon government licenses." Whatever the deficiencies of CBS's newsmen, he said, "they are minor compared to those of a press which would be subservient to the executive power of government."

Leonard H. Goldenson of American Broadcasting Companies (ABC) said ABC news was "fair and objective" and his network would "continue to report the news accurately and fully, confident in the ultimate judgment of the American public."

Concerning the President's Nov. 3 speech, Agnew said it had been "subjected to instant analysis and querulous criticism . . . by a small band of network commentators and self-appointed analysts, the majority of whom expressed in one way or another their hostility to what he [Mr. Nixon] had to say." He cited in particular one instance where Averell Harriman, former U.S. negotiator at the Paris peace talks, was "trotted out" and then presented "a broad range of gratuitous advice challenging and contradicting the policies outlined by the President." Agnew identified Harriman as the negotiator at a time when the U.S. "swapped some of the greatest military concessions in the history of warfare for an enemy agreement on the shape of the bargaining table."

The people had the right, Agnew contended, to "form their own opinions about a Presidential address" without having it "characterized through the prejudices of hostile critics" before it "can even be digested."

While the networks had "often used their power constructively and crea-

tively to awaken the public conscience to critical problems," Agnew said, they had also "elevated Stokely Carmichael and George Lincoln Rockwell from obscurity to national prominence" and, by "a raised eyebrow, an inflection of the voice, a caustic remark," raised "doubts in a million minds about the veracity of a public official or the wisdom of a government policy."

Agnew also objected to the networks' "endless pursuit of controversy." "We should ask," he said, "What is the end value—to enlighten or to profit? What is the end result—to inform or to confuse?. . . . Bad news drives out good news. The irrational is more controversial than the rational. Concurrence can no longer compete with dissent."

Perhaps, Agnew said, "it is time that the networks were made more responsive to the views of the nation and more responsible to the people they serve." He stressed that he was "not asking for government censorship or any other kind of censorship." But he asked "whether a form of censorship already exists when the news that 40 million Americans receive each night is determined by a handful of men responsible only to their corporate employers and is filtered through a handful of commentators who admit to their own set of biases."

The answers to the questions he was raising, Agnew said, must come from the industry—"they are challenged to turn their critical powers on themselves, to direct their energy, their talent and their conviction toward improving the quality and objectivity of news presentation. They are challenged to structure their own civic ethics to relate their great [freedom with their great] responsibilities . . . And the people . . . are challenged . . . to press for responsible news presentations." The people, he said, "can register their complaints on bias through mail to the networks and phone calls to local stations. . . ."

He suggested that the "same wall of separation [should] exist between news and comment on the nation's networks" as in newspapers.

Burch Lauds Agnew View. Federal Communications Commission Chairman

C

D

E

F

G

Dean Burch said Nov. 14 Agnew's remarks were "thoughtful, provocative and deserve careful consideration by the industry and the public." Burch did not consider Agnew's speech intimidating. "Had the vice president suggested that the government censor these networks, that would have been another thing entirely," he said. What Agnew did say, Burch suggested, was that the networks should "examine themselves to see whether they were doing a good job. In other words, 'Physician, heal thyself.' "

Burch also acknowledged Nov. 14, through a spokesman, that he had requested (by telephone Nov. 5) transcripts from the networks of their commentaries after President Nixon's Nov. 3 Vietnam speech. Burch was reported as saying he had "received complaints about the discussion programs following the President's speech."

Nicholas Johnson, one of the FCC commissioners, said Nov. 17 Agnew's speech "has frightened network executives and newsmen in ways that may cause serious and permanent harm to independent journalism and free speech in America." While it was true, he said, "that a handful of men control what the American people see through their television screens," the answer was "not to transfer this power from a handful of men in New York to a handful of men in the White House."

White House View. White House Press Secretary Ronald L. Ziegler told newsmen Nov. 15 President Nixon had "great confidence" in Agnew, who had, the President thought, expressed himself "with great candor." Ziegler said the President had not discussed the speech with Agnew.

Clark R. Mollenhoff, special counsel to the President, said Nov. 15 Agnew's speech "reflected the views of the Administration."

Herbert G. Klein, President Nixon's director of communications, said Nov. 16 (on CBS' "Face the Nation" program) Agnew's speech reflected a widely held view in the top levels of the Administration. Klein added: "I think you can go beyond that. All of the news media needs to re-examine itself in the format it has and its approach to problems of news, to meet the current issues of the day;" "I include the newspapers very thoroughly in this, as well as the networks—if you look at the problems you have today and you fail to continue to examine them, you do invite the government to come in. I would not like to see that happen."

Ziegler Nov. 17 defended the views expressed by Agnew and Klein on the issue but emphasized that the Administration had "absolutely no desire" to censor the news.

Other support for Agnew's comments:

George W. Romney, secretary of housing and urban development, a luncheon speaker Nov. 14 at the Midwest Regional Republican Conference in Des Moines, lauded Agnew as a "champion of the 'old culture' that values historic and democratic principles."

Sen. Hugh Scott (Pa.), GOP Senate leader, said Nov. 14 he thought "the networks deserve a thorough goosing."

GOP National Chairman Rogers C. B. Morton said Nov. 15 Agnew had stated what "had to be said" and "everyone will profit from it."

Agnew Speech Criticized. Former Vice President Hubert H. Humphrey Nov. 17 denounced Agnew's speech as "an obvious and calculated appeal to our people's lesser or baser instincts." Humphrey, attending the first meeting of the Democratic Policy Council (organized in September to speak for the party on national issues) suggested that the Nixon Administration was mounting a coordin-. ated attack on the media and on antiwar demonstrators "or it's one of the most unusual coincidences within the memory of man."

The council later Nov. 17 adopted a resolution denouncing "efforts to stifle criticism of government officials by dissenting citizens and responsible newsmen."

Accompanying Humphrey to his press conference Nov. 17 was W. Averell Harriman, former U.S. negotiator at the Paris peace talks, who said Agnew's comments on news coverage "smacked of a totalitarianism which I don't like at all." (Agnew's criticism of Harriman's commentary after the President's Nov. 3 speech did not mention that Harriman had prefaced his remarks with a disclaimer that "I wouldn't be [so] presumptuous [as] to give a complete analysis of a very carefully thought-out speech by the President of the United States. I'm sure he wants to end this war and no one wishes him well any more than I do." Harriman then discussed his own views on Vietnam and the reasons why he differed with the President on them.)

Other opposition to Agnew's speech:

Senate Democratic Whip Edward M. Kennedy (Mass.) said Nov. 14 "we are now witnessing an attack designed to put American against American—an attack with the ultimate aim of dividing this country into those who support and those who do not support our President's position on Vietnam. If it is allowed to go on, this will be tragic."

National Education Television President James Day said Nov. 13 Agnew's "sweeping remarks . . . both misrepresent and misinterpret the news functions of television."

Thomas P. F. Hoving, chairman of the National Citizens Committee for Broadcasting, said Nov. 13 Agnew's "disgraceful attack . . . officially leads us as a nation into an ugly era of the most fearsome suppression and intimidation."

The American Civil Liberties Union said Nov. 15 Agnew had sounded a "clear and chilling threat" of censorship.

Sigma Delta Chi, the journalistic society, approved at its San Diego convention Nov. 15 a resolution opposing "any effort" by any government official to "control or impede the flow of legitimate comment or analysis of the news."

Six former government officials and the deans of 11 law schools issued a statement in New York Nov. 15 deploring "inflammatory" remarks attributed to Agnew and other high Administration officials in connection with war dissent. Among the officials were Arthur J. Goldberg, Eugene Rostow and William P. Bundy.

Agnew Extends Criticism to Press. Vice President Agnew Nov. 20 extended his criticism of the news media to the press. Addressing the Alabama Chamber of Commerce in Montgomery, Agnew defended his earlier remarks, stressing that "a broader spectrum of national opinion should be represented among the commentators in the network news" and "a high wall of separation should be raised between what is news and what is commentary."

Then he extended his criticism to the press, particularly The New York Times and The Washington Post. "The American people should be made aware," he said, "of the trend toward the monopolization of the great public information vehicles and the concentration of more and more power in fewer and fewer hands."

"Many, many strong, independent voices have been stilled in this country in recent years," Agnew said. "And lacking the vigor of competition, some of those who have survived have—let's face it—grown fat and irresponsible."

He added: "The day when the network commentators and even the gentlemen of The New York Times enjoyed a form of diplomatic immunity from comment and criticism of what they said is over. . . . When they go beyond fair comment and criticism they will be called upon to defend their statements and their positions just as we must defend ours. And when their criticism becomes excessive or unjust, we shall invite them down from their ivory towers to enjoy the rough and tumble of public debate. I don't seek to intimidate the press, or the networks or anyone else from speaking out. But the time for blind acceptance of their opinions is past. And the time for naive belief in their neutrality is gone."

In citing the Post, Agnew pointed out that the same company controlled the Post, Newsweek magazine and a radio and television station in Washington and "all [were] grinding out the same editorial line." He was "not recommending the dismemberment" of the company but "merely point[ing] out that the public should be aware that these four powerful voices hearken to the same master."

Agnew objected to a failure by The Times to carry a story of 300 congressmen and 59 senators signing a letter endorsing President Nixon's Vietnam policy, and Times placement of a story (Nov. 18) of Pope Paul VI's laudatory comments on Mr. Nixon's Vietnam course on Page 11 while a burglary story was on Page 3. He also objected to a Times editorial claiming that "American youth today is far more imbued with idealism, a sense of service and a deep humanitarianism than any generation in recent history, including Mr. Agnew's generation."

Post and Times rebuttal—The Times and Post issued immediate rebuttals Nov. 20 to Agnew's criticism. Arthur Ochs Sulzberger, president and publisher of the Times, denied that the Times "ever sought or enjoyed immunity from comment and criticism" and said "some" of Agnew's statements were "inaccurate." The story Agnew charged was not covered was printed, although, "unfortunately," not in the Washington edition (an early edition). Sulzberger said that was no editorial significance in carrying a story on Page 11 instead of on Page 3.

Mrs. Katharine Graham, president of the Post Co., said Agnew's remarks about the firm were "not supported by the facts." Each Post branch "operated autonomously" and competed "vigorously with one another" and Washington was "one of the most competitive communications cities in America by any objective standards."

(In an article written for the Nov. 28 issue of Life magazine, Agnew said: "The reason I spoke out was because, like the great silent majority, I had had enough. I had endured the didactic inadequacies of the garrulous in silence, hoping for the best but witnessing the worst for many months. And because I am an elected official, I felt I owed it to those I serve to speak the truth.")

Agnew Media Speeches Attacked. Frank Stanton, president of the Columbia Broadcasting System (CBS) accused Vice President Agnew and the Nixon Administration Nov. 25 of an "ominous" attempt to intimidate broadcast journalism. Referring to recent Agnew speeches attacking the news media and to other Administration statements on the subject, Stanton said "the whole pattern of this government intrusion into the substance and methods of the broadcast press, and indeed of all journalism, have the gravest implication." "In the context of this intimidation, the self-serving disavowal interpolations of 'no censorship,' no matter how often repeated, are meaningless," he said.

In a Senate speech Dec. 4, Sen. Charles E. Goodell (R, N.Y.) posed the question "whether the vice president has attempted to use the prestige of his high office to place pressure upon the networks to report the news in a manner more favorable to the Administration." He urged the networks not to react to Agnew's criticism "by compromising in any way their responsibility to offer informative and provocative news analysis and comment."

Herbert G. Klein, director of communications for the Nixon Administration, said Nov. 19 that inquiries had been made at times from the White House to TV stations both before and after Presidential appearances as to their editorial treatment of that appearance. The inquiry, he said, only was "Which side are you on, or something like that." He considered such calls proper.

Nixon backs Agnew's attacks. President Nixon said at a news conference Dec. 8 that Agnew had "rendered a public service in talking in a very dignified and courageous way about a problem that many Americans are concerned about ... the coverage by news media ... of public figures." Agnew, Nixon

declared, "advocated that there should be free expression" and "recognized—as I do—that there should be opinion." Perhaps his point "should be well taken" that TV "might well follow the practice of newspapers of separating news from opinion." These were "useful suggestions. Perhaps the networks disagreed with the criticism, but I would suggest that they should be just as dignified and just as reasonable in answering the criticisms as he was in making them."

Nixon said he thought the news media had "been fair" to his Administration. He had "no complaints," especially about "the extent of the coverage."

Independent council on media urged. Establishment of a "center for media study" that would judge the performance of the press and broadcasters was recommended in a task force report released without comment Jan. 12, 1970 by the National Commission on the Causes and Prevention of Violence. In its 614-page report—"Mass Media and Violence"—the task force said the news media could reduce the potential for violence in America by "functioning as a faithful conduit for intergroup communication, providing a true market place of ideas ... and reducing the incentive to confrontation that sometimes erupts in violence." The independent council on mass media was one of the panel's recommendations to make the media more responsive to the public.

The task force proposed that the center would study the performance of the news media and make recommendations independently of the government, although the President would make initial appointments to the council. The panel noted that such a body had first been advocated 20 years before by the Commission on Freedom of the Press, headed by Dr. Robert M. Hutchins.

A similar recommendation had been made in 1968 by the National Advisory Commission on Civil Disorders.

The task force also criticized the Federal Communications Commission (FCC) for becoming, along with other regulatory agencies, "not guardians of public interest . . . but service agencies for the industries involved." The panel urged the Justice Department and the FCC to use their power over mergers and licenses to avoid "greater concentration of media ownership." The task force also suggested that the FCC clarify its fairness doctrine so that it would not have "a dampening effect on willingness of many broadcast news organizations to treat controversial subjects."

Nixon proposes communications office. President Nixon Feb. 9 submitted to Congress a reorganization plan (automatically effective unless vetoed by either house of Congress within 60 days) creating an Office of Telecommunication Policy within the executive branch to manage the federal telephone and radio network and provide policy recom-

mendations to the President in its field. It was not suggested that the new office would concern itself with the content of broadcasting, and the authority of the Federal Communications Commission over regulatory issues was to be retained.

Agnew renews attack on critics. Vice President Spiro T. Agnew fired a new salvo at his press critics May 22, denouncing by name critical newspapers, magazines, columnists and cartoonists. Speaking at a Republican fund-raising dinner in Houston, Tex., Agnew asserted that "I intend to be heard above the din even if it means raising my voice." He would not temper his language, he said, because "I have sworn I will uphold the Constitution against all enemies, foreign and domestic."

Agnew voiced scorn at "the liberal news media of this country, those really illiberal, self-appointed guardians of our destiny who would like to run the country without ever submitting to the elective process as we in public office must do."

He specifically attacked the editorial writers of the New York Times, Washington Post, Atlanta Constitution, New Republic magazine, I. F. Stone's Bi-Weekly, Post cartoonist Herblock, syndicated columnist Carl T. Rowan and columnists James Reston and Tom Wicker of the Times, Hugh Sidey of Life magazine, Pete Hamill and Harriet Van Horne of the New York Post. He also assailed what he described as "a small hard core of hell-raisers" on college campuses and the "isolationists" in the U.S. Senate.

(Sol M. Linowitz, chairman of the Special Commission on Campus Tensions, reported on ABC's "Issues and Answers" May 31 that many students had informed his group that, "when terms such as 'effete snobs' were hurled, they took their stand with some of the more radical students on campus because this was an attack upon their peers." The commission was formed by the American Council on Education.)

(N.Y. Mayor John V. Lindsay expressed regret May 24 that he had seconded Agnew's nomination for Vice President at the 1968 GOP convention. Appearing on an NBC "Meet the Press" broadcast, Lindsay said neither "the substance or the tactic of attacking youngsters on campuses in general, or members of the press in general, or appealing to lesser instincts, which I believe has been the case, is in the public interest.")

Addressing the International Federation of Newspaper Publishers in Washington June 5, Agnew upheld freedom of the press but said his differences with "some of the news media" had arisen "not over their right to criticize government or public officials but my right to criticize them." He chided the news media in general for not "telling both sides of the story." He particularly objected to coverage of the Vietnam war, which he found "slanted against American involvement . . . without any attempt at balance."

Maddox pickets Atlanta newspapers. Gov. Lester G. Maddox of Georgia picketed the offices of Atlanta's two major newspapers June 4 in a continuing dispute that centered on the papers' opposition to his call for a special session of the Georgia Legislature. While he picketed the offices of the Atlanta Constitution and the Atlanta Journal carrying a placard that denounced the editorial viewpoint of the papers, Maddox said he was just doing his part to help rid the country of "Communists, anarchists and nasty people."

The paper had said editorially they opposed the special session because it would cost about $14,000 daily and accomplish nothing.

Hoover charges Kent news distortion. In a letter reported Aug. 7, Federal Bureau of Investigation (FBI) Director J. Edgar Hoover charged that the Akron Beacon Journal had "distorted" the facts in a July 23 article on an FBI investigation of the shooting of four students at Kent State University in Ohio.

Hoover, in a letter to John S. Knight, president and editor of the Beacon Journal, denied that the FBI "concluded" the shootings were unnecessary, as reported by the newspaper.

Hoover said, "contrary to the misinformation contained in your newspaper," the results of the FBI inquiry had been turned over to the Justice Department "without recommendation or conclusion." Knight, in a letter of reply, said he regretted the paper had used the word "conclude" rather than "report." "But," Knight added, "an exercise in semantics must not be permitted to obscure the fact that our article was essentially correct and not 'distorted,' as you allege."

Newspaper visits. President Nixon visited the editorial offices of the New York Daily News, a supporter of Administration policy, in New York City Aug. 18 and delivered a personal briefing on foreign and domestic issues.

Another newspaper giving general editorial support to Administration policies, the Washington Evening Star, had been given a personal Presidential briefing July 23. The President and other top Administration officials also had briefed a group of editors from Southern states during his New Orleans visit Aug. 14.

Olsen withdrawal. The State Department Aug. 31 announced the withdrawal of Arthur J. Olsen as the department's new press officer.

Newspaper reports said the withdrawal had been made under pressure from Sen. Barry Goldwater (R, Ariz.), who had requested the appointment be dropped in two letters to Secretary of State William P. Rogers. Goldwater had described the appointment as "personally obnoxious" because of a story Olsen

had written for the New York Times during the 1964 presidential campaign, connecting Goldwater with the late right-wing German leader Hans Christoph Seebohm.

Olsen released a statement Aug. 31 in which he said the source for his story had been Seebohm. When Seebohm later retracted the story, Olsen noted that he had reported the denial in the Times.

The State Department Correspondents Association protested the withdrawal to Rogers Sept. 1. The group expressed concern that a "dangerous precedent" had been set whereby any congressman could personally veto appointments not subject to Senate confirmation.

Agnew attacks press 'hate' campaign. In Chicago Oct. 19, Agnew pictured himself as the victim of a "hate" campaign carried unchecked by the nation's press. While his remarks underwent close examination, he said, the press failed to subject the "libelous mouthings" of his opponents to the same scrutiny. Agnew also attacked the Democratic senatorial candidate in Illinois, Adlai E. Stevenson 3d, and said he demeaned the "great name" of his father, the late Adlai Stevenson, former Democratic Presidential candidate.

Federal censor identified. A vice president of the Columbia Broadcasting System, Theodore Koop, was identified Oct. 25 by the Washington Star as being the federal censor who would control broadcast and newspaper reporting during a national emergency. Koop served as assistant director of the government's censorship department during World War II. White House Press Secretary Ronald L. Zeigler said the matter was classified.

Agnew says criticism served purpose. Vice President Spiro Agnew Nov. 20 contended, in a Honolulu speech before the Associated Press Managing Editors Association, that his criticism of the news media had achieved its purpose— to encourage the profession to take a criticial look at itself—and he praised the American news profession as "the fairest and finest journalistic complex in the entire world."

(Newsmen attending the mid-December conference of Republican governors in Sun Valley, Idaho reported that the vice president's feud with the press was a sore point with the governors, many of whom reportedly had privately urged Agnew to end the attacks.)

Canadian police seize U.S. magazine. Montreal police Dec. 12 seized 102,000 copies of Scanlan's magazine, a U.S. monthly whose January issue featured an article on "Guerrilla Warfare." The issue had been sent to Canada for printing after U.S. printers refused the job.

In New York, editor Sidney Zion said the seizure was made at the request of the U.S. government, but Justice Department and Customs Bureau spokesmen denied the charge Dec. 16.

The controversial article reportedly contained a diagram showing how to build a bomb. The diagram was reproduced from a rightist magazine, according to Zion.

Under emergency war measures currently in effect, Canada could suppress the magazine

CBS documentary attacked. Hearings by the House Armed Services Committee were disrupted Feb. 25–March 2, 1971 as its chairman, Rep. F. Edwards Hebert (D, La.), and the Columbia Broadcasting System (CBS) exchanged heated comments on the network's documentary, "The Selling of the Pentagon."

The program, first shown Feb. 23 and rebroadcast Feb. 27, charged that the Pentagon spent nearly $30 million a year to polish its image among Americans by staging elaborate war games, circulating old propaganda-type films and having officers in uniform speak to U.S. audiences about the menace of communism.

After seeing a special Capitol Hill screening of the program, Hebert called it a "vicious piece of propaganda." He said the film left him "with an emptiness in my stomach, nausea . . . to think that an alleged reputable . . . network could lend itself to such a vicious piece."

At one point in his criticism of the documentary, Hebert said, "All I ask is accuracy." CBS News President Richard Salant, answered, "My only comment is: 'He got it.'"

Hebert also took issue with a portion of the program showing him interviewing a Green Beret who had been a prisoner of war. Hebert acknowledged that he provided CBS news with the footage, but charged that he was led to believe that it was to be used for a CBS documentary on prisoners of war.

A CBS official denied Hebert's charge. The spkesman said that in July 1970 CBS asked Hebert's office for use of the film for a documentary on "how the Pentagon presents its message to the American people." According to the CBS official, Hebert's office granted the network permission to use the film or any portion of it.

Talk show accused of bias on SST. The White House and American Broadcasting Company (ABC) talk show host Dick Cavett became involved March 22–24 in a dispute over whether backers of the Super Sonic Transport (SST) were getting enough air time on his late evening show.

A White House aide called ABC March 22 complaining that opponents of the plane were appearing more frequently on the Cavett show than SST supporters. The show's producers then scheduled William M. Magruder, chief of the government's SST office, to debate the merits of the plane with Sen. William Proxmire (D, Wis.), a leader of the anti-SST forces. The White House first agreed, but then said if Proxmire appeared, Magruder would not. ABC then canceled Proxmire and devoted most of the 1½-hour taped March 22 broadcast to Magruder's defense of the plane.

Humphrey blasts Administration on press attacks. Speaking at a meeting of the Democratic party's Policy Council, Sen. Hubert H. Humphrey (Minn.), the party's presidential candidate in 1968, March 24 blamed President Nixon for Vice President Spiro Agnew's "media guerrilla warfare." "Never have the American people encountered," he said, "a national Administration that relied so heavily upon a unique mixture of executive arrogance, public relations gimmickry and the blatant intimidation of the news media."

CBS documentary stirs dispute. The Nixon Administration and some members of Congress, moving to bolster the efforts of defenders of the U.S. military, joined the debate March 18—April 8 over the merits and accuracy of the television documentary, "The Selling of the Pentagon," broadcast by the Columbia Broadcasting System (CBS).

The program, first shown Feb. 23 and rebroadcast Feb. 27, charged that the Pentagon spent nearly $30 million a year to polish its image among Americans by staging elaborate war games, circulating old propaganda-type films and having officers in uniform speak to audiences throughout the U.S. about the menace of communism. The telecast was immediately denounced by Rep. F. Edward Hebert (D, La.), chairman of the House Armed Services Committee, who called it a "vicious piece of propaganda" that left him "with an emptiness in my stomach, nausea . . ."

Vice President Spiro T. Agnew entered the controversy March 18, calling the CBS documentary a "subtle but vicious broadside against the nation's defense establishment." Addressing a Republican club in Boston, Agnew questioned the credibility of the CBS documentary. According to Agnew, two CBS journalists who produced the film on the Pentagon had also taken part in other documentaries involving questionable editing and production techniques.

CBS was also attacked March 19 by Sen. Robert Dole (R, Kan.), who accused it along with two other national television networks of biased news coverage. Dole, chairman of the Republican National Committee, said the news coverage of the National Broadcasting Company (NBC) and the American Broadcasting Company (ABC) was also biased, but said CBS was most guilty of biased reporting.

Agnew said March 20 that CBS had not responded to his March 18 speech in Boston and he challenged the network

to admit or deny his charges "of error and propagandistic manipulation" in the Pentagon documentary and two others.

CBS rebroadcast the documentary March 23, and followed it with the criticism by Agnew, Defense Secretary Melvin R. Laird and Rep. Hebert and a defense of the film by CBS News President Richard S. Salant.

Hebert called the film "one of the most un-American things I've ever seen . . . on the tube." Laird said he thought "there probably could have been a little more professionalism shown in putting the show together."

Salant said in his statement that "no one has refuted the essential accuracy" of the documentary and went on to reply to a number of specific charges made by Agnew and Hebert.

Agnew renewed his criticism of CBS March 24, charging the network with "deliberately publishing untruths." In an interview in St. Louis, the vice president said he was "totally dissatisfied with what the network characterized as a rebuttal on the part of Administration officials, including myself," following the March 23 rebroadcast. He accused CBS of editing some of his earlier remarks and comments of Laird and Hebert "and showed the ones they wanted to show."

House unit subpoenas CBS films—The House Interstate and Foreign Commerce Committee served a subpoena April 8 on CBS to provide for investigation all televised and untelevised materials that were used to produce "The Selling of the Pentagon."

Rep. Harley O. Staggers (D, W. Va.), chairman of the Commerce Committee and its Special Subcommittee on Investigations which served the order, said the sensible course in the controversy was "to get the facts."

Dr. Frank Stanton, president of CBS, said the network would make available only the materials that had actually been broadcast. Stanton and Staggers conferred by telephone April 8 and the congressman said he did not anticipate any problems in obtaining the material his committee wanted.

'Pentagon' TV film subpoenaed again. A House subcommittee probing the production of the television documentary "The Selling of the Pentagon" issued a new subpoena against the Columbia Broadcasting System (CBS) May 26 demanding the appearance of its president and directing that it make available key materials used to make the film.

It was the third time the Special Subcommittee on Investigations of the House Commerce Committee had sought to get the "outtakes" of the CBS film. Outtakes were those portions of film edited out before the broadcast.

The new subpoena replaced one issued by the panel April 7. CBS had refused April 20 to comply with the April 8 order, although it did furnish the subcommittee with the file and transcript of the program as it appeared on tele-

vision. CBS did not, however, provide the panel with the outtakes.

In a letter to Rep. Harley O. Staggers (D, W.Va.), chairman of the subcommittee, CBS said again April 30 that it would not turn over all the materials collected for the documentary. CBS said in the letter that "compliance with the subpoena would have a chilling effect on the ability of journalists at CBS and throughout the profession to report and interpret the news—including of course, the conduct of Government officials."

After learning of the new subpoena a CBS spokesman said that the network's president, Dr. Frank Stanton, would probably appear in compliance with the order. The subpoena called for Stanton's appearance before the panel June 9. The CBS spokesman added, however, that the network would continue to resist efforts to have it make public the film's outtakes.

Nixon said against probe. White House Communications Director Herbert Klein said in a speech in Des Moines, Iowa May 26 that the Nixon Administration did not back the subcommittee's investigation of the CBS program. Klein said of the investigation: "I believe this is wrong and an infringement on freedom of the press. It could lead to further subpoenas of a reporter's notes." Klein added that the President was not "in favor of further restrictions" on the communications media.

Daniel Z. Henkin, assistant secretary of defense for public affairs, criticized CBS May 12 for what he described as misrepresentations in the "Selling" documentary, but he defended the network's right to produce a program critical of the Defense Department's public relations activities.

In testimony before the Special Subcommittee on Investigations, Henkin said: "The Pentagon is not for sale, and not for sale either is the right of a free press to criticize the Pentagon."

Agnew on media 'paranoia.' Vice President Spiro T. Agnew offered another critical assessment of the news media June 1, in a speech to radio station owners affiliated with the Mutual Broadcasting System, who were meeting in the Bahamas.

Agnew said the media had reacted to the "constructive" criticism offered by himself and others in the last 18 months with a "frenzy about intimidation and repression." But "attempts to portray the government as anxious to control or suppress the news media," he said, would "backfire" and compound the "credibility problem" faced by the media.

What the criticism amounted to, Agnew said, was "to call on the free press of this country . . . to police itself against excesses that on occasion have been so blatant they have undermined the confidence of the public in the credibility of the news media as well as the credibility of the government."

Stanton bars TV film data. Frank Stanton, president of the Columbia Broadcasting System (CBS), again refused June 24 to give a Congressional subcommittee all the materials used to produce the television documentary "The Selling of the Pentagon."

Rep. Harley O. Staggers (D, W. Va.), chairman of the House Commerce Committee's Investigations Subcommittee that was looking into the production of the film, told Stanton that his refusal to turn over the raw materials could be viewed as contempt. Staggers threatened to press a contempt citation against the CBS president before the full House.

Stanton told members of the investigations subcommittee that he had refused to show them either the raw materials or the editing procedures used for the film on the grounds that the First Amendment guaranteed freedom-of-the-press privileges. He contended that the vitality of television journalism needed the same freedom from government "surveillance" as that accorded newspapers.

In another development, the board of directors of the National Association of Broadcasters passed a resolution June 25 in support of Stanton's refusal. The board said the resolution was passed "in support of Dr. Stanton in his efforts to establish once and for all that electronic journalism is covered by the same First Amendment guarantee enjoyed by the print media."

CBS rebuffed by Laird—The Pentagon revealed June 19 that Defense Secretary Melvin R. Laird had declined to take part in a taped interview with the Colombia Broadcasting System (CBS) for a documentary on U.S. prisoners of war in Vietnam.

Daniel Z. Henkin, assistant secretary of defense for public affairs, said, however, that Laird "would be pleased to appear on the program if the interview was done live." Henkin said Laird's refusal to do a taped interview was not a "binding role on all interviews," but that the prisoner-of-war issue was very sensitive and only a live interview on it would be acceptable to the Defense Department.

Court uphold press on Pentagon Papers. The Supreme Court upheld by a 6–3 decision June 30 the right of the New York Times and the Washington Post to publish material from a classified Pentagon study of the origins of the Vietnam war. The Nixon Administration had sought to enjoin the papers from publishing the material. [For a detailed review of the case, see chapter two.]

Agnew blasts media again. Speaking during a visit to Singapore, Agnew July 5 again attacked the American press, charging the news media with unintentionally assisting the North Vietnamese by some of their reportage of the Indochina war. He said the North Vietnamese were likely to launch a "high risk, high-casualty" attack when U.S.

forces were sufficiently reduced that would be a "public-relations coup" since the U.S. media would report it "as a failure of the Vietnamization program of the U.S." Agnew added that he was reassuring the leaders of the countries he visited that the Nixon Administration had no intention of leaving a vacuum in Asia or the Middle East and that the U.S. intended to remain a world power despite some "isolationist" voices in Washington.

CBS contempt citation killed. The House refused July 13 to approve a contempt citation against the Columbia Broadcasting System (CBS) and its president, Dr. Frank Stanton, for their failure to cooperate with an investigation into the CBS television documentary "The Selling of the Pentagon." The citation had been recommended by the Commerce Committee.

By a roll-call vote of 226 to 181, the House voted to recommit the proposed citation to the committee. In effect, the recommital killed the proposed citation.

The Commerce Committee had voted July 1 by 25 to 13 to seek the citation after Stanton refused to give its investigating subcommittee all the materials used to produce the documentary. The move was inititated by Rep. Harley O. Staggers (D, W. Va.), chairman of the committee.

Staggers said after the House vote July 13 that he would not raise the matter again. Staggers indicated that he was surprised at the House's action. Never before, Staggers said, had the House denied a contempt citation when requested by a committee and its chairman.

In New York, Stanton said CBS was "very pleased" at the outcome of the vote. He added that "as responsible journalists, we shall continue to do our best to report on public events in a fair and objective manner."

Before the vote, House Speaker Carl Albert had urged Staggers to compromise on the citation, but when he insisted on the vote, Albert announced that he wanted the citation referred to the Judiciary Committee for "official, constitutional study," but instead it was sent back to the Commerce Committee.

In the vote, 131 Democrats and 95 Republicans voted for recommital, 105 Democrats and 76 Republicans voted against.

Agnew attacks media on Attica. Vice President Agnew accused the "radical left" and the nation's news media Sept. 27 of trying to make the bloody prisoners' revolt at the state prison in Attica, N.Y. into "yet another cause celebre in the pantheon of radical revolutionary propaganda."

Agnew also praised Gov. Nelson Rockefeller of New York for his handling of the uprising, which ended Sept. 13 when 1,500 lawmen stormed the prison.

Agnew's remarks were made in a speech to the International Association of Chiefs of Police meeting in Anaheim, Calif. Agnew said that instead of paying tribute to 633 lawmen killed in the U.S. in the last 10 years, there had been "inordinate attention focused on the self-declared and proven enemies of our society."

Agnew attacked the news media for giving wide currency to "the most inflammatory and baseless charges" of convicted criminals and their sympathizers.

Media freedom hearings. Sen. Sam J. Ervin (D, N.C.) convened a series of hearings before his Constitutional Rights Subcommittee Sept. 28–Oct. 20 to investigate the role of the government in the news media. Media representatives, congressmen, scholars and government aides debated charges of federal interference, and a variety of legislative and regulatory changes were recommended.

In announcing the hearings, Ervin warned of "the growing deterioration of the relationship between the press and the government," and "the increasing amount of government control and influence" over broadcast news. He cited the Justice Department's June suit to prevent publication of the Pentagon Papers, a House subcommittee subpoena of materials for a Columbia Broadcasting System (CBS) television documentary, a Federal Communications Commission (FCC) warning against broadcast of drug-related songs, "increased use" of subpoenas to require newsmen to reveal confidential information and the use of false press cards by government investigators.

Several media executives and newsmen complained of government intimidation. New York Times Executive Vice President Harding Bancroft said Sept. 28 that the Pentagon Papers incident, in which his newspaper and the Washington Post had been enjoined from publishing the documents for 15 days, had set "an extremely unfortunate precedent" that might well result in "journalistic timidity or unwarranted self-censorship."

CBS president Frank Stanton (Oct. 29) and CBS newsman Walter Cronkite (Oct. 30) asked for reduced government regulation of the broadcast industry. Stanton said that "over-regulation" by the FCC, especially in its application of the fairness or equal time doctrine, was "beginning to impede the free flow of news." Cronkite asked for an end to government licensing of broadcast stations.

Several witnesses, including FCC members Dean Burch and Nicholas Johnson and National Broadcasting Co. (NBC) newscaster David Brinkley, denied that news freedom had been curtailed. Burch, a Nixon appointee and Johnson, a liberal Democrat, maintained Oct. 20 that the FCC had always avoided judgments about the content of news programs. Johnson said the commission had never tried "to discipline the networks in any way in response to charges of distortion "

Brinkley denied Oct. 19 the criticism by government had hampered his own news coverage.

Criticism of the media as insufficiently free or diverse was expressed by some witnesses, who called for stronger government supervision.

Fred Friendly, former CBS news executive, charged Oct. 12 that the network's profit orientation had acted to impede free and adequate news coverage, and encouraged "the selling of violence and superfluous medicine." George Washington University professor Jerome A. Barron Sept. 30 asked for legislation to require media to accept paid controversial advertising, since "freedom of speech and the press is not the sole possession of those wealthy enough to own a station or a newspaper."

Ervin probes Schorr case. Sen. Sam J. Ervin Jr. (D, N.C.) said Feb. 1 he would introduce legislation to bar Federal Bureau of Investigation (FBI) probes of an individual except in criminal cases. Ervin made the announcement at a hearing of his Constitutional Rights Subcommittee at which CBS newsman Daniel Schorr testified on his own investigation by the agency. The Administration had said the Schorr probe was related to a job he was to be offered, but the newsman testified that he was first contacted by FBI agents one day after being called to the White House to hear criticism of one of his television reports. Ervin said Jan. 31 that the Administration had refused his request that it permit the officials involved to testify, and charged that conflicting accounts of the supposed job had been given by different Administration spokesmen.

The testimony was part of a series of hearings into government-media relations. At a Feb. 8 hearing, Time Inc. board chairman Andrew Heiskell deplored a proposed 142% second class postal rate rise, which he warned might destroy some magazines and small newspapers.

Agnew resumes attacks on press. Vice President Agnew resumed his attacks on media critics of the Administration in a series of speeches in April 1972.

At a meeting of the California GOP Assembly in Palo Alto April 8, Agnew assailed the liberal Eastern press and political critics of the Administration as "demagogues" who pandered to "the leftist radical mob." They denigrated the armed forces and police agencies, he said, "by currying favor with a nest-fouling constituency of home-grown anti-Americans who pervert their constitutional rights in an effort to destroy their country's free institutions."

At an April 11 meeting of the GOP's Capitol Hill Club in Washington, Agnew charged that "latter-day Goebbels of the radical left" were writing and editing anti-Administration bias into reference books. His office said later that he was referring to the Encyclopedia Britannica and to the 1970 Collier's Encyclopedia Yearbook.

At a meeting of the American Society of Newspaper Editors in Washington April 21, Agnew assailed Democratic Senators J. W. Fulbright (Ark.), Hubert H. Humphrey (Minn.), Edward M. Kennedy (Mass.), George McGovern (S.D.), and Edmund S. Muskie (Me.) for having "staked their credibility and some of their political future" on the failure of the President's Vietnam policy. Agnew said such men, "who played a central role in pushing America into an everdeepening involvement in Vietnam, are now charging that the President desires a military victory more than he desires peace." "This is a transparent lie," he charged. Agnew added that "the New York Times, an early and ardent advocate of getting America into Vietnam [was] doing public penance regularly by scourging the President who is getting us out." (Addressing the same meeting later April 21, Times Vice President James Reston asserted that "never since before the last world war, not even in Lyndon Johnson's time, have I seen a trickier Administration than this one.")

Nixon aides score media. White House speechwriter Patrick J. Buchanan and FBI interim director L. Patrick Gray 3rd added their voices April 28 and May 5 to Administration criticism of alleged media news bias.

Buchanan said in a May 5 interview that if the media continued to exercise a news "monopoly" and to "freeze out opposing points of view and opposing information you're going to find something done in the area of antitrust type action," possibly new legislation.

Justice Department acting Assistant Attorney General for the Antitrust Division Walker B. Comegys repeated May 5 the department's denial that its pending antitrust suit against television network entertainment scheduling was related to criticism of news reporting, saying "the antitrust laws would not permit" attacks on news content.

Gray, at that time Nixon's nominee for deputy attorney general, told a bar association meeting in Santa Ana, Calif. April 28 that the media were "becoming too much a part of the culture of disparagement which threatens to destroy all respect for established institutions." He specifically charged that the National Broadcasting Co. (NBC), the Columbia Broadcasting System (CBS), the New York Times and the Washington Post had let "partisan bias and prejudice" influence reporting and editing. Gray said, however, he would "abhor any action by the government to control the press."

Newspapers support Nixon. President Nixon had the editorial support of an overwhelming number of daily newspapers across the country, according to a poll by Editor & Publisher, the weekly news magazine of the newspaper business. In its Nov. 4 issue, the magazine reported Nixon had the editorial support of 753 dailies, or 71.4% of the 1,054 dailies participating in the poll (out of 1,764 in the U.S.), McGovern had the editorial support of 56 dailies, or 5.3%; 245 dailies (23.3%) were uncommitted.

A survey released Nov. 2 by President Nixon's communications director, Herbert G. Klein, reported 1,468 daily and weekly newspapers in the country had endorsed Nixon, 199 had endorsed McGovern.

IPI scores U.S. trend. The annual world review of the International Press Institute (IPI) said in Geneva, Switzerland Dec. 31 that the U.S. government had been trying to "chip away" at press guarantees in order "to make the journalist timid in research for the facts and the public nervous when confronted by a reporter asking for them." IPI conceded, however, that press freedom in the U.S. remained "almost unscathed."

The report singled out for criticism the Supreme Court decision in the Earl Caldwell case, which denied reporters' right to silence before grand juries.

Legislative proposals to prevent government bodies from eliciting information from newsmen was backed at the Sept. 28 hearing by Sen. James B. Pearson (R, Kan.) and Rep. Charles W. Whalen (R, Ohio). [See chapter four for the details of this issue.]

Probe of newsman disputed. Press Secretary Ronald Ziegler admitted Nov. 11 that the White House had ordered an FBI investigation of Columbia Broadcasting System (CBS) correspondent Daniel Schorr, but denied that the probe was related to criticism of Schorr's reporting by President Nixon and Administration aides. Ziegler and Frederic V. Malek, White House personnel aide, said Schorr had been under consideration in August for an unspecified federal job, which occasioned the investigation.

Schorr said Nov. 10 that he had never been told of any job offer, even when he questioned Malek about the probe in October.

Ziegler said the FBI investigation had been started in accord with a "tightly administered procedure," which he said he was unable to explain, with Malek's knowledge. Malek said, however, that the investigation had been "kicked off" by an assistant without his knowledge.

Schorr had been criticized by Nixon, Ziegler and Charles W. Colson, a Presidential aide, for his coverage of the antiballistic missile program, federal aid to parochial schools and Nixon's new economic program.

[For subsequent developments in the conflict between the Nixon Administration and the media, including the impact of the Watergate Affair, see Chapter 3.]

Editorial Comment

The Dallas Morning News
Dallas, Tex., January 20, 1970

"I THINK THE vice-president started a much-needed debate in this country . . . and I honestly do not feel the administration is threatening the freedom of the press."

This comment on Spiro Agnew's analysis of the press is not startling in itself. What makes it unusual is that it was stated by a high official of the Johnson administration, former press secretary George Christian.

Christian can speak on the relations between press and government with some authority, having served on both sides. And his recent remarks to Texas newspaper editors deserve some thought, both from members of the press and from the public at large.

For good reason, the press is first to fight in the cause of free speech and free expression. History shows that the people's freedom to state their beliefs is crucial to the other freedoms —any attempt to impose totalitarian control on a society usually begins with the elimination of free speech and free press.

But those of the press who enjoy freedom of expression can hardly deny the same freedom to the vice-president. He stated his beliefs about the job that the press is doing. And the reaction indicates that there are millions of other Americans who agree with him.

In general, The News believes that Vice-President Agnew made several

points that are valid. Some of his stated opinions, on the other hand, seem to reflect a misunderstanding of the technical requirements imposed by such press problems as deadlines and shortage of space. But there can be no doubt that he has the right, as does every citizen, to say what he thinks about the press and its performance.

The press, after all, has never been shy about making its own opinions known. There is something hypocritical about powerful press agencies' unwillingness to listen to criticism, as well as hand it out.

Of all the hysterical outcry heard in the wake of the Agnew blasts, the line that seemed most unlikely was the charge that the vice-president's oratory was designed to destroy the free press.

The American free press has been in the thick of the great debate in this country for two centuries. If it could be shattered by one official's complaints, that would be a flaw far more serious than any Agnew mentioned.

The press isn't perfect but it is durable. We are convinced that it can defend itself when it believes its critics are wrong and improve itself when it believes its critics are justified.

We agree with friendly press critic George Christian in his belief that "the press is going to survive criticism from worn-out press secretaries and also from presidents and vice-presidents."

TULSA DAILY WORLD
Tulsa, Okla., March 1, 1970

VICE PRESIDENT AGNEW, who has made his reputation taking on effete snobs and supercilious sophisticates, now is going after kooks, demagogues and misfits.

He does have quite a gallery of targets. But note how carefully he has chosen them to hit that same sympathetic nerve in the great majority of Americans. Not many people would stand up and defend the right of the kooks, demagogues and misfits to take advantage of the rest of society.

But the VICE PRESIDENT is more than shrewd. There is, as usual, a bit of truth in what he is saying.

He says the odd characters in our life are getting more than their share of attention in newspapers and on the air. Only somewhat facetiously he suggests that misfits be pursued with butterfly nets instead of television cameras.

This argument against undue coverage of the rebels and oddballs of society was made to the National Governors Conference Thursday. Some will say AGNEW is picking on the news media—and perhaps he is giving our industry more than its share of his critical attention.

But this is not necessarily bad. The press—including all media of information—is of such importance to a free society that it needs to be examined from time. The editors, publishers, newscasters and others in the business do a lot of self-examination, but it should be valuable to get a representative view from outside.

The VICE PRESIDENT'S comments are worth having, not because he is

necessarily right on every point but because he seems to speak the mind of many, many Americans. That should enable us to see how we appear to others.

We don't buy the AGNEW argument in its entirety. A goodly part of the news is written about nonconformists—persons who differ from the majority. This is because the routine often makes dull reading, while the exceptional is more interesting. One banker who embezzles money will get more news attention than the thousands who handle funds every day without netting a dime illicitly.

This goes to human nature and has always been true. But what the VICE PRESIDENT is talking about is the undue attention given persons for no other reason than that they are "antis"—and noisy about it.

Some of these people have learned to take advantage of the news media. They set press conferences or stage their "acts" for the benefit of newsmen and cameras.

To the extent that the media are carried along by these schemers, AGNEW's criticism of the press is true. But most of us in the business are aware when someone tries to use us selfishly. Most—not all—will refuse to lend their facilities to such efforts by the kooks and misfits described by AGNEW.

Every newspaper, wire service, radio or television station must make these decisions on its own. Perhaps the AGNEW speech will keep the press more alert to the danger of being taken for an unsavory ride.

Chicago Tribune

Chicago, Ill., March 2, 1970

When Vice President Agnew accused the television networks and certain newspapers of a left-wing bias in their broadcasts and reportage, the targets of his broadside squealed like a pig stuck in a gate. Now Mr. Agnew has received support from one of the most improbable and most authoritative sources.

Howard K. Smith, Washington-based anchor man for the American Broadcasting company's news department, asserts in an interview with *TV Guide* that most reporters, for television and the other news media, have a "strong leftward bias."

Mr. Smith may be viewed by his liberal colleagues as an intellectual traitor, but the supreme insult in their demonology—"right wing radical"—would sound pretty silly as a label for him. Altho he is a hawk on Viet Nam, he describes himself as a left-of-center liberal. Not long ago he was considered left of liberal.

In 1962, for instance, he put Alger Hiss, an ex-convict who had served a prison term for perjury involving espionage for the Soviet Union, on a television program titled, more hopefully than prophetically, "The Political Obituary of Richard M. Nixon." Hiss, a former state department official, was permitted to denounce Nixon, who had spearheaded a congressional investigation that resulted in Hiss' undoing. Earlier, a book written by Smith, titled "The State of Europe," was praised by the communist Daily Worker.

Thus Smith knows his way around in the fever swamps of liberalism. Mercilessly, he blows the whistle on his liberal colleagues of both press and television. "Our liberal friends today have become dogmatic," he says. "They have a set of dogmatic reactions. . . . Be sure you please your fellows, because that's what's 'good.' They're conventional. They're conformists. They're pleasing Walter Lippmann, they're pleasing the Washington Post, they're pleasing the editors of the New York Times, and they're pleasing one another."

In short, they're knee-jerk liberals.

Smith asserts that President Johnson was "actually politically assassinated" and that the same liberals now "are trying to assassinate President Nixon politically." He says "they hate President Nixon irrationally."

Any newspaper man who has traveled with Presidential candidates in recent campaigns knows that Smith is right. The liberal reporters were as irrational in their hatred of Nixon in the 1960 and 1968 campaigns and in their contempt for Barry Goldwater in the 1964 campaign as they were in their adoration of President Kennedy.

As Smith says, these political activists are "proud of being out of contact with the middle class." He quotes Joseph Kraft as saying in a recent column: "Let's face it, we reporters have very little to do with middle America. They're not our kind of people."

However laughable it may seem, these aspirant Walter Lippmanns consider themselves intellectuals. Actually they are not as stupid as they seem. Just as they discerned with horror, in 1968, that Nixon probably would win, they now perceive, in Kraft's words, a "reactionary tide running in America." If they have very little to do with "middle America," they may soon learn that the American middle class —the great silent majority—has very little to do with them.

ST. LOUIS POST-DISPATCH

St. Louis, Mo., March 13, 1970

The president of NBC has joined the president of CBS in opposing the Nixon Administration's policies toward the news media, as expressed generally in the veiled threats of Vice President Agnew and specifically in the Justice Department's use of blanket subpenas to obtain reporters' notes and TV film clips for use in criminal prosecutions.

It may be dignifying the Agnew-Mitchell tactics too much to call them, as Julian Goodman of NBC does, the greatest attack on the press since 1798. Our own feeling is that what we have here is not so much a conscious plot to shackle the press as a rather bumbling effort to serve the Administration's political purposes in ways which happen to harmonize with Mr. Nixon's resentment of the media dating back to his 1962 "farewell" press conference.

Yet the potential of a serious attack on the independence of the press is there, and it is important that all elements of the press resist it. As direct licensees of the Government, the radio-television industry has a special stake in fighting official dictation of its content, and it is good to see the two leading network executives enlisting in that battle. Also to be welcomed is the formation in Washington of a Reporters' Committee on Freedom of the Press to consider dangers to the news-gathering process in widespread use of the subpena power.

What the public should recognize is that more is involved than a contest between Government and press. In fighting to preserve their independence the newspapers and broadcasters seek not to protect privileges but to safeguard the public's right to free and uncontaminated information on public affairs. If the already overwhelming power of government should ever silence the independent voice and questing mind of non-governmental news media, the losers would be the people.

The press has shortcomings a-plenty, let that be granted. But its faults would be infinitely worse if through law or practice it became an arm of government.

That is the objection to Attorney General Mitchell's policy of issuing blanket subpenas for reporters' notes and TV commentators' film clips, a policy from which he has only slightly retreated in offering to negotiate the scope of the subpenas.

When a reporter or TV cameraman witnesses a crime he is very properly subject to call before the courts to tell what he has seen. But that is an altogether different matter from requiring him to violate the confidentiality of his news sources on a broad and undiscriminating scale. This kind of coercion means making the press an agency of government. It means using the press to do the Government's job of gathering its own evidence for law enforcement. Once this relationship is established with respect to law enforcement, it can all too easily be extended to other fields.

As for Mr. Agnew's recent demand that governors and "other elected officials" join in driving the news of "bizarre extremists" from the TV screens and front pages, some readers have asked how this can be construed as a threat of censorship. It can't, of course, as long as governors and other elected officials maintain the laudable indifference they have so far shown to Mr. Agnew's suggestion. But if they ever followed his advice, somebody would have to decide who is a bizarre extremist, and whoever made that decision would become a censor the moment he tried to impose his decision on the press, whether by law or by pressure.

Unhappy as it may be at times with the news decisions of the news media, the public has an enormous stake in keeping those decisions out of government hands. The broadcasting networks and newspapers are fighting the public's battle, not just their own, in dedicating themselves to that cause.

EVENING HERALD

Rock Hill, S.C., March 7, 1970

Americans, says Vice President Agnew, "need a strong voice to penetrate the cacophony of seditious drivel emanating from the best publicized clowns of our society and from their fans in the Fourth Estate." Going counter to President Nixon's suggestion to the nation, Agnew says he definitely is not going to lower his voice.

That's the vice president's right, just as it is the right of the press to comment on what it thinks is right and wrong with government. True, sometimes there arises one loud voice that would better have been kept stilled, but in nearly every case there is reason behind complaints of the press.

Instead of giving blanket condemnation, perhaps Agnew should be more specific in separating the "drivel" from the truth. Scattergun charges have a way of mixing the truth and drivel into an inseparable mess.

THE ARIZONA REPUBLIC
Phoenix, Ariz., April 1, 1970

Instead of addressing themselves to the serious issues raised by Vice President Spiro Agnew in his speech criticizing the preponderant liberal bias in network television, spokesmen for the industry persist in trying to sidetrack the issue.

Take, as just the latest example, the recent remarks by NBC news broadcaster Chet Huntley in a speech before the George Polk Awards luncheon.

Huntley said that journalists have a right to use judgment about a news story, "to look at facets of it which may not be self-evident, to put it into context, to suggest to his readers or listeners to consider it from points of view which may not be obvious." No one would deny that right to journalists. And Vice President Agnew did not say or imply that anyone should. His entire speech in Des Moines was concerned with the one-sided picture that emerges from network TV because of the closed-shop the industry has erected against other than liberal commentators or reporters.

MR. AGNEW was right, as commentator Howard K. Smith, himself a certified liberal, admitted. What's more, any honest network newscaster knows he was right.

It is human nature to resist relinquishing whatever monopoly situation one enjoys. But it is less than honest to try to shift the focus of the debate from something Mr. Agnew said to something he did not say.

The TV brass, in an apparent effort to curry public sympathy, continues to equate its situation with that of newspapers, magazines, and books. There is no similarity.

TV is a government-regulated monopoly. Anyone is free to publish a newspaper, magazine, or book. But to operate on one of the few available TV channels, one needs government approval. Television channel allotments, in other words, are awarded by the government (i.e. the American public).

That is why, unlike the press, network TV should not be allowed to peddle its nostrums and biases to the exclusion of other ideologies. That is why the operating premise of the networks must be objectivity in all controversial matters. That is why there must be the widest possible range of respectable opinion, evenly balanced at least across that spectrum from liberal to conservative.

BUT ALL THREE NETWORKS have failed abysmally to provide that range of opinion. They have stacked the deck, even if unintentionally, in favor of the liberal ideology. As a result, the millions of Americans who depend on TV for news—and most Americans do depend on TV for news—receive a narrow, incomplete interchange of ideas and opinions.

This is an unacceptable situation. And that is what Mr. Agnew was talking about, not "muzzling the press," or "hamstringing journalists." He was talking about basic fairness, something the TV networks long ago abandoned in their pell-mell pursuit of the truth according to liberalism.

If TV officialdom is genuinely concerned with fairness, it should take positive steps to insure that the liberal ideology no longer dominates its networks. And if it intends to criticize Vice President Agnew, it should do so on the basis of what he actually said, not on the basis of what it would like the public to believe he said.

Pittsburgh Post-Gazette
Pittsburgh, Pa., March 25, 1970

THE ERA of the invisible Vice President of the United States is apparently over. With the emergence of Spiro T. Agnew as a political personality, the Vice President has not only achieved visibility but has also become highly audible. The success of Mr. Agnew as a pitchman for the GOP is a political fact of life to be reckoned with in 1972. The Administration's star salesman is now appearing at fund-raising dinners all over the U.S. and its territories. His free-swinging assaults on Vietnam dissenters and the press have brought joy to the Republican faithful and dyspepsia to the dissident.

The latest foray against the tents of the wicked took place at a $100-a-plate Republican dinner in the Virgin Islands. This time Mr. Agnew aimed his barbed shafts at the mendacious mercenaries of the press who court Pulitzer Prizes by smearing government officials with "tons and tons of innuendos" while glossing over "the evils of communism." The time has come, pontificated Mr. Agnew, when "Our media would be well advised to recognize a new dimension of their responsibility to critically examine our enemies which have no free press to criticize them."

"A new dimension of responsibility" is one of those resounding phrases which, when examined, is found to be meaningless. A news medium has only one primary responsibility—the obligation to report and comment on the news as honestly as possible. This the news media do not always do — mainly because they are operated by human beings who are fallible and not always in possession of all the facts.

The suggestion of the Vice President that there is something essentially pernicious in criticizing the public acts of elective officials is dangerous doctrine. Mr. Agnew would apparently have the free press of this country imitate the controlled press of communist nations. But this would degrade America's free press to the level of the suborned news media of communist states. Much of their effort is aimed at diverting the public attention from the machinations of their rulers by dwelling on the evil designs of "imperialist capitalist powers." The free press would be truly derelict in its democratic responsibility if it abandoned its obligation to scrutinize the actions and utterances of elective officials.

The diatribes of Mr. Agnew might be dismissed as mere fund-raising rhetoric were it not for the suspicion that he speaks with the tacit approval of the Nixon Administration. The sonorous half truths and false analogies of the Vice President could be safely ignored if the Department of Justice had not already demanded that newsmen reveal confidential news sources and had not issued subpenas for the commandeering of files and films.

The concerted campaign against untrammeled freedom of the press makes it imperative that the news media jealously defend their right to criticize the actions of public officials. The man who loves his country, as J. B. Priestly pointed out, is like a loving wife who will do anything for her husband but stop criticizing him.

St. Petersburg Times
St. Petersburg, Fla., May 16, 1970

Television news broadcasters must be totally confused by Vice President Agnew's erratic criticism.

In his first blast on Nov. 13, 1969, Agnew condemned them for presenting only one side of issues. He quoted a congressional committee's criticism that a network "presented a one-sided picture" of the 1968 Chicago demonstrations. He said that "a narrow and distorted picture of America often emerges from the televised news."

So the networks are careful to present both sides.

Now Agnew accuses them of presenting "manufactured news." Writing in TV Guide, he condemns the networks for giving both sides:

"If one point of view is presented, a conscious effort is made to find its opposite and present a new controversy to the public. This raises the question: How much over-emphasized controversy and contrived action can be presented night after night to the American people before reality is clouded by imagery?"

IT ALSO raises some questions about the vice president's consistency as a TV critic.

THE DAILY OKLAHOMAN
Oklahoma City, Okla., April 20, 1970

RIPPLES continue to roll from the splash Vice President Agnew made last fall in charging certain segments of the information media with trimming the news to fit particular ideological biases.

The attack prompted a predictable chorus of protest. That all affected by the charge did not join in, however, seems significant. "I wish," said Turner Catledge recently (he has just retired as chief news executive for the New York Times), "the man had less of a cause." Catledge's statement is particularly interesting in connection with a March 29 Columbia Broadcasting System telecast from Vietnam.

Reporter John Lawrence was interviewing GIs in a combat indoctrination center. The camera focused on one soldier as he stated, in effect, that if he ever got home, no one would ever get him back into a situation like Vietnam again. "Anybody here disagree?" the voice asked as the camera panned the soldiers clustered about him. No one did. That such a gripe session could have taken place no one would seriously question. What is at question is the judgment of those who order, collect, sort, cut, assemble, and schedule the countless bits of news film that go to make up each day's broadcasts. For it would have been just as easy to air an example of GI high morale, discipline, fighting spirit and patriotism.

Rightly or wrongly, many observers — not all of them from the military — believe that television coverage of the war has helped to undermine, wittingly or unwittingly, our national will on Vietnam. That our

will and morale in regard to the war are at an all-time low is unquestioned. And the twin results seem to be an accelerating campaign to protest and discredit the war on one side, and on the other, an equally dangerous tendency to oppose and destroy the protestors. And it is CBS itself, ironically, that has plumbed the degree of danger in this dual trend with a just released poll on American views concerning the basic freedoms guaranteed by the Bill of Rights.

In answer to the question "Do you think everyone should have the right to criticize the government, even if the criticism is damaging to our national interests?" only 42 per cent said yes while 54 per cent said no. In a similar question the right of newspapers, radio and television "to report any story, even if the government feels it's harmful to our national interest" also was affirmed by only 42 per cent while 55 per cent said no.

In short, continuing evidence of justification for the vice president's charge of news media bias would seem to be making many Americans increasingly impatient with unpopular opinions and actions. And this in turn, and more importantly, tends to make them increasingly willing to follow the dangerous course of suspending our precious Bill of Rights freedoms. Thus the lovers of freedom, by hesitating to counsel restraint and self-responsibility on those who abuse it, appear to be stoking a fire of reacton which could, if unchecked, destroy freedom for everyone. Therein lies the real danger.

Honolulu Star-Bulletin
Honolulu, Hawaii, April 6, 1970

Asked recently if he had detected any results from his attacks on television and the other communications media, Vice President Agnew replied: "Sometimes when I look at the tube from time to time, I think I have had a modicum of success."

Walter Cronkite agrees. "I feel that perhaps subconsciously things are happening, but I am trying to rise above it," he said in a recent television discussion. "But I think the industry as a whole is intimidated. Yes, I think that was the intention and I think it worked."

As 6,000 members of the National Association of Broadcasters gather in Chicago this week for their 48th annual convention the posture of the Nixon administration toward them will be very much in their minds.

It should be on the minds of all of us.

Where the Agnew attack amounts to simple criticism it is entirely proper — and perhaps even overdue.

There are those who rate Lyndon Johnson a victim of assassination by the communications media. If Mr. Agnew wants to forestall such a fate for this administration, more power to him.

But where Agnew and others in the administration imply that unfriendly radio and television stations may suffer a loss of license—then we are seeing a wholly improper and dangerous abuse of the tremendous power of the federal establishment.

Tricia Nixon, the President's daughter, is a very intelligent young lady who probably reflects some of the attitudes picked up at the White House dinner table.

It is no comfort that she told a Newsweek interviewer:

"I'm a close watcher of the newspapers and TV. I think they've taken a second look. You can't underestimate the power of fear. They're afraid if they don't shape up. . . ."

ST. LOUIS POST-DISPATCH
St. Louis, Mo., May 25, 1970

Vice President Agnew's latest attack on the news media for stirring up much of the "frenzy" that followed President Nixon's invasion of Cambodia distorts the facts. Such frenzy as occurred was created by Mr. Nixon's escalation of the Indochina war; the press only reported, and commented upon, what happened. Mr. Agnew's attack on Administration critics is equivalent to an admission that there is no substantive defense for what the Administration has done; in such an event, the recourse of certain political types is to attack the critics. It is the red herring tactic.

Mr. Agnew, abetted by right-wing speechwriters, unquestionably speaks for Mr. Nixon, or rather, perhaps, for one segment of Mr. Nixon's complex personality. After he was defeated for Governor of California in 1962 Mr. Nixon severely crticized the press for its campaign coverage and said to reporters, "You won't have Nixon to kick around any more." It would be a mistake to think Mr. Nixon has recovered from his bitterness; they are kicking him around again and through Vice President Agnew he is kicking back.

This is not an edifying spectacle, though the approach seems to have a certain political appeal among the Southern conservatives to whom it is directed. Mr. Agnew appears to forget he is not conducting a back-alley campaign against an opponent who has been calling him names. He is the Vice President, elected by the people, and a spokesman for an Administration pledged to bring people together, not to divide them as he is doing.

It is the historic function of the press to report and to criticize. It should be Mr. Agnew's function (and that of Mr. Nixon) to listen to the critics, responding when necessary with the dignity and restraint befitting high office, but above all taking such constructive action as will meet with popular respect and thus remove the source of criticism.

Mr. Agnew's intemperate attacks on newspaper commentators whose fault is that they are telling the truth demeans his office and that of the presidency.

ALBUQUERQUE JOURNAL
Albuquerque, N.M., May 25, 1970

We're happy to hear the President has not "muzzled" Vice President Agnew despite the latter's efforts to muzzle or at least intimidate the free press in this country. We believe everyone, including the vice president, should continue to enjoy the right to express opinions.

Agnew now not only attacks the "eastern intellectuals" of the press, he has added such "liberal news media in this country" as the highly respected Atlanta Constitution and the Arkansas Gazette and Pulitzer Prize winning newspaper columnists and editorial cartoonists to his list of peeves.

Mrs. Katherine Graham, publisher of the Washington Post and Newsweek, points out the press has come under "some pretty withering crossfire" from political leaders and the radical left alike. She urges the press to continue protecting its "ability to collect the news because that is where the public interest lies."

She makes the valid observation, "Our political leaders may regard us as pernicious enemies but the radical left no less regards us as sycophants and tools of our political enemies. The flak will keep coming at us from both sides and we should not have time to waste whining about it."

Former CBS News president Fred W. Friendly says American journalism has become "so busy defending its honor against attack from all sides" that it is allowing its critics, "whether it is the vice president or the street protestors, the public relations men or the construction workers, to divert us by setting up the agenda for the stories we are covering."

He notes that as a result, "the truly great ground swells which shape our times seem to escape our field of vision remaining slightly out of focus until it is too late to do something about it — My Lai, Kent State, Augusta."

What Mr. Agnew forgets is the news media rarely manufactures or creates news. It reports what is happening where it is occuring. And that is where the public interest lies.

The Charlotte Observer

Charlotte, N.C., May 24, 1970

Vice President Spiro Agnew is still doing what he does best, raising money for the Republican Party by drawing 'em in to $500-a-plate dinners with roasted news media on the bill of fare.

Reports of the death of Agnew's rhetoric by reason of the heated-up situation in the country were completely erroneous. President Nixon may philosophize about "keeping the rhetoric cool when the action is hot," but the vice president was still cooking on the front burner in Houston.

Objections may come this time, not so much for what Agnew had to say about "the liberal news media," but because he left some off his list who will feel that by rights they belong there. What have they done to the vice president to deserve this slight?

At issue in Agnew's speech was criticism of the President's action in sending troops into Cambodia and setting off a wave of protests at home. The vice president roundly denounced the Washington Post and its cartoonist, Herblock, the New York Times, The New Republic, I. F. Stone's Weekly (Izzy Stone should at least send him a free subscription for that plug), the Atlanta Constitution, the Arkansas Gazette, Life magazine, columnist Carl Rowan and the New York Post.

The puzzling thing is that with a few more names Mr. Agnew could have completed the list of practically all the moderate-to-liberal organs in the country, which are in a decided minority. We don't know what he has against the St. Louis Post-Dispatch, the Louisville Courier-Journal, Harper's or Saturday Review. Equal time is in order.

Mr. Agnew's speeches are made up mostly of subjective opinion, not objective reporting. For example, he described those with whom he was unhappy as the "illiberal, self-appointed guardians . . . who would like to run our country without ever submitting to the elective process as we in public office must do."

Not true where publications are concerned. They are subject to the elective process every time their presses turn. Like a politician who doesn't get enough votes, they're out of office if their products aren't elected by enough people. The difference is that people have to wait four years before deciding whether they want to renew a Spiro Agnew.

The news media we are familiar with don't want to "muzzle" Agnew, as he charges. There has never been any question about his right to say anything he likes. There are legitimate questions about the wisdom, accuracy and timing of some of the things he says as the second-ranking elected official in a divided and explosive nation.

Good reporting still demands that the people be reminded that in this country they have many highly conservative to reactionary organs and stations in the media. We assume Mr. Agnew still knows about the jingoistic New York Daily News, the Chicago Tribune, the Indianapolis Star, the San Diego Union, the Oakland Tribune, National Review, columnists William F. Buckley, James Kilpatrick, ad infinitum.

The truth is that the press of the country is overwhelmingly conservative, much of it sympathetic to Nixon, Agnew, Ronald Reagan, et al. And it's really amazing that of all the syndicated columnists in this land he finds fault specifically with only one, Carl Rowan. Those commentators who have backed the Cambodian venture are running out of the nation's ears.

Mr. Agnew is apparently serving the desired purpose of his President and party, so we understand why he is laying it on. But he's a lousy reporter when he doesn't remind folks that Washington has the Evening Star, too, and that Paul Harvey, Jesse Helms and the Charleston News & Courier are in business at their same old stands.

The Washington Post

Washington, D.C., May 26, 1970

Ordinarily it is necessary to retain a high-priced publicity firm to do for you what Vice President Agnew has been doing for The Washington Post over the months—free of charge and sometimes on TV to boot—so we don't want to seem ungrateful. These saturation campaigns, as any publicist will tell you, can cost a pretty penny, and we were, therefore, all the more impressed, upon reading Mr. Agnew's Texas speech, to see how many new accounts he has acquired—Life magazine and its correspondent, Hugh Sidey; Carl Rowan; Harriet Van Horne; the Atlanta Constitution; the Arkansas Gazette. There were other reasons to be impressed: it's not every day of the week, after all, that a national figure rises to rescue from obscurity the growing list of complaints that have been lodged against the administration he serves, proudly trotting out the charges in a seemingly endless vista for the benefit of a party fund-raising dinner. Finally, there is Mr. Agnew's enterprise as a researcher. Surely by now he must preside over the most impressive file of newspaper clippings the world has seen since the Collyer brothers' estate was disposed of.

In view of all this it hardly seems fitting to find trivial fault; therefore we will pass quickly over the fact that it was the Vice President—not we—who construed an editorial assertion that Mr. Nixon was withholding from the public a part of his policy that might make the sudden Cambodian venture seem more rational as meaning (his words) that "the President had lost his sanity." And like everyone else who printed, in their entirety, Mr. Nixon's remarks about the "bums", we were of course pleased, though scarcely chastened, to be told some time after the event (when hell was breaking loose) that the President had actually had some special episode in mind concerning an individual case which he did not see fit to mention at the time. But the snitch-snatch quoting game hardly constitutes our main complaint, and, alas, there is a serious aspect to all this fun. For it is not the selective passages Mr. Agnew chooses to read from his clippings that disturbs us, or even the ingenious interpretation he gives them. Rather it is the special perspective he brings to his files, with which we have quarreled before in editorials that somehow slipped through the Houston fund-raising net.

The problem is the I-me perspective in which Mr. Agnew insists on viewing himself as an issue of some importance. The Atlanta Constitution, he will say, "which doesn't care much for me anyway;" the Arkansas Gazette—"which views me with varying degrees of horror," and so on. Never mind that all this is bending the "Washington-New York axis" out of shape. What Mr. Agnew does not seem to understand in his continuing self-absorption and in the related chatter about whether he will "lower his voice" or go—as now promised—for C above High C, is that the issues are Vietnam-Cambodia, the sliding economy, civil unrest, racial tensions. And, accordingly, the speeches he gives are important as an issue only in that they reflect Mr. Nixon's policies and his views on these matters. There are, to be sure, many persons in the administration who do not share the apparent presidential-vice presidential view that the economy can be saved or the casualty rate in Indochina lowered or civil peace restored if only Harriet Van Horne will shape up, that the critics are at the heart of the administration's troubles, that to characterize their criticism as a threat to the nation akin to that of foreign enemies is sound policy and wise thought. And it is with these persons, as we have said before, that Mr. Agnew's quarrel exists; it is they to whom he is doing his damage and they with whom he must make his peace. Mr. Agnew is a threat to the administration and to its chances of governing wisely and well—he is not a threat to the press.

This brings us to a rather frivolous question which the Vice President has injected into the argument he is pleased to believe concerns himself and his entitlements—namely his First Amendment right of free speech. And this comes up with such regularity, that we think it might be well to dwell for a moment on both his rights and his powers as Vice President. To our knowledge there is no federal or state statute that prevents the Vice President from saying anything he pleases. But he must expect that its relationship to what the administration is doing will be commented upon and judged. For even though he has an incontrovertible right to go around the country calling people and groups of people names, he should be aware that he has no related right to expect that he will be admired in consequence.

That raises the second point: Mr. Agnew's powers and his perks. There is no "right to respect" for government officials written into the Constitution of a country that got its start by spitting in King George's eye and which has done its best ever since to keep its public officials aware that they are serving on public sufferance and often with a minimum of public tolerance. The glory and glamor and trappings of the office itself, in short do not automatically compel either awe or respect—do not presuppose it—and Mr. Agnew's failure to assimilate this idea is somehow akin to the spirit that temporarily foisted upon us the Ruritanian White House uniform—it's all really of a piece.

But if respect does not automatically come with the job or with its outward symbols, the Vice President should nonetheless be heartened to know that he does have certain powers which are wholly unshared with a critical press. For the press and the critics generally may howl their heads off at the administration in office—its policies and its conceits—but the press has no power whatever to degrade or demean the highest offices in the land. Mr. Agnew can rest his fears on that account. The power to demean the presidency or the vice presidency in this nation reposes solely with the men who hold the office.

Arkansas Gazette.
Little Rock, Ark., May 29, 1970

We are indebted to Spiro T. Agnew for compiling, for his speech in Texas last week, one of the best roundups of recent editorial commentary critical of President Nixon and of the vice president himself. It takes some time and effort to bring such material together and, what's more, there is probably no better authority on what has been said about Spiro T. Agnew and Richard Nixon than Spiro T. Agnew.

It is curious how the merit or lack of same in the commentary in question lies in the eye of the beholder. The vice president regards his collection as a sort of chamber of horrible things to say, while we are impressed with how candid and penetrating was the comment that stirred his wrath.

For example, the Washington Post struck to the heart of President Nixon's behaviour in the Cambodia affair when it remarked in one of Agnew's selected editorials that the President's conduct was "erratic and irrational, not to say incomprehensible." Certainly this was an accurate way to describe the President's deeds and words at the time. He was not only committing a blunder that unsettled the nation; he was also dashing off on one occasion to denounce dissenting "bums" before an admiring assemblage of Pentagon lackeys, and on another occasion to talk about football (!!) and Neville Chamberlain to uncomprehending student demonstrators at the Washington monument.

"Erratic" is surely the word, although the President actually had blown his cool just as obviously weeks earlier in a considered tirade against the United States Senate after the Carswell affair.

Mr. Agnew picked up another discerning commentary, worth repeating, from the New York Times's Tom Wicker, who had written that "whatever his motives and his policy, Mr. Nixon relied heavily, in his appearances before the nation, on deception, demagoguery and chauvinism."

Then there was the editorial from the New York Times which said that in the Cambodia campaign Mr. Nixon was sustaining a "military hallucination." The Times went on to observe that "if the President does not promptly pull back from this dangerous adventure, Congress will have to assert its constitutional power of restraint."

Indeed, Mr. Nixon *has* started pulling back from the Cambodian adventure, in apparent response to national dismay and outrage. And the U.S. Senate has been taking up measures to exercise restraint, just as the Times (and incidentally the Arkansas Gazette) had foreseen.

Mr. Agnew spoke in his Texas appearance of a "Washington-New York axis" (the Post and the Times) but he might as well have formally extended it at least to Atlanta, for an Atlanta Constitution editorial on Agnew's Stone Mountain appearance also drew the vice president's fire.

We particularly liked this editorial in which the Constitution, objecting to Agnew's appearance at a dedication of a monument to Generals Lee and Jackson and Jefferson Davis observed:

Honorable men ride that rocky ledge . . . Spiro Agnew has none of these redeeming qualities. He has the grace of a drill sergeant and the understanding of a 19th century prison camp warden.

Agnew's editorial axis extended in several other directions, to include the Luce publication's Life magazine, Columnist Carl Rowan, The New Republic and others, including, of course, the Arkansas Gazette. Life's Hugh Sidey summed up succinctly what the vice president, in the absence of anything constructive to do, has been engaged in over these past several months:

For weeks now Agnew, more than Abbie Hoffman or William Kunstler, has dominated the headlines with a torrent of abuse that served mainly to call attention to all that is bad in our society or what he takes to be bad — laying about with that big careless brush of his against the Administration's lengthening list of enemies.

Portland Press Herald
Portland, Me., May 26, 1970

Vice President Spiro T. Agnew is doing the same disservice to this country as the rabble rousers he denounces for inciting campus riots and disorders.

Mr. Agnew is quite right when he says, as he did in a Texas party speech, that Americans are deluged with "irresponsibility and thoughtlessness." But it isn't all originating with the liberal news media as he charged. Mr. Agnew is originating his share of that deluge.

The Vice President would twist "liberal" into some sort of dirty word. While we have had far more of the liberal incantations than we enjoyed in recent years, we nonetheless defend their right to those views and the privilege of expressing them. Mr. Agnew apparently wants to muzzle all viewpoints but that of the administration while dismissing as nonsense any suggestion that he be more temperate in his own oratory. He is proud of the fact that the President has not told him "what words to use or what tone to take in my speeches" but he is eager to dictate to the whole news media the words and tone they should employ.

Mr. Agnew is little short of absurd when he declares that anyone would attempt to deprive him of the freedom of speech. All that is asked of the Vice President is that he exercise the prestige of that office to stem that deluge of irresponsibility and thoughtlessness; that he practice what he preaches; that he recognize that his passionate rhetoric is no less inflammatory than that which he denounces.

Mr. Agnew could be an effective, persuasive and pacifying voice in defending and, more important, explaining the policies of the administration. But he is reaching only the believers. His vehemence is polarizing just as much as that of the more strident campus voices. The tragedy is that Mr. Agnew is either oblivious to this or deliberately ignores the hazard it creates.

The Des Moines Register
Des Moines, Iowa, May 27, 1970

Vice-President Agnew, who earlier spanked television newscasting and commentary and reporting by newspapers, last week turned his attention to newspaper editorial writers, columnists and a cartoonist. The Vice-President's targets included James Reston, Carl Rowan, Herblock and editorial writers on the Washington Post, New York Times and Atlanta Constitution.

All of the journalists and publications cited by the Vice-President have been critical at times of him or the Administration. Agnew used such terms as "hysterical," "irresponsible," "thoughtless," "sick invective" and "wild, hot rhetoric" to describe their criticism.

The Vice-President must not have intended it to sound that way, but his speech declared in effect that if his critics quit being irresponsible, he would too. Agnew stated: "I have refused to 'cool it' — to use the vernacular — until those self-righteous lower their voices a few decibels." Agnew said the First Amendment belongs to him as much as to the press, and he hoped this would be remembered the next time a "muzzle Agnew" campaign is launched.

No one has suggested that the Vice-President be barred from saying unkind things about the press. The performance of the press is as deserving of critical analysis as that of any American institution.

The Vice-President's attempt to draw an analogy between the function of the press and his function perhaps explains why he is the center of so much controversy. The Vice-President believes he has the right to speak his mind in strong terms just as columnists and editors express their views.

Of course he has that right. But a columnist expresses a personal opinion. A newspaper's editorials reflect the view of a private enterprise. When a President or Vice-President speaks, he speaks for the government. This is why the words of those high officials carry enormous weight, why they are capable of arousing such great passion. The Vice-President's criticisms of students or college admissions practices may be intended to be an expression of personal opinion, but they have an impact and arouse animosity, because of their source, no newspaper editorial ever generated.

Appeals to reason are the best form of argument. Those who have the responsibility of high office have a special obligation to be mindful of their capacity for "bringing people together" or tearing them apart and to keep public discussion at a high, dispassionate level.

New York Post

New York, N.Y., May 25, 1970

Despite all the nobility of intention and gallantry under fire he attributes to himself, Vice President Agnew rendered a dubious service to President Nixon in his latest recital of the sins of critical journalism.

His quotations and citations obviously gave large national exposure to views that remain unpublished in many cities and towns where the press remains in exclusively conservative hands. But most astonishing of all was his interpretation of an editorial in The Washington Post on the Cambodian adventure, which asserted that "there is something so erratic and irrational, not to say incomprehensible, about all this that you have to assume there is more to it than he is telling us."

As far as we know, no one except Spiro Agnew has construed those words as a reflection on the mental health of the President rather than as a severe editorial judgment of an action that lacked convincing defense.

Nor was Mr. Agnew's depiction of a sinister, conspiratorial "Washington-New York axis" fortified by his disclosure that perhaps the harshest words leveled against him had appeared in one of the South's most respected dailies—The Atlanta Constitution.

Rebuttal to the Vice President's newest tirade hardly requires endorsement of every phrase to which he objected—whether published in this newspaper or elsewhere. We take pride in the freedom accorded our columnists, including so dedicated an Agnew adherent as William Buckley.

Mr. Agnew's reappearance in the role of dean of journalism seems a transparent effort to bury issues that have created a national crisis.

Among them are the expansion of the Vietnam war (and the belated admission that we will continue to support South Vietnamese operations in Cambodia after June 30), the incredible inflation-recession haunting our economy, and the deep domestic discords now erupting on Southern battlefields. If there were no voices raised in journalistic protest at the dangerous drift of things, we would be in far more desperate trouble.

It is especially sad that Mr. Agnew chose once again to aim his fire at students—at a time when so many of them have turned to the political process and repudiated the violent fringe. We wonder whether the prospect of such legitimate political opposition is what really scares him. Is he trying to rekindle the fading fires of far-out campus disorder?

Frankly, we believe Mr. Agnew has constituted himself a one-man sideshow to divert attention from the major theaters of political combat—the war, the economy, the resurgence of Southern terrorism, the new student politics. His plaintive plea that he be given only the protection of the First Amendment is a frivolity: no man—including the President—enjoys more free TV time or more extensive coverage of his orations and parenthetical remarks.

But as long as Mr. Agnew chooses to quote so extravagantly from the Administration's critics, he constitutes something of a national asset. It is, after all, a way of insuring equal time.

The News American

Baltimore, Md., August 20, 1970

IT IS NOT without significance that the stable of leftist-liberal lawmakers in Congress keep harping on a curious theme—that the Nixon administration is deliberately trying to harass and intimidate the press.

The latest version came this week from a Senator who shall remain nameless here because what he wants most is his name in the papers.

Here are a couple of his quotes, however, offered because they are so typical of the continuing campaign:

"What we are witnessing is an incredible paradox in which the administration seeks to silence its critics in the media while exploiting the use of the media for its own message to an unprecedented degree."

And:

"The Nixon administration has . . . created a climate of fear, designed to intimidate the media. And when the political leaders of our nation set themselves up as judge and jury, freedom of the press is in danger."

If you play those remarks back, slowly, your sense organs may detect two things. One is the taste of sour grapes. The other is the ripe aroma of fresh manure.

Since when, in the first instance, has any administration in living memory—and probably before that—not tried to put its best foot forward? Where is the "incredible paradox" in accentuating the positive while muting the negative?

In the second instance, if any segment of the press has been intimidated by the Nixon-Agnew-Mitchell cabal so damned by the liberals we—for one—haven't seen any terror-stricken examples. Exactly who is running scared? Exactly how is press freedom being threatened?

The answers are pretty obvious. It is the previously unchallenged, all-wise pooh-bahs who are running scared for a change. They are getting sassed back and for some reason they think it is only they who have the right to challenge and criticize.

In a word, they can dish it out—but they can't take it. Put another way, if it were actually possible to intimidate our press and restrict its freedom of expression to one viewpoint—guess who would be trying to do it.

The Dallas Morning News

Dallas, Tex., October 8, 1970

NEARLY A YEAR ago Vice-President Spiro Agnew blasted the national press with both barrels. The fire was quickly returned by his targets, some of whom accused him of trying to destroy freedom of the press, dissent and progress.

But since then, many members of the press have conceded that Agnew pointed out some real flaws, and there have been noticeable efforts to correct these flaws. Dwight Sargent, former editorial editor of the New York Herald Tribune, is one of those who have publicly acknowledged Agnew's criticism as a help, rather than a hindrance to the American press.

Sargent, who now heads Harvard's Nieman Fellowship program, said in a press conference at SMU Tuesday that newspapers have improved their coverage in areas that drew criticism from Agnew. We agree.

THE VICE-PRESIDENT had two main criticisms of the press that clearly touched a nerve:

He accused the press, particularly the national media, of mixing news reporting and editorial opinion together, often presenting opinion in such a way that the public was led to believe that it was objective fact.

He declared that many of the top news agencies were virtually ignoring the interests and activities of the vast majority of their national audience.

These were serious charges. And if the first reactions from the press were defensive, it quickly became obvious to even the most indignant Fourth Estate types that millions of Americans shared Agnew's views.

Few of those criticized by Agnew have conceded the validity of his criticism by their words. But by their actions they have indicated that they got the message. And that has been good for the press and the public.

In recent months there has been an encouraging trend toward separation of news reporting and editorial opinion, with each being clearly identified. This has benefited both. News coverage has become more objective. Opinion and analysis, presented as such, has become a more useful contribution to national debate of the issues.

ANOTHER encouraging trend is the increased coverage by the national press of middle America and its activities. Though the causes and concerns of the upper-middle-class liberal continue to get much attention, there is also a new interest in the vast majority of citizens who are not radical, revolutionary or riotous. The result is better balance in coverage of the national scene and a better sense of perspective.

We believe that the American press is doing a better job. And in our opinion many of the improvements have resulted because Agnew had the courage to criticize and because many members of the press had the good sense to listen to the criticism and act on those complaints that proved to be valid.

BOSTON HERALD TRAVELER

Boston, Mass., March 20, 1971

No doubt about it: Vice President Spiro Agnew certainly lives up to his billings. His address Thursday night at the Middlesex Republican dinner was entertaining, provocative and controversial. And he proved once again that wherever he goes the crowds will follow—both in protest and (even here in Boston) ardent admiration.

His address at the GOP dinner and his press conferences yesterday morning were devoted almost entirely to criticism of national news media policies and practices, with special emphasis on several network TV documentaries.

Some of Mr. Agnew's complaints are valid, and it is incumbent upon those against whom he has leveled serious charges to answer them adequately. The media is no more immune from criticism than Mr. Agnew, and it is surely no surprise that a man who has been on the receiving end so often has learned to dish it out.

The Vice President, however, might have made a better case than he did against one of his specific targets, the recent CBS documentary, "The Selling of the Pentagon." He scored some points by accusing the network of engaging in the same kind of deception and propaganda, in earlier documentaries, that it says the Defense Department has employed.

But the main thesis of the program was that the Pentagon has been spending a lot of the taxpayer's money, via public relations, to convince him that it is doing a good job. So what else is new?

And what government agency hasn't been doing the same thing for decades?

Mr. Agnew might have asked why a similar documentary wasn't made five, ten or twenty years ago, or when we could expect to have one called "The Selling of HEW" (or the Agriculture Department or the Senate Foreign Relations Committee). He might have inquired whether the sudden interest in the subject, perhaps, stems from biases toward the present occupant of the White House.

Whatever one thinks of the Vice President's blunt and controversial remarks, however, they were not as outrageous as some of the things being said at the meeting, one flight upstairs, which the Ripon Society sponsored as an "alternative" to the Agnew affair.

The Ripon's main speaker, Rep. Paul McCloskey of California, said among other things that crimes committed by the U.S. in Vietnam are "identical" to those for which Nazi Germany was punished at Nuremberg. He also announced that if President Nixon doesn't stop our "immoral" war, he will run against him in the presidential primaries next year.

If one can pose a rational question to those who like to compare this country with Nazi Germany, we would ask Rep. McCloskey and his friends only to imagine what would have happened to him if he had been a member of the Reichstag in 1941, and raised his voice against the immorality of Axis war crimes, threatening to run against Hitler for fuehrer if they weren't stopped.

The Boston Globe

Boston, Mass., March 20, 1971

Vice President Spiro T. Agnew's first speech in Massachusetts in the 26 months he has held national office may not have been, as he had described it, "perhaps the most important I will deliver in my term as Vice President." But it was important, nonetheless.

For one thing, it added to the dialogue, and dialogue is always healthy in a sense, even when one side thinks the other side doesn't know what it is talking about. The point is not to get angry, but to try to be as friendly as possible and keep the dialogue going, even if it is one-sided and at times hard to hear what with the howls of the police dogs outside the hall.

In a way it's much the same on this newspaper, where we all make mistakes too. With Mr. Agnew on the right of us, David Deitch is on the left of us on the opposite page. He says "nobody really believes" in objectivity in news reporting. Well, we do believe in it, but an editorial

or column is somewhat different. So back to the Vice President.

It should be said at the outset that Mr. Agnew scored some points in his attack on the Columbia Broadcasting System, as when he cited a Federal Communications Commission report to show that a baby, described in a 1968 documentary on hunger as dying of starvation, actually died of other causes.

But CBS president Frank Stanton says that Mr. Agnew omitted to mention that the FCC found there was no wrong-doing by CBS News. We frankly don't know who is right. As for another documentary attacked by Mr. Agnew involving an aborted invasion of Haiti, it seems to us irrelevant because it was never broadcast.

Both of these points, however, were used by the Vice President to get at his main target of the evening, the recent documentary entitled "The Selling of the Pentagon." If Mr. Agnew has done nothing else, he has succeeded admirably in drawing attention to the fact that it will be repeated on the CBS network at 10 p.m. next Tuesday. No

highly paid publicist could have done more for it. We think people who missed it last Feb. 23 ought to see it and judge for themselves.

"The Selling of the Pentagon" describes how the Defense Department has been spending at least $30 million a year in propagandizing war and the instruments of war. The Globe praised it editorially Feb. 25. Mr. Agnew apparently sees the chief villain of his alleged conspiracy as an executive producer or a script involved in the documentaries, but we have another idea of where to look for the culprit.

The Vice President clued us in at his press conference Friday morning when, after charging there had been "quite a bit of cut and paste done," he was asked if he could cite any specific instance of it in the Pentagon documenary. "I could but I'm not going to," he said, but then he changed his mind.

Mr. Agnew said the documentary had a colonel saying that if South Vietnam went Communist, Laos would go Communist, too, whereas

these weren't the colonel's words, for he was quoting the Laotian Prime Minister, Souvanna Phouma. Right there we had a thought that here was our old friend the Domino Theory again, and we remembered the author of it—President Eisenhower, back when President Nixon had Mr. Agnew's job. And it struck us that it didn't matter much who said it, the colonel or Souvanna Phouma or Mr. Eisenhower—they all believed it, didn't they?

And then, in checking back, we found that President Eisenhower, who ought to have known all about the Pentagon if anyone ever did, as far back as 1968 had criticized the "defense dollars spent in publicity and influence campaigns in which each service claims superiority over the others and strives for increased appropriations or other congressional favors."

Right there, we think, is Mr. Agnew's real culprit for "The Selling of the Pentagon," and we are sure the John Birch Society will agree that Mr. Agnew ought to go right after him.

The Providence Journal

Providence, R. I., March 24, 1971

Vice President Spiro T. Agnew and Dr. Frank Stanton, president of the Columbia Broadcasting System have been flailing away at each other about the validity of a CBS documentary, *The Selling of the Pentagon*. It's too bad both men have failed to address themselves to the issue with the kind of dedicated attention to the record shown by a Washington magazine editor.

Mr. Agnew criticized the documentary and CBS techniques in the past in the production and editing of the company's documentaries. In a speech in Boston, shortly after the first showing of the Pentagon documentary Feb. 23, Mr. Agnew did offer a few bits and pieces from the record to sustain his argument that CBS distorted reality to make its points.

For his part. Dr. Stanton upheld the validity of the documentary, and it was shown for the second time last night over many CBS stations with added film and talk from critics of the film. But neither Mr. Agnew nor Mr. Stanton so far has approached the issues as did Claude Witze, senior editor of the magazine, *Air Force and Space Digest*.

It may be argued by defenders of CBS that Mr. Witze is part of that military-industrial complex which would be sure to rush to the defense of the Pentagon—in this instance for spending large sums to enlist public support through extensive and expensive public relations activities. But Mr. Witze did not speak or write from a position of special interest.

The Washington editor, a veteran newspaperman who once worked for the *Journal-Bulletin*, simply addressed himself to the record as presented by the film. Then, exercising the function of a good reporter, he checked out what the documentary of-fered and analyzed the way in which the material had been assembled for public presentation.

Mr. Witze did not challenge the right of CBS to look into the Pentagon's public relations activities. But he did challenge the production and editing techniques which went into the making of *The Selling of the Pentagon*—and his findings make grim and shocking reading, findings which CBS so far has not challenged in public. His review disclosed the way in which segments of a presentation by a colonel had been clipped and reassembled, as he says specifically, "to make a presentation sound inept, stupid, wrong, vicious, . . ." Mr. Witze even challenges minor statements of purported fact.

There is no doubt that CBS found a target of commanding interest in the Pentagon's public relations work. But if its employes distorted reality to make a sharper case, as Mr. Witze has charged without challenge, then CBS did more to cast a shadow on its own credibility as a producer of documentaries than did Mr. Agnew.

Mr. Witze put his own feelings succinctly and in a way many TV viewers will adopt. Speaking of the murder of Lee Harvey Oswald "on camera," Mr. Witze said, "Yet, if I saw it today, I would demand confirmation that the event took place at all and that what we saw on the tube was not a clever compilation of film clips, snipped from a wide variety of source material and glued together to make a visual product that could be marketed to some huckster of toothpaste or gasoline and then turn out to be a winner of the Peabody Award."

The nation has heard from Dr. Stanton on Mr. Agnew. How about a word from the doctor now on Mr. Witze?

The Standard-Times

New Bedford, Mass., March 23, 1971

It is difficult to evaluate Vice President Agnew's charge that the Columbia Broadcasting System has been guilty of the same distortion and control of information of which it accused the Pentagon in a recent television documentary.

The difficulty arises because, having accused CBS of manufacturing news in its report, "Selling of the Pentagon," Mr. Agnew failed to cite a single example of alleged misrepresentation of fact or inaccuracy in the program. Instead, he chose examples of alleged inaccuracy or bias from two other TV documentaries, one of which was never broadcast.

In his Boston speech, Mr. Agnew said the CBS program on the Pentagon accused the latter of "a propaganda barrage . . . " It may be, as Air Force magazine maintained, that the CBS report is "the kind of journalistic dishonesty that a reputable newspaper would not tolerate." Yet we submit there is a case to be made for the charge that the Pentagon engages in preparing and distributing propaganda.

Back in the fall of 1968, the Department of the Army circulated two "classified" memoranda among high-ranking officers and civilians. Together, the papers spelled out a coordinated high-pressure public relations campaign aimed at selling the Sentinel anti-ballistic missile to the American people.

The plans fell into the hands of newspapermen and were withdrawn. But they served to reveal the scope of the Pentagon's information machine. The Defense Department has been spending some $30 million a year burnishing its image; although it is lowering its profile somewhat by seeking only $24.2 million for fiscal 1972, it is reasonable to assume the public affairs program will continue almost unchanged.

Nor is this something new. When President Truman set an arbitrary ceiling of $15 billion on the fiscal 1950 defense budget, the armed services were locked in a battle to sell Congress, the president and the public on the merits of their respective roles in the postwar military establishment.

Congressional Quarterly, quoting a 20th-Century Fund report, stated, "For most of the Truman and Eisenhower years, the services used their public relations programs to deflate the claims of other services about competing weapons systems, while inflating the value of their own projects. The biggest battle occurred over the Air Force's request for the B-36 bomber at the expense of the Navy's supercarriers. One Pentagon reporter recalls briefly leaving his chair in a restaurant. When he returned to it, he found detailed plans showing how bombers could neutralize and destroy the Navy's carriers."

In 1958, President Eisenhower decried the "defense dollars spent in publicity and influence campaigns in which each service claims superiority over the other and strives for increased appropriations or other congressional favors."

Neither Mr. Eisenhower's denunciation nor Mr. Agnew's denial seem likely to change much of anything. With funds for defense spending likely to grow tighter as the Vietnam war winds down, we may expect a new publicity battle among the services for a larger share.

Whether this type of activity is called "a propaganda barrage" or, in Mr. Eisenhower's words, "publicity and influence campaigns," doesn't matter very much to the glum taxpayer who has to finance it

THE ANN ARBOR NEWS
Ann Arbor, Mich., March 22, 1971

VICE PRESIDENT Spiro Agnew has criticized the Columbia Broadcasting System for its recent documentary, "The Selling of the Pentagon," and charges CBS with presenting misinformation in two previous documentaries.

We didn't see "The Selling of the Pentagon" so can't comment on it or on the validity of Mr. Agnew's criticism. We would have been much more sympathetic to his complaint, however, if he had eliminated o n e sentence—the one that expressed his "grave doubts" about how much of his comments would be carried by the national news media.

The vice president should never complain about the attention he and his statements get in the communications media, and the more critical they are of the media the more space—if not air time—they seem to get. Undoubtedly the "press" has been more sensitive than it should be in respect to criticism, but we have not observed a tendency to suppress or bury it.

Mr. Agnew's "grave doubts" statement is like the "P.S." frequently found on newspapers' letters to the editor to the effect that "I know you won't print this." It seldom plays any part in the decision as to whether the letter should be used.

Newsday
Long Island, N.Y., March 24, 1971

Vice President Agnew continues to take a strong interest in how the various news media are doing their job. And although his complaints about such excellent TV projects as CBS' "The Selling of the Pentagon" sound like purely defensive carping, there are other statements which deserve considered attention.

For example, Mr. Agnew says that the adversary relationship between the press and government is a fine thing. The press *ought* to be inspecting the affairs of government with as much zealousness as, say, various government spies these days inspect the affairs of liberal senators. If Mr. Agnew is saying that reporters should try to elicit significant information, even at the risk of embarrassing the President with probing questions, he's right. And this is all to the health of the press-government relationship.

On the other hand, the vice president sees the press as overly defensive and says the media have not learned to take criticism. The vice president has a point here, too. Newspapers, TV, magazines are certainly not infallible and must remain open to criticism and admission of error.

In some cities, Chicago, most notably, some journalists have taken to publishing their own criticisms of the newspapers they work for. Most recently, the newsmen at two papers have opposed their papers' endorsement of Mayor Daley.

"The national media are big boys now and they're big enough to stand a little criticism," the vice president says. And we agree. Then he goes on to blast CBS for its probe of the Pentagon. But clearly, the U.S. government and its vice president are also big boys now. They ought to be able to stand a lot of criticism.

THE ARIZONA REPUBLIC
Phoenix, Ariz., March 22, 1971

There is no doubt that the Pentagon is heavily involved in public relations — too heavily involved, as we have pointed out in numerous editorials. In our opinion, the p.r. budget of the Pentagon could and should be heavily slashed.

But it is one thing to object to Pentagon propaganda and another thing to engage in propaganda and distortion in a "documentary" designed to expose Pentagon public relations activities. Yet that is what Vice President Spiro Agnew has charged CBS with doing. And, as the article elsewhere on this page makes clear, that is precisely what the network did.

CBS officials say they stand behind their documentaries. Pray, what else can they say? But the fact remains that almost every documentary that has appeared on that network, that touches upon political or ideological issues, is at best unbalanced, at worst distorted.

That is frequently true of ABC and NBC also. But as Sen. Robert Dole, chairman of the Republican National Committee, pointed out yesterday, CBS is the worst offender.

Network documentaries are not usually as crude as the hatchet job done on the Pentagon, where scenes were spliced, edited, and chopped beyond recognition in order to make the worst possible case against the "military establishment."

Most often the documentaries are simply unbalanced: They set out to present a liberal point of view, and film clips and interviews are carefully selected and arranged so that viewers are left with the desired impression.

This sort of selectivity is totally indefensible in a medium that is licensed by the federal government in the public interest. For while network officials are convinced that heavy doses of liberalism are in the public interest, liberalism is in fact a minority viewpoint in the United States. Yet it is presented on network radio and TV as though it were the only viewpoint — or, after the networks get through with non-liberals, as the only viewpoint that intelligent, respectable people could possibly entertain.

Network television has a great deal to answer for, particularly that day after day it has sought out the kooks, extremists, zanies, and dissenters and presented them — in news programs, talk shows, panel discussions — to the exclusion of voices of moderation. Not content with allowing itself to be used by extremists who manipulate it for their own purposes, TV has at times even instigated and paid for demonstrations when none were immediately available.

CBS itself, whose commentators waxed indignant that the Defense Department did not disclose that a piece of pipeline it displayed at a press conference had been brought back from an earlier, unannounced raid into Laos, financed an invasion of Haiti — an action that violates every journalistic ethic, and violates national and international law.

The problem is that the networks are staffed exclusively with liberals, from such moderate liberals as Mike Wallace to such New Left-types as Alexander Kendrick. Despite all the talk about "professional judgment," given that sort of atmosphere it is no wonder that liberal judgments dominate the airwaves.

The networks have shown themselves incapable of or unwilling to abide by the doctrines of elementary fairness. Perhaps it is time that the Federal Communications Commission, whose chairman Dean Burch knows intimately how unfair the networks are (he was chairman of the GOP National Committee in 1964), forced them to open their closed shop to other than liberal viewpoints.

The New York Times

New York, N.Y., March 25, 1971

The bill of irrelevancies invoked by Vice President Agnew and Defense Secretary Laird against the Columbia Broadcasting System's documentary, "The Selling of the Pentagon," missed the central issue. It is not the Defense Department's flamboyant tactics in advertising its skills with arms and men. It is not the question of profligate spending of taxpayers' money on publicity side-shows and expensive lobbying for the favors of American business leaders. It is not even the repulsive display of "dirty fighting" brutality before audiences including children.

The heart of the matter is the flagrant violation of traditional rules—unmistakably spelled out in Defense Department regulations—which prohibit the military from engaging in political propaganda activities.

Such activities, regardless of their style and substance, run counter to the principle of democratic government. When they embrace the crude primitivism of the films produced by or for the military and exhibited before military and civilian audiences alike, these exhibitions are at once an insult to the nation's intelligence and an appalling breach of faith.

Motion pictures such as "Red Nightmare," which purports to "describe" the Communist take-over of an American town, or "Road to the Wall," a piece of political science-fiction that shows the enemy intent on conquering not only the world but the universe, are a throwback to the hysteria of the Cold War era. They resemble in technique the worst output of totalitarian propaganda.

Even if such appeals to fear and hatred were not repulsive in themselves—indeed, even if their message were more subtle and intelligent—they would still clash head-on with the vital doctrine of a non-political military. This, too, is why it is intolerable for public relations colonels and other officers on active duty to tour the country—as the C.B.S. documentary showed—to tell the American people what policies they ought to support or oppose in Indochina or anywhere, abroad or at home.

When either the armed forces, by pressure or propaganda, or the military intelligence establishment, by secret intrusion into policy-making, arrogate to themselves an activist role in the design of national or international strategy, free government is undermined. This is the issue an American Vice President and Defense Secretary ought to understand. It is at the core of civilian control of the military and of government by an elected leadership, accountable to the people.

BUFFALO EVENING NEWS

Buffalo, N.Y., March 20, 1971

Vice President Agnew's blast at the CBS television network for its recent documentary, "The Selling of the Pentagon," creates a simplistic distraction and avoids what should be his and the public's overriding concern.

Long before the broadcasting of the controversial documentary in late February, it was perfectly obvious that the Pentagon spent a great deal of time and money selling itself to the American public. The vital question is whether all or some of these activities are legitimate.

Unfortunately, the Vice President didn't address himself to that. Without citing any inaccuracies in the program, he simply branded it a "subtle but vicious broadside against the nation's defense establishment." This is pretty shabby argumentation. Unquestionably the CBS documentary had a point of view — that the Pentagon was flooding the public with blatant propaganda — and this, far from being hidden, was explicitly stated.

It's true that some of the cited examples seemed venial sins at worst, but the program scored heavily with other examples: The group of high-level military brass roving the country publicly pushing particular foreign policy views; the admission by a former officer that he had helped mislead a CBS news crew some time ago about actual conditions in Vietnam. Like George Romney, CBS was saying that in this instance its own crew got brainwashed. Thus, grave questions were raised about the candor and suitability of Pentagon salesmanship.

What worries us most about the Vice President here is that he apparently prefers to chide a news organization for raising questions than to hunt for the answers or press for corrections at the Pentagon. He's looking, it seems to us, in the wrong direction.

ST. LOUIS POST-DISPATCH

St. Louis, Mo., March 25, 1971

In resuming his attack on the news media, this time narrow-beamed at Columbia Broadcasting System, Vice President Agnew may or may not have the White House behind him. There is no question that he spoke for President Nixon when he conducted the same vendetta for purposes of the 1970 campaign. But that campaign did not produce notably positive results for the Administration, and Mr. Nixon became a revolutionary, or at least set out to get himself a new "image," shortly afterwards. Mr. Agnew, to the contrary, seems to think that the old Agnew is still good enough for him.

Our theory is that the Vice President senses the possibility of being dropped from the ticket and has launched his own personal campaign to stake out a position of strength with his conservative constituency that will make Mr. Nixon think twice before browsing in other pastures.

For this purpose, Mr. Agnew figures the 1970 snake oil is as good as any for 1972. We can hardly wait to see how it all comes out.

In the meantime CBS and other news media would do well to comprehend the political motives of the performance and to take a bit of Mr. Agnew's own advice by not getting uptight about it. The television networks have nothing to apologize for when they perform the functions of an independent press which declines to regard itself as an agency of the Government.

The significant point about the CBS program "The Selling of the Pentagon," which gave Mr. Agnew the pretext for his latest attack, is the change it may register in television's understanding of its own role as a news medium. Not many years ago, as the program frankly confessed, the networks and their star commentators took it for granted that TV's role was to dispense Government propaganda, especially cold war and military propaganda, in cozy co-operation with the authorities in Washington.

"The Selling of the Pentagon" marks, we hope, a belated discovery that TV news, like the written press, has a duty to express a non-official point of view. When the networks do so, they are bound to incur official displeasure, but instead of bleeding over this they should regard it as a merit badge for duty done.

The Vice President could make so few sustainable criticisms of the Pentagon program that he kept changing the subject to other programs not pertinent to the question of whether or not the armed forces operate an enormous propaganda machine designed to merchandise their views on foreign policy and the military budget. The answer is obvious: of course they do, and CBS performed a valuable public service by saying so with such effectiveness.

DESERET NEWS

Salt Lake City, Utah, March 25, 1971

It's one thing to inform the public — but quite another to try to propagandize it.

That is why the size of the Pentagon's public relations staff and budget is causing concern today in America. This week's second broadcast of the controversial Columbia Broadcasting System's television documentary, "The Selling of the Pentagon," helped to sharpen that concern.

Military public relations is nothing new, of course. In 1890, Admiral Alfred Mahan turned his books on seapower to the task of drumming up support for a modernized American Navy. And General Billy Mitchell used magazine articles as well as bombing demonstrations to show what bombers could do against ships.

But that was a far cry from today's $30 million Madison Avenue approach to public relations in the armed forces. Although the Pentagon's request for fiscal 1972 is only a "modest" $24.2 million, its public affairs program will continue almost unchanged.

The Navy, for example, spends $9.9 million to maintain a public relations staff of 1,086 full-time and 1,600 part-time staffers. The Air Force and Army staffs are somewhat more modest.

At least some of this public relations power is devoted to inter-service squabbling — like the post-World War II battle when the Air Force tried to scuttle the Navy's supercarriers in favor of the B-36 bomber.

More recently, the Army had to withdraw plans for a high-pressure public relations campaign aimed at selling the Sentinel anti-ballistic missile to the American people after the plans fell into the hands of newsmen in the fall of 1968.

Granted, the armed services and the Pentagon need to keep the public informed in such vital matters as defense. But must it be hard-sell of the Pentagon line?

Los Angeles Times

Los Angeles, Calif., March 30, 1971

Vice President Agnew has a human complaint that we all share to a greater extent than he may suspect. The views of the other fellow hardly ever reflect the world as it really is—as we know it is.

The Vice President finds this situation distressing, especially in relation to the news media and government. He has spoken to newspapers about upgrading their performance, and of late he has been concerned with television news. His concern with the news as a government official is in an old tradition that dates from George Washington to the present.

In one of his latest go-rounds, Agnew said "the national news media seem to be able to cloak themselves in a special immunity to criticism," which he then penetrated with ease. He charged that CBS documentaries, "The Selling of the Pentagon" and "Hunger in America" contained distortions. The Vice President also criticized "Project Nassau," a CBS documentary about Haiti that was canceled before it appeared.

Pressing his case, Agnew said it is "timely and in the public interest" to note that personnel connected with "Project Nassau" and "Hunger in America" worked on the Pentagon film. The innuendo against the integrity of the network's news division was plain; the Vice President was unwilling to say specifically what he had in mind, but his purpose was clear: he wanted to stir up vague public suspicion against the network.

The media do not have, nor should they have, any immunity from criticism, and it is nonsense for anyone to claim otherwise. But the media, while pretending no immunity from criticism, will defend their own right to criticize, and, more importantly, the public's right to know.

As long as the Vice President wants to frame the subject in terms of "distortion" and "propaganda," we offer this suggestion: Feed into a computer all the news dispatches from Vietnam and all the government statements on the war and compare them for accuracy. This project, to borrow a phrase from Agnew, would surely be in the public interest.

The Charlotte Observer

Charlotte, N.C., March 25, 1971

A re-run Tuesday night of the CBS-TV documentary, "The Selling of the Pentagon," was an additional public service by the network.

Viewers who missed the first showing in February got to see for themselves what all the fuss was about. Among those taking CBS to task after that first show were Vice President Agnew, Defense Secretary Laird and Rep. Hebert, chairman of the House Armed Services Committee.

Tuesday night's time was devoted not only to the amply documented CBS contention that the Pentagon is engaged in an enormously expensive public relations program that makes a mockery of civilian control. It allowed, too, for opposition statements by Agnew, Laird and Hebert and a CBS response to those complaints.

Putting everything together, CBS won hands down. The factual data in the documentary spoke for itself, the objections by the program's principal critics were weak and the rebuttal by President Richard Salant of CBS News shot the complaints full of holes.

Furthermore, the documentary showed beyond a doubt that the most objectionable public relations practices by the Pentagon have been continued over a number of months in direct contradiction of a policy directive from President Nixon.

In response to the President's order that governmental agencies confine themselves to informational practices, rather than carrying out promotional propaganda campaigns in their own self-interest, the Pentagon has only cut back budgets. It has not stopped the activities complained of.

Arriving at an authoritative figure of how much the Pentagon is spending on public relations and propaganda annually is virtually impossible. The Pentagon's tentacles of promotion and sales effort go in so many different directions and involve so many different kinds of expense that the cost of its self-aggrandizement may never be known.

However, by lumping together such pervasive activities of the Pentagon as preparing press releases, making and distributing films, offering firepower demonstrations to civilians, staging weaponry shows all over the country on the land and in the air, recording radio tapes and TV shows, financing junkets, supplying public speakers, ad infinitum, CBS estimated that the annual cost may go as high as $190 million.

By comparison, the combined annual budgets of the three television networks' news operations amount to $146 million.

Most disappointing in this whole business is the "you're one too!" response of Agnew, Laird and Hebert. They have not spoken to the facts presented and the thesis projected by CBS News. They have chosen instead to impugn the network's motives and assault its character. "Dishonest!" says Agnew. "Unprofessional!" cries Laird. "Un-American!" says Hebert.

There may well be things wrong with CBS News. No news organization is perfect in its selection of, approach to or presentation of facts and opinion. But one thing that is not wrong with CBS News is its documentary, "The Selling of the Pentagon."

The thing that is wrong is that supposedly responsible public officials reacted by choosing to call the network's motives and honesty into question instead of speaking to the critically important features of its presentation.

If this attitude prevails today in Washington, the problem will increase in intensity, not diminish.

The Virginian-Pilot

Norfolk, Va., March 25, 1971

The controversial documentary "The Selling of the Pentagon" was rebroadcast by CBS Tuesday night. The program was followed by criticism from Vice President Agnew, Secretary of Defense Laird, and Representative F. Edward Hebert (D-La.), chairman of the House Armed Services Committee, and then by the network's rebuttal of the charges the critics had made.

"We are proud of 'The Selling of the Pentagon,' and CBS News stands behind it," Richard S. Salant, the president of CBS News, s u m m e d up. "We are confident that when passions die down, it will be recognized as a vital contribution to the people's right to know."

As the program's viewers were able to see for themselves on Tuesday, the outcry from the Pentagon is prompted by the effectiveness and impact of the program. The truth hurts sometimes, and the truth is that the Pentagon spends a lot of money on propaganda, pure and simple. Anyone who has dealt with the military is aware of that. To be sure, a lot of the activity of the flacks for the military is innocent and necessary; there. is also a lot that is unnecessary. It ranges from junkets and lobbying to the hard line, hard-sell spiels of the "anti-communist" evangelists the Pentagon puts on the road. (That is one of the areas where the documentary hit the hardest.) The criticisms of Messrs. Agnew & Co. are mostly quibbles and ignore the main point, which is that Defense Department does indeed spend a lot of money—millions and millions—to propagandize the American people.

As to the criticism from Second District Representative G. William Whitehurst, who parroted the Administration l i n e and then was forced to admit that he hadn't even watched the program, it is best to be charitable. Maybe Dr. Whitehurst will look before he leaps next time.

St. Louis Globe-Democrat

St. Louis, Mo., March 26, 1971

CBS's controversial television program on the Pentagon, rerun in St. Louis this week, offered food for thought, but no thought.

It was a sledgehammer blow designed to discredit the forces that protect America while simultaneously seeking to improve the image of critics who spend their waking hours finding sinister motives behind nearly all Defense Department actions.

This network overkill was demonstrated not only by the filmed tapes of Defense Department promotional material, but also by the narration provided by one of the nation's leading newscasters.

His account was marked by innuendo, antagonistic remarks in the midst of interviews with Pentagon spokesmen, and an openly slanted view of almost everything associated with our defense posture.

What was most significant was the conclusion provided by CBS President Richard Salant. Responding to criticisms of the program by such prominent leaders as Vice President Spiro T. Agnew, Defense Secretary Melvin R. Laird and U.S. Rep. Edward Hebert, Salant made the brunt of his defense a sweeping statement that all of the charges could be refuted.

Yet his answers to most of the specific accusations were evasive.

And, in the end, if it is true that the Pentagon is selling itself and the concept of a strong America, is that a vice? Was Congressman Hebert not correct when he asked: "What do you want them to sell—Communism?"

The Evening Bulletin

Philadelphia, Pa., March 26, 1971

A hot debate is raging in some quarters about the vast armed services' "information" program. It is unnecessary to try to sit in judgment on every aspect of that program to conclude that, in some aspects at least, the military has gotten out of line and perhaps out of hand.

The public has a right to know how the American military establishment works. The Pentagon has a need, even a duty, to so inform it.

But it is inappropriate for the military to use taxpayers' money to propagandize the public on its point of view on ideology and foreign affairs.

And if the viewpoint being "sold" by the military is at variance with the tone of existing national policy — such as peddling a cold war line when the Government is putting stress on negotiating agreements with our adversaries — then this activity is damaging to our political process.

It is to the President, the State Department and the Congress that the public should look to define official attitudes toward the Communist or any other foreign threat to national interests. It is the military's job simply to carry out whatever decisions are made by representatives of the people, not to shape public attitudes.

President Nixon has ordered severe cutbacks, not only in the Pentagon, but in other departments, "in unnecessary information activities, ones which he felt didn't serve a useful public purpose." So says Herbert G. Klein, White House director of communications.

Either the Pentagon is not paying enough attention to the Commander in Chief or there needs to be a more critical study of what constitutes a legitimate public relations program.

THE LINCOLN STAR

Lincoln, Neb., March 25, 1971

The CBS Television news special "The Selling of the Pentagon" — repeated Tuesday following its initial viewing a month ago — brings back to the public eye a controversy left smoldering since the time that attacks on the integrity of the news media, a fashionable pastime of c o n s e r v a t i v e spokesmen, reached their apex over a year ago.

The renewed controversy adds really nothing substantial to either the argument based on the public's right to know or the contention that the public, through the media, is fed an intentionally slanted message.

As the CBS documentary tells it, the Pentagon, in addition to spewing out the flood of press releases normal to any bureaucracy, uses its gigantic public relations machine to glorify war and the arms race, foment jingoism and create a war psychosis among the American people. The Defense Department and its advocates counter that supporting evidence was melded together inaccurately to reach that conclusion; that statements and speeches and events that might stand alone as fact were interwoven to achieve an entirely different context.

The network says it can successfully dispute every claim of inaccuracy lodged against it and the Pentagon says it can document every charge it has. A reasonable observation could be that if the truthfulness and openness of the Pentagon communications apparatus could be doubted before, the Pentagon's defense of criticism could be doubted now. There is also the feeling that the network may have been highhanded in its use of the material at hand; thus the documentary loses some of its authenticity.

But there appears to be little doubt that the Defense Department spends an inordinate amount of money and manpower selling its message. It also is a test of experience that the Pentagon will tell the news media only what it wants to tell them, preventing even the disclosure of information that cannot be deemed essential to the national security. For pointing out that to the public, the network should not be criticized.

Detroit Free Press
Detroit, Mich., March 26, 1971

WE WON'T get embroiled in the argument over methods used in CBS television's documentary, "The Selling of the Pentagon." Both critics and defenders of the program have scored on some points and missed on others. All have had their say, and the public is now left to judge.

But two larger issues do beg for attention. First, the documentary's basic charge has not been successfully challenged, not even attacked in the main. CBS put words and pictures to what many people already knew: That the Pentagon's public information program is, in fact, a multi-million-dollar lobbying tool.

The expense is scandalous, even within the Pentagon's huge budget. And the money is being used to intrude on the formulation of foreign policy, to sway public attitudes on the role of the military, and to influence congressional votes on Pentagon appropriations. Bureaucrats have seized the reins of policy and set off on self-serving missions in widespread violation of their own rules, and in defiance of an explicit policy memorandum from the sitting President.

Headstrong bureaucracy is not new in Washington. But the Pentagon's offense is magnified by its massive spending power and by its blithe meddling in the most basic processes of government. The secretary of Defense, the President, the Congress if necessary, ought to insist that these activities stop.

And the President, for his part, also owes some thought to the administration attitude reflected in Vice President Agnew's behavior. This is the other issue shining in the CBS incident, albeit not for the first time. The administration's persistent antagonism toward its critics in network television is ever more clearly unhealthy.

Is the administration obliged to sit mute when it thinks it sees blatant error in criticism of its activities? Certainly not. However it does seem to us that the administration is obliged to acknowledge the full import of its aggressive complaints.

Vice President Agnew pretends that he is only exercising the rights of debate and rebuttal enjoyed by other citizens and the newsmen he challenges. And he pretends that his expressed ideas need carry no influence beyond what they can earn by their own worth.

But in truth television is not free to debate with him as, say, this newspaper is free to debate. The pronouncements of television are subject to regulation by the government for which Mr. Agnew speaks. In his speaking he has given the country not just several episodes of disagreement, but a drumbeat of accusation that network television, seemingly CBS in particular, pushes a steady diet of falsehood and propaganda.

If the administration believes that network officials are thus abusing their stewardship of the public airways, sworn duty would seem to call for action through established mechanisms, not broadsides on the after-dinner circuit. The administration's evident preference for the latter has persuaded many observers that it is less interested in the overall balance of television than in making the medium say certain things from time to time or qualify things already said.

Whatever the administration intends, there is only one clear message in its behavior. Television figures who cross the White House risk being savaged for the pleasure of political audiences—or subjected to telephone pressure from presidential aides, as in the recent case of ABC's Dick Cavett show, which had hosted several figures opposed to the SST project.

It is difficult to say what would be the perfect relationship in this communications age between government and a major, government-regulated organ of information. But this chronic fever of complaint, cajolery and backdoor pressure is not the blow for open debate that Mr. Agnew pretends, and is nothing the administration need be proud of.

The Dallas Morning News
Dallas, Tex., March 29, 1971

Vice-President Agnew and Rep. F. Edward Hebert, chairman of the House Armed Services Committee, were hopping mad after seeing CBS' first airing of its film, "The Selling of the Pentagon"—a documentary purporting to show how the military enhances its image.

Now the two men are madder than ever after having seen the film a second time. CBS did not comment on their first objections but it edited and added what they said to the film for the second showing.

Both men objected. Agnew said they wouldn't let him edit his own remarks but broadcast only the part of them that CBS wanted to show. Agnew called it a clever manipulation.

Both men had criticized the film as untruthful and as using material supplied for other purposes without asking permission.

Hebert out-Agnewed Agnew, claiming the big-lie technique was used by the network. He complained that a statement made by CBS president Richard S. Salant at the end of the second showing was clearly answered by remarks of his own that had been edited out and which, of course, the public never heard at that time.

Salant said that CBS can refute every charge against the film raised by Agnew, Hebert and Defense Secretary Melvin Laird.

There the matter stands, presumably for keeps. Since a vast audience saw the second showing after the tumult arose, the American people will probably be their own judges of the fairness of the film and the effectiveness of Agnew's and Hebert's rebuttals. The question for air journalism is, how informed will that judgment be?

THE DENVER POST
Denver, Colo., March 29, 1971

WHEN THE NIXON administration and the Defense Establishment have finished quarreling with CBS over the TV documentary, "The Selling of the Pentagon," we suspect that the following propositions will still stand:

● That the Pentagon is spending an excessive amount of the taxpayers' money to convince the taxpayers that the amount being spent on defense is justified and that the taxpayers ought to spend more.

● That the Pentagon is exerting an improper influence on American thinking by providing explosions, shooting, military stunts and demonstrations of adroit ways of killing people as a form of public entertainment.

● That Pentagon propagandists are taking public positions on American foreign policy that are beyond their scope and that are at odds with the position of the government.

Military men have a right to argue their point of view, it is worth emphasizing, but they ought not to do it at public expense. Public funds ought to be used to provide honest information, not propaganda for the Pentagon's position.

We believe the public relations budget of the Pentagon ought to be reduced substantially, that big military shows to entertain and impress civilians ought to be discontinued and that Pentagon spokesmen, on public speaking assignments paid for by the taxpayers, ought not to be pushing their particular views on American foreign policy.

This is an era of financial crisis in the public affairs of the nation.

At such a time, the idea of wasting funds on costly military circuses for business executives or for the public at large is hard to defend. CBS has performed an important public service by calling this matter to public attention.

The Washington Post
Times Herald

Washington, D.C., March 26, 1971

Mr. Agnew versus CBS versus the DOD

The serialized dispute between CBS News, the Pentagon, Congressman Hebert and Vice President Agnew now shows every sign of enjoying the longest airwave run since "One Man's Family." In the beginning, there was only the CBS filmed documentary, "The Selling of the Pentagon," which dealt with the public relations apparatus of the Department of Defense and some highly questionable uses to which it has been put. Since then there have been reruns, rebuttals and rebuttals of rebuttals, and no one can think the dispute is ended yet.

Since threading one's way through the charges is difficult business at best, one point—and a large one—seems worth making at the outset. It is that the documentary film itself constituted a highly valuable and informative exposition of a subject about which the American people should know more—not less.

ↄ⅃ↄ

That some of the criticism of the documentary—in terms of production techniques and occasional inaccuracies—is valid, seems evident to us. It also seems evident that Vice President Agnew, as is his custom, has once again managed to obfuscate and all but wreck that part of the case against CBS that was (and is) based on serious and legitimate questions. In a Boston address last week, the Vice President made his case to rest chiefly on the fact that the writer of one previous CBS documentary and the executive producer of another had each been involved in the same capacity in the production of this one. And each of those two documentaries, Mr. Agnew argued at some length, had had more than an innocent share of subterfuges, falsehoods and/or intentional deceptions behind it. However, even where he was able to raise valid objections to aspects of each production, he so overstated and slanted his case as to render it pointless.

ↄ⅃ↄ

As an example of Mr. Agnew's own production techniques, we will offer you some of his comments in relation to one of the offending documentaries, "Hunger in America." It was the subject of an investigation by the Federal Communications Commission, and Mr. Agnew, quoting from the FCC's report, made much of evidence that had been submitted to the FCC such as that "the CBS crew 'requested that the doors of the commodity distribution office be closed to allow a line of people to form.'" However, Mr. Agnew gave his Boston audience not the merest hint that this and other evidence of wrongdoing had been dismissed by the FCC in the same document. Thus, the FCC on the hoked-up commodity line:

"In view of the statements of the Welfare Department, the fact that CBS shot no film of, and the program gave no indication of, an effort to show a long line of welfare recipients, and the description of the floor plan and modus operandi of the welfare center (room for four persons in a line from the entrance to the food counter), we find no warrant for concluding that CBS sought to slant its news depiction, as charged in this respect."

In our judgment, all this establishes the Vice President as something of an expert on questionable editing; but it does little for his credentials as a critic of the practice. And it is on the subject of editing that we believe CBS may be most vulnerable. That the line between reporting and staging events in this kind of television program is a fine one and also one that is all too easily crossed is a proposition with which we tend to agree. And we think this line in fact is crossed when taped interviews are edited in such a way as to alter the actual response of those of whom questions are asked. Such was the case, for example, in the responses—as they were given and as they appeared—of Assistant Secretary of Defense Daniel Z. Henkin.

Now there are several things to be said about this practice. One is that it is apparently common and customary television procedure to foreshorten and rearrange interviews, to reduce a prolonged interview to a few minutes TV time, and to take considerable liberties with such an interview in terms of both completeness and sequence. And among those who have a hand in these televised documentaries, the procedure is explained as both a necessity of production and a boon to the subject who—it is alleged—generally benefits from the editing in terms of the clarity and relevance of his response.

ↄ⅃ↄ

In our estimation, none of this—the commonness of the practice, the exigencies of production, the effort to "improve upon" a given response—will do to make the practice acceptable or one that anybody should be comfortable with. People who work in the nonelectronic news business know how readily they themselves may distort an event or a remark merely by focusing cameras on the one or failing to provide sufficient context for the other. These dangers are of course multiplied in the production of a televised documentary. The massive presence and the mechanical requirements of TV filming and taping equipment necessarily introduce an element of distortion, and the need to boil down material to make it suitable in terms of time and format introduce the constant danger of another kind of distortion.

Given these built-in problems, the TV producers, it seems to us, should go out of their way to preserve intact and in sequence the response of those they interview, or, at the very least, indicate that something in the sequence has been dropped and/or give the subject of the interview an opportunity to see and approve his revised or altered remarks. To do otherwise does in fact result in a material distortion of the record, especially when the viewer is under the impression that what he is watching is what actually and exactly occurred. It seems a great pity and a waste to let a documentary on such an important subject as that with which "The Selling of the Pentagon" dealt be undermined in terms of credibility and public confidence by these editing techniques—innocent or not.

CBS Replies to Editorial on Pentagon Documentary

March 30, 1971

This letter is in response to your editorial of March 26, in which you start by calling the CBS News documentary, "The Selling of the Pentagon," a "highly valuable and informative exposition of a subject about which the American people should know more," and then proceed to examine in some detail the specific editing of that film and general practices of television news editing technique.

The editorial was obviously written by one who has long labored on the editorial page —and not on the news pages.

You conclude that in some measure (not specified) public confidence and credibility are undermined by our editing techniques "innocent or not."

The question of how a news or documentary broadcast is edited is at least as important as you obviously consider it. It is precisely as important as, and possibly no more complicated than, questions pertaining to editing in the print medium (newspapers and news magazines)—the process by which any journalist rejects or accepts, selects and omits, and almost always compresses material available to him. You do not question the right, indeed the professional obligation of your reporters to do this, nor of your editors to continue the process once the reporter has done his job, nor indeed, of your senior editors to impose their professional judgment upon this same piece of work when or if it comes to them.

But you question not only our right to do the same thing, but also the methods by which we edit, and even our motives ("innocent or not"). You do not, in other words, grant us the right to do precisely what you do—and must do if you are journalists as distinguished from transmission belts.

Why?

The key to why you feel this way is spelled out in your editorial: "People who work in the nonelectronic news business know how readily they themselves may distort an event or a remark . . . these dangers are of course multiplied in the production of a televised documentary."

You are saying that good reporting—fair reporting—is a difficult business, with many pitfalls along the way, that television reporting is a more difficult business with more pitfalls. Fair enough.

Then you go on to suggest, indeed recommend, that our rules should be different than your rules, that sound journalistic ethics and the First Amendment are somehow divisible between rights granted to journalists whose work comes out in ink and somewhat lesser rights for journalists whose work comes out electronically. You say we should go out of our way to "preserve intact and in sequence" the response of those we interview. We both "go out of our way" to be fair and accurate, but we both have limitations of space, and we both seek clarity. Except in verbatim transcripts, neither medium preserves intact or in sequence everything it presents. You say at the very least we should indicate that something in the interview has been dropped. If we asked you to do this, you would properly respond that

Continued on next page

CBS Replies

Continued from preceding page

readers know, without a blizzard of asterisks, that material in your paper is edited, that these are not the complete remarks. Our viewers know it, too. And so do those whom we cover.

But most astonishing of all, you propose that we should give the subject of the interview an opportunity to see and approve his revised remarks. Is that now the policy at The Washington Post? Of course not. You know and I know that this strikes at the very core of independent and free journalism. To grant a subject such a right of review is to remove the basic journalistic function of editing from the hands of the journalist and place it—in the case of the documentary in question—in the hands of the Pentagon. I almost wrote—"tell you what, we'll do it if you'll do it." Then I had a second thought: No, we won't do it even if you should do it.

We are all after the same thing: to be fair, to inform the public fairly and honestly. We do not suggest that we—or any journalistic organization — are free from errors, but nothing in the First Amendment suggests that we must be perfect, or that we are not human. And nothing suggests that if our responsibility is larger, our job tougher of our coverage broader there should be some new set of rules for our kind of journalism, as if to say the First Amendment is fine so long as it doesn't count for much. You don't seem to mind if our end of the dinghy sinks, so long as yours stays afloat.

Fairness is at the root of all this, and fairness can be and always will be debated.

But I submit that we are as careful about editing, as concerned with what is fair and proper and in balance, as rigorous in our internal screening and editorial control processes as any journalistic organization.

The job of ensuring that fairness, that balance and that sense of responsibility is difficult. It is the subject of our constant review and concern. It is not a question that can be solved by a single statement of policy or staff memorandum. It must be, and it is, the daily concern of our working reporters, editors and management.

We believe, as I have said publicly before, that "The Selling of the Pentagon" was edited fairly and honestly. Long after the useful and valuable debate on this broadcast has subsided and perhaps been forgotten we shall be editing other news broadcasts and other documentaries as fairly and as honestly as we know how, and in accordance with established journalistic practice—just as you shall be so editing.

RICHARD S. SALANT,
President, CBS News.
New York.

The Washington Post

Washington, D.C., March 30, 1971

Mr. Salant's Letter

In our letters space today we print a response by Richard Salant of CBS News to our recent editorial concerning the dispute between CBS News, the Pentagon, Vice President Agnew, Congressman Hebert, and now—as it seems—The Washington Post. In time the U.N. may have to be called in, but for now we would like, in a unilateral action, to respond to Mr. Salant's complaint. We think it is off the point. And we think this is so because Mr. Salant invests the term "editing" with functions and freedoms well beyond anything we regard as common or acceptable practice. Mr. Salant taxes us with unfairly recommending two sets of standards in these matters, one for the printed press and another for the electronic. But he reads us wrong. We were and are objecting to the fact that *specifically, in relation to question-and-answer sequences,* two sets of standards *already* exist—and that what he and others in television appear to regard as simple "editing" seems to us to take an excess of unacknowledged liberties with the direct quotations of the principals involved.

Before we go into these, a word might be of use about the editorial practices (and malpractices) common to us both. When a public official or anyone else issues a statement or responds to a series of questions in an interview, the printed media of course exercise an editorial judgment in deciding which part and how much of that material to quote or paraphrase or ignore. The analogy with TV's time limitations, for us, is the limit on space: deciding which of the half million words of news coming into this paper each day shall be among the 80,000 we have room to print. Thus, "Vice President Agnew said last night . . . Mr. Agnew also said . . ." and so on; it is a formulation basic to both the daily paper and the televised newscast.

That bad and misleading judgments can be made by this newspaper in both our presentation and selection of such news goes without saying—or at least it did until we started doing some public soul-searching about it in this newspaper a good while back. There is, for example, a distorting effect in failing to report that certain statements were not unsolicited assertions but responses to a reporter's question. But that we do not confuse the effort to remedy these defects with a waiving of our First Amendment rights or a yielding up of editorial prerogatives should also be obvious to readers of this newspaper—perhaps tediously so by now. What we have in mind, however, when we talk of the license taken by the electronic media in the name of "editing" is something quite different, something this newspaper does not approve and would not leap to defend if it were caught doing. It is the practice of printing highly rearranged material in a Q-and-A sequence as if it were verbatim text, without indicating to the reader that changes had been made and/or without giving the subject an opportunity to approve revisions in the original exchange.

It is, for instance, presenting as a direct six-sentence quotation from a colonel, a "statement" composed of a first sentence from page 55 of his prepared text, followed by a second sentence from page 36, followed by a third and fourth from page 48, and a fifth from page 73, and a sixth from page 88. That occurred in "The Selling of the Pentagon," and we do not see why Mr. Salant should find it difficult to grant that this type of procedure is 1) not "editing" in any conventional sense and 2) likely to undermine both the broadcast's credibility and public confidence in that credibility.

The point here is that "The Selling of the Pentagon" presented this statement as if it were one that had actually been made—verbatim—by the Colonel:

TV can and does simulate an impression of actuality in the way it conveys such rearranged material. Consider, again from the same documentary, a sequence with Daniel Z. Henkin, Assistant Secretary of Defense for Public Affairs. This is how viewers were *shown* Mr. Henkin answering a question:

Roger Mudd: What about your public displays of military equipment at state fairs and shopping centers? What purpose does that serve?
Mr. Henkin: Well, I think it serves the purpose of informing the public about their armed forces. I believe the American public has the right to request information about the armed forces, to have speakers come before them, to ask questions, and to understand the need for our armed forces, why we ask for the funds that we do ask for, how we spend these funds, what are we doing about such problems as drugs—and we do have a drug problem in the armed forces; what are we doing about the racial problem—and we do have a racial problem. I think the public has a valid right to ask us these questions.

This, on the other hand, is how Mr. Henkin *actually* answered the question:

Mr. Henkin: Well, I think it serves the purpose of informing the public about their armed forces. It also has the ancillary benefit, I would hope, of simulating interest in recruiting as we move or try to move to zero draft calls and increased reliance on volunteers for our armed forces. I think it is very important that the American youth have an opportunity to learn about the armed forces.

The answer Mr. Henkin was *shown* to be giving had been transposed from his answer to another question a couple of pages along in the transcribed interview, and one that came out of a sequence dealing not just with military displays but also with the availability of military speakers. At that point in the interview, Roger Mudd asked Mr. Henkin whether the sort of thing he was now talking about — drug problems and racial problems—was "the sort of information that gets passed at state fairs by sergeants who are standing next to rockets." To which Mr. Henkin replied:

Mr. Henkin: No, I didn't—wouldn't limit that to sergeants standing next to any kind of exhibits. I knew—I thought we were discussing speeches and all.

This is how the sequence was *shown* to have occurred, following on Mr. Henkin's transposed reply to the original question:

Mr. Mudd: Well, is that the sort of information about the drug problem you have and the racial problem you have and the budget problems you have—is that the sort of information that gets passed out at state fairs by sergeants who are standing next to rockets.
Mr. Henkin: No, I wouldn't limit that to sergeants standing next to any kind of exhibit. Now, there are those who contend that this is propaganda. I do not agree with this.

The part about discussing "speeches and all" had been omitted; the part about propaganda comes from a few lines above Mr. Henkin's actual answer and was in fact a reference to charges that the Pentagon was using talk of the "increasing Soviet threat" as propaganda to influence the size of the military budget.

Surely, something different from and less cosmic than a challenge to CBS's First Amendment rights is involved in the question of whether or not the subject of such a rearranged interview should not be given a chance to see and approve what he will be demonstrated to have said. And surely this "editing" practice must be conceded—with reason—to have damaging effect on public confidence in what is being shown to have happened—shown to have been said. We agree with Mr. Salant's premise that we are all in the same dinghy. That is why we are so concerned that neither end should sink.

HERALD EXAMINER

Los Angeles, Calif., April 14, 1971

Dr. Frank Stanton, President of the Columbia Broadcasting System, has taken a difficult but highly responsible position in defying portions of a congressional subpoena relating to the network's controversial television documentary, "The Selling of the Pentagon."

This is the program, first broadcast in February and again last month, which has drawn strong criticism from Vice President Agnew, Defense Secretary Laird and other Administration spokesmen. They have lambasted the telecast as a biased attack on the military.

We agree with their assessment. On the other hand we agree wholeheartedly with the reaction of Dr. Stanton to the subpoena served subsequently on his network by the House Interstate and Foreign Commerce Committee. It is important to keep the two issues separate.

The subpoena, returnable on April 20, demanded that CBS proffer the committee not only a copy of the film and text as broadcast but also all the untelevised film and textual materials involved in the undertaking, including contracts and financial records.

Dr. Stanton agreed to produce only the film and text which actually went on the air. Even though radio and TV are federally licensed, he contended, it is an infringement of press freedom for the government to demand confidential material pertaining to editorial judgment.

By his refusal, and the contempt citation it invites, Dr. Stanton has set the stage for a judicial showdown which may wind up in the Supreme Court. Meanwhile he is saying, in effect, that the free press he represents is always subject to criticism and correction, but never to intimidation or influence by licensing authority or any other club the government may lift in threat.

His position, as stated, is sound. The House committee clearly needs only the finished editorial product and the testimony of responsible witnesses to shape its judgment and possible corrective legislation.

Poking through the private files and wastebaskets of TV editors —or of any others in the communications media— is not a proper function of democratic government. Not only television, but all our press —and public— have an important vested interest in the CBS showdown and its result.

The Washington Post
Times Herald

Washington, D. C., April 11, 1971

We had not planned on carrying much further the discussion triggered by that CBS television program, "The Selling of the Pentagon"—almost everybody having had their say, and then some, including ourselves, the networks and a good many congressmen who seem to have enjoyed this aspect of the whole affair as much as they disliked the original program. But the action of Rep. Harley O. Staggers in summoning CBS officials to appear before his committee is so unwarranted and so substantial a threat to the news media of this country that we are obliged to come back to the subject once again.

Mr. Staggers, in his role as chairman of the investigating arm of the House Commerce Committee, has ordered CBS to turn over to that committee not only a film and a transcript of the program itself but also just about everything CBS collected in the process of preparing the program. He wants all the preliminary film, recordings and transcripts used by CBS in getting ready for the program, as well as the names, addresses and fees paid to anyone, other than government officials and regular CBS staff members, who appeared on the program. Apparently in an attempt to demonstrate that his committee is doing more than just reflecting the anger of the Pentagon and Congress over this one program, Mr. Staggers has had a similar order served on NBC in connection with a documentary on the balance of nature.

Frank Stanton, president of CBS, has said that he will provide the committee with a film copy and a written transcript of the program as it appeared on the air and nothing else. We applaud his decision and trust he will stick by it, come what may. CBS deserves to be judged by what it put on the air, not on what it collected and discarded along the way. (Like many others, we have made a judgment about "The Selling of the Pentagon" on that basis. To refresh your memory, we think the program made a substantial contribution in airing an aspect of the Pentagon that sorely needs airing but we thought some of the editing techniques used were open to serious question, mostly because they exposed the show to needless attack. It is remarkable how both defenders and critics of the program have seized on that second point and ignored the first.)

In essence, what Mr. Staggers now wants to do is to sit in judgment, not of the program, but of how CBS operates as a collector and disseminator of information. That, to put it bluntly, is none of his or Congress's business. It is, if we may use an analogy, like demanding that the author of a book produce all his rough drafts, his interview notes, and his correspondence. Or, it is like demanding that the President turn over to Congress all the memos he receives from various government agencies concerning a proposed speech and all the early drafts of that speech. No congressman, we submit, would be so reckless as to propose either. And any congressman who did would be recognized immediately as one who had no respect for and no understanding of the First Amendment or the internal operations of a large organization.

The demand of Mr. Staggers, of course, is founded on the idea that television is somehow so different from the rest of the information media that the Constitution no longer applies. Since the granting of television licenses is a legitimate function of government, the argument goes, the policing of what appears on television is similarly legitimate. No doubt the government can place restricting limits on certain aspects of television; it does on other news media in terms of the laws concerning such matters as libel, obscenity, theft, extortion or business regulations. But government has no general role to play in policing the gathering and presentation of news material, as such, except to guarantee access for competing points of view on a medium, like television, where physical limitations exist.

It is not difficult to imagine the chilling effects on public affairs programing if the course which Mr. Staggers has suggested is followed. It would mean that any television newsman who said anything critical about any governmental official could be called on the carpet to explain how he reached that conclusion. The freedom that has marked the television appearances of such diverse figures as William Buckley and the late Edward R. Murrow would be seriously curtailed. Indeed, the final stop on the road down which Mr. Staggers has embarked is complete governmental control of the content of television news and public affairs programs. While that may be the ideal situation for those who think the government always knows best, it is entirely incompatible with a society in which the government is responsive to the people of the country. Perhaps it would be timely to remind Mr. Staggers and any of his colleagues of like mind and inclination of the words of James Madison on the meaning of freedom for the news media in our system:

Some degree of abuse is inseparable from the proper use of everything, and in no instance is this more true than in that of the press. It has accordingly been decided by the practice of the States, that it is better to leave a few of its noxious branches to their luxuriant growth, than, by pruning them away, to injure the vigour of those yielding the proper fruits. And can the wisdom of this policy be doubted by any who reflect that to the press alone, chequered as it is with abuses, the world is indebted for all the triumphs which have been gained by reason and humanity over error and oppression . . .

AKRON BEACON JOURNAL

Akron, Ohio, April 13, 1971

The big go-round between a House committee and CBS over the honesty and the craftsmanship involved in preparation of CBS News' documentary "The Selling of the Pentagon" raises a basic issue or two that it would pay all of us—inside and outside the news-selling trades—to think about.

The House Interstate and Foreign Commerce Committee subpenaed from CBS, among other things, the unused film clips and tapes and other material discarded in the editing of the show. The only purpose that comes to mind is some sort of new law on the editing of TV journalism.

Dr. Frank Stanton, president of CBS, refused to honor the subpena, and insists that he will fight it in the courts, if necessary, as invasion of his news staff's free press and free speech rights under the Constitution's First Amendment.

We think he is right and the House committee is wrong. And we think the difference is important to everybody who lives in this country.

We don't want to get into argument here about the merits or shortcomings of CBS News in this or any other CBS documentary. Sometimes it's good and sometimes not so good, and honest, intelligent newsmen will differ sharply about when it is which.

The makers of the show have been accused of so editing film and tapes that some of those who appeared on the program were made to seem to say things they didn't actually say.

Sen. Clifford P. Hansen (R-Wyo.), who has been hammering for some time at TV "distortion" of the war in Vietnam in an anti-administration way, took CBS to the woodshed for this.

He did it with some solid support. A large part of his ammunition was a blast from the editorial columns of the aggressive and generally anti-administration Washington Post, and another from the conservative and thorough Barron's Weekly.

And in this week's "Monday," the Republican National Committee's publication, committee chairman Bob Dole, the Kansas senator, is quoted with the question:

"If (CBS) has nothing to hide and if it is as pure as it claims to be . . . why not let Congress see (the disputed material)?"

Granting that the question is serious and important, we vigorously disagree. And if we were similarly subpenaed, we, too, would fight—even if every subpenaed reporter's note, scrap of recorder tape and photo supported fully the finished version of a story we printed.

This is not to whitewash either CBS or us. We know we goof, and we're sure that CBS News is not so superhuman that it can always be right. But we don't think Congressional action is the way to fix it.

Every reporter knows he cannot hope to bring his reader or his watch-er-listener the whole of what he has heard or seen—and he faces a compulsion to make what he tells interesting. He has no captive audience—and you can't tell anything to someone who won't listen or dozes off.

So he selects and he weights, to make a smaller version of the large reality and to focus attention on what is different and interesting—newsworthy —about it. The good craftsman does this carefully, trying to be fair and to make the small finished product essentially like the large original.

It is seldom, for example, that the whole of a speech is printed. And it is undeniable that shortening and selection change emphasis and sharpness—sometimes in ways that will trouble the speaker and some who heard all of what he said.

It is also true that no two reporters or editors ever agree throughout on how best to do this with the least violence to balanced truth and the least chance that the reader or listener will doze off or change channels.

But here the public can inflict a direct penalty for failure. The competing news media, both printed and radio-TV, depend wholly on the public's willingness to believe that, however ineptly, the media are trying to bring them the truth. No newsman can operate very long without awareness that once his readers or watcher-listeners lose this faith in him—he's dead.

As long as there are competing channels to truth, the whip is strong in the public's hands. The deliberate lie, the calculated distortion will become evident, and the offender will get his comeuppance as the public tunes out.

It's different with government, and with some of the most vocal "outside" critics of news media performance. The administration has a special interest—convincing people that its policies are right. So has a political party, or the Pentagon, or any congressman or senator you can name.

The only corresponding long-range "special interest" of the news media is in convincing the public that we are honestly trying to report the truth. That's all we have to sell.

Built into our functions are and must be dissent and criticism of the "ins" from time to time. And as those who insisted on the First Amendment saw, there is no safe way to have Big Brother, no matter how benevolent, ride herd on this.

Public dispute here is good. It can make newsmen more conscious of their shortcomings and push them to work harder to overcome them. But let's have no witchhunts to drive dissent off the tube, and no laws specifying what is "truth" passed and enforced by human beings with partisan interests to promote.

Los Angeles Times

Los Angeles, Calif., April 13, 1971

The media and the government are natural adversaries. The one, if it lives up to its obligation, will try to spread before the public all the relevant facts about the operations of government. Government officials want to see their activities reflected in the best possible light.

The conflict has taken on new dimensions recently in the surge of criticism of television news by Nixon Administration officials and some members of Congress. The House Interstate and Foreign Commerce Committee has initiated the latest move in this struggle by serving a subpoena on the Columbia Broadcasting System in connection with the CBS documentary, "The Selling of the Pentagon." The committee wants the following material:

—All film and sound tape records whether they were used on the air or not.

—The names and addresses of all persons appearing on the documentary, except members of Congress, military personnel and persons who were regular CBS employes as of Jan. 1, 1970.

—A record of disbursement of money to persons who participated.

—Copies or descriptions of contracts or agreements that may have been negotiated with these persons.

The network will supply to the committee a copy of the televised film and a transcript but has refused to yield to the demands listed above. If the dispute reaches the courts and the subpoena is upheld, that would mean, in effect, that the government could bring all television news under surveillance. The end result would be government censorship.

Because the number of broadcasting channels is limited, the government had to become the licensing authority. The government also, under the Federal Communications Act, is responsible for enforcing the "fairness doctrine," which means that broadcasters, having a monopoly, must allow "reasonable opportunity for the discussion of conflicting views of public importance."

Broadcasters are not exempt from criticism from any source, nor is the press, but it is a long jump indeed from this premise to the conclusion that the licensing power of the government gives it the authority to supervise broadcast journalism. Yet the assertion of that power is exactly what is implied by the subpoena served on CBS. The subpoena should not be allowed to stand.

Chicago today American

Chicago, Ill., April 12, 1971

A CLASH between a congressional committee and the Columbia Broadcasting System shows signs of becoming a real test of journalistic independence with Congress on one side and the broadcast media on the other. If such a test does develop, it is one the industry must not lose, because losing it would further strengthen the lethal idea that "truth" is what federal power says it is.

The fight heated up Thursday, when the House Interstate and Foreign Commerce Committee served a subpena on CBS ordering it to show the committee all materials, televised and untelevised, pertaining to the network's controversial show "The Selling of the Pentagon." CBS president Frank Stanton said the committee was welcome to all the material that had been broadcast, but the network would not turn over any film, textual matter or notes that had not appeared on home screens.

The point of the documentary was that the defense department has been spending millions of tax dollars each year to influence public opinion in its favor. This central point can hardly be denied. But critics have charged—evidently with truth—that some misleading techniques were used on the show, such as stringing together unrelated quotes from Pentagon spokesmen to give an inaccurate impression of what they said.

Rep. Harley O. Staggers [D., W. Va.], chairman of the House committee, says his group merely wants to "get the facts" about the controversy. No one can object to a congressional body getting the facts. The trouble is it doesn't just "get" them, it goes on to base judgments and actions on them, and in this case that carries some scary connotations.

It means, in essence, subjecting the editorial judgment of an independent network to that of a government body. It means federal officials telling newsmen, "Now instead of this, you should have shown the public this"—and backing up their views with the implied threat of license revocation. It means setting up a federal standard of truth as being superior to independent judgments of truth. And even if the standards of truth displayed by the federal government were a lot more impressive than they are, that would be a deadly road to follow.

CBS should not budge in its refusal to let congressmen start second-guessing the news media.

THE ROANOKE TIMES

Roanoke, Va., April 14, 1971

Until now, we've purposely said nothing about the flap caused by the CBS news documentary, "The Selling of the Pentagon."

It wasn't that we were disinterested; rather, we saw nothing in the program—either in the initial viewing or at the time of its re-broadcast—to get too exercised about.

True, we didn't like its revelation that the military's massive public-relations budget is used to proselyte the American people in support of a militant anti-Communist foreign policy that no administration has advocated in over a decade.

We were naturally pleased, therefore, when it was subsequently reported that word had quietly gone out from the Pentagon to scrap outdated propaganda films and other materials still being shown the public, and to remind military speakers on the fried-chicken circuit that the law explicitly prohibits them from advocating a particular foreign policy.

On the whole, however, about the only thing noteworthy about the program was that it was ever done in the first place. Here, for a change, was a television network examining a serious public issue in a prime-time viewing period, and utilizing the techniques—still largely unfamiliar to broadcasting—of original, investigative reporting. Were this kind of public service routinely undertaken, the program almost certainly would have passed with little comment.

Suddenly, however, the in-depth CBS report—or, more precisely, the political reaction to its content—is taking on all the earmarks of a serious new attempt at press censorship. For with the decision this past week by the House Interstate and Foreign Commerce Committee to begin an official investigation of the program—even to the extent of serving on CBS a subpoena demanding reporters' notes and untelevised background material—we are seeing once again an all-too-familiar effort by government to intimidate journalists.

Quite possibly, the CBS program did not represent, in overall content, balanced reporting. Moreover, it appears that its producers were careless, or worse, in editing techniques that were applied to a single filmed interview. And, doubtless, the program did not tell the public what the government wished it to be told.

None of these issues, however, is a matter of legitimate concern to a congressional investigating committee. In fact, there is only one question that the government is lawfully empowered to ask of the broadcast industry—and that is whether, given the nation's limited number of available radio-TV outlets, all significant points of view have an opportunity to be heard on a controversial matter. Even that question, however, is one for the Federal Communications Commission—not a congressional committee—to ask. (And, in this dispute, it isn't even a relevant matter; CBS has fully aired the views of the program's critics.)

Wisely, CBS is not allowing the House Commerce Committee to overstep its powers. President Frank Stanton has announced that the network will deliver to the committee only a film and transcript of the program, nothing else. Were he to do more, he in effect would concede government's right to undertake such fishing expeditions at will, exposing reporters' sources, off-the-record notes and other unpublished or un-broadcast materials to official scrutiny. Should that right ever be upheld, freedom of the press will have been irreversibly lost — and, as Jefferson warned nearly 200 years ago, so would every other freedom.

There has never been a clear test of what ought to be a reporter's absolute protection against disclosure of his sources, notes, etc. In fewer than a dozen states is this full protection given legal standing; at the federal level, there is no applicable statute. Yet, as a practical matter, a reporter could not win the confidence and trust of news sources—especially those suspicious, as so many now are, of possible repressive actions by government—if there were even a chance that he might become, indirectly, an investigative agent of government.

This is the fundamental issue that is being posed by the House Interstate Commerce Committee's subpoena against CBS. Similarly, it was the issue that was raised a year or so ago, when several federal grand juries sought in much the same way to misuse subpoena powers against newspaper reporters. Atty. Gen. John Mitchell later apologized for that; even now, however, the Justice Department is before the Supreme Court, balking at having to show "specific compelling need" for seeking secret testimony from reporters.

De Tocqueville recognized, almost two centuries ago, that "in order to enjoy the inestimable benefits that liberty of the press insures, it is necessary to submit to the inevitable evils it creates." That there are occasional abuses of press freedom, we do not deny—although, as even the vice president now affirms, the country's press has never been more responsible than it is today. If CBS was guilty of flawed, perhaps even slanted reporting—as is now being widely debated among professional journalists—the "evil" simply must be submitted to; the far greater evil, most assuredly, would be to allow the government to frighten a basic medium of communications into total silence on national issues—or, worse, to turn it into an opinion-molding cheerleader for whatever political party happens to be in power.

Honolulu Star-Bulletin

Honolulu, Hawaii, April 17, 1971

The question of whether television and radio newsmen are protected by the same constitutional guarantees enjoyed by representatives of the printed media may eventually be decided by the Supreme Court.

The Columbia Broadcasting System, under fire from both the executive and legislative branches for its controversial documentary, "The Selling of the Pentagon," has said it is prepared for a legal battle up to the highest tribunal.

In the words of Dr. Frank Stanton, the network president:

"The fact that television and radio stations are licensed by the government does not deprive the press of First Amendment protection, and the courts have so held. That protection does not depend on whether the government believes we are right or wrong in our news judgment."

Dr. Stanton's position is that the word "press" in the Bill of Rights covers reporters and commentators for television and radio.

CBS has until April 20 to reply to a subpena served on it by the House Interstate and Foreign Commerce Committee. The committee demands all televised and untelevised materials pertaining to "The Selling of the Pentagon." Stanton has said the committee is welcome to material broadcast, but that the network will not make available unused films, textual matter or notes not shown.

The network could be held in contempt of the House. Stanton could be jailed, a punishment he says he would accept rather that accede to the committee's demands.

NBC also has been served a committee subpena in connection with the inclusion of old film in "Say When," a documentary stressing the balance of Nature and decrying the indiscriminate shooting of a mother polar bear. Washington reports indicate the committee is not seriously interested in "Say When"; that it was included to avert allegations that the committee was "picking on" one network.

NBC, like CBS, will go to jail rather than submit.

"The Selling of the Pentagon" may, in fact, turn out to be a milestone in guaranteeing freedom of information in the United States. A Supreme Court decision should have been had long ago on whether freedom of the press extends to television and radio. The networks probably would have made a test case but for the fear that they might lose. Now they appear to be willing to fight for the right and the air, eventually, may be cleared.

The Des Moines Register

Des Moines, Iowa, April 16, 1971

A little over a year ago, the Nixon Administration quit the short-lived practice of issuing catchall subpoenas for the notes, unused pictures and discarded film of reporters, news photographers and television cameramen.

This was a misguided attempt by the Administration to acquire evidence against militant groups that law enforcement agents were unable to obtain. Atty. Gen. John Mitchell admitted the practice was a mistake.

Now the House Interstate and Foreign Commerce Committee has served a subpoena on the Columbia Broadcasting System, demanding the untelevised and televised film pertaining to the network's documentary, "The Selling of the Pentagon." CBS President Frank Stanton said the House of Representatives could have the material that had been broadcast, but the network did not intend to part with unused film, notes or other material that were not part of the documentary.

The incident raises the possibility of congressional intimidation of a television network licensed by the government. The House committee's demand suggests that some congressmen are out to punish CBS because of its exposure of the Pentagon's propaganda excesses.

Systematic government searching for information acquired by journalists, often from confidential sources, could become a serious threat to the public's right to know what government is doing. To attempt to delve into editorial decisions and make journalists into investigative agents of the police by abuse of the subpoena power would be a perversion of the First Amendment guarantee of a free press.

The Courier-Journal

Louisville, Ky., April 17, 1971

ANY SCHOOLBOY, one trusts, recognizes what a different country America would be today if our founding fathers had left its newspapers subject to the licensing whims of government. The first rule of totalitarianism, in fact, is that those editors who will not suppress criticism of the regime must be silenced.

Even Vice President Agnew, for all of his complaints about press fairness and credibility, has not suggested that the First Amendment be repealed. Yet he and some of those who share his views seem bent on doing by indirection, through the back door as it were, what they cannot accomplish by direct assault.

The target now is CBS, which has been commanded by a House subcommittee to hand over all untelevised materials connected with its recent documentary on military public relations, "The Selling of the Pentagon." The subcommittee then proposes to determine for itself whether the editors at CBS were "fair and accurate" in their selection and editing of the film that finally went on the air.

As James Reston commented Thursday on this page, any newspaper served a subpoena demanding its reporters' notes and unused drafts of stories on anything other than a matter of national security could tell the Vice President or the House subcommittee to go climb the Washington Monument. But the journalists in television are still victims of an unresolved double-standard, because their stations and networks are licensed by the government to use "the people's airwaves."

No profiles in courage

During last fall's political campaign, all of us could witness Mr. Agnew's thinly-veiled threats of license-revocation for those stations or networks whose news programs he didn't like. Now we're at the next step on this dangerous ladder: an official governmental demand that a network justify its news judgments to a group of congressmen.

One can be certain of the outcome if this incredible procedure were upheld by the courts. All television editors would work with Congress leaning over their shoulders, and every American could say goodby to any more broadcast criticism of the Pentagon, the FBI, the oil industry or any other sacred cow—and that includes most politicians as well.

In fact, one might as well kiss TV news goodby altogether, since any report on anything except motherhood—and perhaps even on that—will start a controversy somewhere. And if controversy means the risk of no license renewal, so long to controversy and courage.

This is not to argue that television news is always as good or fairly presented as it should be. Like their counterparts on newspapers, many TV journalists have been giving a lot of thought in recent years to the responsibilities that go with their rights, and the better men in both industries are pushing hard for more accuracy, balance and accountability in the news reports they compile.

That's encouraging, and so is a continuing flow of public and official criticism of the job the journalists are doing. But if there comes a time when newsmen must measure what they write or broadcast on the basis of its popularity rather than its truth, don't bother to ask a schoolboy about liberty. If he remembers what it was like, he'll know the danger of babbling about such a dangerous doctrine.

PORTLAND EVENING EXPRESS

Portland, Me., April 26, 1971

The documentary filmed by the Columbia Broadcasting Corporation, "The Selling of the Pentagon", is still a controversial issue at Washington, where the Pentagon and the administration combined to attack it. Later a House subcommittee headed by Rep. Harley Staggers of West Virginia issued a subpoena calling upon CBS to hand over not only the film, but various recordings, film not used in the final product, transcripts, the names of persons who worked on the program, and the disbursement of funds.

Rep. Staggers is a member of the clubby establishment in Congress which always closes ranks to defend its friends and punish its enemies, but outside of a new attempt to discredit the film it's hard to tell what is his purpose. He took the novel attitude, at a subcommittee hearing on Tuesday that the First Amendment did not protect the TV networks, though the courts have held that it does. CBS, on the other hand, insists that its functions do come under the umbrella of the First Amendment's free-press section, and we are pleased to see that the network refused to turn over to Staggers' panel anything but the film and its transcript.

Rep. Staggers had what he thought was a hole card to play when he reminded CBS that the networks "couldn't be operating at all unless the government gave them the right." But who is the "government?" The government is the servant of the American people, and not their master. The "government" does license television, largely for technical reasons, but beyond this responsibility it also has the responsibility of protecting the people's right to know, and it cannot threaten or suppress the networks without jeopardizing the right-to-know principle.

The congressman has given CBS ten days to repent — that is, it must hand over the material demanded or face a contempt citation. We have a feeling that CBS will resist, and we hope it does. Let's have this battle between the bureaucrats and television fought out in the courts on the single question of press freedom, which goes much farther than TV documentaries.

The Wichita Eagle

Wichita, Kans., April 24, 1971

One result of the recent controversial CBS-TV documentary, "The Selling of the Pentagon," is that the House special investigations subcommittee will study whether new laws are needed to protect the public from possible "factually false and misleading filming and edition practices" in making TV news documentaries.

The program drew heavy criticism from the Nixon administration and some members of Congress. However badly or unfairly CBS handled the program, however, its producers should not be subjected to such an investigation.

The subcommittee subpoena calls for all material used in making the film, including background notes and tapes and information not actually used in the final product. The network has agreed to give the subcommittee the finished documentary but no more.

As CBS President Frank Stanton correctly put it, "This subpoena appears to involve no question of alleged violation of criminal law. Rather, the s o l e purpose . . . is to obtain materials which will aid the committee in subjecting to legislative surveillance the news judgments of CBS . . ."

CBS has been accused of using an exaggerated figure on how m u c h the Pentagon spends for its various press, publicity and public-relations activities.

Perhaps the criticism is valid, but it remains a fact that the Pentagon's budget for these purposes is considerable, and the tax paying public has a r i g h t to know about it.

The CBS figures may or may n o t have been overstated, but in response to an inquiry by Senator Fulbright in 1969, the Pentagon admitted that it had an information force of 2,800, with direct salary and operating costs of $27.9 million, a tenfold increase from 1959.

The figure does not include other costly activities, such as Armed Forces Day shows which must also be considered public-relations activities.

So aside from questions of press freedom, journalistic fairness and the other controversies stirred up by the CBS show, the simple fact is that there are large-scale Pentagon publicity outlays at a time when the nation is under pressure to control government costs.

Taxpayers need to know about such expenditures, but aren't likely to learn of them from the government's own information agencies. Only a free press can keep the populace informed.

The subcommittee study is a flagrant case of governmental intervention in the freedom of the press, and it obviously is aimed at intimidating the news media.

It can't be condoned.

The Honolulu Advertiser

Honolulu, Hawaii, April 26, 1971

Criticism is one thing, but if it leads to tactics that are a step towards government censorship, all Americans will be the losers.

No part of the news media should be immune to criticism of its judgment or competence. Vice President Agnew's blasts have prompted, in some cases, a healthy exchange of views.

The CBS documentary, "The Selling of the Pentagon," is controversial, although some feel much of the smoke the military is raising is to fog the film's message about spending for public relations and outright propaganda.

At any rate, the documentary should be judged on the validity of the contents as seen by viewers—the end product offered the public. The same is true of newspaper articles.

THUS THE investigative subcommittee of the House Commerce Committee has gone too far in demanding CBS turn over all material (including unused film, f i n a n c i a l records, names of employes, etc.) connected with the program.

It is all too easy to see how such material can be used to harass, intimidate and raise diversionary questions unrelated to the merits of a program (or news article) as it appears before the public.

Moreover, it is a kind of legislative surveillance that, if allowed, would be a step towards government supervision and censorship.

And there are other aspects. Representative Harley O. Staggers of West Virginia, chairman of the House Commerce Committee, said the investigative subcommittee will also study whether laws are needed to protect the public from possible false and misleading practices in the making of television news documentaries.

NO MATTER HOW you slice it, the request for background materials and Staggers' remarks about "protecting the public" smack of government control over news judgments.

CBS, and NBC in a related case, have refused to provide background materials that were not used on the air, and both networks correctly state that basic constitutional questions of a free broadcast press are involved.

The American Society of Newspaper Editors, in an unusual expression of concern for the well-being of television competitors, has sent a telegram to the House subcommittee accusing it of an open attack on the Fifth Amendment.

THIS PARTICULAR case may well end up in the courts. But it deserves thought from the general public. Americans should realize that what's endangered by the congressional subpoena is not the name of CBS but the people's right to know without the information coming under the shadow of government pressure.

The Miami Herald

Miami, Fla., April 17, 1971

A CONGRESSMAN named Harley Staggers didn't like a Columbia Broadcasting System documentary titled "The Selling of the Pentagon." It is understandable that anyone who feels a kinship with the generals and admirals would not enjoy a TV program that revealed how far and expensively the Pentagon has gone since World War II to justify and glamorize its costly way of life.

There are lots of things on TV we fault. The CBS fakery on a purported invasion of Haiti by "freedom fighters" was a journalistic disgrace. CBS suffered for it in the proper forum of public opinion.

But no matter how unhappy the citizen gets with what appears on the TV screen, he must be less happy with Rep. Staggers' effort to invade an area of journalistic freedom that is and must be kept inviolate.

The congressman is not satisfied to disagree with the CBS documentary on the Pentagon. He is demanding that CBS produce for his committee every bit of raw material that went into the making of the hour-long film. He wants all film that was edited out, along with all transcripts that were used to prepare the show and the names and addresses of all persons who appeared on the program.

CBS has offered to provide the Staggers committee with a tape of the show and a script. We think that is all the congressman is entitled to receive. We see no merit in the argument that TV is government licensed and therefore not entitled to the protection of the First Amendment. The granting of a license by the Federal Communications Commission is the proper business of government, just as the enactment of laws on libel are a proper exercise for the regulation of newspapers.

But when government in Washington can demand that editors and writers of news film and news copy produce all of their source material, including notes and names of all persons interviewed, then the government in Washington will have succeeded in doing what the government in the Soviet Union does each day.

Time and again, the public's interest has been served by information offered in trust to newsmen by individuals who by reason of occupation or personal security cannot afford identification. To remove this trust by congressional fiat would be to close off a source of truths vital to a free nation's self-interest. And the raw material of any reporter's story contains a gathering of unsupportable or unprovable facets, rumors or overzealous suspicions which have no place in a fair report and thus are routinely excised by the writer or editor.

There has been stirred in this country by irresponsible political leaders an unfair and unjustified resentment for those who present the news. There is an effort to sell the idea that there would only be good news about Vietnam, about hunger, about employment and about the environment if it were not for the newspapers and television.

That is shortsighted and it is hogwash.

Certainly there are and have been abuses by some of the tens of thousands of men and women who work each day to tell the people of this country what is happening to their world. But we are reminded by a colleague of The Washington Post of what James Madison said on that subject:

"Some degree of abuse is inseparable from the proper use of everything, and in no instance is this more true than in that of the press. It has accordingly been decided by the practice of the States, that it is better to leave a few of its noxious branches to their luxuriant growth, than, by pruning them away, to injure the vigor of those yielding the proper fruits. And can the wisdom of this policy be doubted by any who reflect that to the press alone, chequered as it is with abuses, the world is indebted for all the triumphs which have been gained by reason and humanity over error and oppression . . ."

The Providence Journal

Providence, R. I., April 17, 1971

The Columbia Broadcasting System is on sound ground in refusing to respond to portions of a congressional subpoena that demanded details of *The Selling of the Pentagon* that were not broadcast. A special House sub-committee wants to browse through every bit of material CBS compiled in the long course of producing the controversial documentary.

No news medium in this country can hope to perform its duties and carry out its responsibilities under the Constitution if it turns over to investigative or prosecuting agencies of government every scrap of material it gathered in pursuit of a story. No news medium, in short, can permit itself to be used as a kind of detective.

There is no question in the CBS case, as in so many similar cases, of alleged violation of criminal law or of government interest in any evidence that might involve criminal prosecution of a third person. The proposed search through CBS records would be—quite simply—a snooping for anything that might interest the subcommittee or one of its members.

These newspapers expressed concern at the way in which CBS handled some of the material that went into the making of the Pentagon documentary. But it strongly supports CBS in its determination to maintain the integrity of its news-gathering operation. We hope CBS fights the case through the United States Supreme Court—if that is necessary.

THE SUN

Baltimore, Md.
April 25, 1971

Chairman Staggers of West Virginia, the chairman of a House Commerce subcommittee, apparently is trying to demonstrate that the First Amendment to the Constitution, guaranteeing freedom of the press, does not apply to television and radio stations licensed by the federal government. Thus he says that the subcommittee's inquiry into a CBS documentary program, "The Selling of the Pentagon," has nothing to do with the First Amendment. He is quoted as explaining that broadcasting companies "couldn't be operating at all unless the government gave them the right. The air waves are licensed by the government, so the government has a right to check on what goes on."

The responsible officers of CBS disagree with Mr. Staggers. They are refusing to comply with portions of a subpoena requiring them to turn over to the subcommittee films and other material obtained or compiled in the preparation of the program, but not actually used. The subcommittee, as Mr. Staggers makes plain, proposes to examine the editing of the program.

In agreeing to submit to the subcommittee the tape and text of the program as it was broadcast but refusing to submit unused material, CBS is relying on the First Amendment. It argues that the purpose of the subpoena is to obtain materials which will aid the subcommittee in subjecting to legislative surveillance the news judgments of CBS, and it holds that the fact that television and radio stations are licensed by the government does not deprive them of First Amendment protection. As CBS said further, no newspaper or magazine could be required constitutionally to comply with such a subpoena.

In our view CBS is correct in its legal position and correct in challenging the subcommittee's authority. There are distinct differences, not to be ignored, between the printed press and radio-television, but in the news coverage television and radio stations should have the basic guarantees of the First Amendment if they are to function effectively. The air waves are licensed for the convenience of the public, not to give the government control over the news or views that are broadcast.

Chicago Tribune

Chicago, Ill., April 17, 1971

The CBS show "The Selling of the Pentagon" has created much more of a hullabaloo than it warranted. We enter the arena now not to engage in any further haggling over a program whose producers evidently were carried away by their biases, but rather to express our astonishment at the extremes to which both its admirers and its critics have gone in their reactions.

Indignation over the program, voiced first in a reasonably subdued and specific manner by Vice President Agnew, last week led a subcommittee of the House Interstate and Foreign Commerce Committee to issue a subpena not only for the televised material but for all films, recordings and transcripts used in preparing the program.

Dr. Frank Stanton, president of CBS,

says he will not comply with the subpena, and he is clearly within his constitutional rights. The subpena is silly. Neither Congress nor anybody else has the right to subpena this sort of material unless it can be demonstrated in court that the material is essential to a case of far greater importance than is involved here and is not available anywhere else. For a committee of Congress to strongarm CBS in this manner will do nobody any good and will only make martyrs of those responsible for the program. If the committee should succeed, it would be a serious blow to freedom of the press.

There was barely time to recover from this indignation when we learned that the show is to be given a special Peabody award next week as an example of "electronic journalism at its finest." The award

is a special one because the show appeared after the normal deadline of Dec. 31 and because the committee feared that to delay the award until next year would lessen its impact. The award is administered by the Henry W. Grady School of Journalism at the University of Georgia.

The ostensible purpose of the CBS program—to focus on the cost of Pentagon public relations—was legitimate enough, but the editing was done with a view to its impact rather than its fairness, and was shabby at best. To give it the Peabody award is more likely to cheapen one of the most prestigious awards in the business than to enhance the prestige of the CBS show. And to call "The Selling of the Pentagon" electronic journalism at its finest is an insult to the profession.

BUFFALO EVENING NEWS

Buffalo, N. Y., April 16, 1971

The welcome support given a federal shield law for newsmen at this week's meeting of the American Society of Newspaper Editors well attests to the stake shared by all news media in protecting a free flow of news vital to the public in a self-governing society.

A bill now in the House would generally shield all newsmen—electronic as well as print — from having to disclose under subpoena confidential sources of information, or from having to submit to official investigative bodies material gathered but not actually published or used on the air.

Several recent court decisions have breached the newsman's code respecting confidentiality of news sources. Such forced disclosures pose an immensely disturbing threat not merely to news-gath-

erers, but to the public interest in bringing forth vital news tips from sources that would clam up in fear of personal exposure. The editors' Freedom of Information Committee warns that "never has the subpoena been used as viciously, as irresponsibly and as often against freedom of the press as it has this year."

While there is thus a clear need for a statutory bulwarking of First Amendment guarantees at the federal level — quite as much as that afforded by the confidentiality laws already enacted in 17 states — no less compelling is the need for safeguarding news media from the growing threat of intimidation by censorial-minded bodies.

The most recent example is the exercise of a House committee's subpoena power to compel the submission of raw notes and film prepared but not used for

two TV documentaries, including the CBS Network's controversial "The Selling of the Pentagon." The shield bill would put a stop to such obnoxious government snooping.

In upholding the free flow of news, the shield bill is appropriately broad in extending protection against improper pressures by the federal courts, grand juries, the Congress and federal agencies. The measure makes exceptions in cases where disclosures of sources or information may be deemed necessary to protect human life or to prevent espionage or foreign aggression. While these exceptions have caused misgivings among some editors, including ourselves, about the possibility of abuse, we are satisfied that the provisions requiring a court showing of necessity for such rare exclusions insures reasonable safeguards.

The Boston Globe

Boston, Mass., April 29, 1971

Every last American — and not merely those who own or have access to a TV set — has or should have a vital interest in the words spoken yesterday by Richard S. Salant, president of CBS News, in receiving a citation from the Boston University School of Public Communication for the TV broadcast, "The Selling of the Pentagon."

For very directly at issue is the freedom of the press — and by "press" we mean not only televised news and documentaries, but the printed media as well. It is about time to bring the First Amendment's guarantee of freedom of the press up-to-date and apply it to television, licensed though it is. For otherwise, the freedom of the press itself will fall by the wayside.

This most basic issue is what is involved in the controversy between CBS News and the House Interstate and Foreign Commerce Committee's Special Subcommittee on Investigations.

The subcommittee has subpoenaed not only the televised film, which had drawn criticism from Vice President Agnew and others, but also all "outtakes" and other raw materials used in preparing the broadcast but not actually broadcast. The purpose transparently is to lay a basis for a claim that the documentary was unfair. CBS has respectfully declined to furnish any other material than what was broadcast.

We think the position of CBS is eternally the right one. Nor does it matter whether "The Selling of the Pentagon" was or was not a fair presentation of the defense establishment's attempts to propagandize itself and the war. We happen to think it was, but we would take the same position on this vital constitutional issue even if we agreed with the criticisms made of the program by Rep. F. Edward Hebert (D-La.), chairman of the House Armed Services Committee.

For the question is not whether

the documentary was fair, but whether government can lay its heavy, censoring hand on the preparation and presentation of such a program, fair or unfair.

Like other newspapers, The Globe must use its best editorial judgment in presenting to readers in print about one-fiftieth of all the material that comes in each day from its reporters, news services and other sources. Sometimes it may make mistakes. But freedom of the press includes the freedom to make those mistakes, and as long as the press is truly free and competitive, there is a built-in assurance that mistakes will be corrected.

How different it would be if the government could oversee and control every detail of the preparation of the news!

The position of broadcast journalism ought to be precisely that of printed journalism. If the House subcommittee goes forward with its nefarious campaign and is backed

by Congress and the courts, then, as Mr. Salant says, "broadcast journalism is excluded from the First Amendment altogether." And the loser is all of the people.

The fact is that because of the threat from government licensing, broadcast journalism is not as good as it could be and should be. There should have been many more documentaries like "The Selling of the Pentagon." They have been all too rare simply because, as Mr. Salant so frankly put it, there are those in the industry who have said, "Let's skip this one, let's not make waves, let's stay out of trouble."

Mr. Salant calls for "a new Bill of Rights for broadcasting," and he is right. It must be supported by the printed press, whose own freedom is being similarly threatened by government encroachment. And it should be supported by all of the public, of every shade of opinion, because the public's very right to know is crucially involved.

The Cincinnati Post

TIMES ⚓ STAR

Cincinnati, Ohio, April 27, 1971

"Congress shall make no law . . . abridging the freedom of speech, or of the press . . ."

This First Amendment clause is one of the bedrock rights of the Republic. But there are ways other than by making laws that those Freedoms may be abridged.

Newspapers are familiar with numerous attempts by authorities to force reporters, under threat of contempt citations, to reveal the sources of their stories, particularly those that may involve criminal activities or be embarrassing to officials.

CONGRESS NOW SEEMS to be trying to do the same thing with the electronic media.

In the aftermath of the controversial Columbia Broadcasting System program, "The Selling of the Pentagon," the Special Subcommittee on Investigations of the House Interstate and Foreign Commerce Committee has subpoenaed not only a film copy and written transcript of the program but all notes, unused film and other materials used in connection with preparing it.

The network has provided the first two items but refused to go further.

"No newspaper, magazine or other part of the press could be required constitutionally to comply with such a subpoena with respect to material gathered by reporters in the course of a journalistic investigation but not published," CBS president Frank Stanton has stated.

"The fact that television and radio stations are licensed by the government does not deprive the broadcast press of First Amendment protection, and the courts have so held. That protection does not depend upon whether the government believes we are right or wrong in our news judgments."

The Federal Communications Commission, which licenses broadcasters, has wisely taken the stance, in this case and in others, that in the absence of overwhelming proofs of deliberate distortion, it will not meddle in journalistic judgments or pose as the arbiter of truth.

Congress might wisely adopt the same stance.

Portland Press Herald

Portland, Me., April 24, 1971

The conflict between the Columbia Broadcasting System and the investigating subcommittee of the House Interstate and Foreign Commerce Committee could strongly influence network news coverage for a long time to come.

It is not without bearing on the other media either. The business of demanding, through subpoena, notes, file material, and all sorts of source matter used in assembling a story is an area for general concern.

It is particularly distasteful in this case because it is related to the CBS documentary, "The Selling of the Pentagon," aired twice already by the network. If it continues in controversy and gets into litigation it may become as durable a feature as "The Wizard of Oz."

The committee did not content itself with demanding a copy of the film and the examination of witnesses. It also ordered CBS to produce "all film, workprints, outtakes, sound tape recordings, written scripts and-or transcripts" whether or not that material was used in the actual broadcasts. It also demanded names and addresses of all persons appearing in the film, exempting network personnel, government officials and members of Congress.

The fact that government does not like having its own indiscretions bared is not sufficient cause for even an implied threat against the news medium. And there is intimidation because television and radio stations are government licensed. They also are beneficiaries of the First Amendment's provisions.

There is no question of a criminal offense here. It is not a matter of obtaining evidence with which to prosecute a third party. It is interference with the dissemination of news, a threat, with no attempt at subtlety, against televised news features which may cast an arm of government in an unfavorable light, however truthful that light may be.

We have suspected on occasions that CBS, or some of its on-camera people, are something less than devoted admirers of the administration. The network's roving eye would be the better for a stronger gleam of objectivity. But it is not to be suppressed or intimidated by a congressional subcommittee, any group of politicians, any legislative body, any department of government, which themselves have disillusioned millions of Americans by their own secret proceedings and often unethical procedures at the expense of the people.

THE BILLINGS GAZETTE

Billings, Mont., April 19, 1971

On Feb. 23, and again a month later, CBS television aired a documentary called "The Selling of the Pentagon," which purported to show the military establishment's public relations effort.

Since then, the documentary has generated enormous controversy, with defenders of the military claiming CBS edited the film in a way that placed the military in the worst possible light.

Even the liberal Washington Post, no friend of the military, editorialized that "It is on the subject of editing that we believe CBS may be most vulnerable. That the line between reporting and staging events in this kind of television program is a fine one and also one that is all too easily crossed is a proposition with which we tend to agree. And we think this line in fact is crossed when taped interviews are edited in such a way as to alter the actual response of those of who questions are asked . . ."

CBS may well be guilty of the same sort of high pressuring that the Pentagon stands accused of. Some congressmen think so, and have subpoenaed the film and all the material that went into it. This was power politics in a city where muscle is the most important asset.

A congressional subpoena, in this case issued by the House Interstate and Foreign Commerce Committee, is not a criminal procedure, but rather an investigative one. Nonetheless, because TV stations are licensed by the Federal Communications Commission, the pressure of a congressional investigation amounts to massive intimidation of the TV newscasters.

There is no chance at all that CBS stations will lose their licenses; that is not the point. Rather, the threat of a license review is being used to pressure CBS into a viewpoint more generous to the federal colossus. The subpoena is, in fact, in itself an abridgement of TV journalism's freedom of expression, and therefor reprehensible.

If the government, or the Pentagon, is convinced that a newscast is distorted, it has the option of making its case public without using muscle tactics to silence the network. But that has not been the tactic. A congressional investigation, with the implied threat to CBS licensees, has been substituted for the free exchange of ideas.

Government is a dangerous master, and a free press (including radio and televsision) is the public's watchdog against a government on a rampage. CBS asked for trouble by apparently biasing its coverage, but that doesn't excuse the sort of strongarm tactics now being employed to make CBS shut up.

HOUSTON CHRONICLE
Houston, Tex., April 12, 1971

Vice-President Spiro T. Agnew is at it again. He seems to be trying to bolster his political standing by browbeating the news media.

This time he charges that the American news media, in the main, have given "preponderantly negative" coverage to the Vietnam war.

Agnew can believe whatever he likes about the news media's performance, of course, but we think he's way off base in his assertion.

If the news media is to be faulted in its coverage of the war, it should be for too ready acceptance of official military and governmental explanations of what was going on.

Columbia Journalism Review devoted a recent issue to press treatment of Vietnam and asked the q u e s t i o n : "What lessons should the media have learned?"

The answer, presented by seven distinguished journalists, was for the press to be more skeptical.

On March 10, 1964, when Sen. Ernest Gruening, Alaska Democrat, delivered the first Senate speech advocating an American withdrawal from Vietnam, it received v i r t u a l l y no press, radio or television coverage.

In retrospect, the government version of North Vietnam's attack on the U.S. destroyers Maddox and C. Turner Joy in the Tonkin Gulf proved highly inaccurate. At the time, only 163 Americans had died in action in Vietnam and the 16,000 American troops there were considered "advisers." Yet the attack on the Maddox and C. Turner Joy moved Congress to vote the

Tonkin resolution, which the Johnson administration considered a functional equivalent of a declaration of war.

L o o k i n g back, the news media should have been much more skeptical of the government account — or as Agnew might put it, more "negative."

Agnew might better have asked why the press didn't forewarn the country of the slow, steady course which led to our deep and unexpected involvement in this war. Why didn't the press tell the people the facts about the war rather than passing along government handouts?

The answer, of course, is that reporters in Vietnam and Washington didn't know the truth. In a war like this, and in a country like Vietnam, the military, political, economic and psychological realities are highly illusive.

We submit, however, that we are closer to the truth about Vietnam today because of hard-digging, dedicated reporters and camera crews who did ask questions and who declined to accept Pentagon handouts at face value.

An editor of the Times of London, Louis Heren, put it in perspective when he said: "Generally speaking, I think the U.S. media, with one or two outstanding exceptions, were slow to question official policy and, indeed, some of the old ideas of patriotism. The majority appear to have been inhibited by the old anti-communist ideology. The slowness to appreciate the situation was the most serious weakness. . ."

BUFFALO EVENING NEWS
Buffalo, N.Y., May 7, 1971

The news media have been getting a lot of flak from a lot of politicians lately. While some of it is no doubt deserved, much of it reflects widespread distress over the unpleasant nature of so much of the news being reported, and some is pure-and-simple political scapegoating.

A good example of the latter is California Gov. Ronald Reagan's red-faced bluster against Sacramento newsmen for "invading his privacy" by asking him about the report that he had paid no state income tax. Someone in the tax office, it seems, had leaked the fact that the governor's reported business losses more than offset any tax due on his $44,100 salary and other income, so that he paid nothing on 1970 income despite his philosophy that "taxes should hurt." But instead of just admitting the facts and explaining the circumstances, Gov. Reagan angrily turned his reply into a cheap shot at the newsmen.

A similar cheap shot was that of the

Republican national chairman, Sen. Robert Dole of Kansas, in charging that the "big production" the media made of recent anti-war demonstrations in Washington "gives our friends — and our enemies — around the world a false picture of a weak, divided nation." Is Sen. Dole claiming that the happenings in the national capital which resulted in over 12,000 arrests should NOT have been treated as a major news story by the press and the broadcasters? If he is, he it should have been ignored? If he is, he shows abysmal news judgment and would do better hereafter to just fight Democrats and leave the media-baiting to Spiro Agnew.

What's most ironic about the Dole complaint, in any case, is that nearly all the coverage we saw of the most recent Washington demonstrations made the police and the Nixon administration — Sen. Dole's team—look pretty good. But a fine lot of gratitude he shows for it!

CHICAGO Sun-Times
Chicago, Ill., July 14, 1971

Having lost a courtroom round in his battle to force the news media to spread only good cheer, President Nixon has returned to the old tactic of sending Vice President Spiro T. Agnew into the fray as front man.

And once again, Agnew is using the jawbone of an ass. In Singapore, he said that if the press reported a military defeat for the Saigon government, it would be "a public relations coup" for Hanoi. In Addis Ababa, he said world leaders were "just appalled" at the publication of the Pentagon papers.

In the first instance, Agnew and his boss are trying to blame the press in advance for reporting the events, not the events themselves.

In the second instance, we think it appalling that Agnew feels he must apologize for a free press in countries which do not have one. But it is hardly unexpected, given the administration's contempt for and ignorance of the Bill of Rights, as evidenced in such things as advocacy of preventive detention.

If one wishes to add to the list, there is Atty. Gen. John N. Mitchell's crusade to use wiretaps on dissident political groups, "no-knock" legislation and Agnew's broadsides against the electronic media.

Yesterday's Sun-Times carried a story on a related matter which also deserves comment as an example of administration bungling. By its attempts before a federal grand jury in Boston to see whether it has a criminal case against the newspapers which published the Pentagon papers, the Justice Department is acting as it should have done in the first place. Newspapers of course are not above the law, whether it be libel or espionage. What they are immune from under the First Amendment is prior restraint from publication, a right subsequently upheld by the U.S. Supreme Court, and Messrs. Nixon and Mitchell should have known this.

Mr. Nixon's popularity is low — only 46 per cent of the people, according to the Gallup Poll, approve generally of his policies. Why? Because people are confused. They do not know which to believe—the media which report events as they happen, or Mr. Nixon and Agnew, who try to gloss over and distort those events.

The Courier-Journal

Louisville, Ky., July 13, 1971

AH, THE SADNESS of it. The newspapers' publication of the Pentagon papers has damaged the United States in the eyes of every government he's visited on his current trot around the globe, Vice President Agnew tells us. The leaders of those countries are "a little jumpy about the United States," he says, and they've asked him not to tell reporters too much about their conversations with him.

Things must be in a truly distressing state. For if the leaders of such bastions of democracy as South Korea, Singapore, Kuwait, Saudi Arabia and Ethiopia are disturbed by the arrogance of the American press, then everybody else probably is, too. Even our beloved ally, Generalissimo Franco, might have to step away from the brink of candor when Mr. Agnew and all those reporters arrive in Spain Saturday.

During their private conversations, though, all these friends of the United States in Asia and Africa could be whispering a few helpful tips into the Vice President's ear. Prime Minister Lee Kuan Yew of Singapore, for instance, knows how to avoid the disclosure of embarrassing information about his government in the popular press. Just a few days before Mr. Agnew's arrival, the Prime Minister shut down two newspapers and jailed the editors of a third for criticizing him. And General Franco—well, the freedom of the Spanish press is practically legendary.

His burdens are many

But alas, the irresponsibility of the American press is only a part of the burden the Vice President is bearing for us in those far-off lands. Not only do the leaders think our press is irresponsible, he says; they also think our Congress is irresponsible. They were awfully upset, he says, by Congress' refusal to continue development of the SST. "They do not see," he says, "how a great country—a technological giant—can continue to be great if it turns its back on its responsibilities." And Mr. Agnew agrees wholeheartedly with them.

In retrospect, it *is* shameful that our irresponsible Congress and the irresponsible voters Congress represents have conspired to deprive the Ethiopians of supersonic transportation. It's all part of our "neo-isolationism" and our "wave of retreat from responsibility," probably. We've become so wrapped up in our own petty problems that we've given scarcely a thought to our obligations to the sheiks and prime ministers and generalissimos who stand guard for us on those far frontiers.

But, thank goodness, our friends know where the blame should be placed. The "wave of retreat from responsibility" isn't the fault of the Nixon administration. They understand, Mr. Agnew says, that the President has no intention of keeping troops "everywhere in the world," but they fully expect the United States to give them the money and arms they need to resist aggression.

If dollars and guns will soothe the minds of the anxious potentates, they almost certainly will get them. If we give them enough, perhaps they'll forget how irresponsible we are. Perhaps they'll even forgive us for junking the SST.

If Mr. Agnew's diplomacy can accomplish that, even the most irresponsible among us will be forced to confess that his trip has been well worthwhile.

St. Louis Globe-Democrat

St. Louis, Mo., July 8, 1971

A newspaper, radio station or television station is not presenting an objective, fair picture of the American scene if it persistently reports only the problems plaguing the United States.

If you add to this an obvious hate-Nixon bias that afflicts much of the liberal press, the end product is about as representative of the United States as a page from Pravda.

The news media do have an obligation to tell the public what is right with the country as well as what is wrong. When they religiously omit all mention of the positive and dwell exclusively on the negative the result is a badly flawed representation of the whole, a grossly distorted national image.

President Nixon, who like other Presidents, must bear the brunt of much of this "look-how-terrible-everything-is" attitude, pointed out that a steady, relentless diet of problems can be dangerous to the country.

* * *

"Don't let the problems of the moment obscure the great and good things that are going on in this country," said Mr. Nixon.

"When a society comes to the point where there is negativism, defeatism, a sense of alienation, it is inevitable that younger people will give up. They will turn to drugs and other activities disruptive of society."

Many critics of the Vietnam war seem to enjoy trying to find fault with every move our country made in the war. Much of this literary masochism goes unchallenged even though it often is pure fiction.

The truth is that the United States' motives in going into Vietnam were and are the best. We made mistakes, but our goal from the beginning was to repel the invading North Vietnamese and preserve the freedom of the South Vietnamese.

In retrospect it can be seen the price was too high.

But then when we look back at World War I, World War II and Korea, when hasn't it been?

President Nixon, in our opinion, has done about as good a job of ending the war on an honorable basis as any man could have done. The situation he inherited from President Johnson was a nightmare. President Johnson had committed about 540,000 American men to Vietnam with no set plan for winning or ending the war.

* * *

By now about 300,000 troops have come home. There probably will be less than 50,000 in Vietnam by the end of this year as South Vietnam assumes nearly complete control of its own defense.

Why then this terrible recrimination, this endlessly searching for scapegoats in Vietnam, the positive fetish for pouring over the slanted, carefully selected Pentagon papers that were gathered by men who admit they were disillusioned with the war?

This pathetically biased study's main contribution may be to make it almost impossible to examine the war in a scholarly, objective manner until many years have passed.

* * *

We see this same negativism when some look at the problems of crime and drug abuse. Some gloom-sayers conclude the nation is beyond saving.

The fact is that in 1970 the nation saw its first sizable decrease in crime in most of our larger cities, including St. Louis, in more than a decade. The drug problem is serious but again the prognosis is optimistic.

Strong counter-measures are everywhere in evidence from the federal to the local level. The Army has set up a program for identifying and treating addicts coming back from Vietnam. It is finding that addiction is not as widespread as some critics claim.

To imply that any but a small fraction of young people are hooked on drugs is an unwarranted slur on the younger generation that, by and large, is as intelligent, humane and dedicated to democratic ideals as any previous generation.

* * *

There are a great many things that are right in the United States, the greatest of which is the freedom we all enjoy to express our opinions without fear of reprisal.

Our economy, despite its problems, dwarfs that of any other nation in the world. In 1970 Americans produced goods and services worth $977 billion, more than twice the amount of the world's second-largest producer, the Soviet Union.

In fact, wherever one looks, he can see great new and exciting programs taking shape — an unparalleled national effort to clean up the environment, a new federal program for reforming welfare, a national commitment to build housing that is beginning to roll into high gear after years of planning, an unprecedented de-segregation of schools, the granting of the ballot to those 18, 19 and 20, and a developing foreign policy aimed at negotiation rather than confrontation.

One could go on, but this should suffice to put the picture more in perspective. Keep some of these things in mind the next time you read or hear an exaggerated account of what's wrong with our country.

NEW ORLEANS STATES-ITEM
New Orleans, La., July 13, 1971

Vice President Agnew is either incapable of understanding the role of the press in a free society, or he simply doesn't want to understand.

He reports from Ethiopia with a degree of vengeance that world leaders are "just appalled" at the publication by The New York Times of the now famous "Pentagon Papers" on the Vietnam war.

The vice president is quick to add that his own talks with Asian and African leaders have not been jeopardized because they know he feels the same way they do on the matter.

We are appalled, too, but for a different reason. We are appalled that Mr. Agnew, who purports to be on a diplomatic mission, does not sufficiently understand the greatness of America to explain to world leaders the role of the press, an integral part of that greatness.

Mr. Agnew need not be appalled. He should, as a representative of this nation, interpret the function of a free press for those who do not understand. He might make these points in his travels abroad:

The primary function of the American press is that of independent, unfettered watchdog acting on behalf of the people it serves.

The Founding Fathers believed so absolutely in the concept of a free press that three justices of the Supreme Court found in a ruling on behalf of The New York Times and other newspapers that the First Amendment leaves no room for government restraint at all.

The decision of The New York Times to expose the conduct of the Vietnam war is a classic example of the role the press should play in the democratic process.

Justice Hugo Black made this point in his observations concerning publication of the Pentagon Papers:

"Far from deserving condemnation for their courageous reporting, The New York Times, the Washington Post and other newspapers should be commended for serving the purpose that the Founding Fathers saw so clearly. In revealing the workings of government that led to the Vietnam war, the newspapers nobly did precisely that which the founders hoped and trusted they would do."

Mr. Agnew might also read the words of retired Justice Tom Clark from an earlier ruling on the role of the press.

"A vigorous and dauntless press is a chief source feeding the flow of democratic expression and controversy which maintains the institutions of a free society.

"By interpreting to the citizen the policies of his government and vigilantly scrutinizing the official conduct of those who administer the state, an independent press stimulates free discussion and focuses public opinion on issues and officials as a potent check on arbitrary action or abuse.

"The press, in fact, 'serves one of the most vital of all general interests: The dissemination of news from as many different sources, and with as many different facets and colors as is possible. That interest is closely akin to, if indeed it is not the same as, the interest protected by the First Amendment; it presupposes that right conclusions are more likely to be gathered out of a multitude of tongues, than through all kinds of authoritative selection. To many this is, and always will be, folly; but we have staked upon it our all.' "

The final words are worth repeating.

". . . but we have staked upon it our all."

THE SUN
Baltimore, Md., July 7, 1971

Vice President Agnew, talking to American reporters at Singapore during his world trip, has introduced a novel concept of news evaluation into his discussion of the American press. Mr. Agnew offers what might be called a prior criticism of news dispatches. He seems to anticipate events in Vietnam that have not yet occurred and undertakes to warn the public against the way in which they may be reported in the press.

Mr. Agnew was quoted in Peter J. Kumpa's news dispatch as saying:

We're in a very vulnerable situation with respect to American opinion because it's completely possible for the North Vietnamese, in a very high-risk, high-casualty effort, to launch a pinpointed attack which will unquestionably—if it's successful, regardless of North Vietnamese casualties—be played heavily as a failure of the Vietnamization program in the United States.

Mr. Kumpa reported that Mr. Agnew said that the United States military believe such an attack is likely and expected. He quoted Mr. Agnew further:

Success in a military sense is a lot different from a public relations coup, which is easily achieved because so many of our people in the national media are too ready to assist the North Vietnamese by their over-emphasis on what's taking place. I don't think they mean to assist them, but we've gone through this terrible, introspective, almost masochistic, twinge of conscience in our country regarding the Vietnam war where we look with favor on anything good that happens to the enemy.

Mr. Agnew told the reporters at Singapore that he thought the South Vietnamese, eventually if not immediately, could defeat such a Communist attack. To this he added: "The point is, will the attack be related to the American people in perspective or will it be distorted as a complete defeat for the Vietnamization program?"

The Vice President's analysis of this news-to-come can be appraised to some extent by his recollection of the way in which the Cambodian invasion was reported. Mr. Agnew said the American press has reported the invasion miserably and inaccurately, treating it "as a total escalation of the war, as a defeat, and it turned out to be one of the smartest things we've done in Vietnam, without which we couldn't continue with our withdrawals."

In fact the American press reported in detail President Nixon's advance appraisal of the Cambodian operation as a turning point in the war and reported in detail the government's accounts of the developments in Cambodia. The invasion was accurately reported as a widening of the war, but not as a "total escalation" or as a "defeat." The government's claim as to its ultimate importance has been reported often. It might be added that the government has yet to give anything like a detailed report on the later invasion of Laos by South Vietnamese forces, although some government officials have claimed that the information gathered by reporters was incomplete.

In the case of events yet to occur in Vietnam the press will continue to report the facts as fully and accurately as it can obtain them, and it will report the statements made by Mr. Nixon and other American officials. Mr. Agnew takes a singularly narrow view of the broad scope of American journalism and of the way in which a free press functions in a free society. He shows, moreover, a remarkable lack of confidence in the ability of the public to grasp facts and form its own judgment.

Des Moines Tribune
Des Moines, Iowa, July 13, 1971

Vice-President Spiro Agnew, who has been touring Asian and African countries, told reporters in a press conference in Ethiopia that world leaders were "just appalled" at the publication of the Pentagon papers on Vietnam. He said these world leaders feel that the United States cannot continue as a world power if every secret is leaked.

Agnew said the people he talked to were not concerned about whether the Pentagon papers should have been declassified but whether private persons outside the government should be able to declassify the material.

This is a common reaction of many persons who do not understand the American system of democracy and the Bill of Rights. We hope Vice-President Agnew took the opportunity to explain that the First Amendment prohibits censorship (prior restraint) by the government against speech or publication — with the exception of extreme, immediate danger to the state, in the opinion of a majority of the Supreme Court — and that this doctrine was upheld by the court in the specific case of the Pentagon papers. (Newspapers are not protected against violation of espionage laws, of course, and may be prosecuted in court for having published secrets, on the ground that the national security was harmed.)

Agnew might well have pointed out that this does not make the U.S. government powerless to hide secrets. But he ought to have explained, further, that leaking "secrets" to the press is an old and familiar practice in the U.S. system of government. Presidents, secretaries of state and defense and others in officialdom make a regular practice of releasing "secret" material for their own purposes.

It isn't newspaper enterprise or irresponsibility that causes most of the secrets to get out. It is the conflicts in political opinion, which are the heart of a democratic system.

Public officials are always leaking secrets to reporters, who are sworn to protect the identity of their informants, including presidents. The officials do this for all kinds of purposes, including their own political advantage.

The Washington Post revealed in 1957, for example, the contents of the secret Gaither report on U.S. military preparedness. The Democrats used it in advocating heavy arms spending in the early 1960s. The Eisenhower Administration released the Yalta Big Three conference papers. Actually, some of the 1964 Vietnam contingency plans, which the New York Times published and which the government went to court to keep from the public, were published in 1964 by reporters who were "leaked" the information.

▸ ▸ ▸

We hope that Agnew pointed out that there have been few cases of truly vital secrets spilled as the result of newspaper publication. The atomic bomb secrets were not published but were given to Russia by spies. Newspapers did not reveal important military secrets (such as troop movements and battle plans) in World War II, the Korean war or the Vietnam war.

Agnew might have told the foreign leaders that our experience with the First Amendment is that there is less risk in letting the people know what their government is doing than in giving officials arbitrary power to censor.

He could have added that we have had more difficulty in foreign relations as the result of *successful* secrecy in military affairs and diplomacy than the other way around.

BUFFALO EVENING NEWS
Buffalo, N.Y., September 29, 1971

Why is it that, whenever there is any news story of social consequence, the Vice President of the United States can be depended upon to turn it into another excuse for an attack on the press?

What is he really gunning for, that he works so diligently to undermine the credibility of the only institution the free people of this nation have for informing themselves of what is taking place in their own country and abroad?

Now it is the Attica prison riot for which he condemns the press. His complaint, typically, was that the news media — not any particular ones, but in general — focused "inordinate attention . . . on the self-declared and proven enemies of our soceity."

Yet what is the biggest lesson Mr. Agnew himself draws from Attica? "It is that Americans who value our system and its free institutions cannot underestimate the potential for violence and destruction inherent in any radical militant movement." So how, pray tell, can he fault the press for overplaying the very element in the case he warns us never to underestimate?

Mr. Agnew's attack on the press for its Attica coverage happens to concern an event that was close to home for us, and one that The News covered thoroughly and at first hand. We are tremendously proud of the job our news staff did, working to exhaustion against every conceivable barrier to learn what was going on inside those walls and to tell the story as honestly and in as fair a perspective as they possibly could.

Certainly it was not a pleasant story to tell, and there were aspects which, by their nature, provoked furious reactions. There were the widest kinds of variations in the coverage, too, depending on which particular account you read, heard or saw, or which angry witness or participant was sounding off. But by and large, the news media did their utmost to tell the story accurately and in depth.

Whatever Mr. Agnew knows of the Attica facts, he must have learned mainly from the news media. Somehow, for example, they must have given him a basis for his judgment that "the litany of anti-American hate preached by radical propagandists" in the Attica aftermath "is a dagger at the heart of our country's free institutions." On this, we do not disagree. But what worries us almost as much is the litany of anti-media hate which (to use the same mixed metaphor) the vice president keeps brandishing, like a "dagger at the heart" of one of the most crucial of those very free institutions—the free press.

What is behind these constant, authoritarian-style attacks on all elements of the news media? A former president of the American Society of Newspaper Editors, Norman E. Isaacs, now of the Columbia University journalism faculty, hit all too close to home, we fear, in appearing yesterday before the Senate Subcommittee on Constitutional Rights: "I can only consider this (Agnew attack) another broadside from an administration determined to lower the public regard for the press and to create a public mood by which the news media can be forced into a subservient role."

OREGON JOURNAL
Portland, Ore., September 30, 1971

Many governments believe that they must censor the press in order to control their systems.

The American system was based on just the reverse: The government needs censors, and therefore the press must be free.

Sen. Sam J. Ervin Jr., D-N.C., the 75-year-old champion of freedoms guaranteed by the Constitution, opened Senate hearings of American press freedom by quoting Thomas Jefferson to that effect: "No government ought to be without censors and where the press is free, no one ever will."

Bear in mind that freedom of the press is not an exclusive privilege of newspapers. It is a right of all citizens, not just those who are in the business of publishing, to print what they want to say. The accompanying right is that of the citizen to avail himself of a wide range of information to educate himself and to form opinion.

Newspapers, which rely on that same freedom that belongs to everyone, by and large have assumed a responsibility to strive for accuracy; to try to distinguish between factual reports and opinion, and to try to be fair and informed in setting forth both fact and opinion. In their relationship with government, the press and other media sometimes serve as go-betweens — between people and government, and between government and people — and also as watch-dogs to guard against the misuse of power through the exposure of the printed or spoken word.

Thomas Jefferson's "censors" thus are also informers and interpreters. The risk of error is wide, the chance to be wrong is great, the curse of omission ever present.

But, says Sen. Ervin, "Most Americans have come to understand that the irritating excesses of the press are a small price to pay for a press independent of government control."

He sees, however, a "general time of crisis" in this country, in which freedom of the press is being challenged by high government officials who "appear to believe that the purpose of the press is to present the government's policies and programs to the public in the best possible light."

Whether censorship is imposed by government or is self-imposed under intimidation through governmental power, the result is the same and the consequences are frightful.

So Ervin has called on his Constitutional Rights subcommittee to undertake three weeks of hearings to investigate the attempt to prevent publication of the Pentagon Papers; the subpoenaing of reporters and their notes; the use of phony press credentials by government agents, and the threat of governmental control of material presented by broadcast media.

While Ervin was opening his hearings, the most strident voice of those high government officials — that of Vice President Agnew — again was using a broad brush to attack the "liberal press" for its coverage and analysis of the Attica prison revolt, making "heroes" out of criminals and promoting the "celebrated radical left causes."

The press, like the other segments of this society, should be subject to criticism. That criticism should be fair, informed and specific, but the media lumped together under the single label of the "press" is no monolith; it is made up of thousands of individual elements. It is time to hoist the danger signs when someone speaking from the exalted position of the vice presidency would blackjack the press as a single institution.

Thinking back to Jefferson's concept of the free press and government, Agnew's own comment might apply: "When those who protect us are attacked, we are all attacked. When those who safeguard our institutions are endangered, our institutions are endangered."

Needless to say, he was not talking about the guarantees of the First Amendment. But his words fly back at him. Perhaps Sen. Ervin's hearings come none too soon.

PORTLAND EVENING EXPRESS
Portland, Me., September 30, 1971

The press, says Ronald L. Ziegler, White House press secretary, displays "too much sensitivity" to criticism and threats of government intimidation.

On the element of sensitivity to criticism, we are inclined to agree with him. The press, like government, is people. And people very often react to criticism defensively. They tend toward an instinctive effort to deny or to direct blame to another source. What would be far better, of course, is calm appraisal of the criticism and an effort to make constructive application of it.

It would be reasonable to apply that procedure to government reaction to press criticism as well as press reaction to government criticism.

Of all people, a press aide to Richard Nixon would be aware that there are times when people in government are excessively sensitive to press criticism. On the other hand, there are as many times when government sources seem quite insensitive to that criticism.

However, on the matter of threats of government intimidation, we wonder if there is any such thing as "too much sensitivity." It seems vital that the press be constantly sensitive to any such danger.

Politicians have been known to regard frequent press criticism as harassment or evidence of animosity. That might explain why frequent criticism of the news media by the Vice President of the United States might by construed by the press as a threat of government intimidation.

Arkansas Gazette.

Little Rock, Ark., October 1, 1971

Spiro T. Agnew has been unloosed again after a period of months in which he had said very little, for reasons that no one knows without being privy to the inner counsels at the White House. Mr. Agnew, like other vice presidents, does what he is told; he speaks or he remains silent at the President's pleasure.

Agnew's prime target this time around appears to be the familiar one, that old devil, the press. It would be a temptation to dismiss out of hand, from pure boredom, Agnew's renewed attempt to blame the nation's ills, most recently "Attica," on the press. However, there may be more here than meets the eye; indeed the unloosing of Agnew may portend an assault upon the press on a grander scale than anything yet conceived. If it is conceded that public officials and the press are natural adversaries, and that all presidents try to "manage" and sometimes intimidate the press, there has still been no administration in this century with the Nixon administration's "instinct for the jugular" in this kind of confrontation, nor any administration so hostile to the Bill of Rights as a whole.

What has changed since Spiro last in the dooryard gloomed? The Supreme Court has changed. Hugo Black, the greatest champion of the First Amendment, is dead. John Marshall Harlan, a respected conservative, is retired. And Richard Nixon will have two more nominees for the nine-member court to join the two members he has already appointed, both of whom have taken a restrictive view of the rights of the press under the First Amendment.

If Mr. Nixon's next two appointees take as jaundiced a view of the press as his first two, then the press—which is to say radio and TV as well as the newspapers and magazines—may be in for more trouble than it has known in this century.

The reemergence of Agnew, hatchet in either hand, might even signify that the administration is preparing to initiate broadside new prosecutions in connection with the "Pentagon papers" affair. Both of the Nixon justices on the Supreme Court in dissenting opinions acidly criticised the New York Times and Washington Post for daring to reveal information which the government had royally decreed to be "top secret." The decision upholding the two newspapers' position and the First Amendment was divided 6-3 and, as Mr. Nixon adds appointees to the Court, the margin of support for the First Amendment in key cases may become perilous indeed.

At the time that the Court handed down the decision in the Times case, many of us hailed it as a victory, which it was in one way. But in another way the news was rather evocative of the joke about the Sunday School class president who told an ailing member that the class had voted 6 to 3 to pray for his recovery. The Pyrrhic nature of the victory in the Times case was emphasized by the fact that three justices in the six-member majority indicated that they might have ruled differently if Congress had passed some legislation in the field, which would be the American equivalent of the notorious "official secrets" act in Britain.

As it happened, the reappearance of Agnew on the speaking circuit coincided with the opening of U. S. Senate hearings in which the officers of the American Society of Newspaper Editors and other newspaper executives have testified against the precedent set in the government's action on the Pentagon papers, and against other dangers to press freedom. The entry of the ASNE is the congressional argument is timely, to say the least.

Yet, as for the press in general, we are not sure how thorough and widespread is the realization of the threat to the press posed by this administration, especially now that it is changing the complexion of the Supreme Court. Nearly all the U. S. newspapers supported the New York Times and Washington Post in the Pentagon papers case, and yet, when the general election comes next year, it is a better than even bet that a majority of the newspapers will trot dutifully down the line again to endorse Richard Nixon for president, disregarding knowledge of what a bitter enemy he is, and has been, of the free press principle. There are, alas, many publishers who are Republicans before they are newspapermen.

Richard Nixon has always been very good at conning newspaper executives at conventions and in background sessions with selected press lords. One day the newspapers may wake up to realize that Nixon is trying to put them out of business, or at least trying to shut them up so effectively that it would not matter much whether they were in business or not. We would hope that the awakening would come in time.

The Charleston Gazette

Charleston, W. Va., November 22, 1971

We suppose there are a few people somewhere who believe the FBI was conducting an investigation of CBS correspondent Daniel Schorr because the White House was thinking about offering him a job.

This is the implausible excuse which was offered when Schorr complained about the investigation and suggested he was being harassed because the White House didn't think well of his news reporting and had so said on several occasions.

The excuse is implausible because Schorr wasn't notified that he was being considered for a job in the federal government, had never sought a job in the federal government, and was highly likely to reject a job in the federal government if one were offered him. Further, it was no secret that the government distrusted Schorr. Why would the government want to employ a man it didn't trust?

The circumstances suggest that a clumsy attempt to intimidate the newsman had been mounted, just as Schorr claimed, and that the White House was caught with egg on its face.

It is acceptable procedure, if the White House is thinking of offering someone a job, to begin by telling him so. This gives him a chance to turn it down at once, saving the expense of an investigation. If he is receptive, the security check can be made with his consent.

The FBI check on Schorr was furtive, but not furtive enough to prevent him from learning that the FBI was looking into his background. This is an ancient tool of terror, commonplace in totalitarian societies. It has no place in America.

Personal liberty seems to be a concept beyond the comprehension of the Nixon administration, which more than any other ostensibly peacetime administrations has sought to regulate citizen behavior by police threat.

Detroit Free Press

Detroit, Mich., November 22, 1971

WHEN THE White House got caught siccing the FBI on Daniel Schorr of CBS News, one of the underlings explained that Mr. Schorr was being considered for a federal appointment.

Unfortunately, the government has so far been unwilling or unable to say which job, and the story continues to have the telltale smell of little fishes. It is, though, an ingenious device, and it opens up all sorts of possibilities for harassment of government critics.

Sylvia Porter had best be wary of her criticism lest she find herself on one of those celebrated lists for secretary of the Treasury.

Jack Anderson will surely make the semi-finals of the competition for deputy chief of the CIA. Bill Buckley is a possibility for the job of ambassador to Peking, something we're sure to need in a year or so.

And if there is ever an opening for court jester, Art Buchwald and Russell Baker can expect to have their every step dogged by slue-footed FBI agents. ("Was he ever known to drop insulting one-liners about the vice president?").

Such possibilities are not, of course, really so far-fetched. An administration that has too short a fuse and is too likely to react vindictively to criticism has abused a legitimate tool of government—the security check for prospective employees—and it will have to be watched constantly lest it do so again.

Moreover, there is a danger that the tactic will be extended to the general populace rather than just the White House press corps.

So if a little man in a blue suit comes nosing around telling your neighbors you may be the next Supreme Court appointee, watch out, folks. The President has these lists.

Minneapolis Tribune

Minneapolis, Minn., November 16, 1971

We find it not at all disturbing when an administration has its differences with the press. On the contrary, we'd find it disturbing if the two didn't have any differences, for if the press is performing its role properly, it's bound to question policies the government is trying to promote and publicize things the government would rather be kept quiet.

The Nixon administration, however, has gone beyond grumbling about the news media, and even beyond Trumanesque or Johnsonian outbursts directed at individual reporters or commentators. There have been attempts to discredit the news media, most notably those of Vice-President Agnew. There have been efforts, in the Pentagon Papers case, to abrogate some of the fundamental freedoms guaranteed by the First Amendment. Now there appears to have been an effort to harass and intimidate Daniel Schorr, a Washington correspondent for the Columbia Broadcasting System, who has clashed frequently with the White House over his reporting.

Schorr, it seems, has been investigated by the FBI, which was acting on orders from the White House. The investigation began in August, after presidential aides disputed Schorr's report of a Nixon speech. Two days later, the FBI was questioning Schorr's supervisors, his neighbors and even his brother's neighbors.

A White House official, asked about the investigation, said Schorr "was under consideration . . . for a high position in the environmental area." But he refused to identify the post. Schorr says he "checked every source who might know, without the slightest indication that I was ever considered for any post." He also noted that the usual procedure is for the government to notify a person that he's under consideration for a job before beginning to investigate him. No one, however, discussed a job with Schorr. We might add that it seems unlikely that the administration would consider "a high position" for a reporter whose fairness and accuracy it had so frequently questioned.

Sen. Ervin of North Carolina, declaring that a government attempt to discourage anyone from commenting on public affairs would be "a gross violation of the First Amendment," has said that his judiciary subcommittee will look into the FBI investigation of Schorr. We welcome the senator's decision. The White House might have been acting in good faith; there might have been a job for which Schorr was being considered. But until the facts are known, the investigation will continue to look like an attempt to harass a reporter into silence. That alone could discourage other potential critics. And that alone is disturbing.

The Virginian-Pilot

Norfolk, Va., November 16, 1971

Whoever ordered the FBI to investigate Daniel Schorr seems to have succeeded in Nader-izing the CBS newsman.

Ralph Nader was unknown until General Motors put private detectives on his trail when he began crusading about auto safety, you may recall. The end result was that the biggest corporation in the world was brought to its knees by Mr. Nader, who was institutionalized into a contemporary St. George the dragon-killer in the process.

Mr. Schorr isn't exactly unknown. But who knows—and who cares?—what he said to cause faceless lieutenants in the White House to order him to be snooped upon? Once the fact that the FBI had been investigating Mr. Schorr was made public, the White House let it be known that he was being considered for a Government job in the environmental field. There was never any attempt to harass or intimidate Mr. Schorr, the White House said—who could ever think such a thing?

Well, yes. But Mr. Schorr says he was never offered any Government position and he doesn't think he was ever considered for one. It would be difficult to find anyone outside the White House who is willing to swallow the official version. The matter "was handled in a clumsy way," admits Press Secretary Ron Ziegler.

It certainly was. The issue now is whether the Administration is engaged in another attack upon the press, and Senator Sam Ervin, the defender of the faith from North Carolina, has invited Mr. Schorr to testify when his Senate subcommittee holds its next round of hearings on freedom of the press in January. Mr. Ervin also has invited Communications Director Herbert Klein and other Administration aides to testify. If Mr. Klein & Co. invoke "executive privilege" to beg off, as expected, Mr. Ervin might read into the record some of Mr. Klein's speeches about the Nixon Administration's candor with the press and public. They are always good for laughs.

AKRON BEACON JOURNAL

Akron, Ohio, November 16, 1971

It could be true, of course, that the FBI investigated CBS reporter Daniel Schorr because the White House wanted to offer Schorr a job. It could be true despite the facts that the White House had complained to C B S about Schorr's reporting, that it didn't tell Schorr about the job or the investigation, and couldn't, when queried, quite remember what job it had in mind.

It also could be true, and seems much more likely, that the administration has substituted a Sherlockian stealth for Agnew's blunderbuss in an effort to chill criticism of the President. It seems more likely because the Nixon administration, like the man who heads it, is a very "private" administration, supersensitive to what is said or written about it.

★

Although early on Mr. Nixon made some ceremony of removing from his office the battery of television sets that Lyndon Johnson monitored, he didn't give the sets to Goodwill. They are in another room. Someone else does the watching, and the reckoning of which commentators are "for" the President and which are "against." It seems reasonable to assume that these scorecards are kept for some purpose.

That purpose hardly squares, as James Reston has noted, with Mr. Nixon's 1968 pledge of "an open administration — open to ideas from people, and open with its communication with the people — an administration of open doors, open eyes and open minds."

It suggests something quite different — namely an administration intent on, if not always adept at, manipulating images. One remembers Attorney General Mitchell's injunction to reporters to "watch what we do instead of what we say." And remembers as well his real — or feigned — wrath over revelation of a list of possible Supreme Court nominees who failed to pass muster by the American Bar Association. Did the leak originate in the ABA, which denied it, or with an administration which wanted credit in reactionary quarters for trying to put on the court men it knew the Senate would not confirm?

★

Mr. Nixon always has resented what he considered to be an animosity toward him on the part of the press. The Schorr episode suggests that he or those around him consider the correct relationship to be one of permanent hostility.

If that impression is correct, a tragic misjudgment has been made, for the Nixon administration has had, on the whole, a friendly press.

Its major embarrassments have resulted from factual reporting of deeds such as the Carswell nomination, the Cambodian "incursion," and the somersault on wage-price controls, rather than from carping examination of what the President has said.

The resort to use of the FBI for purposes that must be assumed amount to intimidation is a sign of a saddening insecurity.

The Pentagon Papers & Government Secrecy

The Pentagon Papers case was the climax of the struggle between the Administration and the news media. The publication of the secret documents confirmed the suspicions of many in the Administration that certain segments of the press were irresponsible or even disloyal. To many journalists, the government's attempts to suppress publication of the Pentagon Papers proved that the Nixon Administration was determined to stifle freedom of the press.

The Supreme Court checked the attempt to block publication of the documents, but another crucial issue raised by the case could not be resolved by the courts: What justification had there been for stamping so many documents top secret?

Most of the information contained in the study was known to diligent newspaper readers and certainly to the Vietnamese Communists. Few, if any, of the facts revealed were manifestly worthy of official concealment. In the Pentagon Papers case, as on so many previous occasions, the classification system seemed to have been used to hide official errors rather than to protect genuine secrets.

Stolen FBI files disseminated. Stolen Federal Bureau of Investigation (FBI) intelligence files were received March 22, 1971 by Sen. George McGovern (D, S.D.) and Rep. Parren J. Mitchell (D, Md.). The documents, most of them relating to peace and black activist groups, were sent by the Citizens Commission to Investigate the FBI, which admitted stealing the files after breaking into the FBI office at Media, Pa. March 8.

Both McGovern and Mitchell returned the documents immediately. McGovern said he refused to be associated with "this illegal action by a private group" and said he favored Congressional investigation of the bureau. Mitchell said in a speech March 23 that burglary was a crime and should be dealt with as such. However, he added that "the investigation and surveillance of individuals, peace groups and black student groups," as indicated by the files, was also criminal.

Attorney General John N. Mitchell said March 23 that copies of the stolen records had also been distributed to the press. He urged that the information be withheld so as not to "endanger the lives or cause other serious harm to persons engaged in investigative activities on behalf of the United States." He also said disclosure of national defense information "could endanger the United States and give aid to foreign governments whose interests might be inimical to those of the United States."

The Washington Post, which received the documents March 23, published a description of the files in its March 24 editions but omitted most names and specific locations. Copies were also received by the New York Times and the Los Angeles Times.

According to a Justice Department source, the 14 documents distributed were among nearly 800 stolen. Most of them were marked "United States Government Memorandum."

One was a Nov. 4, 1970 memorandum by FBI Director J. Edgar Hoover ordering investigations of all groups "organized to project the demands of black students." The memo said, "Increased campus disorders involving black students pose a definite threat to the nation's stability and security and indicate need for increase in both the quality and quantity of intelligence information on Black Student Unions and similar groups which are targets for influence and control by violence-prone Black Panther party and other extremists."

Another document, a newsletter from the Philadelphia FBI office, encouraged agents to increase interviews with dissenters "for plenty of reasons, chief of which are it will enhance the paranoia endemic in these circles and will further serve to get the point across there is an FBI agent behind every mailbox." The document, dated Sept. 16, 1970, added, "some will be overcome by the overwhelming personalities of the contacting agent and volunteer to tell all—perhaps on a continuing basis."

One of the documents related to a philosophy professor at a Philadelphia-area college evidently suspected of harboring fugitives. The file indicated that a college switchboard operator had agreed to report on long distance calls received by the professor and that the agent had the cooperation of a campus security guard. Another reported attempts to infiltrate a 1969 war-resisters' conference at Haverford (Pa.) College and a 1970 convention of the National Association of Black Students at Wayne State University (Detroit). The documents contained a report from the Swarthmore (Pa.) police department on black militant activities at Swarthmore College.

Publication of secrets halted. The New York Times halted publication June 15 of a series of Vietnam war articles drawn from a secret Pentagon study after the Justice Department obtained a temporary court order barring publication of the articles.

The Pentagon study, traced increasing U.S. involvement in the Vietnam war and covering a period ending in 1968. The study contained some startling developments, such as Johnson Administration plans for major American military action against North Vietnam almost five months before the 1964 Tonkin Gulf incident, a covert commitment of U.S. ground combat troops to the war and an anxiety lest the escalation become publicized.

The Times printed three installments of the series June 13–15 covering 18 pages of newsprint with documents and analysis drawn from the Pentagon study. The study itself consisted of 3,000 pages of analysis and 4,000 pages of official documents on the policy decisions which led to U.S. involvement in the war. The Pentagon papers did not include Presidential papers and included only those State Department documents that turned up in the Defense Department files.

Commissioned by then-Defense Secretary Robert S. McNamara, the study was held confidential—only 15 copies reportedly were produced initially when it was written in 1968—and eventually committed by McNamara to the federal archives. The Times came into possession of 39 of its 40 book-length volumes.

Nixon Administration reaction—The Nixon Administration took the position on the Times articles that they involved unauthorized release of classified defense material. White House Press Secretary Ronald L. Ziegler pointed out June 14 that President Nixon had developed a "new Vietnam policy" and had decided upon assuming office in 1968 "not to engage . . . in a continuation or justification" of earlier policies. Questions about disclosure of the material were referred to the Defense Department.

The Pentagon issued a statement June 14 citing its concern about "the disclosure of publication of highly classified information affecting national security" and saying it had called "this violation of security" to the attention of the Justice Department. The material, it said, "remains classified and sensitive" despite its coverage of a period ending in 1968 and the government had "the responsibility to determine what individual or individuals, if any, violated the laws relating to national security information by unauthorized disclosure of classified material."

Earlier June 14, Defense Secretary Melvin R. Laird, appearing at a Senate hearing on foreign aid, called the disclosure of the Pentagon material "unauthorized" and a violation of security regulations. He opposed Sen. Stuart Symington's (D, Mo.) intention to seek a "full examination of the origins of the war" with the objection that it "would not serve the interests of the country and would not help us disengage from Vietnam." Laird said the documents would remain classified and would not be made available to the Senate panel, although Symington found it "shocking" that Congress had been uninformed about the material.

Following the hearing, Symington put in the record letters in which Laird had refused a November 1969 request from Sen. J. W. Fulbright (D, Ark.) for the McNamara report to be made available to his Foreign Relations Committee.

Later June 14, Assistant Attorney General Robert C. Mardian, head of the internal security division, telephoned the Times to request that publication of the series be halted. He said court action would follow lack of compliance. The call came about two hours before press time for the edition scheduled to carry the third installment of the Vietnam series. An hour before press time, the Times received a telegram from Attorney General John N. Mitchell asking it to refrain from publishing any "further information of this character" on the ground it would "cause irreparable injury to the defense interests" of the U.S. Mitchell requested return of the documents to the Defense Department. The information, he said, related to national defense and "bears a top secret classification" and "as such," publication was "directly prohibited by the provisions of the Espionage Law."

The Times refused. "It is in the interest of the people of this country to be informed of the material contained in this series of articles," it replied. The newspaper said it would oppose a U.S. court action but would "abide by the final decision of the court."

News curb debated—The Justice Department filed a civil suit June 15 to seek permanent enjoinment against publication of the articles. At a hearing before U.S. District Judge Murray I. Gurfein in New York that day, U.S. Attorney Michael D. Hess contended that the newspaper had violated a statute making it a crime for persons having "unauthorized possession" of federal documents to disclose their contents in a way that "could be used to the injury of the United States or to the advantage of any foreign nation." He cited a reference by Secretary of State William P. Rogers to concern over the disclosures expressed by several friendly nations. If the government was facing "irreparable injury" in its international relations, he said, it was not unreasonable to order a "slight delay" in the Times' publication schedule until the case could be further resolved.

At a news conference that day, Rogers had said the material had elicited diplomatic inquiries from foreign governments and could cause "a great deal of difficulty." "If governments can't deal with us in any degree of confidentiality," he said, "it's going to be a very serious matter."

The Times' attorney, Alexander M. Bickel, a Yale University professor, told Gurfein June 15 the issue involved was a "classic case of censorship" that was forbidden by the First Amendment's guarantee of a free press. He said court action to bar publication of an article was unprecedented in the U.S. and that the government's case, in any event, was based on an anti-espionage law never intended by Congress to be used against the press. "A newspaper exists to publish, not to submit its publishing schedule to the United States government," Bickel argued.

Gurfein urged the Times to consent to halt publication of the articles, but the Times, holding that this would be a precedent for federal action to curb news publications, refused.

Court hearings set—Gurfein agreed with the U.S. position that the temporary harm done to the Times would be "far outweighed by the irreparable harm that could be done" to the interests of the U.S. He ordered the Times June 15 to halt publication of the articles for four days, and he set a hearing for June 18 on the issue of continuing the ban. He declined at that time to order the Times to return the Pentagon material.

But Gurfein June 16 set another hearing on the Justice Department's request for an order to have the Times relinquish its Pentagon papers for government inspection, a procedure it held "important" to presentation of its case.

Public Senate hearings announced. Senate Democratic Leader Mike Mansfield (Mont.) said June 15 a Senate committee would hold public hearings on how the U.S. became involved in the war. The purpose would not be to find "scapegoats" concerning publication by the Times of the classified material, Mansfield said, but to "lay out the whole story" in the hope it would lead to closer cooperation between Congress and the Executive branch on foreign policy and thus "prevent future Vietnams." Mansfield expressed himself as "delighted" that the Times had been publishing the series.

Senate Republican Leader Hugh Scott (Pa.), while terming release of the Pentagon material "a bad thing, . . . a federal crime," viewed the articles June 14 as being "very instructive and somewhat shocking."

There was little immediate Congressional comment on the Times' articles. Sen. George S. McGovern (D, S.D.) said June 14 the series revealed an "almost incredible deception" of Congress and the public by the highest officials in government, including the President. McGovern cautioned that it would be a mistake to assume such deception "began and ended with the Johnson Administration" and was of the opinion that it would no longer be tenable for any senator to permit the Executive branch to make foreign policy alone. McGovern June 16 denounced the Justice Department effort to "harry the New York Times" and shut off "a free flow of vital information to the public."

Rep. Paul N. McCloskey Jr. (R, Calif.) commented June 14 that "the issue of truthfulness in government is a problem as serious as that of ending the war itself."

Sen. Gaylord P. Nelson (D, Wis.) asserted June 15 the documents "clearly show that those who made the decisions to deepen our involvement in the war in Vietnam were not only deluding the American public but deluding themselves as well." He did not consider release of the material a danger to national security. While the documents contained information "embarrassing to the political and military leadership of the country," he said, that was "no reason to deny the public information it is clearly entitled to have."

Congressional reaction builds. Reaction to the Times' articles and the U.S. action to curb them began building among members of Congress by June 16. Letters were sent by 62 representatives, most of them liberal Democrats, to the Defense and Justice Departments requesting the secret papers be made available to Congress and protesting "harassment" of the Times. The move was initiated by Rep. Jonathan B. Bingham (D, N.Y.).

Hearings on the government's classification procedures were announced by a House Government Operations subcommittee headed by Rep. William S. Moorhead (D, Pa.), who said the classification of the Pentagon papers involved in the dispute "was done not so much to save the security of the United States but to save some red faces."

Fulbright and McCloskey June 16 requested from the Times copies of unpublished material in the projected series, which the Times refused. Fulbright, traveling in England at the time, said in London the articles confirmed a "deliberate and flagrant deception" by the Johnson Administration that had done "serious injury" to the roles of Congress and the public in dealing with the issues of war and peace.

Sen. John G. Tower (R, Tex.) described the Times' articles June 16 as "particularly interesting" but questioned the propriety of publishing the information.

Articles barred pending appeals. The controversy touched off by the New York Times' publication of Vietnam articles based on a secret Pentagon report was broadened June 18–22 when three other newspapers published similar material and, like the Times, were constrained to halt publication under court orders obtained by the Justice Department. The restraints against publication of the material, despite several decisions upholding the newspapers' right to publish it, were extended by the various courts pending appeals, which were expected to reach the Supreme Court.

The Times was under court order not to continue its Vietnam series when the Washington Post began publishing June 18 a series of articles based on the same classified Pentagon papers. The Justice Department sought and obtained a court order stopping the series after its second installment the next day, although the Post article was distributed by the Washington Post-Los Angeles Times News Service to its 345 clients and was described in accounts carried by the New York Times, which was barred from carrying its own series, the Associated Press and United Press International, which were available to almost all the daily newspapers in the country, and by radio and television newscasters.

Publication of material, then barred in the Times and Post, spread June 22 to the Boston Globe, which published four and a half pages of material drawn from the secret Pentagon study of the Vietnam war. A Justice Department suit to bar further articles was immediately filed with U.S. District Judge Anthony Julian, who issued a temporary restraining order later June 22 against further publication of such articles because of the possibility of "immediate and irreparable injury" to U.S. security. The judge, in a step not taken by the courts in New York and Washington, also ordered the documents or material from which the article was drawn impounded. He revised this requirement June 23 to permit the documents to be placed by the Globe in a bank safe deposit vault with restricted access.

Publication of the material continued to spread. The Chicago Sun-Times June 23 published material it said it had received from "sources involving the Pentagon study," and the Knight newspaper group published in eight of its 11 newspapers June 23 stories claimed to be drawn from the controversial Pentagon study. The Justice Department made inquiry to the Sun-Times about its material but took no immediate action to bar further publication on a preliminary finding that the base documents had been declassified in 1968.

The court action against the New York Times and Washington Post, meanwhile, continued. These were among the developments:

New York Times—The Times obeyed an order by U.S. District Judge Murray I. Gurfein June 15 to halt publication of its Vietnam series. The Justice Department sought return of the Pentagon papers from the newspaper for examination, contending it could not support its case that the national interest would be harmed by publication unless it knew what the newspaper planned to publish. The Times contended the government had copies of the material and inspection of the Times' material, much of it copied, could compromise its confidential source by facilitating identification of that source.

Gurfein ruled against what he termed a federal "fishing expedition into the files of any newspaper" June 17 and suggested the Times give the court and the Justice Department a list of descriptive headings of the documents in its possession. The Times complied.

Three Washington officials traveled to New York June 18 to present testimony to the court in secret. During the day Gurfein suggested the Times "ought to be willing to sit down" with the Justice Department and "as a matter of simple patriotism" determine whether publication of any of the classified documents "is or is not dangerous to the national security." But the Times attorney resisted with the point this would lead to self-censorship by the press or government censorship.

Gurfein June 19 denied an injunction against the Times series but extended the restraining order against publication pending appeal. While publication might cause "some embarrassment to the government in security aspects," Gurfein held, security "also lies in the value of our free institutions," such as the free press. He found "no cogent reasons" advanced, aside from the overall embarrassment aspect, that public knowledge of the material would be a vital security breach.

Gurfein also rejected a contention that the case constituted a violation of espionage laws barring transmission of secret data with intent to harm the country. The Times' effort, he said, had been "in good faith" and for "the right of the public to know."

The restraining order against the Times was continued later June 19 by Judge Irving R. Kaufman to permit consideration of the issue by a three-judge panel of his 2nd Circuit Court of Appeals.

Further extension of the restraining order was effected June 21 by the three-judge panel, because of the "extraordinary importance" of the issue, to carry the case before the entire eight-member court. In a brief presented by U.S. Attorney Whitney N. Seymour Jr., the government contended that "national defense documents, properly classified by the Executive, are an exception to an absolute freedom of the press and should be protected by the government against unauthorized disclosure." Seymour also submitted a sealed list of items in the Pentagon papers the government claimed would be security impairments if disclosed.

The appeals court issued a 5–3 decision June 23 that the Times could resume publication of the series after June 25 but could not use any material that the government held vital to national security. The court instructed Gurfein to hold secret hearings to determine what parts of the Pentagon papers posed "such grave and immediate danger" to U.S. security as to warrant enjoinment of publication.

Washington Post—The Post published articles in its June 18 and 19 editions on the involvement of the U.S. in the Vietnam war, the series based on a classified Pentagon study. As in the case of the Times, the Justice Department sought court restraint after the Post refused June 18 to voluntarily halt such publication.

U.S. District Judge Gerhard A. Gesell in Washington refused June 18 to sanction prior restraint of the articles with the observation "the court has before it no precise information suggesting in what respects, if any, the publication of this information will injure" the country. The proper recourse of the government in case of a security violation would be a criminal suit, he said.

Gesell regretted that the Post had refused his request for a delay in publishing the material to further weigh the issues involved. The Post's position, presented by its attorney, Roger A. Clark, was that the court would be "treading on dangerous ground if it tries to determine what is news."

Gesell's ruling was reversed June 19 by the U.S. Court of Appeals for the District of Columbia, which held in a 2–1 decision that the articles should be barred, pending a full hearing, and that "freedom of the press, as important as it is, is not boundless." The majority claimed precedent for the government's position that prior restraint on publication might be appropriate in a case involving national security.

The dissenter was Judge J. Skelly Wright, who said "to allow a government to suppress free speech simply through a system of bureaucratic classification would sell our heritage far, far too cheaply." Any impairment of the country's image inherent in revelation of the documents, he said, would be "miniscule compared to the lack of faith in our government engendered in our people from their suppression."

After further hearings, some parts of which were secret at the government's request, much the same scenario was repeated. Gesell June 21 upheld the Post against prior restraint, permitting resumption of the articles, but the appellate court later June 21 continued the press curb and ordered a hearing before the full nine-man court. In rejecting the government's argument that "an immediate grave threat to the national security" was involved, Gesell noted his opposition to adjustment of the free-press guarantee to views of protesting foreign governments.

Hearings before the full appeals court, including secret sessions, were held June 22–23. U.S. Solicitor General Erwin N. Griswold entered the case for the first time June 22 and announced he had been authorized by the secretaries of state and defense and the military chiefs of staff to offer the solution of a "joint task force" to examine the documents involved for possible declassification within 45 days. The Post opposed such procedure with the view it would constitute "government by handout." In his presentation, Griswold stressed the gravity of the issue, which involved, he said, "the integrity of the institution of the presidency" itself.

The Appeals Court June 23 rejected the government's case that continued publication of the material would jeopardize security and upheld the Post's constitutional right to publish the articles. However, it continued the curb against the series to permit appeal.

In its ruling, concurred in by seven of the nine judges, the court referred to the Supreme Court's establishment of the "vitality of the principle that any prior restraint on publication comes into court under a heavy presumption against its constitutional validity." The appellate court said its rejection of the government's case was "fortified" by consideration of "the massive character of the 'leak' which has occurred," a reference to the number of newspapers carrying the material. This raised "substantial doubt," it said, "that effective relief of the kind sought by the government can be provided by the judiciary."

Nixon to release documents to Congress. President Nixon informed Senate Majority Leader Mike Mansfield June 23 that he would release to Congress two top-secret studies it had requested. The two documents were a 47-volume report on U.S. involvement in Vietnam covering the period 1940–1968 and a 1965 Defense Department study of the Gulf of Tonkin incident.

According to White House Press Secretary Ronald L. Ziegler, the President specified that he was releasing the documents, which retained their top-secret classification, with the understanding that they would not be made public until their classification had been reviewed by the executive branch.

A Presidential directive Jan. 15, which the White House declined to make public

because it was an "internal paper," had instructed government agencies to review existing classification procedures. Acting on that directive, Defense Secretary Melvin R. Laird disclosed June 22 that he had ordered a review of the controversial documents to determine which could be made public.

The same day, federal lawyers made an offer before appellate courts in Washington and New York to begin an interagency review of the already published documents to determine how much could be declassified. The lawyers were contesting lower court decisions upholding the right of the New York Times and Washington Post to publish the Pentagon study.

Despite Nixon's action, Reps. John E. Moss (D, Calif.) and Ogden R. Reid (R, N.Y.) said they would press a court suit filed June 23 in Washington's U.S. district court to force Laird to make all or part of the documents public under the Freedom of Information Act of 1966 for which they had been principal sponsors. Moss, a member of the Foreign Operations and Government Information subcommittee of the House Government Operations Committee, had objected that the papers released by the President were referred to the House Armed Services Committee where members could read but not copy them.

The documents released to Congress were to be held by the secretary of the Senate pending a decision on how the Senate would conduct hearings on the origins of the war.

Meanwhile, the Senate leadership moved toward creating a special joint panel composed of eight members from the Foreign Relations Committee and eight from the Armed Services Committee. The select committee was a compromise (to avoid jurisdictional disputes) worked out by Mansfield with ranking Democratic and Republican members of the Foreign Relations Committee, a leading war opponent, and Armed Services, which had generally supported Johnson and Nixon Administration policies. The committee was expected to begin hearings in the fall. The Foreign Relations Committee said it still planned its own inquiry.

In related developments, Sen. Edmund S. Muskie (D, Me.) (June 20) and Sen. Hubert H. Humphrey (D, Minn.) (June 23) announced plans to introduce legislation to create boards that would have authority to declassify secret government documents.

Arthur J. Goldberg, former Supreme Court justice and secretary of labor, was the leadoff witness June 23 at a series of hearings by the House Subcommittee on Foreign Operations and Government Information on whether information that should go to the public and Congress from the executive branch was being obstructed. Goldberg proposed creation of an independent board to review classified material. Conceding the need to preserve national security secrets, Goldberg said the executive branch nevertheless should

not be permitted to use the classification stamp to conceal mistakes and prevent political embarrassment.

Ellsberg speaks out. Daniel Ellsberg, 40, a senior research associate at the Massachusetts Institute of Technology widely identified as the New York Times' source for the Pentagon documents in a TV appearance June 23, made his first public statement since he disappeared June 16. He was interviewed by Walter Cronkite of Columbia Broadcasting System at a secret location.

Ellsberg did not mention his suggested role in the release of the documents. Cronkite indicated that Ellsberg's delicate legal position prevented him from speaking directly on the subject.

Ellsberg, who had drafted a section of the controversial study, said one reason for the documents to be made public at this time was the possibility that "we were in for a replay of the year 1964."

Ellsberg had been named as the Times' source by Sidney Zion, a former Times reporter, on a WMCA radio program in New York June 16, and the next day in an article from the Washington bureau of the St. Louis-Post Dispatch.

Ellsberg reportedly was the principal object of an FBI investigation begun June 14 seeking the source which gave the Times the secret study. Two FBI agents had sought out Ellsberg at his home in Cambridge, Mass. June 17 after he had dropped out of sight. Justice Department officials stressed there was no warrant for his arrest.

The search for Ellsberg also led FBI agents June 22 to the office of Rep. Paul N. McCloskey (R, Calif.), a prominent war critic, who had disclosed June 17 that Ellsberg had given him a month ago copies of documents dealing with the U.S. involvement in the war. McCloskey said he could not determine whether his copy was part of the Times' series. He said the agents had asked him about his conversations with Ellsberg, which he declined to reveal.

In Los Angeles June 23, a federal grand jury, also conducting an investigation into how the documents reached the Times, subpoenaed as a witness a close friend of Ellsberg who had been associated with him at the Rand Corp. in Santa Monica, Calif. The witness, Anthony J. Russo, an economist and engineer no longer employed at Rand, refused to testify and was ordered to appear before Judge William P. Gray June 25 to show cause why he should not be held in contempt of court.

Restraint on press rebuffed. The Supreme Court upheld by a 6–3 decision June 30 the New York Times and the Washington Post against the government's attempt to halt their publication of material from a classified Pentagon study of the origins of the Vietnam war. Prior federal court stays against publication of the material were vacated.

The Times and Post resumed publication of the articles with their July 1 editions. Similar material was being published by other newspapers, although only four—The Boston Globe and the St. Louis Post-Dispatch in addition to the Times and Post—had been under federal court restraint not to publish the material. The Pentagon study in question also was being read in an open session of a Congressional panel by Sen. Mike Gravel (D, Alaska) although the study had been delivered, as promised by President Nixon, to both houses of Congress without removal of its security classification. [See below]

The Supreme Court decision was the climax of the controversy initiated June 13 when the Times began publication of the Pentagon documents. The Times articles were halted June 15 after the Justice Department obtained a federal court order against further publication. The Washington Post articles were published June 18 and 19 and halted under similar circumstances.

The decision—The court's decision was brief and unsigned. It quoted precedents that "any system of prior restraints of expression comes to this court bearing a heavy presumption against its constitutional validity" and that the government "thus carries a heavy burden of showing justification for the enforcement of such a restraint." It said that the district courts in New York and Washington and the appellate court in Washington had "held that the government had not met that burden" and "we agree."

Three members of the majority held that the First Amendment's free press guarantee was unassailable and the courts lacked the power to suppress press publication, no matter what threat to national security might be posed. Two of the three—Hugo L. Black and William O. Douglas—considered judicial restraint of the press altogether prohibited under the First Amendment. The third, Thurgood Marshall, stressed the principle of separation of powers, noting that prior restraint had never been authorized by Congress and Congress specifically had rejected bills to authorize restraint in 1917 and 1957.

A second group within the majority—Justices William J. Brennan Jr., Potter Stewart and Byron R. White—asserted that the press could not be curbed except to prevent immediate and irreparable damage to the nation. They held that the material in question in this case did not pose such a threat.

Brennan held that the temporary restraints should not have been imposed because the government had alleged only in general terms that security breaches might occur.

Both Stewart and White, who concurred in their opinions, believed that publication of the documents was not in the national interest although publication could not constitutionally be prevented. Stewart held that protection of state secrets was "the duty of the executive" and not the duty of the courts

through the banning of news articles. If publication would cause "direct, immediate and irreparable damage to our nation or its people," he said, he would uphold prior restraint, but he did not find that situation to exist in this case.

The Times and Post and other newspapers publishing the material were lauded by Black, who said they "should be commended for serving the purpose that the Founding Fathers saw so clearly" in the First Amendment's declaration that "Congress shall make no law . . . abridging the freedom of the press." A primary responsibility of the press, he said, was "to prevent any part of the government from deceiving the people." "In revealing the workings of government that led to the Vietnam war," he said, "the newspapers nobly did precisely that which the founders hoped and trusted they would do."

Justice Douglas said that the First Amendment's aim was to prevent "governmental suppression of embarrassing information." He said the temporary restraints on publication in the case "constitute a flouting of the principles of the First Amendment."

The separation-of-powers principle also was stressed by Brennan, Stewart and White, who held that the courts could not restrain publications except under extraordinary and extreme circumstances. Four justices commented on the issue of criminal laws, including the espionage laws, and their possible application of these to the case. White said that "the newspapers are presumably now on full notice" that federal prosecutions could be brought for violation of such laws. He added that he "would have no difficulty in sustaining convictions" in such an event even if the security breach were not sufficient to justify prior restraint.

The dissents—The three dissenting justices were Chief Justice Warren E. Burger and Justices Harry A. Blackmun and John M. Harlan.

The three held that the decision was too precipitous—Burger referred to the "frenetic haste" of the case—and that the issue should be returned to trial with restraints upon publication continued. They asserted that the courts should uphold the executive branch's contention, at the cabinet level, that material should be kept confidential on a matter affecting foreign relations.

Burger and Blackmun were critical of the Times for failing to give sufficient time for proper consideration to the case. Burger said it was a breach of "the duty of an honorable press" not to have inquired about possible security violations before publishing the material. Burger said he had found this failing "hardly believable" and he saw no harm resulting if the issue were returned for additional testimony.

Blackmun asserted that if the war were prolonged and the return of American war prisoners were delayed as a result of the publication of the material, "then the nation's people will know

where the responsibility for these sad consequences rests."

The third dissenter, Harlan, said: "The judiciary must review the initial executive determination to the point of satisfying itself that the subject matter of the dispute does lie within the proper compass of the President's foreign policy relations power. . .The judiciary may properly insist that the determination that disclosure of the subject matter would irreparably impair the national security be made by the head of the executive department concerned. . . . But in my judgment, the judiciary may not properly go beyond these two inquiries and redetermine for itself the probable impact of disclosure on the national security."

High court's acceptance of case—The New York Times brought its case before the Supreme Court June 24 with the argument that the court-ordered restraint on publishing the material already constituted a violation of the First Amendment. It pointed out that the Post had been freed to resume publication of the material and its articles, if they did resume, plus such articles appearing in other newspapers, would inflict "irreparable harm" on the Times' interests. It cited in addition the doctrine of separation of powers and the lack of Congressional sanction for courts to impose prior restraint on newspaper publication.

In the Post case, the Court of Appeals in Washington June 24 denied the Justice Department's request for a rehearing on the case and the court reaffirmed its June 23 ruling that the government had not demonstrated any grounds for preventing publication of the material. Both appellate decisions, the denial and the reaffirmation of its ruling, were by 7–2 votes. "The matter is now ripe for presentation to the Supreme Court," it said.

The Supreme Court accepted the Times and Post cases June 25. Because of the restraint continued upon the Times but not the Post from appellate decisions, it put both newspapers under equal publication restraints pending an ultimate decision. It marked the first time the Supreme Court had restrained publication of a newspaper article, and four justices —Black, Douglas, Brennan and Marshall —dissented in favor of freeing both papers to print the articles without hearing arguments. Although the court's order permitted both newspapers to publish information from the Pentagon study, it proscribed items the government considered "dangerous" to national security. A listing of such dangerous items was requested from the Justice Department to be filed with the court. Both newspapers declined the opportunity to resume the articles under such circumstances, which they considered tantamount to government censorship.

With Burger, Blackmun and Harlan dissenting, the court June 26 rejected the government's request for a secret hearing for presentation of details that publication of the material would be harmful to the national interest.

In a two-hour hearing June 26, the government presented its case that publication of the "top secret" documents could be barred as violations of the espionage laws and of statutes and executive orders under which the president had sole authority to control classified material. The power of the courts to block publication of government secrets that posed a "grave and irrevocable" security threat was claimed. And the government held that publication of the Pentagon study involved diplomatic jeopardy because of the loss of confidentiality.

The government urged adoption of a standard permitting federal court intervention to halt publication whenever it would "affect lives," the "termination of the war" or "the process of recovering our prisoners of war."

In its consideration of the case, the Supreme Court extended its session beyond its last scheduled meeting of the current term June 28.

Other newspapers publish material. Two more newspapers published material drawn from the controversial Pentagon study on American involvement in Vietnam June 25 and 28 and one was restrained by court order. The other was not.

The St. Louis Post-Dispatch published material June 25 it said was based on the Pentagon report and U.S. District Judge James H. Meredith, after the newspaper refused to halt publication voluntarily, issued a restraining order June 26 at the request of the Justice Department.

The Christian Science Monitor published June 29 what it said were excerpts from the Pentagon papers. The U.S. Attorney for the District of Massachusetts, Herbert F. Travers Jr., telephoned the Monitor, asked that two more planned articles not be published and was refused. The Justice Department announced later June 29 it would not seek to enjoin the future articles since the material did not include any "designated by the United States as potentially injurious to the national defense."

Monitor editor Erwin D. Canham said he had informed Travers that the future material consisted of an "analytical piece" on Ho Chi Minh, dating from the 1940s, and U.S. relations in the Far East in the mid-40s.

The Justice Department announced June 24 that no legal action would be taken "at this time" against the Los Angeles Times or Knight newspapers which published articles that day on the Pentagon papers. The articles had been reviewed and the decision made that the contents did not constitute a security threat.

Congress gets documents. Two copies of the 47-volume Pentagon study were delivered to Congress June 28 on President Nixon's order and placed in locked vaults under 24-hour guard. A letter of transmittal from Defense Secretary Melvin R. Laird accompanied the documents,

warning that disclosure of the contents would pose "grave and immediate danger to the national security."

The documents were received by Rep. F. Edward Hebert (D, La.), chairman of the Armed Services Committee, for the House, and Sen. Allen J. Ellender (D, La.), president pro tem of the Senate. Hebert said rules which he would issue to House members would bar note-taking or disclosure of the contents.

In related developments, seven members of a House Government Operations subcommittee, acting under a 1928 statute, demanded that the Pentagon give the committee copies of the study, in addition to a report on the Gulf of Tonkin incident. The subcommittee, headed by Rep. William S. Moorhead (D, Pa.), was investigating government information and secrecy policies. The 1928 law required any executive agency to submit requested information pertaining to matters within a committee's jurisdiction.

A former Pentagon security expert had testified before the committee June 24 that the government was spending $50 million a year to guard classified defense documents, only .5% of which should have been kept from the public. William G. Florence, who had retired May 31, said the defense classification system was "literally clogged" because of the widespread view in the Pentagon that "information is born classified" and should only be made public after proof that it would be of no interest to another country.

A panel of newsmen appeared before the subcommittee June 25 to defend the newspapers that had published parts of the Pentagon study and to criticize what they described as the government's excessive secrecy.

The House Armed Services Committee June 29 rejected 25–2 a resolution by Rep. Bella Abzug (D, N.Y.) that would make the study available to all House members and security-cleared staff members and permit them to take notes. Despite committee disapproval, the resolution of inquiry would be submitted for a House vote.

Gravel reads papers to press—Sen. Mike Gravel (D, Alaska) read aloud to newsmen for over three hours June 29 portions of the Pentagon study. The act was deplored by many Republican colleagues, but Majority Leader Mike Mansfield refused to take disciplinary action against the freshman senator.

Gravel had intended to read the documents to the Senate in an all-night speech, but the Republican leadership thwarted attempts to raise the necessary quorum. Undaunted, Gravel hastily called a meeting of the Senate Public Works subcommittee of which he was chairman. Gravel chose the hearing as a forum to gain Congressional immunity from possible prosecution.

Gravel said he had received about half of the Pentagon study June 24 from an unidentified private source.

With Rep. John G. Dow (D, N.Y.) in the witness chair, Gravel began the hearing with the explanation, "I will not accept the notion that the President of the United States can manipulate the United States Senate into silence. It is my constitutional obligation to protect the security of the people by fostering the free flow of information absolutely essential to their democratic decision-making."

Gravel said he was convinced his action was "in no way jeopardizing this nation's security." During the reading, Gravel omitted supporting papers he considered sensitive material.

The documents disclosed by Gravel contained substantial material that had already been published.

Visibly exhausted, Gravel stopped reading at 1:12 a.m. June 30 after he had broken into tears several times during the session. He then read an impassioned speech against the war. His staff made copies of the remaining papers available to the press.

Republican senators opened the Senate June 30 with heated demands that Gravel be disciplined for violating Rule 36 prohibiting senators from disclosing confidential information emanating from the executive branch. After meeting with Senate Minority Leader Hugh Scott (R, Pa.) and Minority Whip Robert P. Griffin (R, Mich.), Majority Leader Mansfield noted Gravel's sincere convictions and said he would take no action other than to have a "friendly talk" with Gravel.

Ellsberg indicted, admits giving papers. Daniel Ellsberg, the former Defense Department aide widely cited as the source of the Pentagon study first published in the New York Times, surrendered to the U.S. attorney in Boston June 28 after admitting that he had leaked the documents to the press.

After his arrest and arraignment on charges of unauthorized possession of secret documents, Ellsberg was released on $50,000 bail.

Later in the day, a Los Angeles federal grand jury indicted Ellsberg on two counts, violation of the Espionage Act and theft of government property.

Before surrendering at 10 a.m. as his lawyers had promised June 26, Ellsberg told newsmen that he had given the information contained in the documents to Sen. J. W. Fulbright (D, Ark.), chairman of the Senate Foreign Relations Committee. Ellsberg, accompanied by his wife Patricia, said his only regret was that he had not acted sooner in releasing the information to the press. He added: "I did this clearly at my own jeopardy and I am prepared to answer to all the consequences of these decisions. That includes the personal consequences to me and my family, whatever these may be." Interviewed later in the day at his home in Cambridge, Mass., Ellsberg refused to divulge whether he was the Times' source for the documents because of litigation in process before the Supreme Court. He also said he would not have released the documents if he had thought a single page "would do grave damage to the national interests."

On the advice of his lawyers, Ellsberg had eluded an intensive search by the Federal Bureau of Investigation after a warrant for his arrest was issued in Los Angeles late June 25. The warrant charged Ellsberg specifically with possession and failure to return the secret papers, under Title 18, Section 793E, of the U.S. Code. He was not charged with transmitting the documents to anyone else. The indictment June 28 briefly noted that Ellsberg in September and October 1969 had "had access to and control over copies of certain documents and writings relating to the national defense." The period described coincided with Ellsberg's employment at Rand Corp. in Santa Monica, Calif., the research organization that had received two of the 15 original copies of the 47-volume Pentagon study.

(Lynda R. Sinay, a freelance advertising agent described as a close friend of Ellsberg, had testified before the grand jury June 24 that Ellsberg had paid her $150 to Xerox copies of certain documents, but she said she did not know their contents.)

The second count of the indictment cited Section 641 of the U.S. Code and charged that Ellsberg had "willfully, knowingly and unlawfully" retained the Pentagon study and had failed to deliver it to the proper recipient. Each count carried a maximum 10-year prison term and/or a $10,000 fine.

Mitchell threatens prosecutions. Attorney General John N. Mitchell said July 1 that the Justice Department would prosecute "all those who have violated federal criminal laws" in connection with the disclosure of the secret Pentagon papers. Mitchell said the government was pursuing its investigation into how the papers were leaked to the press.

The attorney general's warning was made in a press release issued by the Justice Department. A department spokesman declined to go beyond Mitchell's prepared statement.

The spokesman indicated, however, that the statement was intended to show that the Supreme Court's June 30 ruling that the New York Times and Washington Post could not be restrained from publishing the Pentagon papers did not affect possible criminal prosecution of lawbreakers. The Mitchell statement said that "a review of the Court's opinions indicate that there is nothing in them to affect this situation."

In a later development July 1, Secretary of State William P. Rogers told newsmen that he hoped the press would "recognize an obligation to refrain from the publication of information" in the Pentagon papers harmful to the nation's security. He said that the government was prepared "to lend its assistance in identifying documents" that could do such harm.

(The New York Times, responding to Rogers' statement, said July 1 that the newspaper had taken "the interest of the country, including national security, into account at all times in our editing and reporting of the documents.")

U.S. tightens Rand security. Defense Secretary Melvin R. Laird ordered Air Force security personnel July 1 to take custody of all secret documents at the Rand Corporation, the private research institute in Santa Monica, Calif.

Dr. Daniel Ellsberg, who said June 28 that he had leaked the Pentagon papers to the press, was a former Rand employe.

Gravel defends reading. Sen. Mike Gravel (D, Alaska) defended on the Senate floor July 6 his public reading June 29 of portions of the Pentagon papers. Gravel declared that he had publicly read the top-secret papers because he deemed it "in the best interests of this nation we all love." He conceded that "perhaps I did not approach the matter with the same degree of delicacy another would employ."

Majority Leader Mike Mansfield (D, Mont.), who met with Gravel June 30 to discuss the incident, said later that he would oppose any move to censure or punish him.

Congressional developments. The Defense Department denied July 1 that it had promised to provide every member of Congress with a complete 47-volume set of the Pentagon war study.

Jerry W. Freidheim, the department's press officer, said that the Pentagon's view was that the documents had been made available to the House and Senate leadership and that individual congressmen should request the materials from congressional leaders.

Freidheim acknowledged, however, that the Pentagon was considering printing a sanitized version of the 47-volume study which might eventually be made available on a general basis.

In refusing to provide a copy of the report to each congressmen, the Pentagon in effect turned down a demand by Rep. William S. Moorhead (D, Pa.), chairman of the House Foreign Operations and Government Information Subcommittee. Moorhead had asked the Pentagon to furnish his panel with complete copies of both the Vietnam papers and of the government's study of the Gulf of Tonkin incident.

After learning of the Pentagon's refusal, Moorhead said that the Defense Department was "in violation of the law and setting a poor example to our citizenry." He renewed his demand for the full sets of the studies.

Burger comments on Pentagon papers case. Chief Justice Warren Burger said in a television interview broadcast July 5 that in the 6–3 ruling on the case the justices were "actually unanimous" on the "basic problems of First Amendment rights of newspapers." He said the proliferation of opinions—one for each justice—was due to the "pressure" of the case, since "the simplest thing to do in getting it out in a hurry is each justice states what is on his mind."

Intelligence data sought. Sen. John Sherman Cooper (R, Ky.) introduced legislation July 7 to require the Central Intelligence Agency (CIA) to regularly provide Congress with up-to-date and detailed intelligence information.

Cooper, a member of the Foreign Relations Committee, said that Congress needed the CIA's evaluation and analysis of the intelligence data to participate effectively in the formation of foreign policy. At the present time, only the executive branch had access to CIA intelligence reports.

An aide to Cooper said that the senator had been considering the legislation for three years but that disclosure of the Pentagon papers had given his proposal new impetus.

Limit on clearances sought. A White House press aide acknowledged July 7 that President Nixon had ordered all government departments and agencies to compile at once lists of all persons who had authority to see top-security materials.

Gerald L. Warren, assistant White House press secretary, said in response to newsmen's questions that a confidential memorandum had been sent out June 30 directing federal agencies to prepare the lists. Warren, speaking to reporters at the Western White House in San Clemente, Calif., said that the memorandum was signed by Brig. Gen. Alexander M. Haig Jr., deputy assistant to the President for national security.

Existence of the Haig memorandum was first disclosed by the Washington Post July 6.

According to the Post's account, all federal departments and agencies, including the White House, had to submit by July 10 lists of the numbers of government workers, outside consultants and private contractors who held clearance for top-secret information and the "various categories of compartmented intelligence data." By the end of July, the Post said, the government agencies were expected to provide the White House with the names of those who held security clearances and whether they were employed by the government or outside firms.

Warren neither confirmed nor denied the Post's account of the memorandum's details. Other government officials said, however, that the order was part of Administration plans to reduce the number of persons in and out of government holding security clearances.

In Washington, a Pentagon spokesman said July 7 that the Defense Department had already begun compiling its list. The spokesman, Brig. Gen. Daniel James Jr., said that the department was unable to say how many persons in the defense establishment had access to top-secret material.

Rostow defends U.S. role. Walt W. Rostow, one of President Johnson's key advisors on Vietnam, said July 11, in a meeting with newsmen, that "the first initial effect" of publication of the Pentagon papers was to undermine faith in the presidency and strengthen an emerging mood of isolationism. Rostow added that he believed the publication of the documents distorted the truth about how the U.S. went to war in Vietnam.

Rostow singled out for criticism the New York Times for its part in the documents controversy. He said he regarded the Times' "performance" in its series of articles on the documents "as the shoddiest piece of journalism since I had any experience in public life, in 1941."

Rostow said that the Times' "headline writers, lead writers, editorial writers and columnists went beyond the Pentagon papers in purveying a sense of deceit by a President of the United States."

Grand jury probes disclosure. A federal grand jury in Boston was reported July 12 to be investigating possible criminal charges against the New York Times, the Washington Post and the Boston Globe in connection with their publication of the secret Pentagon papers.

The jury, which had been sitting on other matters, was called back into session July 7 amid tight security measures.

The Washington Post reported that in addition to the three papers, the jury was considering criminal charges against Neil Sheehan, the Times' reporter credited with breaking the story about the war documents.

According to published reports, the grand jury was seeking to determine where the documents were copied and who conveyed them to the three newspapers. The government was also investigating whether the papers violated interstate theft statutes in receiving the documents.

Dr. Daniel Ellsberg, who said that he had given the papers to the press, was reportedly also under investigation by the Boston grand jury.

According to one report, the grand jury was looking into whether Ellsberg had been aided by others in making the secret study available to the press. Ellsberg was presently a research associate at the Massachusetts Institute of Technology.

Boston jury dismissed. The Justice Department was reported July 20 to have dismissed a federal grand jury in Boston that was looking into the publication of the secret Pentagon war papers because of a leak to the press. According to published reports, a new jury was empaneled at once to continue the investigation.

The original grand jury was reportedly dismissed because the Justice Department believed one or more of the jurors had violated their oath of secrecy by talking with the press. U.S. court officials in Boston, however, denied that the jury had been discharged over a press leak.

The new grand jury was believed to have picked up the first panel's investigation of how New York Times' reporter Neil Sheehan came into possession of the war study. Sheehan was credited with breaking the story.

Buckley admits papers' hoax. William F. Buckley Jr., editor in chief of the National Review, said July 21 that his magazine's publication of "highly classified documents" dealing with U.S. involvement in Vietnam was a hoax.

The National Review, a conservative weekly magazine, published July 20 more than 14 pages of what it described as government memorandums "not published by the New York Times and Washington Post" in their series in June and July based on the Pentagon war study.

At a news conference in New York, Buckley said "we admit we proceeded in something of an ethical vacuum." He said National Review editors had composed the "documents" in their offices.

Buckley said the purpose of the hoax was to show that "forged documents would be widely accepted as genuine, provided their content was inherently plausible."

Among the so-called "documents" published by the Review was a memorandum suggesting a "demonstration drop" of a nuclear device over North Vietnam if Hanoi did not respond to U.S. peace feelers. Another called for "employing atomic weapons whenever advantageous."

FBI probe at State Department. A State Department spokesman, in response to questions at a press briefing Sept. 2, confirmed that Federal Bureau of Investigation (FBI) agents had questioned State Department personnel recently in a probe of unauthorized news leaks. Sources established that "three or four" officials had voluntarily submitted to lie detector tests concerning a July 23, New York Times story on U.S. negotiating positions at the American-Soviet strategic arms limitation talks (SALT).

Secretary of State William P. Rogers said Sept. 3 that the investigation had been launched because "it looked on the surface as if there might be" a crime. He added, "I don't believe there was a crime." Rogers said it "was an investigation of a violation of law, and it wasn't directed at the State Department. In fact, it wasn't even started here."

A Justice Department official had said Sept. 2 that the questioning had extended to Defense Department officials. The Times story was written by William Beecher, the newspaper's Pentagon reporter.

The investigation reportedly caused distress among some personnel at the State Department, where, officials said, the FBI had not been involved since the wholesale loyalty-security investigations of the 1950s on charges of Communist infiltration raised by the late Sen. Joseph R. McCarthy. The department had its own division empowered to investigate security leaks. An internal study by the State Department in 1970 had dealt with lingering bitterness and inhibitions at the department because of the McCarthy experience.

Rogers said Sept. 3, "I think it is a fact that the State Department had suffered from the scars of those [McCarthy] days." He said he had met "with my top assistants" to insure that a "policy of openness, which is so essential to a free nation, will be continued." But he said such an investigation could not be curtailed "because it might reawaken those fears." Rogers said he had reservations about lie detector tests "in terms of proof," but he said they could help establish innocence.

At the press briefing Sept. 2, State Department spokesman Robert J. McCloskey admitted that some topics had been placed temporarily off limits for discussion with reporters, such as the President's proposed China trip and the South Vietnamese presidential elections. But he said there had been no attempt to limit contacts with the press and that department personnel had only been asked to "use their common sense in dealing with the journalists."

Suit against Globe dropped. A suit brought by the Justice Department against the Boston Globe over its publication of the Pentagon papers was dismissed Sept. 8 in U.S. district court in Boston.

Source of leak investigated. Publication of secret material pertaining to formulation of the Nixon Administration's policy on the Indian-Pakistani war was continued Jan. 3-5, 1972 by columnist Jack Anderson. He released some of the material to wire services and newspapers Jan. 5 and offered to make it available to a Congressional committee. Anderson, whose column itself was syndicated to 700 newspapers, had initiated the controversy with reports, based on the secret material, published Dec. 30-31, 1971.

An Administration and FBI investigation into the source of the leak was under way. White House spokesmen declined to comment on the issue, other than to say that President Nixon was aware of it. Henry A. Kissinger, the President's national security adviser, had said Jan. 3 that Anderson had taken remarks indicating the Administration was against India "out of context."

The Anderson columns were based largely on classified material, stamped "secret sensitive," from meetings of the Washington Special Action Group (WSAG), a top-level strategy panel assembled during crises. Anderson said Jan. 5 his sources were "some of their [the Administration's] own boys" and "if they want to finger them, they're going to wind up with bubble gum all over their faces." His purpose in publishing the material, he said Jan. 3, was "to force a showdown with the Administration over their classification system," which he did not consider "in the public interest in a democracy."

Nixon acts on security leaks. White House Press Secretary Ronald L. Ziegler said Jan. 17 that steps had been taken under President Nixon's direction to prevent leaks of information on national security matters. He said recent publication of data from secret policy discussions had caused "great concern" in the White House.

While the public should be kept informed of foreign policy, Ziegler said, "subordinates of the President, in order to make recommendations to him, must be able to discuss freely the issues and options for policy."

The recent publication of such material, mostly pertaining to the Indian-Pakistani war, had been initiated by columnist Jack Anderson.

Anderson releases secret text—Saying several newspapers had requested it, Anderson Jan. 14 released the full text of minutes of a Dec. 8, 1971 White House strategy session on the Pakistan crisis. Material from it and other such meetings had been appearing in publications over the past month.

Stolen FBI papers printed. "A virtually complete collection" of 271 documents on political surveillance stolen from the FBI's Media, Pa. office in March 1971 was printed in the March issue of Win, an antiwar magazine, which received the documents from the secret Citizens' Commission to Investigate the FBI.

The documents, some of which had been released earlier, further detailed FBI surveillance of peace, student and black groups. According to a statement by the commission included in the Win article, over 200 documents concerned "left or liberal" groups, while only two referred to "right-wing" groups, the Philadelphia branches of the Ku Klux Klan and the Jewish Defense League.

Document classification curbed. President Nixon signed an executive order March 8 to limit the practice of classifying government documents as secret, and to speed the process of declassification. Meanwhile, two House committees considered measures to assert a Congressional role in secrecy control.

While the President's order would limit the number of agencies and individuals with classification powers, punish abuses for non-security purposes and require routine disclosure of most secret papers within six to ten years, Nixon admitted that any improvement in information flow would depend "upon the good judgment of individuals throughout the government," and remain strictly under executive control.

Under the order, no document could be restrictively classified unless its release "could reasonably be expected" to damage the national interest. The number of agencies in possession of a "top secret" stamp would be reduced from 24 to 12, and only 13 others could use the "secret" stamp. Only 1,860 officials would have "top secret" classification power compared with about 5,100 in the past. "Repeated abuse" of such power, such as "to conceal inefficiency or administrative error," could result in "administrative action."

In general, "top secret" papers would automatically drop to "secret" status after two years; "secret" documents would be downgraded to the "confidential" category after two years, and all "confidential" material would be released after six years.

Exceptions, which would undergo automatic review after 10 years, included documents supplied in confidence by foreign sovereignties, lawfully protected information such as atomic energy data, information damaging to spies, and information "the continuing protection of which is essential to the national security." An agency withholding such data would have to explain its action to anyone requesting a specific paper.

After 30 years, all documents would be declassified unless countermanded in writing by the head of the originating agency. Presidential papers, however, would remain undisclosed unless released by the individual president.

The entire procedure would be supervised by an interagency review committee under the National Security Council.

Nixon also announced March 8 that he had ordered Secretary of State William P. Rogers to speed publication of the department's document series, "Foreign Relations of the United States," which currently lagged 26 years behind events, with a goal of six years of data to be published in the next three years.

House hearings. A House Armed Services subcommittee began hearings March 8 on a proposal by Committee Chairman F. Edward Hebert (D, La.)

and ranking Republican Leslie Arends (Ill.) to set up an executive-legislative-judicial secrecy review commission.

The Government Information Subcommittee of the House Government Operations Committee began hearings March 6 on secrecy practices. George Reedy, former press secretary to President Lyndon Johnson, advised Congress to probe the centralization of executive activities at the White House, where they were protected from Congressional scrutiny by Presidential privilege.

James C. Hagerty, former press secretary to President Dwight Eisenhower, said the classification system had been used "as a matter of rote, or imagined protection from error." He recommended high-level classification reviews within each agency, with periodic reviews from a higher level.

Subcommittee Chairman William S. Moorhead (D, Pa.) said March 8 that Congress might prefer a statutory law rather than the President's executive order.

Pulitzer Prizes. The 56th annual Pulitzer Prizes in journalism, letters and music were presented in New York City May 1 amid sharp criticism from the board of trustees of Columbia University, which sponsored the competition. The trustees for the first time issued a statement chiding the selection panel, composed mostly of newspaper editors, saying they "had deep reservations about the timeliness and suitability of certain of the journalism awards." The 23-man board added that "had the selections been those of the trustees alone, certain of the recipients would not have been chosen."

The strongly-worded statement was believed to have been prompted by two awards—one to The New York Times for public service and the other to Jack Anderson for national reporting. In both cases classified government documents were the basis for the award-winning stories.

The Times, which had published Pentagon papers detailing U.S. involvement in the Vietnam war, also came under attack from Vice President Agnew. Speaking in Charleston, S.C. May 3, the vice president said the award to the Times had "demeaned" the Pulitzer Prizes.

Anderson received his prize for disclosures of Administration policymaking during the India-Pakistan war.

Eisenhower to chair declassification panel. John D. Eisenhower, 49, son of the late Dwight D. Eisenhower and former ambassador to Belgium, was appointed May 17 to chair a new interagency watchdog committee on government secrets. The committee, established by executive order March 8 as a result of the Pentagon Papers controversy, implemented a new declassification schedule and heard appeals for speedier declassification of specific documents.

1965–68 documents disclosed. More secret material from the Pentagon Papers, a government study of U.S. involvement in Vietnam, was made public by syndicated columnist Jack Anderson June 26. Material from 43 of 47 volumes of the papers had been disclosed in 1971.

The newly-released material was in volumes covering Johnson Administration efforts in 1965–68 to get peace talks started.

In releasing the top secret material, Anderson said President Nixon had made public "even more sensitive negotiations." Much of the material had already been made public by other means, such as in President Lyndon B. Johnson's memoirs. Some items had appeared in Anderson's columns the previous three weeks.

This had led to government complaints at the "Pentagon Papers" trial of Daniel Ellsberg and Anthony J. Russo Jr. in Los Angeles of "a high likelihood" that the defense had leaked the latest four volumes to Anderson, an activity denied by Anderson and the defendants.

Report on classification changes. The White House announced Aug. 3 that a government report had shown that the number of federal employes authorized to classify U.S. documents "top secret," "secret" or "confidential" had been reduced by 63% in the past 60 days.

The cutback was one part of the Nixon Administration's program to streamline the government's security classification system.

The report was presented by John Eisenhower, chairman of the new Interagency Classification Review Committee.

According to the report, the number of government employes authorized to classify national security information had been reduced from 43,586 to 16,238 since May 17.

According to the report, there was a 53% reduction in the number of officials who could classify materials "top secret," the highest security classification. There was a 39% drop in the number of officials who could classify documents as "secret," and a 76% drop in those who could label materials "confidential," the lowest security classification.

The report showed that the biggest reduction was at the Pentagon, where the number of employes who could classify materials dropped from 30,542 to 8,809.

End to secrecy proposed. Sen. Lawton Chiles (D, Fla.) proposed a bill Aug. 4 that would virtually end all secret meetings in Congress and at the executive level. Chiles described his proposal as a "government in the sunshine" law.

Chiles's bill would require an open-door policy for all Congressional commitee meetings and government agencies except in matters relating to national security and defense, matters required by law to be kept confidential, matters relating to the internal management of agencies and disciplinary actions that would adversely affect a person's reputation.

Ellsberg trial delayed. The Supreme Court Aug. 5 refused a government request to convene a special summer session to consider overturning Justice William O. Douglas's stay of the trial of Daniel Ellsberg and Anthony J. Russo Jr. in the Pentagon papers case.

The Justice Department had asked the court to vacate Douglas' order so that the trial of the defendants, charged with leaking the secret war study to the press, could resume in Los Angeles. A legal controversy over a government wiretap had led to a halt in the proceedings July 26.

With Douglas's stay in force, it was unlikely that the trial would resume before October.

Douglas stay halts trial—Douglas stayed the opening of the trial July 29, 48 hours before opening arguments were to be heard. Douglas said he was granting the stay to allow attorneys for Ellsberg and Russo to appeal to the Supreme Court their contention that the government be required to divulge details of a wiretapped conversation involving a defense lawyer or consultant.

Douglas gave defense attorneys until Aug. 28 to file a petition for review of the wiretap question by the full court. If the court agreed to hear the appeal when it convened Oct. 2, the opening of the trial could be delayed until 1973.

At issue in the wiretap controversy was whether the defendants had a right to see transcripts of a telephone conversation involving a member of the Ellsberg-Russo defense team that was monitored by the government as part of a "foreign intelligence" investigation unrelated to the Pentagon papers case.

The government had refused to make available to defense attorneys the details of that wiretap on the ground that it was not related to the Ellsberg-Russo trial.

Ellsberg appeal rejected. The Supreme Court cleared the way Nov. 13 for the government to resume its prosecution of Daniel Ellsberg and Anthony J. Russo Jr., who were accused of making public the Pentagon Papers.

With two justices dissenting, the court refused to hear the defendants' appeal that the presiding trial judge should have allowed them to see the transcript of a defense lawyer's conversation that had been monitored by a government wiretap.

The decision in effect dissolved a stay issued by Justice William O. Douglas July 29 that stopped the trial in Los Angeles 48 hours before opening arguments were to be heard.

In a related development, the court had refused Nov. 10 to stay the jailing of a Harvard University professor for his refusal to answer questions about the Pentagon Papers case.

Samuel L. Popkin, a political scientist, had been sentenced to 18 months in jail for contempt after he declined to answer seven questions before a U.S. grand jury in Boston in March. Popkin was a friend of Ellsberg.

The 1st Circuit Court of Appeals upheld Popkin's right to refuse replies to four of the seven questions. Those four had to do with his opinions of who might have had copies of the 47-volume war study. But the appeals court ruled that the three others were germane and should have been answered. Only Douglas dissented in the court's 8–1 decision.

Old documents still unavailable. Despite a presidential directive to ease the public's access to once-secret data, problems remained for those interested in seeing that information, according to a New York Times report Nov. 21.

In June, President Nixon had pledged to "lift the veil of secrecy" from needlessly classified official papers. To that end, he ordered that access to secret and confidential papers more than 10 years old be made easier. But despite his order, the output of such information was still no more than a trickle, according to historians, other scholars and newsmen. More requests for documents had been denied or labeled "pending" than had been granted.

Prohibitive costs, bureaucratic red tape and general confusion over Nixon's directive were said to be behind the apparent slowness in making the documents more available.

Popkin freed in contempt case. Prof. Samuel L. Popkin, the Harvard scholar who was jailed for refusing to answer certain questions about the Pentagon papers, was released from a Dedham, Mass. jail Nov. 28 in a surprise move by the government.

Popkin gained his freedom when the Justice Department unexpectedly dismissed the Boston grand jury before which he had refused to answer the questions. He was jailed for contempt Nov. 21 and had been expected to remain there until Jan. 12 when the jury was to end its investigation into the Pentagon papers case.

The U.S. attorney's office in Boston said the jury was dismissed to avoid any conflict with the government's case against Daniel Ellsberg and Anthony J. Russo Jr. on criminal charges involving the once-secret war study.

According to published reports, the decision to dismiss the jury and in effect free Popkin was made within the Justice Department's Internal Security Division. During the week that Popkin was imprisoned, Harvard officials, including President Derek C. Bok, sought to have Popkin released.

Popkin's release did not necessarily mean that the government was no longer interested in the information he withheld from the grand jury. If the government wanted to continue its investigation into the distribution of the Pentagon papers, it could impanel a new grand jury to ask Popkin the same questions he refused to answer before. They dealt with identification of government officials and others who had talked confidentially with him during his research on Vietnam.

Mistrial declared in Ellsberg case. The judge in the Pentagon Papers trial in Los Angeles declared a mistrial Dec. 8 because of an unparalleled lapse between the time a jury was seated and the actual opening of the trial.

Attorneys for Daniel Ellsberg and Anthony J. Russo Jr., principal defendants in the case, had sought a mistrial on different grounds.

Federal District Court Judge William M. Byrne Jr. announced his decision and dismissed the jury after Ellsberg and Russo had waived their double jeopardy protection.

Pentagon Papers defense begins case. The defense in the Pentagon Papers trial began its case Feb. 27, 1973, promising to show that the controversial documents had no relationship to the national security and that they were "needed by the country" in order to evaluate the war in Vietnam.

Time charges wiretaps by FBI. Time magazine charged in its March 5 issue that the White House ordered over a period of more than two years the Federal Bureau of Investigation (FBI) to tap the telephones of "six or seven" newsmen and a number of White House aides in order to pinpoint a news leak in the executive staff. Time attributed the story to "four different sources in the government." It declined, however, to name the sources or the newsmen involved. The magazine said the late J. Edgar Hoover, then director of the FBI, at first balked at using wiretaps, but was ordered by then Attorney General John Mitchell to follow White House orders.

Time said the wiretapping actually kept Hoover in office. Mitchell's deputy Richard Kleindienst, the present attorney general, wanted Hoover to retire, but quickly dropped the issue when Hoover threatened to expose the wiretaps to Congress. Time said the taps failed to uncover any leaks.

Kleindienst issued a statement Feb. 26 denying the Time magazine charges with regard to both himself and Mitchell.

Taps on Times reporters disclosed. The phones of at least two reporters for the New York Times were tapped by members of the Nixon Administration in connection with the Pentagon Papers disclosure, the Washington Post reported May 3.

The Post cited one highly placed Administration source as saying the wiretapping was supervised by Watergate co-conspirators E. Howard Hunt Jr. and G. Gordon Liddy, and that former Attorney General John N. Mitchell authorized the taps.

The source said the team of wiretappers, supervised by Hunt and Liddy, operated independently of the FBI, the agency normally responsible for electronic surveillance.

According to Post sources, the wiretaps followed earlier White House-ordered taps of other reporters, the purpose of which was to discover leaks of information about the strategic arms limitation talks to the news media.

The sources also said the home or office phones of at least 10 White House staffers were tapped in an effort to stem other news leaks.

Charges against Ellsberg, Russo dismissed. Government charges of espionage, theft and conspiracy against Pentagon Papers trial defendants Daniel Ellsberg and Anthony J. Russo Jr. were dismissed by presiding Judge William M. Byrne in Los Angeles May 11. Byrne worded the dismissal so as to preclude retrial.

In granting the dismissal, Byrne was highly critical of government conduct during the case. "Bizarre events have incurably infected the prosecution of this case," he said. "The totality of the circumstances . . . offend 'a sense of justice,' " he added.

1969 phone taps reported. The Nixon Administration, concerned over leaks of classified information—especially with regard to the strategic arms limitations talks beginning in 1969—ordered wiretaps placed on the telephones of reporters from three newspapers and at least one government official, the New York Times reported May 11.

Times sources said reporters placed under surveillance were William Beecher and Hedrick Smith of the New York Times, and Henry Brandon, a Washington-based correspondent for the Sunday Times of London. Phones of unidentified reporters for the Washington Post also were tapped, the Times said.

The government official was Morton H. Halperin, a member of the National Security Council until 1971. The tap on his home phone was revealed in a memo given May 9 by Acting FBI Director William Ruckelshaus to Pentagon Papers trial Judge William M. Byrne

According to the account supplied by Times sources, former Attorney General John N. Mitchell called the late director of the FBI, J. Edgar Hoover, in the spring of 1969, requesting that the taps be placed.

Hoover refused to comply without written authorization from Mitchell, who subsequently sent the late FBI chief an unspecified number of forms used to request "national security" wiretaps. (The Supreme Court had ruled in 1972 the government needed court orders before it could install wiretaps in national security cases, except where foreign connections were involved.

According to Times sources, Mitchell and Assistant Attorney General Richard Kleindienst, sometime after, suggested to Hoover, for reasons that were unclear, that a Congressional committee be allowed to investigate the FBI. Hoover refused consent, saying he might be asked about the wiretap installations.

In September 1971, the Justice Department retrieved the forms.

Ruckelshaus ordered an investigation of the 1969-71 buggings, but had not been able to determine if records still existed, the Times said.

Nixon authorized wiretaps. The White House May 16 acknowledged that President Nixon personally authorized the use of 17 wiretaps against 13 members of his own Administration and four newsmen.

The New York Times reported May 17 that Henry A. Kissinger, assistant to the President for national security affairs, personally provided the FBI with the names of a number of his aides on the National Security Council (NSC), whom he wanted wiretapped. The Times cited Justice Department officials as its source.

The White House, in formally acknowledging the existence of the wiretaps, said they were made in 1969 after publication in the Times May 9, 1969 of an article by William Beecher disclosing American B-52s were bombing Cambodia. (Beecher was appointed deputy assistant secretary of defense for public affairs April 20.)

Among those tapped was Helmut Sonnenfeldt, a former NSC official, who was nominated April 10 to be undersecretary of the Treasury.

Times sources revealed that Marvin Kalb, a diplomatic correspondent for the Columbia Broadcasting System (CBS), was under surveillance.

Kissinger, in an interview with the Times May 14, confirmed he had seen summaries of the wiretaps, but he said he had not asked that they be installed nor had he specifically approved them in advance. He also admitted he held one or two conversations with Hoover in 1969 in which he expressed "very great concern" that national security information be fully safeguarded.

The Washington Post reported May 18 that specific wiretaps had also been authorized by H. R. Haldeman, Nixon's former chief of staff.

Other former NSC officials whose phones were reported tapped were Anthony Lake, Daniel I. Davidson, and Winston Lord. Lord, a personal aide to Kissinger during the Paris peace talks and during his visits to Peking and Moscow, was on a one-year leave from the NSC.

Nixon affirms right to secrecy. President Nixon May 24 affirmed the government's right to secrecy in national security matters and denounced "those who steal secrets and publish them in the newspapers."

The latter remark, a reference to publication of the Pentagon Papers, drew a standing ovation from his audience of more than 600 recently returned prisoners of war. The scene was a State Department briefing for the POWs while their wives attended a reception elsewhere in the department with Mrs. Nixon. Later, the group attended a banquet and entertainment on the White House lawn.

"I want to be quite blunt," Nixon continued. "Had we not had secrecy, had we not had secret negotiations" with the North Vietnamese, Soviet and Chinese leaders, ". . . there would have been no China initiative, there would have been no limitation of arms for the Soviet Union and no summit, and had we not had that kind of security, and that kind of secrecy that allowed for the kind of exchange that is essential, you men would still be in Hanoi rather than Washington today.

"And let me say, I think it is time in this country to quit making national heroes out of those who steal secrets and publish them in the newspapers.

"Because, gentlemen, you see, in order to continue these great initiatives for peace, we must have confidentiality, we must have secret communications."

Ellsberg wiretap revealed. The Washington Post reported June 14 that the White House in 1971 received information from wiretaps—previously undisclosed—on Pentagon Papers defendant Daniel Ellsberg and New York Times reporters Neil Sheehan and Tad Szulc.

Despite demands by Pentagon Papers trial Judge William M. Byrne Jr., the taps were not disclosed by the government.

Post sources said federal investigators were trying to determine who authorized the wiretaps and why they were not reported to Judge Byrne.

According to Post sources, the wiretap information was received in the White House as early as May 1971—one month before the Pentagon Papers were published in the New York Times and one month before the White House "plumbers group" was set up on orders from President Nixon.

The Federal Bureau of Investigation said it had no record of any such electronic surveillance.

Post sources said they were unable to relate these taps to ones President Nixon said had been discontinued in February 1971.

The tap on Ellsberg continued for at least four months. The surveillance of the other two was irregular and lasted over several months, the Post said.

White House aides David R. Young Jr. and Egil Krogh Jr. were already involved in the investigation of Ellsberg's possession of a copy of the Pentagon Papers when the tap against Ellsberg was begun, the Post said.

Sheehan prepared the Pentagon Papers for publication by the Times.

Guidelines set for U.S. information. The right of the federal government to withhold data under the Freedom of Information Act was defined in a ruling by the U.S. Court of Appeals for the District of Columbia Aug. 20.

The decision came in a case in which consumer advocate Ralph Nader's Freedom of Information Clearinghouse had sought access to Civil Service Commission records concerning efficiency of federal agencies. A federal trial court had dismissed the case without hearing arguments.

The three-judge appeals panel set the following guidelines:

■ When refusing to disclose information, federal agencies would have to give a court detailed reasons for doing so.

■ Government agencies were ordered to establish an indexing system which divided documents into managable parts that were cross-referenced.

■ Trial courts would be able to designate special examiners, called masters, to examine documents and evaluate an agency's contention of exemption so the

court could handle "the enormous document-generating capacity of government agencies."

The appeals panel said the government's refusal to disclose data "seriously distorts the traditional adversary nature" of the legal system "because the person with the greatest interest in obtaining disclosure is at a loss to argue with desirable legal precision for the revelation of the concealed information."

The case was returned to the original trial court for a decision based on the new guidelines.

Kissinger confirmation hearings. Henry A. Kissinger's role in the 1969–71 wiretapping of government officials and newsmen* became the major question before the Senate Foreign Relations Committee as it opened public confirmation hearings Sept. 7 on Kissinger's nomination as secretary of state.

Kissinger defended the wiretapping as necessary to stop leaks to the press. He said he had consented to the practice in 1969 on the advice of then Attorney General John N. Mitchell and the late director of the Federal Bureau of Investigation (FBI), J. Edgar Hoover. He disclaimed deep involvement in the operation and said his office's involvement ended by the summer of 1970. Kissinger urged the committee to deal directly with Attorney General Elliot L. Richardson in further pursuit of the matter. In response to a question, he said "there were cases in which the sources of some leaks were discovered and corrective action taken."

---

*Disclosure of the identities of the 13 government officials and four newsmen subjected to the wiretapping was completed Aug. 31 when the New York Times identified three more officials on the list. They were James W. McLane, then on the White House Domestic Council staff, currently deputy director of the Cost of Living Council; John P. Sears, then deputy White House counsel and a former law partner of President Nixon; and Lt. Gen. Robert E. Pursley, then a colonel and military aide to the defense secretary, currently commander of American forces in Japan. Among those identified previously were Richard Moose, then on the National Security Council, currently a consultant to the Senate Foreign Relations Committee; and William Safire, then a presidential speechwriter, currently a columnist for the New York Times.

Editorial
Comment

The New York Times

New York, N.Y., June 16, 1971

In an unprecedented example of censorship, the Attorney General of the United States has temporarily succeeded in preventing The New York Times from continuing to publish documentary and other material taken from a secret Pentagon study of the decisions affecting American participation in the Vietnam War.

Through a temporary restraining order issued by a Federal District judge yesterday, we are prevented from publishing, at least through the end of the week, any new chapters in this massive documentary history of American involvement in the war. But The Times will continue to fight to the fullest possible extent of the law what we believe to be an unconstitutional prior restraint imposed by the Attorney General.

What was the reason that impelled The Times to publish this material in the first place? The basic reason is, as was stated in our original reply to Mr. Mitchell, that we believe "that it is in the interest of the people of this country to be informed. . . ." A fundamental responsibility of the press in this democracy is to publish infor-

mation that helps the people of the United States to understand the processes of their own government, especially when those processes have been clouded over in a hazy veil of public dissimulation and even deception.

As a newspaper that takes seriously its obligation and its responsibilities to the public, we believe that, once this material fell into our hands, it was not only in the interests of the American people to publish it but, even more emphatically, it would have been an abnegation of responsibility and a renunciation of our obligations under the First Amendment not to have published it. Obviously, The Times would not have made this decision, if there had been any reason to believe that publication would have endangered the life of a single American soldier or in any way threatened the security of our country or the peace of the world.

The documents in question belong to history. They refer to the development of American interest and participation in Indochina from the post-World War II period up to mid-1968, which is now almost three years ago.

Their publication could not conceivably damage American security interests, much less the lives of Americans in Indochinese. We therefore felt it incumbent to take ourselves the responsibility for their publication, and doing so raise once again the question of the Government's propensity for over-classification and mis-classification of documents that by any reasonable scale values have long since belonged in the public domain.

We publish the documents and related running account not to prove any debater's point about the origins a development of American participation in the war, to place the finger of blame on any individuals, civili or military, but to present to the American public a h tory—admittedly incomplete—of decision-making at t highest levels of government on one of the most vi issues that has ever affected "our lives, our fortunes a our sacred honor"—an issue on which the Americ people and their duly elected representatives in Congre have been largely curtained off from the truth.

It is the effort to expose and elucidate that truth th is the very essence of freedom of the press.

The Washington Post
Times Herald

Washington, D.C., June 17, 1971

Tuesday, in his first day on the bench, Federal Judge Murray I. Gurfein presided over a case in which the federal government, for what seems to be the first time in history, was asking a judge to order a newspaper not to print a particular piece of news. In such a situation, it is hardly surprising that Judge Gurfein issued a temporary restraining order barring The New York Times from printing the remainder of its series on the secret Pentagon study of the development of U.S. involvement in the Vietnam war. Such orders are often issued to maintain the status quo while the merits of a case are more fully considered, especially when maintaining the status quo does no harm to the party against whom the order is directed. And the Times has not been hurt by the four-day delay in its publishing plans. But the Times, the press as a whole, and the country itself would be badly hurt if, by some peculiar quirk of reasoning, Judge Gurfein, or any other judge, should attempt to make this order (or any similar order) permanent.

We say that because the federal government does not have a constitutional leg to stand on in its effort to censor the contents of a newspaper. Indeed, the history of the United States, the con-

stitutional interpretations consistently applied to the First Amendment for almost two centuries, and the theory of American government are so devoid of any precedents or any logic to support the government's position that we think it is fair to surmise that matters other than a desire to suppress the remainder of the Times's series must lie behind this lawsuit.

One of the things that every law student learns about the First Amendment is that its language guaranteeing freedom of speech and of the press means *at least* that no prior restraints shall be laid by government on the publication of any information. This idea is not new and was not new when it was expressed in the American Constitution; it grew directly out of British experience, and Sir William Blackstone had set down the rule as it was understood before the American Revolution:

The liberty of the press is indeed essential to the nature of a free state; but this consists in laying no previous restraints upon publications, and not in freedom from censure for criminal matter when published. Every free man has an undoubted right to lay what sentiments he pleases before the public: to forbid this is to destroy the freedom of the press: but if he

publishes what is improper, mischievous, or illegal, he must take the consequences of his own temerity.

The argument about freedom of the press in the years since Blackstone wrote has rarely involved his commentary on "previous restraints." Instead, it has revolved about how much more freedom than the standard he set out was granted by the First Amendment, about what kind of publications —if any—could be punished after they were printed. We are aware of only one case in which the Supreme Court ever addressed itself to the question of pre-publication censorship, and in it the court struck down an effort by the State of Minnesota to suppress a local scandal sheet.

It is evident, then, that unless the courts are now prepared to throw some 200 years of history and precedent out the window, the government will lose its case and the Times will be free, come Sunday, to resume publication of these documents. That is as it should be. A press that can be formally prevented by government from printing what it will—forbidden to print it in advance —is no more than a tool of government and one that can be used as the government may wish to deceive and to mislead.

THE MIAMI NEWS

Miami, Fla., June 17, 1971

Lest attention be diverted by the Federal government's attempt to censor The New York Times, the focal point of the Pentagon Papers in no wise has been altered.

Our troubles in Vietnam began with the Harry Truman administration, w e r e helped along by Dwight Eisenhower and John Foster Dulles, spurred by John F. Kennedy and escalated by Lyndon Baines Johnson. This is the sorry record of history as related in official documents and thus far unchallenged.

The Nixon Administration, while it had no hand in the early blunders which piled upon blunders, nevertheless is not home scot-free because it has been fostering a secret war in Laos — a war which is talked about only behind the closed doors of the U.S. Senate, but a war in which American lives are being lost.

The Pentagon documents, stolen or not, confirm that the United States' highest executives broadened a war 10,000 miles from home in the jungles of southeast Asia and then proceeded to lie to the American people when questioned about its record. One must wonder whether the security of the country really is endangered by publication of what is history. More likely, the government fears that the revelations will intensify the questioning of why our role in Vietnam is prolonged.

The New York Times will be criticized in some circles for its disclosures (which appeared in abridged form in The Miami News) but it has performed in the highest tradition of a free press. It is unfortunate that, for the first time in the history of this democracy, a newspaper has been prevented by court injunction from complete discharge of its duty to fully inform the public.

Censorship is the initial step towards loss of other basic freedoms.

The Boston Globe

Boston, Mass., June 16, 1971

There are some things which no government should or will confide to anyone outside of its own inner circle. This is not because all things are not indeed the citizen's business. They are and must be if government is to be the servant, not the master of the people. It is because the business of surviving as a nation may be at stake.

The nation's plans for resisting invasion clearly are and must be government's secret. The way to build an A-bomb or an N-bomb or even, who knows?, an XYZ bomb is not ever going to be released to the nation's press, and the newspapers themselves would be the first to demand some official scalps were this to occur.

But certainly the New York Times's disclosures on the machinations and deceptions connected with American participation in the Indochinese war do not fit the description of a national security violation. It can be argued, to the contrary, that government efforts to prevent further disclosure are themselves a threat to the national security. However strained the rationale may appear to be, what the government is saying, nevertheless, is that official conniving and duplicity or, perhaps, simple stupidity, are none of the American people's business even when the cost is 55,000 American lives and a frightening torn country. The Times's disclosures pertain only to prior Administrations.

The Times's revelations, says the Department of Justice (and a Federal court has at least temporarily concurred), "will cause irreparable damage to the defense interests of the United States." On the contrary, however, irreparable damage is done to the nation when such disclosures are suppressed.

The people's confidence in either their government's integrity or its wisdom or perhaps both may be shaken all the more when government persists in the outlandish view that how the nation was conned into this war, and conned illegally at that, and how it could similarly be plunged into another, is none of the public's business. Where it is shown that past Presidents can and do err as grievously as has been demonstrated (either because they were too self-willed or were the victims of advisers) the motives of incumbent administrators who would conceal the facts then themselves inevitably become suspect.

The Nixon Administration takes the curious position that it was a breach of security to disclose that the Gulf of Tonkin resolution was drafted three months before the incident on which it was based. But the real outrage is the resolution itself and the suppression of this vital information until now. Had the Congress and the American people then known what they know now, we would have been out of Indochina long before this. The Nixon Administration's abhorrence of the disclosures does not exactly put to rest all doubts of the legitimacy of its own purposes in continuing the war into which the nation was apparently tricked.

Mr. Nixon speaks of saving the lives of American "boys," just as President Johnson did, and he is indeed bringing them home in numbers. But there are still more than 200,000 of them over there, and he stubbornly resists all efforts to bring them home now and thus save their lives. In leaving them there he is prompted by the same dubious reasons that prompted President Johnson to send them there in the first place. If ever there were arguments that should convince wavering senators that passage of the McGovern-Hatfield resolution is vital, the Times's disclosures and the Administration's reaction to them is it. It is not only the integrity of the Johnson Administration that is at stake. It is the integrity of the Nixon Administration. The Times's disclosures of what happened four, five, 10 or 20 years ago "do irreparable injury to the defense interests of the United States" in the same way that those interests were impaired by disclosures that George Washington's false teeth were ill-fitting.

What happens when a government bottles up legitimate information, or tries to, has been demonstrated time and again. It was not until 13 months had passed, for example, that the nation learned that peace was possible in 1964, if Mr. Johnson had wanted it, which he did not—and, seemingly, this Administration does not now because the time is not ripe. The Thieu government is not yet sufficiently entrenched.

The virtues of the fullest possible disclosures were put down in 1968 in the preface to a collection of his speeches by none other than the former Secretary of Defense Robert S. McNamara—and never mind that he was one of those who kept Mr. Johnson's secrets:

"The people of this nation, in whose name and by whose ultimate consent all high government officials serve, have both the need and the right to be thoroughly informed on decisions. The only narrow and necessary exceptions are those matters restricted by the irreducible requirements of intelligence collection or battlefield security."

The late President Kennedy was even more to the point after the Cuban Bay of Pigs fiasco on which the Times eliminated vital information in its exclusive account of the invasion then planned.

"If you had printed more about the operation," Mr. Kennedy later told Turner Catledge, then a Times editor, "you would have saved us from a colossal mistake."

The Times, in our view, has performed a singular public service, and should be rewarded rather than denigrated by the Nixon Administration. It is significant that no Administration official, and no one else, for that matter, challenges the authenticity of the Times's revelations. The only Washington complaint is that it has unearthed facts which Washington wanted to keep locked in one of its dark closets.

The whole truth, when it is brought to light, can only help the people to know what they need to know, for their security and that of the nation.

Newsday

Long Island, N.Y., June 16, 1971

The critical issue in the case of the United States vs. the New York Times is: Does the Nixon administration fear the effect of the extraordinary "Vietnam papers" on the enemy or on the American people?

Under terms of a ruling by a federal judge appointed four days ago by President Nixon, it will be at least Sunday before the public can learn the next chapter in the incredible history of duplicity and misinformation that accompanied the nation's descent into the Vietnam morass.

This delay, if not the complete suppression of these startling documents, is the responsibility of the Nixon administration, which sought the restraining order on the grounds that publication could "result in irreparable injury to the national defense." It again widens the breach between the White House and those who question, criticize or dissent from the government's handling of the Vietnam war.

The administration's position seems singularly untenable at this point since the papers in the Times' possession do not cover any activities beyond mid-1968—three years ago—and therefore would appear in no way to jeopardize the lives or performance of any present U.S. military forces.

What the documents do jeopardize, of course, is the familiar governmental assurance that it is telling the truth, keeping the people informed and acting in their best interests.

And while the material appearing in the Times dealt only with previous administrations—and primarily with the Johnson years of escalation—this attempt at suppression by President Nixon and Attorney General Mitchell perpetuates the spirit of obfuscation and concealment that permeates the official behavior described in the published accounts.

The present controversy also emphasizes the role of the press in public affairs. Although the Nixon administration frequently has criticized the media for its negative attitude toward government, the Vietnam papers underline the necessity for skepticism. The current revelations surely would not have created such an impact had the American press pursued its mission more vigorously when the Johnson administration was selling the war to the American people.

The Times has done a distinct public service in publishing this heretofore secret history of U.S. involvement in Vietnam from the end of World War II. Unsettling as the disclosures may be to those who have insisted upon the right of the government not to be questioned, publication of the report fulfills an essential need of democracy—the right of the people to know.

In this history, which was undertaken by Pentagon analysts at the behest of former Defense Secretary McNamara, it is made clear that our participation in Vietnamese affairs has, again and again, been marked by Machiavellian counterplay, by a disregard for public honesty and by the conviction that a small group of White House policymakers can stage-manage domestic opinion and do whatever else they think necessary to justify their narrow concept of American self-interest.

The famous Tonkin Gulf incident, for instance, according to the government's own account, did not occur in the vacuum suggested by the Johnson administration. The August, 1964, "attack" on two U.S. destroyers by North Vietnam followed months of provocative action by U.S.-supported Vietnamese forces and the development of a battle plan for escalating the war. Congress, lacking this knowledge, was so outraged by the administration's report of the Tonkin Gulf affair that it passed a resolution essentially ceding war-waging powers to President Johnson in Southeast Asia. And, on that basis, Washington unleashed its formidable air power on North Vietnam with, as the study notes, "virtually no domestic criticism."

The implications of this study—and its release and attempted suppression—must not be minimized. Central to the matter is the power of the presidency, particularly as it applies in decisions affecting war and peace. Obviously, according to disclosures made by the Times, the people and the Congress were willing, albeit unknowing accomplices, to a series of decisions that saw this nation go from a provider of military aid in the Truman era to a major combatant during the Johnson years—all the time without really understanding the implications of our Vietnamese adventure. Yesterday, the Times reported that President Johnson decided to undertake an offensive ground war in April, 1965, despite the existing policy that counseled against another Korean-type land war in Asia. Mr. Johnson made this momentous choice and then, according to the Pentagon history, ordered that the decision be kept secret.

Although the study does not allude to the Nixon administration, there is no reason to believe that the presidency has become less a repository of power under the present leadership. But, whoever occupies the White House, Republican or Democrat, the people should have a basic assurance that their fate—and the fate of this nation—will not be decided precipitately by an over-enthusiastic exercise of power or, simply, by an administrative misjudgment or executive blunder. In order to limit presidential war-making power, a bill introduced last month by Sen. John C. Stennis (D-Miss.) merits enactment. The proposed measure would allow the President to dispatch troops only to ward off invasion or protect Americans abroad. If, after 30 days, the Congress had not ratified that presidential action, the troops would return—immediately.

In defending its right to publish the Vietnam chronicle, the Times stated that "it is in the best interest of the people of this country to be informed of the material . . ." To say the least, we agree. If the government is unwilling to level with the people, the press must perform that service. Rep. Paul N. McCloskey (R-Calif.), a critic of the Vietnam war, said after the Times series began that "the issue of truthfulness of government is a problem as serious as that of ending the war itself." Too often, he said, government cover-ups are "not a matter of protecting secret information from the enemy." Rather, he said, the "intention is to conceal information from the people of the United States as if we were the enemy."

Secrecy may, at times, be necessary in the administration of even the most open of societies. But when it becomes a substitute for honesty and when deception becomes synonymous with diplomacy, the goals of this nation are compromised. The Times case should be a signal to us all that power has been misused in Washington. The people should take every step to see that the abuse does not continue.

Senate Majority Leader Mike Mansfield (D-Mont.) already has suggested the possibility of hearings into the disclosures. They should be held. As in the case of congressional inquiries into American war crimes, which this newspaper has proposed, the need for the American people to know what has been done in their name is essential if we are to prevent future Vietnams and regain the sense of national pride and purpose that are vital to our survival as a democratic society.

THE MILWAUKEE JOURNAL

Milwaukee, Wis., June 16, 1971

What the American people have been getting through the publication by The New York Times of an official analysis of the Vietnam War is the story of suppressed truth and government duplicity.

It is a tragic story of how we went deeper and deeper into an unnecessary war for the wrong reasons under a cloak of deep secrecy. It documents what has been evident for a long time — that former President Johnson was planning bombing assaults on North Vietnam and enlargement of our military commitment at the very time he was conducting a campaign for election with a promise not to widen the war, while labeling his opponent a warmonger.

The Nixon administration has obtained a temporary court order to stop publication of the secret survey until the legality can be decided. It claims that national security has been breached, that foreign relations have been harmed and that irreparable damage has been done to national defense.

These protests are weak. The main result of the publication so far has been to embarrass those who ran our government from 1964 through 1968 and those who

run it now, who have continued the same course of misleading the American people. The survey ends with the year 1968 and covers mainly the period when President Johnson took us secretly into an ever widening war. But the same kind of secrecy has continued since — as Cambodia and the invasion of Laos underlined dramatically. The present administration continued to draw the veil over clandestine machinations in Laos that its predecessor started.

The American people have been gulled and have the right to know it. The disclosure of the survey does not affect national security except to the extent that it lessens public confidence in the government. Confidence is vital to a democracy. The story of duplicity over Vietnam merely confirms what the majority of Americans have increasingly felt when polled — that they were being misled from the start on Vietnam. It is amazing that Secretary of State Rogers, in commenting on the survey, could say with some wonder: "There is still a view in large segments of the American public that the government somehow isn't coming clean."

The government has taken the unprecedented step of seeking an injunction against continued publication of the documents. This

will be a precedent setting test, for it involves the use of "prior restraint" to curb a newspaper. That, as the late Chief Justice Hughes once said, "is the essence of censorship." The normal and proper procedure is to punish an illegal expression rather than to suppress it in advance. If the government obtains the right to determine what may or may not be printed before the fact, then it obtains the power of full censorship.

The arbitrary classification of a document as "top secret" does not necessarily make it so, and under the First Amendment the press has the right of judgment—subject to subsequent action if it proves wrong.

The argument that our international relations are damaged is relevant only in that other governments joined ours in secrecy and duplicity and now stand embarrassed, too. There are, of course, instances of secret agreements with other governments that are necessary for security. But in this case the secrecy shielded wrongdoing.

At stake here is the public's right to know and the duty of the press to inform. That what is being disclosed is shameful and stigmatic is unfortunate — but disclosure is vital as a curb on future wrongdoing and duplicity.

THE KNICKERBOCKER NEWS
*** UNION-STAR ***

Albany, N.Y., June 16, 1971

The Justice Department has accused the New York Times, in effect, of violating the Espionage Law with its publication of a long report and condensation of a Pentagon study on the United States involvement in the Vietnam War.

The department first sought to halt the publication by request (although some might characterize the tone of the department's request as intimidation). The department told the Times if it did not cease publication it would seek a court order compelling it to do so. Subsequently it obtained a temporary injunction halting publication for four days.

The Times has refused the request, said it will oppose in court any efforts to make the temporary injunction permanent, and said if the court issues a permanent injunction it will obey it.

The Justice Department contends the publication of exerpts from the defense study "will cause irreparable injury to

the defense interests of the United States."

All this leaves various matters to consider.

One is the predilection of the defense establishment for secrecy. Any upper level military bureaucrat can use his "Secret" stamp with virtual abandon. He can use the word security as a synonym of sorts for embarrassment.

A second is whether the publication of this document, dealing with matters of several years ago, actually imperils the "defense interests" of the United States or merely causes that embarrassment. The evidence is strong that it causes embarrassment.

A third is whether publication is a violation of the law. There is some doubt that it is, although it is more evident that those who supplied the Times with the

Pentagon report violated regulations ruling their conduct.

It is important to recall that at the time of the Bay of Pigs, the Times had information in its possession concerning plans for the Cuban "invasion." At that time it considered it to be its duty to remain silent. History may well have led it to regret its decision. But that situation was different from the current one. Then the Times was aware of something about to happen. This time it is reporting history.

We commend the Times for its courage in printing the summary of the Pentagon report on Vietnam. We commend it for refusing to be intimidated and for being prepared to present its case against a permanent injunction in court. We commend it equally for its announcement that it will obey any court decision.

In all these things, the Times is performing a service to the American people.

Long Island Press

New York, N.Y., June 16, 1971

Two far-reaching, separate sets of questions are involved in the New York Times' publication of a secret Pentagon study of the Vietnam War.

One has to do with the First Amendment right of a newspaper to print such information. The other has to do with the ramifications of the substance of the revelations.

This case is devolping into one of the most significant in the long history of the great American dilemma raised by the conflict between the public's right to know and the governments privilege of confidentiality.

No one seriously questions the need for classified information in military matters. As State Secretary Rogers pointed out yesterday, publication of secret documents can also, by violating confidences, cause serious breaches in trust in our relations with other governments. The difficulty, however, is that there can be no absolute determination of where security begins and ends. All too often, secrecy has been used to disguise error and questionable policies rather than preserve security.

Atty. Gen. Mitchell in obtaining a temporary injunction against the Times yesterday, charged that publication of the Vietnam report "has prejudiced the defense interests of the United States" and that further publication would "result in irreparable injury to the national defense." It is now incumbent on him to make overwhelmingly convincing case before such an awesome and unprecedented decision be made permanent. Indeed, it should go all the way, if need be, to the Supreme Court.

Mr. Mitchell's case is not clearcut so far. The events dealt with in the report occurred several years ago. Much of the information merely documents what has since, in general terms, become public knowledge, illuminating—sometimes shockingly—the nation's drift into war.

Considering the lives lost, the pain to so many millions of individuals and the extent to which the war has torn the fabric of American society, every responsible attempt to let the public know is not only the exercise of an American right, but an exercise in American wisdom.

While such publication may be a sign of our vulnerability, it is also a sign of our strength.

Even as the demonologists are busy picking through the dirty linen for their favorite bad guys, a fact that seems to be overlooked is that the study was not prepared by the accusers, but by the principals themselves.

There is much that is damning, particularly the cynical failure to inform both Congress and the public of national life-and-death decisions. It is also distressing to note the fallibility of leaders. Operating in what they considered the highest national interest, they threw all their talents and energy into an effort that demeaned American power instead of enhancing it, and contributed so to the economic and social turmoil at home.

They thought they were fighting a limited war, and in a sense, they were right; our full military potential was never unleashed. The result, however, was the opposite of the intention to end the fighting; it was a tragic miscalculation in which enough force was used to kill and maim thousands of people and generate a domestic disaster, but not enough to deter the other side's force and terror.

All this documentation, however, is still the raw stuff of history, not history itself, which is the evaluation and understanding of such material. For those who rush to judgment, there must be words of caution. There is much material that has not yet appeared—the reports of other agencies and other leaders and, most significantly, material that may never appear, the documents about the inner workings of Hanoi, Peking, Moscow and other protagonists in this frightful struggle.

As the brilliant book by John Toland, "The Rising Sun," reveals in its analysis of World War II as seen through Japanese sources, opinions and prejudices are easy to come by, but awareness of broad historical truths takes patient study of all sides.

Instead of trying to bottle this up through the courts, the administration should cooperate with Senate Democratic Leader Mike Mansfield's intention to hold open hearings, "to see the whole story laid out .. ." because "the congress and the people are entitled to all the elements pertaining to this tragedy."

DENVER POST

Denver, Colo., June 16, 1971

THIS NEWSPAPER believes that the interests of the United States will be strengthened—not harmed—by making available to the American people the contents of a secret Pentagon study on the origins of U.S. involvement in the Vietnam war.

For that reason, we are publishing a New York Times series on the Pentagon study; and, in today's Denver Post, we complete the publication of all the material so far made available by The Times.

A New York court, acting in response to a U.S. Justice Department plea, has issued a temporary order restraining The Times from publishing the last two articles in its series until the merits of the government's objections can be considered.

But we doubt that the series will be held up beyond the termination of the restraining order at 1 p.m. Saturday, EDT. Unless the First Amendment's protection of freedom of the press has lost its meaning, The Times will be freed to publish and distribute the balance of the series after that time, and we intend to publish it also.

What the series has revealed thus far has been embarrassing to the administration of former President Lyndon Johnson, disturbing to the Congress and the people, and damaging to public confidence in the government and our war policy.

But the exposure of past mistakes does not damage our present security. Instead, it places us in a position to strengthen our system so that we can avoid similar mistakes in the future. Our country would be

damaged, not by the dissemination of information, but by the supression of it.

The Vietnam war has troubled the mind and conscience of the United States for years. In a poll reported by the Gallup organization this week, Vietnam is listed as the Number One issue bothering the American people.

IN THIS SITUATION, every bit of information that can be provided on how and why we got involved in Vietnam is useful in helping to understand the problems and come to conclusions about the future.

The first step toward overcoming the national agony that Vietnam has caused us is to face the truth, and the Pentagon study helps us to do that. As long as the reports on that study are made available to us, we intend to publish them.

The Evening Bulletin

Philadelphia, Pa., June 17, 1971

There are many reasons why the Government would feel bound to move as it did in court to halt publication by the New York Times of a secret Pentagon study of U. S. involvement in the Vietnam war up to May, 1968 and the decision-making process that led to it.

None of these reasons, from the viewpoint of the responsibility of the free press to this democratic nation, overrides the obligation the Times felt in laying the historic record before the American people.

The federal judge who issued a temporary restraining order against the Times spoke of the importance of the case and its involvement "with the history of the relationship between the security of the Government and a free press."

No doubt about it, the Times took upon itself a heavy responsibility in putting into print secret information derived from the files of the Government.

There are statutes dealing with revelations of secret material, and penalties, although whether they apply here is a disputed question still to be decided. Constitutional liberty is also involved.

• • •

The Government, on its part, has a legitimate need for privacy in security matters, although the abuses of government secrecy are well known. It is possible that foreign countries could gather useful intelligence data on internal procedures and communications from the publication even of secret material that is not current. Diplomacy may be handicapped if foreign governments fear they cannot communicate with Washington on a confidential basis.

Against any such considerations, however, place one which could loom larger: the protection of the nation from the abuses and mistakes of its servants in government which may be shielded by official secrecy.

Government was never seen by the founding fathers as a perfect instrument above challenge. They wrote their checks and balances in the Constitution to protect American liberty against governmental abuse.

It is the obligation of a free press to inform the public to the best of its ability about the truth of vital government decisions that affect the life, the well-being, and the future of U.S. citizens and their form of government.

This, in the last analysis, is the justification for the freedom granted the press under the Constitution, the basic law of the land. It is a freedom that has to be deserved, used, earned, and defended in every generation if democratic self-government itself is to survive.

• • •

So the editors of the Times made a decision in publishing this record of the past. They staked their reputations and their fortunes and made themselves subject to legal action by the Government to put documents before the public, some of which raise grave questions about the integrity of previous government officials in their dealings with the American public on the Vietnam War.

There may be lessons to be learned from these old documents that will serve Americans well, strengthening democratic government processes, preventing the repetition of mistakes, and so restoring the shaken faith of people in government. Such faith is a greater support for national defense than any secrecy stamp on years-old documents.

The decision of the courts in this particular case is still to be made. And whether or not the Times' procedure has made it in some way legally vulnerable remains to be seen. All the circumstances surrounding the disclosure and all their implications are not yet known. But, nonetheless, the Times acted in the spirit of a great tradition. Its courage as a newspaper commands respect.

ST. LOUIS POST-DISPATCH

St. Louis, Mo., June 17, 1971

The Nixon Administration has given disturbing signs of its basic hostility to freedom of the press and of its own sense of political insecurity by its frenzied efforts to prevent *The New York Times* from continuing publication of a Pentagon history of how the United States got involved in the Vietnam war.

In the light of demonstrated animosity toward *The New York Times* in particular and toward media critics of the Administration in general by Vice President Agnew and other Administration spokesmen, this case ominously reflects the Administration's failure to understand that the role of the press is to be observer and monitor of government and not a handmaiden to promote its policies. Since the Pentagon papers in question all deal with the actions of past Administrations, three years and more ago, the Nixon Administration's ham-fisted attempts to keep them secret also lends plausibility to a belief that it fears a publication which could set a precedent for subsequent disclosure of its own deception of Congress and the public.

The Administration would have conveyed a much better sense of proportion and sureness if, once the classified documents were out, the President had quietly declassified the material and let the public judge their historical significance and their import for the performance of the officials involved.

Any dispassionate reading of the classified material acquired and partially published by *The Times* could lead only to the conclusion that at most it would seriously embarrass those officials of the Johnson and previous administrations who planned and persisted in calamitous military policies in Indochina and who misled the American people and their legislators as to what they were doing. But it is not the duty of the press to save the U.S. government from embarrassment, or to preserve its virtuous image in the eyes of foreign governments, which is what some Administration spokesmen have suggested is at stake.

The only justifiable reason for withholding publication of this historical material would be that its revelation would jeopardize lives or, in a broader sense, threaten American security. But as *The Times* has emphatically pointed out, publication of these documents "could not conceivably damage American security interests, much less the lives of Americans or Indochinese."

The Nixon Administration has so far offered no credible case to the contrary. It is unconvincing when it contends that publication of the verbatim texts of messages originally transmitted in coded cablegrams might enable hostile governments to decipher the code and learn the contents of messages on other subjects which they have intercepted. To give credence to such a theory, one would have to assure that other governments are incredibly efficient in intercepting and storing messages for possible future use, and assume also that the U. S. government does not follow the normally prudent practices of constantly changing codes and of using different ones for highly sensitive messages.

The whole process of easy classification and cumbersome declassification is called into question by the furor over the publication of classified documents, the chief direct effect of which is to discomfit government officials whose miscalculations are thus brought to light. The lesson of this case is that secret classifications should automatically be dissolved after a stipulated brief period except for documents which have a direct and continuing bearing on existing military security. Otherwise, government officials will use the classified stamp as a device to cover up their mistakes and their egregious pursuit of wrong-headed policies; and the press will be impeded in its proper function of letting the people know how their officials are making and carrying out policies.

In making what the Justice Department itself said was a historically unprecedented move to stop a newspaper from publishing prepared articles, the Nixon Administration is launching a frontal assault on the First Amendment, which grew out of the founders' abhorrence of prior restraints on the press by government. In unlimbering such a heavy legal weapon against *The Times* in a New York federal court, the Administration is giving the impression that it is less concerned with security than it is with continuing a vendetta against its media critics and at the same time preventing the public from having information to which it is entitled.

Los Angeles Times

Los Angeles, Calif., June 17, 1971

Publication of the War Papers

The publication by the New York Times of secret government documents about the Vietnam war, and the government's attempt to prevent the New York Times from publishing them, raise three questions of great importance to the people of this country.

Those questions are: the documents themselves and what they reveal about the war; the judgment of the New York Times in publishing them even though they were classified "Secret" and "Top Secret"; and judgment of the government in attempting to stop the publication of further articles.

To the first, what the documents show, the answer is that they show not much that is wholly astonishing. The arguments of the principals within the Johnson Administration about the war are seen pretty much as they have been understood.

But the documents published to date do indeed show details that were not known before. Incomplete as they are, the documents show that the men of that administration moved sooner than the public knew toward an involvement in the war deeper than the public knew. They show further that the Johnson Administration engaged in, at best, dissimulation, and, on a few occasions, deliberate deception of the people of the United States, in a course of action of great importance to those people. The documents document the "credibility gap."

★

It was, as we all know by now, a tragic series of acts by the government, tragic in the real sense because what the government did in those years was done from the highest motives of idealism, of patriotism. How it was done, and what can be learned from the way it was done, and how to avoid doing anything like it in the future as best we can avoid it—these are the questions illuminated by the publication of those documents. That they are accurate, and that they touch on the deepest issues confronting the people—war and peace—no one can deny.

The question then is the judgment of the New York Times in publishing them. The New York Times argued simply that "it is in the interest of the people of this country to be informed." The American government is the servant of the people; what the

government does is the public's business. With that general statement no one can quarrel. To protect the freedom of the citizens to know what their government is doing, and to dispute it if they wish, and to keep the government in the hands of the citizens to whom it is responsible—it was for these purposes that the First Amendment to the U.S. Constitution was adopted. Not for the press as an industry, but for the citizens.

Is the press then at liberty to publish whatever it wants to no matter what the consequences? Of course not. It is restrained by the laws of libel; it is restrained by sensible governmental regulations—and it is restrained finally by its own good judgment and sense of fairness.

The record of the American press in refraining from publishing confidential information affecting the security of the country and the lives of its citizens is, we can say in all candor, excellent. With one lamentable exception, the press went through the Second World War, when censorship was a reasonable and necessary regulation, without breaching security; so too, on the whole, in the Vietnam war, where there is no censorship.

No newspaper we know of would knowingly compromise the national security interest of the country or the lives of its citizens; and the government has its "Secret" and "Top Secret" and other classifications to keep confidential that kind of information. The Executive Orders establishing those classifications are specific and reasonable about what kind of information is not to be made public.

By no standard of either those classifications or of common sense can the documents published by the New York Times yet be said to endanger the security of the country or the lives of its citizens. The documents are past history. They reveal old arguments, not present intentions or future operations.

Yet the Justice Department contends in its suit that with the continued publication of the information, the "nation's security will suffer immediate and irreparable harm."

Some embarrassment, yes; some personal anguish, certainly. But there is no evidence yet offered to show that the security

of the country is in any way endangered by the publication.

Unnamed government spokesmen have suggested that the verbatim publication of actual messages exchanged abroad may enable the Soviet Union to break American codes. If so, and if the government asserts and proves that in court, it would be a different matter; then the argument could well be made that the publication of the texts verbatim did indeed endanger national security.

The government claims also that the publication endangers the confidentiality of communications with other governments. That is a consideration. It would be much more a consideration if democratic governments around the world did not continually spill the diplomatic beans about their negotiations; and if officials of the American government, from Presidents down, did not tell state secrets as they saw fit and for their purposes.

★

Which is what the present controversy is all about, really; the history of the war in Vietnam, and how we got into it. It is a history already being told, in part, in books and memoirs. The current publication of documents merely adds more pieces to that history. It is all coming out, anyway; and it will continue to, as the participants to those decisions tell their versions of one of the most difficult episodes in the American experience.

It was astonishing, therefore, that the government sought to stop publication. On the arguments so far brought by the government, there is no evidence that the national security is endangered. There is only the evidence that the government does not like what is being published.

That, in a word, is censorship. The government is relying on the Espionage Act to enforce against the newspaper a law that perhaps was never intended to be used against the press; that certainly never has been so used; and that, we firmly believe, cannot, under the Constitution, be so used in this case.

The government's action is almost without parallel in the history of the nation. It is a sweeping assertion of government power, and, on the evidence produced so far, an assertion of power that challenges the basic right of the people to be informed about the activities of their government.

Tulsa, Okla., June 17, 1971

SUBSTANTIAL and controversial questions spurt quickly out of the furor over the NEW YORK TIMES' publication of secret DEFENSE DEPARTMENT documents relating to the origins and escalation of the Vietnam war.

Almost certainly the U.S. SUPREME COURT will have to rule on the legal issues, such as the right of a newspaper to publish any information it can get its hands on and the right of the Government to stop it.

There are questions of journalistic ethics, for almost all newspapermen dealing with the Pentagon or other sensitive offices have seen classified material without putting it into public print. How did the TIMES justify its decision here?

A judgment factor enters into this case, for it could hardly be an accident that an antiwar newspaper could suddenly come into possession of secret documents calculated to weaken the U.S. case for being in Vietnam.

That raises the issue of political intent, which colors the entire incident. For at this particular moment the conduct of the war is perhaps the most sensitive pressure on the NIXON Administration. The TIMES could have printed classified material on other topics without getting the JUSTICE DEPARTMENT on its neck, but this one is hot, hot, hot.

Anyone can see how the disclosures may affect decisions still to be made in Congress and elsewhere. Senate Majority Leader MIKE MANSFIELD and other antiwar lawmakers are already on record calling for full Senate investigation of the determinations leading to the U.S. involvement in Vietnam.

It can be argued, with some merit, that the American people should have all pertinent facts that led to this bloody and protracted war. But isn't it equally true that the secret processes of Government—if they are sensitive enough to be classified—can be released only at the risk of embarrassing the nation and possibly harming its foreign relations?

We have a hunch the Senate's self-righteous investigation is inevitable now—and in turn it could have a strong effect on future judgments regarding Indochina. The leak to the NEW YORK TIMES has opened a particularly squirmy can of worms.

The Seattle Times

Seattle, Wash., June 17, 1971

THE controversy over news publication of a secret Pentagon study of steps and missteps leading to America's over-involvement in the Vietnam war puts in sharp focus an old and knotty question.

What is the responsibility of the news media to make known publicly information on matters in which the national security may be jeopardized?

In obtaining a temporary restraining order against further publication of basic information in the Pentagon study, the federal government has contended that security was being breached.

As defendant in the court action, The New York Times has rejected the charge of a security breach, insists that the press has an inherent responsibility to make the information known publicly, and argues the point of constitutional invalidity of prior-publication censorship.

AS we view the information published so far, little if anything has been forthcoming that was not made known to the public, directly or by interpretation during the period in which the events were taking place.

Yet the cohesive manner by which those events have been inter-related and given their due emphasis by the Pentagon study provides shocking perspective of disgraceful double-talk by high officials in government at that time.

It is now disclosed that at the very time during the 1964 presidential election campaign that the Republican nominee, Barry Goldwater, was being depicted by President Johnson's supporters as a "war-happy hawk," the incumbent President himself was entertaining recommendations for the major military involvement which subsequently turned so sour, even disastrous.

MOREOVER, the study puts into historical perspective the first American involvement from President Eisenhower's policies of economic and advisory assistance to the beginning of overt military involvement during President Kennedy's administration—and on to Mr. Johnson's throwing away all pretenses by ordering the all-out American escalation which now has cost the lives of about 50,000 Americans.

Is this perspective to be denied to the American people? The Seattle Times holds that the news media would be conducting themselves as indecently as the high government officials have done if they flinched in the responsibility to make available to the people information which the people should have.

AS to the United States attorney general's assertions — and he doubtless speaks for the White House, too — that national security has been breached, we say this has yet to be proved, if it can be proved without an actual violation of security.

This poses a most intriguing procedural question — namely, how does one go about arguing secret security matters in court proceedings without divulging all of the secret details?

We suggest that the federal government would have been well advised not to attempt the legal restraint on publication of the Pentagon document. By its action the government has widened the controversy and has attracted additional national and world-wide attention to valid reasons for the American credibility gap between its government and its people.

THE ARIZONA REPUBLIC

Phoenix, Ariz., June 17, 1971

There isn't much doubt that the New York Times decided to publish its series about the Pentagon study on the origins of the Vietnam war because the study satisfies the Times's ideological passions.

The revelations don't really tell us an awful lot that wasn't already known about the Johnson administration's lack of candor toward Congress and toward the American people. But they reinforce the themes so prevalent in the Times editorial page: That the government cannot be trusted, that the Vietnam war has corrupted our nation, that the most honorable thing we can now do is get out of Vietnam as fast as possible.

But motives aside, we disagree with government contentions that publication of the documents will cause irreparable injury to the defense interests of the U.S. The leak may cause concern in foreign chancelleries about the ability of Washington to keep secret negotiations secret, but that consideration must remain subordinate to the public's right to know. Therefore the Times's revelations are in the public interest.

Why shouldn't the American public, whose sons are fighting and dying in Vietnam, be allowed to know the origins of the war? Why should Congress be denied legitimate documents? Why should the Nixon administration cover up for the Johnson administration by perpetuating a cloak of secrecy?

The Times and other dove spokesmen frequently imply that secrecy is unique with the Johnson administration and with the Vietnam war. In fact, official secrecy through the very same device of classifying official documents surrounded U.S. diplomacy before and during World War II, the Korean War, and the Bay of Pigs fiasco in Cuba.

Yet the Times and its enthusiasts never say that the public has a right to know how President Franklin Roosevelt was less than candid with the American people. (Cong. Clare Boothe Luce charged that FDR "lied us into war," and such esteemed historians as Charles Beard explained in detail just exactly how.) They never reprimanded JFK aide Arthur Sylvester, when he said that the government had a right to lie. And they acquiesced in the bald deception, since admitted by former New Frontiersmen, that the money raised to ransom captives from the Bay of Pigs invasion came from private rather than government sources.

Governments, even democratic governments, do lie—not just to protect the national interest but to cover up their mistakes and machinations. Since New Deal days, administrations have elevated lying and deception to a highly refined art, in large part because they understood that they would not be challenged by a medium that shared a common ideology. Indeed, the failure of the press to challenge the news management of the Kennedy administration will stand as the nadir of journalism in our lifetime.

But the news management of the Johnson administration has now been challenged by the Times. And although we question the Times's motives in doing so, we nevertheless hope that the government's request for a preliminary injunction against that newspaper will be denied.

THE DALLAS TIMES HERALD

Dallas, Tex., June 17, 1971

FROM A practical standpoint, it may not matter that a federal judge has temporarily barred the New York Times from continuing to publish a top-secret report on the Vietnam war.

Mike Mansfield, the Senate Democratic leader, says he will hold congressional hearings, and on his own hook, divulge whatever is in the documents.

Even so, this shouldn't obscure the issue raised by the episode, which issue, of course, is the propriety of anyone's revealing the contents of government documents that touch on the national security.

The Times takes its stand on the people's right to know. Does this suffice, however? In an orderly society, rights entail responsibility. And surely it is not altogether responsible to publish information which the government wants to withhold in the interest of national security. If nothing else, the theft of that information is a serious federal crime.

So far we don't know everything contained in the Pentagon's 47-volume, 7,000-page study. But the government declares that its contents are top-secret.

Who are the editors of the Times to dispute that? Do Arthur Ochs Sulzberger and A. M. Rosenthal have a clearer idea of what is essential to national security than does Melvin Laird?

To cite only one specific instance of how publication could jeopardize our security, government officials are quoted by United Press International as saying that the verbatim publication of diplomatic and military cable texts "might allow the Soviet Union to crack the code of other U.S. communications transmitted during the early 1960s." How would the New York Times like *that?*

Nor is security the only problem here. What we may be seeing is the opening phase of a movement to influence public opinion through stolen documents. Earlier this year, sneak thieves made off with some confidential FBI files that disclosed the role of G-men in keeping an eye on Earth Day demonstrators. It was correctly pointed out by no less a personage than Vice President Agnew that the agents were only attending a public rally at which New Left types like Rennie Davis were slated to speak. Still, the FBI's prestige may have suffered, and that, after all, was the purpose of the thefts.

We can't say with certainty what motives the New York Times entertained in acquiring and publishing the Pentagon study. The Times, however, makes a habit of discrediting the U.S. war effort. And certain it is that the report, which reveals such tidbits as how President Johnson quietly escalated the ground war, will discomfit the government and delight the antiwar faction.

It is not that such matters should never come to light. They should—but only at such time as the authors of the documents seems judge expedient in the national interest.

The British have a rule that the most important of government papers may not be opened to the public for 50 years. And the British have been doing business as a free and functioning nation far longer than we. What must they, and other civilized peoples, think of us as we writhe in embarrassment over the leakage of vital information about a crisis that still is going on?

Herald News

Fall River, Mass., June 17, 1971

The controversy over the publication of documents relating to the Vietnam War by the New York Times is no longer confined to the war itself. The Department of Justice has sought an injunction against the Times to prevent further publication of the documents, and a temporary injunction has been granted. The issue is therefore no longer merely the lack of candor of the Johnson administration in relation to the conduct of the war; it is now also the issue of freedom of the press to publish the documents, which amounts to the right of the American people to know the truth about how they got involved in Vietnam so deeply and so tragically.

The Department of Justice, at the instance of the State Department, charged that "injury could be done to the United States" if more documents are published. United States District Judge Murray Garfein who granted the temporary injunction against the Times said that "irreparable harm could be done to the interests of the United States" if the publication continued. On Friday both the Department of Justice and the Times will present the arguments for and against making the injunction permanent.

Certainly, if the Times is forbidden to publish any more documents, there is bound to be real damage to the government of the United States, since the ban is bound to arouse the valid suspicion on the public's part that it is being misled by one administration after another. The credibility gap has already injured the United States. A permanent injunction against the Times will widen that gap still further. In a democracy loss of faith in the government can be fatal.

The damage to the interests of the country by further publication, the public is in no position to estimate. The judge, whose position is far from enviable, will have to decide. But it is hard to see on the basis of what has already been published how the reputation of the country can be much more tarnished than it already is.

It is no secret that successive administrations determined to defend southeast Asia against the likelihood of a Communist takeover. Whether it was right or wrong, this was the decision taken during the Eisenhower administration, and implemented by Presidents Kennedy, Johnson and Nixon. Furthermore, this is open knowledge. Unhappily, the way in which the succeeding administrations went about defending southeast Asia was more or less concealed from the American people. Had the war proved rapid or inconsequential, the concealment would, in all probability, have created little or no stir. Instead, the war proved prolonged, costly and inconclusive.

As a result, the concealment practiced by successive administrations (and by most other countries in terms of war strategy) has caused widespread mistrust of the executive branch of our government. At this late date, facing up to the facts would seem to be the best policy for the government. A permanent injunction against the Times would hinder the public from knowing the facts, and therefore from facing them. It would simply make present suspicions worse.

THE RICHMOND NEWS LEADER

Richmond, Va., June 17, 1971

In a simpler age, the New York Times' publication of classified Pentagon documents would be considered an act of treason in time of war. But we are sophisticated now, and the blood of 45,000 Americans dead in Vietnam does not constitute a war, while the revelation of state secrets is an exercise of the freedom of the press, and the peddling of half-truths to a disaffected America is a defense of the public's "right to know."

For the moment, a Federal court injunction is preventing the Times from publishing more articles in its "Vietnam Archive" series. That legal blockade probably will crumble shortly, or be circumvented by other events. The Times' mouthpiece, James Reston, has implied as much: According to Reston, the documents "are now being quietly circulated in Washington...(and) are now in the hands of some Congressmen and Presidential candidates...." Moreover, says Reston, "many...in possession of the facts, and a few...in possession of the documents...would gladly go to jail rather than submit to the suppression of their information." So in one way or another, every document probably will be made public.

At that point — whether reprimanded by a court or not — the Times will have much to answer for. Why, for example, did the Times prepare its series in total secrecy? Why didn't the Times consult with the government when it came into possession of highly classified documents? Why did the Times release its series on Sunday, just four days prior to the Senate's vote on the Hatfield-McGovern "end-the-war" amendment?

The Times will slough off such questions by focusing the controversy on First Amendment prerogatives and alleged governmental suppression. And in the eyes of the public, the Times undoubtedly will score a major victory over the government, because the Nixon Administration now finds itself in a classic damned-if-you-do, damned-if-you-don't situation.

If the Nixon Administration had sat on the sidelines and watched the Times go its merry way, then the principle of the Federal right to secrecy would have dissolved; a precedent for further unauthorized disclosures in the press would have been established; other documents of unknown sensitivity would have been released. The sensitivity of the papers probably is the Administration's central concern. While none of the documents reflects on current members of the government, their publication poses numerous problems for the Nixon Administration.

First — and this is where the Nixon Administration must take the blame — the obvious breech of highest-level security can undermine the Administration's ability to conduct diplomacy with both allies and enemies. Second, the documents contain numerous embarrassing references to friendly governments which may, to say the least, strain America's relations with certain countries. Third, the large number of contingency plans among the papers will give America's enemies instructive insights into the thought processes typical of the United States government. These problems are no less real because the documents were produced several years ago by a different administration.

But with this Administration's attempts to return the papers to secrecy, the damage that has been done — and that might be done — will lose its significance in the eyes of the American public. The Times and its defenders will point to the sensational aspects of the "Vietnam Archive," and they will contend that the Nixon Administration is attempting to cover-up past blunders and deceptions. But as the Times admits, the documents do not tell the whole story. Indeed, the papers present bad history at best, and afford no opportunity for the men who wrote them to justify their actions. With the present mood of the country, each sensational item will be cast in the worst possible light.

Consider. The covert operations sponsored by the United States in Laos and North Vietnam prior to the Gulf of Tonkin incidents will be seen as acts of American aggression, even though they were in response to original acts of aggression by the North Vietnamese. The wide-ranging contingency planning for moves against North Vietnam will be seen as deliberate attempts to involve the United States in war, even though it would be the height of governmental irresponsibility not to produce such plans at all times for all areas of the world. And the surreptitious slide into ground combat in Vietnam will be seen as the attempt of a war-mongering President to bypass an unwilling public and an unapproving Congress — even though Lyndon Johnson's own thoughts and motivations have not begun to be revealed.

By moving against the Times, the Nixon Administration will bear the onus of these one-sided interpretations of the Pentagon documents. The distinction between the Nixon and Johnson Administrations already is becoming hazy, and President Nixon soon may find himself described as the man who has continued Johnson's policies — not as the man who has changed them. Most important, the media considers the documents as proof of the so-called Johnson "credibility gap." The more that the Pentagon papers are associated with President Nixon, the more the Johnson credibility gap will be associated with President Nixon, too. The fact will be lost that President Nixon has done everything he said he would do with regard to Vietnam.

There just may be no way out of the box the Nixon Administration now occupies, courtesy of the New York Times. As the controversy continues — which it will do for the foreseeable future — the President may pay dearly for the alleged sins of another President: Allies and enemies may turn their backs on his attempts at peace; the Congress may force him to retreat from Vietnam; and the American public may force him — in the manner of Lyndon Johnson — to abandon his office.

Potentially, the consequences of the publication of the Pentagon documents are that grave — and ultimately may be graver still.

Portland Press Herald

Portland, Me., June 17, 1971

"All The News That's Fit To Print."

The New York Times made that motto famous. It still adorns its front page. Right now there is a great debate as to whether that standard was applied in the decision to print what the government claims to be a top secret defense document.

A newspaper's instinct is to leap into print in defense of one of the family with a ringing cry about the people's right to know who did what in getting this nation bogged down in an Asian land war.

But the issue here, like the war itself, is not all that simple. It is difficult to offer an unqualified defense of anyone who may be involved in an unlawful act even if it is in the public interest. And in this case, even the public interest is not indisputably defined.

If publication of the Pentagon study stiffens Communist resistance to honest negotiation, if it does injury to the national defense, if it complicates diplomatic functions in a manner disadvantageous to this nation or harmful to world peace, it is not in the public interest.

The manner in which the document was obtained, and the publication of it, may be unlawful. This discolors even the purest of motives.

On the other hand, government sources have been known to employ the secret classification for purposes more to their personal advantage than to the national welfare.

The distant observer makes hard and fast judgments here at his peril for there is too much detail on both sides of the issue to which he does not have access. At the moment, the wisest course seems that of the judge who temporarily suspended publication until a more thorough briefing is held.

THE BLADE

Toledo, Ohio, June 17, 1971

As THE Government moved to force the New York Times to cease publishing the massive study of why and how this nation got involved in Indochina, Attorney General Mitchell said that precedent-setting step was necessary because the disclosures would do "irreparable injury to the defense interests of the United States."

It will now be up to the Government, of course, to prove that contention in court. Even as that possibility looms, this unusual effort by the Nixon administration to, in effect, censor this publication may be somewhat academic in view of Senate Majority Leader Mansfield's announcement that the secret report on the Vietnam war will be brought out in congressional hearings. Thus, it seems certain that regardless of what the federal court decrees, the American people will in time see the full story of how our participation in Vietnam evolved, as compiled by 30 to 40 authors working under orders from former Defense Secretary McNamara.

At this point, and having only the first three installments of the supposedly classified study available for perusing, one is led to conclude that there is little that has been revealed thus far that would strike the layman as endangering our defense interests. The material documented in what has been published deals with the moves and decisions from the post-World War II period to mid-1968 that plunged this nation ever deeper into the tragedy of Vietnam. It is a shocking record; it may be embarrassing to officials involved; it is a detailed chronicle of a long series of miscalculations, errors in judgment, and perfidious deception that tends to further erode public confidence in our Government. But

none of that should be confused with our defense interests or, indeed, national security.

Basically, this year-long analysis of the story of Vietnam will add disturbing substance to the deep mood of distrust and suspicion with which the public has viewed the justification for our involvment for years—and which, for that matter, we have long and sharply questioned editorially. In that sense, it is understandably upsetting to an Administration that has gone along with previous defenses of our commitments even while moving slowly to extricate us from the Indochinese quagmire.

The tangled web of secrecy, if not duplicity, that covers the long and bloody trail into Vietnam runs through the Truman, Eisenhower, and Kennedy administrations. But at least in those early years, the efforts to meet commitments were on a limited scale that absorbed money and materiel but not men. It was, as this chilling documentary brings out, under the administration of Lyndon Baines Johnson that the coldly calculated escalation effort was devised even as the American people were being told by President Johnson that he would never send our boys 10,000 miles away to fight a battle that Asian boys should be fighting.

It is shocking, to say the least, to note that while Mr. Johnson was campaigning in 1964 as the candidate opposed to expanding the war, he and his inner circle of advisers were planning to do just that. It is an eternal blot on his veracity that he is shown to have been lying to the American people time and again, that the Gulf of Tonkin resolution was drawn up three months before the alleged attack that insured its passage, that U.S. strategy as devised by the Johnson administration de-

pended upon finding an appropriate "incident" to justify carrying the bombing into North Vietnam, and that such terms as "carefully orchestrated" were applied to the military hopes for accelerating the fighting.

A bitter cynicism wells up upon reading instructions to top officials in a National Security Action Memorandum of April 6, 1965—less than three months after Mr. Johnson, the self-proclaimed peace candidate, began his first full term—that the sizable expansion of combat action ordered by the President be kept from the American public. "The President desires that . . . premature publicity be avoided by all possible precautions," the memo says. "The actions themselves should be taken as rapidly as practicable, but in ways that should minimize any appearance of sudden changes in policy . . . The President's desire is that these movements and changes should be understood as being gradual and wholly consistent with existing policy." In fact, they were none of those.

The United States has lost more than 50,000 of its finest young men in Vietnam, including more than 45,000 in combat. We have frittered away hundreds of billions of dollars, and brought about intense disruptions to our domestic economy and society. No court should now stand in the way of newspaper publication of the germane parts of this secret examination of the decision-making process that led us to our greatest international disaster.

The American people have, at the very least, the right to know how they were misled and by whom. And history deserves nothing more than this essential information to carve out Lyndon Johnson's proper but scarcely glorious niche for posterity.

LEDGER-STAR

Norfolk, Va., June 17, 1971

A federal district judge has ordered The New York Times not to print any more of the top secret documentation of the origin and conduct of the American involvement in the Vietnam war pending arguments before his court tomorrow.

The restraining order was issued at the request of Attorney General John Mitchell on the ground that publication of the material on June 13 and 14 had already prejudiced the defense interests of the United States and that additional publication would further prejudice those interests and result also in "irreparable injury" to the country. The government further claimed that the Times had violated Title 18 of the U. S. Code, Section 793, for which maximum punishment is 10 years in jail and/or $10,000 fine for: ". . . Having unauthorized possession of, access to, or control over any document . . . relating to the national defense, or information relating to the national defense . . . that could be used to the injury of the United States or the advantage of any foreign nation."

The Times replies that "once this material fell into our hands" it became the newspaper's responsibility to publish it because "of our obligations under the First Amendment . . ."

Thus was set what might turn out to be a historic struggle between the right of a government to determine what is injurious to itself and advantageous to a foreign nation, and the right of a newspaper to decide whether the government has any such right, and to break the law in so deciding.

★ ★ ★ ★

The argument that the First Amendment "obligated" the Times to publish this top secret material is unconvincing, and has the ring of after-the-fact rationale. The First Amendment does not oblige the Times to publish anything; as the newspaper's motto makes plain, it prints the news it thinks fit to print.

Equally unconvincing insofar as propriety is concerned is the argu-

ment of the Times that it felt it had to print the material "once it fell into our hands." If such an obligation exists, does not a corollary obligation require that the Times seek out top secret and other classified material that it does not happen to come by quite so fortuitously?

★ ★ ★ ★

Where the Times argues that what has been printed is history, it is, we think, arguing correctly; most of these facts are known; certainly what took place in Vietnam is known; what these documents do is to show the options discussed and the reasons for and against their implementation. Sometimes policies were postponed until after elections; the effect of decisions on elections seems to be an occupational hazard of Presidents, and if Democrats have let upcoming elections affect the implementation of decisions more than have Republicans, it is only that the Democrats were more often in the seat of

power. Nor is deception unknown among Presidents, more's the pity.

But what bothers us as much as any other aspect of this confrontation is the seeming attitude of the Times that it is above the law, a government within a government with the power of arbitrary reversal of government decisions. If the Times places itself above the law for the sake of the people, who then is obliged among the people to observe the law?

The material that fell into the hands of the newspaper was classified top secret. Perhaps the classification was no longer justified by the passing of the years; we are certainly inclined to believe so from what we have read. But classifications can be changed on official documents, and this study of the causes and escalation of the American presence in Vietnam could have been declassified. Would it not have been acting more responsibly if the Times had first sought declassification? But then, of course, it may have lost the story.

San Francisco Chronicle

San Francisco, Calif., June 17, 1971

ATTORNEY GENERAL MITCHELL'S successful effort to persuade a court to stop the New York Times from publishing the last installments of its series on decision-making in the Vietnam war is an act of Government censorship by unprecedented means and an utterly deplorable interference with press freedom.

Freedom of the press as guaranteed by the First Amendment to the Constitution means, and has always meant, the freedom of a newspaper to publish without prior restraint by any official or judge.

It is clear that this freedom has been denied to the New York Times by the issuance of a Federal Court's temporary restraining order. A publisher either has freedom to publish, or he doesn't have it. If a court, at the instance of the executive, can step in and take it away from him, even temporarily, the whole principle of press freedom is in danger. In this case, the order of the Federal Court to restrain publication is admittedly issued for the first time in the Nation's history. That will be found to be a mistake of historic magnitude.

★ ★ ★

THE PUBLISHER, executives, editors and reporters of the New York Times who have been haled to court in this action are of course complying with the order while resisting its continuance. We wholeheartedly support them in this. It was their judgment that the historical material contained in the Pentagon's 47-volume study on Vietnam should be divulged. They have stated that they believed that it is "a fundamental responsibility of the press . . . to publish information that helps the people of the United States to understand the processes of their own government, especially when those processes have been clouded over in a veil of public dissimulation and even deception."

The editors of the New York Times are careful, responsible newspapermen. They recognized the documents in question, all dating back to 1967 or earlier, as belonging to history. They were fully aware that many of the documents were classified "secret" or "top secret," but they were convinced, as we are, that the papers were overclassified or misclassified so far as concerns their sensitiveness in this year 1971. So they made the decision to publish, confident that this endangered the life of not a single American soldier and threatened neither the security of the country nor the peace of the world.

★ ★ ★

THIS CASE PRESENTS the military versus the press, the military with its ever-ready ability to stamp papers and so put them out of public view. But the story of Vietnam — how we blundered into it, how the escalation of the war was arranged, how Congress and the people were deceived and left in the dark — is a story that belongs to the public, even if it had to be wrested from the hands of the Pentagon establishment.

The Government's allegation that the divulgence of this story has done and can do "irreparable injury" to the United States and its security is legal lingo and won't hold water. The events and decisions disclosed do not concern things in the future; they have already happened four years ago and longer. If the Government wanted to pick a case for testing its ability, through the courts, to suppress the official public record of a war, it certainly picked the wrong time, the wrong war, and the wrong newspaper.

The Cincinnati Post

TIMES ⬩ STAR

Cincinnati, Ohio, June 16, 1971

The dispute between the Justice Department and the New York Times over that newspaper's publishing top secret Pentagon documents on Vietman probably has a long future in the courts.

At least two important rights are involved. One is the constitutional guarantee of freedom of the press, which the Times cites to justify its action. The other is the government's undoubted right to protect its secrets in the interest of national security.

The clash of these competing rights may well go to the Supreme Court and we cannot foresee the outcome. But there are a number of points that are clear already.

The first among them is that somebody, possibly a present or former government official, stole or misappropriated large sections of a 47-volume study of U.S. involvement in Vietnam that was ordered by Defense Secretary Robert S. McNamara in 1967.

Turning over this highly classified material to the Times was a flagrant violation of the espionage law. The person or persons who betrayed their trust should be identified and tried.

THE LAW IS LESS CLEAR about the Times' action in publishing the secret documents. The newspaper says it resolved its doubts in favor of "the public's right to know," and that contention is difficult for another newspaper to criticize.

In general, governments keep matters secret for real reasons of security or to cover up official blunders and incompetence. In the latter case, it is the duty of the press to ferret out the story and make it public.

In the material published so far by the Times, there is nothing startlingly new. The documents rightly stress that our unhappy involvement with Vietnam started under the Truman administration and was steadily deepened by the Eisenhower, Kennedy and Johnson administrations.

Some of the official papers suggest that President Johnson was deceitful as he led the country into massive involvement in Vietnam. But if Johnsonian trickiness is news to any citizen today, he has not been paying attention.

The papers also may be embarrassing in exposing the arrogance of the McNamaras, Bundys, Rostows and other individuals who were not military experts but overconfidently went to war with a people they did not understand. That too is hardly a breach of high security.

There were things, however, that should better have been left unpublished. The documents may have exposed some of our codes and military strategy. They "blew the cover" of a Canadian official who undertook missions for us to Hanoi. This could make foreign diplomats wary about helping out in the future.

Finally, there is the question of timing. The Times says it had the documents for three months. It started publishing them just days before the vote in the Senate on the McGovern-Hatfield amendment to order withdrawal of all U.S. troops from Vietnam by Dec. 31.

We would like to think that the material could not be edited any sooner, that it was published only because "the public has a right to know" and not to help antiwar senators pull the rug out from under President Nixon's Vietnam policy.

CHICAGO DAILY NEWS

Chicago, Ill., June 18, 1971

The government's action in censoring the New York Times' serialized presentation of a classified Pentagon report on the Vietnam War is so extraordinary as to have no discoverable precedent. So deeply ingrained is the principle of press freedom that even in wartime, prior censorship within the continental limits has been voluntary; only in the field has the military censored news dispatches, and that for the express purpose of denying aid and comfort to the enemy.

One must assume, then, that the administration felt it had compelling reason to enjoin the Times from publishing the final instalments of the series. It implied it had such reason when it charged that such publication "would further prejudice the defense interests of the United States and result in irreparable injury to the United States."

The burden of proof is squarely upon the government to demonstrate just how those results might have come about. Otherwise it invites the presumption that its motives were far less lofty: that it sought to avoid political embarrassment by suppressing the material.

The presumption is not avoided by

Vice President Agnew's saying the judgment of what is fit to print should be left to "the professionals" (presumably the military and the politicans) and that "no government can conduct its diplomacy on the pages of a newspaper — or in the glare of public scrunity." We would judge the editors of the Times at least as "professional" as the generals or politicans in the field of responsible news judgment; it was the Times that suppressed the Bay of Pigs story (and was later chided for it by President Kennedy) precisely because it concluded that publication would breach security.

But in this case the "top secret' label is surely frivolous in its implication of national security involvement. The events discussed occurred far enough back that they can have no possible relevance to current military operations. Neither can they relate directly to anything the Nixon administration has undertaken in the diplomatic area; their time-span ends before Mr. Nixon's election. If there was any possibility of compromising secret codes, that is academic: codes are subject to constant shifting around, and a key in use half a dozen years ago would hardly be still used today.

Then why "top secret"? What "irreparable damage"?

We can only conclude that the prospective harm is considered to be in the area of our national dignity, or "face."

But is the administration seriously arguing that saving "face" justifies denying the public the truth about the way the national leadership bumbled its arrogant, wrongheaded way into a disastrous war, systematically deceiving the people as to what it was secretly up to? That says something chilling about the judgment, if not the character, of the architects of the policy that led to censoring the Times.

But now that the issue is joined, it should be pursued to its ultimate conclusions.

For there is something curious here that draws the warring, opposite ends of the political establishment into common cause, with the "ins" stoutly defending the right of the "outs" to perpetual asylum, perpetual cloaking of their misdeeds. Either in the injunction proceedings, which the Times promises to carry, if necessary, to the Supreme Court, or in the congressional investigation, we hope the truth will out.

The Greenville News

Greenville, S.C., June 18, 1971

Legal proceedings arising from publication by the New York Times of top-secret official documents on America's involvement in the Vietnam war revolve around a profound issue, one much deeper than the very serious questions raised by information contained in the documents so far made public.

Discussion of the policies of the Kennedy and Johnson administrations as exposed by the so-called McNamara papers can come later. At the moment the basic issue is the right of the Times to publish the material.

The case already has made history. For the first time a federal judge has ordered an American newspaper to withhold publication of information in its posession. The order is temporary and effective only until Saturday. A full hearing is scheduled today. The Times is complying with the temporary order but will contest the right of the government and the courts to forbid publication.

At this point the First Amendment to the Constitution

forbidding Congress to pass any law abridging the freedom of the press is tested against a law forbidding publication of information "prejudicial to the safety or interest of the United States or for the benefit of any foreign government to the detriment of the United States ..."

The government, of course, must prove that information already published and still unpublished is prejudicial to the national security. Its case apparently is based upon a contention that publication impairs national defense and diplomatic relations with friendly foreign governments.

Without doubt, information already published by the Times embarrasses the government at home and abroad. All sorts of official duplicity and failure to heed warnings based upon sound information is laid bare. Exposure of intelligence and diplomatic mechanisms could be considered damaging to national security.

Even if the government proves that the statute has been violated and that publication of the rest of the documents will make defense and diplomacy more difficult, the constitutional right of the people to know about official

blunders in important matters still is involved.

It is ironic that a Republican administration is seeking to suppress information discrediting its Democratic predecessors. This would indicate that the government does view the material as highly prejudicial to basic national interests, transcending politics and going beyond mere embarrassment.

But the real question goes to the basic foundation of national security in a free nation.

There is no such thing as national security for the United States without broad and deep public confidence in the government. A government or a political party which deliberately deceives the people on matters of vital interest is itself a threat to national security because that government or that party undermines public confidence in official processes.

The right of a free people and a free press to monitor the processes of government and of politics and to expose and correct

blatant governmental or political duplicity and blundering is, therefore, a fundamental part of national security.

Although information published by the Times and presumably information still to be published is embarrassing, distressing and perhaps damaging, suppressing it would be even more dangerous to American liberty and American security.

In addition, the right of America's news media to publish such information, once it has been obtained, is basic. A free press, guaranteed to the American people by the Constitution, cannot remain free if it has to operate under threat of injunction against exploring the workings of government.

Only in cases of impending national disaster should any form of legal censorship be imposed upon the American press. On the basis of information made public so far, publication of the McNamara papers in full would not cause sufficient security damage to justify the terrible dangers of censorship and suppression of information, with resulting loss of confidence in government itself.

SUN-TIMES

Chicago, Ill., July 1, 1971

It is being called "historic" and a "landmark," this decision that the New York Times and the Washington Post have the right to publish the classified documents known as the Pentagon papers. It was, in a way, neither of these things. Rather, it was a reaffirmation by the Supreme Court of what had been assumed to be true between the time the First Amendment went into effect and the time President Nixon and Atty. Gen. John N. Mitchell came along. This a s s u m p t i o n, not lightly held, was that government could not dictate in advance what the free press might publish.

"Any system of prior restraints," said the six justices in their majority opinion, "comes to this court bearing a heavy presumption against its con-

stitutional validity." The government, they said, failed in its "heavy burden" of showing that publication of the Pentagon study of the Indochina war would do grave and immediate harm to the country's safety.

Nor, the ruling meant, had the two newspapers violated the Espionage Act, since the law requires the government to show wilful intent to harm the national security.

In a concurring opinion, Associate Justice Potter Stewart made a point long held by editors. "In the absence of governmental checks and balances present in other areas of our national life," he wrote, "the only effective restraint upon executive power and policy in the areas of national defense and international affairs may be

in an enlightened citizenry — in an informed and critical public opinion which alone can here protect the values of democratic government." But, he added, "without an informed and free press, there cannot be an enlightened people."

Other justices had other things of great importance to say, and we shall look further at them tomorrow. For the moment, it is enough to say that the world shall now know what went on in those secret, tragic years, and will be the better for it. As Associate Justice Hugo L. Black wrote: "The guarding of military and diplomatic secrets at the expense of informed representative government provides no real security for our Republic." The best guarantee of that is an informed citizenry.

The New York Times

New York, N.Y., July 1, 1971

The historic decision of the Supreme Court in the case of the United States Government vs. The New York Times and The Washington Post is a ringing victory for freedom under law. By lifting the restraining order that had prevented this and other newspapers from publishing the hitherto secret Pentagon Papers, the nation's highest tribunal strongly reaffirmed the guarantee of the people's right to know, implicit in the First Amendment to the Constitution of the United States.

This was the essence of what The New York Times and other newspapers were fighting for and this is the essence of the Court's majority opinions. The basic question, which goes to the very core of the American political system, involved the weighing by the Court of the First Amendment's guarantee of freedom against the Government's power to restrict that freedom in the name of national security. The Supreme Court did not hold that the First Amendment gave an absolute right to publish anything under all circumstances. Nor did The Times seek that right. What The Times sought, and what the Court upheld, was the right to publish these particular documents at this particular time without prior Governmental restraint.

The crux of the problem lay indeed in this question of prior restraint. For the first time in the history of the United States, the Federal Government had sought through the courts to prevent publication of material that it maintained would do "irreparable injury" to the national security if spread before the public. The Times, supported in this instance by the overwhelming majority of the American press, held on the contrary that it was in the national interest to publish this information, which was of historic rather than current operational nature.

If the documents had involved troop movements, ship sailings, imminent military plans, the case might have been quite different; and in fact The Times would not have endeavored to publish such material. But this was not the case; the documents and accompanying analysis are historic, in no instance going beyond 1968, and incapable in 1971 of harming the life of a single human being

or interfering with any current military operation. The majority of the Court clearly recognized that embarrassment of public officials in the past—or even in the present—is insufficient reason to overturn what Justice White described as "the concededly extraordinary pro-

tection against prior restraint under our constitutional system."

So far as the Government's classification of the material is concerned, it is quite true, as some of our critics have observed, that "no one elected The Times" to declassify it. But it is also true, as the Court implicitly recognizes, that the public interest is not served by classification and retention in secret form of vast amounts of information, 99.5 per cent of which a retired senior civil servant recently testified "could not be prejudicial to the defense interests of the nation."

Out of this case should surely come a total revision of governmental procedures and practice in the entire area of classification of documents. Everyone who has ever had anything to do with such documents knows that for many years the classification procedures have been hopelessly muddled by inertia, timidity and sometimes even stupidity and venality.

Beyond all this, one may hope that the entire exercise will induce the present Administration to re-examine its own attitudes toward secrecy, suppression and restriction of the liberties of free man in a free society. The issue the Supreme Court decided yesterday touched the heart of this republic; and we fully realize that this is not so much a victory for any particular newspaper as it is for the basic principles of freedom on which the American form of government rests. This is really the profound message of yesterday's decision, in which this newspaper rejoices with humility and with the consciousness that the freedom thus reaffirmed carries with it, as always, the reciprocal obligation to present the truth to the American public so far as it can be determined. That is, in fact, why the Pentagon material had to be published. It is only with the fullest possible understanding of the facts and of the background of any policy decision that the American people can be expected to play the role required of them in this democracy.

It would be well for the present Administration, in the light of yesterday's decision, to reconsider with far more care and understanding than it has in the past, the fundamental importance of individual freedoms—including especially freedom of speech, of the press, of assembly—to the life of the American democracy. "Without an informed and free press," as Justice Stewart said, "there cannot be an enlightened people."

ST. LOUIS POST-DISPATCH

St. Louis, Mo., July 1, 1971

The state shall be my governors but not my critics; they may be mistaken in the choice of a licensor as easily as this licensor may be mistaken in an author . . . For though a licensor should happen to be judicious more than ordinary . . . yet his very office and his commission enjoins him to let pass nothing but what is vulgarly received already.

John Milton's words of more than 300 years ago ought to r e s o u n d over and above the Supreme Court's 6-3 decision that the Government cannot restrain publication of a secret Pentagon study of the Vietnam war.

What the English poet said easily predicts the kind of secrecy classifications lately practice: when in doubt, classify. But the words are more important because they distill Anglo-Saxon experience into the reasons for the First Amendment, guaranteeing freedom of the press.

In one of the nine opinions issued by the individual Justices, Justice Black observed that this Amendment, and the whole Bill of Rights, were adopted after the original Constitution simply to protect the people's rights from the Government established there. He could imagine "no greater perversion of history" than the minority argument that general governmental powers limited the Bill of Rights.

Yet that is what Chief Justice Burger did

seem to contend. He held that the imperative of a free press was colliding with the effective functioning of a complex government. And thus the issue was joined, between freedom on one side and balancing freedom on the other.

We believe Justice Black has far the better of the argument historically. Apart from that, however, there is little evidence that the principle of a free press was colliding with or endangering the operation of a complex government in any way whatsoever. The Pentagon papers printed by *The New York Times*, the *Washington Post* and the *St. Louis Post-Dispatch* reveal history, not military secrets.

Since no more than that was involved, the Administration had little r e a s o n to claim secrecy, and far, far less to claim the right of precensorship of what the newspapers told the people.

In substance, the Administration had no case. Justices Black, Douglas, Brennan and Marshall were right the first time, last Friday, when they noted that they would have set aside all restraints on the newspapers without further 'ado. Upon hearings, Justices White and Stewart joined them in the final decision.

What is unfortunate is that the Administration even tried to make a case. Justice Black asserted that this was the first time in 182 years of the Republic that "the federal courts are

asked to hold that the First Amendment does not mean what it says, but rather means that the Government can halt the publication of current news of vital importance to the people . . ."

It is remarkable that this first big claim to precensorship should be made on so flimsy a basis, concerning old documents about a war never declared. The Administration's position here adds an absurdity to Attorney General Mitchell's previous record of constitutional ineptitude about wiretapping, preventive detention, no-knock raids and so on. Surely a President concerned with the reputation and effectiveness of his Administration would question whether such a legal adviser should remain. We feel strongly he should not.

As matters stand, the Nixon Administration's blundering maneuvers can only reflect more on its own credibility. If this Administration does not even want to let the people know how previous Administrations mired them in the Vietnam war, how much confidence can there be in present avowed efforts to extricate the country?

Freedom of the press, we firmly believe, was bound to win against so unprecedented and irrational an attack. What is saddening is that a President and Attorney General sworn to uphold the Constitution would so misunderstand it.

The Boston Globe

Boston, Mass., July 1, 1971

It is with no sense of gloating, nor even with the feeling that a great and lasting victory has been won, that we welcome the historic 6-to-3 decision of the United States Supreme Court allowing newspapers to publish the secret Pentagon study of the Vietnam war.

That the victory is a great one—as great in many ways as the acquittal of John Peter Zenger in 1735—there can be no doubt. But it will not be a lasting one, in these days of repressive measures in every area of the public domain, unless not only the press but the public it serves maintains an eternal vigilance.

And any thoughts of elation must be brought up short immediately with the realization that this immoral war, which a truly free press and a diligently responsible Congress could and should have prevented, still grinds on and exacts its grisly daily toll of Asian and American lives.

It is important for the public to know what was involved and what was not involved in **N.Y. Times vs. the United States** and the cases involving the Washington Post, the Boston Globe and others. Unless this

is made clear, the impression will spread that the press, protected by the First Amendment, has been given carte blanche to print government secrets. And that is simply not the case.

Newspapers, as we said last Friday, enjoy no special exemption from the laws of the land. They can be, and have been, held accountable in court for what they publish. And this is as it should be.

What was involved in the landmark case decided Wednesday was what the lawyers call "prior restraint"—whether a judge can legally order a newspaper not to print something. The nation's highest court held that in this case, at least, he could not do so. The First Amendment prevents it. And the people, whom that basic amendment of the Bill of Rights protects, can be grateful for it.

The decision means that newspapers may not be barred from publishing. But, as always, they publish at their peril, and can be brought to account for it in court. But at least they can publish.

How important this principle is, and in what grave danger our American democracy found itself in recent

days, can be realized by a glance at our nation's history. It shows that never before had the government succeeded by order of a court in preventing a newspaper from publishing.

John Peter Zenger was jailed for almost 10 months **after** he had published, not before, and he was acquitted after his counsel appealed over the head of the judge, pleading truth as a defense, to a jury of his peers.

Even under the Alien and Sedition Acts, editors were jailed, not for what they were about to print, but for what they had already printed.

Not until last June 16th, in all the centuries of America's existence, had a government and a judge succeeded in preventing a newspaper from printing a story it deemed the public had a right to know.

Now our highest court has said this is unconstitutional. Yet it is a measure of the repression of our times that the Justice Department saw fit to press this case at all, and that as many as three Supreme Court Justices could be found to support the repression.

It is also a measure of that repression that not even the lawyers for the newspapers, at least in our opinion, made as strong a case as they could have in the arguments before the high court last Saturday.

Nor is the danger confined to newspapers versus the Justice Department. Unless the full House Commerce Committee has the sense and the courage to reverse its subcommittee today and to refuse to cite Dr. Frank Stanton for contempt, or unless Congress itself has that sense and that courage, the case of the Columbia Broadcasting System's "Selling of the Pentagon" may present the Supreme Court with the next historic test of freedom of the press.

Yet one has the feeling that at last the tide may have turned. Newspapers, at least, are again free to publish—and to take the consequences. We have no doubt that the Pentagon papers which they can now print may not tell the whole story that the public needs to know. Some, in fact, may give wrong impressions. But at least the whole story is now free to be told without censorship.

And that is an accomplishment in which all Americans have a right to feel great pride.

The Washington Post
Times Herald

Washington, D.C., July 1, 1971

The Pentagon Papers: Free–At Last

"Our democracy depends for its future on the informed will of the majority, and it is the purpose and the effect of the First Amendment to expose to the public the maximum amount of information on which sound judgment can be made by the electorate. The equities favor disclosure, not suppression. No one can measure the effects of even a momentary delay."

This passage from the ruling of U.S. District Court Judge Gerhard Gesell on June 21, 1971, comes close to summing up our own views in the case of the United States Government vs. The Washington Post—and, frankly, we would have preferred to leave it at that. Instead, the issue moved up to the Supreme Court and yesterday the government's plea for a restraining order against this newspaper and The New York Times was dismissed by a vote of 6-to-3. Perhaps the best way we can express our gratification with the outcome is to refer you to page one where we are resuming publication today of material from the Pentagon papers, otherwise known as the "History of U.S. Decision-Making Process on Vietnam Policy." That we are again free to print this material is an undoubted gain if only because to have remained under restraint would have been an immeasurable loss not for us alone, nor for the press alone, but for the public, and for the country, and for the democratic processes: *It is the purpose and the effect of the First Amendment to expose to the public the maximum amount of information on which sound judgment can be made by the electorate.*

But it has to be added that from the beginning of this unprecedented confrontation between press and government, the issue has not only been *what* we could print but also *when*. So it cannot be forgotten now that for a period of more than two weeks, in the case of The Times, and ten days in the case of The Post, and for shorter spans in the case of the Boston Globe and the St. Louis Post Dispatch, newspapers in this country, abiding by court orders, have, in effect, been prevented by government from publishing certain material. It is not enough to say that the material in question was historical (and therefore hardly urgent) because even history, freshly authenticated and in compelling detail, has the capacity to shape contemporary events. Another time we might be dealing with information of far greater urgency and *no one can measure the effects of even a momentary delay.*

It can hardly be said, then, that yesterday's Supreme Court opinion, together with six separate concurrences and three separate dissents, effectively comes to terms with the tormenting issue at the heart of this dispute—the government's right of prior restraint of the press. It does not resolve the dilemma posed by the First Amendment's protections of the press, on the one hand, and the government's undoubted right to protect security on the other. For what the court majority seems to be saying, without attempting in this space to take into account the many conflicting conclusions stated by all nine justices, is that the government failed to make its point—*not* that a point was not necessarily there to be made. Some justices saw merit in the government's argument, as to the facts, and others were at pains to suggest that the government's point might better be made in a different way—through criminal penalties for publication of at least some parts of this material.

So there is not all that much comfort, let alone clearcut law, to be found in yesterday's outcome, though in fairness to the Court and to the government, the affair of the Pentagon papers was an exceedingly difficult case on which to rest broad principles of law; it involved a breakdown of government security of such scope and magnitude that relief from the courts, in any practical sense, was probably never within the government's reach. It seems doubtful, in short, that we will see its likes again, and this says several, in some ways contradictory, things to us, not least of which is that the losses and gains on both sides can best be measured, not in theoretical law, but in real and practical terms.

We were dealing here, presumably, with 7,000 pages of classified material, some of it rated exceedingly sensitive. So it is not entirely surprising that the courts should have been reluctant to dismiss the government's plea out of hand—although the District Court here did just that. On the other hand, the sheer bulk of the material and the manifest insensitivity, in any real sense, of so much of it, necessarily undermined the government's argument, which came down in the end to a plea for highly selective restraints by the courts against only a small portion of the whole. Out of this process, perhaps, may come a positive boon in terms of a thorough re-examination of the classification procedures of the government; for even the government's counsel, as well as the administration, conceded along the way that the existing practices result in massive over-classification of material, for far too long a time.

But the real lesson of this affair, in practical terms, lies elsewhere, or so it seems to us, for what we have been witnessing over the past two weeks has been a belated and very nearly frantic effort by the government to remove from the public domain what should never have been lost—and under circumstances that are quite unlikely to repeat themselves. It has not been often in our history that a newspaper has found itself in possession of so prodigious an amount of classified material, and has begun to publish it, with a clear statement of what it had in hand, and a plain forewarning of what was still to come; such an opportunity for prior restraint does not normally present itself. And neither, for that matter does the government often bundle together quite such an extraordinary load of classified material and leave it lying around quite so negligently.

The very uniqueness of this affair, in other words, has grossly distorted the realities, which are that the government has a very broad grant of authority to conduct its activities in secret, and enormous powers to preserve its essential secrets, and an impressive record of doing so. That it failed to do so in this case was never an argument, in our view, for suspending the First Amendment rights of the press or for limiting the prerogative of the press to exercise its own judgement in the handling of these documents. Still less was it an argument for denying the public its right to be informed.

Chicago Tribune

Chicago, Ill., July 1, 1971

The Supreme Court has probably reached the most sensible conclusion it could reach under the circumstances — namely that the so-called Pentagon Papers do not contain material which would so jeopardize the national security as to justify prior restraint by the government against their publication. The New York Times and the Washington Post — and other papers, too, for that matter — may therefore resume printing them if they wish.

This doesn't mean that the Nixon administration wasn't justified in bringing action against the papers. The government could not have sat by and done nothing while documents which were officially labeled as top-secret — rightly or wrongly — were being spread across the front pages of the country. For self-serving reasons, the administration might have welcomed the publication of evidence which has proved embarrassing to previous Democratic administrations and to many others who are now among Mr. Nixon's critics. But Atty. Gen. Mitchell did what the law required him to do.

The dissenting opinions of three conservative justices, especially Chief Justice Burger, suggest with some validity that the matter deserves more study than the liberal justices were willing to give it. But the outcome, we believe, was inescapable.

Nor does yesterday's decision vindicate Dr. Daniel Ellsberg or anybody else who may have been involved in transmitting the papers to the press. As a former government employe, and as a man once authorized to have access to the papers, Dr. Ellsberg was under obligations and restrictions beyond those applying to the press.

If the decision is a rebuke to anyone, it is to the succession of burocrats who have undermined the security system by overclassifying documents, often only to protect their own reputations, and by failing to declassify them or lower their classification when this should have been done.

Had this been done years ago, the papers would never have attracted the interest they did. Many of them would have deserved little more than a yawn. And Alaska's Sen. Mike Gravel might have been denied a chance to demonstrate his histrionic skills by calling a meeting of his own subcommittee on Capitol buildings and grounds and reading from the secret documents until the early hours of the morning.

It is unlikely that his performance had any influence on the Supreme Court, which was faced simply with a conflict between the freedom of the press and the power of the government to suppress material which, in the court's opinion, should not be suppressed. The court ruled for a free press.

Chicago today American

Chicago, Ill., July 1, 1971

WE ARE enjoying to the full a heady feeling that the fortunate peoples of the earth can enjoy now and then: The feeling that we live in a country where freedom really is understood and safeguarded, that we have a Constitution that means what it says and a judiciary that insists on its being respected, and that officials of our government will not succeed with their efforts— even their well-meant, ever-so-reasonable efforts—to cramp and limit freedom for greater "security."

For this exhilarating feeling we are indebted to the Six Supreme court justices who ruled yesterday that the New York Times and the Washington Post could go on publishing stories based on a secret Pentagon study of the Viet Nam war. The Justice Department had tried to prevent them from publishing more of this material, claiming that publication might endanger national security. The 6-to-3 majority held that the government, in trying to enjoin newspapers from printing facts in their possession, was taking a step unprecedented in the nation's history and had failed to show justification for it; the broad claim of "national security" was not enough.

Justice Potter Stewart, in fact, singled out national defense and international dealings as areas in which "an informed and free press" is especially vital. These "sensitive" areas are the very ones, he observed, in which the Executive branch has accumulated vast powers—where the governmental checks and balances present in other fields are lacking, and must be supplied by an alert press and public.

Clearly, the justices are not saying that the government can never, under any circumstances, restrain publication beforehand. They are saying only that it must have overwhelmingly strong and specific reasons for doing so, and that merely invoking a secrecy law does not justify prior restraint. The point evidently needs to be hammered home repeatedly.

The government, thru Congress, is free to enact laws forbidding certain actions and providing penalties for those who choose to break the law. But it is not free to restrain people even from choosing; to declare that free choice is too dangerous to be entrusted to citizens.

Yesterday's decision firmly plants that principle in the area of press freedom, and we believe it will stand as a landmark of constitutional law. It may also help to bring about a healthier, more open relationship between the federal government on one hand, the press and the people on the other. Over the last 30 years or so, a fog of secrecy has been deepening around governmental doings; this ruling may be the refreshing gust that blows it away.

DAILY ■ NEWS

New York, N.Y., July 1, 1971

PRESS FREEDOM WINS AGAIN

In a 6-3, nine-opinion decision handed down yesterday, the U.S. Supreme Court ruled that the N.Y. Times and the Washington Post may continue publication—interrupted by government-obtained restraining order

Potter Stewart   **Byron White**

—of passages from the world-famous top secret Pentagon report on the Vietnam war.

We are, of course, happy to see the principle of freedom of the press win once more in its unending battle to continue as a U.S. constitutional cornerstone.

However, there were many interesting angles and aspects to this tremendous episode.

Chief Justice Warren E. Burger and Associate Justices Harry A. Blackmun and John M. Harlan dissented, all three complaining of the haste with which these complex cases were rushed through the courts.

Justices Hugo L. Black and William O. Douglas, to nobody's surprise, said that government, under the Constitution's First Amendment, should have no right to prior restraint of publication.

These two old gentlemen's extremism was offset in large part, as we see the matter, by the common sense of the other four members of the majority, particularly Justices—

STEWART AND WHITE

—in their separate opinions.

Justice Stewart observed that "without an informed and free press there cannot be an enlightened people," and felt that there must be some checkreins on the huge power which the Executive branch of the government has acquired in recent decades.

Justice White said he thought the First Amendment would not prevent issuance of restraining orders in all cases where publication of some material would endanger the nation, and added:

Nor, after examining the materials the government characterizes as the most sensitive and destructive, can I deny that revelation of these documents will do substantial damage to the public interest. Indeed, I am confident that their disclosure will have that result.

Evidently, however, Justice White did not think their publication would pose a clear and present threat to the nation's safety; so he went along with the majority.

It remained for—

CHIEF JUSTICE BURGER

—to pay some highly interesting respects, if that is the word, to the N.Y. Times for printing this material which Daniel Ellsberg says he stole from the government.

Said the Chief Justice in part:

To me, it is hardly believable that a newspaper long regarded as a great institution in American life would fail to perform one of the basic and simple duties of every citizen with respect to the discovery or possession of stolen property or secret government documents.

That duty, I had thought—perhaps naively—was to report forthwith to responsible public officers. This duty rests on taxi drivers, justices, and the New York Times.

So ends this chapter in the story of the Purloined Pentagon Papers—a story which has shaken the nation, stirred up the fiercest passions and hatreds, and conceivably hampered President Richard M. Nixon in his effort to end U.S. participation in the Vietnam war with honor to the nation.

Where the story goes from here, who knows? Let's hope it takes a turn for the better, not for the worse.

Arkansas Gazette.

Little Rock, Ark., July 1, 1971

IT IS rarely safe to predict the outcome of a case in the United States Supreme Court even when the merits appear as transparent as they have appeared in the case of the government vs. the New York Times and the Washington Post. So it was that none of us supporting the right of the Times and the Post to publish the celebrated "Pentagon papers" could rest easy until the decision was actually handed down, as it was, finally, yesterday afternoon.

In the end, in any case, the newspapers won—and it was a historic victory for the First Amendment, the embattled cornerstone of individual guarantees in the American Republic. The margin of victory was comfortable, at 6 to 3, although not overwhelming, as the Court upheld the right of a free press to publish as it chooses without prior restraint in the absence of any provable threat to national security. The Court found that the government had failed to prove any such threat in trying to make a security case out of a three-year-old secret Pentagon study of how the United States blundered into the Vietnam war.

It was a great day for freedom of the press, which is to say a great day for the American system of democratic government.

If there is any sobering reflection, it would have to be over the curious dissenting votes of Mr. Chief Justice Burger, Mr. Justice Blackmun and Mr. Justice Harlan. The Pentagon papers, commissioned by then Secretary of Defense McNamara obviously have no military secrets other than the kind of secrets that embarrass the men and the government that made the dreadful blunders in Vietnam. The major disclosures go back six and seven years, into a war that was never declared and which the government claims to be getting out of now. The Pentagon papers belong to history and to the American public, which has a right to know the full truth about the war into which it was led so deceitfully.

The dissenting vote of the Chief Justice, for its part, tends to confirm again the view of some of us who never shared the early enthusiasm for Mr. Burger's appointment to the Court. Indeed, if Burger looks the part and has a grand presence, he is surely the most overrated Chief Justice in this century. It is all too obvious, moreover, that two of the three dissenting votes were cast by the Nixon appointees to the Court—the "Minnesota Twins," Burger and Blackmun. And it must be remembered that these were the "good" Nixon nominees, not the ones that the U.S. Senate refused to confirm!

THE MAJORITY decision, in its prior turn, is a boon to the country in more ways than one. First of all, of course, it is a splendid reassurance to have the Court shoring up the First Amendment to the Constitution against the government's attack. But let us consider as well what an absurd situation would have obtained if the Court had issued permanent injunctions against the Times and the Post in the matter of the Pentagon papers.

These "top secret" papers, in fact, have been wandering all over the countryside. There is no telling how many copies, and copies of copies, of the Pentagon report are in existence. A score of newspapers have been publishing articles based on sections of the Pentagon study, and the whole report has been made available (under pressure) to the entire body of Congress.

Even as the Supreme Court was preparing to hand down its ruling, a United States Senator in a public hearing was reading before the television cameras his own selection of excerpts from the secret study! The Court itself would have been left in a ludicrous position if it had enjoined newspapers from publishing material which has become, for all good reason, the worst kept "secret" in American history.

Honolulu Star-Bulletin

Honolulu, Hawaii, July 1, 1971

Although the Supreme Court's opinion in the case of the secret Pentagon papers represents a tremendous victory for the right of the press to publish and the right of the people to know what their government does, it is not as far-reaching as it might appear at first glance.

The reason is that, by ordering the presses of the New York Times, the Washington Post and other newspapers to be shut down, in effect, while a court decision could be reached, the Supreme Court did, in fact, by a 5-4 decision establish a precedent of prior restraint.

In rendering their dissent, Chief Justice Warren E. Burger and Justices John M. Harlan and Harry A. Blackmun protested the haste with which the constitutional controversy had been passed through the courts. Further, one of the six-man majority in freeing the newspapers to publish, Justice Byron R. White, said "I do not say that in no circumstances would the First Amendment permit an injunction against publishing information about government plans of operations."

Thus the high court, even though by only a one man margin — in the 5-4 vote to hold up publication while the court considered — established a precedent of prior restraint which will stand until, perhaps, it is reversed by some future court. The precedent overrules the positions taken by Justices William O. Douglas and Hugo L. Black that the First Amendment "leaves no room for a governmental restraint on the press."

Although Douglas, Black, William J. Brennan Jr., and Thurgood Marshall took the position in the 5-4 restraint decision that the courts infringed the Constitution by delaying publication, the majority — Burger, White, Harlan, Blackmun and Potter Stewart — ruled that publication could be at least temporarily suppressed.

These are aspects of the Times and Post cases which may be argued if at any time in the future the government decides that, for whatever reason, it will go to court to prevent publication. In the cases at hand the Justice Department claimed continued publication of the Pentagon papers would cause "irreparable damage" to the national security. In the Times case the federal court for the southern district of New York and the District of Columbia Court of Appeals, in the Post case, held that the government had failed to prove its point. The Supreme Court has now agreed.

The court order issued Wednesday did note the following:

"Any system of prior restraint of expression comes to this court bearing a heavy presumption against its constitutional validity. The government thus carries a heavy burden of showing justification of the enforcement of such restraint."

Nonetheless, the court held in effect that the courts are open to the government to attempt to prevent publication and to delay publication while the case is being heard. It is not censorship, but it is in fact a system of prior restraint which waters down the First Amendment's guarantee that "Congress shall make no law . . . abridging the freedom of speech, or of the press . . ."

ARKANSAS DEMOCRAT

Little Rock, Ark., July 1, 1971

Naturally, we are gratified that the Supreme Court ruled yesterday that the government could not forbid newspapers to continue printing the so-called Pentagon papers. What really bothered us was that the court took so long to decide that the first amendment really means what it says: "Congress shall make no law . . . abridging the freedom . . . of the press . . ."

If prior restraint on the press were allowed in this instance, it could be allowed in others, and the result would be that the newspapers in this country would be no different that those in a totalitarian countries, where the press prints just what the government wants printed and no more.

Now, as to punishment AFTER publication, that is another matter. We are as bothered as anyone about the theft and printing of top-secret documents. There are laws that make that a crime and the laws ought to be enforced — or repealed. This is the legal action the Nixon administration should have been pushing, in our opinion, instead of trying to get a court to allow it to tell newspapers what to print. Franklin Roosevelt, who deeply resented newspaper criticism and who was President during a world war, would not even try this, although he was tempted to do so. Especially when the Chicago Tribune, his severest critic, got hold of some secret war plans and started publishing them.

As far as the Pentagon papers are concerned, we think far too much has been made of them. They are one-sided, incomplete reports, written by people who opposed our involvement in Vietnam and published (first) by those newspapers that also oppose it. But as to whether the newspapers had a right to publish them, the answer must be, yes, just as the Supreme Court said. We're only sorry it didn't say it unanimously, instead of 6 to 3.

The San Diego Union

San Diego, Calif., July 1, 1971

Humpty Dumpty, in "Alice-in-Wonderland," when asked the meaning of a word, replied, "It means just what I choose it to mean; neither more nor less." Humpty Dumpty's conclusion has much in common with the Supreme Court decision of yesterday on the case of the Government versus the New York Times and the Washington Post.

The Times and other newspapers which had published documents classified as top secret will interpret the court's words as a great victory.

Others, of more sober mind, will see the decision as a very narrow one, reflecting only the conclusion of six members of the Supreme Court that publication of the documents in question will not gravely damage the United States of America.

Certainly, the real issue in yesterday's ruling was not freedom of the press. Nobody would seriously contend that freedom of the press includes the publication of documents critical to national security. The issue tested by the court was simply whether or not the documents in the hands of the Times and its colleagues were properly characterized as top secret The Supreme Court declared that they were not. That is a decision and we all abide by it.

However, the Times and others who rejoice in the Supreme Court decision must also be willing to acknowledge that the court did not touch upon other critical matters, such as the real limits of the powers of the attorney general, the injunctive powers of the Executive Branch as they relate to the First Amendment or the powers of the Executive relating to classification of state documents.

Most significantly, the court did not touch in any way upon the grave criminal aspects of this whole unhappy affair.

The court, for instance, did not exonerate Mr. Ellsberg for purloining the papers. It did not even touch on espionage.

The court did not excuse the New York Times for its incredible action in receiving stolen property, holding it for several months, and failing to report having the stolen property in its possession. Nor did the court excuse the similar action of the Washington Post and other newspapers.

It is plain now that the federal government took the wrong case before the bar. It permitted the issue to be argued on the fuzzy grounds of how secret a secret is rather than on the basis of whether the laws involving theft and receipt of stolen property apply to everyone.

Chief Justice Burger, in his stirring dissent, declared that they do, saying that the duty to report the receipt of stolen goods "rests on taxi drivers, justices and the New York Times."

There must be a gnawing feeling in the souls of all Americans hungry to be assured that nobody can be above the law in our Republic. On this basis, the people of the United States of America deserve to see the criminal aspects of this case pursued to their ultimate end.

St. Petersburg Times

St. Petersburg, Fla., July 1, 1971

In the long history of man's struggle for freedom, June 30, 1971, will be recorded as an important date.

It was then the United States Supreme Court struck down an unprecedented attempt by the federal government to restrict the people's right to a press free of prior government restraint.

WHEN THE government attempts such censorship, said the six-justice majority, it carries a heavy burden of showing that publication represents a grave and immediate danger to the United States. Other federal judges had ruled that in these cases the Nixon Administration had not met that burden. "We agree," said the highest court of law in the land.

This great issue did not just spring before the court. It was brought there — forced into the arena — by the poor judgment and remarkable presumption of power of the Nixon Administration.

No other national administration has claimed it possessed an "inherent power" to restrict publication. President Nixon's basic mistake was to allow the prosecution of this case, which was without statutory authority or legal precedent. He should have done what Franklin Roosevelt did in 1941 when, three days before the attack on Pearl Harbor, the Chicago Tribune and Washington Sun-Times printed the government's secret war mobilization plans. There was an investigation, but no injunctions, no indictments.

Joining this issue was not an isolated mistake. It follows the trend of this Administration showing little regard for many fundamental American liberties: the right of free speech, the right of privacy, the right to reasonable bail, freedom from unlawful arrest and the presumption of innocence until proven guilty.

BY ITS error, the Administration thrust a heavy burden upon the Supreme Court. The court responded admirably. Strictly constructing the Bill of Rights, it said the government could make no law abridging freedom of the press. It rejected the claim of an "inherent power" to do otherwise.

Still, the court's division was somewhat unsettling. The dissenters were Justice John M. Harlan, a hard-line conservative nominated by President Eisenhower in 1955; Chief Justice Warren E. Burger and Justice Harry A. Blackmun, both nominated by Mr. Nixon.

Does their dissent represent the future thinking of the court?

Mr. Nixon promised in 1968 to change the direction of the Supreme Court. If this means that his appointees will lightly discard civil liberties, we expect many Americans soon will be having some second thoughts.

When threatened, it becomes clearer that freedom itself imposes a heavy burden upon those who enjoy it. Liberty is ours because other Americans exercised it, defended it and gave up their lives for it. Presidents and justices will come and go in Washington, but always remaining is the responsibility of the American people to pass on to the future, and to enlarge, the freedoms they inherited.

The Hartford Courant

Hartford, Conn., July 1, 1971

The Supreme Court of the United States has upheld, although by a split vote of 6 to 3, the right of the New York Times, the Washington Post, and by implication, other publications to publish articles based on the top-secret Pentagon study of the Vietnam war. Its decision upholding two federal district court judges and the Washington federal Court of Appeals is hardly surprising in view of the fact that the Government's attempt to suppress the articles before they were published was the first of its kind in the nation's history, as Justice Brennan observed. To many informed observers, the major surprise was not the act that the Court upheld the publication of the papers but rather that Chief Justice Burger and Justices Blckman and Harlan dissented.

The court did not rule, and could not have ruled, that the press has the absolute liberty to publish secret documents of all kinds and at all times. But the majority maintained, we believe properly, that the Government must be able to establish that prior restraint of publication is justified by the urgent national interest. The Government, the majority ruled, had failed to show that publication would result in that "irreparable harm" which the attorneys for the Justice Department had claimed to be the case.

It is also important to note two other fields into which the majority opinion did not enter. One of these, of course, is the possibility that the newspapers that publish the top secret documents may be subject to prosecution for violating the law establishing the security regulations of the United States. The First Amendment says that Congress shall make no law abridging the freedom of the press. But the Bill of Rights gives the press no license for irresponsibility. While this same Supreme Court has broadened the definition of libel as applied to persons who are not public officials, it has not and could not give it the right to publish without taking the responsibility for the publication.

There is another field into which the Court's decision did not enter. That is the question of whether or not the documents were legally acquired by the newspapers that published them. It seems to be established now that some of the newspapers at least were the beneficiaries of Dr. Ellsberg's generosity. Chief Justice Burger, in his personal opinion, referred to the documents as having been "purloined." If the documents are, in fact, stolen goods, it is at least conceivable that the receivers are open to prosecution.

But the important thing is what the majority of Court did say. It clearly established again that the Government carries a heavy burden of showing justification for censorship of the press, or indeed of violating any of the constitutional guarantees of the Bill of Rights. And that is clearly as it should be.

THE DENVER POST

Denver, Colo., July 1, 1971

THE SUPREME COURT of the United States has done more than strike the fetters from two Eastern newspapers—the New York Times and the Washington Post—and allow them to print information about the origins of America's involvement in the Vietnam war.

It has rescued the First Amendment from attack, reaffirmed the paramount position of freedom of expression in our constitutional system and rebuffed the efforts of the government to keep important information out of the American marketplace.

THE COURT RULED, in a six to three decision, that the government had not met the "heavy burden" of justifying the imposition of previous restraint—censorship—on newspapers. Whatever harm might be done to the nation by publication of additional stories on the Pentagon papers, the court deemed it insufficient to override the right of the press to publish and of the people to know.

Although the majority opinion was brief, the justices wrote individual concurring and dissenting opinions examining at length some of the broad and difficult questions raised by this rare government challenge to freedom of the press.

Justice Black, who complained that the government "seems to have forgotten . . . the essential purpose and history" of the First Amendment, discussed the cases in terms of the role of the press in a free society.

"In the First Amendment," he wrote, "the founding fathers gave the free press the protection it must have to fulfill its essential role in our democracy. The press was to serve the governed, not the governors. . . .

"And paramount among the responsibilities of a free press is the duty to prevent any part of the government from deceiving the people and sending them off to distant lands to die of foreign fevers and foreign shot and shell.

"In revealing the workings of government that led to the Vietnam war, the newspapers nobly did precisely that which the founders hoped and trusted they would do."

THE THREE DISSENTERS—Justices Burger, Blackmun and Harlan—did not argue that the government had proved that publication would pose a peril to the nation so great as to overbalance the freedom of the press.

They argued merely that the judicial system had dealt with the case too swiftly—"with frenetic haste"—and that the government had not been given enough time to prove that publication would bring substantial harm to the nation.

The view this newspaper has expressed is that the courts moved, not too swiftly, but at a pace so slow that they allowed the freedom of the press to be abridged for 15 days.

We do not take the position, as Justices Black and Douglas did, that the First Amendment does not allow *any* previous restraint on newspapers, no matter how great the peril to American lives and the national safety.

But we say that the danger must be so vast, so specific and so clear that the courts can recognize it immediately or else the press ought not to be restrained at all. Despite Wednesday's decision, we do not consider that freedom of the press is secure when the government can prevent publication for 15 days.

BY KEEPING information out of the marketplace of ideas at a crucial stage in decision-making, the government can steer the country down a path that might be spurned if the information were available at the right time.

Even though the court might rule later that the information could be published, the country might already be committed and the damage might already be done.

If danger to the national interest is so indirect and so difficult to perceive as to require extended court deliberations, then it is not the kind of danger to overrride the First Amendment.

The majority agreed with two district court judges and two panels of appeals court judges in finding no such overriding danger in these cases. The dissenters could not find it either, but would have been content to keep the press under fetters while they continued the search.

Justice Stewart observed in his concurring opinion that "the only effective restraint upon executive policy and power in the areas of national defense and international affairs may lie in an enlightened citizenry—in an informed and critical public opinion which alone can here protect the values of democratic government."

In the light of the court's decision, the newspapers are free to take up once again the task of fostering the "enlightened citizenry" and the "critical public opinion" that a democratic society needs.

THIS NEWSPAPER intends to do that responsibly by providing as much information as it can, subject only to the voluntary restraint it would exercise to protect lives and the security of the society.

We do not believe the decision offers any encouragement to the press to exceed the rights that the court reaffirmed. And we do not intend to violate the principle that a free press must be a responsible press, dedicated to serving the nation's vital interests.

Wednesday's decision has left us and the rest of the American press in a better position to do our jobs. But the victory in the case belongs, not so much to the press, as to the people who use the information effectively to run their country and their lives.

St. Louis Globe-Democrat

St. Louis, Mo., July 1, 1971

In one of the most momentous decisions the United States Supreme Court has made in this century, the tribunal upheld by a vote of 6 to 3 the paramount right of the press to publish material without censorship or restriction by government.

If shorn of this freedom, the Constitution and ultimately the democratic principles that have obtained in America for 180 years would have been doomed.

The First Amendment was soundly fortified by the decision, which bars abridgment of free speech and the right of the people to be informed.

Citizens of the nation were deeply concerned in this issue. Regardless of their opinions about the Pentagon Papers or individual publications, their political ties or ideologies, people rejected the threat to unfettered reporting of government.

Many may object or have reservations over the way these "purloined" papers were obtained. And perhaps they are also justified in resenting the apparent bias with which the Pentagon data was revealed. But no one wants government dictating what can or cannot be published.

This was the first time in the history of the Republic the federal government has sued to enjoin the press from publishing. It should be the last.

* * *

What the government asked in its demand for injunction was "prior restraint," prohibition before the documents were printed. The majority opinion declared the government had not shown justification for restraint, which it was their burden to prove. That means the New York Times and Washington Post, and inferentially all other news organs, have liberty to publish the Pentagon commentaries, marked "secret" by federal officials.

Justice Hugo L. Black, who was particularly blunt, wrote in his opinion, "It is unfortunate that some of my brethren are apparently willing to hold that publication of news may sometimes be enjoined. Such a holding would make a shambles of the "First Amendment." Justice Black added the "guarding of military secrets and diplomatic secrets at the expense of informed government provides no real security" for the nation. Justice Potter Stewart noted "that without an informed and free press there cannot be an enlightened people."

The basis of the government's argument was, primarily, because revelation of the documents would endanger national security. The papers, ordered compiled by former Defense Secretary Robert S. McNamara, were certain records, analyses and personal interpretations of events leading up to and through the Vietnam war—but all prior to 1968.

Justice Thurgood Marshall observed the issue in the case was not, as the government contended, hazard to the nation's essential interests—the issue was whether "this court or Congress has the right to make law."

The establishment of press freedom—which is not a franchise for newspapers or any other media, but a right of the people—is obviously a constitutional endowment carrying obligations. Every right bears definite responsibility. The press has a duty to avoid publication of material, especially in time of war, that could imperil defense, the security of government functions and of the nation's people.

In past times, this duty has been clearly recognized by publishers and editors, who meticulously guarded defense secrets and military plans. But this, as in World War II, was done with voluntary censorship by the press. The system worked adequately. There have been occasions when "top secret" data have been leaked by editors; there have also been occasions when such secrets have been blabbed by high national officials.

With all the errata under such conditions, the obligations in this regard have worked rather well. Certainly such a system is infinitely preferable to Big Brother deciding what shall or shall not be printed.

Such an avenue can lead all too obviously to government dictatorship — hiding mistakes behind a "secret" stamp and setting a federal brake on free circulation of information.

* * *

The right to publish, as we have previously observed, must be maintained, but not at the risk of long-term security and peace of the world. The government in this case did not show that the Pentagon Papers would involve such risks.

No doubt difficulty will arise in obtaining frank diplomatic discussions with foreign leaders, who might fear their comments one day would be published. This presents something of a dilemma.

Yet it is probably reasonable to assume diplomats abroad will talk to the United States if it is in their interests regardless of possible secrecy breaks. Besides, White House "sources" or State Department "authorities" often leak their own "top secrets" for various purposes.

One of the great problems about the "secret" stamp of federal government is its ubiquitous and unwarranted use. It can be a screen to hide political purpose and all kinds of mistakes, as well as matters that should perhaps not be broadcast.

Publisher John S. Knight of Detroit, who served in the Bureau of Censorship at home and abroad during World War II, has said that in many instances documents were stamped indiscriminately "top secret" which had absolutely no relationship to national security. This habit has been enormously expanded since.

Chief Justice Warren E. Burger, who dissented to the majority opinion along with Justices Harry A. Blackmun and John M. Harlan, charged the Times had unauthorized possession of "purloined documents." There is remedy for this outside the injunctive process.

LEDGER-STAR

Norfolk, Va., July 1, 1971

The Supreme Court decided yesterday 6 to 3 that the government had not proved a strong enough case to override the historic prohibition in the Constitution that prevents interference with a newspaper's right to publish without prior restraint.

The majority held that the government had not met the burden of showing justification for restraint, which seems to suggest that under different circumstances, in different days and times, there might very well be reason to prevent a newspaper from publishing material the government knows a newspaper has and is about to disseminate.

★ ★ ★ ★

But Mr. Justice Black did not admit to any prior restraint under any circumstances. He wrote:

"The guarding of military or diplomatic secrets at the expense of informed representative government provides no real security for our Republic."

According to Justice Black there should exist no national security safeguards whatsoever when the right of a newspaper to publish and the right of a government, representing the people, to protect itself and them in time of war, revolution, riot or what have you, clash head-on. While this is an extraordinarily broad reaffirmation of the First Amendment, it is also a dangerous doctrine, in our view; for what it promulgates is the philosophy that the American people must be told now what is going on even in wartime and even if the knowledge leads an e n e m y to knowledge that can be destructive of or seriously damaging to American interests.

★ ★ ★ ★

Moreover, at least one justice who voted with the majority says that in these Pentagon Papers there is no question in his mind that "revelation of (the most sensitive and destructive) of these documents will do substantial damage to public interest. Indeed," wrote Justice White, "I am confident that their disclosure will have that result." Nonetheless, he concurred with the majority view that the government had not proved its case, and based his decision on ". . . the concededly extraordinary protection against prior restraints enjoyed by the press under our Constitutional system."

In fact, a number of the justices in their written views said that if the newspapers print materials truly jeopardizing U. S. military or diplomatic positions on Vietnam, they could be tried for criminal violations of the Espionage Act.

To be sure, this is a landmark case in law. But to the extent that it so broadens the right to print without prior restraint that it may be interpreted as a danger to the nation's security, the chances are that the emphasis will not remain where Justice Black conceives it to be. Congress, we think, will not stand by while military and diplom a t i c secrets remain unguarded and endangered; and we do not think the men who wrote the First Amendment's prohibition against laws affecting a free press meant it to be that way.

The Evening Gazette

Worcester, Mass., July 1, 1971

San Francisco Chronicle

San Francisco, Calif.

July 1, 1971

IN UPHOLDING the right of the New York Times and other newspapers to publish the classified Pentagon Papers, the 6-to-3 majority of the Supreme Court leaned heavily upon the First Amendment and the lack of any legislation that would permit the President — or the Court — to restrain such publication.

Said Justice Black, in a concurring opinion: "In revealing the workings of government that led to the Vietnam war, the newspapers did precisely what the founders hoped and trusted they would do."

The dissenters held that the First Amendment's guarantee of freedom of the press is not absolute. Justice White agreed with the dissenters in this respect and pointedly observed that certain circumstances might well justify an order to withhold publication of information about Government plans and operations.

SUCH CIRCUMSTANCES the majority found, did not exist in the current case. The Government provided no proof that the publication would endanger national security, it said, and the Government was attempting to act beyond its established authority and in the absence of any law permitting the contemplated action.

Justice Marshall, for instance, suggested that the ultimate issue before the court was whether it, rather than Congress, has the power to make law. He noted that Congress has specifically refused to pass laws that would permit the President to restrain publication of documents which he can legally classify as "secret" or "top secret." Therefore, he said, it was not for the Supreme Court to overrule Congress, and, in effect fashion such a law for application in this case.

JUSTICE BLACKMUN, dissenting, called for development of legal standards to fix "the broad right of the right of the press to print and the very narrow right of the Government to prevent." Various opinions alluded to existing law which makes it a crime to "receive, disclose, communicate, withhold and publish certain documents" — a law which the lower court found does not refer to the publication of newspaper stories.

Nevertheless, and despite the flat declaration of Justice Brennan that the First Amendment "stands as an absolute bar against the imposition of judicial restraints" in the matters here involved, a reading of the opinions, concurring and dissenting, leaves the layman with a feeling that the newspapers, while left free to print the Pentagon Papers, have been silently warned to avoid printing any that might indeed imperil national security, if by any lapse of editorial judgment, they might decide to do so.

In his dissenting opinion yesterday on the Pentagon Papers, Chief Justice Warren Burger summed up the grave issues at stake:

He said that the "imperative of a free and unfettered press" was in collision "with another imperative, the effective functioning of a complex modern government and specifically the effective exercise of certain constitutional powers of the executive — the President."

That was the far-reaching question the judges had to decide hastily and under unprecedented pressure. The right of the people to know vs. the duty of elected officials to protect the national security.

Perhaps never before in the 195 years of this Republic has the issue been posed so dramatically. Never before has the government gone to the courts to stop a newspaper from publishing information it already had in its possession. But perhaps never before has any newspaper had unauthorized possession of so extensive and sensitive a collection of top secret documents from government files as The Washington Post and The New York Times did in recent weeks.

It is our conviction that the majority of the court ruled correctly in lifting the restraining orders against the two newspapers, thereby allowing them to continue publishing the secret papers. But we find it difficult to go along with those who seem to think that the government had no case at all, and that only feelings of embarrassment were involved. The question of national security cannot be so easily brushed aside.

There is also the gnawing question of whether these documents were "stolen." Are government documents "private property" that can be stolen or are they, on the face of the matter, essentially the property of the public? If Lyndon Johnson has a copy of the Pentagon history, as he supposedly has in Austin, is that "stolen?" Were the two copies at the Rand Corporation "stolen?" were these papers taken in the dark of night and handed over to newspapers? Or were they, like so many other classified government documents, handed over to reporters by government officials or past government officials? When is that stealing and when is it not? These are hard questions, to which answers must be found.

Justice Byron White, who concurred with the majority, said he did so "only because of the concededly extraordinary protection against prior restraints enjoyed by the press under our constitutional system." White said he was sure that the documents were so sensitive that their disclosure "will do substantial damage to the public interest."

White may be wrong in that view, as the government may be wrong. But it should be conceded that responsible and fair-minded men do hold that opinion. It certainly is conceivable that some government secrets could not be revealed without hurting the national security. In a case like that — if a newspaper somehow got hold of a dangerously compromising document — we cannot imagine that either a responsible editor or a responsible judge could approve the publishing of it.

But from what we have seen of the Pentagon Papers, they do not fall into that category. Some of them deal with events of 20 years ago, and none is less than three years old. It seems doubtful in the extreme that anything in them can seriously compromise the security of the United States.

The risk in that must be weighed against the risk from the other side — that a government victory in this case might have altered the status of newsgathering and news-dissemination in this country in a far-reaching and dangerous fashion. There is in the best of governments a fundamental instinct of self-preservation that leads public officials to constantly put a good face on things and hide the mistakes. The best way to hide the mistakes is to use the "Top-Secret" stamp. If nothing else, this whole episode has pointed up the glaring need for the government to revise its security and classification procedures.

There is still another reason why the Pentagon Papers should be released for public scrutiny. As they have come out thus far, in bits and pieces, they have fueled the fires of the antiwar factions in this country to a white heat. Every Vietnam critic has found support for his view that the war was the result of an evil conspiracy in high places, where decisions were made in collusion and in secret.

A more balanced view is essential, and it most probably can be found in the 47 volumes. These documents are a vast compendium of conversations, memos, contingency plans, speculations, and comments. To sort out what actual decisions were arrived at, and how, is going to be no easy feat. But it must be done.

There is little question that the Pentagon Papers case will go down as a historical development of considerable importance. As Chief Justice Burger pointed out, great claims and principles can sometimes be in collision. There are times and circumstances that might some day lead the Supreme Court to a different decision from the one announced yesterday.

But a strong precedent has been established that the freedom of the press must be sustained even under circumstance that may risk harm to national interests. It is an awesome responsibility that the newspapers of this nation have under the Constitution, as affirmed again yesterday by the Supreme Court.

Minneapolis Tribune

Minneapolis, Minn., July 1, 1971

The decision by the U.S. Supreme Court Wednesday in the Pentagon Papers cases was much more than a victory for the New York Times, the Washington Post and journalists everywhere. It was the victory for the constitutional right of the American people to be informed about their government and its actions.

The effort of the Nixon administration to prevent the Times and the Post from publishing material from the Pentagon Papers brought into conflict two values: the nation's security and the freedom of its people. The high court's majority accepted the judgment of the two newspapers and of three lower courts that the material in the Pentagon Papers, which are more than three years old, would not endanger national security if published.

This was a landmark issue, for it was the first time in the nation's history that the court was asked to rule on whether it should restrain newspapers on grounds of national security. The Nixon administration clearly failed to justify the court's tampering with the First Amendment, which guarantees freedom of speech and of the press. Had the Times and the Post lost their cases, the concept of "prior restraint" upon newspaper publication — press censorship — would have achieved court sanction. The court has previously held that prior restraints on publications were in conflict with the First Amendment, except in exceptional cases, such as current battle plans or troop movements. Restraints mean, of course, limitations on the free flow of information necessary in a democratic society.

After the court issued its decision, the Post's attorney said he felt it would have the future effect of discouraging the government from seeking to restrain newspapers. We hope he is right. Even though the Nixon administration lost in this instance, it did create the precedent of such suits against newspapers and it did succeed in obtaining temporary restraining orders.

But even though we disagree with the Nixon administration in this case, we recognize the government's need to maintain the privacy of much of its security planning and internal communication. At a minimum, the administration and C o n g r e s s must move to adopt a more rational, defensible system of classifying government documents — a system that separates the nation's legitimate security needs from the self-serving desire of many politicians and government employees to cover up their mistakes or embarrassment. One former classification official says that 99 percent of the material now classified doesn't need to be.

With the court's ruling, the American people will continue to get the information contained in the Pentagon Papers. The portions published so far have shown the deceit of the Johnson administration. As the public now learns more about the origins of American involvement and escalation in this terrible war, we all may be helped toward a greater wisdom about the conflict. And such wisdom, in turn, could help this country throw off the seemingly endless burden it now bears in Vietnam.

THE NASHVILLE TENNESSEAN

Nashville, Tenn., July 1, 1971

THE UNITED States Supreme Court—in one of the great landmark decisions of American history—ruled yesterday the government did not have the power to prevent newspapers from publishing the "Pentagon Papers" describing the background of the nation's involvement in the Vietnam War.

* * *

The issue hinged on an interpretation of the First Amendment, which expressly prohibits Congress from passing any law that would put a restraint on a newspaper before publication. The court majority decided the amendment meant what it said.

"Any system of prior restraints of expression comes to this court bearing a h e a v y presumption against its constitutional validity," the majority opinion said. "The government thus carries a heavy burden of showing justification" in preventing publication of the material. The majority decided the government did not show such justification.

The decision was 6 to 3 against the position of President Nixon and Attorney General John Mitchell, who had sought to prevent the New York Times and the Washington Post from publishing the "Pentagon Papers."

Among the dissenters were two justices who were appointed to the court by President Nixon—Chief Justice Warren Burger and Justice Harry A. Blackmun.

Justices Burger and Blackmun were placed on the court to bolster Mr. Nixon's stated intention of molding the court into a "strict constructionist" pattern—that is, one that would decide cases more on a literal interpretation of the Constitution.

But in this case, it was the older members of the court who held the line against adventuring and decided the issue on a literal interpretation of the Constitution.

The majority's decision is much more than a convenience to the press. It is a victory for the right of every American citizen to be informed by a free press about the actions of his government. Only by obtaining such information can a free people govern itself intelligently.

This was the main issue of the case—not the government's claim that publication of the "Pentagon Papers" would endanger the national security. The courts—from the district level up to the Supreme Court—rejected this claim as unjustified. The government simply did not prove its case. It could not show that the papers, declared secret in the past, pose any danger to the national security today. In fact, the court found, the papers are not in any sense a threat to national security.

The larger question presented by this case is how the public can be protected from the bureaucratic practice of classifying documents "secret" when the people should know what is in them. Congress is considering how to handle that problem.

But yesterday's ruling stands out in the great tradition of a country which believes that only an informed people can govern themselves.

In 1730—even before the American colonies rebelled against the tyranny of a British king—freedom of the press was established in this country by virtue of a court case. It was in New York where a Governor of the Colony had been embarrassed by articles published in a newspaper of a printer named John Peter Zenger.

A distinguished lawyer, Andrew Hamilton, pleaded the Zenger case successfully to a jury. The press, he argued, must have the right to tell the people about how their government operates.

* * *

He argued: "The question before the Court and you gentlemen of the jury is not of small nor private concern. It is not the cause of a poor printer, nor of New York alone, which you are now trying. . . . It is the best cause. It is the cause of liberty."

In the same tradition the founding fathers decided that Congress would pass no law abridging freedom of the press.

The ruling of the Supreme Court yesterday was in the same tradition and for the best cause—the cause of liberty.

DESERET NEWS

Salt Lake City, Utah, July 1, 1971

The green light that the U.S. Supreme Court gave Wednesday to the publication of the controversial Pentagon study on the origins of the Vietnam war is a testimonial to the responsibility with which the free press traditionally operates in America.

The high court's ruling also is a clear indication that the executive branch of the federal establishment is often too quick to stamp "secret" on government documents, to conclude that their publication will impair national security, and to insist that such information be kept even from Congress.

With doubts on these matters finally resolved and the legality of publication clearly established, the Deseret News today begins publishing extensive excerpts of the Pentagon study as its 47 volumes are summarized and released.

But Americans still need to be careful not to read too much into either the Supreme Court's ruling or the Pentagon study itself.

The high court's decision is not a license for the press to declare open season on disclosing all sorts of classified government documents, many of which would indeed put the nation in peril if publicized.

In this particular case, the press was right and the government was wrong. Even so, the press is not always the best judge of what impairs national security. Indeed, when it comes to keeping the country safe and secure, it is normally best to err on the side of too much caution rather than too little.

Moreover, the ruling is not a vindication of the accuracy and objectivity of the Pentagon study. We still don't know the identity of all the authors of the Pentagon papers — and some 40 different writers were involved. We don't know what was left out of the study, much less the condensed versions being published. Even the exhaustive New York Times is able to print only about 5 percent of the Pentagon documents.

While the immediate victors in Wednesday's Supreme Court decision were the newspapers involved, the ultimate winners are the American people. By this verdict they have obtained the lawful opportunity to look closely at information purchased with their tax dollars and, in a sense, with Americans' blood spilled in Vietnam.

But it may be a limited and short-lived victory unless there's a change to make sure that secret information isn't mis-classified, that even legitimate secrets aren't kept under wraps longer than they need to be, and that when information can't be told to the general public it is still available to all the government officials who need it to carry out their duties.

Certainly Congress cannot effectively do its part in this nation's system of checks and balances when key lawmakers are denied information, like the Pentagon study, which is available to the executive branch and can serve as a basis for making important policy decisions.

These are among the points our readers should keep in mind as they sift among the details of the Pentagon study.

New York Post

New York, N.Y., July 1, 1971

Despite every frantic, frenzied argument that the Nixon Administration sought to contrive, the sanctity of the Pentagon Papers is vastly less crucial to the safety of this nation than the freedom of its newspapers.

That is perhaps the essential meaning of yesterday's reassuring 6-3 ruling by the U.S. Supreme Court—affirming the First Amendment and the right of The New York Times and The Washington Post to publish the long-suppressed documentary history of the American tragedy in Vietnam.

Only three judges in the majority—Black, Douglas and Marshall—clearly and unequivocally rejected the notion of "prior restraint" and remained "strict constructionists" in the realm of liberty. Justices Brennan, Stewart and White held in essence that the government had not met the burden of showing clear and present danger. But the immediate effect of the decision is to halt the censorship drive and discourage any reckless new onslaught.

We are all—press and public alike—indebted to the men and women at The Times and The Washington Post who from the outset refused to be intimidated and vowed to fight the case through to a legal finish. It is not merely our liberty to print that has been reaffirmed; it is your right to read.

But for those in our profession the decision imposes a special responsibility to continue to seek out the truth about the war—not only the past history of its origins and escalation but the tangled obscurities of the present.

In his dissent yesterday, Chief Justice Burger suggested that the "effective functioning" of modern government, particularly the Executive Branch, would be damaged by the disclosures of the war history. In reality, it is tragically misguided policy that has inflicted the damage and the press that may be credited with helping to begin to restore effective, humane functioning of government. That mission is not yet accomplished.

* * *

Not long before the court's judgment was handed down, Attorney General Mitchell appeared before graduates of the FBI's National Academy to complain that a "tidal wave of legalisms" had engulfed the nation's criminal prosecutors. His words were echoed soon afterward by the President. Had they received advance news of their defeat in the Supreme Court?

Although it was deciding a civil case, the court's majority opinion also stands as a momentous rebuke to these and all other government officials who share a punitive, pinched conception of the Constitution and the laws to which it gives vitality and meaning.

For in these cases, the government was not seriously addressing itself to Constitutional right or broadened legal interpretation. Its case was shadowed from the start by a determination to conceal a damning account of official error and shame and to protect future pretense.

The secrecy obsession is not unique to any single administration or any party power—as the Vietnam documents prove only too convincingly. It remains the solemn obligation of the press and of the courts to contend against it when it appears—as they joined to do on this occasion.

Baltimore, Md., July 1, 1971

IN ITS momentous 6-3 ruling on the secret Pentagon papers controversy, the Supreme Court rendered a tremendous service to the cause of American democracy.

What the court affirmed, in essence, it that freedom of the nation's press is so vital that its preservation normally must take priority over all other considerations.

The other considerations in this case were grave indeed. It had been charged by the United States government that printing of the stolen Pentagon documents constituted a definite threat to the national security.

In the head-on court collision which ensued, the government attempted a seldom-invoked form of censorship—moving to restrain publication of disputed material in advance. The publishers contested the action.

Now, by ruling against the government, the Supreme Court has adjudged that—generally speaking—even classified material is exempt from pre-publication censorship by government authorities.

This is the nub of the decision—a point which tends to be obscured by all the side arguments in a matter which has many other moral and legal ramifications.

The Supreme Court did not decide whether or not the editors who defied the government by printing the Pentagon papers acted responsibly.

If they and their informant or informants are guilty of breaking specific laws, they still can be punished—as they should be.

The historic importance of the Supreme Court decision transcends such considerations, just as it transcends the conflicting value judgments on the Vietnam war which are involved.

What was proclaimed—once and for all, we hope—was a warning to government that the principle of a free press in this nation is all but sacrosanct.

Long Island Press

New York, N.Y., July 1, 1971

The Supreme Court's decision yesterday to permit the New York Times and the Washington Post to print the Pentagon study of the Vietnam War was an historic reaffirmation of political freedom.

The court majority, in ruling that the government failed to meet the "heavy burden of showing justification" for blocking publication, made it clear this nation remains committed to the still quite revolutionary principle that only the most overwhelming consideration of national security may be considered a reason for government to tell anyone what he may say, think or print.

The decision does not answer all the legal and moral questions raised by the publication of these papers. We must still deal with the question of the government's legitimate right to confidentiality.

But after a long, long season of self hate by far too many Americans of small faith in their own freedom, the nation can stand proud in the knowledge that no other great power reveres so highly the principle that government, no matter how big and how strong, remains subject to the people, not the other way around.

In recent years the power of our executive branch has grown perforce under the imperatives of meeting great needs at home and abroad. The result has been the gradual, almost imperceptible assumption of powers by President after President to the point where the public will has tended to be ignored.

How this has led to the Indochina tragedy · is only too painfully evident. It might have been averted had the government dealt more openly with the people. Thanks to the New York Times for its bold decision, not just to print but, perhaps more significantly, to challenge the powers to which government had so dangerously become accustomed, the nation has been jolted back to a new awareness of its first principles.

To live free is a most difficult yet the most promising form of human society. The key to freedom is an enlightened people who can check and balance the enormous power entrusted to public officials. As Justice Potter Stewart observed, "the only effective restraint upon executive policy and power in the area of national defense and international affairs may lie . . . in an informed and critical public opinion which alone can here protect the values of democratic government."

THE WALL STREET JOURNAL.

New York, N.Y., July 1, 1971

The Supreme Court, in the Pentagon-papers case, has upheld the Constitutional stricture against press censorship and left The New York Times, The Washington Post and other newspapers free to publish material from the controversial documents.

But the way in which the court acted, with an unsigned decision to which three justices dissented and with each justice writing a separate opinion, shows that, while the legal question has been resolved for now, philosophical questions remain. The nine justices are almost as diverse in their views of this historic confrontation between press and government as the public obviously has been.

Yet the justices in their separate ways have provided some philosophical guideposts. Three propositions in particular are worthy of careful note.

The conflict, of course, was between the public's right to know and the government's right to conceal in the interests of national security. Mr. Justice Black stated the fundamental proposition—as embodied in the First Amendment to the Constitution—eloquently.

"In the First Amendment," he wrote in his opinion, "the founding fathers gave the free press the protection it must have to fulfill its essential role in our democracy. The press was to serve the governed, not the governors. The government's power to censor the press was abolished so that the press would remain forever free to censure the government."

This is a fundamental principle of the American system. The press and government are meant to be separate and sometimes in conflict with each other. The citizen can decide which he chooses to trust or believe—an option he would not have if the two worked hand in glove. To change this principle would be to radically change the system.

A second proposition was offered by Mr. Justice Stewart and it merits deep consideration by the public, the press, the Congress and the·administration. He suggested that the best way for the government to protect secrecy that is truly vital to the national security is to avoid secrecy that is not vital.

"For when everything is classified, then nothing is classified, and the system becomes one to be disregarded by the cynical and careless and to be manipulated by those intent on self-protection or self-promotion," Mr. Justice Stewart wrote. The hallmark of a truly effective security system; he said, "would be the maximum possible disclosure, recognizing that secrecy can best be preserved when credibility is truly maintained."

The State Department and some other branches of this administration claim that they already are reviewing their classification policies and we can only hope that it will prove to be a really serious effort. We would hope that Congress will also exert strong pressure for greater disclosure and there are signs that it will do just that. Unwarranted secrecy and the failure to inform the public and Congress in advance of vital policy decisions has seriously weakened the credibility of the United States government.

Restoring that credibility may well be more vital to the nation's security than anything else the government could do. Substantive action, not mere salesmanship, will be needed and one of the most effective actions would be wholesale declassification of information that should long ago have been in the public domain.

The third guidepost was offered in the dissenting opinion of Mr. Justice Blackmun, who is concerned, as are many Americans, about possible disclosure by the press of government information that might directly affect national security. He argued, as did the two other dissenting justices, Messrs. Burger and Harlan, not that the majority decision was necessarily a misinterpretation of Constitution or law, but that it was too hasty in light of the national-security questions involved.

Mr. Justice Blackmun noted that the court's ruling against censorship places a heavy responsibility upon the press to exercise care in its own judgments of whether to disclose information. If press disclosures should have the effect of jeopardizing troops, disrupting sensitive negotiations in matters of war and peace or other consequences of such dimensions the public has the right to hold the press responsible.

We have seen nothing in the Pentagon papers published so far that would even remotely endanger national security, and the government was obviously unable to make a convincing case that the papers contain any such information. But the press can never escape the fact that its freedom from censorship entails responsibilities to the nation.

Newspapermen might wish that the full court could have been unequivocal in upholding the freedom guaranteed by the First Amendment. The freedom was upheld, however, and that is what matters for the moment. If it all has led to a better understanding of where the nation's security really lies then it has all been worthwhile.

In our view, the nation's security lies in a continuing willingness of its people to face unpleasant facts, to engage in full and earnest debate and to protect the free, democratic institutions that make those things possible.

The Courier-Journal

Louisville, Ky., July 2, 1971

Secrecy: A hasty battle, a narrow victory

In the First Amendment the Founding Fathers gave the press the protection it must have to fulfill its essential role in our democracy. The press was to serve the governed, not the governors. The government's power to censor the press was abolished so that the press would remain forever free to censure the government. The press was protected so that it could bare the secrets of government and inform the people. Only a free and unrestrained press can effectively expose deception in government.

—Justice Hugo Black

THE SUPREME COURT'S ruling that the government may not restrain publication of the hitherto secret Pentagon documents concerning our involvement in the Vietnam war is of course a victory for freedom of the press and the people's right to know. Had Justice Black's words been included in the Court's order, it would have been a great victory. Instead, the Court decided merely that a gadfly press may not be swatted by the government before it stings—this time.

The right of *The New York Times* and *The Washington Post*—and hence other newspapers as well—to publish anything contained in the secret Pentagon study was tersely affirmed. "Any system of prior restraints of expression comes to this court bearing a heavy presumption against its constitutional validity," the order read. "The government thus carries a heavy burden of showing justification of the enforcement of such a restraint."

Future standards unclear

The Court then simply upheld the opinion of two lower courts that the government failed to show that justification. The 180-word formal order—the only opinion in the case that stands for legal precedent in the future—does not condemn the government's effort to muzzle the press, nor does it clarify the boundary line between the government's right to secrecy and the public's right to information. It does not prohibit future attempts at censorship. It sets no standard by which future quarrels between the press and the would-be censors may be adjudicated.

The individual opinions handed down by the nine Justices ranged from ringing opposition to prior restraint of press or speech under any circumstances to support of a ban on publication of the Pentagon documents. Only three Justices flatly stated that the lower courts were wrong to impose even a temporary restraint on the newspapers' right to publish the documents, and none of them commented on the propriety of secret judicial hearings on a newspaper's right to publish. Those who indicated they would support censorship under circumstances posing a "direct," "immediate" and "grave" danger to national security set no standard by which the government would be required to prove such danger in order to censor the press in the future.

These grave omissions may be blamed on what Chief Justice Burger called the "frenetic haste" of the two cases' movement through the courts. The Chief Justice and his two colleagues in dissent, Justices Harlan and Blackmun, all declared that the two weeks during which the courts had suspended the newspapers' right to publish the secret documents was too brief a time to build a case upon which vital constitutional opinion could be hung.

Such a precipitous pace may justify the narrow importance of the Court's decision in these cases, and the Justices may have been wise to defer the broader constitutional questions to another, more leisurely time. But the minority's view—that the lower courts' restraint upon the newspapers should be continued while the Supreme Court studied the issues in a quiet atmosphere—would have established a far more dangerous precedent than the majority was willing to permit. Had the minority prevailed, an unsympathetic court could keep vital information out of print for months on the ground that speed would mean irresponsibility.

Nor did the haste justify Chief Justice Burger's intemperate attack on *The New York Times*—an attack which did not address the legal issues at hand. His declaration that the newspaper should have consulted with the government before publishing the Pentagon documents suggests a surprising naivete about the lengths to which government agencies and officials—including presidents—will go to hide or suppress facts that are embarrassing to themselves.

Who'll be responsible?

And what of Justice Blackmun's strange conclusion that if the war is prolonged and a delay in the return of American POWs results from publication, "then the nation's people will know where the responsibility for these sad consequences rests"? Could not one say with greater justification that if the American people had not been kept in the dark all these years about Vietnam they might have ended the war a long time ago, or never joined it in the first place? If there are "sad consequences" still to come, shall we blame those who expose how decisions are made in Washington; or shall we blame the fact that decisions are made by men too well shielded by secrecy from any kind of public accountability?

If this constitutional crisis makes it more difficult for the government to operate in such dark and broad secrecy in the future, that alone will have made it worth the trouble. "When everything is classified, then nothing is classified," Justice Stewart said, "and the system becomes one to be disregarded by the cynical or the careless, and to be manipulated by those intent on self-protection or self-promotion."

That has been the *modus operandi* of too many of our public servants for too long, and it is a grave threat to our representative democracy, which cannot be preserved by a citizenry benighted by unnecessary secrecy and false information. "Without an informed and free press," Justice Stewart said, "there cannot be an enlightened people."

The Court has relit the light for a while.

The Times-Picayune

New Orleans, La., July 2, 1971

The United States Supreme Court's historic decision for freedom of the press in the case of the publication of Pentagon papers by The New York Times and The Washington Post is a precedent that will be a beginning in many ways.

A trickle, if not stream, of variously branded classified materials may well start flowing to newspaper or magazine publishers eager or willing to disseminate what they feel the public has a right to know and what, in their judgment, does not endanger national security in some way.

The high court's 6-3 decision, not as broad as some would think, resolved the key legal question of whether the Times should initially have been stopped from publishing the stolen Vietnam data on June 15. The formal, one-page ruling says simply the administration did not meet the "burden of showing justification" for a printing ban.

Extent of publication of future spirited materials — spirited in the sense of stolen as well as potentially controversial — might depend on the outcome of the Justice Department case against Daniel Ellsberg, suspected of having unlawfully taken the classified papers on Vietnam and delivered them to the Times. Conviction and sentencing could discourage others from like ventures — despite what their stricken or sensitive consciences might dictate.

Resolution of Mr. Ellsberg's case may indeed develop a dilemma in the whole affair. For if it is illegal and punishable to steal government data, can it be justifiable to receive and keep it? Or as dissenting Chief Justice Warren Burger put it: The New York Times had the duty to report it had possession of stolen property; "this duty rests on taxi drivers, justices, and The New York Times."

Another beginning that the court case might prompt is a thorough overhaul of the Pentagon or other agency systems for determining what should be confidential or secret and what should be in the public domain.

Congress may consider a range of legislation to clear the situation but in the interim the executive branch will surely take steps toward tightening government security and developing a logical system for classifying and de-classifying information.

The Supreme Court has not rent the legitimate veil of official secrecy. It has, with the administration's failure to prove its case to a majority of the jurists, stripped away cloaks behind which a bureaucracy likes to take refuge in self-protection.

The Detroit News

Detroit, Mich., July 2, 1971

The Supreme Court decision that permitted the New York Times and the Washington Post to resume publication of articles based on the Pentagon papers may not be quite the historic action in defense of freedom of the press that some of our newspaper colleagues read into it.

Indeed, it could, in the long run, lead to the imposition of new restraints on freedom of the press more severe than those proposed by the Nixon administration to halt publication of the purloined Pentagon papers.

In finding for the newspapers, a majority of the court, in its 6 to 3 decision, held that "the government has not met" the heavy burden of presumption against the constitutionality of any attempt by the government to halt publication.

But a majority of the justices also said, either in their concurring or dissenting decisions, that freedom of the press is not absolute and that there is at least a narrow class of cases in which the First Amendment's apparent ban on prior judicial restraint may be overridden.

Some justices cited cases in which it had been held that freedom of speech did not encompass the shouting of fire in a crowded theater and that in time of war freedom of the press did not permit such matters as the sailing dates of transports or the number and location of troops to be published.

Other justices held that no prior restraint could be imposed on any publication because Congress had explicitly refused to pass legislation to limit such publication. But their thinking implied that if Congress should pass such legislation, the court then might change its mind and permit prior restraint.

Even the newspaper attorneys in their argument before the court indicated that there are situations in which restraint is in order and is constitutional. In e f f e c t, they argued, and successfully, that the necessity of such restraint was not proved in the instance of the purloined Pentagon papers published by the two newspapers.

In short, what was decided by the Supreme Court was the narrow point that national security was not sufficiently imperiled by the publication by the New York Times and the Washington Post of the secret Pentagon papers to warrant any permanent ban on their publication.

But as a result of the decision by the Times and the Post to publish these papers, it is likely there will be future cases involving irresponsible publication of national secrets and, consequently, new efforts at legislation to spell out what can and what cannot be published.

Indeed, in warning the editors of the Times and the Post to be "fully aware of their ultimate responsibilities to the United States" in resuming publication of the papers, Justice Harry Blackman said:

"If, however, damage has been done, and if, with the court's action today, these newspapers proceed to publish the critical documents and there results therefrom 'the death of soldiers, the destruction of alliances, the greatly increased difficulty of negotiation with our enemies, the inability of our diplomats to negotiate,' to which list I might add the factors of prolongation of the war and of further delay in the freeing of U.S. prisoners, then the nation's people will know where the responsibility for these sad consequences rests."

This warning not only says that if these terrible events ensue, the public would blame the newspapers but it also implies public demand for government control of the press that would far exceed that which the Nixon administration sought to impose on the Pentagon papers in the interests of national security.

The Times and the Post have thus opened up a Pandora's box which in the long run may do more to oppress the free press than to protect it from government control.

The Philadelphia Inquirer

Philadelphia, Pa., July 2, 1971

The unprecedented outpouring of separate opinions in the Supreme Court case on the Pentagon papers not only adds up to a historic victory for press freedom but offers some eloquent and timely reminders of why that guarantee was written into the Constitution in the first place.

As The New York Times itself has observed in an editorial, ". . . this is not so much a victory for any particular newspaper as it is for the basic principles of freedom on which the American form of government rests."

That message came through loud and clear in some of the concurring opinions as the justices took the occasion of this landmark decision to teach a history lesson.

★ ★ ★

Press freedom, they reminded the nation, was embodied in the Constitution not for the protection of newspaper editors as some privileged class but for the protection of their readers —the American people.

"In the First Amendment," said Mr. Justice Black, "the Founding Fathers gave the free press the protection it must have to fulfill its essential role in our democracy. The press was to serve the governed, not the governors . . . The press was protected so that it could bare the secrets of government and inform the people."

Mr. Justice Douglas similarly delved into history when he recalled:

"The dominant purpose of the First Amendment was to prohibit the widespread practice of governmental suppression of embarrassing information. It is common knowledge that the First Amendment was adopted against the widespread use of the common law of seditious libel to punish the dissemination of material that is embarrassing to the powers-that-be."

And Mr. Justice Stewart applied all this history to our own sensitive and complex times in this observation:

"In the absence of the governmental checks and balances present in other areas of our national life, the only effective restraint upon executive policy and power in the areas of national defense and international affairs may lie in an enlightened citizenry—in an informed and critical public opinion which alone can here protect the values of democratic government. For this reason, it is perhaps here that a press that is alert, aware and free most vitally serves the basic purpose of the First Amendment. For without an informed and free press there cannot be an enlightened people."

The ringing reaffirmation of these fundamentals, we hope, will make an impression upon those critics of the press who have charged that publication of the Pentagon papers was simply a sensational and self-serving scheme to "sell papers."

Beyond that, we should like to think that within government itself it will lead to a prompt review and reform of a classification system which fails to discriminate betweeen legitimate state secrets and information to which the public is entitled.

"When everything is classified," Mr. Justice Steward pointed out, "then nothing is classified, and the system becomes one to be disregarded by the cynical or the careless, and to be manipulated by those intent on self-protection or self-promotion . . . Secrecy can best be preserved only when credibility is truly maintained."

Such credibility cannot be maintained by stamping everything in sight with a "top secret" label and then trying to apply prior governmental restraint to publication of material which does not justify that designation.

In not only balking such an attempt in this instance but providing the historical context for its decision, the Supreme Court has served the nation well and helped to keep it free.

THE KNICKERBOCKER NEWS
★★★ UNION-STAR ★★★
Albany, N.Y., July 2, 1971

The Constitution of the United States says:

"Congress shall make no law . . . abridging the freedom of speech, or of the press. . . ."

Nor has Congress made such a law. Indeed, on two occasions, in the World War I days of 1917 and again in 1957, when administrations asked Congress for laws that would have put only modest restraints on the press, the Congress refused to pass the requested legislation.

The constitutional mandate has been maintained through American history.

Now, once again, press freedom has been preserved. This time by the Supreme Court, whose split decision permitted the New York Times and Washington Post to resume publication of secret Pentagon studies of our involvement in the Vietnam war. The court ruled the government had not proved that publication of the documents threatened national security.

THE FULL IMPACT of the court's ruling will be determined in the future. Only three of the nine justices ruled absolutely that the press is free. Three others qualified their finding by saying that the press could be muted only to prevent immediate and irreparable damage to the nation, and that in the instance before it there was no such danger. The three justices dissenting from the majority complained of the speed with which the case was decided, implied that the Times and the Post should have asked the govern-

ment if security would be endangered by publication of the documents, and gravely sought to place on the newspapers responsibility for any prolongation of the Vietnam war that might result from the publication.

The court, as a whole, gave no absolute decision on the matter of "prior restraint," that is prevention of publication by government fiat. The decision did, however, take note of a previous ruling stating "any system of prior restraints of expression comes to this court bearing a heavy presumption against its constitutional validity."

THE VICTORY of the press cannot be considered complete, although in the narrower confines of the case at issue the victory was a great one. The decision makes clear that the government must be on the strongest of grounds in matters of the utmost seriousness to the nation before it can stop the presses again.

Some of the opinions are critical of the newspapers that published the documents in question and, indeed, critical of the press in general. One justice took occasion to note that the press can be held accountable for its acts. The press is, of course, well aware of that. Its mention by the justice might be considered indicative of a mood in Washington that has come to be epitomized by Vice President Agnew in his frequent castigations of the press.

ON THE OTHER SIDE of the coin is the stand voiced by Justice Potter Stewart in his opinion in the case. Said the justice, in part:

"The only effective restraint upon executive policy and power in the areas of national defense and international affairs may lie in an enlightened citizenry—in an informed and critical public opinion which alone can here protect the values of democratic government. For this reason, it is perhaps here that a press that is alert, aware and free most vitally serves the basic purpose of the First Amendment. For without an informed and free press there cannot be an enlightened people."

Likewise, Justice William O. Douglas, in an opinion in which Justice Hugo L. Black joined, said:

"SECRECY IN GOVERNMENT is fundamentally undemocratic, perpetuating bureaucratic errors. Open debate and discussion of public issues are vital to our national health."

To which we must add that open debate and discussion can come only from a people that is kept informed by its press.

What we have in this decision of the court is not a declaration that the people always have the right to know, but that in this particular instance they had the right to know.

And that is victory indeed for both people and the press. It must serve as well as a reminder that, for both people and press, freedom long will continue to be a hard bought thing.

RAPID CITY JOURNAL—
Rapid City, S.D., July 2, 1971

The euphoria which America's media are experiencing as a result of this week's Supreme Court decision is understandable.

Two of the most prestigious newspapers in the land took on the federal government on the issue of publishing material the government would rather not have citizens know. The newspapers won and the Fourth Estate is now applauding a decision that confirms its understanding of the First Amendment.

The court ruled that the government had not proved the national security would be damaged if certain classified documents from a 47-volume Pentagon war study were published.

Without doubt, the decision is one of the most important on free-

dom of the press for more than 200 years.

On the whole, we cannot help but feel America will profit from this unusual occurrence. Among other things, it should discourage some of the secrecy in government, which, as Stanley Karnow points out on this page today, should be the servant of the people. It ought also produce more candor from those in positions of leadership.

Aside from the visceral issue, the point is manifest that there has been too liberal use of the stamp marked "secret," and for too long. What has been hidden behind this label, apparently, is history, plus the embarrassment of those whose judgment, in hindsight, was not so good.

America's security apparently has not been compromised by unlocking these secrets, but, admittedly, neither has our bargaining position with North Vietnam been strengthened by what has happened. The state of national morale is not exceptionally high, either, but it will recover. We concur with those who say had the war been a success, these secrets on how the war was orchestrated would be much less interesting.

In the cacaphony, we hear those who remind us that much of what the Pentagon papers portend to say for the first time was reported or alluded to earlier. But few recognized its meaning at the time.

Therefore we should question whether the nation need wallow

in mascochism and finger-pointing, when there's blame enough to go all around, including the press.

To be seen is whether the public, which has tended to blame the press for much of what's wrong with America, will recognize that it, too, is the beneficiary of the decision. Emerging equally are the peoples' right to know and the press' right to publish.

But regardless of the ruling, the press and government will always dance around the secrecy question, which boils down to a matter of responsibility and judgment of both.

The court has given a vote of confidence to the press on both scores.

THE ARIZONA REPUBLIC
Phoenix, Ariz., July 2, 1971

The Supreme Court's 6 to 3 decision, rejecting the government's request for an injunction to block publication of stories based on a secret Pentagon study of U.S. involvement in the Vietnam war, does not come anywhere near revealing the doubt and confusion the individual justices felt over the many grave q u e s t i o n s involved.

In fact, the nine separate opinions covered almost the entire range of arguments on the question of the First Amendment guarantee of a free press and the government's historic right to protect national security.

We believe the majority decision was the only one acceptable in a free society. Although several justices ranged far afield developing extraneous ideological positions, the vital question before the court was whether the press can be prevented in advance from publishing classified information.

The answer, thankfully, is that it cannot. Nevertheless, five of the justices implied that if newspapers print materials that could actually jeopardize the U.S. military or diplomatic stance, the papers and their editors could be tried for criminal violations of the Espionage Act.

In other words, the court said that the government cannot exercise prior restraint, but in exercising their professional judgment editors must be prepared to accept the consequences.

This is hardly a revolutionary doctrine. It is the guiding principle of any free press, whose editors are daily faced with decisions involving judgment, possible libel, and taste.

From the beginning we have defended the right of the New York Times and Washington Post to publish the stories. We frankly question their motives for doing so, since the predictable result of the disclosures complements the ideological positions of both papers by embarrassing the government and casting doubt on a foreign venture of which they disapprove. But their motives were never at issue in this case, and neither paper should have to answer for them.

Nevertheless, we s h a r e Chief Justice Warren Burger's astonishment that the newspapers (particularly the Times, which originally broke the story), failed to perform "one of the basic and simple duties of every citizen with respect to the discovery or possession of stolen property or secret documents" — namely, withholding publication until their executives conferred with government officials to see if an agreement could be reached about publication.

By placing the responsibility on the shoulders of newspapers, the S u p r e m e Court has reaffirmed that editors have a solemn public responsibility. And that, it seems to us, is what the First Amendment is all about.

Herald News
Fall River, Mass., July 2, 1971

The Supreme Court's decision to permit the New York Times and other newspapers to continue publication of Pentagon documents concerning the Vietnam war is based on a realistic appraisal of what, if any, damage will be done to the nation's interests by allowing them to be read. This was the contention of the government: that the country would be damaged by their publication. The Supreme Court evidently disagrees with the State Department and the Department of Justice.

It is a fact that up to date the sections of the Pentagon papers that have been published have divulged little that was not known or inferred years ago. The national interest may have been hurt by the Vietnam war, although this is still debatable. But it is hard to think it will be hurt by the compilation of old documents and memoranda which prove how reluctantly and painfully one administration after another permitted the Vietnam involvement to grow worse. Anyone who read the newspapers of those years knew that this was so.

The concealment from the public of strategic plans is nothing new, nor especially reprehensible. Nor has there been evidence of anything that can be reasonably called a conspiracy to get us deeper into what has turned out to be an especially unproductive war.

The papers are embarrassing to individuals who made wrong guesses, and their number includes almost everyone principally involved. But again, the fact that wrong guesses were made is hardly surprising in view of the way the war has turned out. The Justice Department failed to prove its contention to the satisfaction of the Supreme Court, and on the whole, most Americans will agree with the court's decision.

Furthermore, now that publication has begun, to halt it would create even more suspicion and rumors of double-dealing in Washington. As the Supreme Court has indicated, the best thing for the nation and the government is to permit the publication to resume.

THE DAILY OKLAHOMAN
Oklahoma City, Okla. July 2, 1971

BY a 6-3 vote, the Supreme Court ruled the government hadn't proved that the national interest would be damaged by further publication of parts of the now celebrated Pentagon papers.

Since the case turned on this point and not on the clear violation of the Espionage Act that occurred, an interesting question arises. Does the ruling mean that the burden of proof rests on the government in every conceivable future challenge affecting the millions of classified documents in its possession?

Like so many other thorny questions arising under representative government, the case of the purloined papers involves issues that never will be resolved to the satisfaction of everybody.

There are times certainly when a government requires secrecy in its diplomatic and military affairs, and must withhold information it considers inimical to national security. But it is equally apparent that overclassification is used often to cover mistaken judgments as well as to protect legitimate secrets. And if these mistaken judgments — however well intended — never are brought to light, the officials responsible for them never are required to answer to the public.

As Thomas Jefferson once observed, "Honest error must be arrested where its toleration leads to public ruin." But how is error to be arrested if it's never disclosed? On balance, therefore, the national interest was best served by the majority ruling which recognized the importance of an informed citizenry and refused to impose prior restraint on the newspapers.

For the way will be open to complete censorship if the government ever is empowered to prevent publication of whatever it suspects a newspaper intends to print. The newspapers still are accountable under the Espionage Act, and the Justice Department is free to bring criminal charges, but only after publication and not before.

In his dissent to the majority opinion, Chief Justice Warren Burger oversimplified the issue by viewing it in terms of stolen goods. Information is more than merchandise and a newspaper is worth more than the paper it's printed on.

"In proportion as the structure of government gives force to public opinion," said George Washington, "it is essential that public opinion should be enlightened." The history of American government is replete with similar expressions, and they properly dominate the majority opinion in the present case.

THE INDIANAPOLIS STAR
Indianapolis, Ind., July 2, 1971

The freedom of the press, for 15 taut days caught in the middle between the competitive bad judgments of the New York Times and several collaborative newspapers on the one hand and the administration on the other, has survived.

The United States Supreme Court has ruled against the government's suit to prohibit publication of the top-secret Pentagon Vietnam war study which had come into possession of the Times. The court cited a previous decision holding that "any system of prior restraints of expression comes to this court bearing a heavy presumption against its constitutional validity." It held that the government had failed to show an impending danger to the nation sufficient to override that constitutional consideration.

This is the status quo ante. The American press is still free.

We said before and we still believe the Times used very bad judgment in deciding to publish material from the Pentagon Papers at this time. We can see no good to be accomplished by doing so. The action simply provided additional nasty fodder for those who try to paint the United States as a completely wicked, conscienceless ogre.

The administration showed matching bad judgment in going to court in an attempt to block the publication. By doing so it brought on blaring international publicity for a drab rehearsal of past history that otherwise would have drawn more yawns than attention.

What's worse, the administration put itself in the position of seeking to establish a gag on the press that is one of the trappings of dictatorship.

If the government could suppress the truth simply by stamping it "secret," then the government would be able to cover up all manner of blunders, thefts, bribery, conspiracies and lies. Newspapers would not be permitted to publish the truth when they discover it. Television and radio stations would not be able to broadcast it.

A people denied the truth about its government is a people that can be readily enslaved. Our republican form of government could be swept away by a dictatorship of bureaucrats with a rubber stamp, and the people would not know it until too late.

The freedom of the press is for the protection of the people. It safeguards them against the establishment of tyranny by stealth and subterfuge.

THE STATES-ITEM
New Orleans, La., July 2, 1971

Truth has triumphed in one of the most dramatic confrontations in American history.

The United States Supreme Court, by a 6-3 vote, ruled Wednesday that The New York Times, The Washington Post and, by implication, other newspapers, could resume publication of a heretofore secret Pentagon study of the origin and development of the American involvement in Vietnam.

Thus ended before the Supreme Court, which has known controversy before, the confrontation between the government of the United States and two of the nation's great newspapers over the issue of freedom of the press.

Because there was disagreement on the court, with no single opinion being able to command a majority, the case did not produce a landmark decision. Instead it produced a three-paragraph ruling which, on its face, would appear limited to the facts of the particular case.

The court chose not to meet head-on the issue of prior publication restraint. It avoided the issue by stating that any attempt by the government to block news articles prior to publication bears "a heavy burden of presumption against its constitutional validity." In this case — the first effort by the government in the history of the United States to enjoin publication in a newspaper on grounds of national security — the court declared "the government has not met that burden."

However, by stating the burden had not been met in this case, the court raised the possibility that it might sanction prior restraint under certain c o n d i t i o n s. Indeed, three of the six justices who voted for the newspapers—Brennan, Stewart and White — indicated they might vote for restraint under certain circumstances, i.e., w h e r e there was a danger of direct, immediate, and irreparable harm to the nation's security.

Thus the court did not preclude the possibility of enjoining publication of different information under different circumstances. Indeed, if these three justices had voted with the three dissenting justices in this case—Burger, Blackmun and Harland — the vote would be exactly opposite.

The other three judges who voted for the newspapers — Black. Douglas and Marshall — said the First Amendment leaves no room for government restraint of any kind.

Justice Black, who throughout his long and distinguished career on the nation's highest court has steadfastly maintained that the freedoms guaranteed by the First Amendment are absolute, summed it up best, in our opinion:

"Far from deserving condemnation for their courageous reporting, The New York Times, The Washington Post and other newspapers should be commended for s e r v i n g the purpose that the Founding Fathers saw so clearly. In revealing the workings of government that led to the Vietnam war, the newspapers nobly did precisely that which the founders hoped and trusted they would do."

Portland Press Herald
Portland, Me., July 2, 1971

The decision of the U.S. Supreme Court in the case of the Pentagon Papers should not be received with great elation by the news media.

The reaffirmation of the freedom of the press is important. It is welcome and just. But it does not free the New York Times, where the issue was initiated, from the taint of unethical and irresponsible behavior. There can be no complete satisfaction in employing wrong methods to reveal another wrong.

There was a significant difference in approach among the six in the majority. While four held that the First Amendment, by its very wording, barred restraints on the newspapers, two of the six found as they did because no law authorizes such restraints. These justices made it very clear that they were

not saying that under no circumstance could an injunction be issued to halt publication of government plans or operations.

We should be equally attentive to the admonition of such as Chief Justice Warren E. Burger who noted that free speech rights are not absolute and that the Times should have reported to the government that it was in possession of "purloined documents."

The Times needn't have sacrificed its "scoop" in the interest of propriety. It could have published an article indicating the possession of the documents and their content and insisted that they be declassified. The court judgment could have been accomplished via that route and the stature of the newspaper would have been enhanced.

When national security is in dispute we do not believe the authority for declassification of "secret" material rests with a group of newspaper editors.

On the other side of the issue, the federal government should find some lesson in all this too. Pentagon filing cabinets, and those of m a n y other departments and agencies, undoubtedly are bursting with classified documents the content of which in no way reflects on national security. Much of that material probably would be of little interest to the people. But some would be.

The "confidential," "secret," and "top secret" classifications undoubtedly are abused and this case should promote a sincere effort to eliminate this abuse. Government,

even in the most scrupulous of democratic concepts cannot operate without some secrecy. But it is very easily overdone.

There can be no positive security against the possibility that a person in a sensitive role will one day violate that trust. The promise of personal gain or the threat of personal damage may make a man turn traitor. Another may experience a change in personal convictions to the degree that he will make his own judgment superior to all others and violate the trust he once enjoyed.

The press exceeds its rights when it becomes a party to such action even though, as in this instance, the highest tribunal may ultimately decide that the national security is not in jeopardy.

The Salt Lake Tribune

Salt Lake City, Utah, July 2, 1971

Once again the people's right to know has been upheld. By refusing to permit the government to block news articles prior to publication, the Supreme Court has served notice that the First Amendment's guarantee of a free press means exactly what it says.

In a response said to be without precedent, all nine justices wrote opinions. Six supported and three opposed the New York Times' and Washington Post's right to publish a Pentagon study of the Vietnam War which had been declared top secret by the government.

In their reasoning the justices divided roughly into three groups: Black, Marshall and Douglas held that the First Amendment's guarantee of a free press forbids any judicial restraint; Brennen, White and Stewart said the press could not be muzzled except to prevent immediate and irreparable damage to the nation. and Burger, Blackmun and Harlan said the court should not refuse to enforce the executive branch's conclusion that the material should be kept confidential — so long as a cabinet level officer had personally decided that it should be.

Justice Stewart put basic responsibility for protecting state secrets precisely where it belongs — on the executive branch. "It is the duty of the executive," he wrote, "to protect state secrets through its own security measures and not the duty of the courts to do it by banning news articles."

So much material is now classified as secret the government cannot possibly guard it all. If only the genuinely sensitive material were so classified the executive could keep better track of it and newspapers and other responsible media would once more respect the "secret" label.

Although the immediate result of the decision permits resumed publication of the Pentagon papers, the long-term effects are uncertain. Did the Supreme Court, by permitting prior restraint of publication while it heard appeals from lower courts, set a precedent for some degree of new government control over the press? Or did the court's decision speak so clearly that no district court judge would dare attempt prior restraint again unless a direct threat of dire and irreparable harm was alleged?

This was the first attempt of the government to enjoin publication on grounds of national security. As noted, three justices upheld the press' right to publish regardless of national security considerations but three others — enough to swing a future case — said restraint was justified if a genuine threat to national security was posed. In the Pentagon papers case they concluded no such threat existed and thus voted to permit publication.

The basic issue of the government's right to exert prior restraint for national security reasons remains unsettled. Possibly it always will be and for the same reason the Pentagon papers case was the first such test. That reason is simply that the American press, for all its failings, is not irresponsible.

The fact that never before has it been taken to court on a charge of endangering national security is ample evidence of the press' good judgment and voluntary self restraint in such matters. That reputation is further enhanced by this week's Supreme Court decision.

The Oregonian

Portland, Ore., July 2, 1971

The Supreme Court split 6-3 on the crucial issue in the government's historic case to stop publication of the Pentagon papers. The key question was: Does the Constitution permit prior restraint of publication? The majority held that, at least in this instance, the government had not shown that such publication would "surely result in direct, immediate and irreparable damage" to the national interest. The minority of three justices, including Chief Justice Warren Burger, argued that the case had been considered in "feverish" haste and that, in any event, the constitutional powers of the executive weighed against an absolute application of the First Amendment's provision that "Congress shall make no law . . . abridging the freedom of the press."

Thus, the case turned on one issue — prior restraint. But the extraordinary abundance of opinions — one by each member of the court — provides interesting insights on other matters. The court is shown to be at considerable variance on the interpretation of the First Amendment. On the other hand, it appears to be in general agreement that publication of classified documents in the press is an entirely different matter than their revelation to unauthorized persons in the manner implied in the case against Dr. Daniel Ellsberg.

Three members of the court — Justices Black, Douglas and Brennen — see the First Amendment as a bar to prior restraint of the press and object even to temporary injunctions such as delayed publication of the reports in some newspapers. On the contrary, the three in the minority — Chief Justice Burger and Justices Blackmun and Harlan — see such restraint as essential in some cases in consideration of the constitutional powers of the executive in matters of foreign affairs and national defense.

The swing men on the court on prior restraint and related issues are revealed to be Justices White and Stewart, each of whom joined in the other's opinion concurring in the majority ruling. They were not convinced of the government's real need for an injunction in this case, but they dwelt at some length on the need for a certain degree of secrecy in national affairs. Moreover, they imply that their votes might have gone against the newspapers if the government's charge had been a criminal one involving publication of material protected in the nation's criminal code. Justice Marshall, the sixth member of the majority, objected to what he called the government's effort to get the court, not Congress, to make law.

Justice White, with Justice Stewart's concurrence, put emphasis on the distinction between the newspaper case and the Ellsberg case, although he did not mention Ellsberg. It is "a criminal act," he pointed out, "for any unauthorized possessor of a document relating to national defense either (1) willfully to communicate or cause to be communicated that document to any person not entitled to receive it or (2) willfully to retain the document and fail to deliver it to an officer of the United States entitled to receive it."

Significantly, the three justices in the minority made record of their endorsement of Justice White's opinion on this point. That puts five justices, a majority, on record as recognizing a basis for prosecution of someone in Dr. Ellsberg's self-confessed position.

These nine opinions, although hastily drawn, constitute the most authoritative statement available on the government's power in relation to the press. It was a historic case in that the U. S. government had never heretofore sought to restrain newspaper publication by court injunction. And the majority opinion is historic in its reaffirmation of the real purpose of the freedom of the press clause in the First Amendment.

In the words of Justice Stewart: "The only effective restraint upon executive policy and power in the areas of national defense and international affairs may lie in an enlightened citizenry — in an informed and critical public opinion which alone can here protect the values of democratic government."

But those who may have the erroneous impression that this decision gives free rein to the press or any individual to reveal secret documents indiscriminately and with impunity had better read these opinions. They are not comforting for anyone who would, on his own, release material that might pose a grave and immediate danger to the security of the United States.

Los Angeles Times

Los Angeles, Calif., March 10, 1972

Too much secrecy in government breeds error and deception and undermines public confidence upon which a democratic government rests. But the ideal of no secrecy presupposes a different kind of world than the one we live in.

The people must be as fully informed as possible; the government must protect the confidentiality of some of its processes, especially in foreign affairs and in matters affecting national security. The problem is to reconcile these two equally valid principles.

Since the beginning of World War II, the equation has been out of balance. Through the system of classification of millions of documents, secrecy has been pervasive in government. As a result, public debate has been crippled and sometimes foreclosed on national policy of the utmost importance; momentous decisions have been made in secrecy or with only enough information dribbled to the people to entice public support.

In view of this, President Nixon's decision to reform the classification of sensitive documents is welcome. The significance of the action was underscored by the President's statement that it was "designed to lift the veil of secrecy which now enshrouds altogether too many papers written by employes of the federal establishment . . ."

The details of the executive order suggest that the President is making more than a polite bow to the increasing public protest of recent years against government secrecy. He cut in half—to 12—the number of agencies authorized to stamp documents top secret. He reduced from 5,100 to 1,860 the number of persons authorized to use that stamp. He imposed stricter criteria for classifying papers. More significantly, the official wielding the stamp must be prepared to justify the action.

The extent to which secrecy—to use the President's word—"enshrouds" the government can be understood by the fact that 160 million pages of government documents were marked top secret, secret or confidential from 1946 to 1954. Under the new order, top secret papers can become public after 10 years. The process can be halted only by an official with top secret classifying authority, who must supply written reasons.

The four exemptions to the new procedure come well within the President's authority to protect information supplied by a foreign government and to guard security information such as atomic secrets, codes, intelligence operations and related areas. But even in military matters, secrecy has gone beyond reason. Last year a retired Pentagon security officer estimated the Pentagon files contained about 20 million classified documents of which he said only 1% to 5% "must legitimately be guarded in the national interest."

Illegitimate secrecy divides the people from their government; it is corrupting and dangerous and leads to disaster. The problem in this age of the hydrogen bomb is complex, but it can be brought under control if tackled with intelligence and determination.

THE COMMERCIAL APPEAL

Memphis, Tenn., March 10, 1972

A PROBLEM OF confidence has assumed crisis proportions between the government and the American people with unsettling frequency during the last 10 years — unsettling to both sides in what should be a stable if not ecstatic affair of state. President Nixon, a victim of the so-called "credibility gap" and the shock effect of the Pentagon Papers, has moved to limit secrecy surrounding government documents.

In an executive order signed Wednesday, the President directed that greater restraint be used in classifying documents and that those already classified be made public on a quicker schedule than in the past.

Administration spokesmen acknowledged that the success of the order will depend largely on both the discretion and the commitment of many officials: The fine line between "national security" and the "public's right to know" still must be drawn by human beings, most of whom are bureaucrats. If they ignore the spirit of the President's order after June 1, when it goes into effect, its impact will be severely reduced.

AT THIS POINT, however, a measure of optimism is not unwarranted. The President sounded like he meant business. "The many abuses of the security system," he said, "can no longer be tolerated. Fundamental to our way of life is the belief that when information which properly belongs to the public is systematically withheld by those in power, the people soon become ignorant of their own affairs, distrustful of those who manage them, and — eventually — incapable of determining their own destinies."

These words apply not only to the federal government in Washington but also to every other government, whether at the state or local level. Members of the Memphis City Council and Board of Education, who haven't been able to shake off the crutch of closed meetings, should take note.

The problem of confidence is nothing new in American government or politics. George Washington is said to have hated the press until his death, although he vehemently espoused the need for an informed public. President Polk had his "Gulf of Tonkin" when he went to war with Mexico in 1846. Just before America entered World War II, Roosevelt declared for political reasons that it would never happen. Then there were flimsy coverups by Eisenhower over the U2 flights and by John Kennedy over the Bay of Pigs, before Lyndon Johnson went what some consider the last mile of deceit over Vietnam.

Nixon's order may create an atmosphere more conducive to openness, even if it doesn't complement honesty with trust in one magic night under an election-year moon.

Had the order been in effect last summer, many of the documents in the Pentagon Papers would have been declassified when they were published. Large numbers of documents from the Truman and Eisenhower administrations should become available. Papers dealing with the Bay of Pigs and the Cuban missile crisis will be eligible for inspection unless the government can prove that they would adversely affect the national interest.

Fewer departments and many fewer officials will be empowered to classify documents. In fact, the opportunity for the bureaucrats to make work with their red stamps will be reduced by more than 50 per cent.

Some officials believe that national policies, especially in defense and foreign affairs, have become so complex that the public should be satisfied to let the experts take care of things without being asked a lot of ignorant and bothersome questions.

BUT WHEN the public's right to know becomes bad for national welfare, except in cases of national security, the kind of government in question ceases to be a democracy. And even cases of security offer room for argument. If rumors and half-complete reports about the Bay of Pigs had been published before the invasion, as they could have been by at least one major newspaper, the United States probably would have been spared an international embarrassment.

Moreover, the very complexity of our society and world demand that greater efforts be made to inform the public because it becomes more difficult to do so. Information must flow freely if the nation is to maintain a system of freedom.

ALBUQUERQUE JOURNAL

Albuquerque, N.M., March 9, 1972

We hope President Nixon's new rules for classification of government documents will do what he expects—"lift the veils of secrecy which now enshroud altogether too many papers written by employes of the federal establishment."

The President cut in half—from 24 to 12—the number of departments and agencies which can use the "Top Secret" designation. Formerly 5 1 0 0 employes of the State Department, Pentagon and Central Intelligence Agency were authorized to make the classification. Now approximately 1860 will have the power.

The President makes it clear that some government information will continue to be kept secret for years if national security is involved. But he also ordered a review and possible reclassification of an estimated 460 million pages of classified documents that have accumulated since the beginning of World War II. He also provided for the automatic declassification for material after the passage of time—generally from six to 10 years.

The new rules permit use of the "Top Secret" stamp only if disclosure "could reasonably be expected to damage national security." Previously such a designation was permitted if the originator of the material had even a remote expectation of damage to the national security.

Nixon firmly believes the new rules will prevent classification of material "to conceal inefficiency or administrative error" in government.

At least part of the President's action must be attributed to the outcry which resulted from publication of the Pentagon Papers and the Anderson Papers and court decisions which grew out of the Pentagon Papers issue.

Members of the House Government Information subcommittee conducting hearings into government classification procedures with an eye to strengthening the Freedom of Information Act were miffed by the President's executive order because of the absence of opportunity for Congress to consider alternatives.

While cheering the President's new order, we would also hope the subcommittee does not end its work. The order changing classification rules was long overdue but even more must be done to assure the public of its right to know what its elected government is doing.

Long Island Press

New York, N.Y., March 12, 1972

The public's ability to get the information it needs to make decisions—it's right to know what's happening — is basic to the health of American democracy. Perhaps more than anything else, it sets us apart from totalitarian systems.

To assure that this right shall not be abridged, the founding fathers wrote into the Bill of Rights that "Congress shall make no law respecting . . . the freedom of speech, or of the press . . ." Though freedom of the press has often been attacked it has happily survived, in principle at least.

The most recent example, of course, was the Pentagon Papers dispute, in which the late Supreme Court Justice Hugo Black, in one of his last and most important decisions, wrote: "The press was to serve the governed, not the governors . . . the press was protected so that it could bare the secrets of government and inform the people."

But while the press' right to print and to inform endures, so do the attacks—some frontal, some devious, all dangerous. These include hiding embarrassing information behind "classified" and "top secret" labels, the increased subpenaing of journalists by grand juries and congressional committees, efforts to impose pre-publication censorship and threats of new regulations.

* * *

President Nixon, therefore, has taken a major, and most welcome, step to limit the secrecy surrounding government documents. In the first major overhaul of classification procedures since 1953,

Mr. Nixon last week signed an executive order, effective June 1, which would reduce the number of documents that can be hidden behind classified labels and speed the declassification of secret papers.

"The major abuses of the security system can no longer be tolerated," Mr. Nixon said. "Fundamental to our way of life is the belief that when information which properly belongs to the public is systematically withheld by those in power, the people soon become ignorant of their own words, distrustful of those who manage them, and—eventually—incapable of determining their own destinies."

It remains to be seen, of course, if Mr. Nixon's aides put into practice what the boss preaches. The success of the program still depends on the discretion of officials who head the major governmental agencies—and in the past, under Democratic and Republican administrations alike, have shown disturbing tendency to enshroud their errors in a veil of secrecy.

As Rep. William S. Moorhead, chairman of a panel probing bureaucratic secrecy practices, said, it still is possible for a president to hide embarrassing documents until he is out of office . . . succeeded, perhaps by another who might not have won if the facts were known.

While Mr. Nixon has moved in the right direction, the best answer remains a non-partisan, professional classification and declassification board to make the final decision. The memory of the Pentagon Papers and the Anderson Papers on the India-Pakistan War is too fresh to settle for less.

* * *

The increased subpenaing of newsmen by grand juries and congressional committees is another way to harass journalists and impede their search for news.

Based on a survey of more than 1,000 newsmen and an analysis of constitutional law and subpena practices, a University of Michigan legal scholar concludes that newsmen should be granted "absolute" and "unconditional" immunity from such subpena.

The study by Prof. Vincent A. Blasi was released by the Reporters Committee for Freedom of the Press, which requested the report but had no part in the research or writing.

Prof. Blasi notes the importance of protecting confidential sources, which are essential to the writers of in-depth, interpretive news—none involving grand jury or investigative panels—and sees few instances in which newsmen should be required to disclose such sources.

Thirteen states already have passed statutes giving newsmen immunity to protect their sources. The other states and the Congress should follow the example. The news sources aren't the real issue; the public's right to know is.

ST. LOUIS POST-DISPATCH
St. Louis, Mo., March 10, 1972

In issuing an executive order designed to reduce secrecy in government, President Nixon succinctly summed up the dangers in a system of excessive classification. "When information which properly belongs to the public is systematically withheld by those in power," he said, "the people soon become ignorant of their own affairs, distrustful of those who manage them, and—eventually—incapable of determining their own destinies."

Despite the antidemocratic implications of secrecy, the trend has continued under every President for the past 30 years—until now the Government has a mountainous store of documents walled off from public access, most of them put there through the tendency of bureaucrats to follow the maxim: when in doubt, classify. The system, as Mr. Nixon said, "has frequently served to conceal bureaucratic mistakes or to prevent 'embarrassment to officials and the Administration.

That is exactly what was involved in attempts to maintain the secrecy of the Pentagon history of the Vietnam War, an effort to which the Nixon Administration, paradoxically, lent its full resources despite the fact that the mistakes and the deceptions being covered up were those of the previous Administration. Now Mr. Nixon has issued a welcome executive order to reduce secrecy by establishing timetables for automatic declassification and by cutting down on the number of officials and agencies entitled to classify government documents. But judgment as to the effect of the order should be withheld in view of doubts about it expressed in Congress. The order incidentally makes the continued investigation of Pentagon Papers leaks inconsistent with the Administration's stated philosophy on secrecy.

So is the Administration's resistance to a suit by 33 members of Congress challenging the scope of the power claimed by the Government to withhold from Congress and the public documents relating to last fall's underground nuclear test in Alaska. The U.S. Court of Appeals for the District of Columbia has already ruled that the entire file on the test cannot be kept secret simply because some of the material in it is sensitive. The Justice Department is saying that the judgment as to what should be secret is solely within the discretion of the Executive Branch. The Supreme Court has agreed to review the case.

The most charitable explanation of the Administration's conflicting words and acts—its avowed commitment to greater openness in government, on the one hand, and its vigorous defense of secrecy in the courts, on the other—is that the Executive Branch favors a relaxation of secrecy only on its own terms. No act of Congress clearly authorizes the massive application of secrecy stamps that has been undertaken. The classification system is based on such a flimsy legal foundation and has been so flagrantly abused that the whole concept ought to be overhauled—not just by executive order but by a congressional statute limiting the kinds of data that may be kept secret.

New York Post
New York, N.Y., March 9, 1972

It is hard to shake off a certain skepticism about President Nixon's latest pledge to "lift the veil of secrecy" concealing classified federal documents. Apparently the staged process of disclosure may take considerably longer than Salome's dance—which involved no fewer than seven veils—but is not guaranteed to be as revealing.

There is no question that the fundamental issue is timely. The House government information subcommittee has been conducting hearings on the subject, and the U.S. Supreme Court has just accepted a case in which official secrecy is at issue.

Indeed, it seems obvious that the President's executive order, embellished with many eloquent affirmations of the people's right to know, was issued at this time to suggest deepening executive concern about the problem—and also to disarm increasingly vocal critics.

These are the practical plans: the number of departments, agencies and personnel authorized to classify material will be substantially reduced and provision will be made for phased declassification of many documents.

Even so, disclosure that "could reasonably be expected" to impair "national security" may be forbidden and the earliest a "confidential" document might be made public would be six years after classification. "Top secret" material would be reduced on a timetable to "secret," then "confidential" status, to be aired after 10 years.

Those are remarkably restrictive margins for the self-described "open Administration" originally introduced by the President. The classification decisions are not apparently subject to any process of independent review. Broader "freedom of information" questions are given no thoughful reappraisal; there is nothing, for instance, that would impel Henry A. Kissinger to appear for public questioning by the Senate Foreign Relations Committee.

In other words, the executive order from the White House on information policy flunks many tests of basic credibility. Congress and the courts may be able to define the limits of secrecy with larger vision and detachment.

The Times-Picayune
New Orleans, La., March 10, 1972

Simultaneous with House hearings on freedom of information, President Nixon signed an executive order this week to cut down on governmental secrecy and to speed up the release of classified documents.

With announcement of his action he asserted, "The many abuses of the security system can no longer be tolerated." After declaring the present federal system of classifying documents does not "meet the standards of an open and democratic society," he said too many papers have been classified for too long a time.

Mr. Nixon will find popular support for any sincere effort to facilitate the right of the public to know what goes on in its government, but we'd guess there will be intramural opposition in the bureaucracy.

In saying that "classification has frequently served to conceal bureaucratic mistakes," the President virtually lifted the words of those who complain about the shortcomings of the Freedom of Information Act which became effective five years ago.

By terms of the new executive order, as of June 1 papers are to be stamped as classified only if unauthorized release of the contents "could reasonably be expected to damage the national security." This new expression may be enough to improve some discretionary judgments.

But Mr. Nixon needs to speak out on some of the other irritating barriers erected by bureaucrats to conceal public records. Ralph Nader's Center for Study of Responsive Law lists some of the artifices for concealing, and most investigative newsmen, we would suppose, have encountered some of them.

These include such subterfuges as the allegation that private trade secrets are involved when they aren't; high fees for copies of information; mingling of unclassified material with that which is, causing all to remain secret; needlessly protracted delays in making information available and concealment in investigation files.

Mr. Nixon, whose administration has been burned several times on "secret" documents, takes a desirable step toward loosening up information. He could have gone farther without breaching propriety.

Des Moines Tribune

Des Moines, Iowa, March 11, 1972

President Nixon has issued an executive order relaxing secrecy rules. Accompanying the order was a statement in which Nixon promised to put the "full force of my office" behind a revised system of classifying government documents.

Under the new plan, which will go into effect June 1, the number of federal departments and agencies authorized to classify documents will be reduced from 24 to 12, and the number of individuals entitled to put a "top secret" stamp on documents will be cut from 5,100 to 1,860.

Unless exempted for "national security" reasons, classified documents are to be downgraded automatically over a period of years and eventually declassified. "Top secret" documents, for example, will fall into the "secret" category after two years, then fall to "confidential" after another two years before removal from classification after a total of 10 years.

That is a very large "unless" "National security"

has been the reason for almost all the secrecy which has denied the public important knowledge of its government's operations since World War II. With that exception unlimited, all the changes in classification and classifiers could mean very little.

Nixon acknowledged that present secrecy rules have "frequently served to conceal bureaucratic mistakes or to prevent embarrassment to officials and administrations." He insisted that his order provided for a "critically important shift" in the classification system by putting the "burden of proof" on the administrators who want to classify materials rather than on the citizens who claim a right to know what the government is doing.

This sounds fine. But government documents deemed particularly sensitive to national security still could be classified for as long as 30 years, possibly longer. After 10 years, a citizen could request a review of the classified material, provided he could describe the record "with sufficient partic-

ularity that it may be identified" and, furthermore, that the materials could be "obtained with a reasonable amount of effort." This provision, it seems to us, puts the burden on the citizen rather than the bureaucrat.

Under the revised classification system, the American people would still need a Daniel Ellsberg to pry the Pentagon Papers out from under official secrecy.

The Nixon Administration, like the Johnson Administration before it, has been criticized repeatedly for resorting to executive orders and classification authority to hide information and documents which are politically embarrassing.

The smaller number of bureaucrats empowered in the new order to classify could hide just as much information as ever, as arbitrarily as ever. Whether they do depends on how President Nixon puts the "full force of his office" behind freedom of information in letter and spirit.

The Cincinnati Post

TIMES ⭑ STAR

Cincinnati, Ohio, March 11, 1972

It is possible a "showdown" of sorts over the 1967 federal "freedom of information" law may be in the works.

This law supposedly opens up government records to the public eye, with some loosely defined exceptions.

But hardly any government agency gives up information without a struggle. Under cover of such excuses as "It is not in the public interest" or "It would serve no useful purpose," bureaucrats continually withhold documents and other information.

President Nixon now has issued a new order, designed to "lift the veil of secrecy which now shrouds too many papers."

A House committee is investigating the effectiveness of the 1967 law over the last five years.

And the Supreme Court has agreed to hear an appeal from the Nixon Administration's refusal to let go of a series of reports submitted to the President in advance of last fall's atomic test at Amchitka, Alaska.

None of these things may turn the trick, but they could help.

Nixon's order, if taken literally, could open up a good many records needlessly stamped "top secret" or "confidential." The President drastically has reduced the number of officials entitled to "classify" government documents, tightened the reasons for such action and automatically declassified masses of papers. And he has put the onus for classifying records on the man who does it.

The 1967 law permits any citizen denied information by a government agency to go to court and sue for it. It is such a case the Supreme Court now will decide.

The House committee can add to the pressure for freer information by the testimony and evidence it produces.

ONE OF THE FIRST WITNESSES was James C. Hagerty, press secretary to President Eisenhower (and a good one).

Hagerty said that during his eight years in office he constantly was confronted with restrictions on information he was ready to release.

"I would then actually have to take these papers to the President," he said, "and have him declassify them on the spot.

"The only thing that was 'top secret' about that was what he would say when he had to go through this nonsense."

FEW PRESIDENTS have taken that attitude, and it is the ingrown nature of the bureaucracy to cover up.

Perhaps Nixon's new order, or pressure from Congress, or even a Supreme Court decision, may not change things much. But they might.

And while the House committee is at it, it should use its influence to break the logjam on information from Congress — which was careful to exempt itself from the provisions of the "freedom of information" law that it passed.

The Hartford Courant

Hartford, Conn., March 11, 1972

President Nixon has just issued a badly-needed executive order placing strict limits on the authority of government agencies to classify documents and keep them secret.

The order, which takes effect June 1, is of course, an outgrowth of the leak of the Pentagon Papers. That incident served to put the spotlight on widespread overuse of secrecy stamps and the lack of an effective means to declassify documents once the secrecy is no longer needed.

The President's order has two main effects. First, it cuts by as much as two thirds the numbers of agencies and officials empowered to classify documents, particularly in the upper-drawer "secret" and "top secret" categories.

Second, it provides for automatic declassification of a document after a fixed period of time unless the government can bear the burden of proving that the secrecy is still needed. That will reverse the present system under which a document, once classified, stays that way unless, in a rare event, someone declassifies it.

There should be no doubt by now that action of this sort is not only necessary but long overdue. Overclassification has for too long been a tool of bureaucrats seeking to hide their mistakes or avoid sticky questions. Both the availability of public information and the credibility of the government have suffered as a result.

The lack of an effective declassification system may present an even more serious problem. We have already set a precedent under which an individual can see some sense of moral duty in undertaking do-it-yourself declassification for what he sees as a public service. It means that the most effective declassification machinery is not the government's. Instead, the decisions are in the hands of anyone with access to classified files and a copying machine.

The leaks of the Pentagon Papers and other documents in similar incidents appear to have done little damage to national security, but we cannot hope that the leaders' judgment will always be as

good. It is almost inevitable that should the practice continue, someone some day, either through bad judgment or less noble instincts, will put out something that is really damaging.

The government can help curb that practice by putting its own house in order and restoring confidence in its use of secrecy stamps. There is no temptation to leak overclassified material if there is no overclassified material to leak.

The President's order will not, of course, immediately produce that degree of perfection. It is, however, a giant step forward. Congress is considering parallel action that would add the force of statutory law to the President's action and could possibly create a review agency to guard against future abuses.

All are necessary steps that should have been taken long ago. As a case in point, had the President's order been in effect last year, most of the Pentagon Papers would already have been public information.

Watergate
& the Media

The investigation and coverage of the Watergate Affair and related scandals intensified the conflict between the Nixon Administration and the mass media.

Initially, the Watergate break-in was covered as a curious but purely local crime. But persistent investigation by two Washington Post reporters, Bob Woodward and Carl Bernstein, uncovered crucial links in the chain leading from the burglars to high officials in the Committee to Re-Elect the President and the White House.

Most of the media continued to treat the scandal as a minor story until James McCord, one of the men captured inside the Democratic offices, implicated higher-ups in the planning and cover-up of the affair in March 1973.

Stung by the revelations that began appearing in the press, Nixon Administration officials charged the media with inflating the affair to impair or even destroy President Nixon's ability to govern.

Nixon aides deny Post's charges. Nixon Administration officials Oct. 16, 1972 rebutted charges made in the Washington Post that a political sabotage and spying effort involved high Nixon aides. White House Press Secretary Ronald L. Ziegler called the charges "hearsay, innuendo and guilt by association" and said he refused to "dignify" them by discussing them. Clark MacGregor, chairman of the Nixon re-election effort, attacked the Post for using "unsubstantiated charges" to "maliciously" link the White House to Watergate.

Neither spokesman would discuss specific items of the charges. MacGregor left the room after reading his statement, although Ziegler denied that Segretti had ever worked for the White House and MacGregor said he had not worked for either the political or financial branches of the campaign structure.

The Post's executive editor, Benjamin C. Bradlee, said later that none of the facts in its investigative reports about Watergate had been "successfully challenged."

White House denies charge against Haldeman. A Washington Post report linking H.R. Haldeman, President Nixon's White House chief of staff, with a "secret" campaign fund used to finance political espionage was denied Oct. 25 in a statement by the White House press office.

The story also was denied Oct. 25 by White House Press Secretary Ronald L. Ziegler and Nixon campaign director Clark MacGregor. Ziegler said Haldeman never had access to such a fund and, in fact, such a fund never existed. MacGregor said he had been assured by Haldeman that he had never had authority to disburse campaign funds for the President's re-election.

Ziegler also attacked the Post for a "political effort," "character assassination" and "the shoddiest type of journalism."

Newsman jailed. John F. Lawrence, chief of the Washington bureau of the Los Angeles Times, was jailed for several hours Dec. 19 after refusing to turn over to the U.S. district court in the District of Columbia tape recordings of an interview with a key government witness in the case involving the break-in at the Democratic party headquarters at the Watergate building.

The tapes recorded an interview with Alfred C. Baldwin 3rd, who said he had played a role in the break-in. The interview was conducted by Los Angeles Times reporters Jack Nelson and Ronald J. Ostrow and articles based on the interview, naming Baldwin as the source, were published. Lawyers for one of the seven defendants arrested in the break-in, E. Howard Hunt Jr., requested the court to order the Times to produce the tapes for the possible impeachment of Baldwin when he testified in the trial, which was scheduled to begin Jan. 8, 1973.

The request, made Dec. 11, was upheld Dec. 14 by Chief Judge John J. Sirica of the Washington court, who approved subpoenas for Lawrence, as the paper's representative, and for Nelson and Ostrow. Baldwin had advised the court he had destroyed his own recordings of the interview.

The Times and the reporters asked the court to quash the subpoenas to protect "the people's right" to information. The interview, they said, had been obtained on the promise that the material would be held confidential unless Baldwin consented to disclosure.

Since the two interviewers disclosed they had turned over the tapes to the Times, Lawrence, who had played no direct part in the interview, became responsible for producing the tapes. Lawrence declined to surrender them Dec. 19, on the grounds it would be a violation of the First Amendment's guarantee of a free press. He was held in contempt of court and ordered by Sirica to be held in custody until he produced the tapes. The custody lasted for more than two hours until a three-judge panel of the U.S. court of appeals ordered his release pending a hearing the next day. The appeals court Dec. 20 continued the stay of sentence pending an appeal to the Supreme Court. But the contempt action was voided Dec. 21 when Baldwin released the Times from the pledge of confidentiality and the newspaper surrendered the tape recordings to Sirica for private inspection.

Lawrence became the fourth newsman jailed during 1972 for refusing to disclose confidential information. [For further details on confidentiality issue see Chapter 4.]

Nixon comments on TV newsmen. In an interview conducted by Saul Pett of the Associated Press in the Oval Office Dec. 20, President Nixon made several critical remarks about television news commentators. The report of the interview was published Jan. 14, 1973. Among Nixon's remarks:

"I could go up the wall watching TV commentators. I don't. I get my news from the news summary the staff prepares every day and it's great, it gives me all sides. I never watch TV commentators or the news shows when they are about me. That's because I don't want decisions influenced by personal emotional reactions.

"Decision-makers can't be affected by current opinion, by TV barking at you and commentators banging away with the idea that World War III is coming because of the mining of Haiphong. Nor can decisions be affected by the demonstrators outside.

"The major weakness of inexperienced people is that they take things personally, especially in politics, and that can destroy you.

Reporter accuses Justice Department. Jack Nelson, a reporter for the Los Angeles Times, testified Feb. 5 before a House Judiciary subcommittee holding hearings on a news shield law that the Department of Justice tried to suppress an interview concerning the Watergate bugging of Democratic headquarters. He said the Justice Department had threatened to take away immunity from prosecution from Alfred C. Baldwin 3rd if the tapes of the interview were not released to the Justice Department. Nelson called Baldwin the key government witness in the trial.

Butz attacks urban press. Agriculture Secretary Earl L. Butz Feb. 20 attacked the "big city newspapers and urban press" for sensationalizing the price jumps by reporting "grossly unfair and phoney" statistics of annual rate increases. Computation of annual rates, which roughly represent the monthly increase multiplied by 12, often failed to reflect seasonal variations, Butz charged. He singled out press reports of the January Wholesale Price Index.

"Use of such statistics is like saying that if you have a cold this week, it is at the annual rate of 52 colds a year. This kind of arithmetic is preposterous," Butz declared.

Aides to the secretary said Feb. 22 that they had discovered only two newspapers—the Wall Street Journal and the Washington Post—which regularly had reported annual rates of increases.

Watergate subpoenas issued. Subpoenas were issued Feb. 26 for 12 reporters and news executives to relinquish to the Committee to Re-Elect the President their notes or other private material relating to their Watergate articles. The subpoenas were obtained by the committee in connection with civil suits on the case. Five of the subpoenas were issued for Washington Post personnel: publisher Katharine Graham, managing editor Howard Simons and three reporters. Four were directed at Washington Star-News reporters. Others subpoenaed were reporters at the New York Times and Time magazine reporters and Walter J. Sheridan, a former network correspondent.

Court quashes press subpoenas. U.S. District Court Judge Charles R. Richey for the District of Columbia March 21 quashed subpoenas served on representatives of news organizations by the Nixon re-election committee to compel their unpublished material on the Watergate case.

Richey based his action on the 1st Amendment's guarantee of freedom of the press. "This court cannot blind itself to the possible chilling effect the enforcement of . . . these subpoenas would have on the press and the public," he said.

While he did not hold that journalists had an absolute privilege against testifying, Richey said, the courts "must be flexible to some extent" and the particular instances before him were "all exceptional." He also said the committee had failed to show that other sources of evidence "have been exhausted or even approached" or that the material demanded of the journalists was "central to the case."

The news organizations involved were the New York Times, the Washington Post, the Washington Star-News and Time magazine.

One of those subpoenaed, Walter J. Sheridan, a former network correspondent, complied with the subpoena because he did not possess the press privilege at the time.

Nixon's statements called 'inoperative.' Following President Nixon's April 17 announcement that there had been "major developments" from a "new" inquiry he had ordered into the Watergate case, White House Press Secretary Ronald L. Ziegler said the President's previous statements denying Watergate involvement by White House staff members* were now "inoperative" since they were based on "investigations prior to the developments announced today."

The statement drew an angry accusation at the press briefing April 18 from Clark Mollenhoff, reporter for the Des Moines (Iowa) Register and Tribune and former White House aide. "Do you feel free to stand up there," he asked Ziegler, "and lie and put out misinformation and then come around later and say it's all 'inoperative'? That's what you're doing. You're not entitled to any credibility at all."

In reply, Ziegler said of the White House policy on Watergate that he was "not in a position to answer any questions no matter how they are phrased on the subject" since it "could very well prejudice the prosecution or the rights of innocent individuals or indeed the judicial process itself."

AFL-CIO American Newspaper Guild President Charles A. Perlik Jr. sent a telegram to the White House April 18 demanding an apology from the President to the press "on behalf of yourself and all

---

*President Nixon's previous statements on the Watergate case:

At a news conference Aug. 29, 1972, he disclosed that his own staff had investigated the affair and he could "categorically" state that the probe "indicates that no one in the White House staff, no one in this Administration, presently employed, was involved in this very bizarre incident."

The President, at a news conference March 2, reiterated that the White House investigation of Watergate indicated that no one on the White House staff at the time the investigation was conducted was involved "or had knowledge of the Watergate matter."

President Nixon, at an impromptu news conference March 15, said he had confidence in all the White House staffers who had been linked to Watergate.

those in your Administration who have so willingly and freely heaped calumny" on the news media for its coverage of the Watergate case.

Anderson stops publishing grand jury leaks. Syndicated columnist Jack Anderson agreed April 25 after a meeting with federal prosecutors to their request that he stop publishing excerpts of secret testimony before the federal grand jury probing the Watergate Affair.

Anderson had shown other reporters and newsmen copies of grand jury transcripts he had obtained and used as the basis for several columns on the case since April 16. Watergate prosecution sources indicated the material was authentic, and Chief Judge John J. Sirica of the federal court in Washington April 22 ordered an investigation into the leaks. (All grand jury deliberations are secret.) Anderson said he would return transcripts to the court. He said he acted out of "great respect" for Sirica.

Nixon lauds press on Watergate. In a speech in which he accepted responsibility for the Watergate affair while denying any personal involvement in it, President Nixon April 30 paid tribute to the press as part of "the system" that had "brought facts to light" and would "bring those guilty to justice." The system included "a determined grand jury, honest prosecutors, a courageous judge—John Sirica—and a vigorous free press." He said it was necessary now that "we place our faith in that system, and especially in the judicial system."

Shortly after making his speech, President Nixon appeared in the White House press room where some 15 reporters and photographers were gathered. "Ladies and gentlemen of the press," he told them, "we have had our differences in the past, and I hope you give me hell every time you think I'm wrong. I hope I'm worthy of your trust." Then he left.

White House Press Secretary Ronald L. Ziegler, in response to a reporter's question whether he would apologize to the Washington Post for previous denunciations of its Watergate coverage, said May 1 that he would do so. Ziegler had accused the Post and its reporters of "shabby journalism" and "a blatant effort at character assassination."

He said Post reporters Bob Woodward and Carl Bernstein had vigorously pursued the story and deserved the credit they were receiving.

"When we're wrong, we're wrong," Ziegler said, "and I would have to say I was in that case and other cases."

The apology was accepted by Post publisher Katharine Graham later May 1. "We appreciate it and accept it with pleasure," she said, commenting that "the Administration was trying to undermine the credibility of the press for the last 10 months."

Post wins journalism awards. The Washington Post was awarded May 7 the Pulitzer Prize for distinguished public service in journalism for its investigation of the Watergate case. (Two Post reporters assigned to the Watergate case, Carl Bernstein and Bob Woodward, had received the George Polk Memorial Award for national reporting Jan. 31.)

Agnew scores press 'techniques.' Vice President Agnew deplored Watergate reporting "techniques" of the media May 8 as "a very short jump from McCarthyism."

Saying there had been "a great amount of hearsay" and use of material from unnamed sources, Agnew chided the press for being "overzealous" on Watergate. "I applaud the efforts and I applaud the results," he said, "but I cannot applaud the techniques being used."

Proxmire says press unfair to Nixon. Sen. William Proxmire (D, Wis.) charged in a Senate speech May 8 that the press was being "grossly unfair" to President Nixon. He was being "tried, sentenced and executed by rumor and allegation" and this was analogous to "McCarthyistic destruction," Proxmire said.

Proxmire also praised the press for a "superb job" in uncovering the Watergate scandal.

Proxmire's private view that Nixon was "involved in Watergate up to his ears" and possibly unable to extricate himself, also was reported the same day from conversations Proxmire had with several home-state editors.

1969 phone taps reported. The Nixon Administration, concerned over leaks of classified information—especially with regard to the strategic arms limitations talks beginning in 1969—ordered wiretaps placed on the telephones of reporters from three newspapers and at least one government official, the New York Times reported May 11.

Times sources said reporters placed under surveillance were William Beecher and Hedrick Smith of the New York Times, and Henry Brandon, a Washington-based correspondent for the Sunday Times of London. Phones of unidentified reporters for the Washington Post also were tapped, the Times said.

According to the account supplied by Times sources, former Attorney General John N. Mitchell called the late director of the FBI, J. Edgar Hoover, in the spring of 1969, requesting that the taps be placed. Hoover refused to comply without written authorization from Mitchell, who subsequently sent the late FBI chief an unspecified number of forms used to request "national security" wiretaps. (The Supreme Court had ruled in 1972 the government needed court orders before it could install wiretaps in national security cases, except where foreign connections were involved.)

According to Times sources, Mitchell and Assistant Attorney General Richard Kleindienst, sometime after, suggested to Hoover, for reasons that were unclear, that a Congressional committee be allowed to investigate the FBI. Hoover refused consent, saying he might be asked about the wiretap installations.

In September 1971, the Justice Department retrieved the forms.

Acting FBI Director William B. Ruckelshaus ordered an investigation of the 1969–71 buggings, but had not been able to determine if records still existed, the Times said.

Nixon authorized wiretaps. The White House May 16 acknowledged that President Nixon personally authorized the use of 17 wiretaps against 13 members of his own Administration and four newsmen.

The New York Times reported May 17 that Henry A. Kissinger, assistant to the President for national security affairs, personally provided the FBI with the names of a number of his aides on the National Security Council (NSC), whom he wanted wiretapped. The Times cited Justice Department officials as its source.

The White House, in formally acknowledging the existence of the wire taps, said they were made in 1969 after publication in the Times May 9, 1969 of an article by William Beecher disclosing American B-52s were bombing Cambodia. (Beecher was appointed deputy assistant secretary of defense for public affairs April 20.)

Among those tapped was Helmut Sonnenfeldt, a former NSC official, who was nominated April 10 to be undersecretary of the Treasury.

Times sources revealed that Marvin Kalb, a diplomatic correspondent for the Columbia Broadcasting System (CBS), was under surveillance.

Kissinger, in an interview with the Times May 14, confirmed he had seen summaries of the wiretaps, but he said he had not asked that they be installed nor had he specifically approved them in advance. He also admitted he held one or two conversations with Hoover in 1969 in which he expressed "very great concern" that national security information be fully safeguarded.

The Washington Post reported May 18 that specific wiretaps had also been authorized by H. R. Haldeman, Nixon's former chief of staff.

Vast Administration plot since 1969. The Washington Post reported May 17 that since 1969 the Nixon Administration had engaged in a wide pattern of illegal and quasi-legal activities against radical leaders, students, demonstrators, news reporters, Democratic candidates for president and vice president, the Congress and Nixon Administration officials suspected of leaking information to the press.

Reporters Carl Bernstein and Bob Woodward quoted "highly placed sources in the executive branch" who said that although most of the clandestine operations were political in nature, they were conducted by the Federal Bureau of Investigation (FBI), the Secret Service and special teams working for the White House and the Justice Department under the guise of "national security."

Included in the list of activities reported by the Post was the organization by White House aide Charles W. Colson of a group of 30 Nixon supporters to "attack" news correspondents through use of write-in, telephone and telegraph campaigns.

Another instance of covert activity directed against newsmen was the 1971 investigation of Columbia Broadcasting System correspondent Daniel Schorr. Haldeman personally ordered the FBI probe, the Post reported.

Times reports break-in. A 1969 break-in by FBI agents at the offices of the underground newspaper, the Washington Free Press, was disclosed by the New York Times June 1. Aiding the FBI were members of the Army's 116th Military Intelligence Detachment, the Times said. The raid took place just before the Nixon inauguration, when there was concern about a series of planned counter-inaugural activities. The FBI June 1 admitted entering with a search warrant, but a spokesman claimed agents had been given a key by the building landlord.

CBS drops 'instant analysis.' The Columbia Broadcasting System (CBS) announced June 6 that its radio and television networks would no longer broadcast analyses of presidential speeches immediately after their delivery. The analyses by news commentators had been the target of Vice President Spiro T. Agnew's "instant analysis and querulous criticism" speech in 1969.

The statement by CBS board chairman William S. Paley said that in the future, commentary on Presidential speeches would be carried on normal news programs.

After a speech about which there might be "significant national disagreement," CBS said, its networks would give free time, usually within a week, to the holders of opposing views.

A CBS spokesman said those chosen to reply would not necessarily be members of the opposing political party. The free time policy would be suspended during Presidential election years in deference to the Federal Communications Commission's equal-time regulations.

Spokesmen for the other two major networks, American Broadcasting Co. and National Broadcasting Co., said their commentary policies on presidential speeches would not change.

Press coverage criticized. A Gallup poll released June 13 reported that 44% of those polled believed that the press had given too much coverage to the Watergate affair, while 38% said coverage had been "about right," and 11% said there had been too little.

The poll found opinion on the issue to be highly partisan: 66% of the Republicans interviewed responded "too much" coverage; 31% of the Democrats agreed. The poll was taken June 1-4.

In other press developments, the Times of London and Mayor John V. Lindsay of New York City criticized Watergate coverage primarily for publishing material which might be prejudicial in later proceedings and for overlooking the principle of due process.

In an editorial June 5, the London newspaper gave credit to the press for "forcing the Watergate affair into the open" but said newspaper revelations of grand jury leaks and the televising of Senate committee hearings had given "enormous publicity" to hearsay evidence and subjected President Nixon to a form of "lynch law." The Times was especially critical of the publication of statements by former presidential counsel John W. Dean 3rd to Senate investigators.

In a commencement address in New York June 12, Lindsay accused the Nixon Administration of "outrageous abuse of executive power," while charging the press with disregarding grand jury secrecy and catering to "investigators who leak their suspicions before going to trial."

Dean testifies on press 'enemies.' Former Presidential Counsel John W. Dean 3rd testified before the Senate Select Committee on Presidential Campaign Activities June 25-29 on the alleged cover-up of the Watergate Affair. Much of his testimony concerned the attitude of the Nixon Administration toward the media.

In his opening statement June 25 Dean said that there was deep concern at the White House about news leaks. He said that White House security aide John Caulfield had told him that John Ehrlichman, the President's principal advisor on domestic affairs, had directed him to tap columnist Joseph Kraft's telephone "in pursuit of a leak" even when J. Edgar Hoover, then FBI director, "was unwilling."

This concern "took a quantum jump" when the Pentagon Papers were published in June 1971. In late June or early July, 1971, Caulfield told Dean that White House special counsel Charles W. Colson had instructed him, "at Ehrlichman's direction," to burglarize the Brookings Institution to see if "they had certain leaked documents." The instruction was "to plant a fire bomb in the building and retrieve the documents during the commotion." Dean told Ehrlichman the plan was "insane" and it was called off.

Almost a year later, Robert C. Mardian, then assistant attorney general, told Dean he "had gone to see the President to get instructions regarding the disposition of wiretap logs that related to

newsmen and White House staffers who were suspected of leaking." But, "about Feb. 22 or 23 of this year, Time magazine notified the White House it was going to print a story that the White House had undertaken wiretaps of newsmen and White House staff and requested a response. The White House press office notified me of this inquiry.

"I then called Mr. Ehrlichman and told him about the forthcoming story in Time magazine. I asked him how Mr. Ziegler should handle it. He said Mr. Ziegler should flatly deny it—period."

During cross-examination June 26 by Sen. Lowell P. Weicker Jr. (R, Conn.), Dean revealed that the White House maintained "what was called an 'enemies list,' which was rather extensive and continually being updated."

Dean also told Weicker that Nixon's chief of staff, H. R. Haldeman, had once requested an FBI investigation of CBS newsman Daniel Schorr. The investigation "proceeded," but, "to the dismay of the White House," it was "sort of a full field wide open investigation and this became very apparent. So this put the White House in a rather scrambling position to explain what had happened. The long and short of the explanation was that Mr. Schorr was being considered for a post and that this was a part of a preliminary investigation."

Dean related another incident involving Nixon's close personal friend, Charles (Bebe) Rebozo. After an article unfavorable to Rebozo had appeared in Newsday, the Long Island, N.Y. newspaper, Dean said he got "instructions that one of the authors of the article should have some problems" with the Internal Revenue Service. Dean said he arranged that the writer be subjected to an income tax audit.

Among documents Dean submitted in evidence June 27 were lists of Nixon's "political enemies." An original list of 20 names included Schorr, described as "a real media enemy," Ed Guthman, the national editor of the Los Angeles Times who was described as a former Kennedy aide and "a highly sophisticated hatchetman against us in '68," and Mary McGrory, a Washington columnist described as the author of "daily hate Nixon articles."

An updated "master list" of political opponents that Dean provided to the committee listed the following as media enemies:

Jack Anderson, columnist, "Washington Merry-Go-Round"
Jim Bishop, author, columnist, King Features Syndicate
Thomas Braden, columnist, Los Angeles Times Syndicate
D.J.R. Bruckner, Los Angeles Times Syndicate
Marquis Childs, chief Washington correspondent, St. Louis Post Dispatch
James Deakin, White House correspondent, St. Louis Post Dispatch
James Doyle, Washington Star
Richard Dudman, St. Louis Post Dispatch
William Eaton, Chicago Daily News
Rowland Evans Jr., syndicated columnist, Publishers Hall
Saul Friedmann, Knight Newspapers, syndicated columnist
Clayton Fritchey, syndicated columnist, Washington correspondent, Harpers

George Frazier, Boston Globe
Pete Hamill, New York Post
Michael Harrington, author and journalist; member, executive committee Socialist party
Sydney Harris, columnist, drama critic and writer of 'Strictly Personal,' syndicated Publishers Hall
Robert Healy, Boston Globe
William Hines, Jr., journalist; science and education, Chicago Sun times
Stanley Karnow, foreign correspondent, Washington Post
Ted Knap, syndicated columnist, New York Daily News
Edwin Knoll, Progressive
Morton Kondracke, Chicago Sun Times
Joseph Kraft, syndicated columnist, Publishers Hall
James Laird, Philadelphia Inquirer
Max Lerner, syndicated columnist, New York Post; author, lecturer, professor (Brandeis University)
Stanley Levey, Scripps Howard
Flora Lewis, syndicated columnist on economics
Stuart Loory, Los Angeles Times
Mary McGrory, syndicated columnist on New Left
Frank Mankiewicz, syndicated columnist Los Angeles Times
James Millstone, St. Louis Post Disptach
Martin Nolan, Boston Globe
Ed Guthman, Los Angeles Times
Thomas O'Neill, Baltimore Sun [died in April 1971]
John Pierson, Wall Street Journal
William Prochnau, Seattle Times
James Reston, New York Times
Carl Rowan, syndicated columnist, Publishers Hall
Warren Unna, Washington Post, NET
Harriet Van Horne, columnist, New York Post
Milton Viorst, reporter, author, writer
James Wechsler, New York Post
Tom Wicker, New York Times
Gary Wills, syndicated columnist, author of "Nixon-Agonistes."
The New York Times
Washington Post
St. Louis Post Dispatch
Jules Duscha, Washingtonian
Robert Manning, editor, Atlantic
John Osborne, New Republic
Richard Rovere, New Yorker
Robert Sherrill, Nation
Paul Samuelson, Newsweek
Julian Goodman, chief executive officer, NBC
John Macy, Jr., president, Public Broadcasting Corp.; former Civil Service Commission
Marvin Kalb, CBS
Daniel Schorr, CBS
Lem Tucker, NBC
Sander Vanocur, NBC

Dean also provided the committee with a memo to him from Colson dated Nov. 17, 1972 concerning columnist Jack Anderson. The text of the memo was as follows:

Second Colson Memo to Dean
(Nov. 17, 1972)
I have received from an informer some interesting information on Jack Anderson, including a report that Jack Anderson was found in a room with wiretap equipment and a private investigator in connection with the Dodd investigation. Anderson, according to my source, had the wiretap equipment supplied to him by a Washington, D.C., man.

According to the same source, Anderson and Drew Pearson were paid $100,000 in 1958 by Batista to write favorable articles about the former Cuban dictator. In 1961 Anderson wrote several very favorable articles on Fidel Castro. Fredo de la Campo, Batista's Under Secretary of State, sent Anderson a telegram saying "I hope you were paid well, as well for the Castro articles as you were for the Batista articles." My source has a copy of the telegram.

You know my personal feelings about Jack Anderson. After his incredibly sloppy and malicious reporting on Eagleton, his credibility has diminished. It now appears as if we have the opportunity to destroy it. Do you agree that we should pursue this activity?

USIA facilities barred. The U.S. Information Agency (USIA) announced June 26 that foreign newsmen would not be permitted to use USIA facilities to broadcast feature programs on the Watergate case to television stations abroad.

Although the facilities had been provided "as a courtesy" in the past, agency spokesmen said, "It is not the function of the USIA to extend a story that may be detrimental to U.S. interest by duplicating and furthering dissemination of feature material."

The British Broadcasting Corp. specifically had been denied permission to use USIA studios in order to broadcast a "call in" interview with Sen. Daniel K. Inouye (D, Hawaii), a member of the Senate Watergate committee.

The Voice of America was continuing to provide "factual coverage of the news about Watergate," USIA spokesmen added.

Nixon displays anger at press. President Nixon showed his anger at the press Aug. 20 as he was entering a New Orleans hall for a speech to the Veterans of Foreign Wars. Nixon turned around abruptly, grabbed White House Press Secretary Ronald L. Ziegler by the shoulders and shoved him towards newsmen following them. According to reports and filmed accounts, Nixon told Ziegler: "I don't want any press with me and you take care of it." The newsmen were directed to another entrance.

Vice president denounces leaks. Vice President Spiro T. Agnew Aug. 21 denounced leaks to the press on the federal investigation in Baltimore concerning possible violations by him of certain criminal statutes.

In a nationally televised statement, Agnew said he could only assume from such press accounts "that some Justice Department officials have decided to indict me in the press whether or not the evidence supports their position."

This was "a clear and outrageous effort to influence the outcome of possible grand jury deliberations," Agnew charged.

He specifically referred to an article in the Aug. 27 issue of Time magazine, published Aug. 20, reporting the view of unidentified Justice Department officials that the case against Agnew was "growing steadily stronger and that an indictment appears inevitable."

Referring to his press conference Aug. 8 to rebut press allegations against him "coming from people who were actually participating in the investigation," Agnew said "since then the leaks have continued unabated." It had become clear, he said, "that sources so frequently quoted—were indeed that—persons involved in the investigatory process." Agnew deplored "the impact which this smear publicity may have on the rights of others, particularly private citizens who have been swept into this highly publicized investigation."

Agnew said he had asked Attorney General Elliot L. Richardson to fulfill his promise and "vigorously" pursue an investigation of the possibility that his de-

partment was the source of such leaks. Agnew referred to a denial by Richardson Aug. 19 that any of the leaks came from his department.

In a reference to his earlier offer to meet with the U.S. Attorney George Beall conducting the investigation in Baltimore, Agnew was critical of Beall's handling of the case. Beall said "that he's not sure whether he even wishes to question me," Agnew said. "I suppose that if he only wants to hear one side of the story that's up to him. I will say only that it seems to me a very strange way to run an investigation."

Richardson statement—In his Aug. 19 statement, made on the ABC-TV "Issues and Answers" broadcast, Richardson said leaks about the Agnew case had caused him "considerable distress" but an investigation had satisfied him that Beall and his staff were not responsible for them. Richardson said he would discipline any department employe found culpable in the matter.

After Agnew's Aug. 21 statement demanding a probe of departmental leaks, Richardson himself read a brief statement later Aug. 21 reaffirming his stand "that every reasonable step is being taken to assure" that the department "has not been and will not be the source of such publicity." While he "fully shared" Agnew's "concern about unfair and inaccurate publicity," Richardson said, there was no "firm basis for the assumption that the information which has appeared in the press has come from law enforcement officials."

In any case, Richardson continued, "any plausible lead implicating" the department "will be pursued vigorously and appropriate disciplinary action will be taken against any department employe found to be responsible."

Beall also denied Aug. 21 that his prosecutors were "in any way" the source of the leaks.

Watergate issue dominates session. President Nixon fielded an intense barrage of questions on Watergate during most of a 50-minute news conference Aug. 22 on the lawn of his San Clemente, Calif. home. It was Nixon's first news conference in five months and his first televised news conference in 14 months.

In the course of the questioning, Nixon accepted all responsibility for the Watergate scandal, said he would not resign and pledged a strong term of office.

He attacked his Watergate critics, said he would abide by a "definitive" Supreme Court decision to make public his taped recordings of conversations being withheld from Watergate investigators and strongly defended Vice President Spiro T. Agnew.

The questioning was intensely personal, even on the non-Watergate topics. The President was asked if he would expect Agnew to resign if he were indicted, and whether Nixon owed the American people

an apology on the secret Cambodia bombing in light of his public statement to the contrary.

On Watergate, Nixon was asked how much blame he accepted for its abuses, whether an action represented the appearance of a lack of moral leadership, whether he ever considered resigning and why he had not informed prosecutors of information given him of criminal wrongdoing.

The President appeared nervous, but stumbled less over his words than during his appearance two days before in New Orleans, when his delivery and angry shoving of an aid drew press comment and subsequent White House reassurance that the President possessed a positive attitude and could govern.

(Deputy White House Press Secretary Gerald L. Warren said Aug. 20 that "the past few months have been periods of pressure on the President.")

At his news conference, Nixon drew laughter with a reference to the pushing incident, saying at one point he "would have blown my stack, just as I did at [Press Secretary Ronald] Ziegler the other day."

No thought of resigning—Nixon was asked "at any time during the Watergate crisis have you ever considered resigning? Would you consider resigning if you felt that your capacity to govern had been seriously weakened? And in that connection, how much do you think your capacity to govern has been weakened?" He replied:

The answer to the first two questions is no. The answer to the third question is that it is true that as far as the capacity to govern is concerned, that to be under a constant barrage—12 to 15 minutes a night on each of the three major networks for four months—tends to raise some questions in the people's minds with regard to the President; and it may raise some questions with regard to the capacity to govern.

But I also know this: I was elected to do a job. Watergate is an episode that I deeply deplore; and, had I been running the campaign—other than trying to run the country, and particularly the foreign policy of this country at this time—it would never have happened. But that's water under the bridge. Let's go on now.

Agnew's status—"My confidence in his integrity has not been shaken," Nixon said of Agnew, "and in fact it has been strengthened by his courageous conduct and his ability." Nixon said the charges against Agnew were "made about activities that occurred before he became vice president." It would be "improper" to comment on the charges, but not upon "the outrageous leak in information from either the grand jury or the prosecutors or the Department of Justice or all three." He said he had requested a full investigation by the department.

Not only "trying" an individual but "convicting him in the headlines and on television before he's had a chance to present his case in court is completely contrary to the American tradition. Even a vice president has a right to some ... consideration in this respect, let alone the ordinary individual," the President said, and added, any federal employe who had leaked such information "will be summarily dismissed."

Political opponents scored—Nixon was asked who he was referring to in his recent remark about "those who would exploit Watergate to keep you from doing your job?" He replied:

I would suggest that where the shoe fits, people should wear it. I would think that some political figures, some members of the press perhaps, some members of the television, perhaps, would exploit it. I don't impute, interestingly enough, motives, however, that are improper interests, because here's what is involved.

There are a great number of people in this country that would prefer that I do resign. There are a great number of people in this country that didn't accept the mandate of 1972. After all, I know that most of the members of the press corps were not enthusiastic. And I understand that about either my election in '68 or '72. That's not unusual. Frankly, if I had always followed what the press predicted or the polls predicted, I would have never been elected President.

But what I am saying is this. People who did not accept the mandate of '72, who do not want the strong America that I want to build, who do not want the foreign policy leadership that I want to give, who do not want to cut down the size of this Government bureaucracy that burdens us so greatly and to give more of our Government back to the people, people who do not want these things naturally would exploit any issues. If it weren't Watergate, anything else in order to keep the President from doing his job.

Nixon holds 2nd press conference. President Nixon, holding his second news conference in two weeks Sept. 5, admitted he had a problem of rebuilding confidence in his leadership. He said it was "rather difficult" to have the President "attacked in every way" on television for four months "without having some of that confidence being worn away." He described the attack as "by innuendo, by leak, by, frankly, leers and sneers of commentators," adding that was "their perfect right."

Poll reports press support. A Louis Harris poll published Sept. 8 found a substantial majority, 66%–24%, did not believe the "press is just out to get President Nixon on Watergate" but a majority, 50%–44%, thought "the press and television have given Watergate more attention than it deserves." The latter represented a turnaround from a 46%–40% plurality found in July which felt that media attention to Watergate was "not excessive."

Memos on press campaign released. The Senate Watergate committee released Sept. 26 memos disclosing an extensive operation by the White House to draft letters and telegrams of support for the President to be sent to "opinion leaders" throughout the country over other persons' signatures. The "opinion leaders" included editors, publishers and business leaders. Under the system, the news media was denounced following a presidential press conference.

A Dec. 11, 1970 memo from Jeb Stuart Magruder, then White House aide, to H. R. Haldeman, then White House chief of staff, listed action taken following the press conference. Among the actions:

"Ten telegrams have been drafted by Buchanan. They will be sent to Time and Newsweek by 20 names around the country from our letter-writing system"; an op-ed page statement for the New York Times was being drafted by two aides and Herbert Klein, then the President's director of communications, was recommended as the "best signatory" for the article.

According to another memo, Nixon tried to influence the public interpretation of New York Mayor John V. Lindsay's re-election in 1969. In a memo to Haldeman, Nixon wrote that "the press, of course, will try to interpret this as a referendum on Vietnam" and "it is vitally important that this be nailed prior to the election and, of course, be nailed immediately afterwards as strongly as possible." He suggested "it would be helpful" if conservative columnists could "hit" the issue "and better still if some more in the center were to do so."

Agnew attacks prosecution. In a speech delivered in Los Angeles Sept. 29, Vice President Agnew reasserted his innocence of criminal charges and issued a bitter denunciation of the Justice Department's handling of his case.

Speaking to a cheering, sympathetic audience at the convention of the National Federation of Republican Women, Agnew said that because of "these tactics which have been employed against me, . . . I will not resign if indicted."

Agnew first delivered a prepared text devoted to a general discussion of the need for secrecy in grand jury proceedings, the violation of which, he said, had led "during the past few months" to a "cruel form of trial in the media."

In the informal remarks which followed, Agnew said—without naming Assistant Attorney General Henry E. Petersen directly—that "conduct of high individuals in the Department of Justice, particularly the conduct of the chief of the criminal investigation division, is unprofessional and malicious and outrageous, if I am to believe what has been printed in the news magazines and said on the television networks. . . ."

Agnew said he intended to use the courts in an attempt "to examine under oath those people who are trying to destroy me politically through the abuse of the criminal justice system. . . ." If department employes were found to "have abused their sacred trust and forsaken their professional standards," Agnew added, he would ask President Nixon to "summarily discharge" them.

In a statement released later Sept. 29, Attorney General Elliot L. Richardson defended Petersen as a "distinguished government lawyer" who was "constrained from defending himself" against Agnew's attack "by the ethical standards governing a criminal investigation." Final responsibility for the department's conduct of the Agnew investigation, Richardson added, rested with the attorney general.

Deputy White House Press Secretary Gerald L. Warren said Oct. 1 that Richardson had assured Nixon that Petersen was not the source of the "we've got the evidence. We've got it cold" quote which had reportedly angered Agnew.

Further clarification was offered by Fred P. Graham, the Columbia Broadcasting System reporter who had cited Petersen's remarks. In a letter to the New York Times Oct. 1, Graham said Petersen "has never discussed the merits" of the Agnew case with him. Graham said he had made it clear in his broadcast that an unnamed "source close to the negotiations" had told him Petersen had made the comment during a meeting with Agnew's lawyers.

Deputy Attorney General William D. Ruckelshaus said later that Petersen did not recall making the comment, nor did Richardson remember hearing it. And, asked Ruckelshaus, "who stands to lose the most" from the incident? He added that the Justice Department would suffer if the case were harmed by prejudicial publicity.

In a letter to the Washington Post Oct. 3, Agnew criticized newspaper misuse of Graham's television report, saying it did not "make a great deal of difference who in the Justice Department dropped this little morsel in the hands of Mr. Graham. The fact remains that four newspapers of considerable circulation left the distinct impression . . . that Mr. Petersen made this improper, unprofessional and highly prejudicial comment."

Agnew said he had since become concerned over the Justice Department implications that the leak of Petersen's remark had come from Agnew's own attorneys. He said his attorneys were "willing to sign affidavits that they did not discuss anything concerning the meeting with the news media."

Judge grants Agnew subpoena power on leaks. Judge Walter E. Hoffman, who had been assigned to oversee the investigation of Vice President Agnew, in an unusual action Oct. 3 authorized Agnew's attorneys to investigate—with full powers of subpoena—the alleged news leaks by Justice Department officials. Under Hoffman's order, the lawyers could privately question under oath and take sworn depositions from any persons they deemed "appropriate and necessary."

Agnew's attorneys had charged the Justice Department with conducting "a deliberate campaign" of news leaks "calculated and intended to deprive [Agnew] of his basic rights to due process and fair hearing." In a suit they had asked the court to bar the department from "discussing with or disclosing to any person any such testimony, documents or materials."

Hoffman ordered that transcripts of the depositions be sealed and kept from public court records, and all lawyers involved in the case were directed to withhold comment on the depositions. Hoffman also required that Agnew's attorneys notify the Justice Department 48 hours before witnesses were questioned.

Some lawyers were quoted Oct. 4 as believing that Hoffman's order was unprecedented in that a person under criminal investigation but not yet under indictment was granted such broad authority to question prosecutors and others involved.

The order was also seen as a potential source of further constitutional issues in the Agnew case if reporters questioned by his attorneys refused to reveal their sources.

In another action Oct. 3, Judge Hoffman summoned the grand jurors to an open session and delivered a special charge cautioning them to "disregard totally any comments you might have seen or heard from any source, save and except what you have heard or seen in your grand jury room while in official session."

Hoffman called the press "integral and necessary," but added that "unfortunately, in the present-day grab for priority in getting news items, the news media frequently overlook the rights of others, especially where criminal matters are involved."

Agnew's attorneys, acting on Hoffman's authority, issued subpoenas Oct. 5 to reporters and news organizations allegedly involved in receiving leaks on the Agnew case from the Justice Department. Subpoenas for "all writings and other forms of record (including drafts)" reflecting on sources were served on Richard M. Cohen, Washington Post; Nicholas Gage, New York Times; Ronald Sarro and Robert Walters, Washington Star-News; William Sherman, New York Daily News; Stephen Lesher, Newsweek magazine; Ronald Nessen, National Broadcasting Company; and Fred P. Graham, Columbia Broadcasting System.

Newsweek and Time magazines were subpoenaed for the testimony of all staff members who had written or contributed to certain stories on Agnew. Justice Department officials were also subpoenaed, and all were scheduled to appear for questioning Oct. 11, in Hoffman's presence.

Spokesmen for the news organizations were unanimous in their determination to fight the subpoenas on First Amendment grounds. They noted that in the 1972 Supreme Court decision subjecting newsmen to subpoena on confidential information, Associate Justice Lewis F. Powell Jr. had said the courts were "available to newsmen in instances where legitimate First Amendment interests are in question and require protection." Lawyers also noted that the 1972 case involved newsmen who were allegedly direct witnesses to criminal acts, while the current subpoenas were a part of Agnew's civil action to halt the grand jury investigation by proving potentially prejudicial news leaks.

Replying to the Agnew suit Oct. 8, the Justice Department branded as "frivolous" Agnew's charges of a deliberate campaign of news leaks and accused the Agnew defense of a "fishing expedition" in subpoenaing newsmen.

The department also submitted the results of its internal investigation of Agnew's charges, which, the department said, indicated that Justice officials were not necessarily the source of leaks. "There appears to be," the document stated, "a high correlation between the facts transmitted by the Department of Justice to the White House and/or the vice president and the disclosures which have appeared in the press."

Newsmen and their lawyers were in Baltimore Oct. 10, prepared to argue motions which had been filed to quash their subpoenas when Agnew appeared at a dramatic courtroom hearing before Judge Hoffman, entered a plea of no contest (nolo contendere) to one count of income tax evasion and announced his resignation. Agnew's plea rendered the litigation on the question of news leaks moot.

Senate committee hears Segretti. The Senate Watergate committee took testimony Oct. 3 from Donald H. Segretti on the "dirty tricks" he played on Democratic candidates seeking the presidential nomination in 1972.

Looking back, Segretti said he realized his activities were wrong and regretted any harm caused by them. He apologized for one "scurrilous letter" he faked purporting sexual misconduct to two Democratic candidates. But he said his activities had been exaggerated "out of all proportion" by the news media and he had suffered abuse by "rumor, character assassination, innuendo" and invasion of privacy.

Kelley promises open FBI news policy. Clarence M. Kelley, director of the Federal Bureau of Investigation (FBI), said Oct. 11 that his agency would adopt an "open stance" policy toward the press.

He promised a "complete candidness and willingness to answer press inquiries, recognizing the right of the press in our democratic society to obtain information for the enlightenment of the public." Kelley said he had set up a three-member press section to answer newsmen's questions. Under the late FBI Director J. Edgar Hoover, the FBI had no press office.

Nixon duels with press. President Nixon held a televised news conference at the White House Oct. 26 to answer questions arising from his dismissal of Special Watergate Prosecutor Archibald Cox and the military alert during the Middle East crisis. The press conference was marked by presidential displeasure with the news media, especially television, which surfaced in half a dozen answers. At one point, asked what it was that aroused his anger at television

coverage, Nixon, denying anger, remarked, "You see, one can only be angry with those he respects."

He began showing his anger when one reporter asked him "what goes through your mind when you hear of people who love this country and people who believe in you say, reluctantly, that perhaps you should resign or be impeached."

"I'm glad we don't take the vote of this room," Nixon began, then referred to "the most difficult decision of my first term"—the bombing of North Vietnam in December 1972. At that time, he said, "exactly the same words were used on the networks . . . that were used now—tyrant, dictator, he's lost his senses, he should resign, he should be impeached. But I stuck it out and as a result of that we not only got our prisoners of war home . . . on their feet rather than on their knees, but we brought peace to Vietnam, something we haven't had and didn't for over 12 years."

"As far as what goes through my mind," he said, "I will simply say that I intend to continue to carry out to the best of my ability the responsibilities I was elected to carry out last November. The events of this past week I know, for example, in your head office in New York [CBS-TV] some thought it was simply a blown-up exercise, there wasn't a real [Middle East] crisis. I wish it had been that. It was a real crisis. It was the most difficult crisis we've had since the Cuban confrontation of 1962.

Other tough questions—Nixon was asked other tough questions: whether he thought America was at the point of rebellion over "too many shocks"; how he was bearing up emotionally "under the stress"; how he could regain the confidence of the people; if he could explain the rationale of a law and order Administration covering up "primafacie evidence" of high crimes and misdemeanors. He was asked if the Administration's story was "credible" that a close friend had not told him for three years that he had a $100,000 cash contribution from billionaire Howard Hughes. "Well, it's obviously not credible to you," Nixon began his answer to the newsman.

'Vicious reporting' cited—The American people "can ride through the shocks that they have," Nixon said. But he observed a "difference" between now and earlier days—"the electronic media."

"I have never heard or seen," he continued, "such outrageous, vicious, distorted reporting in 27 years of public life. I'm not blaming anybody for that. Perhaps what happened is that what we did brought it about, and therefore the media decided that they would have to take that particular line. But when people are pounded night after night with that kind of frantic, hysterical reporting, it naturally shakes their confidence.

"And yet I should point out that even in this week when many thought that the President was shellshocked, unable to act, the President acted decisively in the interests of peace and the interests of the country, and I can assure you that whatever shocks gentlemen of the press may have, or others—political people—these shocks will not affect me and my doing my job."

As to how he was "bearing up emotionally under the stress of recent events," Nixon replied:

"Well, those who saw me during the Middle East crisis thought I bore up rather well. . . . I have a quality which is, I guess I must have inherited it from my Midwestern mother and father, which is that the tougher it gets the cooler I get. Of course it isn't pleasant to get criticism; some of it is justified, of course. It isn't pleasant to find your honesty questioned, it isn't pleasant to find for example that, speaking of my friend, Mr. Rebozo, that despite the fact that those who printed it and those who said it knew it was untrue—said that he had a million-dollar trust fund for me that he was handling—it was nevertheless put on one of the networks, knowing it was untrue. It isn't pleasant, for example, to hear, or read, that a million dollars in campaign funds went into my San Clemente property, and even after we have a complete audit, to have it repeated.

"Those are things which of course do tend to get under the skin of the man who holds this office. But as far as I'm concerned, I have learned to expect it. It has been my lot throughout my political life, and I suppose because I've been through so much, that maybe one of the reasons is when I have to face an international crisis, I have what it takes."

A reporter questioned him about his criticism of television reporting.

Q. Mr. President, you've lambasted the television networks pretty well. Could I ask you, at the risk of reopening an obvious wound—you say, after you've put on a lot of heat, that you don't blame anyone. I find that a little puzzling. What is it about the television coverage of you in these past weeks and months that has so aroused your anger? **A. Don't get the impression that you arouse my anger. Q. I have that impression. A. You see, one can only be angry with those he respects.**

Later in the conference, Nixon returned to the subject. He did not want to leave an impression with his "good friends from CBS," he said, "that I don't respect the reporters. What I was simply saying was this: That when a commentator takes a bit of news and then with knowledge of what the facts are distorts it viciously, I have no respect for that individual."

As for regaining the peoples' confidence, Nixon expected "to move forward in building a structure of peace in the world." His European initiative and continued initiatives with the Soviet Union and China, he said, "will be the major legacy of this Administration." He also spoke of "moving forward at home" in the battle against the high cost of living and the "deplorable" campaign abuses uncovered in the Watergate matter.

Nixon attempted to banter with one of his former aides, Clark Mollenhoff, who said he had to be loud to gain recognition "because you happen to dodge my questions all the time." He was asked for an explanation of "the rationale of a law and order Administration covering up evidence, primafacie evidence, of high crimes and misdemeanors."

Nixon responded: "Well, I should point out that perhaps all the other reporters in the room are aware of the fact we have waived executive privilege on all individuals within the Administration—it's been the greatest waiver of executive privilege in the whole history of this nation—and as far as any other matters are concerned, the matters of the tapes, the matters of Presidential conversations, those are matters in which the President has the responsibility to defend this office, which I shall continue to do."

Media officials rebut attack. Network executives rebutted President Nixon's news conference criticism of television reporting Oct. 27.

NBC News President Richard C. Wald said he felt the President was "making a mistake—the old mistake of blaming the messenger for the message."

CBS News President Richard Salant said "we are professionally obligated to try not to be directly involved in a dispute with the President" and "we are convinced that none of the network reporting justifies the adjectives" used by Nixon.

Elmer Lower, the president of ABC News, said "we have never knowingly broadcast anything false" and he stood by his network's record "for fairness and balance."

Bos Johnson, president of the Radio-Television News Director's Association, said Oct. 30 in Huntington, W.Va. that the news media did not create the issues but reported them.

Other reactions—Vice President-designate Gerald R. Ford commented Oct. 27 he believed the President, "on second thought, probably wished he hadn't" made the remark that "one can only be angry with those he respects." He said he thought Nixon was "totally on top of the job."

Assistant Senate GOP Leader Robert P. Griffin (Mich.) said Oct.26 that Nixon had given "a cool, reassuring performance in a very tense and hostile atmosphere [that] demolished myths about his ability to govern under fire."

Sen. Edmund S. Muskie (D, Me.) said Oct. 26 that Nixon had tried to "divert our attention" from his political and legal problems by overstating developments in the Middle East and by attacking the media.

White House presses media attack—President Nixon's attack on the news media was elaborated by spokesmen Oct. 29 and 30.

Deputy Press Secretary Gerald L. Warren lectured White House correspondents Oct. 29 on the President's insistence on

"perspective" in their reports. He indicated his displeasure with specific television broadcasts. Warren again assailed TV networks Oct. 30.

Nixon speechwriter Patrick Buchanan appeared on the CBS morning news program Oct. 29. He likened the mood at the Nixon press conference to that in a bull ring and gave his "personal" recommendation that the Administration make a legislative effort "to break the power of the networks."

Nixon's son-in-law, David Eisenhower, appeared on a morning NBC-TV interview Oct. 30 to assert there was too much "reporting without applying any perspective to it at all." In his view, the "irresponsibility" of the media had been "matched by the irresponsibility of the people they may quote."

(An official of the Veterans of Foreign Wars disclosed Oct. 25 that a White House aide had approached him to solicit statements of support for Nixon following the President's news conference, originally scheduled for that day. A spokesman for the National Association of Manufacturers said the organization's lobbyist had been contacted by "a lower echelon" White House official who suggested "we might want to make a comment" after the Nixon press session.)

Editorials urge resignation. The Detroit News, which supported Nixon for re-election in 1972, called for his resignation in an editorial Nov. 4. Another newspaper which also supported Nixon's re-election, the Denver Post, also called upon the President to resign.

Editorials calling for Nixon's resignation appeared in the New York Times Nov. 4 and the Nov. 12 issue of Time magazine (published Nov. 4), the first editorial in Time's 50-year history.

Resignation also was advocated Nov. 2 by syndicated columnist Joseph Alsop, long a Nixon supporter on defense and Vietnam policies, and the same week by ABC-TV anchor man Howard K. Smith. Conservative spokesman William F. Buckley Jr. told a Kansas State University audience Nov. 2 he believed Nixon would resign upon the urging of Republicans and friends.

An editorial in the Long Island, N.Y. newspaper Newsday Nov. 9 called for Nixon's impeachment "as soon as possible."

Plans against news media revealed. A Senate Watergate Committee member, Sen. Lowell P. Weicker Jr. (R, Conn.), released Oct. 31 and Nov. 1 a series of White House memoranda that suggested means to counter what the President viewed as unfavorable coverage by the news media.

One memorandum, from former White House aide Jeb Stuart Magruder to the President's Chief of Staff, H. R. Haldeman, said that efforts "to get" the media on a case by case basis were "very unfruitful and wasteful of our time." Instead, Magruder said in the memo, dated Oct. 17, 1969, "a major impact" could be made if the Administration: had the Federal Communications Commission (FCC) monitor the networks to prove bias on their part; threatened antitrust action against major news organizations; threatened an Internal Revenue Service (IRS) investigation of "the various organizations that we are most concerned about"; gave exclusive information to favorable newsmen; conducted major letter writing campaigns through the Republican National Committee.

Attached to the memorandum was a log of 21 requests made by President Nixon between mid-September and mid-October, 1969. Among Nixon's requests, White House Communications Director Herbert G. Klein was asked "to take appropriate action to counter biased TV coverage over the summer."

Peter M. Flanigan, a top White House aide, was asked by Nixon to "take action to counter" a report by Dan Rather, a reporter for the Columbia Broadcasting System (CBS), that Gen. Lewis B. Hershey had been fired as head of the Selective Service System because of student protests. In another memo to Klein, Nixon asked "to have the Chicago Tribune hit Senator [Charles H.] Percy (R, Ill.) hard on his ties with the peace group."

Commenting on the Magruder memorandum and others he had released, Weicker said there "was no way to know" if White House officials had acted on any of the proposals, but "it shows the type of thinking that was going on at the White House."

Weicker also made public a memorandum from former White House Counsel Charles W. Colson to Haldeman that was dated Sept. 25, 1970. Colson wrote that officials of the major television networks were "very much afraid of us and are trying hard to prove they are good guys." Colson had met with network executives to urge them to resist requests by Democrats for free air time to counter televised statements made by Nixon.

Colson added that he would ask FCC Chairman Dean Burch to consider issuing "an interpretive ruling" on the fairness doctrine after the Republicans had obtained a majority on the FCC.

White House compiles press 'sins'. The New York Times reported Nov. 5 that the White House had been compiling a list of alleged "sins" committed by the press, especially television, against President Nixon. The Times suggested that the list had been the basis for Nixon's attack on the press Oct. 26.

Among the items on the list was an analysis of news coverage by the three television networks Oct. 22, the first weekday subsequent to the firing of Archibald Cox, the special Watergate prosecutor. The programs contained 19 spots the White House considered unfavorable to Nixon, two spots it considered favorable and one spot it judged neutral, the Times reported.

Ken W. Clawson, director of the White House Office of Communications, said: "Were those 19 television spots reporting, or were they creating an impeachment atmosphere? That day on television was probably the last straw for the President—the outcries for impeachment on television in the wake of the Cox firing."

In a related development, the Washington Post reported Nov. 5 it had obtained a White House memorandum that called for a campaign of "pestering" the Post and its publisher, Katharine Graham.

In the May 6, 1970 memo to former White House Chief of Staff H.R. Haldeman, Jeb Stuart Magruder, then a White House aide, said a letter writing team was calling and writing the Post every day to complain about the paper's "childish, ridiculous and overboard" critical attitude toward President Nixon. As a second measure against the Post, Magruder suggested that White House aide Lyn Nofziger "work out with someone in the House a round robin letter to the Post that says we live in Washington D.C. and read the D.C. papers, but fortunately we also have the opportunity to read the papers from our home districts and are appalled by the biased coverage the people of Washington receive of the news, compared to that in the rest of the country."

CBS restores 'instant analysis.' The Columbia Broadcasting System (CBS) announced Nov. 12 that after a five-month trial it was rescinding its ban on analyses of presidential speeches immediately after their delivery.

CBS Chairman William S. Paley explained that while the additional time for reflection and research might enhance the network's coverage, the "rapid series of exceptionally newsworthy events" had made it clear that "postponing news analysis under all circumstances may impair a journalistic service of far greater value to the public than we had realized."

Paley said the network would continue its policy of providing free time to qualified spokesmen for opposing views.

Guild calls for impeachment. The Internal Executive Board of the AFL-CIO Newspaper Guild adopted a resolution Nov. 15 calling for initiation of impeachment proceedings against Nixon "without further delay." Wire service groups dissociated themselves from the resolution, and there was some dissent within the guild that the action would compromise editorial objectivity. The resolution itself passed by a 15–1 vote.

Declares 'I am not a crook.' President Nixon actively campaigned to mute his Watergate and credibility problems with a four-day round of public appearances in the South Nov. 17–20.

One of the appearances was a question-and-answer session before newspaper executives nationally telecast from Disney World, Fla. Nov. 17. He said "people have got to know whether or not their President is a crook—well, I'm not a crook."

'Slapping' incident reported. As Nixon was departing from McCoy Air Force Base near Orlando Nov. 17, moving among a small group of well-wishers, he approached Air Force m., Sgt. Edward Kleizo standing beside his son. Nixon asked him if he was the boy's "mother or his grandmother," his vision apparently obscured by bright floodlights. Kleizo replied he was neither. "Of course you're not," Nixon said, checking closer. Then he gave Kleizo a slap or pat on the cheek, apparently to make up for his mistake. Several reporters who witnessed the incident dismissed it as trivial, but it was reported as a slapping incident by several newspapers. The White House denounced these as "irresponsible." The witnessing reporters put out a statement describing the slap as a "light" one that "had the velocity that a man might use in slapping shaving lotion on his own face." They said the President was not angry. Kleizo agreed; he considered the President's gesture "the greatest honor that I've ever had."

News Council unable to get data. The National News Council said the White House had failed to respond to numerous requests for documentation of President Nixon's Oct. 27 criticism of television network newscasts, it was reported Nov. 24.

In his press conference Oct. 27, Nixon accused the network newscasters of "vicious" and "distorted" reporting. Ken W. Clawson, director of the White House Office of Communications, later confirmed to the New York Times that an Administration list of press "sins" committed against the President had been compiled.

William Arthur, director of the council, said he had asked White House Press Secretary Ronald L. Ziegler to enumerate instances of "hysterical" or "distorted" reporting, but there had been no response.

The National News Council was created by the Twentieth Century Fund to monitor the press.

Nixon aide blasts media. White House aide Bruce Herschensohn criticized the national media in its Watergate reporting Nov. 24 as "a kangaroo court" whose "verdict is very clear from the outset." The media, he said, "should be subject to the same scrutiny as they give their target, the President." Herschensohn was addressing a "Support the President" rally in Albuquerque attended by about 600 persons.

CIA uses journalists to obtain data. The Washington Star-News reported Nov. 30 that William E. Colby, director of the Central Intelligence Agency (CIA), had ordered a review of the agency's use of journalists as sources of foreign intelligence data.

According to the Star-News, CIA officials had determined, after a review of their files, that about 40 full-time reporters, free-lance journalists and correspondents for trade publications—all stationed abroad—were regular undercover contacts who were paid for supplying data to CIA field agents.

It was understood, the Star-News said, that Colby had decided to sever CIA connections with at least five journalists who were employed full-time by general circulation news-gathering organizations. However, the agency intended to maintain its ties with the other undercover journalists as well as journalists who on an informal, unpaid basis from time to time had supplied the CIA with information, the Star-News reported.

CBS charges reprisal in suits. In a brief filed in response to federal antitrust suits against the three television networks, CBS charged Dec. 21 that the government had embarked on "an unlawful plan" to "restrain, intimidate and inhibit criticism of the President of the United States and his appointees."

CBS, along with NBC and the American Broadcasting Co. (ABC), responded in federal district court in Los Angeles to antitrust suits filed in April 1972 which sought to prevent the networks from producing their own serials and feature films and from obtaining financial interests in independent production operations.

Both NBC and ABC asserted defenses based on First Amendment rights, but—according to network sources—neither was as explicit as CBS.

The CBS brief argued that "as early as October 1969" the Nixon Administration had prepared plans to "use the power and machinery of the federal government" to stifle television news coverage. The purpose of the suits, CBS contended, was not to enforce antitrust law, but to threaten or punish news organizations.

Ziegler promises more briefings. White House Press Secretary Ronald L. Ziegler met with reporters Jan. 22, 1974 to tell them of President Nixon's determination to serve out his term and not be "consumed another year by the Watergate matter."

Ziegler, an infrequent spokesman at the regular White House press briefings for six months, said he would conduct the briefings "more often" in the future. The practice had largely been turned over to Deputy Press Secretary Gerald L. Warren.

Ziegler attributed Nixon's low poll standing largely to the impact of "unsupported charges" against him. "The mistakes of Watergate" had an impact, he said, "but I think this other element [unsupported charges] has had even a more substantial impact."

Ziegler said Nixon had been "under massive attacks" and been "substantially maligned" over the past year but he [Nixon] knew he had "not been involved in any wrongdoing." Ziegler said the President believed that "we have had almost a year of extensive investigation of Watergate . . . and that it's time to wrap this matter up and conclude it."

Ziegler defended a new White House requirement that presidential aides report all press contacts to him. Reporters feared an inhibiting effect from the practice. It would produce more comment on the record, Ziegler said, and less for background. "Source stories have been getting somewhat out of hand," he said, referring to stories attributed to "sources" and not individuals. Warren, confirming the requirement Jan. 21, said it had been adopted about 10 days previously.

Ziegler denies comment on Post report. Ziegler refused to comment on a Feb. 1 Washington Post report that President Nixon had continued to maintain a close association with three of his former key aides who were targets of Watergate investigations: former domestic affairs adviser John D. Ehrlichman, former chief of staff H. R. Haldeman and former counsel Charles W. Colson. Ziegler said he was "not going to respond to a story which was generated in that way and contains a mixture of supposed discussions, many of them out of context."

(Ziegler said at the same news briefing that the new White House press policy would be to turn aside questions on Watergate and concentrate on "the business of government." The only exceptions, Ziegler said, would be when a formal statement was necessary or when White House lawyers wished to "provide relevant answers.")

Nixon recalls attacks on Lincoln. Speaking at the Lincoln Memorial in Washington Feb. 12, President Nixon drew a parallel between his own ordeal and that of President Abraham Lincoln's. "No President in history has been more vilified or was more vilified during the time he was President," he said, "than Lincoln. Those who knew him, his secretaries, have written that he was very deeply hurt by what was said about him and drawn about him, but on the other hand, Lincoln had the great strength of character never to display it, always to stand tall and strong and firm no matter how harsh or unfair the criticism might be."

Longworth birthday party—Nixon visited the 90th birthday celebration Feb. 12 for Alice Roosevelt Longworth, a daughter of Theodore Roosevelt. Later, he attributed her longevity to "not being obsessed by the Washington scene." "If she had spent all of her time reading the [Washington] Post or the [Washington] Star [-News] she would have been dead by now," he told reporters. "Mrs.

Longworth keeps young by not being obsessed with the miserable political things that all of us unfortunately think about in Washington, by thinking about those great issues that will affect the future of the world, which the Post, unfortunately seldom writes about in a responsible way."

St. Clair attacks Post story. Special presidential counsel James D. St. Clair Feb. 17 attacked the "inaccuracy and innuendo" of a Washington Post report that said that the court-appointed panel of technical experts examining the Watergate tapes had found "technical indications" that two of the tapes might be re-recordings rather than the originals said to have been surrendered by the White House. St. Clair said he would ask for a Justice Department investigation into the "person or persons who may have violated legal restraints" in referring to matters before the grand jury.

Nixon disparages Washington reporting. Addressing an "Honor America Day" rally in Huntsville, Ala. Feb. 18, President Nixon disparaged news reporting in Washington. There was a tendency there, he said, "for partisanship to take over from statesmanship, . . . a tendency in the reporting of news—I do not say this critically, it's simply a fact of life— that bad news is news and good news is not news." As a result, he continued, "those of us who work there and try to develop the policies of the nation may get a distorted view of what is America and what it is really like. It is there that you hear more than any other place in America that America is sick, that there is something wrong with America that cannot be corrected."

Atlanta editor kidnapped. J. Reginald Murphy, 40, editor of the Atlanta Constitution, was kidnapped Feb. 20 by members of a group calling itself the American Revolutionary Army. He was lured from his home by a man, who had asked for aid from the newspaper in distributing $100,000 worth of heating oil to Atlanta's needy.

The abductors subsequently contacted the Constitution by a tape recorded message by Murphy. He said his kidnappers were demanding a ransom of $700,000. A spokesman for the Constitution said the newspaper would pay the ransom as soon as it learned the method and site of the delivery.

Murphy described the members of the American Revolutionary Army as men who said they were displeased with the U.S. news media, which they labeled "too leftist and too liberal." He said the group was "quite strong" across the U.S. and that in the future it "intends to go into guerrilla warfare."

Although it was not part of their ransom demand, Murphy said, the kidnappers were calling for the resignation of all members of Congress and "free elections" that "would return the American government to the American people."

"The American Revolutionary Army tells me that they intend in the future to engage in guerrilla warfare throughout the country. They don't intend to engage in bloodshed at this time. One of their significant demands is that all federal government officials resign and that free elections be held in the future. To make that clear, they mean the senators and congressmen, they are not talking about the people who have worked in the federal agencies in the past, they're talking about elected officials."

Murphy also said his abduction had been planned at the same time as, but not in concert with, the Symbionese Liberation Army's kidnapping of Patricia Hearst, daughter of Randolph A. Hearst, publisher and editor of the San Francisco Examiner. Neither group shared the same goals nor did they work in the same way, Murphy said.

Murphy was released by his captors Feb. 23 following the payment of the $700,000 ransom by his newspaper. Six hours later police arrested a suburban Atlanta couple in connection with the case.

Held in an Atlanta jail in lieu of bail totaling $1.5 million were building contractor William A. H. Williams, 33, and his wife, Betty Ruth, 26. An agent for the Federal Bureau of Investigation (FBI) said suitcases filled with $700,000 had been found in their Lilburn, Ga. home.

According to Murphy, who wrote an account of the kidnapping for his newspaper, a man calling himself "Lamont Woods" asked for help in distributing anonymously $300,000 worth of fuel oil to the needy. The man picked up Murphy the evening of Feb. 20 and drove north from Atlanta, supposedly to sign papers for the fuel distribution. As they drove, the man pulled out a gun and said: "Mr. Murphy, you have been kidnapped. We're going to straighten out this damn country. We're going to stop these lying, leftist, liberal news media."

Nixon holds news conference. At his first White House news conference in several months, President Nixon Feb. 25 said his interpretation of the Constitution required a criminal offense by a president for impeachment. The news session was marked by less open rancor between Nixon and the press than at previous post-Watergate press conferences.

Editorial Comment

The Burlington Free Press

Burlington, Vt., April 25, 1973

THIS EDITORIAL IS surely the most difficult one this writer has attempted in a 15-year career of newspapering. It will please few, if any, of our colleagues in the newspaper profession. But popularity of position, either among our peers in the profession or among friends and acquaintances outside, was never a goal of honest editorial writing.

What is important is the matter of integrity; if a newspaperman does not have integrity and is not willing to defend it against all the pressures of this hectic life, then he has nothing. This editorial, then, is a statement of conscience.

* * *

A LARGE PORTION of the American press (and here we include newspapers, television, radio and magazines) is carrying on an anti-Nixon vendetta in the coverage of the so-called "Watergate scandal." There is simply and absolutely no excuse whatever

for the sensational, mostly unsubstantiated, reckless and distorted reportage of this unhappy affair. It is a reportage of hatred against a man, a President of the United States, and this writer hereby condemns it and completely disassociates himself from it.

The "bugging" of Democratic Party headquarters at the Watergate complex in Washington cannot be condoned, and we make no effort to do so. But neither can it be projected honestly into a scandal of historic proportions. There have been many political scandals of more far-reaching significance, unfortunately, in our nation's history — but never heretofore has blind hatred on the part of the press compelled such coverage of clear and unashamed recrimination. The 1960 Presidential election is a case in point, when "lost" and destroyed ballots in Illinois and Texas and Missouri actually swung the election. Or, of more recent vintage, the Bobby Baker scandal of the 1960s whose implications were far more serious than the

Watergate "bugging" and associated activities.

But the American press did not devote a fraction of its considerable energies and talents to those scandals that it has to the Watergate case. And why not? We can only conclude that the name and the personality of the man in the Oval Office makes all the difference, and this is a damning indictment of a large portion of the nation's press whose sense of purpose and responsibility has been mangled.

* * *

IF THE PRESS continues in its zealous overkill on this affair, it is not likely to destroy either President Nixon or the Nixon Administration but it will gravely injure something more important: The faith of the people in our system of government and all that it provides and protects — including, most pointedly, freedom of the press.

In short, the American press is becoming its own worst enemy. The

champions of press freedom are becomin the practitioners of press McCarthyism, an the end result could be far more devastatin to this nation than most of our colleague seem to realize.

A "herd psychology" pervades the pres most evident in Washington, and th psychology must be overcome by men an women of courage from within th profession itself who will cry out for hone and compassionate reportage. Otherwis most certainly this period will b remembered — with more sadness tha outrage — as the darkest chapter in the lor history of American press freedom.

As this writer noted at the beginnin this editorial is a personal statement conscience which may or may not reflect t views of some others in our profession. B integrity — a newspaperman's integrity compels its publication here and now.
Franklin B. Smith

The News and Courier

Charleston, S.C., April 25, 1973

As Watergate probers get closer to the nerve centers of the Nixon administration, White House morale and prestige continue to suffer. So does effective government of the United States.

The darker the second Nixon term is tarnished, the worse for the American people. They desperately need the kind of leadership that Richard Nixon is peculiarly fitted to supply. The irony of wrecking the executive branch over a scandalous but relatively unimportant issue should not be overlooked in eagerness to smear Tricky Dick and his gang of telephone buggers.

While denouncing underhand methods of gathering political intelligence during the 1972 campaign, some probers themselves are under attack. On Monday the U. S. District Court

in Washington ordered investigation of leaks in secret testimony before the grand jury. An emergency meeting of the court's judges, The Associated Press reported, was prompted by columnist Jack Anderson's accounts of verbatim testimony before the grand jury investigating Watergate.

So far nothing has been said about bugging the grand jury room. Anderson retorted that it is the constitutional right of a free press to publish information beneficial to the public. He attributed President Nixon's opening of White House sources to "our access to the grand jury findings."

The extent to which secrets should be disclosed is one of the continuing issues of our time. The Pentagon Papers were an

example, and the trial of David Ellsberg has grown out of that case. Some of the defenders of Ellsberg, who stole Defense Dept. secrets and gave them to the press, are among the most vituperative attackers of Watergate bugging.

Other critics — among them David Brinkley — seem more concerned over stupidity than moral, legal and ethical guilt. Nixon had it made before Watergate, these critics argue, and his campaigners did not need to risk a scandal to pick over Democratic secrets.

Now the critics are more upset over the cover-up than Watergate itself. We confess that we no longer know whom to believe on any side of this case. A Gallup Poll reported that four out of 10 people it questioned believe President Nixon knew in ad-

vance about Watergate: Responses indicated that 53 per cent believe it was "just politics", and 31 per cent call it "corruption". The rest had no opinion or hadn't heard of the case.

The Watergate probe now has gathered so much momentum that it will have to run its course. Meanwhile the wheels of government are clogged, and public trust is shaken. Things that need to be done are neglected. President Nixon may have to organize a new White House staff as a result of this case.

Whether one regards the episode as stupid, corrupt or "just politics" blown out of proportion, the damage to the country could be grave. At best, poor judgment in high places has been disclosed. We see no profit in wrecking national interests, however, over Watergate.

THE RICHMOND NEWS LEADER
Richmond, Va., April 26, 1973

Watergate promises to linger for months, but some tentative conclusions may be drawn now:

Conservatives and pro-Nixon moderates stunningly misjudged the extent of Nixon administration involvement in the Watergate fiasco. Two primary assumptions led Nixon supporters astray: (1) that no one closely connected to the President would be so criminally stupid as to take part in the Watergate operation; (2) that the nation's heavily anti-Nixon press was incapable of producing more fact than fiction. Both assumptions were reasonable, but neither proved accurate.

Because of their abiding detestation of Mr. Nixon, certain leftists in the media have consistently opted for a presumption of guilt in evaluating the President's motives and actions. If he bombed, it was often described as genocide—not an attempt to end the war. If he said an unkind word about the press, it was described as repression—not an appeal for fair treatment. If he asked the FBI or the Justice Department to investigate a bomb-lobbing radical, it was incipient gestapo-ism—not an attempt to have a criminal locked up. There has been a consistent imputation of deliberate evil on a grand scale, no matter how scanty the corroborative evidence. So it was not surprising that these same reporters assumed that Watergate was a White House-level conspiracy that demanded further investigation.

For the wrong reasons the leftist press made evidently correct assumptions about Watergate. They lucked out, and therein lies one of the unnoticed tragedies of this tawdry affair. Watergate constitutes the single vindication of leftist assumption relating to the Nixon administration. Yet henceforward Watergate will overshadow the countless reportorial excesses of the past. In their zeal for Mr. Nixon's neck, even now they are going beyond the limits of journalistic propriety. Last Thursday, for example, *The Washington Post* ran a double-decker banner headline across the top of page 1: "Mitchell, Dean Approved Watergate, Payoffs, Magruder Reportedly Says." Neither Mitchell nor Dean had been—or has been—indicted or tried or convicted for any crime.

How far the anti-Nixonite press will go in the future depends on the President. He alone can salvage both the potential of his second term and the dignity of the presidency itself. If he does not—in the military term—"seize the initiative," then Watergate may become his Waterloo, for nothing he does in the remaining years of his presidency will be free of the innuendo-encrusted sniping engendered by the spectacle of his staff stumbling across the front pages of the daily newspaper. Now-or-never situations seldom arise in politics, but the President surely confronts one today. His supporters must be reassured. His enemies must be sidetracked. His nation must know that it is guided by leadership above reproach. Failure could well force the President to a political Elba from which he could never return.

THE ARIZONA REPUBLIC
Phoenix, Ariz., April 25, 1973

Jack Anderson is about to tangle with the law in an entirely new way. The Washington columnist, in a long career of peephole journalism, has been able to print bits and pieces of secret documents slipped to him by disgruntled Washington bureaucrats.

This gave him the aura of an all-wise journalist who was in everyone's confidence. If anyone wanted to know where he received his information, he c l a i m e d a newsman's right not to divulge the sources of his news. Only rarely, as in the Sen. Tom Eagleton affair, did he have the grace to admit that his sources could be wrong.

Now, h o w e v e r, Anderson has gone beyond the limits usually permitted a newspaper reporter. He has printed verbatim portions of testimony given to the Watergate grand jury in Washington.

Judge John J. Sirica, who presided over the Watergate grand jury, has called a second grand jury to investigate the leaks from the first grand jury. The other 14 judges in the U.S. district court supported Judge Sirica's move.

Anderson promptly announced he would depend on the Constitution to protect his rights as a newspaperman.

One wonders — what rights?

A grand jury is called to determine whether a crime has been committed and whether there is probable cause to bring formal charges. By their very nature, proceedings of a grand jury must remain secret. Anyone can go before a grand jury and make the most outrageous charges. If Jack Anderson or anyone else can print those charges under the protective umbrella of the First Amendment (freedom of the press), then a grand jury can be used for the most vicious sort of character assassination.

Material submitted to a grand jury is raw, unrefined, and unverified information. When the late Sen. Joe McCarthy used the same sort of information from FBI and other files, the word McCarthyism was coined as an epithet. Perhaps the time has come to talk about Andersonism.

In cold fact, the second grand jury is far more likely to return indictments against those who leaked the information from the first grand jury than it is to seek to punish those who published it. If Anderson is called before the grand jury, as he almost certainly will be, we will watch with interest to see whether he leaks his own testimony to a fellow columnist, thus placing himself in the same jeopardy that those who leaked information to him now find themselves.

The constitutional guarantees of a free press are under assault across the country. A federal court in Louisiana recently upheld a contempt conviction against reporters who printed testimony given in open court. An Indiana circuit court judge threw the press out of a murder trial. Tennessee and Texas have both just passed shield laws (much like the one Arizona has) to give reporters qualified protection against being f o r c e d to reveal their news sources.

We submit that the c u r r e n t wave of anti-press sentiment has been created largely by the irresponsibility of such gossip purveyors as Jack Anderson. In publishing stolen transcripts from the Watergate grand jury, Anderson did a disservice to himself, to his profession, and to the administration of justice.

Some high officials in the Nixon administration are learning how serious a matter it is to try to steal secrets from a campaign headquarters. American journalism will be the better if Jack Anderson learns how serious it is to publish secrets of a grand jury.

The Evening Gazette
Worcester, Mass., April 18, 1973

The federal Bureau of Investigation was out of line in some of its recent efforts to discover the news sources of columnist Jack Anderson.

Anderson's reporting has not always brought glory to the newspaper business. But the FBI brought no glory on itself by tracing 96 telephone calls to Anderson through subpoenaed toll records.

Attacks on the confidential aspects of newsgathering have been questionable enough, but checking phone calls is an invasion of privacy even more difficult to justify.

U.S. District Court Judge John J. Sirica issued a temporary injunction ordering that the FBI quit using telephone records in this case.

The FBI, in its current shadowy role in the Watergate affair, would do well to keep meticulously clear of politics. Faith in the bureau's strictly nonpolitical posture needs to be restored — and prying into personal telephone conversations of newsmen doesn't help that posture.

THE SACRAMENTO BEE
Sacramento, Calif., April 27, 1973

Pulitzer prize-winning columnist Jack Anderson showed good judgment and a sense of responsibility in agreeing he will no longer quote secret Grand Jury testimony on the Watergate case in his nationally syndicated columns.

It is the constitutional right of the press to publish any and all news generated by the White House, the Congress or the courts. Court rules or federal rules of criminal procedure do not supersede the Constitution.

However, Anderson quite properly took into consideration the United States attorneys' pleas that the prosecution was having trouble getting witnesses to testify because the witnesses said they were afraid anything they said could end up in Anderson's columns.

As Anderson said in agreeing to voluntarily turn over his copies of secret testimony to Chief US District Judge John J. Sirica: "We are working for the same purposes, to get to the bottom of Watergate."

In reporting and investigating the Watergate matter Anderson, whose columns appear in The Bee, has done this nation a valuable service. White House sources told Anderson one factor which persuaded the President to throw open the Watergate investigation was Anderson's access to the Grand Jury testimony.

Because of the dogged investigation by Anderson and the thorough reporting job done by the Washington Post, the disquieting significance of the Watergate bugging and burglary was brought home to the public, instead of being dismissed as a "third-rate burglary," as a White House press secretary termed it.

It is good for this country to have gadflies like Anderson in Washington. In the long run his unstinting devotion to the people's right to know may serve to keep the government officials more honest than they might be otherwise.

Pittsburgh Post-Gazette
Pittsburgh, Pa., April 27, 1973

THE STORY, uncovered by The Washington Post, about an alleged campaign of grand-scale deception by Richard Nixon's re-election committee last May comes at the worst possible time for the beleaguered President and his White House staff. The almost hourly revelations and accusations concerning the White House's involvement in the Watergate scandal are increasingly taking their toll in eroding the people's confidence in their government.

Mr. Ziegler

But The Post's report about a supposed effort by Mr. Nixon's campaign committee to fake the public's response to the mining of North Vietnamese harbors verges on the incredible.

* * *

That Mr. Nixon's committee would pay for telegrams to be sent to the White House in support of the mining and for the placing of a deceptive and possibly illegal advertisement in the May 17 New York Times smacks of the kind of banana republic political tactics which most citizens of the United States cannot readily believe of their own government.

According to The Post, a re-election committee official said that the grand deception included "petition drives, organizing rallies, bringing people in buses to Washington, organizing calls to the White House, getting voters to call their congressmen." The purpose? "We felt (the decision to mine Haiphong harbor) could make or break the President," the unnamed official said.

White House Press Secretary Ron Ziegler told the nation on May 10 that telegrams, letters and phone calls were running 5 or 6 to 1 in support of Mr. Nixon's action and cited them as indicating "substantial support" in Congress and among voters for the mining, said The Post story.

It also reported that a former Nixon campaign official said that the Committee to Re-elect the President was "totally mobilized for the biggest piece of deception—we never do anything honestly. Imagine, the President sending himself telegrams, patting himself on the back."

The apparent involvement of two convicted Watergate conspirators, Bernard Barker and Frank Sturgis, in the campaign to fake support for Mr. Nixon's mining decision adds a cinematic gangland twist to a barely credible plot.

On top of all that, the ad in The Times, says The Post story, was signed by people passing themselves off as representing citizens' support for Mr. Nixon's harbor-mining decision.

The most damning piece of evidence apparently is the reported admission by an executive of the group handling the Nixon committee's advertising that the ad was paid for with 44 one-hundred dollar bills sent from the President's re-election committee in Washington.

* * *

That the Watergate crimes seemingly were perpetrated in adherence to the re-election committee's and White House staff's apparent belief that victory in the presidential election was worth any cost is unfortunately consonant, moreover, with the reported fake-support campaign in May.

What defies our understanding of logic, finally, is how any of Mr. Nixon's advisers could have believed that such criminal deception could justify the risk of dishonoring the very office which they fought so hard to win.

The Miami Herald
Miami, Fla., April 26, 1973

MAY 1972 was the time when the Nixon administration evened it up with the lying media — the newspapers, the TV, the radio — all the print and talk people who thought the war in Vietnam was unwise and who thought the people thought so, too.

On May 8 President Nixon announced he had ordered the mining of Haiphong harbor and six other North Vietnamese ports. On May 9 it was done.

Next day, May 10, White House Press Secretary Ronald Ziegler announced that telegrams, letters and phone calls were running 5 or 6 to 1 supporting the Presidential action. A $4,400 signed ad denouncing that newspaper appeared in The New York Times May 17.

Over the next two weeks busloads of approving citizens descended on Washington. There were pro-Nixon rallies in several cities, including Miami. Petitions were circulated. People telegraphed their congressmen. A Harris Poll showed that 59 per cent of Americans approved the war action.

But this was no spontaneous, popular reaction. It was organized, set up, staged, rigged, manipulated by a quasi-governmental organization, the Committee for the Reelection of the President (CREP), perhaps the most fateful albatross ever to light on the White House.

CREP has spilled its guts to the press it once denounced as biased and out of touch with the thinking of the people. One former campaign official told The Washington Post that the organization was "totally mobilized for the biggest piece of deception — we never do anything honestly. Imagine, the President sending himself telegrams, patting himself on the back."

There is nothing wrong in urging citizens to become articulate on government or any of its issues. This is done every day, and if it is done honestly it is wholesome.

The involvement of the government itself in such an exercise, however, is quite another matter. It smacks almost of Herr Dr. Goebbels, promoting the Fuehrer Prinzip through his Reichministry of Propaganda and Enlightenment.

The technique may well call in question other evidences of spontaneity in public reaction to government doings. What are we left to believe?

Of all the revelations of the weeks past this is the most disappointing, the most disheartening.

Other governments have maintained corps of publicity men grinding out releases designed to place the boss in the best light.

But to put words in the mouths of people with money — surely some of it tax money — is the ultimate desecration of free, untrammeled speech. It is the greening of American public opinion, and in sadness we deplore it.

Chicago Tribune

Chicago, Ill., June 13, 1973

The Ervin committee yesterday rejected Maurice Stans' request for a postponement of his appearance in the Watergate hearings, just as it had earlier rejected Special Prosecutor Archibald Cox's request that the whole proceedings be delayed—or at least conducted in private. Both requests were based on the legitimate argument that the present televised hearings might interfere with a fair trial when and if the witnesses appear in court in connection with Watergate.

And yet the committee was right in rejecting the requests. The most eloquent criticism of the committee hearings has come from Britain—notably the London Times—and from Mr. Cox himself, who is a staunch admirer of the British system of justice. In one of the longest editorials it has ever printed, the Times described the publicity attending the hearings as "so prejudicial that it alone would seem to preclude the possibility of a fair trial for any accused, even including the President himself if there were impeachment proceedings."

There is much to admire about British justice, especially its speed and precision compared with our dilatory, meandering process which can be manipulated endlessly by clever defense lawyers. Perhaps if the courts functioned here as they do in Britain, we, too, could afford to abandon grand juries and muzzle the investigators. But they don't. The sad fact is that few of our scandals would ever have reached the surface if we had sat back and relied on "due process of law," British-style. Teapot Dome was aired in a Congressional hearing. The Watergate facts were dug up largely by the press. The Kerner and Barrett evidence was produced mainly before grand juries.

In Britain, the press is effectively prevented from undertaking "investigative reporting" as we know it. The courts treat as contempt the publication of anything which might be regarded as prejudicial. The British Press Council is ready to chastise any paper that oversteps the bounds of propriety. The only evidence that is likely to be produced is that gathered by the prosecution or the court.

The fact that political scandals are relatively rare in Britain [and, when they do occur, relatively frivolous] may be the result of Britain's system of justice or it may reflect the traditionally higher standards of public service in Britain. But whatever the reason for our poor showing, it is not going to be improved by calling off the dogs. The press and the legislatures and grand juries are likely to be essential to American justice for a long time to come.

Senators Ervin and Baker gave well reasoned arguments in favor of continuing with the hearings despite Mr. Stans' request. The hearings have been conducted with restraint. Incidentally, the London Times' "most damaging example" of prejudicial publicity arose not from the public hearings, but from secret testimony.

The committee hearings should continue because they remind us all that American office-holders are answerable not just to prosecutors and judges, but to the country as a whole. But to say this is not to say that the hearings should run wild. The senators must be judicious in their questioning and must do their best to see that those named have a chance to answer the charges made against them. We're thinking not so much of the President, who can get all the publicity he wants whenever he wants it, but of lesser men who may be innocent and yet may be unable to clear their names in court because of the difficulty of getting a fair trial.

Richmond Times-Dispatch

Richmond, Va., June 12, 1973

More and more people are suggesting that if President Nixon would only hold a press conference on the Watergate scandal, many of his troubles related to the affair would vanish. This implies that the President's remarks to a gathering of reporters would be more credible than the statements he already has issued on the matter.

Those who hold this point of view argue that by agreeing to submit to questions from newsmen, the President would show that he really has nothing to hide and that he is willing to promote full disclosure of the White House's role in the affair. Theoretically, this should contribute to the restoration of public confidence in the Nixon administration.

Conducted under proper procedures, a press conference might serve some constructive purposes. But the procedures that ordinarily govern presidential press conferences probably would not be desirable. With scores of reporters vying for the President's attention, the questions would lack continuity and depth and the answers, if Mr. Nixon wished to avoid the possibility that two or three newsmen would monopolize the conference, would have to be brief. A better approach would be for the President to meet with a small group of reporters on a pool basis, an arrangement that would permit both the questions and the answers to be thorough and precise.

Even under the best of conditions, however, a press conference on Watergate might be of only limited and temporary value. In his public statements on the affair, Mr. Nixon has insisted that he had no prior knowledge of the Watergate operation and that he was not personally involved in subsequent efforts to conceal the facts about it. It is unlikely that he would say anything substantially different from this at a press conference. On the contrary, he probably would be more adamant than ever in protesting his innocence.

This might strengthen the faith of his supporters, but it probably would not mollify his severest critics in the press and in Congress. Nothing will satisfy them except (a) a complete confession of guilt from Mr. Nixon or (b) proof of his innocence from *non-presidential sources*. His word, whether given in statements or press conferences, is not good enough for these people. Their suspicions will remain alive until those former presidential aides who have personal knowledge of the President's involvement or non-involvement in Watergate—John Mitchell, John Dean, John Ehrlichman and H. R. Haldeman—present public testimony that results in the President's exoneration.

So while a strong case can be made for a presidential press conference, it is possible to expect too much from one. The quickest and most effective way to resolve doubts about the President is to bring Mitchell, Dean, Ehrlichman and Haldeman before the Senate Watergate committee and let them tell their stories.

THE RICHMOND NEWS LEADER

Richmond, Va., June 14, 1973

Speaking for the CBS radio network, correspondent Dallas Townsend recently took umbrage with a *London Times* editorial that accused the American press, the Ervin Committee, and the Watergate grand jury of acting out "a Washington variant of lynch law." Not so, said Townsend, as he noted that the *Times* editorial "discredited... every institution that has had anything to do with bringing the scandal into the light of day. . ." But then Townsend sought to slough off the *Times'* charge that the Ervin Committee is obstructing justice by publicly prejudicing cases against potential defendants: "The fact is," said Townsend, "that justice, in this case, is not the overriding concern."

What is the "overriding concern"? According to Townsend, it "is one of high national issues, political as well as legal, one of ethics as of law. It is a case of a democracy being able to learn the scope of grave and dangerous flaws in its political

system and thereby learn[ing] how to correct them." Up to a point, Townsend's opinion is justifiable: The government has failed to bring all the alleged Watergate participants to swift justice, and if, in order to know the full truth of Watergate, some of the guilty must have their cases so prejudiced as to escape justice, then that is the way the game must now be played.

But what Townsend ignores, and what the *Times* implies in its references to "lynch law," is the possible loss of justice for the *innocent* as well as the guilty. As an example, consider the performance before the Ervin Committee of former Secretary of Commerce Maurice Stans: In the face of an avalanche of innuendo in the press, Stans so plausibly professed his innocence that several Senators were visibly annoyed by their inability to nail his hide to the wall. Viewing the confrontation between

Stans and the Ervin Committee, one could almost hear some of the Senators say in exasperated anger, "But you're supposed to be guilty!"

In a court of law, Stans' innocence would be assumed until he had been found guilty beyond reasonable doubt. Through a combination of grand jury leaks, press hearsay and speculation, and Ervin Committee publicity, Stans' innocence not only is not assumed — it is regarded as inconceivable. And that is why the *Times* spoke of "lynch law." So Dallas Townsend erred in completely dismissing justice as the "overriding issue." Perhaps the search for truth can override justice for the guilty. But the nation should not sanction any twisting of the truth that will render justice for the innocent consequently impossible. For in the long run, to do so would constitute a crime far worse than Watergate itself.

Detroit Free Press
Detroit, Mich., June 30, 1973

EVERYONE KEEPS a list, written or mental, of people they don't like, and the White House is no exception. Most, however, refer to it in more earthy terms than "enemies list" used by the administration. As entertainer Bill Cosby noted, "Nixon was on my list long before I was on Nixon's list."

Most of the 173 people named on the enemies list supplied to the Senate Watergate Committee by former presidential counsel John Dean III felt more honored than outraged, although the list was pretty outrageous.

For example, there was that noted political commentator from Beaver Falls, Pa., Joe Namath, somewhat ignominiously traded by the White House from the New York Jets to the rival Giants. Who would have thought Broadway Joe could get away from booze, broads and knee surgeons long enough to become anyone's political enemy?

As befitting the lofty heights of the presidency, the list was bipartisan. It included Wally Hickel, a former Republican governor, Charles Goodell, a former Republican senator, and John Lindsay, a former Republican.

Paul Newman, who made a better Hud than did George Romney, thought he had won a Richard. "And I would like to thank John Mitchell, Jeb Magruder, John Dean III and Maurice Stans for making this award possible."

The presidents of Yale and MIT were on the list, but not the president of Harvard. There would be gloom in the Square except Harvard's law school dean and three faculty members made it.

Ed Guthman made the list as managing editor of the Los Angeles Times, which prompted a New York Times staff writer to note:

"Alas, Mr. Guthman is not the managing editor, but the national editor, and the citation by itself does not make him eligible for promotion." It probably doesn't eliminate him from future consideration though, so no harm's done.

The list was remarkable both for those included and those excluded. Columnist Sydney Harris, who gives innocuous word tests, made it, but Herblock, who does scathing political cartoons, did not.

Barbra Streisand made it, but neither Shirley McLaine nor her brother, Warren Beatty, did.

Sen. Howard Baker, R-Tenn., reported that Watergate Committee Chairman Sam Ervin, D-N.C., leaned over as the list was made public and said, "I think I'm going to demand a recount. There are more enemies than we got votes."

The list was rather exclusive. It threatens to replace the Social Register in Washington.

THE KANSAS CITY STAR
Kansas City, Mo., June 19, 1973

A recent Gallup poll shows that 44 per cent of the people questioned—more than 4 out of 10 —believe that newspapers, magazines, television and radio are paying too much attention to Watergate and related subjects. The poll isn't surprising and we would guess that it is accurate: A high percentage of the American people are tired of Watergate and wish it would go away for various reasons.

We cannot agree, however, that the press should reduce coverage or let the issues fade away no matter how unpopular the recital becomes. It is the obligation of the media to provide information to the people no matter how distasteful it might be. The First Amendment to the Constitution guaranteeing freedom of the press is not there by accident; a free press is an integral part of the system and the chief value of the media is not in the entertainment it furnishes but as a purveyor of information.

People who are disenchanted with Watergate can be divided into three broad categories:

The least important group comprises those who are unhappy if a soap opera is supplanted occasionally or who are not much interested in anything that doesn't concern movies, sports or TV personalities. These individuals take little, if any, interest in public affairs. If they vote, it almost always is an uninformed act. But they seldom vote, and democracy's loss is small.

A second group is composed of those who are very interested in government, but from a blindly partisan and very narrow view that often reflects a fundamental self-interest. They resent any unfavorable reporting on the President or his party as unpatriotic, if not disloyal. They consider it a personal attack upon themselves, so strongly do they identify. Right now these people are a certain type of Republican. If the occupant of the White House happened to be a Democrat, they would be a certain type of Democrat.

The third and probably biggest group tired of Watergate are concerned people who dread the implications of presidential involvement and would rather not think of this breakdown of a system they revere and honor. It is frightening to imagine that a large majority might have been fooled in the campaign into voting for people who do not believe in the system at all. The alarm and uneasiness of this group is understandable. They wish it had never happened and want to act as if it didn't—somewhat in the manner of trying to ignore a doctor's bad report.

But why is full coverage of governmental failures important at all? For the answer, the essentials of representative government must be recalled. If such government is a pact between the rulers and the ruled, with the people claiming the right to change rulers, then the inviolability of the electoral system must be reasonably assured. The system is a peaceful means of change, of revolution. Rather than behead unsatisfactory Presidents, governors, mayors or representatives, we vote them out of office periodically and replace them with others.

The obvious key to representative government is the electoral system, and the essence of the electoral system must be a free choice arrived at through observation, information and the formation of clear opinion.

If one political group secures an unfair advantage over others, and if that advantage is secured by breaking the law, then it is best that the people know of it. If polls are rigged, if phony letters and telegrams are used to indicate support or disapproval or to disrupt a campaign, then the whole system is debased and the people are voting a lie.

Most important of all, if trusted institutions of government and sensitive offices—the Justice Department, the Federal Bureau of Investigation or the Central Intelligence Agency—are used to further the political cause of incumbents, then the basic concept of representative government is betrayed and an ugly corruption is being created.

All of which is why the American people do not dare to dismiss or ignore Watergate and its associated bad news—no matter how painful it becomes.

Los Angeles Times
Los Angeles , Calif., June 28, 1973

The list of White House "enemies," which John W. Dean III turned over to the Senate Watergate committee, makes a bizarrely disparate collection of names. Probably it marks the first time that Gov. George C. Wallace and Jane Fonda have found themselves in the same company. Included were senators and congressmen, newspapermen and Democratic political contributors.

Dean says the list was continually updated and embellished. It is not yet known what, if anything, was done with the list.

But it is known what was intended to be done with the list. White House memos proposed to use the power of the Internal Revenue Service to harass persons the White House thought of as enemies.

This plan was as shocking a proposal as we have encountered in the Watergate affair, for it was a proposal to use the great power of the government to intimidate citizens it considered unfriendly.

Most disturbing was the allegation by Dean that the White House arranged for the IRS to do a special audit on the tax returns of the Newsday editor in charge of an investigative series on the President's financial dealings with his friend, C. G. (Bebe) Rebozo. The editor, Robert Greene, confirmed that an audit had in fact been done and that no errors were found in his tax returns.

This charge requires the most thorough investigation. Required also is a thorough inquiry into whether any aspect of the plan proposed was put into effect. It is incumbent on the IRS to answer, and fast.

It will be most useful also to hear the results of the investigation ordered by Rep. Wilbur D. Mills (D-Ark.), chairman of the Joint Committee on Internal Revenue Taxation.

These memos illustrate again what had been glimpsed before the Watergate case broke, what has become glaringly obtrusive since then, that there were men in the Nixon Administration—and not just a few—who had absolutely no business being trusted with power, because they were simply incapable of understanding the necessary limits which law imposes on the exercise of power.

The list released by Dean was feverishly indiscriminating, a fact that speaks volumes about the cast of mind behind it. To Mr. Nixon's aides who compiled the list there seemed to be only "them" and "us," and that division having been settled, the next step, in the words of one of the memos accompanying the list, was simply to decide "how we can use the available federal machinery to screw our political enemies." The high-mindedness of that comment, the respect for due process and fair play it implies, pretty well sums things up.

What is one to make of the eager readiness of men in authority to exploit the police power of the state for petty and corrupt political purposes, a readiness that constituted a whole pattern of behavior? That is one question among the many that have emerged this week that the President has an obligation to respond to. His personal involvement in wrongdoing is for now an unproven allegation, but his overall responsibility for what has occurred in his Administration is a fact, and that fact must be addressed with greater candor and thoroughness than we have yet heard.

THE CHRISTIAN SCIENCE MONITOR

Boston, Mass., August 24, 1973

President Nixon strengthened his position in fielding all questions on Watergate shot at him by the press Wednesday in San Clemente.

It was the kind of performance his friends and critics have been urging. Apart from an early nervousness, he showed a resilience of spirit, an adroitness, that should be an answer to reports that the President's composure, as well as public support, had been weakened by the Watergate ordeal.

True, there were problems with the format the President chose for his first open press session in five months. The press were summoned almost by surprise. There was the usual lack of opportunity to follow up on questions. And a press conference, as Senator Ervin pointed out after listening to

the President's performance, still fails to offer the kind of cross-examination needed to get an exact fix on Watergate.

But it was a press conference. And it does mark a significant turn toward conciliation and away from counterattack. A start toward resolving the Watergate tangle, and toward rebuilding the President's standing among the American people, could stem from it.

The President, in acceding to demands for a press conference, did not give ground on most of the key elements of his defense. While he was speaking in San Clemente, his lawyer Charles Alan Wright was defending before Judge Sirica in Washington the President's right to keep the Watergate tapes from Congress and the courts. On the issue of wiretaps and illegal

entry, the President agreed the Ellsberg break-in was wrong specifically but did not back off from his right to do whatever he thought necessary under his "inherent power" as President to defend national security. He did not yield over the propriety of meeting the Ellsberg trial judge for the FBI chief vacancy.

Nor did the President close the door on his opportunities for counterattack. He still portrayed — here and in New Orleans — as out to get him all those who disagree with his policies on Vietnam, social reforms, and so forth. This is an unfortunate device of Mr. Nixon's. Indeed, there are many Americans who may disagree with the President on Southeast Asia, busing, aid to parochial schools, and yet wish him no political or personal harm. They want him to survive. They know

that when the President is in trouble the country is in trouble.

The tendency to cast opponents as enemies has been one of the themes behind the Watergate revelations. But leaving Watergate aside, it is a principle of democracy that opposing views exist and have a right to be heard and weighed and ultimately voted upon.

The President availed himself of the right to present his case through the press Wednesday. How far he will have convinced doubters about Watergate remains to be seen — we expect that the polls will show a favorable public response. But by openly accepting tough leading Watergate questions he has brought himself back more in touch with the American people. He has made himself less remote.

THE TENNESSEAN

Nashville, Tenn., August 25, 1973

AT HIS news conference in San Clemente, President Nixon was almost his old combative self as he dealt with the press in barely controlled fury, fielding its questions on Watergate while criticizing the preoccupation with it.

* * *

He had at least stopped sitting behind a wall of silence. If the tension between him and the press corps skirted the breaking point a few times, he nevertheless answered its questions.

In the process, he managed to contradict the testimony of his former White House counsel, the acting FBI director, the attorney general, the former attorney general and the statements of his daughter.

It was clear enough he had opened the counterattack against his critics in a bid for public support to put Watergate behind and get on with other things. If the opening gun was in New Orleans, where he spoke to the VFW, his press conference was a salvo with the underlying thread of a persecuted president whom the press had never liked or supported and of many others who had never accepted his mandate of 1972.

Mr. Nixon's verbal self portrait is of a man surrrounded by enemies, even some on his own staff who played fast and loose with him while he was trying to get the truth out. Other unnamed people don't want him to give strong leadership and cut the size of bureaucracy.

The President's defense of his own actions and that of others is curious. He had tapes at the White House because he found the capability already there. He re-

fuses to give them up because other presidents have so refused. If there is something wrong with wiretapping, well, the Kennedy administration had far more than his. And, the President opened a new can of worms by claiming that government-authorized burglaries took place on "a very large scale" during the Kennedy and Johnson administrations.

This is the kind of unsupported claims that Mr. Nixon deplores in others. But the point is, previous wrongs do not make something right. What another president did, if wrong, is not an excuse for Mr. Nixon''s administration to do likewise.

Throughout his long political career, when he has found himself in a squeeze, Mr. Nixon has countered criticism of his excesses by saying that others do it too, by attacking imaginary enemies, persons or institutions, if vulnerable, and by deflecting the argument into another area.

In New Orleans, while defending the duplicity of secret bombings in Cambodia, Mr. Nixon said, "I find that some politicians and some members of the press who enthusiastically supported the administration which got us into Vietnam 10 years ago are now critical of what I did to get us out." That is a debaters' ploy, and it doesn't answer the problem about deceiving the American people.

* * *

It is an interesting counteroffensive, but what is sad is that Mr. Nixon does not yet seem to grasp what is at the heart of the nation's worst political scandal, which he thinks "is water under the bridge."

The Dallas Morning News

Dallas, Tex., August 24, 1973

THE PRESIDENT has now gone through his long-awaited grilling by the national press corps. His critics' disappointed reaction to this event, which they've been demanding for months, reminds us of an old World War II story.

It seems there was a draftee who spent all his time wandering around the barracks area, picking up every piece of paper he could find. He would look at each scrap of paper, mutter "that's not it," and throw it away. He would then go on to the next find, mutter, "that's not it," and continue the search. After days of this, he was finally taken to the post psychiatrist, who examined the searcher, ruled him psychologically incapacitated and presented him with a certificate of medical discharge.

The draftee seized this paper, read it and then joyously exclaimed, "THAT'S it!"

A SIMILAR single-mindedness seems to motivate the total behavior of the President's most dedicated critics. Saying that the truth must be served, first they demanded that he remove the shield of executive privilege from his aides, so that they could be questioned by the Senate panel. The President did. But then the critics declared that these were only underlings and, in the interest of finding the truth, the President himself should speak on the issue.

He did. But the critics declared that this speech was too vague and self-serving. In the interest of truth, they said, he should make a more detailed answer to the questions that were being raised during the TV hearings. He postponed meeting this demand until the hearings recessed, but he then spoke again to the nation, taking responsibility, deploring the incident and asking Americans to let him get on with his job.

The critics immediately branded this as mere window-dressing and issue-dodging. They declared that, in the interest of truth, the President should subject himself to some really probing questions from the professional interviewers of the Washington press corps.

He has now done that, fielding the toughest questions before live TV.

His critics' reaction? Need you ask? They've instantly ruled that he has not really faced up to the crucial questions and that something more will have to be done.

The big step that is demanded in the interest of truth at this point is a complete airing of the President's confidential tapes and papers. If only that were done, the critics say, the truth would out, the matter would be settled and the country could move on to other problems.

That, of course, is exactly what they have said about all the other steps that they have demanded the President take—all those other steps that, once taken, they have immediately dismissed as empty and meaningless.

We suspect that the tapes, too, will be similarly shrugged off if they are released and fail to serve the critics' true purpose. That purpose is not to bring out the truth, but to humiliate Richard Nixon completely, destroy his mandate from the voters and drive him out of the presidency.

THE ONLY way that President Nixon can really satisfy most of his critics is to grovel before the nation's voters, confess total guilt on every charge that his critics have thought up and announce his resignation.

Somehow we get the feeling that if the President took that unlikely action, a coast-to-coast chorus of critics would shout in harmony, "THAT'S it!"

The Washington Post
Times Herald

Washington, D.C., October 7, 1973

Tulsa, Okla.
October 6, 1973

VICE PRESIDENT AGNEW through his attorneys, has declared war on the press in a move that can only obscure the central question that lies before the Grand Jury investigating him.

The subpoenas served on reporters and news media yesterday also set up what must surely become a landmark case before the U.S. SUPREME COURT. For only the highest Court in the land can resolve the essential issue in this conflict of Constitutional principles.

The confrontation is between the right of the free flow of information and the right to a fair trial. We are not ready to say that the VICE PRESIDENT has been denied a fair trial by the stories that have appeared about him—although undoubtedly he has been hurt politically.

But is it the "leaks" that have hurt him, or the fact he is under investigation by a Grand Jury? He has not been charged with any crime, but the mere fact that a man in so high an office is involved in such an investigation is bound to be sensational news. It cannot be kept a secret and it cannot be treated as a routine story.

AGNEW is understandably upset by some of the leaks and the speculation, which he believes to have come from the JUSTICE DEPARTMENT. But his subpoenas, authorized by the Federal Judge in charge of the Grand Jury at Baltimore, are not directed at the possible *sources* but at the *intermediary*—the press.

The newsmen and the media will have to fight this attack as a crippling abridgment of the FIRST AMENDMENT guarantee of free expression. If it is allowed to continue unchecked, the whole area of investigative reporting will be undermined, for no one would give confidential information if he knew the origin could be revealed by Court order.

It boils down to this: Should any Judge, at his own discretion, be the arbiter of what may be printed or broadcast—through the weapons of subpoena power, the threat of contempt citations and other leverage held by his Court? This is a direction in which our society already is moving, and no more serious threat to freedom of the press exists.

Meanwhile, what of AGNEW? If there is evidence against him to warrant a charge, that will be the central issue: Guilt or innocence. Who told what to a reporter must not be allowed to divert attention from that question. If the VICE PRESIDENT has done nothing wrong, as he states, he is entitled to be freed of suspicion and suspense. If there is serious evidence against him, then it should be presented in Court.

We have deplored irresponsible leaking of misinformation—and still believe it is wrong. But the harm here is in trampling one part of the Bill of Rights to try to preserve another.

The current administration has a genius for pushing the country into situations which place undue and unwelcome stress on our durable old Constitution. The latest in the line of a seemingly unending stream of sharp constitutional tests has been posed by Vice President Agnew's assertion that the Department of Justice has engaged in a systematic and deliberate campaign of leaking information to the press in an effort to destroy him politically, in the course of destroying any chance he may have of receiving a fair hearing before a grand or petit jury. This has led to issuance by Mr. Agnew's lawyers of subpoenas to reporters from The Washington Post, The Washington Star News, The New York Times, The New York Daily News, CBS News, NBC News, and Newsweek and Time magazines. All of this presages a monumental and, in our view, an entirely avoidable constitutional confrontation over the First Amendment.

Mr. Agnew revealed on Aug. 6 that he had been informed that he was the target of a federal grand jury investigation. There can be no doubt that since that time numerous stories based on information from sources close to the investigation have appeared concerning the nature of the charges being made against the Vice President, the names of the witnesses against him, his state of mind and the nature of the negotiations between his lawyers and the Department of Justice. From this, his lawyers have drawn the conclusion that "a number of officials in the prosecutorial arm of our government have misused their offices in an immoral and illegal attempt to drive the Vice President from the office to which he was elected, and to assure his conviction."

Since Judge Walter E. Hoffman issued no opinion on the motion in which this argument was made, one cannot know with certainty just how he reacted to that rather startling assertion. He gave two pretty clear indications of his thinking, however. First, he granted the Vice President's lawyers extraordinary authority to take depositions in a criminal proceeding prior to the conclusion of grand jury deliberations and he gave them subpoena power to make the taking of those depositions possible. The second hint came in his very strong admonition to the grand jury to consider only the evidence presented to it and to disregard press reports in the case. In the course of that statement, Judge Hoffman went on to say:

We are rapidly approaching the day when the perpetual conflict between the news media, operating as they do under freedom of speech and freedom of the press and the judicial system, charged with protecting the rights of persons under investigation for criminal acts must be resolved.

The first question is whether such a conflict really does exist. And the next question is whether this case offers the best occasion for resolving it. We believe that the answer to both questions is, no. The Constitution is full of useful ambiguity which through our history has permitted reasonable men to reconcile conflicting rights and interests in a spirit of accommodation which preserves the essence of the Constitution without placing unbearable stress on our nation's institutions. Constitutional clashes have generally been avoided, and wisely so, whenever possible. Such a clash could have been avoided here.

Mr. Agnew's argument is that he should not be indicted because, among other things, the prosecutors have fatally flawed their case by filling news pages and the airwaves with prejudicial information against him. While he has every right to assert that claim, we would doubt that it has much substance. The fact that the trials of Sirhan Sirhan, Angela Davis, Jack Ruby and Bobby Seale were successfully concluded indicates that American judges know very well how to pick juries in highly publicized criminal cases and we do not see how Mr. Agnew's trial—if it ever comes to that—would be all that much more vulnerable to prejudicial pre-trial publicity, especially since the publicity has clearly cut both ways.

At the most, his assertions, if supported by the facts, might indicate that other prosecutors or another special prosecutor should be named to handle his case.

And that is the heart of the matter. Mr. Agnew's grievance is with the Department of Justice and not—as he himself has acknowledged—with the press. The press is peripheral to his argument. Attorney General Elliot L. Richardson has conducted an investigation into the leaks alleged to have come from his department. Mr. Agnew's lawyers can—as they may well have already done—subpoena the Attorney General and any officials working for him, including the FBI agents who have questioned federal prosecutors. It is hard to believe that Mr. Agnew's highly skilled defense team, building upon the information already developed within the department, cannot ferret out the information they need by means of interrogations conducted under oath.

To go beyond that by asking reporters to reveal the names of sources who gave information under a pledge of confidentiality is to jeopardize an extraordinarily important constitutional principle by use of a legal ploy that is not only premature but probably marginal in the case at hand. The First Amendment right of freedom of the press is not a right flowing to newsmen individually or collectively. It is, rather, grounded on the founding fathers' belief that only a people free to receive the greatest possible flow of information could govern themselves wisely. Thus, the right put into jeopardy here is the reader's right or the viewer's right to receive as much information as newsmen—by the exercise of their best judgment rather than that of some governmental instrumentality—can conscientiously gather and responsibly present to them.

The Agnew case illustrates the point. The professional obligation of the press is to question the veracity and probable accuracy of the information their sources have revealed. And a further mission of the press is to provide the public with as much information as possible about the fitness of elected officers to conduct the people's business; this is fundamental to public participation in the democratic process.

The ability to assure confidentiality to sources is vitally important to this mission. That ability was severely jeopardized in *Branzburg v. Hayes*, in which the Supreme Court decided that pledges of secrecy made by reporters did not outweigh the obligation to respond to a grand jury subpoena and to answer questions in a criminal investigation. If the press' ability to guarantee confidentiality is limited even more, the capacity to inform the public will be severely, if not irreparably, impaired.

This newspaper has long believed that the words of the First Amendment were sufficient unto themselves and that judicial or legislative efforts to define or codify these freedoms in precise and detailed terms are potentially damaging to the freest possible flow of information to the public. For years prior to the Branzburg decision, informal accommodations which served the interests of justice and preserved the principle of freedom of the press were possible. With the Branzburg decision on the books, each new situation presents yet another threat to the free functioning of the press. Lawyers like to say that hard cases make bad law. It can likewise be said that incautious challenges to broad constitutional principles can lead, not to greater clarity and precision, but to bad constitutional precedents—to the progressive erosion, in short, of fundamental rights which, by their very sweep and breadth, have served us well for almost two centuries.

Los Angeles Times
Los Angeles, Calif., October 5, 1973

The order issued by U.S. Dist. Judge Walter E. Hoffman, at the request of attorneys for Vice President Agnew, was an extraordinary assertion of judicial power. It gave the Vice President, through his attorneys, authority to conduct his own investigation, backed by the power of subpoena, of his own charges that the Department of Justice has made a "malicious, immoral and illegal" attack on him.

The order, if it stands (the Justice Department so far has given no hint as to its position), would cover Atty. Gen. Elliot L. Richardson and his aides. Hoffman said Agnew's attorneys could subpoena and question under oath any persons they deemed "appropriate and necessary."

"Astonishing," one constitutional scholar said of Hoffman's action. Other lawyers called it unprecedented for a person under criminal investigation, but not indicted, to be given the power to question prosecutors.

The order has opened a wide new area of controversy and probably new litigation, with the Vice President—in effect and with the assistance of Hoffman—putting the government on trial before the Justice Department has completed presenting evidence to the grand jury and before the department has reached a decision on whether or not to actually seek an indictment.

This raises the question, among others, as to whether the grand jury action can be concluded before Agnew's lawyers can complete depositions from a large number of persons they apparently will question. The depositions will be sealed and kept secret under Hoffman's order, and will be withheld from public court records.

Another aspect of Hoffman's action is its implicit attack on the right of news reporters to protect the confidentiality of their sources. Agnew's lawyers are said to be prepared to subpoena a number of reporters for various news-gathering organizations. If they refuse to disclose their sources, they will face the possibility of jail for contempt of court.

Hoffman, in his special charge to the grand jury investigating allegations against Agnew, said, "The perpetual conflict between the news media . . . and the judicial system . . . must be resolved."

Implicit in this view and the way it was stated is the baseless notion that criminal proceedings conducted in secret assure a fair trial. Implicit also in his charge is the equally wrong notion that jurors are not sufficiently intelligent or conscientious to reach decisions solely on the evidence. Hoffman asked any juror who felt that his "mind has been improperly influenced by the news media" to advise him promptly. None has.

On the face of it, Hoffman's order was too broad. It rests on unfounded assumptions that the grand jury will shirk its duty. But more than that, it assumes that the courts can set aside the First Amendment protections of press and speech. And, finally, it falsely assumes that open public scrutiny of the judicial process is inherently in conflict with a fair trial.

The Times-Picayune
New Orleans, La., October 7, 1973

The right of freedom of the press is not absolute. That is, it is no more absolute than the freedom of speech which precludes, in Justice Oliver Wendell Holmes' classic example, the guiltless shouting of "Fire!" in a crowded theater.

For if press freedom were absolute, libelous stories, which may not be prevented from publication by prior judicial restraint, could likewise not be punished by the courts. But courts can and do.

Thus freedom to publish does not excuse, exempt or otherwise exonerate one from breaking the law against malicious slander.

That brings us to another area in which press freedom is not synonymous with license to break the law with impunity; that is, with liberty to aid and abet those who violate the secrecy of the grand jury.

Vice President Spiro Agnew may be guilty of taking kickbacks from contractors doing business in Maryland, as has been variously alleged in massive leaks caught like a bucket brigade by the news media; or he may be victim, as he contends, of a vicious frameup initiated by others under fire who sought his influence in vain to stifle a Justice Department investigation.

All of which has led to what is apparently unprecedented subpoena power granted to the vice president's lawyers to ferret out the sources of news leaks related to the federal grand jury probe. His defense attorneys may question under oath anyone "they deem appropriate or necessary, upon 48-hour notice to the Justice Department.

In issuing the order, U.S. District Court Judge Walter E. Hoffman charged that "Such depositions . . ." (from newsmen, lawyers, Justice officials and past or present friends of Mr. Agnew) "shall be sealed and not be made part of any public file." Secrecy is to apply even to the names of those subpoenaed or testifying.

Organizations of newsmen who may be subpoenaed may renew a familiar cry of "chilling effect" on freedom of the press, but in doing so some may have to coldly admit being party to illegal acts that chill another American freedom — the right, as President Nixon put it, "not to be tried and convicted in the press and on television by leaks and innuendos and the rest."

Cautioning the jurors not to be "improperly influenced by the news media," whose stories about the inquiry "frequently are wholly or partially inaccurate," Judge Hoffman stated what may start a wholesome new round on the dimensions of press freedom and press responsibility.

"We are rapidly approaching the day when the perpetual conflict between the news media, operating as they do under freedom of speech and freedom of the press, and the judicial system charged with protecting the rights of persons under investigation for criminal acts, must be resolved."

For Vice President Agnew, that day may have already passed, at least as far as his political future is concerned.

HOUSTON CHRONICLE
Houston, Tex., October 7, 1973

United States Dist. Judge Walter E. Hoffman has taken a common-sense approach to Vice-President Spiro Agnew's complaints that he has been the victim of "malicious, immoral and illegal" attacks by federal prosecutors. The vice-president accuses the prosecutors of being the source of constant leaks of information and accusations concerning his alleged involvement in kickbacks from Maryland contractors.

Judge Hoffman is correct in moving to protect Agnew's constitutional rights in this respect. The judge, assigned to the case from his normal Norfolk, Va., base, has chosen the direct course of authorizing the vice-president's lawyers to subpoena sworn testimony from anyone they think has information about the news leaks.

The judge's broad order is relatively unprecedented, just as is the situation from which it flows. The order's implications and consequences can be far-reaching and it is in this respect that we are concerned about the undue emphasis which is being placed on the news media rather than whoever is doing the leaking.

Judge Hoffman made a public charge to the grand jury hearing testimony about the vice-president the same day he authorized the probe into leaks of information. Its tenor was to emphasize a judicial confrontation with the media which printed news about the leaks rather than concern with those leaking information for their own purposes.

Actions by the vice-president's attorneys have also tended to shift the emphasis from those culpable of the leaks to those who tried to keep the public informed of the consequences of the leaks. Agnew's attorneys, in what seems a vindictive and propagandistic act, have served subpoenaes on newsmen in an attempt to force them to reveal sources of the leaks. This not only aims at the wrong target but throws a smokescreen over the clear issues by embroiling them with the constitutional question of confidentiality of a reporter's sources as a necessity of a free press.

The fault in this situation lies with whatever government officials are serving whatever purposes they have in leaks of information. It does not lie in the news media whose obligation is to tell the public what its officials are up to.

It is the responsibility of prosecutors not to attempt to influence the course of justice by leaking selected information. It is charges of this action which are being investigated and this is where the emphasis should lie.

The Pittsburgh Press
Pittsburgh, Pa., October 7, 1973

What does Vice President Agnew, under investigation for allegedly accepting bribes and kickbacks, expect to accomplish by trying to force reporters covering the story to divulge their confidential sources of information?

It very much looks as though the vice president, by putting members of the press on the spot, hopes to divert attention from his own uncomfortable predicament.

Federal Judge Walter E. Hoffman of Norfolk abetted this sorry business by permitting Mr. Agnew's lawyers to serve subpoenas on Washington newsmen in an effort to find out who leaked what information to w h o m and why.

★ ★ ★

The central issue in the Agnew case is not where newsmen are getting their stories about the investigation.

The central issue is whether the allegations of bribery, extortion, tax fraud and conspiracy against the vice president are true or false.

And the best place to resolve that issue is within the judicial system, as quickly as possible, rather than having it go on and on.

Mr. Agnew is being unrealistic if he believes a federal investigation of the vice president of the United States c a n be conducted without news coverage and editorial comment.

Newsmen had (and have) a responsibility to tell the country what was happening, even if it meant quoting unnamed b u t reliable sources to get at the facts.

There is no overriding public interest in forcing reporters to identify their sources in the Agnew investigation. Without such sources, reporters — and their readers — would be unaware and uninformed.

Nor is there any public interest in sending newsmen to jail for refusing to testify, as now seems likely if the questioning is pursued.

★ ★ ★

All of this re-emphasizes the need for a federal shield law for news sources so information can flow to the public without fear of reprisal or harassment.

It also re-emphasizes the need to stop cluttering the Agnew investigation with extraneous side issues that can only delay and detract from the swift and fair disposition of the case.

Oakland Tribune
Oakland, Calif., October 9, 1973

The issuance of subpoenas by a U.S. District Court in an attempt to force reporters to reveal sources of news leaks in the Agnew kickback probe is a broad and serious threat to freedom of the press.

Such action again points to the need for Congress to pass legislation which would give reporters the right to refuse to name sources of their stories, if those sources desire to go unnamed. Various bills have been introduced, but they have been lying idle for months because lawmakers have failed to agree on whether newsmen should have unqualified protection of the law.

If anything good comes from the subpoenas, it could be that interest in these bills will be revived.

Once Congress realizes the implications of this broadside assault on a free press, members may be spurred to action. For this is not an isolated case aimed at one reporter. Rather it is directed at newspaper, magazine and television reporters for a number of stories by a number of newsmen.

The U.S. Supreme Court ruled in June, 1972 that newsmen have no inherent constitutional right to refuse to disclose sources. The court, however, invited Congress to draft legislation which would give them that right.

In filing this civil litigation, Agnew's attorneys apparently are relying on that decision and the failure of Congress to act, to help them discover just who is leaking the information. Their ultimate purpose is not clear.

Should they be upheld and reporters forced to give them the information requested, investigative reporting by the news media could be greatly jeopardized. In turn, such restrictions on news gathering would seriously impair the people's right to know about matters that concern them.

For a free flow of information is essential to preserving our republic. And certainly, in this case, the activities surrounding the vice president of the United States are of vital interest to a nation which desires to effectively govern itself.

Congress must act soon before there are any more assaults on the ability of the media to fulfill its functions of informing the public.

Until Congress does so, the media—and their sources—must not be intimidated in their attempts to keep the public informed. Newsmen must fight in every conceivable way to protect the people's access to a free press.

San Jose Mercury
San Jose, Calif., October 10, 1973

It remains fashionable to slay the messenger who brings bad news. That, in substance, is what lawyers for Vice President Spiro T. Agnew are attempting to do in issuing subpoenas to reporters who have written stories about the federal investigation of Agnew.

The reporters will not reveal the sources of their information. They can't.

Once a reporter reveals the source of confidentially revealed information he is dead. No longer will anyone trust him with sensitive information. And other persons, perhaps with information that could blow the lid off public or private graft, are given reason to pause before they consider sharing it with a member of the press.

The result is less information for the public.

True, the use of confidential sources can be abused. But bogus reports are soon found out, just as a reporter quickly discovers who is most likely to be honest with him and who isn't. This inexact way of sorting out truth certainly is preferable to dark clouds of secrecy under which misconduct thrives because no ones dares reveal it.

We believe the public has the right to know about the investigations of high governmental officials at the first inkling of such an undertaking. The official is not left without a forum.

We do not believe an open society negates the opportunity for a person to have a fair trial or hearing.

These convictions are central to the perpetuation of a free press in America. It is ironic, but perhaps appropriate, that they are again being tested this particular week National Newspaper Week.

THE ARIZONA REPUBLIC
Phoenix, Ariz., October 9, 1973

V i c e President Spiro Agnew made a serious mistake when he issued subpoenas to half a dozen Eastern Seaboard newspaper and television reporters in an effort to force t h e m to divulge news sources.

Agnew may be right in his claim that massive pretrial publicity makes it impossible for him to get a fair trial. But the simple truth of the matter is that he has not yet been indicted, nor officially accused, of any crime.

Nor is there any reason for the vice president to believe the reporters are covering up crimes which will be divulged by airing their unpublished notes and revealing their secret contacts.

As it happens, we think Agnew has gotten a bad deal in the publicity field. If Assistant Attorney General Henry F. Petersen told CBS newsman F r e d Graham, "We've got the evidence, we've got it cold," it is obvious that the Agnew case was being prejudged.

Since The Washington Post has once attributed the quote to Petersen and on another occasion to unidentified lawyers, we'd like to see that issue settled in a court of law.

But looking at Graham's notebooks or listening to his tapes isn't the way to settle the issue. Agnew should tell his lawyers to take action against Petersen for libel or slander.

The F i r s t Amendment (free press) and the Fifth Amendment (fair trial) have existed side by side in the Constitution for nearly 200 years. Neither has priority over the other.

A reporter's unpublished notes or a television man's unused tapes are his own, and (unless they are proof that a crime has been committed) should not be taken from him without his consent.

Vice President Agnew has been given a bad deal by someone who leaked questionable information to the press. But the fault lies with the people who leaked the information, not with the press that used it.

Hitting at the very foundations of America's press freedom won't help Agnew. It will hurt an institution on which our freedom is based.

Pittsburgh Post-Gazette

Pittsburgh, Pa., October 10, 1973

ACTING on the time-tested premise that a strong offense is the best defense, Vice President Agnew's lawyers are about to try the federal prosecutors. They have obtained from federal Judge Walter E. Hoffman the unusual right to subpena and question under oath Department of Justice prosecutors, newsmen or anyone else they think might know about leaks in the government's case against the Vice President.

If the defense lawyers can string these and other legal maneuvers out long enough they might hope that the five-year statute of limitations on some of the allegations against Mr. Agnew will expire on Oct. 26 without an indictment having been returned.

Since they are in a race against time, top Justice Department officials are prepared to give sworn depositions denying a department campaign of news leaks which Mr. Agnew contends have destroyed him politically and deprived him of his basic rights to due process and a fair hearing.

* * *

The Justice Department has reported that 134 of its officials were in positions to know details of its case against Mr. Agnew and that all have denied leaking information. But how is one to know how widespread information is in this age of photostats or how long it would take to run down and check out all of the possibilities for leaks?

Even if all of the Justice Department's extensive plumbing were shown to have sprung no leaks, could not Mr. Agnew's lawyers turn then to other sources? In its legal arguments the department has noted a "high correlation" between the information relayed to persons on the White House and vice presidential staffs and subsequent published reports.

In other words, the department seems to be saying, the leaks might be traced to the White House or to Mr. Agnew's own staff. Thus the potential for Mr. Agnew's lawyers to probe for leaks would appear to be boundless.

When it comes to the newsmen who served as conduits for the leaks, however, Mr. Agnew has chosen the wrong target. The newsmen didn't invent the stories about Mr. Agnew's troubles with the government; they simply reported them and protected sources which, for obvious reasons, didn't want to be identified. The Justice Department has quite properly asked Judge Hoffman to reverse his decision allowing newsmen to be subpenaed and he should do it.

If high and presumably responsible public officials tell reporters that the Vice President of the United States is considering a deal with the Justice Department in which he would plead guilty to a criminal charge, then that is news of the first magnitude. While it is damaging to the Vice President, the culprits are not the reporters but the people who, for their own reasons, leak the news.

The reporters are simply informing the public, which has a right to know what its officials are up to. If the officials have a strong case against Mr. Agnew, they should be able to make it stick in court, where only evidence — not hearsay — is admissable. Mr. Agnew, meanwhile, has rightly taken advantage of every forum to proclaim his innocence and to build public sympathy.

If the subpenaed reporters refuse to testify and are subjected to contempt proceedings, they must rely upon the First Amendment guarantee of a free press to see them through. Thus the ancient but unresolved issue of free press vs. fair trial will become part of what promises to be one of the most complicated legal struggles in the nation's history.

The Evening Bulletin

Philadelphia, Pa., October 10, 1973

A peculiar situation has developed in the Agnew case, with Federal Judge Walter E. Hoffman granting Vice President Agnew's lawyers apparently unprecedented authority to make their own investigation into alleged leaks to the press from the Justice Department.

The judge seems to think that this is the proper occasion for a showdown between the news media, operating under the constitutional guarantee of free press, and the courts, as the protector of the constitutional rights of persons under investigation for criminal acts.

But is it really? Or could it prove to be a diversion, along with so many others in recent months, from the task of trying to establish the facts about the conduct of the highest officials in American Government?

And after Watergate's demonstration of the vital role of the free press in such a situation, and the absolute indispensability of newsmen being able to keep confidential their sources to do their job, isn't it passing strange to witness now an attempt to force them to destroy their effectiveness by betraying their trust?

Of course the press is not going to roll over and play dead when confronted by this kind of challenge. The public should realize what is at stake.

If the public ever has a right to know, and the press ever has a duty to inform the public, it is surely in a case involving an official a heartbeat away from the Presidency.

Surely the press has to dig out everything it can in such a case when the machinery of a government in crisis — including the administration of justice — is being operated by men at odds with one another over such a grave development.

There is justifiable sympathy with the Vice President's predicament, as reports have poured forth that lack the backing of an indictment, much less the substance of a conviction. He may even benefit from a backlash of sympathy because of the impropriety of some of the "leaking," particularly any violations of grand jury secrecy.

But Mr. Agnew and his supporters have not been silent, either, in a play for support in what amounts in some of its aspects to an intra-Republican donnybrook. It is a Republican federal attorney in Maryland who has investigated the Republican Vice President under the oversight of a Republican attorney general appointed by a Republican President.

Mr. Agnew's anger at those he regards as trying to do him in is understandable. So is his effort to nail them. However, it isn't going to help him, and it certainly isn't going to help the country, to try to strike a crippling blow at the press. That won't settle his guilt or innocence.

The nation's political life, as well as Mr. Agnew's personal future, is involved.

Whatever Mr. Agnew has suffered, the country has suffered more from coverup.

The Vice President, as others involved in highly and even irresponsibly publicized cases, can receive justice at the hands of the courts and his fellow citizens as jurors if it comes to that.

The courts are not without their safeguards nor are jurors without good judgment. That's been shown time and again, often to the discomfort of the present administration.

Of course news media sometimes do not meet their responsibilities. There are abuses of free press.

But the country would be without the protection of a free press against official wrongs if reporting was throttled by enforced disclosure of confidential news sources—news sources which in some cases may well represent the conscience of individuals fearful of deals and coverups.

What's needed now is to remove the element of doubt that hangs over the conduct of the Vice President, not to put reporters on the rack about who leaked what to whom.

THE SAGINAW NEWS

Saginaw, Mich., October 30, 1973

In the aftermath of his latest televised news conference the President has put more distance, not less, between himself and the people, the Congress and the nation's mass media.

In common parlance, Mr. Nixon blew it Friday night with a shabby attack on the press and an unheeding response to the federal legislative branch of government.

While the nation was reassured about Mr. Nixon's apparent state of good health and the power of the President to deal effectively with international crisis, there was no assurance that Mr. Nixon can soon bring about a domestic reconciliation which his badly shaken administration so sorely needs.

Rather than projecting the image of a national leader who truly understands the width of the credibility gap that now confronts his administration, the President proceeded along old but familiar lines.

This was the old Richard M. Nixon we were seeing — the old Richard Nixon who has never made his peace with the press, the old-new Richard Nixon who wants Watergate cleaned up on his own terms, the old-new Richard Nixon who seemingly fails to comprehend the public's dismay as those he has chosen to draw closest to him disappear one after another into the jaws of probes.

Unfortunately the President did little the other night to restore public confidence in the present administration.

It was almost unreal.

Here is the nation and the Congress still reeling from the now infamous "Saturday night purge" of Archibald Cox, Elliot L. Richardson and William Ruckelshaus — and there is the President describing Mr. Cox as a troublemaker who had to go. But there is the promise of a new Watergate special prosecutor with not an iota of assurance that the new one will have any freer hand than the fired one. Incredible.

Here is an investigation building around the President's pal, C. G. (Bebe) Rebozo involving the sale of securities which threatens Mr. Rebozo's job as the head of a Key Biscayne, Fla. bank — and there is the President defending Mr. Rebozo as an honorable man who used sound judgment in returning a $100,000 campaign gift from the Hughes Corp. after sitting on it for three years.

And finally here is the President, who advised the press only a few weeks ago to "give us hell when you think we deserve it," giving the press hell for doing the job it is obligated to do.

As for Mr. Nixon's unbridled attack on the television networks —

which included some backtracking to include the printed media — the news gatherers can live with that. There is no law anywhere that declares the media immune from presidential criticism.

In Mr. Nixon's present situation, however, it came across as a desperate attempt to once again discredit the press when things are going badly. It's an old trick in politics. Slay the bearer of the message. Only this time it doesn't wash except among those prone to blame the media for the President's troubles. With them it wins the President some scattered applause. For the most part, however, it will only lower the President's standing in public esteem.

We really don't know what it is that Mr. Nixon expects from the press any more. But one thing he cannot expect is that it become part of a cover up. Moreover, in light of the fact that the press and the electronic media are vigorously pursuing leads which, up to now, have proved anything but false, it is distressing that Mr. Nixon has chosen to characterize Watergate coverage as "outrageous, vicious and distorted."

These problems the press did not create for Mr. Nixon. Its chief guilt up to now has been reporting the problems that have beset the President and exposing the scandals that have cast his administration in such bad light.

Yet even for Mr. Nixon such an attack as the one he unloaded the other night reached an uncharacteristic high.

The bad part of it is that turned a news conference into a confrontation — one of the worst confrontations the public has ever been privy to witnessing between a President and the press before the glaring eye of TV cameras. Worse, we may now wonder when, if ever, Mr. Nixon can again meet with the press under any other conditions but confrontation.

Whether that was the worst of the three tactical mistakes Mr. Nixon made the other night is, to be sure, debatable. While there can be no question that the President has further truncated his already strained relations with the media in this country, the public isn't going to get all upset over that.

The public's more legitimate concern is that he has also managed to harden the resolve of Congress to look into the possibility of impeachment proceedings and forced the Senate to reject out of hand an administration-appointed Watergate prosecutor investigating the administration.

Each of these things raises grave questions about Mr. Nixon's future

relationships with Congress and his ability to govern effectively.

Mr. Nixon has projected not the image of a President behind whom the people are ready to unite but rather the image of one whose actions and utterances simply cloud the air with still more doubt. The President did nothing to clear

away the heavy cloud the other night.

Investigation has become a way of life for the Nixon administration. That is truly tragic. The people have reached the point where they are wondering every day — what next? And eventually there is something. That is equally tragic.

THE NASHVILLE TENNESSEAN

Nashville, Tenn., October 28, 1973

THE TRAGEDY for the country is that President Nixon perceives his difficulties, but won't concede that absolute candor is his admit that absolute candor is his only route to rescue.

The chief executive can suggest that the doubts and suspicious and cynicism about his leadership arise from the impact of the television screens. But that is an irrational viewpoint, for television didn't bring on the Watergate avalanche, or Mr. Nixon's private housing arrangements, or the Agnew resignation.

*   *   *

The networks didn't fire Special Prosecutor Archibald Cox and wipe out, with a single stroke, two of the top men at the Justice Department who were trying to salvage some integrity for this administration.

Incredibly, Mr. Nixon now proposes to recreate the office of Special Prosecutor which he did away with in a fit of anger. Thus he not only ignores the destruction which he left at Justice, but suggests with a straight face that his administration will investigate itself up to, but not including the President.

Since Mr. Nixon has reiterated his authority to fire such a prosecutor at any time, what attorney in his right mind is going to accept such a post? If one did, where would there be any credibility of prosecution in a situation where the prosecutor is expected to be sweetly reasonable to White House suggestions?

If there is a Special Prosecutor, he must be independent of the White House with full authority, if necessary, to take the President into court. The Congress and the Courts cannot be a party to a whitewash of Watergate, or depend on Mr. Nixon's latest promise of full cooperation. He pledged that before, and he broke that pledge.

Mr. Nixon was right in saying that "Justice delayed is justice denied," but it has been the White House which has forced delay and confrontation. It was the White House which used every legal strategem, tactic and loophole to resist giving up the tapes and documents necessary for any court proceedings.

And, the President made clear, it will continue to resist further such demands. Therein lies the curious paradox of Mr. Nixon's words of wanting "an expeditious concluson" and his deeds of blocking just that.

Mr. Nixon moves to command headlines, influence events, and to try to project the image if the "cool" leader, statesman and peacemaker. Yet it comes off badly and with deepened suspicions, simply because he is devious when there is no need.

In his discussion of the Cox firing, Mr. Nixon said of his so-called compromise: "Atty. Gen. (Elliot) Richardson approved of this proposition." Mr. Richardson and his associates have both indicated he did not approve. Which are we to believe?

Mr. Nixon spoke of cooperation with a special prosecutor, yet Mr. Cox in his news conference told of an absolute lack of cooperation form the White House. Which are we to believe?

In commenting on the Middle East, Mr. Nixon said, ". . . I know for example in your head office in New York, some thought it was simply a blown-up exercise . . . It was a real crisis, the most difficult since the Cuban confrontation of 1962."

Communist leader Leonid Brezhnev suggested Friday that Washington had intensified the Middle East situation and reacted irresponsibly by circulating "fantastic rumors" about Soviet intentions. Mr. Nixon said it was a real crisis, and Mr. Brezhnev indicated it wasn't.

*   *   *

Well, one could go on and on itemizing Mr. Nixon's positions which seem in disagreement with the facts, or at least in a state of ambiguity. If there is a crisis of confidence in his leadership, it stems not from the television news or the printed pages, but from Mr. Nixon's inability to be direct and candid.

Mr. Nixon will not solve his problem by attacking his critics, or lead the nation out of the wilderness of Watergate by glossing over the gravity of damage he has done himself. Mr. Nixon boasted of his "coolness" at his news conference. Would that the nation could also boast of his candor.

Confidentiality
& the Courts

The conflict between a reporter's need to protect his confidential sources and the government's need to gather evidence of criminal activity is not a new one. The flurry of subpoenas issued during the early 1970s, however, was a clear-cut break with previous practice. Between 1900 and 1970 the issue of the "newsman's privilege" was raised in only a handful of cases. Government subpoenas for information gleaned from confidential sources had been issued to newsmen in less than a dozen cases during this period.

The rash of recent subpoenas cannot be assigned to any single cause. Some prosecutors have argued that the press has become more recalcitrant, refusing to comply with discreet and non-compulsory requests for information. Spokesmen for the news media claim that the Administration's attacks on the media have created a climate that encourages prosecutors to take an aggressive attitude toward newsmen.

Various proposals have been made to resolve the conflict. Some 14 states already have news shield laws on their books, offering complete or partial immunity to reporters who refuse to disclose their sources. At least eight separate bills have been introduced in Congress to create a federal news shield law. Major questions have been raised by these competing legislative proposals: Should the newsmen's privilege be absolute or qualified? How is the privilege to be claimed? Who is covered by the shield? Problems such as these have led some newsmen and legal authorities to warn that by defining privileges any news shield law will tend to dilute the guarantees of freedom of the press set forth in the First Amendment.

Government to get TV film. The Columbia Broadcasting System (CBS) announced Jan. 26, 1970 that it would comply with a government subpoena for the unused portions of a TV program dealing with the Black Panthers, including an interview with their leader-in-exile, Eldridge Cleaver. The subpoena was served Jan. 8 by government agents who requested that CBS turn over the films used to produce the broadcast

which was shown Jan. 6 in the CBS series, "60 Minutes."

It was reported that the government sought to show the films to a federal grand jury in San Francisco which was considering an indictment against a Panther leader, David Hilliard, accused of threatening the life of President Nixon.

U.S. subpoenas challenged. A Justice Department spokesman disclosed Feb. 7 that Attorney General John N. Mitchell had offered to meet with representatives of the nation's news media to dispel their fears that the government was using its subpoena powers injudiciously. The uneasiness among the news media executives was caused by the government's recent series of wide-ranging subpoenas to newsmen covering the activities of radical political groups.

Data on Panthers sought. Mike Wallace, a TV news correspondent for the Columbia Broadcasting System (CBS), said Feb. 23 that the Justice Department had asked him to testify voluntarily before a federal grand jury in New Haven, Conn. investigating the activities of the Black Panthers. It was the third time the government had sought data on the Panthers from CBS's news files.

Wallace had interviewed Eldridge Cleaver, the party's self-exiled minister of information for a Jan. 6 telecast. Wallace said Paul Loewenwater, the producer of the Jan. 6 program, was also asked to appear before the grand jury.

A spokesman for the Justice Department confirmed Feb. 21 that contacts had been made with certain CBS personnel and acknowledged the possibility of serving them with subpoenaes. The spokesman said Attorney General John N. Mitchell did not think the contacts conflicted with his Feb. 5 statement that no further subpoenas would be issued to those associated with national media without an attempt first to negotiate an agreement on their scope.

The first subpoena was served to the Columbia Broadcasting System (CBS) Jan. 8 for the out-takes (unused portions)

of a film dealing with the activities of the Black Panther party. CBS was served with a second subpoena Jan. 29, demanding that the network turn over to the Secret Service and the Federal Bureau of Investigation (FBI) a complete record of all the materials used to produce the film, including the recorded tapes of an interview with Eldridge Cleaver, the party's self-exiled minister of information.

Representatives of Time, Life and Newsweek magazines revealed Feb. 1 that the government had subpoenaed the unedited files and unused photographs dealing with the movements of the militant Weatherman faction of the Students for a Democratic Society (SDS) during four days of civil disturbances in Chicago Oct. 8–11, 1969. Spokesmen for the three magazines said the subpoenas were served shortly after the disorders.

The New York Times reported Feb. 2 that one of its reporters, Earl Caldwell, had been subpoenaed to testify before a federal grand jury in San Francisco investigating the activities of the Black Panthers. The subpoena directed Caldwell to appear before the grand jury with his "notes and tape recordings" regarding the activities and personnel of the Panther party.

Executives representing The New York Times, CBS, Time and Newsweek Feb. 4 issued statements assailing the government's apparent policy of using subpoenas to collect information about radical political groups.

Attorney General Mitchell said Feb. 5 that the Justice Department was initiating steps to assure the nation's news media that no subpoenas would be issued to newsmen without an attempt to first reach agreement on the scope of the subpoenas.

Lindsay urges fight vs. repression. New York Mayor John V. Lindsay, in a speech April 2 at the University of California's Berkeley campus, denounced Justice Department subpoenas of newsmen's notes and an attempt by the Administration to curtail demonstrations near the White House.

C

D

E

F

G

A

News disclosures limited. U.S. District Court Judge Alfonzo J. Zirpoli signed a court order in San Francisco April 9 limiting the government's power of subpoena on a New York Times correspondant who had been covering the activities of the Black Panthers and other militant black groups. The order was issued after a hearing before Zirpoli April 3 at which attorneys for Earl Caldwell, the Times' newsman, asked the court to quash a subpoena that had directed Caldwell to appear before a grand jury that had been investigating the activities of black militants.

B

Zirpoli's order held that Caldwell should not be required to disclose confidential information or sources developed in his newspaper work. The order specifically protected Caldwell's right to defend his confidential relationships with Black Panther leaders as news sources. Zirpoli declined to strike down the subpoena, but he ordered that Caldwell could consult his attorney during his testimony before the grand jury. The judge also left open to the government the right to prove in a new hearing that the national interest required Caldwell's testimony, if data he had could be obtained in no other way.

C

In signing the order, Zirpoli restated his earlier opinion that Caldwell and his employers had legal standing to resist the attempt to subpoena confidential information from him. He said that to require testimony from Caldwell based on his confidential relationships with his sources would "damage and impair" the professional activities of other Times reporters and other news agencies.

D

In other related developments:

■Thirteen newspaper, television and magazine reporters announced March 8 the formation of a professional committee to examine and defend their profession's rights in answering the subpoenas of government investigators.

■Federal Communications Commissioner Nicholas Johnson said Feb. 12 that the nation's news media had an "absolute right" to refuse the demands of government investigators for reporters' confidential information and unused television film. Johnson criticized the Nixon Administration and the Justice Department for what he termed a "wave of government subpoenas . . ." He charged that the subpoenas, "together with other manipulations of the press, have placed the freedom and integrity of this country's news media in serious jeopardy." He also attacked the media's management for what he called its "acquiescence."

E

F

G

Court rejects claim of prejudicial publicity. The Supreme Court June 29 unanimously and without comment rejected an appeal by Thomas C. Wansley, a Lynchburg, Va. Negro convicted of rape and sentenced to life in prison. Wansley had claimed that a confession attributed to him was invalid and that Lynchburg newspaper stories had prejudiced the case.

Newsman guilty in contempt case. Earl Caldwell, a reporter for the New York Times, was found guilty June 5 of civil contempt by a federal district court judge in San Francisco for refusing to testify before a grand jury investigating the activities of black militant organizations.

Judge Alfonso J. Zirpoli allowed Caldwell, 32, to remain free pending an appeal of the contempt order. The judge issued the order staying the execution of the judgment over the objections lodged by Victor C. Woerheide, an assistant U.S. attorney. The judgment required that Caldwell be held in jail until he agreed to testify before the grand jury or until such time as the grand jury completed its inquiry and was dismissed.

Woerheide argued that the "object of civil contempt is to force compliance. If he [Caldwell] is at large pending appeal, that will vitiate the court's finding of contempt."

Caldwell had refused to testify because he felt his relationship with his news sources would be destroyed by his appearance before a closed grand jury session.

Mitchell sets news subpoena rules. Attorney General John N. Mitchell issued guidelines to the Justice Department Aug. 10 that barred government lawyers from seeking subpoenas to force testimony from newsmen in criminal cases without his personal approval.

In a speech before the American Bar Association's House of Delegates in St. Louis, Mitchell said the guidelines were "reasonable and workable" and "represent a genuine effort . . . to accommodate the respective responsibilities of the news media and the federal prosecutor."

Mitchell conceded that some disputed subpoenas had been issued "in haste" without considering the effects on freedom of the press, but he also emphasized the department would retain its right to use the subpoena where "fair administration of justice requires it."

The guidelines warned that if subpoenas were obtained without prior approval by the attorney general, the department would move to quash the action. According to the new rules, in considering use of the subpoena, the government would balance the possible limit to exercise of First Amendment rights against the public interest in justice. All reasonable attempts to obtain information from nonpress sources would precede use of the subpoena. The guidelines also required negotiations with newsmen before resorting to the subpoena.

The guidelines included the following principles: that the press should not be used as a "springboard" for investigations and subpoenas should only be used if a crime were indicated by sources outside the press; the subpoena should only be used to gain essential information that the government had unsuccessfully tried to gain from nonpress sources;

normally the subpoena should only be used for the verification of published information and great caution should be observed when unpublished material was involved; and material sought should be of a limited nature—in subject matter, time covered and volume.

Press subpoenas limited. The U.S. Court of Appeals for the Ninth Circuit, in a San Francisco ruling Nov. 17, vacated a contempt judgment against New York Times reporter Earl Caldwell, who had refused to testify in a grand jury investigation of the Black Panthers. The appeals court, which also reversed an order requiring Caldwell to testify, said that the federal government must demonstrate that evidence is necessary and otherwise unobtainable before a journalist can be forced to testify.

The appeals court said: "Where it has been shown that the public's First Amendment right to be informed would be jeopardized by requiring a journalist to submit to secret grand jury interrogation, the government must respond by demonstrating a compelling need for the witness' presence before judicial process properly can issue to require attendance." The court said, however, that the Caldwell case was unique in that "it is not every news source that is as sensitive as the Black Panther party. . . . It is not every reporter who so uniquely enjoys the trust and confidence of his sensitive news source."

The ruling set conditions for permissible press subpoenas that were similar to guidelines issued in August by Attorney General John N. Mitchell. Nevertheless, the Justice Department announced Dec. 4 that it would ask for Supreme Court review of the appeals court ruling. A department spokesman said the case raised questions sufficiently important for a high court review.

Jailing of editor upheld. The jailing of Mark Knops, the editor of an underground newspaper who refused to testify before a grand jury investigating a bombing at the University of Wisconsin Aug. 24, was upheld Feb. 2, 1971 by the Wisconsin Supreme Court. The court said the public's "overriding need to know" what Knops might be able to tell the Walworth County grand jury outweighed his right as a journalist to conceal his sources.

Knops, who had been ordered to jail in September 1970 for contempt, had asserted his right against self-incrimination and was granted immunity. He then refused to answer on the ground that he could keep secret his journalistic sources.

Among related developments:

■ An appeals court in Frankfort, Ky. ruled Jan. 22 that a newsman could keep a source of information secret but would have to disclose the information itself before a grand jury. Paul Branzburg had refused to testify before a Jefferson

County grand jury on an article on marijuana and hashish published in the Louisville Courier-Journal. Supreme Court Justice Potter Stewart granted Branzburg's plea Jan. 26 to block for 30 days his appearance before grand juries in Jefferson and Franklin Counties to give him time to appeal the summonses to the Supreme Court on grounds that they violated freedom of the press.

■ The Massachusetts Supreme Court ruled Jan. 29 that "Massachusetts, unlike certain other states, has created no statutory privilege protecting news sources." The ruling came in the case of Paul Pappas, a TV newsman, who refused to answer certain questions concerning the Black Panthers before a grand jury investigating July 1970 racial disturbances in New Bedford. The court said, "We adhere to the view that there exists no constitutional newsman's privilege, either qualified or absolute, to refuse to appear and testify before a court of grand jury."

Nixon opposes subpoenas. President Nixon said at a news conference May 1 that he took "a very jaundiced view" of subpoena of reporters' notes or requiring revelation of sources unless it involved information dealing with a major crime. He did not support exertion of federal pressure on broadcast networks, although he believed that public figures had a right "to indicate when we think the news coverage has been fair or unfair."

Burger urges 'civility.' Chief Justice Warren E. Burger, in a Washington speech May 18, assailed "adrenaline-fueled lawyers" who disrupted courtrooms and insulted judges. Extending his criticism to overzealous journalists and demonstrators as well as lawyers, Burger spoke of "the necessity for civility if we are to keep the jungle from closing in on us."

Burger said the press had a "crucial" role and added, "sometimes their highest service is to reflect precisely the conduct of the brash and swaggering lawyer or intemperate, blustering judge." But he deplored incidents of incivility when "Speakers are shouted down or prevented from speaking. Editorials tend to become shrill with invective and political cartoons are savagely reminiscent of a century past."

Judge says public gets one view. A federal judge in Buffalo said Oct. 1 that the public was getting a "one-sided view" of what happened during the Sept. 9–13 uprising at Attica because state correction authorities had barred newsmen from interviewing inmates about the revolt.

Federal Judge John T. Curtin criticized the ban on news interviews in a case brought by several newsmen in

March to force state prison officials to permit reporters to talk with inmates.

During procedural arguments involving attorneys for both sides, Judge Curtin repeatedly asked Assistant Attorney General Joseph J. Ricotta to explain why newsmen should not be allowed into Attica to interview prisoners. Ricotta said Russell G. Oswald, state commissioner of corrections, had suspended the "guidelines" for newsmen under a provision of the regulations providing that newsmen could be excluded if it was deemed that the security of the prison would be threatened.

Newsmen right to silence curbed. The Supreme Court ruled 5–4 June 29, 1972 that journalists had no constitutional right to refuse to testify before grand juries about information they obtained in confidence.

Justice White, in the majority opinion joined by the four Nixon appointees, said "the public interest in pursuing and prosecuting those crimes reported to the press" took precedence over the public interest in some future news that might not be divulged to reporters if confidentiality were compromised. He wrote that establishing a First Amendment "newsman's privilege" would require still further rulings about pamphleteers, lecturers, pollsters and scholarly researchers. Only bad faith attempts by prosecutors to harass reporters could come under constitutional censure, White wrote.

In response to a dissenting opinion by Justice Stewart warning that governments might try "to annex the jounalistic profession as an investigative arm of government," Justice Powell wrote in a separate opinion that "the solicitude repeatedly shown by this court for First Amendment freedoms" should dispel such fears.

The ruling was made in three cases, one concerning the civil contempt conviction of New York Times reporter Earl Caldwell, who refused in 1970 to enter a grand jury room where the Black Panther party was under investigation. The Panthers also figured in the second case, in which Paul Pappas, a New Bedford, Mass. television newsman had refused to reveal to a grand jury what transpired at a Panther headquarters he had visited. The third case involved Paul M. Branzburg of the Louisville (Ky.) Courier-Journal, who refused to testify before grand juries about illegal drug use he had witnessed.

Laws in 18 states gave some protection to journalists against disclosing confidential information, as did pending Congressional legislation.

Reporter loses plea; jailed. The court refused Oct. 3 to stay the jailing of a former Newark Evening News reporter who had refused to answer grand jury questions about an alleged bribe to a Newark Housing Authority official.

The reporter, Peter J. Bridge, surrendered in Newark Oct. 4 to begin an indeterminate sentence for contempt of court. Bridge was the first reporter to serve a jail term since the court ruled June 29 that newsmen did not enjoy constitutional protection against having to reveal confidential sources of information to a grand jury.

The court's 8–1 decision to deny an appeal by Bridge was disclosed to newsmen in a two-sentence statement. The statement said Justice William O. Douglas would have granted the stay.

Bridge had been ordered to serve a contempt of court sentence for refusing to answer five questions asked by a county grand jury investigating alleged corruption in the Newark Housing Authority. The questions he refused to answer dealt with a reported bribe attempt, what the bribe was for and whether any Newark housing officials had been harassed.

N.J. reporter freed. Reporter Peter J. Bridge was released from a county jail in Newark, N.J. Oct. 24, 21 days after he was imprisoned for refusing to answer a grand jury's questions about a story he wrote.

Bridge was the first newsman to be jailed since the Supreme Court ruled in June that journalists could be compelled to answer grand jury questions regarding criminal questions. At the time of his release, Bridge was serving a contempt sentence after he declined to answer questions about an alleged bribe to a Newark official.

In a related development, another reporter, William T. Farr of the Los Angeles Times, was sent to jail in Los Angeles Nov. 16 for his refusal to disclose the sources for a 1970 news story he wrote about the Charles Manson murder case.

But later Nov. 16 Farr was released from jail on his own recognizance on an order by a state appeals court, which agreed to rule on a petition to free him.

Supreme Court refuses contempt review. The Supreme Court refused Nov. 13 to review a contempt citation against William Farr, a California newspaperman, for his refusal to tell the trial judge in the 1970 Charles Manson murder case the source of confidential information about a witness's statement to the prosecution.

Only Douglas dissented as the court let stand the contempt citation against William T. Farr, a former reporter for the Los Angeles Herald-Examiner. Farr, now with the Los Angeles Times, faced an indefinite jail term for contempt.

The case grew out of an article by Farr involving restricted court information that at the time had not been admitted into evidence. Farr refused to tell Judge Charles H. Older who had given him a copy of that statement.

Prison visits curbed. The California Supreme Court refused Nov. 16 to review a lower court decision denying an interview by a reporter with Ruchel Magee, a murder trial defendant incarcerated at San Quentin prison. The lower court had ruled that the state could refuse interviews or disclosures of prison records for "the legitimate purposes of maintaining prison security, discipline and orderly administration."

Popkin freed in contempt case. Prof. Samuel L. Popkin, the Harvard scholar who was jailed for refusing to answer certain questions about the Pentagon papers, was released from a Dedham, Mass. jail Nov. 28 in a surprise move by the government.

Popkin gained his freedom when the Justice Department unexpectedly dismissed the Boston grand jury before which he had refused to answer the questions. He was jailed for contempt Nov. 21 and had been expected to remain there until Jan. 12 when the jury was to end its investigation into the Pentagon papers case.

The U.S. attorney's office in Boston said the jury was dismissed to avoid any conflict with the government's case against Daniel Ellsberg and Anthony J. Russo Jr. on criminal charges involving the once-secret war study.

The Supreme Court had refused Nov. 10 to stay Popkin's jailing. The 1st Circuit Court of Appeals upheld Popkin's right to refuse replies to four of the seven questions. Those four had to do with his opinions of who might have had copies of the 47-volume war study. But the appeals court ruled that the three others were germane and should have been answered. Only Justice William O. Douglas dissented in the Supreme Court's 8–1 decision.

Civil case privilege backed. A three-judge panel of the 2nd U.S. Circuit Court of Appeals upheld a lower court ruling backing a newsman who refused to disclose the name of a news source in connection with a civil case, it was reported Dec. 8.

Black plaintiffs in a Chicago civil suit had sought to force Alfred Balk to identify the real estate agent who supplied information for his 1962 Saturday Evening Post article about racial block busting. The appeals court cited press privilege laws in Illinois and New York, where the article was written, and said the case did not present "a concern so compelling as to override" First Amendment rights.

New Jersey law backs newsmen. The New Jersey legislature passed Dec. 14 what was called the nation's strongest press privilege law. The measure would allow anyone who gathered news for any news media to refuse to disclose any information about the story or its sources to any judicial or investigative body, whether or not the information was actually published. The measure would continue to protect a newsman even if he left the profession after the information was gathered. Passage was sparked by the October jailing of a Newark reporter.

Newsman jailed. John F. Lawrence, chief of the Washington bureau of the Los Angeles Times, was jailed for several hours Dec. 19 after refusing to turn over to the U.S. district court in the District of Columbia tape recordings of an interview with a key government witness in the case involving the break-in at the Democratic party headquarters at the Watergate building.

The tapes recorded an interview with Alfred C. Baldwin 3rd, who said he had played a role in the break-in. The interview was conducted by Los Angeles Times reporters Jack Nelson and Ronald J. Ostrow and articles based on the interview, naming Baldwin as the source, were published. Lawyers for one of the seven defendants arrested in the break-in, E. Howard Hunt Jr., requested the court to order the Times to produce the tapes for the possible impeachment of Baldwin when he testified in the trial, which was scheduled to begin Jan. 8, 1973.

The request, made Dec. 11, was upheld Dec. 14 by Chief Judge John J. Sirica of the Washington court, who approved subpoenas for Lawrence, as the paper's representative, and for Nelson and Ostrow. Baldwin had advised the court he had destroyed his own recordings of the interview.

The Times and the reporters asked the court to quash the subpoenas to protect "the people's right" to information. The interview, they said, had been obtained on the promise that the material would be held confidential unless Baldwin consented to disclosure.

Since the two interviewers disclosed they had turned over the tapes to the Times, Lawrence, who had played no direct part in the interview, became responsible for producing the tapes. Lawrence declined to surrender them Dec. 19, on the grounds it would be a violation of the First Amendment's guarantee of a free press. He was held in contempt of court and ordered by Sirica to be held in custody until he produced the tapes. The custody lasted for more than two hours until a three-judge panel of the U.S. court of appeals ordered his release pending a hearing the next day. The appeals court Dec. 20 continued the stay of sentence pending an appeal to the Supreme Court. But the contempt action was voided Dec. 21 when Baldwin released the Times from the pledge of confidentiality and the newspaper surrendered the tape recordings to Sirica for private inspection.

Lawrence became the fourth newsman jailed during the year for refusing to disclose confidential information. One of them, William T. Farr, also a Los Angeles Times reporter, had been imprisoned since Nov. 27 for refusing to disclose the source of an article on the Charles Manson murder trial. In addition to Lawrence and Farr, Newark Evening News reporter Peter Bridge was imprisoned for 20 days in October and Edwin A. Goodman of WBAI-FM radio station in New York served 44 hours of a 30-day sentence March 3–4.

The Reporters Committee for the Freedom of the Press protested Dec. 21 that the latest case "represents a further serious erosion" of the First Amendment. The only reason Lawrence "escaped further imprisonment," it said, "was not by the protection of the First Amendment but because a news source backed down on the confidentiality privilege."

Farr jailed. U.S. District Court Judge Robert J. Kelleher refused Dec. 19 to free Los Angeles newsman William T. Farr, jailed since Nov. 27 for refusing to reveal the source of a news story he wrote during the Charles Manson murder trial.

Kelleher sent the case back to the state courts, to determine whether trial judge Charles C. Older was biased when he jailed Farr under an indefinite prison sentence for contempt. Kelleher cited a Supreme Court decision refusing to extend protection to newsmen during grand jury proceedings, and said Farr's "lurid" stories demonstrated the "compelling need to protect the defendant against prejudicial publicity."

During the trial, Farr had been protected by a state newsman privilege law, but when he left the Los Angeles Herald-Examiner after the trial, Older ordered him to reveal his source.

IPI scores U.S. trend. The annual world review of the International Press Institute (IPI) said in Geneva, Switzerland Dec. 31 that the U.S. government had been trying to "chip away" at press guarantees in order "to make the journalist timid in research for the facts and the public nervous when confronted by a reporter asking for them." IPI conceded, however, that press freedom in the U.S. remained "almost unscathed."

The report singled out for criticism the Supreme Court decision in the Earl Caldwell case, which denied reporters' right to silence before grand juries.

Farr released. Supreme Court Justice William O. Douglas Jan. 11, 1973 ordered the release of Los Angeles newsman William T. Farr after 48 days in jail, pending review of his case by a federal appeals court.

The Supreme Court had refused, over Douglas' dissent, to review an earlier appeal by Farr against a contempt citation for concealing the names of sources for news articles about the murder trial of Charles Manson. Farr had since begun a second court challenge based on the alleged bias of the trial judge, the judge's alleged assurances to Farr before the controversial articles appeared that the reporter was protected by California's newsman privilege law, and the lack of a serious judicial need for the names of his informants.

Gov. Ronald Reagan had signed a bill Dec. 30, 1972 strengthening the state's law guarding newsmen's rights to refuse to disclose their sources to grand juries.

La. convictions appealed. The Reporters' Committee for Freedom of the Press filed a brief in 5th U.S. Circuit Court of Appeals in New Orleans Jan. 15 in support of two Baton Rouge reporters who had been fined $300 each for contempt of court after disobeying a federal judge's order against news coverage of a public civil rights hearing.

The brief said the case was "the first in history" in which the Justice Department claimed "that the courts may criminally punish newsmen for reporting public events." The government position, the brief charged, would allow judges to impose temporary censorship whenever they deemed fit.

The Justice Department, in its own brief, said the reporters should have obeyed the order unless it was later overturned in court, and cited four newspapers who had obeyed a temporary court injunction in the Pentagon Papers case. The Reporters' Committee said newsmen had the right to ignore "a clearly unconstitutional prior restraint," and presented affidavits supporting that position from the four newspapers cited by the Justice Department—the New York Times, the Washington Post, the Boston Globe and the St. Louis Post Dispatch.

Immunity law hearings begin. A House Judiciary subcommittee opened hearings Feb. 5 on a federal law to protect newsmen from being forced to reveal confidential information. The Supreme Court had ruled June 29, 1972 that newsmen were not automatically protected from being made to testify before a grand jury.

The subcommittee, chaired by Rep. Robert W. Kastenmeier (D, Wis.) had before it more than 30 bills offering varying degrees of immunity.

The hearing began with the testimony of two newsmen who claimed they were harassed by government agencies for refusing to reveal confidential information. Earl Caldwell of the New York Times said he was "hounded" by the Federal Bureau of Investigation because he would not talk about conversations he had with

the Black Panthers. It was he who was compelled by the June 29 Supreme Court ruling to testify.

Los Angeles Times reporter Jack Nelson testified Feb. 5 that the Department of Justice tried to suppress an interview concerning the Watergate bugging of Democratic headquarters. He said the Justice Department had threatened to take away immunity from prosecution from Alfred C. Baldwin 3rd if the tapes of the interview were not released to the Justice Department. Nelson called Baldwin the key government witness in the trial.

Peter J. Bridge, a former reporter with the defunct Newark Evening News, testified Feb. 7 that any law that had qualifications attached would invite further inroads by the courts and "tend to destroy immunity." Bridge was jailed for 21 days for refusing to testify before a grand jury.

Richard C. Wald, president of NBC News, called for absolute immunity the same day. Without it, he said, newsmen could be turned into policemen without badges.

The Justice Department, however, was not in agreement with the newsmen about the need for absolute immunity. Assistant Attorney General Roger C. Cramton argued Feb. 7 that once an immunity law was enacted there would be cries that it was being abused and used irresponsibly. "Step by step, what started out as being a privilege or a favor to the news media can turn out to be a species of regulation." Cramton added that such a law would "unduly subordinate to the interests of the press the vital national interest in vigorous law enforcement."

University of Michigan law professor Vincent A. Blasi, commissioned by the Reporters' Committee on Freedom of the Press to do a two-year study on the immunity issue, took a middle stand Feb. 8. He opposed an all-or-nothing attitude and called for qualified immunity against disclosure of information. Newsmen could fend off investigative subpoenas by submitting affidavits saying their testimony would break "an explicit promise of confidentiality" or "damage an important ongoing source."

Blasi said trial subpoenas could be dealt with in the same way, although this could be abridged if it were shown in court that the reporter's testimony was absolutely necessary. Blasi said such immunity would extend only to those individuals who were deemed professional journalists.

Reporter, activists freed. A federal grand jury refused Feb. 15 to indict Washington reporter Leslie H. Whitten on charges of illegally possessing documents stolen from the Bureau of Indian Affairs in November 1972. After the jury's decision, the Department of Justice moved to dismiss the charges against Whitten, who collaborated with columnist Jack Anderson in a syndicated column.

Similar charges were dismissed against Indian activists Hank Adams and Anita Collins.

Whitten and Adams were arrested in Washington by the FBI Jan. 31 as they carried three boxes of documents to Whitten's car. The pair claimed they were returning the papers to the FBI and did not intend making use of them. Collins was arrested for picking up the documents at the Washington bus station the night before.

Watergate subpoenas. Subpoenas were issued Feb. 26 for 12 reporters and news executives to relinquish to the Nixon re-election committee their notes or other private material relating to their Watergate articles. The subpoenas were obtained by the committee in connection with civil suits on the case. Five of the subpoenas were issued for Washington Post personnel: publisher Katharine Graham, managing editor Howard Simons and three reporters. Four were directed at Washington Star-News reporters. Others subpoenaed were reporters at the New York Times and Time magazine reporters and Walter J. Sheridan, a former network correspondent.

Contempt citation quashed. A contempt citation issued by a San Andreas, Calif. judge against a newspaper publisher who criticized him, was thrown out of court by a state appellate court judge March 2. Superior Court Judge Ralph McGee said the editorial against Justice Court Judge Howard Blewett was protected by the First Amendment. Therefore, he said, publisher Oscar Mellin could not be held in contempt. Blewett, not an attorney, was angered by a series of editorials by Mellin that criticized the California practice of allowing non attorneys to serve as judges.

Committees consider immunity laws. Congressional subcommittees continued to hear testimony from newspapermen and political leaders as they considered a course of action on a press immunity law.

House Subcommittee No. 3 of the Judiciary Committee heard a second round of testimony beginning with Gov. Thomas J. Meskill (R, Conn.), who said March 1 that a law giving newsmen absolute immunity from being forced to reveal confidential sources would give them license to defame public officials and shield criminals.

Clark R. Mollenhoff, former special counsel to President Nixon and present Washington bureau chief for the Des Moines Register, urged the subcommittee March 7 to pass no law and instead allow the press to rely on the First Amendment on a case-by-case basis.

Other subcommittee witnesses, however, were not as sanguine about the future of news reporting as long as newsmen had no protection. A. M. Rosenthal, managing editor of the New York Times, warned that more restrictions on newsmen were in the offing if an absolute immunity law were not passed. In his March 5 testimony, he reminded the committee that he had been expelled from Poland 14 years earlier for probing "too deeply into the internal affairs of the government, the party and the leadership." Now, he said, he was involved in a debate about being allowed to do in the U.S. what led to his expulsion from Poland.

Robert G. Fichenberg, chairman of the Freedom of Information Committee of the American Society of Newspaper Editors (ASNE), said March 12 before the House unit that the ASNE, previously on record as favoring a limited immunity law, now felt "a dangerous assault" was developing against newsmen and their confidential sources. A limited law was not sufficient to safeguard the press, he said.

Meanwhile, Sen. Sam J. Ervin (D, N.C.) chairman of the Senate Judiciary Committee's Subcommittee on Constitutional Rights, held similar hearings. Ervin said Feb. 20 he was offering a bill guaranteeing limited immunity from forced testimony. A bill giving absolute immunity had no chance of passage in Congress, Irvin said.

Among those testifying was Sen. Thomas F. Eagleton (D, Mo.), former vice presidential candidate and a victim of erroneous reporting in 1972, who urged Feb. 21 a law that allowed newsmen to keep their sources confidential, even in cases of libel. "Erroneous journalism . . . is a price which simply must be paid in order not to jeopardize the free flow of news."

William Cahn, past president of the National District Attorneys Association, testified Feb. 27 that newspapers often published articles that gave law enforcement officials leads regarding crimes. Although he said the immunity law in his state (New York) had never interfered with justice, he urged Congress not to pass a law that would block all subpoenas.

Court upholds campus press freedom. The Supreme Court ruled 6-3 March 19 that state colleges and universities could not expel a student for distributing literature on campus they found offensive, regardless of whether it was in good taste. The University of Missouri was ordered to reinstate Barbara S. Papish, a graduate student in journalism, who was dismissed in 1969 for distributing on campus an underground newspaper that contained the words "m-----f-----." The majority opinion said state colleges and universities were not "enclaves immune from the sweep of the 1st Amendment." The minority opinion argued that the majority improperly treated the case as a criminal prosecution rather than an administrative action.

Court rejects Bridge case. The Supreme Court March 19 declined to review the conviction of reporter Peter Bridge, who spent 20 days in jail because he would not answer grand jury questions on confidential information given him by a Newark, N.J. housing official. Justice William O. Douglas noted the case was moot since Bridge had already served his sentence.

Court quashes press subpoenas. U.S. District Court Judge Charles R. Richey for the District of Columbia March 21 quashed subpoenas served on representatives of news organizations by the Nixon re-election committee to compel their unpublished material on the Watergate case.

Richey based his action on the 1st Amendment's guarantee of freedom of the press. "This court cannot blind itself to the possible chilling effect the enforcement of . . . these subpoenas would have on the press and the public," he said.

While he did not hold that journalists had an absolute privilege against testifying, Richey said, the courts "must be flexible to some extent" and the particular instances before him were "all exceptional." He also said the committee had failed to show that other sources of evidence "have been exhausted or even approached" or that the material demanded of the journalists was "central to the case."

The news organizations involved were the New York Times, the Washington Post, the Washington Star-News and Time magazine.

One of those subpoenaed, Walter J. Sheridan, a former network correspondent, complied with the subpoena because he did not possess the press privilege at the time.

Court rejects Maryland case. With only Justice William O. Douglas dissenting, the Supreme Court April 23 refused to review a Maryland court ruling against Baltimore Evening Sun reporter David Lightman, who was ordered to reveal details of an article he wrote about the availability of drugs in the Maryland resort town of Ocean City. Since he had not identified himself as a reporter to a tobacco shop salesgirl offering to sell him marijuana, Lightman was not entitled to protection of the confidentiality of his source material, the Maryland Supreme Court had ruled.

Court upholds Chicago writer. The Supreme Court May 7 declined to disturb lower court decisions permitting magazine writer Alfred W. Balk to refuse to disclose the source of an article on blockbusting in Chicago. Balk, author of an article—"Confessions of a Blockbuster"—in the defunct Saturday Evening Post, was being asked to testify in a civil suit brought by 3,000 Chicago blacks against 60 real estate firms, whom they charged with 20 years of excessive pricing and promotion of panic selling.

TV crew arrested at Wounded Knee. Four members of a Columbia Broadcasting System television film crew were arrested by federal agents when a 70-day confrontation between militant indians and federal officials ended at Wounded Knee, S.D. May 8. The four men were charged with "aiding a civil disorder."

Watergate stalls press shield bill. The Watergate affair was said to have halted Congressional action on legislation protecting newsmen from revealing confidential sources, the New York Times reported July 1.

The Times said many congressmen were posing the question: "If the press did not need a federal shield law to break Watergate, why does it need a shield law at all?" The Times also noted that any press shield bill would have to be considered by the Senate Judiciary Committee's Subcommittee on Constitutional Rights. The panel's chairman, Sen. Sam J. Ervin Jr. (D, N.C.), was occupied with the public hearings on the Watergate case.

A House Judiciary Committee subcommittee reported a partial shield law to the full committee June 14. The bill freed a newsman from having to disclose his news source to a grand jury; included a similar provision for civil or criminal trials, except when compelling or overriding public interest was involved; and defined a newsman as anyone involved in "obtaining, writing, reviewing, editing or otherwise preparing information in any form for any medium of communication to the public." The bill would not preclude state press immunity laws, nor would it apply in certain cases involving libel.

Alabama gets press ethics law. Alabama Gov. George C. Wallace (D) Sept. 14 signed into law a bill requiring all newsmen to make complete personal financial disclosures before being allowed to cover state government. Sponsors of the bill felt that newsmen were in a position to influence legislation and as a result should be required to disclose conflicts of interest.

Immediately after Wallace signed the bill, Jesse J. Lewis, publisher of the weekly Birmingham Times, initiated a class action suit in federal district court in Birmingham to have the law struck down.

Richardson to widen press protection. A Justice Department spokesman said Oct. 4 that Attorney General Elliot L. Richardson would sign a directive "which would require his specific approval before any newsman could be questioned, arrested or indicted for any offense which the reporter was suspected of having committed while covering or investigating a news story." The spokesman predicted the new guidelines would "quickly put an end" to the wall that was growing between the media and the Justice Department as a result of the arrests of Boston Globe reporter Thomas Oliphant [See below] and investigative reporter Les Whitten.

The directive would apply to all Justice Department officials, including U.S. marshals and agents for the Federal Bureau of Investigation, the spokesman said.

Charges against Oliphant dropped—The Justice Department July 5 dropped charges against Boston Globe reporter Thomas Oliphant, accused of crossing state lines to participate in a riot, obstructing a federal officer during a riot and conspiracy to so obstruct, after he flew in a light plane that dropped food supplies to Indians occupying Wounded Knee, S.D. April 17.

A Justice Department spokesman cited "lack of evidence" as the reason for the dismissal.

Judge grants Agnew subpoena power. Judge Walter E. Hoffman, presiding over the Maryland grand jury investigation of Vice President Spiro T. Agnew, Oct. 3 authorized Agnew's attorneys to subpoena reporters to determine the source of leaks about the investigation. Although subpoenas were issued, the litigation was made moot when Agnew pleaded nolo contendere to one count of income tax evasion Oct. 10. [For further details, see pp. 98–99.]

Court lets La. fines stand. Over the objection of Justice William O. Douglas, the Supreme Court Oct. 23 let stand $300 fines levied against two Baton Rouge, La. reporters, who wrote articles about open court hearings, in defiance of an order by a federal judge. Reporters Larry Dickinson of the Baton Rouge Advocate and Gibbs Adams of the State Times were fined by U.S. District Court Judge C. Harold Cox after their newspapers printed stories about a civil rights worker who was seeking to block prosecution on a murder conspiracy charge.

The 5th U.S. Circuit Court of Appeals, conceding the order against Dickinson and Adams violated their 1st Amendment rights, upheld the fine on the ground that the reporters had a duty to obey the order until it was overturned by a higher court. The Supreme Court concurred in this ruling.

Alabama press disclosure law struck down. A panel of three federal judges in Montgomery, Ala. Dec. 21 declared that part of a recently enacted Alabama law requiring reporters to disclose the sources of their incomes was unconstitutional.

The court ruled that if newsmen were made to disclose their finances to an ethics commission in order to gain accreditation to cover state government, they would be denied reasonable access to the news.

In a related development, U.S. District Court Judge Gerhard A. Gesell ruled Oct. 11 that the Periodical Correspondents Association could not deny press credentials to cover Congress to the Washington editor of the magazine Consumer Reports—a consumer protection publication—if it had issued credentials to correspondents for other specialized groups.

AT&T cites law on call disclosures. American Telephone & Telegraph Co. (AT&T) informed representatives of 10 news organizations and the Reporters Committee for Freedom of the Press Dec. 24 that the Communications Act of 1934 required the company to disclose records of telephone calls by reporters when requested by government agencies.

ABA opposes newsman shield law. The American Bar Association (ABA) House of Delegates Feb. 4, 1974 went on record by 157–122 vote opposing bills before Congress that would grant reporters the right to refuse to reveal confidential sources of information to investigators, prosecutors or judges.

Proponents of the shield law resolution told the delegates that newsmen needed such a law to expose corruption in government. Without it, they said, news sources could not talk without fear of public exposure. Warning that such a privilege would verge on the absolute and cover a wide and indistinct class, opponents argued that newsmen's privilege would encourage grand jury secrecy violations, hamper the ability of victims of libel to protect themselves against irresponsible reporting and ultimately cause the public to demand regulation of the press.

IRS returns Times phone records. The Internal Revenue Service (IRS) Feb. 13 returned to the Chesapeake and Potomac Telephone Co. (C&P) telephone records of the Washington bureau of the New York Times that it had secretly subpoenaed Jan. 8. Not among the returned records, however, were logs of toll calls made from the Maryland home of Washington-based Times reporter David E. Rosenbaum, whose name had appeared on the Jan. 8 IRS subpoena for the Times records. (Rosenbaum said Feb. 12 that the IRS might have been interested in the calls he made when he was investigating charges of tax evasion against a major contributor to President Nixon's 1972 campaign.)

The IRS said it had subpoenaed the records as part of an investigation into a leak of information by an IRS employe. The records were procured by an "administrative summons," a legal instrument normally reserved for tax evasion cases and one not giving notice to the person or organization under scrutiny.

Reporters' panel to seek injunction—The Reporters Committee for Freedom of the Press said Feb. 11 it would seek a court order enjoining the American Telephone & Telegraph Co. (AT&T) from secretly providing law enforcement agencies with telephone records of newsmen.

The suit, aimed at insuring newsmen of notice of service so they would be able to fight the subpoenas in court, followed disclosure by the St. Louis Post-Dispatch Feb. 1 that the Justice Department had issued secret subpoenas in 1971 for the telephone records of the Post-Dispatch, Knight Newspapers Inc. and Leslie H. Whitten, an associate of syndicated columnist Jack Anderson.

AT&T promises notice of subpoenas—AT&T announced Feb. 15 that it would notify its customers when records of their long distance phone calls were subpoenaed by government investigators. The phone company also agreed to supply the records only in response to subpoenas, not simply to written requests as had been the policy in the past. However, AT&T qualified its announcement, saying subscribers would be notified in all cases except when "the agency requesting the records directs the company not to disclose, certifying that such a notification could impede its investigation and interfere with enforcement of the law."

A spokesman for the Reporters Committee for Freedom of the Press said the exception potentially nullified AT&T's entire commitment to advance notification.

Editorial

Comment

𝔓𝔦𝔱𝔱𝔰𝔟𝔲𝔯𝔤𝔥 𝔓𝔬𝔰𝔱-𝔊𝔞𝔷𝔢𝔱𝔱𝔢
Pittsburgh, Pa., January 30, 1970

THE FEDERAL government can't go around subpoenaing reporters and unused portions of television news stories and expect the press to remain free to inform the people. The government is NOT the people but rather the other party to the social contract. Either the government knows everything and the people know next to nothing or the people, through their news media, maintain their right to know. You can't have it both ways.

And you won't, if what the government is doing to the Columbia Broadcasting System is allowed to go on. Within 48 hours after CBS aired a news-feature on the Black Panthers, including an interview with Panther leader Eldridge Cleaver, two men identifying themselves as from the government dropped a subpoena on the desk of Richard S. Salant, president of CBS News. The government, it seems, wants the complete video tape, not just the portions CBS decided to televise, of the Panther story, plus a complete record of all correspondence, memoranda, notes and telephone calls made in connection with arranging the Panther program.

* * *

Unfortunately, the network, after balking initially on the video tape demand, caved in but is still holding out on the other ridiculous demands for what amounts to a federal super-snooperama.

Subpoenaing video tapes and reporters' notes and memoranda for grand juries, congressional investigating committees or local police inspection will mean two things:

▶ News media people will understandably drop the whole idea of intensive, expensive investigative and in-depth reporting because (1) many of them will not wish to become extensions of the Secret Service, the FBI or the police; nor (2) will they wish to tie up their reportorial, clerical and executive personnel in meeting subpoena requirements and in appearances before juries and governmental investigating committees.

▶ Controversial persons and groups will tell establishment media reporters to get lost. So would you if you were involved in something you believed worthwhile but knew was unpopular with the government, the police or large segments of the population. That is, if you knew everything you told a reporter would be revealed not at his discretion but at the discretion of the government, you wouldn't talk.

If every "far-out" group clammed up to the news media, we would be much less — dangerously less — well informed. The same holds true if the news media's motivation for enterprising reporting were inhibited. A free press is as much a part of the checks and balances system of our government as are the House, the Senate, the Court and the Executive. A press (linear and electronic) which is merely a tool of government is as about as effective a check as a President who can't veto, a House and a Senate whose members are the same persons and a Supreme Court made up of congressional committee chairmen. Whatever the role of government snoops, it must never be one of looking ove rthe shoulders of reporters.

THE INDIANAPOLIS NEWS
Indianapolis, Ind., February 19, 1970

We hope Nixon administration has indeed backed off from the idea of subpenaing press notes, tapes, and other records as a method of clamping down on crime.

As frequently occurs in the pulling and hauling of the American system, the press and the people it serves are in danger of getting caught in the middle. And the simple fact of the matter is that journalists cannot simultaneously fulfill their task of serving the public by gathering information on subjects of common interest and perform as an arm of the law-enforcement process.

In saying this, we are not claiming special privileges for journalists as citizens. In the course of their daily lives, they are and should be as subject to the full workings of the police procedure as anyone else. But we do suggest that there are in the journalistic field as in others such things as privileged relationships which cannot be overriden without destroying the profession.

This sort of relationship is recognized, for example, between doctors and patients, lawyers and their clients. It is understood that these professionals could not perform the services the public expects of them unless confidential disclosures can be kept that way. The same is true, in a general sense, of the press. If matters disclosed to a reporter in confidence cannot be kept confidential, the reporter in very short order will not have anything disclosed to him.

The result would be the drying up of news sources depriving the public of information it had previously been able to obtain. The reporters themselves would not be harmed greatly in a personal sense; but the reading public which looks to them for facts about important events will be harmed. And the material the Justice Department wants to obtain would no longer exist.

We grant the relationship of the press to the legal process is a complicated one. Recently it was the defense side of the argument which, under the guise of protecting the rights of the accused, wanted to cut down on journalistic prerogatives; now it is the prosecution side. We believe the interests of defense and prosecution alike, along with those of the public generally, are best served when the press is able to perform its appropriate functions without undue interference.

The Hartford Courant
Hartford, Conn., February 7, 1970

In at least three cities, New York, Chicago and San Francisco, the Department of Justice has sought to subpoena confidential records and notes of newspapers, radio and TV stations and networks and news magazines as part of what appear to be blanket grand jury investigations of Black Panther and Weathermen activities. It seems reasonably well established that the Department is seeking to pull a dragnet through the confidential files of the news organizations in the hope of dredging up damaging information against individuals and organizations it suspects of illegal activities. And in so far as it may be a dragnet, we believe the operation should be viewed by both public and press with very serious concern.

This newspaper has always maintained that the press has no rights or privileges that the general public does not share, except for the single guarantee in the First Amendment of the Constitution that "Congress shall make no law abridging . . . the freedom of speech or of the press."

We have held that the rights of access to information under Connecticut's Right to Know Law were granted, not to the press, but to the public. We believe, and have consistently held on this page, and our representatives have so testified before legislative committees, that a reporter has no more right to read a public record or to attend a meeting of public officials than has any other citizen.

We also have consistently maintained that a newspaper or any other news medium has the same obligation as other individuals and organizations to cooperate in the processes of justice, at least up to the point of revealing confidential sources of information.

Following protests from the news organizations whose confidential material had been sought by subpoena, the Justice Department, which had authorized the dragnet procedure, has indicated that it will at least negotiate with newsmen concerning the release of the material it has been seeking. This may or may not be a satisfactory solution, depending on the willingness of the government's attorneys to accept the newsmen's opinion of what should be held in confidence.

In any event, the original procedure, which may now be modified, posed a real threat to both the public and the press in two important respects. First, it threatened to dry up the confidential sources of legitimate news. Off-the-record conversations provide a considerable part of the news any medium publishes—and not only news about crime. These sources talk only because they know their identities will not be disclosed in any circumstances.

Second, and not less important, the attempt to use confidential news material could contribute to the highly dangerous impression that the press is in effect an investigative arm of the government, which it is not and can never be without destroying one of the fundamental foundations of our society. On both grounds the procedure ought to be condemned.

THE RICHMOND NEWS LEADER
Richmond, Va., February 10, 1970

Freedom of the press, one of the chief safeguards of liberty, never has had a satisfactory definition in philosophy or in law. Yet most persons understand generally what it is, just as most persons understand generally that it always stands in jeopardy of government. The press historically has had to stave off constant efforts of governments to intrude into the realm of the press; last week, the Federal government and some of the nation's major media collided on the issue of freedom of the press once more. Fortunately, by the weekend, the government had beaten a hasty retreat.

The question at issue was whether the government has the right to subpoena the unshown film of CBS, the unpublished files of *Time* and *Newsweek*, and the private jottings and tape recordings of a reporter for the New York *Times*. The Justice Department had subpoenaed just such material in connection with its investigations of the Black Panthers and other pro-Communist groups such as the Students for a Democratic Society. The Justice Department contended that freedom of the press does not relieve the media of certain obligations of citizenship — i.e., the duty to surrender information potentially helpful to the courts.

The media refused. They argued that to comply with the subpoenas could lead—indeed, *would* lead—to a permanent loss of information that the public deserves to have. Reporters require the freedom to seek out news sources without fear that what they are told in confidence, and what they see and hear in places to which they are admitted in trust, one day will have to be spilled to a judge or to the cops. Otherwise news sources, fearing possible persecution, prosecution, or other retribution, very likely will clam up — to the public's detriment.

The right of the press to withhold information never has been tested in the courts, and the Justice Department, to its credit, retreated in its demands last week precisely because it feared a court confrontation that might have diminished the freedom of the press. In common law, attorneys have the right to protect the secrecy of their dealings with their clients, but journalists — like doctors and ministers — operate in a gray area. Twelve States, however, do grant reporters the statutory right to withhold names of confidential informants under specified circumstances.

To assure the free flow of news, journalists must have the right to withhold certain information they cull as well as the names of their sources, even when the subjects involved are as pernicious as the Black Panthers and SDS. Yet this particular freedom of the press puts a burden on the press itself. That is to say, the press must not allow itself to be used as a publicity vehicle for every revolutionary group that comes down the road. For if the press permits itself to be so used, it will cease to serve the public interest and will be self-serving only. And should that happen, a disgruntled public very likely would conclude that a press that serves only itself has no rights at all.

Detroit Free Press
Detroit, Mich., February 8, 1970

THE NEWS media are resisting the Justice Department demands for unedited tapes and files for reasons that have less to do with the Black Panthers and Weatherman than with the rights of men in a free society to know the world around them.

The Panthers are unpopular; the Weatherman behave like adolescent political vandals. But they — and middle-class drug users, draft resisters, other radical action groups—are part of the forces challenging American society today. How much would Americans know about them if their members regarded newsmen solely as investigative agents of the federal government?

And that's precisely what the newsmen would become if they bent to the Justice Department's demands.

The issue is not the Panthers today, but a whole network of news sources tomorrow. The greatest news stories and the most basic daily information on government often begin with information given confidentially to a reporter. If the federal government had the snooping powers it has been trying to command, few diplomats or officials would dare explain to the press the impact of foreign policy or military decisions.

If southern officials could have forced reporters to divulge the names of local Negro activists, they could have broken the back of the civil rights movement in the '60s.

Much of the information the federal government itself releases is skeletal, incomplete, impenetrable. Often Americans don't find out what's going on from press releases but from the reporter who finds someone to speak off the record—a method where an informed or reliable source can transmit information without exposing himself to retribution.

Would Americans ever know of the corruption in Saigon, the inefficiency of the Vietnamese army, the potential fire danger in color TV sets, the special tax advantages conferred on specific companies if someone hadn't said to a reporter, "Don't quote me, but . . ." and sent him off on a search for the information?

Once the federal government arrogates to itself the power to force newsmen to divulge their sources, will future sources risk harassment, investigation, perhaps demotion or firing by talking to reporters?

The Justice Department has backed down on its original demand, calling it a "misunderstanding." About one thing, however, there should be no misunderstanding. It is not just a reporter's notebook or a news magazine's privilege that has been at stake this week, but the free flow of information and ideas in a democratic society: Your right to know. The immediate target may have been the Panthers and the Weatherman, but the ultimate victim would have been the American people themselves.

TULSA DAILY WORLD

Tulsa, Okla., February 8, 1970

DO NEWSMEN have any right to protect their sources of confidential information against official inquiry—from policemen, investigators and grand juries?

That question is at the heart of a growing concern in the news industry about demands for material not printed or broadcast — reporters' notes, tape recordings and film.

Subpoenas have been served, in recent days, on such major news gatherers as the NEW YORK TIMES, the COLUMBIA BROADCASTING SYSTEM and TIME and NEWSWEEK magazines. All were after this kind of material, collected by newsmen but not used in public reports.

The press people—and that includes the broadcast media—protested against giving up their source material to a Federal Grand Jury, for example, investigating Black Panthers.

This did not necessarily mean the media were trying to protect the Panthers or expressing sympathy with their cause. Their anxiety is to keep from destroying or harming the basic relationship between reporters and their news sources.

We believe it is important that the public understand this special relationship, because it is so vital to the functioning of a free press.

In their broad coverage of news, reporters and editors deal with many kinds of people—not as friends or allies but as professionals seeking the raw materials of their business.

A tremendous amount of information comes from persons who would not give it if their names were divulged or if they could not trust the newsmen in whom they confide. This is a confidential relationship; there is no other way to describe it. Once the faith is broken, the source dries up.

It is impossible to overstate the importance of these informants and this kind of information in the news-seeking business. Without it, reporters would have to rely more and more on official versions of what is going on—versions that often leave out as much as they include.

There is nothing new about protecting sources, it has been going on ever since the first newspaper was printed. Newsmen have always resisted efforts to pry loose the identities of their informants. Some have gone to jail rather than break their word.

Of course, there is a limit to this kind of obligation. If a reporter knew something that would endanger lives or imperil national security, certainly he would not be justified in clinging to a code of silence.

But in everyday dealings with news sources—including some on the shady side of the law—no newsman can function unless he can be trusted to respect confidences—even in the face of Grand Jury subpoenas.

The Courier-Journal

Louisville, Ky., February 3, 1970

THIS is an awkward period, when so many Americans not only respond to, but actually seem to seek, simplistic answers to complex problems. The press is one of those institutions caught in the middle of this overcharged atmosphere. There are moments when we are reminded of the Greek legend that the messenger who brought bad news was killed merely for the delivery of it.

Uncomfortable or not, the press has to continue to remind the citizenry of the dangers involved when official actions border on the breaching of Constitutional rights.

At this moment all the branches of the press are under pressure from federal agencies to produce information gathered in confidence. The CBS network has acquiesced, although reluctantly. So have *Time* and *Life* magazines. The Chicago newspapers, including the conservative *Tribune*, are doing the proper thing of conceding civic duty, but asking the court to define and superintend what matter should be released.

It is a complex field. One subpoena action seeks data about a threat on the President's life. We agree instantly that this is information which no member of the press should keep from the proper government agencies. Not all of the demands being made on the press are so clear, however.

Should everything the news agencies have gathered about the Black Panthers and the Weathermen be turned over without question? These are two organizations detested by many people and for which this newspaper holds no brief. There have been other organizations in the past which were equally despised. There will be more in the future. Do we accept our traditional rule of law—of due process—or do we accept whatever short cuts seem handy? Is there not some line which has to be carefully drawn?

Like all others, the Chicago newspapers have long gathered much information by protecting sources. We have, too. Many scandalous episodes of official malfeasance have come to light as the result of some office holder willing to provide the key information, provided his identity was not disclosed. Indeed, the American people still might not know about the Pinkville massacre. That tip came from a Pentagon source. It isn't difficult to imagine the kinds of retribution angry general officers could impose were they to discover the source. The Chicago Newspaper Publishers Association is quite right in describing the government's request for the raw material about the Weathermen and the Panthers as "a fishing expedition."

The CBS subpoena strikes us as sweepingly loose. It calls not only for all the "out-takes," the portions of film not shown to the public, but a complete record of all correspondence, memoranda, notes and telephone conversations made in connection with arranging the Black Panther program shown January 6. The subpoena covers the period from mid-1968 to 1970.

A Self-Defeating Process

The basic point is that let it become a rule of law that everyone in communications must divulge all raw material and all sources, no matter what the provocation, and the flow of information to the American people will swiftly dry up.

We have stated all this as dispassionately as we can. The fact is that we are deeply disturbed about the loose and casual nature of some of these proceedings. We concede the primacy of civic duty under any "clear and present danger" to the national security. We do not concede that the way to get at the militant groups—upon which we also happen to frown—is to sabotage the rights of the press. We believe there is a "clear and present danger" in the subpoena processes being employed. We fear it could well unsettle a substantive part of the American freedoms.

BUFFALO EVENING NEWS

Buffalo, N.Y., February 5, 1970

The sudden ominous flurry of federal court subpoenas to elicit information from news media in criminal proceedings has disturbing implications that should concern the public at large as well as every professional newsman.

A San Francisco correspondent for the New York Times has been ordered to appear before a federal grand jury investigating the Black Panther party. In that same investigation, the Columbia Broadcasting System has been ordered to produce not only film sequences actually broadcast, but also unused portions of films and a complete record of all notes, correspondence, memoranda and records of telephone calls made in arranging its program on the Black Panthers. Similarly, in an investigation of student radicals, a federal court has subpoenaed unedited files and unused pictures from three magazines.

Responding to protests, the Justice Department is now backtracking somewhat from its wide-ranging demands. Welcome though this is, the threat posed at the federal level in the effort to force disclosure of reporters' confidential notes and news sources is only tentatively eased, and at the state level it remains as critical as ever.

Newsmen, of course, are obliged as citizens to respect the judicial process. But newsmen also have a well-recognized obligation, as a matter of professional conscience and ethics, to respect any good-faith pledge they have given not to divulge the source of information obtained in confidence. This long-standing tradition of newsmen protecting the confidentiality of their sources has served the public very well over the years by bringing to light countless scandals which never would have been made known if the informants had to fear personal involvement or exposure.

Thus, for the print and electronic media alike, the danger in this new dragnet subpoenaing of newsmen's raw files is two-fold — on the one hand, it is that news sources will be dried up by the fear of exposure; and on the other hand, that newsmen in protecting the traditional confidentiality of their sources will face a greatly increased hazard of being jailed for contempt for refusing to comply with the blanket subpoenaes.

The latter threat is felt with particular intensity by the working reporters — a point given force by a petition from 23 reporters for the Wall Street Journal to their editors, urging the Journal and the entire journalistic profession to resist an inquisitorial practice "which could be used to make us betray virtually any source."

This is a new version of an old issue, and one clothed with broad public concern, as The News has reiterated over many years in urging statutory protection of a newsman's confidential sources. At least 12 states grant this protection on the same public-interest basis as they recognize the confidentiality of the doctor-patient and lawyer-client relationship. The New York Legislature has seemed on the verge of passing such legislation in each of the last two years, but it has always ended up pigeonholed in the final adjournment rush. Let us hope the latest episodes will trigger enough renewed concern among all the media as well as the public at large to put it through this year.

Chicago Tribune

Chicago, Ill., February 6, 1970

Dragnet subpenas obtained by federal prosecutors for newspaper, news magazine, and television network files, films tape recordings, reporters' notes, and other material were ascribed by a justice department spokesman yesterday to a "communications breakdown" in the department. This explanation is scarcely credible, but the policy affirmed by the department, if carried out in good faith, will serve the public interest without violating the constitutional guarantee of a free press.

The spokesman said that recent subpenas demanding any and all source material, used or unused, about the activities of radical groups that might be in the files of the news media went far beyond the intent of the justice department's policy. The policy, he said, is to negotiate with the news media for specific information and material and to issue subpenas only as a last resort.

There is a vast difference between this declared policy and recent practice. After the riots in Chicago during the Democratic convention in 1968 not only federal and state prosecutors and grand juries but also defense attorneys obtained "fishing expedition" subpenas for material and information possessed by the news media. Similar demands were made after the S. D. S.-Weatherman rampage in the Chicago Loop last October and again after the gun battle between the police and Black Panthers in December. In January, after David Hilliard, a Black Panther leader, was charged with threatening to kill President Nixon, one television network was ordered to produce all its correspondence and interoffice memoranda relating to the Black Panthers since mid-1968.

When television networks cover riots and other public events in which crimes may have been committed, the video tape, whether used or unused, may be affected by a public interest, in which case there can be no valid objection to a subpena for its use by proper authorities. Newspaper reporters who have information that may be pertinent to the proof of guilt or innocence of persons accused of crime have the same duty to cooperate with the authorities or serve as witnesses.

Whether information obtained by a reporter in confidence should be divulged depends upon the circumstances. The reporter has no right to withhold information relating to the commission of a crime, but in other matters his ability to serve the public interest may depend upon confidential sources who trust him with "off the record" information. If reporters and the news media generally could be compelled in any circumstances to disclose confidential information, including the identity of their sources, they would be severely handicapped. They would be regarded as arms of the police or the government, and even good friends would be afraid to talk to them.

Most newsmen and most public officials, including judges, well know that there is a reasonable basis on which all of them can discharge their public responsibilities without violating constitutional protections on which the public interest depends. The justice department now seems committed to such a policy.

HOUSTON CHRONICLE

Houston, Tex., February 10, 1970

When a news photographer takes pictures of a disturbance of a riot, he is not acting as an agent of the police.

When a newspaper reporter makes an investigation into a possibly illegal movement, or when he interviews persons who may have engaged in radical actions, he is reporting the news. He is not acting as an agent of law enforcement.

It hardly needs to be said that news reporters and photographers are normally happy to cooperate with the police. But if they ever become identified as informal agents of the police, or of gatherers of information which may later be used in court, then obviously their task of covering the news will be greatly inhibited.

We mention this because the San Francisco correspondent for the New York Times has been subpoenaed to appear before a federal grand jury investigating the Black Panther party. He has been ordered to appear with "notes and tape recordings of interviews covered the period from Jan. 1, 1969, to date, reflecting statements made for publication by officers and spokesmen for the Black Panther party concerning the aims and purposes of said organization and the activities of said organization, its offices, staff, personnel and members . . ."

Columbia Broadcasting System recently was served a similar subpoena by federal agents and ordered to produce its tapes and unused film takes for a CBS program concerning the Black Panthers.

Federal subpoenas have also been served on Time, Life and Newsweek magazines, seeking their unedited files and unused pictures dealing with the militant Weatherman organization.

The government is putting these news representatives is a difficult spot. If reporters and photographers are to be compelled to give evidence against those they interview, obviously they won't be interviewing any more Black Panthers in the future— or anyone else who might fear that their statements may be later used against them.

In the short run, the New York Times and the CBS information may be useful in the case against the Black Panthers. In the long run, the nation will suffer if reporters are not allowed to protect their sources of information, especially when the stories involve radical or possibly illegal activities.

New York Post

New York, N.Y., February 6, 1970

Foreshadowing the spirit of Vice President Agnew's enthusiastic media-baiting, the Dept. of Justice set out last fall on a fishing trip of its own. In recent days, however, the waters have become somewhat troubled and the dragnet snagged. The haul promises to be poor.

As belatedly acknowledged by Attorney General Mitchell yesterday in a statement apologizing for the salvo of subpenas loosed by his department at newspapers, newsmagazines and a TV network, it has long been the government's practice to negotiate with the press for unpublished material that might possibly be useful in legal actions.

In that connection, reporters have often helped the government. The issue at hand, by contrast, was the attempt of government investigators to help themselves—with both hands—before talking the matter over with publishers, reporters and broadcasters. By resisting the Mitchell invasion, the media have demonstrated a clearer comprehension of Constitutional liberties than the purported professionals at the Justice Dept.

The fact that it took so long for Mitchell to recall past policy—it was last October that Chicago papers were targeted for the first subpenas—indicates clearly that the government was more determined on a test of wills than a test case.

The lessons of the outcome this time ought to be plain, not only to news officials who were intimidated by Agnew's assaults but to the Vice President as well. Since the Attorney General has not developed any substantial reputation as a civil libertarian, it is apparent that the Nixon Administration has been obliged to back off for other reasons—primarily the resistance of newsmen who would not allow it to bull, or bully, through. That awareness, to cite a well-worn phrase of the President's, may open up an era of negotiation instead of confrontation. But the battle against Agnewism is not over.

CHICAGO Sun-Times

Chicago, Ill., August 13, 1970

New guidelines delineated by Atty. Gen. John N. Mitchell concerning the subpenaing of newsmen's records are equitable and workable. They follow generally the philosophy we have expressed on a number of occasions and that of Judge Louis B. Garippo of the Cook County Criminal Court who last May established sound precedent concerning such subpenas in a ruling of national significance. The Field Newspapers, through their counsel, Daniel Feldman, of Isham, Lincoln and Beale, were parties to that suit.

Until Judge Garippo's decision—and earlier ones by Judge Saul A. Epton

and U.S. District Judge Alfonzo J. Zirpoli of San Francisco—some defense and prosecuting attorneys attempted "fishing expeditions" by arbitrarily summoning news files, photographs and reporters' memoranda in their search for evidence.

Judge Garippo said this had a "chilling effect" on the news media's First Amendment rights. We note with appreciation Mitchell's own use of the words "chilling effect" in giving the background for the new guidelines.

Mitchell said subpenas should be sought only after negotiations with the press failed to produce desired material. He himself must be satisfied the material is essential; it cannot consist of peripheral or speculative information and should be confined to verification of published information. Even this should be avoided if non-press sources are available.

Mitchell said the news media is not exempt from subpena and we agree that newspapers have an obligation to co-operate in the due process of law. But the law must not inhibit newspapers in their duty to keep the public informed. The court rulings and Mitchell's guidelines protect both the public and the press.

St. Louis Globe-Democrat

St. Louis, Mo., April 9, 1970

The ruling by a federal district judge in California, that in the absence of "an overriding national interest," a reporter may not be compelled to reveal confidential information to a grand jury investigation, is said to be the first court declaration that newsmen have a First Amendment privilege not to answer questions based on confidential associations.

The ruling is a mixed blessing.

We believe that reporters and editors, just as any other citizens, have no right to shield c r i m i n a l s by withholding information that might lead to their conviction and punishment.

We believe just as strongly that there are times when sources of information need to be protected.

For example if a newspaper is spearheading an investigation into alleged corruption in some agency of government, a reporter should not be forced to betray his source of information.

This presupposes that the informant is an innocent person who is only interested in being protected from reprisal while aiding the investigation.

The press can serve as an honest watchdog only if its members themselves are incorruptible. No reporter in conscience can protect someone guilty of crime or conspiracy to commit crime on the grounds of "confidential association." That is just a high-sounding name for complicity.

DESERET NEWS

Salt Lake City, Utah, March 23, 1970

Two years ago this page urged Congress to seriously consider adopting a law to protect reporters from being forced to disclose the sources of confidential information.

We did so because unless confidential news sources are protected, wrongdoing may go unexposed and the public can be deprived of the facts it needs to reach sound decisions.

Recent efforts by federal prosecutors to subpoena reporters' notes and TV tapes re-emphasize the need for legal safeguards, and appropriate legislation has been introduced in both houses of Congress.

While 16 states already have laws protecting confidential communications to news media, there is no such protection under the federal system.

Yet an Associated Press executive is quoted as estimating that at least half of the information disseminated by that world-wide news service comes from sources which were "originally and continuingly confidential."

Among those already shielded by law from divulging confidential communications are physicians, lawyers, clergymen, accountants, social workers, psychologists, grand jurors, and what informers tell prosecutors and police.

The proposed new law, of course, would not repeal the laws against libel and slander or the other restrictions to make newsmen responsible.

Indeed, the measure specifically provides that newsmen cannot be shielded from divulging their sources in a civil action for libel, in grand jury or other proceedings required by law to be secret, or in cases involving national security as determined by court order.

As The New Republic magazine observes, "A newsman cannot be expected to learn what the Black Panthers or Weathermen or heroin users are doing unless he operates in an atmosphere of reciprocal confidentiality. . . .

"The sources and the information protected today may involve Black Panthers and the SDS. Tomorrow, they may involve disclosure of corruption or abuse of power among public officials or corporate executives."

The main beneficiary, then, of the proposed new law would not be newsmen or their confidential sources so much as it would be the general public.

St. Petersburg Times

St. Petersburg, Fla., February 3, 1970

This is a conservative editorial.

It calls for strict observance of constitutional principles.

It seeks, in the classic Webster definition of conservatism, "to preserve what is established."

Ours has proved a great constitution, and the wisdom it embodies should be conserved through good times and bad, through peace and through war, through poverty and prosperity and through apathy and rebellion.

THAT IS WHY no citizen who truly deserves to call himself "patriot" can tolerate government attempts to butcher the First Amendment. That is why no responsible editor will bow to federal court subpoenas of the unedited notes, tapes, films and files which news organizations have collected on militant revolutionaries.

To do so violates the law of the land . . . specifically the constitutional ban on abridging freedom of the press.

It is perfectly legal for newsmen to volunteer crime-fighting information to the police and the courts. They have been doing that for years and continue to do so, even in this day of law-and-order diatribes against the press.

But when reporters are forced, not asked, to reveal information given to them in confidence, forced to reveal sources who trusted them, forced to function as quasi-spies for the government, freedom of the press has been abridged.

Outside sources soon refuse to talk. Newsmen must take all their information from the government (since it's the only information available). Reports naturally become one-sided; the government controls all that the people know.

THAT IS how it is done.

That is how the news is presented in Russia.

That is why American newsmen are so conservative on the First Amendment.

It is a cornerstone of freedom.

The Boston Globe

Boston, Mass., August 2, 1970

No matter how it is cut, and despite his best intentions, United States Attorney General John N. Mitchell's latest formula for extracting confidential information from newsmen is a threat to the widest possible gathering and dissemination of news on which the welfare of the nation depends.

This is a point which it is not easy to make clear to those not in the news gathering business, for it always falsely appears that newsmen, by insisting on their right to freedom from outside controls, especially government control, are demanding privileges not granted to other citizens. What needs to be understood is that newsmen are asking nothing for themselves. What they seek to preserve, even at the risk of being jailed, is the public's unfettered right to the published facts they dig up in any and all vital matters.

It is this right on which Mr. Mitchell would impinge in the guidelines he has issued for subpoening newsmen's confidential notes, tapes, photos and other records in matters that law enforcement agencies and grand juries are investigating. Mr. Mitchell argues that the withholding of such information abets crime and criminals. This is a low blow. What really would abet crime and criminals would be the drying up of those confidential sources of information on which the disclosure of wrong doing, as often as not in government itself, depends. If a newsman's confidences were to be violated on government demand, that would be the end of them. Ended, too, would be all disclosures that did not have government's imprimatur. Newsmen would find themselves impressed into service as a secret police agency, and that would be the end of their independence and their usefulness.

Sixteen progressive states have recognized this with laws protecting such confidences. It is recognized also in Washington where a Newsman's Privilege Act has been introduced in both Houses of Congress. Mr. Mitchell himself seems to recognize it with at least one part of his mind. He has pledged that no confidential records would be subpoened without his personal approval. But by thus restricting the subpoena power, he assents to the dangers that are inherent in it. And if he now were to be accorded what some think is a personal violation of the First Amendment, what then of the Attorneys General who come after him?

It is not newsmen whose name would be mud after fear of disclosure had dried up confidential news sources. It is the public and its right to know—whether government wants it to know or not.

WORCESTER TELEGRAM.

Worcester, Mass., August 13, 1970

Atty, Gen. John Mitchell's guidelines on limiting federal authority to require newsmen to testify in criminal cases may limit potential conflicts in a touchy area. It is a conciliatory move to allay the media's concern and "avoid a confrontation and an imposed settlement" of the issue by the courts.

The guidelines make it clear that newsmen and photographers will not be subpoenaed unless their testimony is crucial and cannot be obtained elsewhere. Stressing that the press must not be considered "an investigative arm of the government," Mitchell says federal authorities must try to obtain information through nonpress sources before a subpoena for newsmen can be authorized by the attorney general himself. The disclosure of crime must come from other than press sources, and "great caution" is to be observed in requesting subpoena authorization by the attorney general for unpublished information.

The new guidelines may be flexible enough to protect the media's free access to news sources and satisfy the need for criminal justice at the same time. If applied with caution, they may resolve the conflict created by a newsman's duty as a citizen to testify and his commitment to the public.

In implementing the new guidelines, however, government lawyers ought to proceed with extreme care. The First Amendment is the lifeblood of our free and democratic society. The maintenance of confidential news sources is essential to carry out the duties and responsibilities of free media.

Says Frank Stanton, president of the Columbia Broadcasting System: "Broad, unrestricted access to reporters' notes, notebooks and other materials not published or broadcast can have a direct and seriously adverse effect on the free flow of information and access to news sources."

Seventeen of the 50 states have laws recognizing the confidentiality of reporters' notes and contacts. Massachusetts is not one of them. A newsman here can go to jail for refusing to disclose everything he may know in connection with a court case.

Mitchell's guidelines are not likely to resolve the touchy issue for good. In Washington, for example, a Newsman's Privilege Act has been introduced in both houses of Congress. But the attorney general's blueprint may bring some uniformity. to the interpretation of the government's interest vs. newsmen's right to protect their sources of information. As it is, different judges in various federal courts apply different measuring sticks.

If the all-important separation of press and government is preserved and the free gathering and dissemination of news protected, Mitchell's guidelines can serve a useful purpose.

The Providence Journal

Providence, R.I., August 14, 1970

In a move that U.S. Atty. Gen. John N. Mitchell describes as conciliatory to the nation's press, guidelines have been established to control the use of subpoena power to obtain reporter's notes, news photographs and television film.

After months of controversy, Mr. Mitchell has adopted a course that may well ease the difficulties he has encountered up to now. If closely adhered to, the guidelines should serve to curtail an extreme practice resorted to with increasing frequency under the Nixon administration. It was obvious to many news executives that their resources had become the target of government exploitation—a reservoir of information, so to speak, in which the federal authorities were wont to go a-fishing.

First Amendment protection of a free press was cited repeatedly as the nation's news media rose to do battle. The press, it was argued, was being used improperly to perform a function assigned to law enforcement agencies, thus endangering the confidential relationship between journalists and their news sources. There is considerable merit in such reasoning. When the news-gathering process becomes vulnerable to review by the agents of law enforcement, theoretical dangers of government interference enter the realm of actuality, and it becomes increasingly difficult for the news media to perform in its independent role.

Henceforth, the subpoena will be used more sparingly, the attorney general suggests. The guidelines acknowledge that the "compulsory process in some circumstances may have a limiting effect on First Amendment rights" and offer assurance that "the Department of Justice does not consider the press 'an investigative arm of the government.' "

Whether the new policy will satisfy most newsgathering organizations and restore an element of tranquillity to the tense relationship existing between Mr. Mitchell and the press will be known only after a fair test. Whether Mr. Mitchell will have his wish to "avoid a confrontation and an imposed settlement" of the issue by the courts is even more difficult to say. It may depend on how effective the guidelines are in limiting compulsion and how far any journalistic organization now engaged in litigation feels obliged to go for legal clarification.

Doctors, lawyers and clergymen are granted a privileged relationship in the work they do, and that is as it should be to preserve confidences that otherwise would be impossible. Conceivably, the day may come when informing the public and enforcing the laws face an intolerable degree of incompatability on these same grounds, at which point the Supreme Court will be forced to find a way to preserve the integrity and effectiveness of both sides in the dispute.

Mr. Mitchell is right to seek an improved basis of understanding so long as conciliatory words are the prologue to meaningful change. The press must defend what it construes to be its constitutional rights and if forced to the limit would have no choice but to carry its appeal to the highest court for an ultimate decision, as undesirable as such an uncompromising course may be.

Portland Press Herald
Portland, Me., August 13, 1970

Attorney General John N. Mitchell has reiterated his intention to force newsmen, under court order if necessary, to testify, submit their notes and other information in certain criminal proceedings.

Mr. Mitchell told the American Bar Association that the government will attempt to negotiate with news sources in such instances but will use the power of subpoena if necessary. He said the government sees the use of subpoenas against the press as an "authorized and proper exercise of the federal grand jury power to obtain facts" in criminal cases.

The Attorney General also told the lawyers that the press as well as the government has the obligation to see that justice is accomplished through "our established legal procedure."

There can be no denying that. There are many instances when the press has been far more attentive to that obligation than has the government. It is devotion to that precise obligation which prompts responsible newspapers and other news gathering organizations to investigate when government agencies sometimes seem uninterested; it is that obligation which prompts newsmen to ferret out misconduct within the government's own house; it is that obligation which compels newsmen to acquire the information the government wants.

In short, in very many instances in which the subpoena might be used against the press, a newsman or news team has done a job that the government was unwilling or unable to do. Rarely would a newsman be reluctant to share his information with an investigator or grand jury. Sharing it is his purpose in acquiring it. What he may wish to protect, however, are his sources and methods.

Promising that protection may have been his only means of access to some information. Violating that promise may deprive him of that source permanently and make it more difficult to cultivate new sources. In that event, he and the government are deprived of information which might be used in accomplishment of justice in other matters.

The formula is applied consistently and properly by policemen. Prosecutors are willing to forego justice in some cases in order to approach it more confidently in others. People involved at least indirectly in major crimes are given immunity from prosecution in exchange for their testimony. That is one method of discharging an obligation to justice.

The sort of information that would be forcibly extracted from a newsman under subpoena could serve justice only temporarily. Its ultimate effect would be to retard justice.

THE ARIZONA REPUBLIC
Phoenix, Ariz., November 25, 1970

Arizona law clearly protects a reporter from being forced to reveal the sources of his information. Unfortunately, no such protection exists in federal law. So we were naturally pleased when a federal appeals court in San Francisco held that New York Timesman Earl Caldwell was not guilty of contempt when he refused to appear before a grand jury last June.

Caldwell had been given some information about the Black Panther movement on the promise that he would not reveal his source. Had he been forced to appear before the grand jury, he could have been subjected to a line of questioning that would have forced him to break his promise.

While we have no use for the Panthers, a revolutionary group dedicated to the destruction of the government, the principle involved is important. The press provides far too valuable a check on government officials to permit it to be turned into an investigative arm of the government.

There was one important reservation in the decision of the federal appeals court. If the government can demonstrate "a compelling need for the witnesses's presence," then a reporter can be forced to appear before a grand jury. In other words, if there exists "a clear and imminent danger" that the Black Panthers are going to strike, and if a reporter has knowledge of such a plan, he can be called before a grand jury.

Short of any such national danger, however, the public will be better served by protecting the reporter and his sources.

The Washington Post
Washington, D.C., August 13, 1970

From our point of view—which is admittedly and obviously an interested one—approximately two cheers seem to be in order for Attorney General Mitchell's statement respecting the issuance of subpoenas for news media personnel or property. During the past year or so, federal prosecutors have taken to issuing subpoenas to newsmen and their employers with a kind of reckless abandon that seems to us full of peril for the freedom of the press. Newsmen who are forced to turn informer in the name of law enforcement, forced to tell in public what they were told in confidence and forced, in addition perhaps, to divulge the sources of their information, are likely to be heavily handicapped in the gathering of news. And the burden of that handicap is certain to be borne by the readers who depend upon them for information.

One cheer is due Mr. Mitchell for his recognition that the issuance of subpoenas to newsmen has an important impact on First Amendment freedoms. The guidelines promulgated by the Department of Justice acknowledge that the "compulsory process in some circumstances may have a limiting effect on the exercise of First Amendment rights." That's an understatement; but it's better than a flat denial. A second cheer is due for Mr. Mitchell's evident desire to be discriminating and restrained in authorizing subpoenas. They are to be authorized, the guidelines say, only when they are requisite to the fair administration of justice, only after negotiations with the media, only when other attempts to get the needed information have failed and only with his express personal approval.

This newspaper is convinced, nevertheless, as we have said in an *amicus* brief filed in the Earl Caldwell case, that "the First Amendment grants to newsmen a constitutional privilege, absolute and unqualified, to refuse in all circumstances, without penalty, to divulge to anyone any information or source, confidential or otherwise, which they obtain in the course of their professional newsgathering activities."

Undoubtedly, such an absolute privilege may entail a loss under some circumstances to law enforcement and the administration of justice. The same may be said about exercise of the Fifth Amendment privilege against self-incrimination, about the privilege generally extended to communications between husbands and wives, lawyers and clients, doctors and patients, priests and penitents and about the exclusion of evidence obtained unlawfully. All these are sometimes used as justification for withholding from a grand jury or a court information which might be of very considerable value. But the community has deemed the cost to justice a price worth paying for the vital social values conserved by the granting of the privilege.

A privileged status for newsmen in the discharge of their professional duties serves even more important social values. For as Supreme Court Justice Frank Murphy said 20-odd years ago, "A free press lies at the heart of our democracy and its preservation is essential to the survival of liberty. Any inroad made upon the constitutional protection of a free press tends to undermine the freedom of all men to print and to read the truth."

If newsmen began to act as informers or as investigative agents of the government, invaluable sources of information would cease to trust them. The free flow of news has not dried up before now for two reasons. One is that prosecutors and policemen have generally respected the special situation of newsmen, have acted as though the First Amendment privilege was a fact. The other reason is that newsmen have traditionally accepted fine or imprisonment rather than disclose confidential sources or information when prosecutors have tried to breach the privilege. Whenever newsmen have thus defied constituted authority, the public has tended to honor rather than to condemn them, as though this martyrdom were a sort of noblesse oblige of their calling. But it is at once foolish and unfair to impose such punishment on persons serving the public interest. Besides, news sources may not always rely on the willingness of newsmen to go to prison.

The preservation of a free press should not depend upon the caprice of government officials or upon the readiness of individual newsmen to sacrifice themselves for the sake of their sources. Rather, the responsibility for preserving a freely functioning press should be assumed by the government, and particularly by the courts, as guardians of a Constitution which guaranteed an independent press because such a press was deemed indispensable to a free and self-governing society.

The Miami Herald
Miami, Fla., August 13, 1970

ISSUING subpenas to newsmen, said Attorney General John Mitchell, may have a "limiting effect" on constitutional guarantees of a free press.

Well said, Mr. Mitchell. We agree.

That freedom was included in the First Amendment because the founders believed there could be no other freedoms without it.

Yet now Mr. Mitchell proposes "to weigh that limiting effect against the public interest to be served in the fair administration of justice."

We strongly disagree with his proposal. "The public interest" is what that First Amendment is all about. It cannot be limited without penalizing the public.

What Mr. Mitchell advocates is limiting freedoms to make the fight against crime easier. This is a dangerous course. Would he limit other freedoms to solve other problems?

Democracy as this nation practices it is not the most efficient form of government, of course. There are more authoritarian types that can get things done faster. But Americans always have believed those cost more liberty than they wished to pay.

If reporters manage to turn up information on criminal activities which the government with its vast machinery and skills does not have, it will be there in the newspaper for all to read or on the air for all to hear. So informed, cannot the government then make its case without subpenaing the reporters into government service?

In the case of unpublished information, for the government to subpena this would in effect make it the monitor and perhaps the public arbiter of what the newspaper or broadcasting station should publish or should not publish. The same is true in the case of confidential informants. This in many cases would destroy the role of the press as auditor of public affairs.

Mr. Mitchell's guidelines for issuing subpenas to newsmen, as he expressed them before the American Bar Association, are hedged by such phrases as "all reasonable attempts" and "should make clear" and "The department does not approve of utilizing the press as a springboard for investigations."

These same guidelines speak of what the government "should do," of "great caution" necessary, of what "should normally" be the practice. These broad words leave much to judgment.

The founders of the Constitution quite clearly did not believe this basic freedom could exist if it rested solely upon the discretion of a federal prosecutor, or even the attorney general.

Neither do we.

THE DALLAS TIMES HERALD
Dallas, Tex., August 13, 1970

ATTY. GEN. John N. Mitchell appears to be having some difficulty in making up his mind about the role a free press plays, or ought to play, in a democratic society.

On the one hand, he staunchly affirms the right of the Justice Department to subpoena newsmen and their files. On the other, he says he will not oppose legislation granting some type of reporter-informant privilege similar to the lawyer-client relationship.

Mitchell told the House of Delegates of the American Bar Association this week that the controversy over free press-free trial was "one of the most difficult problems I have faced as attorney general." The problem existed before he took office but the practice of summoning newsmen to trials has been expanded during his tenure.

"Serious journalists from all the media have told me privately they would rather go to prison than comply with subpoenas," Mitchell said. "The press views subpoenas as an effort by the government to use them as quasi-governmental investigators."

Mitchell appeared to confirm the press' view of subpoenas by noting that more and more news organizations are covering controversial events and that newsmen occasionally have more information than the government is able to obtain.

He continues to ignore the fact that if newsmen's sources are not protected, either by law or by the insistence of the media, reporters will be severely handicapped in obtaining the news which the attorney general finds helpful.

The controversy should be eased somewhat by Mitchell's new guidelines, which stress negotiations between prosecutors and newsmen. If negotiations fail, subpoenas will be issued only with the express authorization of the attorney general.

The guidelines require that investigators first try to obtain information needed for prosecutors from nonpress sources. Also, Mitchell said, caution should be observed in requesting unpublished information where a serious claim of confidentiality is alleged.

The final answer to the problem lies in specific legislation protecting the reporter-informant relationship. Lawyers are not subpoenaed to testify about their clients. Neither should reporters be required to testify about their informants.

OREGON JOURNAL
Portland, Ore., August 13, 1970

The issue of subpoenaing newsmen, which John N. Mitchell this week called "one of the most difficult problems I have faced as attorney general," is also a difficult problem for the newsmen themselves.

Democratic government cannot work without a free and responsible press to keep the voters informed. There is a real risk that newsmen will lose valuable sources of information if the source believes that an over-eager prosecutor can cause the reporter to identify him in court or before a grand jury.

But the Constitution gives no special privileges to the news profession. The First Amendment's guarantees of freedom of speech and of the press apply to every citizen, not just to persons with a job on a newspaper or broadcasting station. Ordinarily a citizen has a duty to testify, and testify truthfully, in response to a subpoena.

Some states have adopted a shield law giving what passes between a newsman and his sources a confidential status comparable to communications between a doctor and his patient, a lawyer and his client, or a priest and his confessant. Some editors favor such a law for Oregon, and for the United States.

But those editors ignore the problem of how to define a professional newsman, since under the Constitution every citizen has a right to gather and spread information. Doctors and lawyers are licensed, and ministers are registered. Licensing of newsmen would give whoever controls the process an unthinkable means of control over the press.

The situation is better left in the indefinite area where it now rests. In his speech this week to the American Bar Association's House of Delegates, Atty. Gen. Mitchell stated what he called temporary guidelines for federal prosecutors which seem to strike an acceptable note. All reasonable attempts should be made to obtain the information from non-press sources. The attorney general himself must authorize each subpoena, and the request for that authorization must show that the information sought is essential and cannot be obtained from non-press sources. Negotiations with the press should be attempted when a subpoena is being considered.

That is a more sensible and sensitive attitude than Mr. Mitchell's Justice Department has displayed in some alarming cases since the Nixon administration came into office. It suggests that the attorney general has listened to the protests the press has made about them.

Inevitably there still may be cases where a newsman may feel he has to resist a subpoena to protect his sources, even at the risk of punishment for contempt of court. That's one of the hazards of the news business, although the motives of a public official who would put a newsman in that position should be and assuredly will be questioned.

But newsmen ought not ask for special protections from the law. The same law that tells them what they can do may also tell them what they can't do, and then goodby freedom of the press.

CHICAGO DAILY NEWS
Chicago, Ill., November 19, 1970

The role of a news reporter is often difficult in these troubled times. In carrying out his function of keeping the public informed, he may gain access to news sources that are closed to the agencies of government. Can he then be forced to reveal those sources, betray confidences and in effect serve as a tool of the government?

Such a case arose in San Francisco, where a New York Times reporter, Earl Caldwell, wrote stories based on his contacts with members of the Black Panther Party. He was ordered to bring notes and tape recordings before a federal grand jury. He refused, on the ground that appearing before the grand jury, even in secret session, would cut him off from sources that had confidence in him. He was cited for contempt.

But the 9th U.S. Circuit Court of Appeals has now vacated that judgment, and in the process contributed valuable insights on basic rights and the role of the press. The court said the government had failed to show any "compelling need" for Caldwell's appearance before the grand jury.

"Where it has been shown that the public's First Amendment right to be informed would be jeopardized by requiring a journalist to submit to secret grand jury interrogation, the government must respond by demonstrating a compelling need for the witness' presence," the court held.

The opinion also noted that if a grand jury could force a newsman to reveal "information obtained by him as a newsgatherer," the effect would be to convert the reporter into "an investigative agent of the government."

"The very concept of a free press," the court added, "requires that the news media be accorded a measure of autonomy; that they should be free to pursue their own investigation to their own ends without fear of governmental interference, and that they should be able to protect their investigative processes."

This is the heart of the matter. And while the court made clear its ruling in the Caldwell case was "a narrow one," it still will stand as a landmark decision in guiding future action in this sensitive area. All too often, in recent years, prosecutors have tended to subpena reporters and photographers in what amounted to fishing expeditions for any information they might use. The press has resisted, and to his credit Atty. Gen. Mitchell recently issued his own guidelines counseling restraint in such matters.

The First Amendment guarantee of press freedom must of course be viewed in context with other basic rights under the Constitution. When those rights come in conflict a resolution is sometimes difficult. There may well be times when the "compelling needs" of society outweigh a reporter's need to protect his confidential sources of information. But as the appeals court has now made clear, the need must be real and demonstrable, and not merely a gleam in an eager prosecutor's eye.

The Evening Bulletin
Philadelphia, Pa., November 22, 1970

A U. S. appeals court in California has reaffirmed and expanded the right of newsmen to guard the confidentiality of their news sources.

Not only may they do so by refusing to testify or turn over their notes; there are instances when they might refuse even to appear before a judicial proceeding.

The 9th Circuit Court held that where the public's right to information may be jeopardized, only a "compelling need" for the newsman's presence before a judicial process may justify the government requiring his appearance. The opinion said:

"The very concept of a free press requires that (reporters) ... be free to pursue their own investigation to their own ends without fear of governmental interference, and that they should be able to protect their investigative processes."

This was admittedly a landmark case from the start because it points up a new facet of the race problem confronting America, the distrust which certain minorities tend to hold for the "establishment."

It involves Earl Caldwell, a black reporter for the New York Times, who did a series of articles about the Black Panthers. Last January, Mr. Caldwell was ordered to appear and bring notes to substantiate his stories to a secret grand jury. He refused.

U. S. District Judge Alfonso J. Zirpoli later modified the order, permitting Mr. Caldwell to bring his own attorney to the hearing and to withhold certain confidential information.

The newsman again refused, contending that his credibility in the black community would be undermined, his news sources would dry up, if he even appeared in secret session. There would be no way for him ever to disprove suspicions that he revealed what he had promised not to divulge.

Mr. Caldwell feared, in short, that he would be considered a black spy for the "white press." He did, however, offer to testify in public, and the New York Times backed him in this stand.

What is at issue here is more than the trials of a reporter seeking to protect his livelihood, or the tribulations of the press trying to report the news without harassment of government officials.

Communication across the lines of conflict in our society is essential if today's problems are to be understood and dealt with effectively. Reporters such as Mr. Caldwell fulfill a vital function in that they can bridge the gap; they are trusted, more or less, by both sides.

If this trust is undermined, and the bridge destroyed, all right-thinking citizens will be the losers.

The News American
Baltimore, Md., November 24, 1970

WHICH IS more important — the frequent need of a free press to keep its sources of information in confidence, or the right of a grand jury to demand disclosure of such sources for the purpose of law enforcement?

In this question is summarized an old and still unresolved collision of basic concerns in our democracy. It is imperative to protect the public from dangers to its well-being. But it is equally important to ferret out and expose those dangers in the first place.

The men of vision who guaranteed a free press by writing the First Amendment understood that a free press is the surest safeguard against evil. They failed, however, to specify if that freedom should be subject to abridgement in the course of correcting the very evils it may have disclosed.

Depending on the whims of various judges, untold numbers of reporters have been jailed for contempt when they have refused to divulge the identity of persons whose anonymity was vital for further information. Whether the press can be trusted was always the key concern.

Now, in San Francisco, a United States Court of Appeals has finally come up with a ruling which could and should solve the problem once and for all. It involves a reporter cited for contempt for refusing to divulge sources in his disclosures of Black Panther activities.

While the case was pending, Attorney General John Mitchell conceded that the public's First Amendment right to be informed should not normally be jeopardized. Accordingly, he said, whenever an impasse arises over whether a reporter should be compelled to give evidence that is both vital and otherwise unobtainable — the attorney general personally would decide which consideration is to take precedence.

In its ruling, the 9th Circuit Court also sustained the general inviolability of press freedom. But it held that in cases of conflict the government must show "a compelling need for the witness' (reporter's) presence before judicial process properly can issue to require attendance."

That, in non-legal jargon, means that a court should decide whenever there is a question as to which will serve the public interest best — a reporter's need to protect his sources or the need of enforcement agents to get otherwise unobtainable information.

The court's ruling makes a lot more sense than Mr. Mitchell's solution which, in effect, would give one of two adversaries the final say. Judicial resolution of these continuing deadlocks, whenever they occur, is the only fair and proper recourse — and it is to be hoped the San Francisco ruling will be sustained by the Supreme Court.

ST. LOUIS POST-DISPATCH

St. Louis, Mo., November 20, 1970

The Ninth Circuit Court of Appeals at San Francisco has powerfully buttressed the First Amendment with its reversal of a contempt conviction against Earl Caldwell, the *New York Times* reporter who refused to appear before a grand jury investigating the Black Panthers. Backed by his newspaper, Mr. Caldwell, who is black himself, said going before the jury would destroy his credibility with news sources among black militants, and thus impede the flow of information through the press. The lower court held that he might refuse to answer certain questions by the grand jury, but was compelled to appear before it. Now the Circuit Court says even an appearance cannot be compelled unless the Government demonstrates an "overriding national interest" which justifies violating "the public's First Amendment right to be informed."

It is well that the Court put the issue that way, in terms of the public's right to be informed, rather than the press's right to inform it. For it is the public, not only the press, that suffers with the erosion of this right.

Newsmen have no wish to avoid doing their duty as citizens, but in some cases they occupy a special position which makes it impossible for them both to testify before a grand jury and to maintain the integrity of their news sources. In such cases, when the Government insists that a reporter become in effect a part of the law enforcement apparatus it is insisting that he abandon his function and responsibilities as a reporter. Let the Government prosecute its own cases with its own investigators, its own witnesses, its own policemen. As Mr. Caldwell says, it has no business asking newsmen to "play on both sides of the street."

THE MILWAUKEE JOURNAL

Milwaukee, Wis., November 22, 1970

A free press and the public's right to be informed are inseparable. So there is a broadly beneficial significance to a Federal Court of Appeals decision in San Francisco that the government must show a pressing need for evidence before compelling a journalist to submit to secret grand jury interrogation.

The case involves a New York Times reporter and a federal grand jury investigation of Black Panthers. While a lower court had conceded that the reporter had a limited right to shield the identity of confidential sources, it ruled that he could not refuse completely to testify. The reporter argued that he was willing to make statements in open court but that mere appearance at a secret proceeding would irreparably damage the unique trust and confidence he had built up with his sources. After all, how could they know what he really divulged?

In supporting the reporter, the appeals court emphasized that the case was "a narrow one." A reporter would have to show that a grand jury appearance would jeopardize his relationship with sources and cripple his capacity to report news. Then it would be up to the government to prove a "compelling need for the witness' presence" before attendance could be required. Fair enough. For journalists, such protection against indiscriminate use of the subpena power has never been enunciated before by so high a court.

The ruling is immediately relevant in Wisconsin, where an underground newspaper editor, Mark Knops, is still in jail for contempt of court after refusing to tell a grand jury about his news sources. Plainly, Knops' claim to a degree of journalistic immunity is not frivolous and he should at least be out on bail until the Wisconsin Supreme Court has a chance to consider his appeal on Dec. 2. Anything less is unjust.

THE NASHVILLE TENNESSEAN

Nashville, Tenn., November 19, 1970

A U.S. COURT of appeals in San Francisco has ruled that the government cannot force a reporter to testify before a federal grand jury unless it can prove "a compelling need" for his testimony.

The three-judge court—in a unanimous decision—voided a lower court contempt citation against Mr. Earl Caldwell, a New York Times reporter who had refused to testify before a San Francisco grand jury investigating the Black Panther Party.

★ ★ ★

The lower court judge—like the appeals court—had held that Mr. Caldwell had a "journalist's right" to refuse to answer questions about his news sources unless the government could prove a compelling national interest to force him to disclose such information. But the district judge had held the reporter in contempt for refusing to appear before the grand jury.

However, the appeals court went a step further and wiped out the contempt citation against Mr. Caldwell for refusing to appear, holding that "the need for an untrammeled press takes on special urgency in times of widespread protest and dissent."

In such times, the appeals court said, the First Amendment protections of a free press exist for the purpose of maintaining communications with dissenting groups and to provide the public with a wide range of information about the nature of protest.

The Justice Department under Attorney General John Mitchell has been pressing for a policy to force newsmen to disclose to the courts information they have received from possible lawbreakers in confidence.

No doubt, the department's aim is to improve law enforcement. But it is a misguided aim, unless the real goal is to completely isolate dissidents and to cut off their opportunity to express a point of view.

A newsman is granted freedom under the U.S. Constitution not because he is a critic of any one segment of society, but because he is able to be a critic of the total society, including institutions of government, even the police and law enforcement authorities.

It should be assumed that any so-called underground source a newsman develops the law enforcement establishment, through its techniques, also should be able to develop. To demand that a working reporter cut his ties with sources is to demand that he give up his constitutional mandate to freedom to gather and report news without government interference or license.

The court seems to be saying that this freedom of the reporter is not limitless; that there is an extremity of national interest to which the citizen must respond. But it does not lay any ground rules for where that extremity lies.

It is clear that government cannot be imprecise in making demands on reporters. There is the strong suspicion that in Mr. Caldwell's case he would have gone to jail before he divulged the confidences of his sources. In some other case at some other time some other reporter might make another determination.

But in this case the court says the government has not demonstrated its need to know. The right of a free press and its free representative has been protected by this decision of the courts.

The constitutional protections of a free press do not exist for the convenience of the reporter or the private advantage of the press. They exist for the purpose of keeping the public informed on all areas of life and alerting the people to threatening trends and movements which would not become known otherwise. History has proven that government itself can threaten freedom.

★ ★ ★

The press can operate to the public benefit only when it is free to report on all developments without official interference. When attempts are made to force reporters to do for the police what the police fail to do for themselves the public's right to be informed is threatened.

ALBUQUERQUE JOURNAL

Albuquerque, N.M., November 21, 1970

Another victory has been scored for a free press in the highly susceptible area of protecting news sources.

It came in a 9th U.S. Circuit Court of Appeals ruling that a newsman cannot be ordered to appear before a secret U.S. grand jury session unless the government demonstrates a "compelling public need" for his presence.

That decision purges Earl Caldwell, a New York Times reporter, of contempt for failing to appear last June before a federal grand jury investigating Black Panther activities.

Two months earlier U.S. District Judge Alfonse Zirpoli had held that a newsman must appear although entitled to refuse to answer certain grand jury questions until the government showed "a compelling and overriding national interest" requiring his testimony.

While Zirpoli's decision was regarded by many as a free press victory, Caldwell didn't agree and he refused to appear, drawing a contempt citation.

The appellate court's decision overturning Zirpoli's touched the nerve center of Reporter Caldwell's dilemma. It declared that if a newsman were compelled to testify in secret his sources "might very understandably fear that the reporter's resolve to protect them would crumble in the pressures of the secret hearing."

The opinion also noted that if the grand jury could require Caldwell to disclose information obtained as a news gatherer, "then the grand jury and the Department of Justice have the power to appropriate appellant's (Caldwell's) investigative efforts to their own behalf."

In other words federal snoopers should get off their duffs and do their own investigating.

The New York Times

New York, N.Y., July 15, 1972

A subtle trend toward erosion of the Bill of Rights is among the points of concern raised by the shift in the Supreme Court. Specifically, the decision denying reporters the right to refuse to reveal their sources of confidential information to a grand jury reflects, as Justice Stewart pointedly observed in his sharp dissent, "a disturbing insensitivity to the critical role of an independent press in our society."

In the cases involving three newsmen—including a reporter for The New York Times—who maintained their right to protect their sources of information, the Court's majority seemed oblivious of the chilling effect of its decision on the press's freedom to investigate, to expose, and to report without fear of governmental sanctions. The decision is an assault on the public's right to know. By forcing newsmen to reveal their sources of information to a grand jury, the Court is in fact undermining the whole basis of the confidential relationship between a reporter and his sources, which is the only basis on which much information of vital importance to the public can ever be revealed.

It is the public, rather than the media or the reporters, that will be the principal victim of this amazingly constricted viewpoint of the Court. For it will be infinitely more difficult henceforth to obtain and publish information involving criminal matters that, perhaps for ulterior motives, governmental bodies may wish to conceal. "As the years pass, the power of government becomes more and more pervasive," Justice Douglas noted in his dissent. "It is a power to suffocate both people and causes."

The newsmen did not claim "an absolute privilege against official interrogation in all circumstances"—after all, newsmen do have the normal obligations of citizenship—but they did claim, and are now denied, protection against grand jury questioning except when there was special reason to believe that they possessed relevant information for which there was "compelling" need. In eighteen states including New York, reporters have this special and needed right to the privacy of communications; and Justice Powell's "enigmatic" opinion, concurring with the majority, specifically notes that newsmen do have constitutional rights "in safeguarding their sources," and that governmental authorities are not free to "annex" the news media as "an investigative arm of government."

Yet the purport of the prevailing opinion raises exactly this danger, especially insofar as two of the three cases themselves involved reportorial activities with such an unpopular and suspect group as the Black Panthers, and the third was concerned with the equally unpopular and generally suspect "drug culture." Obviously the decision opens a way to fishing expeditions on the part of grand juries and prosecuting attorneys, at the expense of newsmen's ability to maintain independent and confidential relationships with persons in possession of useful information who fear loss of jobs, harassment or other reprisals if their identity is disclosed.

It seems evident that Federal legislation to restore to reporters some reasonable protection from grand juries of their right to confidentiality—along the lines proposed by Senator Cranston of California and Representatives Koch and Reid of New York—is now essential.

Chicago Tribune

Chicago, Ill., July 8, 1972

The United States Supreme Court last week solemnly acknowledged the virtues of a free press and the need to protect it, and it then just as solemnly declined to do so.

The 5 to 4 opinion involved three cases in which newspaper reporters had been subpenaed to divulge the nature and sources of information which they had gained in confidence. The most notable of the cases was that of Earl Caldwell, a New York Times reporter who established a confidential relationship with the Black Panthers in California and was then ordered by a grand jury to tell it what he had learned about the Panthers and their plans.

The majority opinion, written by Justice White, cited case after case in which the courts have recognized the dangers which unrestrained power in the hands of officials can create for a free press. The Court held that these dangers were not present in the cases before it; it then went on to minimize the dangers in general and to criticize what it seems to regard as a journalistic theory "that it is better to write about crime than to do something about it." It wound up by sidestepping the whole issue, leaving reporters completely at the mercy of prosecutors and grand juries. To define the conditions under which a reporter might be subpenaed, it said, would involve "a long and difficult journey."

"In each instance where a reporter is subpenaed to testify," the court said, "the courts would also be embroiled in preliminary factual and legal determinations with respect to whether the proper predicate had been laid for the reporter's appearance: Is there probable cause to believe that a crime has been committed? Is it likely that the reporter has useful information gained in confidence? Could the grand jury obtain the information elsewhere? Is the official interest sufficient to outweigh the claimed privilege?"

For heaven's sake, these are precisely the sort of questions the courts must undertake to answer if the First Amendment is to mean anything at all. The reporters involved, and their employers, were not demanding absolute immunity, even tho some editors and some politicians [such as California's liberal Sen. Alan Cranston] have proposed it. They were not putting the interests of a free press above the interests of justice.

They were merely asking the Court to acknowledge that the power of subpena can be abused and that the courts have a duty to prevent such abuse.

As for the suggestion that newspapers are more interested in printing stories about crime than in doing anything about it, it is so naive as to be astonishing. The type of crime most often involved in the confidences we're talking about is corruption in government. Who would ever stop it if it were not exposed in the press? How would the press be able to expose it without the help of confidential informants who were willing to tell what they knew to reporters whom they trusted? The Supreme Court's blanket ruling will certainly make these people think twice before they talk to a reporter, and to that extent the Court has turned itself into the protector of corruption and incompetence in government. Any reputable newspaper's purpose in exposing corruption is precisely to see that something is done about it.

In a concurring opinion, Justice Powell offered the hollow consolation that "no harassment of newsmen will be tolerated" and that the courts "will still be available" to them. In view of the majority opinion, it is hard to see what the courts will be able to do about it.

In the main dissenting opinion, Justice Stewart deplored that the Court had overlooked the precedent of prior cases and had "failed to recognize that under the guise of 'investigating crime' vindictive prosecutors can . . . explore the newsman's sources at will, with no serious law enforcement purpose" and can demand information about informants "who have neither committed crimes nor have information about crime."

So where do we go from here? We have to go someplace, because if the present opinion stands, it will promote neither justice nor freedom of the press. Legislation might help, but the task of interpreting any laws is going to fall to the courts anyway. The better solution is to see that another case is brought before the Supreme Court, one in which there is less justification for a subpena. Justice Powell, for one, would presumably then have to change his position. Last week's dissenters would become the new majority, voicing a doctrine upholding both justice and the First Amendment.

LEDGER-STAR

Norfolk, Va., July 3, 1972

In ruling against any special immunity for n e w s m e n, when it c o m e s to grand jury subpoenas and the supplying of information in criminal cases, the Supreme Court followed what is surely the only possible course. This is true whether the term of reference is the public's stake in effective legal action against crime or, simply, the equal application of the laws to all individuals.

The argument that there is special citizen concern in giving the press wide latitude and protection for news channels—to insure its usefulness—is not so persuasive as to override all other considerations. Most especially it must not

override the duly established legal processes which protect *all* the people. And it would be wrong in the extreme to establish the principle of reporters' immunity from court or jury action as a stated legal exemption.

One of the immediate obstacles to any such formal i m m u n i t y would be the difficulty in determining who is to be so shielded. Can anyone who claims to work for any publication or broadcast operation of any kind assert such immunity? And what would prevent the deliberate use of this device by a conniving lawbreaker—simply establishing some temporary or largely phoney "publication" — to put

himself beyond reach of the courts?

No, the refusal to divulge a news source or information to a proper authority is an act for which the refusing newsman or publication must a c c e p t the legal consequences just like anybody else.

There should be nothing in law, just as the court says there is nothing under the Constitution's freedom-of-the-press guarantee, which gives the newsman any special escape from the processes of justice. In this regard, he is simply an American citizen, to be treated in the same way as any o t h e r American citizen.

The Burlington Free Press
Burlington, Vt., July 1, 1972

WE DO NOT always join others of the press in claiming special privileges for newsmen. We do not believe, for example, that newsmen are beyond the laws protecting national security. Nor can they be excused for breaking and entering, wiretapping, theft and the like, even though they may break the law to get information.

The press is justified in its outcry against the Supreme Court decision that newsmen must obey calls to testify before grand juries or face the possibility of contempt penalties.

The court reasons that there is no justification for relieving newsmen of the obligation to testify, shared by all citizens.

We hope that Congress and the state legislatures will specifically grant newsmen the privilege of remaining quiet.

We maintain that there is reason and that it lies in the newsman's function. It is the reporter's primary function to get information, including that which the government may not know and that which the government may know and does not want anybody to know that it knows.

If a newsman cannot guarantee his sources anonymity, he will be greatly hampered in his work as a fact-getting watchdog. This function of a reporter is generally recognized as worthwhile.

TULSA DAILY WORLD
Tulsa, Okla., July 1, 1972

"THE CONSTITUTION does not . . . exempt the newsman from performing the citizen's normal duty. . . ."

With those words, the U.S. SUPREME COURT Thursday held that reporters have no special right to refuse to testify before Grand Juries.

Reluctantly, with some reservations and at the risk of ostracism within the journalistic lodge, we concur.

The Court's decision involved appeals from reporters who claimed that they had a Constitutional right to keep their sources of information confidential and that, therefore, they had a Constitutional right to refuse to testify.

While agreeing with the Court, our sympathies are with the newsmen. Few who have been in this business for any length of time have not been in a similar spot with regard to confidential informants. In order to penetrate vital secrets for his readers, the reporter sometimes must keep a less important secret himself—namely, the source of his information.

This little hypocrisy is a practical necessity at times. Some States (Oklahoma not among them) recognize it and, by statute, exempt newsmen from revealing confidential sources under certain circumstances. Such limited immunity, granted as a statutory privilege, may serve the public. But we think it must be considered a privilege, given by the grace of the State, and not a Constitutional Right.

The FIRST AMENDMENT guarantees freedom of speech and not just to bona fide news reporters employed by newspapers and broadcasters. It applies to every person who wants to speak, write or publish his views. It covers equally the newspaper with millions of dollars worth of presses and the fellow down the street who wants to distribute a few handbills.

The SUPREME COURT correctly held that the publishing and broadcasting industries and their employes enjoy the same rights of free press and free speech as everyone else and no more.

THE CINCINNATI ENQUIRER
Cincinnati, Ohio, July 5, 1972

THE SUPREME COURT has held that the Constitution does not immunize members of the press from being required to testify before grand juries, even though their testimony may entail identifying confidential sources or information given to them in confidence.

The ink was scarcely dry on the court's view, written by Justice Byron R. White, before Sen. Alan Cranston (D-Calif.) was offering legislation in Congress to define by statute a First Amendment corollary whose existence had rarely, over the years, been questioned.

A number of states, including Ohio, long ago recognized the indispensability of confidentiality as a tool of the journalistic profession. Ohio journalists, as a result, could not be compelled to offer testimony that might impair their sources of information.

Such a form of journalistic immunity is not an arbitrary privilege the nation's newspapermen invented for themselves. They do not, in short, regard their profession as being apart from the rest of American life. They believe, instead, that their ability to safeguard confidences is crucial to their capacity to inform the public.

No one could have defined the issues more clearly than did Associate Justice Potter Stewart in his vigorous dissent:

"Not only will this decision impair performance of the press' constitutionally protected functions, but it will, I am convinced, in the long run, harm rather than help the administration of justice."

Justice Stewart added: "The press has a preferred position in our constitutional scheme not to enable it to make money, not to set newspapers apart as a favored class, but to bring fulfillment to the public's right to know. The right to know is crucial to the governing powers of the people . . . Knowledge is essential to informed decisions."

Congress has been considering for several years a proposal to establish nationally the same safeguards a number of states have already established within their own confines. The Supreme Court's ruling will — and should — give fresh urgency to that goal.

THE PLAIN DEALER
Cleveland, Ohio, July 1, 1972

That the news media have enjoyed preferential treatment under the U.S. Constitution is undeniable.

Also, there is little question that the privileged status of the American press was greatly diminished by this week's ruling of the U.S. Supreme Court denying newsmen immunity from testifying before a grand jury.

What seems unclear in many minds, however, is that it is not newspapers and news broadcasting organizations that ultimately will be most injured by the court decision. To be sure, the ruling will impair the ability of newsmen to gather and disseminate information.

But the injured party, knowingly or not, is the American public.

The press was granted privileged status under the Constitution to assure the free flow of ideas and information necessary in a democracy. By the ruling, the news media will be hampered in presenting this information.

The Supreme Court ruled that newsmen cannot refuse to reveal the names of confidential sources to grand juries in criminal investigations. This immunity specifically had been written into law in 17 states.

Specters of undesirable possibilities appear:

• A journalistic investigation into political shenanigans could be effectively ended by a judge or prosecutor in sympathy with the politicians involved.

• Underworld figures would be reluctant to speak because they know newsmen cannot protect their anonymity.

• Dissident organizations, fearful of political reprisal, would refuse press scrutiny. The list goes on.

And, in the end, it is the public that loses. It is the public that is not told of the political hanky-panky. It is the public that is not told of the crime syndicate. It is the public that is not told of the plans of the radical organization.

As Justice William O. Douglas stated in a dissenting opinion: "The press has a preferred position in our constitutional scheme not to enable it to make money, not to set newsmen apart as a favored class, but to bring fulfillment to the public's right to know. The right to know is crucial to the governing powers of the people."

By removing the protection of the 1st Amendment, Justice Potter Stewart correctly argued in his dissenting opinion, "The court thus invites state and federal authorities to undermine the historic independence of the press by attempting to annex the journalistic profession as an investigative arm of the government."

U.S. Sen. Alan Cranston, D-Calif., yesterday introduced a bill that would give newsmen the right to refuse to disclose confidential sources of information to Congress, federal courts and other federal agencies. Its passage would be helpful to newsmen. Its passage is vital to the public.

The Topeka Daily Capital
Topeka, Kans., July 5, 1972

Once again, the U.S. Supreme Court has turned to legislating, utilizing to the last its 5-4 liberal majority.

Until the court voted by that narrowest of margins to abridge the First Amendment's guarantee of a free press in the U.S. Constitution, reporters for all news media labored under the unquestioned impression they not only had the right, but, indeed, the responsibility, to protect their news sources.

The federal government, the states and the local governments all have sufficient police and investigative personnel without assuming reporters are an extension of these police arms.

But despite the long-held opinion, the high court decided the First Amendment, which the free press has guarded zealously against all attacks, is just fine, but means nothing without special legislation to carry out the principle of press freedom.

Justice Potter Stewart dissented from the court's opinion. He said "the right to gather news . . . implies a right to a confidential relationship between a reporter and his source. . . .It is obvious that informants are necessary to the newsgathering process. If it is to perform its constitutional mission, the press must do far more than merely print public statements or publish prepared handouts. It is equally obvious that the promise of confidentiality may be a prerequisite to a productive relationship between a newsman and his informants. An officeholder may fear his superior; a member of the bureaucracy his associates; a dissident, the scorn of majority opinion."

The court, by its decision opened the way for federal grand juries and grand juries in 36 of the 50 states to compel reporters to reveal news sources and information given them in confidence.

Sen. Alan Cranston, D-Calif., has introduced a bill which would give the newspapers and other news media the protection they should have to meet their responsibilities in a free and open society.

The California senator's bill cannot reach beyond the federal level into the states. There are 14 states including Cranston's California, with laws protecting newsmen from compulsory disclosure of confidential sources. Others are Arizona, Alabama, Arkansas, Indiana, Kentucky, Maryland, Michigan, Montana, Georgia, New Jersey, Ohio, Pennsylvania and New York.

Notably absent from the list of states which protect the professional relationship of news reporters with their sources is Kansas.

In the interest of the public's right to know without the possible strictures inherent in the high court's decision, the Congress should move quickly to enact the Cranston Bill, and state legislatures should move with equal speed to pass similar legislation at the state level.

Oakland Tribune
Oakland, Calif., July 4, 1972

When the U.S. Supreme Court ruled that newsmen have no special right to refuse to cooperate with grand juries, it struck a serious blow at freedom of the press.

The 5-4 decision leaves grand juries open to compel newsmen to divulge confidential sources they have used in gathering news stories.

The result may be that sources who once would have trusted reporters not to reveal their names may now clam up under threat that those newsmen may be forced to tell all to a grand jury.

Fortunately, Justice Byron R. White, who cast the swing vote in the decision, suggested that congressional action be taken to grant reporters immunity from the probing questions of grand juries.

In his written opinion, Justice White said Congress is free to determine whether a statutory newsman's privilege is necessary and desirable.

Sen. Alan Cranston, D-Calif., himself a one time newsman, took the hint and has introduced a bill which would block the Federal Government from forcing reporters to disclose their confidential sources.

Cranston said his proposed legislation would provide "the legal protection they (newsmen) need and should have to meet their responsibilities in a free and open society."

Without immunity from compelled testimony, reporters may find it difficult to ferret out news stories about major and consequential activities and circumstances.

It is not a matter of putting the press above the law or granting it privileges not available to the general public. Rather it is assuring the constitutional right of a free people to be adequately informed.

Fourteen states, including California, have seen it that way and have afforded the press the privilege of immunity. There is little reason why the Federal Government cannot extend the same rights.

The Court merely found the press does not have the inherent right to protection from revealing news sources under the First Amendment, but that it could be secured by federal law.

By adopting Cranston's bill, Congress would be doing more than making it easier for newsmen to do their jobs. It would be helping to keep information flowing freely to people who have the constitutional right to know about events that affect their lives.

The Evening Star
Washington, D.C., July 3, 1972

It is always a little awkward to argue one's own case, particularly when the issue involved is one of special constitutional privilege. Yet the Supreme Court decision holding that newsmen have no right under the First Amendment to refuse to give confidential information and names of informants to grand juries strikes not only at the interests of newspapers but at the interests of the public as a whole.

No one claims, of course, that newspapers are above the law or that reporters do not share the obligations of other citizens. To require reporters to reveal their confidential sources of information, however, is automatically inhibiting on the whole process of newsgathering. Even if sparingly enforced it will seriously damage the ability of any newspaper to keep its readers informed.

Although Justice Powell, in his concurring opinion, strongly denied any intention by the court to make the press into an investigative branch of the government, this is an unavoidable implication of the majority decision. If, along with the testimony of reporters, notes, tapes and films can also be subpoenaed by federal and local authorities, the problem of newsgathering will not only be made more difficult but also more hazardous. What editor would send out his photographers to cover a riot, for example, if the evidence, published or unpublished, had to be made available to investigating authorities? How much investigative reporting would be possible, particularly in the area of crime, if confidential sources were routinely exposed?

Fortunately, the effect of the ruling is somewhat mitigated by Justice Powell's opinion in voting with the five-man majority. It holds, in effect, that the majority opinion is limited in its nature, that the intent is to strike a balance between the freedom of the press and the obligation of all citizens to give relevant testimony in criminal cases, and that this balance should be determined on a case-by-case basis. According to this interpretation, a majority holds that the courts may still protect journalistic confidentiality in many cases.

Fortunately also, the majority opinion written by Justice White is an open invitation to Congress and state legislatures to write the necessary protections into law. Many states indeed have already done so and Senator Ervin of North Carolina has been conducting a long series of hearings bearing most directly on the question of reporters' privilege. The court's ruling makes it the more imperative that federal legislation be enacted as soon as possible, guaranteeing once and for all the basic rights of a free press.

Newsday
Long Island, N.Y., July 2, 1972

The Supreme Court ruled last week that despite First Amendment guarantees, a grand jury may compel newsmen to reveal confidential conversations and the identity of sources. The narrow 5-4 decision apparently does not rule out lower courts making some exceptions. And moves are already under way to provide by legislation this safeguard just denied by the Supreme Court. Nevertheless, some citizens may feel the Court has made it difficult or even dangerous for them to talk to newspapermen in confidence.

So let's make one thing clear so far as Newsday is concerned: Where the public interest is at stake, we will continue to respect and protect the confidentiality of our informants to the fullest of our ability.

We mean no disrespect for grand juries or prosecutors or the Supreme Court. It is, fortunately, a rare occasion when the citizen's only avenue to justice lies in confiding to a trusted reporter. But there are sufficient instances to demonstrate that this occasional privilege can be a vital means of safeguarding the freedoms we cherish.

The danger in the Supreme Court's ruling is not that it directly restricts freedom of the press, but that it might intimidate someone with a *legitimate* need to communicate to the press in confidence. And we emphasize "legitimate."

That's why Newsday will do everything possible to protect the confidentiality of its sources and will work to have this safeguard written into law by Congress.

HERALD EXAMINER
Los Angeles, Calif., July 11, 1972

"Congress shall make no law respecting an establishment of religion, or prohibiting the free exercise thereof; or abridging the freedom of speech, or of the press; or the right of the people peaceably to assemble, and to petition the Government for a redress of grievances." — First amendment to the U.S. Constitution.

The Supreme Court decision that newsmen must reveal their confidential sources when asked by a grand jury, or face jail for contempt, is bound to cause more abuses than it will cure.

Most important is the ruling's effect on freedom of speech and the press, as guaranteed by the First Amendment. The guarantee is made not only to publishers but to every citizen.

Journalists are the living links between the public and the printing press: The public speaks through journalists and the public listens through journalists. The nation thus learns from itself about itself.

The First Amendment offers freedom of speech and press to all — the guilty as well as the innocent, the culpable as well as the righteous, the discontented as well as the fat cat.

This Supreme Court ruling tends to limit access to the press to official sources in most situations. Only rarely will it apply to criminal situations. Criminals do not contact newsmen to chat about their activities. Most public officials, however, like nothing better.

Many political and diplomatic stories are derived from anonymous leaks, on information given because the source is confident he will not be revealed. This involves situations such as the Pentagon Papers or it might be the revelation of graft in the office of a small town mayor.

To argue the specifics is to argue interminably. What is paramount is that an inalienable right need not be diminished in order to deal with its abuses; if it is lessened, it is no longer inalienable.

The abuse of a fundamental right is part of the price a free society pays to remain free. That is why laws dealing with these abuses are also designed to protect rights, not to erode them.

Robert G. Fichenberg, chairman of the Freedom of Information Committee of the American Society of Newspaper Editors, has charged that the court ruling leaves a newsman in the position of becoming "an agent for the government" when involved in investigative reporting.

"The Court's narrow view . . . of the scope of the First Amendment cannot help but have a chilling effect on the relations between newsmen and their sources, drying up the free flow of news and depriving the public of an indispensable check on the operations of the government," he said.

That would appear to tell it all.

THE DALLAS TIMES HERALD
Dallas, Tex., July 11, 1972

CREDIBLE newspapers and broadcasters, the committed guardians of the people, look gravely upon the recent U.S. Supreme Court opinion that could dam the flow of information imperative to a nation's life.

The court, by narrow 5-to-4 decision, imposed shackling restrictions on the free and independent press. More importantly, it dimmed the light of knowledge for all of the people.

It ruled that newsmen can be called by grand juries, forced to divulge names of news sources and answer any questions that the jury might decide are relevant to the case involved. If the newsman refuses to answer in protection of his source, he can be imprisoned.

The nation's press asks no special concessions. No favors . . . just honored continuance of First Amendment guarantees that have served well to this disturbing point.

There are multiple dangers in the court's thin majority conclusion. Not to newspaper or broadcasting station, but to the people. It stifles, dries up sources of information who inform for the public good. The court's ruling is a direct warning to citizen sources that if they convey information to a newsman, they could be identified and stripped of the anonymity that encouraged them to reveal in the first place.

To use the language of another concerned newspaper, Newsday, The Times Herald assures that where the public interest is at stake, it will continue to respect and protect the confidentiality of informants to the fullest of our ability.

Many, many times The Times Herald has used citizen knowledge, passed in respected confidence, to find and reveal corruption, assist in the capture of law violators and otherwise serve the public good.

It has not kept score, but it respects this citizen-newspaper relationship for community betterment which, after all, is what this is all about. It would not want to see intimidation of citizen sources who contact the press with valid information.

Justice Byron R. White's testy opinion roamed outside the basic issue itself when it concluded that "newsmen have no constitutional right of access to scenes of crime or disaster when the general public is excluded, and they may be prohibited from attending or publishing information about trials if such restrictions are necessary to assure a defendant a fair trial before an impartial tribunal."

Justice White is assuming a whole lot. The U.S. press has never contended that it is above the law. It follows the directives of local police and fire officials in covering crime and disaster in covering crime and disaster, —and it is proud to be the only alerting service for unprotected citizens on tornado, flood and turbulent weather warnings.

And it will fight tenaciously to maintain its right to trial coverage. Secret trials in this country? Unthinkable.

Wisconsin ▲ State Journal
Madison, Wis., July 5, 1972

Many newspaper editors and professional journalistic g r o u p s are w r i n g i n g their hands over the United States Supreme Court decision which held that newsmen, like all citizens, have an obligation to answer Grand Jury subpoenas and supply information in criminal investigations.

The American Society of Newspaper Editors called the decision a "direct blow at the right of the people to be fully i n f o r m e d without hindrance by the government. Other predicted "harassment" of reporters by grand juries and prosecutors will increase.

We believe there is considerable overreaction to t h e decision and doubt if all the dire predictions to a free press will result.

Justice Lewis F. Powell Jr., writing a concurring opinion said judges may still use the "balancing" technique of weighing the First Amendment considerations in each case against the citizens' obligation to give information to grand juries.

Justice Powell emphasized t h a t the majority opinion does not hold that newsmen, subpoenaed to testify before a grand jury, are without constitutional rights with respect to the gathering of news or in safeguarding their sources.

The high court stated that "no harassment of newsmen will be tolerated," Justice Powell said as he denied the contention in a dissenting opinion that state and federal authorities are free to "annex" the news m e d i a as "an investigative arm of government."

In the narrow 5 to 4 decision, Justice Powell's views i n d i c a t e the court may alter its opinion in some future cases, but in any event, the final d e c i s i o n will have to come from Congress and state l e g i s l a tures to give reporters the necessary protection of the confidentialty of their sources.

If this protection is so vital to a free press and the public it serves, lawmakers s h o u l d spell it out in clear and concise language so it will not be subject to a narrow 5 to 4 interpretation.

St. Petersburg Times
St. Petersburg, Fla., July 3, 1972

Question: If you, a citizen, are believed to have information that may be helpful to a government investigation, would you be required to testify? Yes, is the answer. You may be jailed if you refuse.

Question: Why, then, should news reporters be treated differently? They shouldn't, was the Supreme Court answer last week; reporters ought to be required to testify just like everyone else.

WE DISAGREE, and here's why.

The argument begins with the Constitution and First Amendment rights for press freedom. The nation's founders awarded special importance to the public's right to unrestricted information. Democracy could not work, they felt, where the public was uninformed.

The press, they concluded, was the best way to inform. The question here is, how does that principle apply to grand jury, congressional or other government investigation.

IN THIS WAY: Reporters will be restricted in their information - gathering if their news sources know that everything they say in confidence can be forced from the reporter under threat of a jail sentence.

It follows that if reporters' sources are cut off, information to the public is similarly restricted. If public access is restricted, constitutional guarantees have been abrogated.

Take for example, the case of New York Times reporter Earl Caldwell, considered by the Supreme Court in its ruling last week. Caldwell had been in California talking to Black Panthers and writing stories.

The public read those stories avidly, eager to learn the thinking behind a sometimes v i o l e n t, emerging political power in the black community, seeking to understand how that phenomenon might influence current politics or touch their personal lives.

MEANWHILE, a California grand jury was also expressing interest in Panther activities. No crime was alleged; the jury was conducting an investigation in response to public alarm, and wanted the information on Caldwell's notes and tapes. Caldwell refused.

In overturning a contempt conviction against Caldwell (Nov. 1970) the Ninth Circuit Court of Appeals ruled that "Where it has been shown the public's First Amendment right to be informed would be joepardized by requiring a journalist to submit to secret grand jury interrogation, the government must respond by demonstrating a compelling need for the witness' presence . . ."

The question, then, is not really freedom of the press; it is the public's right to information. That right suffered a severe blow when the Supreme Court struck down the reasonable "compelling need" compromise offered by the Ninth Circuit Court.

THE ATLANTA CONSTITUTION
Atlanta, Ga., July 3, 1972

There is a portion of the U.S. Supreme Court's decision saying that newsmen must supply information to grand juries in criminal investigations with which we agree. As Justice Byron R. White's opinion for the 5.4 majority put it, the U.S. Constitution does not exempt a newsman from "performing the citizen's normal duty of appearing and furnishing information relevant to the grand jury's task'"

But we think the high court erred drastically in failing to apply the First A m e n d m e n t 's guarantees of free speech and free press to the special situation of protecting a reporter from disclosing information obtained from confidential sources.

As Justice Potter Stewart wrote, in dissent, this ruling "invites state and federal authorities to undermine the historic independence of the press by attempting to annex the journalistic profession as an investigative arm of government."

Doctors, lawyers, and priests, are by tradition and sometimes by law protected in the right to honor a confidence offered to them in their professional capacities. In the case of the priest, this takes on a sacred and religious aspect.

We believe the right of the free press involves directly the right of the newsman to, on occasion, talk to confidential sources with the implicit guarantee that such sources will remain confidential. We agree with the American Society of Newspaper Editors who called the ruling a "direct blow at the right of the people to be fully informed without hindrance by the government." Sigma Delta Chi, the national professional journalistic society, has endorsed a similar stand.

"What was at issue here," said Robert Fichenberg, chairman of the Freedom of Information Committee of the editor's group, "was whether a reporter can be compelled to reveal his sources for a story in which the government may have an interest. If he can, he becomes in effect an agent for the government."

We hope, with all due respect, that the Supreme Court may see fit to affirm the right of the free press in whatever rulings may be necessary to clarify the effect of last week's ruling on the role of a reporter in a free society.

BOSTON HERALD TRAVELER

Sunday Advertiser

Boston, Mass., October 8, 1972

Another news reporter was clapped in jail last week in harsh reprisal for his defense of what many prominent jurists consider a constitutional right, the preservation of the freedom and independence of the press from government sanction.

And it is inevitable that others will follow, unless Congress, and in this state the legislature, adopt the kind of "shield" laws necessary to protect the press — and consequently, the public — from the threat of interference and limitation by bureaucracy, which restricts the press from investigating and holding up to public inspection what is inimical to the public interest.

Legislation to that end is pending in Washington now; and was defeated on Beacon Hill during the past session. So long as it is delayed, just so long will the erosion of the priceless and irreplaceable rights continue unabated. For the principal issue at stake here is not only the right of the press to publish, although that is important, but the right of the public to know.

The insidious significance of the latest incidence of repression of the press is, as columnist Tom Wicker pointed out, that the newsman, or in this case former newsman, did not refuse to testify before a New Jersey grand jury as he was ordered to do. What Peter J. Bridge, who had been a reporter for the now-defunct Newark News, was guilty of was refusal to go on a fishing expedition with the authorities, who already knew the source of his information.

For that he was found in contempt; whereas the grand jury and the county attorney were the ones really at fault in their failure to go to the source for the information they sought.

This is demonstrative of how swiftly the deterioration of rights sets in when they are subjected, like the drops of water in the Chinese torture, to repeated infringements. As seen here, the interference with the right of confidentiality which every reporter and every publisher needs to protect the sources of otherwise unobtainable information, has now been extended in an attempt to make the independent press a tool and extension of law enforcement.

The first amendment to the U.S. Constitution is quite explicit in its declaration that "Congress shall make no law . . . abridging the freedom . . . of the press"; but the U.S. Supreme Court last summer, in a similar case, ruled that newsmen must reveal their confidential sources when asked by a grand jury.

That decision was a divided one, and the margin (5-4) was the narrowest possible. The dissent was strong, particularly that voiced by Justices Potter and Stewart. Justice Potter warned that to subvert the historical position of the independent press would "not only impair the performance of its constitutionally protected functions but will in the long run harm, rather than help the administration of justice." And already we have seen his prophetic words come true.

Justice Stewart went even further. He held that the right to publish was "central to the first amendment and basic to the existence of constitutional democracy. The full flow of information to the public protected by the free press guarantee would be severely curtailed if no protection whatever were afforded to the process by which news is assembled . . . for without freedom to acquire information, the right to publish would be impermissibly compromised."

At the time of the Supreme Court action we suggested that it would cause more abuses than it would cure. That feeling is stronger than ever. The hope for protecting this and other traditional rights against the constant invasion of government, lies in the fact that the division of the court has become a challenge for the legislative branch to act.

With Congress rushing towards prorogation, it may be too much to expect immediate action. But the longer it postpones action, the greater the threat to civil liberty, which is too steep a price to pay.

The Star-Ledger

Newark, N.J., October 4, 1972

A newspaperman is scheduled to go to jail today because he refused to compromise a principle, an unswerving belief that the constitutional protections of a free press should not be violated, even for an instant.

In declining to accede to an edict of the court requiring him to testify before a grand jury, Peter Bridge will suffer a personal loss of freedom. But there should not be the slightest doubt that this newpaperman does not stand alone in this ordeal; he is a resolute surrogate for colleagues in the communications media who share his conviction that the First Admendment shields a free press against institutional incursions and oppressive, stifling influences.

The case against Mr. Bridge, a reporter for the defunct Evening News, has a shaky statutory premise. A lower court found a defect in the existing law on press privilege, expressly designed to protect the confidentiality of news sources.

The court held that the newsman had automatically waived his exemption from testifying before a grand jury when he identified his source for an article about the Newark Housing Authority and a purported bribe to influence a vote for an executive director.

This is a totally unacceptable premise for the news media. It would have grave implications for the press in the future, generating a chilling effect on news gathering, if the constitutional shield on confidentiality of news sources is vulnerable to official harassment.

This inherent danger was acknowledged by the State Senate by its passage of a bill sponsored by Sen. James H. Wallwork that would afford full protection against indiscriminate disclosure of news sources.

Unfortunately, the Assembly did not get to consider the measure because of extended debate on tax reform. The bill will come up again next month, when the Legislature reconvenes. It should be given swift confirmation by the Assembly.

This action, of course, would be too late for Mr. Bridge, but it would constitute a needed affirmation by the Legislature, belatedly shoring up statutory frailities that would have a critical inhibiting effect on news enterprise, especially investigative reporting

THE INDIANAPOLIS STAR

Indianapolis, Ind., October 9, 1972

However the legalities were spun out in the courts, the power to corrupt was the ultimate winner in the controversy that has led to the imprisonment of a 36-year-old newspaper reporter for refusing to betray confidential sources.

The courts may well have followed lines of the purest legality in the dispute, but the ultimate results could prove foul.

In an article last May, in the now defunct Newark Evening News, reporter Peter Bridge quoted a member of the Newark Housing Authority as saying he was offered a $10,000 bribe by an unknown man to "vote right" in the election for authority director.

A grand jury investigation was held during which Bridge, as a witness, answered 80 questions but refused to answer five questions on grounds they would compromise confidential information sources. A superior court judge cited him for contempt and sentenced him to jail.

The United States Supreme Court, which had ruled June 29, in the case of another newsman, that newsmen may not withhold confidential information from grand juries, refused to hear Bridge's appeal of the jailing, and Bridge began serving the sentence this week.

The housing authority election investigation ended, to all intents and purposes, with the bribe charge never having been proved, which should not be particularly surprising, for big-stake corruption charges are exceedingly hard to prove.

Corruption involving huge stakes, such as millions of dollars in municipal, state or Federal contracts, is most often carried out by highly skilled professional contact men protected against exposure or effective prosecution by a carefully arranged series of "fixes" at key points.

The pattern has been made clear in numerous cases where prosecution was successful.

The drawback is that many potential witnesses capable of lifting the lid on such cases fear to do so because of the danger of retaliation, against which even the most powerful governmental authorities cannot offer a foolproof guarantee.

There is less constraint on the part of such potential witnesses if they can give information to newsmen whom they trust, with the assurance that details which could endanger their safety or lives will be held confidential.

Witnesses fearing reprisals are unlikely to talk to anyone at all, including reporters, if they are aware their identity and statements are subject to transmission through the very machinery of government powerful corruptors infiltrate to carry out their schemes.

Consequently the U.S. Supreme Court has, unwittingly, no doubt, destroyed a lever of great value in prying open lids to expose large-scale corruption.

New York Post

New York, N.Y., October 5, 1972

A government official, talking with a reporter, says: "Look, we'll have to go off the record for a minute." A legislative committee chairman announces a closed-door hearing. A diplomat declines comment while "private negotiations" are in progress. And a press secretary tells reporters there will be a "backgrounder" briefing by a high source who cannot be identified.

In all these instances of dealing with the press, government routinely insists for one reason or another on confidentiality, arguing that certain public business must sometimes be conducted privately. Yet some of the same officials who claim that right now object that it is inappropriate for reporters to insist on protecting their sources.

The issue is particularly acute right now as 1) reporter Peter Bridge, who worked for the Newark Evening News, begins an indefinite jail term for refusing to answer a grand jury's questions —it was seeking *unpublished* material —and as 2) Congress weighs a number of related bills filed since the U. S. Supreme Court decided this summer that reporters have no special Constitutional right to keep confidential data or the names of sources from grand juries.

The authority of Congress to legislate on the matter is not in dispute.

The question is how the legitimate interests of both the press and the government can be fairly accommodated in a new law, conceding that conflicts are bound to arise periodically.

Rights and responsibilities in this realm are not easy to define without disagreement. But it is obvious that a reporter or editor has the same legal obligations, generally speaking, as any other citizen—and the same direct interest in seeing justice done. A reporter who witnessed an act of violent crime could scarcely maintain that the authorities had no right to seek his testimony because he was in the news business.

It does not follow that a reporter should be compelled to serve as an agent of the police or other investigative force. The journalist does not carry credentials as a detective or district attorney and has no subpena power. The press may, and often does, direct the attention of the authorities to apparent violations of law; that is one of its functions. It is not an agency of prosecution. Police do not make a practice of publicly identifying their informants —for good reason. Why should the press be required to do so?

Questions of this sort are most important in framing an acceptable new law. They invite sensible answers from Congress.

BUFFALO EVENING NEWS

Buffalo, N.Y., October 5, 1972

In a recent 5-to-4 decision, the U. S. Supreme Court denied any constitutional protection against forced disclosure of newsmen's confidential sources and information. At the same time, while the court majority was unwilling to read the First Amendment as implying the same privilege for newsmen as those long recognized for doctor-patient and lawyer-client relationships, it virtually invited the legislative branch to "fashion standards and rules as narrow or broad as deemed necessary to address the evil discerned . . ."

Appropriately, then, Congress now is conducting hearings on bills to provide "broad but not unlimited" statutory protection against government harassment by subpoena, for which five major journalistic organizations turned to Congress in seeking relief.

The case for a newsmen's "shield law" couldn't have been stated with more force than it was in the eloquent dissenting opinion of Justice Potter Stewart. The protection sought, he said, is not a privilege merely for journalists but for the fundamental protection of "the broad societal interest in a full and free flow of information to the public." As he explained:

"The right to publish is central to the First Amendment . . . A corollary of the right to publish must be the right to gather news. The full flow of information to the public . . . would be severely curtailed if no protection whatever were afforded to the process by which news is assembled and disseminated. The right to gather news implies, in turn, a right to a confidential relationship between a reporter and his sources . . ."

The effort to obtain clearly-defined statutory protection, regrettably, appears jeopardized by opposition from the Justice Department. Roger C. Cramton, an assistant attorney general, contends that adoption of the department's own internal guidelines governing the subpoena of newsmen makes a newsmen's privilege law unnecessary.

We strongly disagree. It may well be true that "only seven" subpoenas have been issued against journalists since former Atty. Gen. Mitchell established stricter rules two years ago requiring that all other non-press sources of information be exhausted before seeking to compel confidential testimony from newsmen — and then only with the attorney general's approval.

But this begs the question of whether the threat of contempt action was justified in the cases of those newsmen from whom the government has admittedly sought forced disclosures. Worse, the Justice Department's trust-us doctrine asks reporters to put their fate — not in a judicial guarantee of due process — but in administrative officials to decide the indispensability of what they know in cases in which the government itself is the prosecutor.

In matters risking restrictions on the free flow of information — where the public is as much the loser as a vigilant investigative press — the tenuous reliance of newsmen on the rule-reading power of transient administrators is no substitute for a clear-cut statutory rule affording court protection against some prosecutor's fishing expedition. The subpoena power is far too awesome to be left to "iffy" guidelines.

THE ATLANTA CONSTITUTION
Atlanta, Ga., October 7, 1972

Newspaper people have been tangling with Officialdom since 1690 when Benjamin Harris published Publick Occurences Both Foreign and Domestick. That was the first newspaper in the American colonies, and it was suppressed by the authorities after one edition.

The latest hassle involves a newspaperman named Peter J. Bridge who worked for the now defunct Newark Evening News. Bridge's offense was that he refused to answer a grand jury's questions about some information he may have obtained in confidence while working on a story. He DID confirm the truth of the story he had written (about bribery of officials and other matters); what he refused to answer were matters he had NOT written about and had not himself witnessed. That refusal, a court decided, amounted to contempt. And now the U.S. Supreme Court has refused to intervene in that decision.

This case has been blown up by some into a major challenge to freedom of the press. It is seen by others as another sinister effort by the government to scrap Constitutional rights. We can't go that far. But we do suggest that the continuing historical conflict between the press and governmental or civic agencies is based on disagreement over the role of the press. Should that role be what the press thinks it is — to inform the public without fear or favor? Or should it be what Officialdom apparently conceives it to be — to publish what Officialdom wants published and not much else? Or should it perhaps be something in between?

Bridge is going to jail for an indefinite stay because he believes a free press requires some leeway in gathering information from sources who insist on being confidential. Eliminate confidential information by requiring reporters to divulge sources when called upon to do so and you severely restrict the power of the press to keep itself and you informed on what is going on. You — the reading public — may some day end up reading nothing but government handouts and press releases. That, let us assure you, is worse than going to jail.

WORCESTER TELEGRAM
Worcester, Mass., October 8, 1972

The growing threat to press freedom — and everyone's freedom — has gained momention with the case of Peter J. Bridge. Once a reporter for the Newark Evening News, he was jailed for contempt of court in connection with a story he wrote on municipal corruption. The U.S. Supreme Court refused to postpone his sentence.

In the recent Earl Caldwell case, the majority of the Supreme Court ruled that a reporter may not refuse to appear before a federal grand jury to answer questions about the sources of information. Concurrently, in the case of Paul Branzburg, five justices held that a newsman may not refuse to answer questions about illegal activity to which he was a witness.

But Bridge went to jail for neither of those offenses. He was punished because he refused to answer questions about facts he had not published to which he may not even know the answers. This was harassment.

On May 5, he wrote a story, quoting a member of the Newark Housing Authority who said that she was offered a bribe. Bridge was forced to testify and repeated his account. He answered 80 questions. But he declined to answer five questions about who had offered the bribe, what the person may have looked like or other details of the scandal not included in his news story. He contended that the grand jury was conducting a fishing expedition — far beyond determining the source of confidential information or asking for a reporter's personal observation of illegal activities. Indeed, the jury demanded something that may or may not be in Bridge's notebook. And the reporter argued that the state had shown no compelling need for whatever information he might have — one of the criteria set by the Supreme Court in limiting press freedom.

The New Jersey court threw the book at Bridge. It reasoned that the state's law protecting the confidentiality of a reporter's source covers only the "identity" of the source, not the information itself. This appears to leave open the possibility, in the words of columnist Tom Wicker, that Bridge would have escaped jail if he had only written his story this way: "Informed sources said today that Mrs. Beatty said someone had tried to bribe her."

After the June 29 Supreme Court decision on Caldwell, Justice Lewis O. Powell attempted to reassure the press: "If the newsman is called upon to give information bearing only a remote and tenuous relationship to the subject of the investigation, or if he has some other reason to believe that his testimony implicates confidential source relationship without a legitimate need of law enforcement, he will have access to the court on a motion to quash and an appropriate protective order may be entered."

He was wrong. The New Jersey case makes those words empty. It underscores the minority opinion, expressed by Justice Potter Stewart: "The court's crabbed view of the First Amendment reflects a disturbing insensitivity to the critical role of an independent press in our society."

Indeed, the danger is serious. While it may be easy for a prosecutor to fall back on a testimony by a reporter, that can discourage other newsmen from seeking essential information for the public. An intiidated press is not a free press. And without the free flow of expression, there is no free society. The Communist states provide grim evidence of that.

The case of Peter Bridge should open everyone's eyes and prompt legislation to reverse a disturbing trend.

THE ROANOKE TIMES
Roanoke, Va., October 7, 1972

When a news reporter misuses his sources (or has none at all), the rest of the news media will help drag the truth out. That was shown in the case of Jack Anderson's monumental blunder, to use a mild word for it, in reporting without verifiable sources that Senator Eagleton had had some drunken driving arrests. With that in mind, the general public should consider favorably a bill by Sen. Alan Cranston, D-Calif., which reads:

A person connected with or employed by a news media or press cannot be required by a court, a legislature, or any administrative body to disclose before the Congress or any federal court or agency any information or the source of any information proposed for publication or broadcast.

The purpose of the bill is to protect a reporter's right to associate with all kinds of people and reach the sources which put him on the trail of news in the public interest. In the absence of such a law the Supreme Court recently ruled, 5-4, that the reporter had no such protection.

For every Jack Anderson blooper there can be cited hundreds of cases where newsmen have revealed stories of crookedness in government, unions and business; or where they cast new light on organization of public concern. In almost every case of this sort, the reporter had to have a tip—somebody who clued him in to where the body was buried. If he must reveal the source, the source will dry up.

These investigations are in the public interest. There are several bills coming before Congress but Senator Cranston, perhaps because he is a former newspaper man (for International News Service), has written the best of them. Voters should look kindly upon it; Congressmen should vote for it—and candidates ought to make their views known. The Anderson-Eagleton affair shows that when things really go wrong, the responsible media jump in to make things right.

ARKANSAS DEMOCRAT
Little Rock, Ark., October 13, 1972

Until last week the problem of protecting newsmen's sources was important but not urgent. All that changed when Peter Bridge, a 36-year-old reporter with two kids, a pregnant wife and no job, was sent to jail in Newark, N.J., because he refused to answer questions before a grand jury.

There was much irony in the incident. First, New Jersey is one of 18 states (Arkansas is another one) that has a shield law, which is the customary term for a law that grants journalists a right to refuse to identify the sources of their information. Unfortunately, the judge decided that Bridge, by trying to be as cooperative as he could, had waived his immunity. Secondly, the newspaper in which the story appeared, the Newark Evening News, went out of business a month ago.

Out of a job, a new baby expected momentarily, Bridge could not have been blamed if he told the grand jury what it wanted to know and gone home. But to Bridge it's not that simple. "I am neither a martyr nor a masochist," he said. "I worry about my family, but I also worry about the impact on my kids if I give up on what I know is right." He is a man of principle and a professional journalist. He's covered crime in New Jersey (in that state, this probably doesn't even qualify him to be called a specialist) for 11 years. He knows that once he starts talking to a grand jury and no matter what questions are asked, every source he has will dry up. For a reporter, that's as deadly as it is for an oil driller; all he can do is start over in another part of the country.

Earl Caldwell, the investigatory reporter for the New York Times, says that a reporter's career is over even if he walks to the door of the grand jury room. Since its deliberations are secret, his sources have no way of knowing what the reporter said once he goes inside those doors. But Caldwell's argument was not persuasive. It was his case that led the Supreme Court in June to rule 5 to 4 that the first amendment did not protect a reporter from going before a federal grand jury. Bridge is the first journalist to go to jail since this decision, and although he was jailed by a state court, the Supreme Court's decision unquestionably had a bearing on the action taken by the New Jersey judge. Although the Supreme Court decision was devastating, the opinion held out hope by saying that the Congress had the power to give some kind of immunity to reporters.

Since then more than 20 bills have been introduced, and probably one would have passed if the journalists could get together on what they want. Some demand total immunity; others, like us, think it should be qualified at least to the extent that before making a reporter testify a prosecutor would have to prove in court that (1) the information was essential to solving a specific crime important to the nation's interest and (2) there was no other way to get the information. In a poll, most of the members of the Arkansas delegation have said that they would vote for such a bill. Rep. Wilbur Mills added "with enthusiasm," and Sen. J. W. Fulbright is a co-sponsor with Sen. Sam Ervin, D-N.C., of SB3925, which may be the best of all those thrown in the hopper so far.

Maybe when the Congress reconvenes in January, the different journalism organizations and the members of Congress will have come to some agreement.

It's not the journalist but the public that will be the real loser if a bill isn't passed, setting a national standard for dealing with this problem. People must be able to talk to the journalist in confidence. What government underling would point to corruption on a high level, or what radical group would admit a reporter to its inner councils, if they knew that by doing so they risked their jobs or their freedom? Worse yet, how many reporters would continue to go after these important, controversial stories if they thought they might wind up like Peter Bridge?

THE COMMERCIAL APPEAL
Memphis, Tenn., October 8, 1972

THE JAILING OF reporter Peter J. Bridge of New Jersey for refusing to reveal all the details he supposedly knew about a bribe case to a grand jury again brings to the forefront the need for specific federal and state legislation to protect a newsman's sources.

The fact that Bridge, 36, was willing to go to jail on this principle, even though his wife is momentarily expecting their third child, is indication enough of how important he regards the question of privileged information.

It reminds us, too, that just last month reporter Joseph Weiler of The Commercial Appeal stood up to a threat of jail from a state Senate committee. He has been ordered to show cause on Nov. 13 why he should not be held in contempt of the Senate for refusing to divulge the sources of tips concerning child abuse at the Arlington Hospital and School for Retarded Children, although the committee has closed the case.

TRADITIONALLY the protection of news sources has been considered safe under the First Amendment. But last June, in a 5-4 decision, the Supreme Court ruled this did not hold true in grand jury hearings. Justice Byron White, writing the majority opinion, said, "We do not hold . . . that state and federal authorities are free to 'annex' the news media as 'an investigative arm of government.'" However, Justice Potter Stewart, in one of two dissenting opinions, charged the majority was threatening "to undermine the historic independence of the press by attempting" just that. "Not only will this decision impair performance of the press' constitutionally protected functions, but it will, I am convinced, in the long run, harm rather than help the administration of justice," wrote Stewart.

Stewart also said the "right to publish is central to the First Amendment" with the right to gather news as a corollary. "The right to gather news implies, in turn, a right to a confidential relationship between a reporter and his source."

That does not alter the fact that the majority ruling prevails, and in it Justice White wrote: "The sole issue . . . is the obligation of reporters to respond to grand jury subpenas as other citizens do and to answer questions relevant to an investigation into the commission of crime."

This is a key point. The role of the journalist is hardly the same as "other citizens" who might lack the time, inclination or ability to dig out information concerning the public welfare. It is rare that one finds a private citizen ferreting out crime, corruption, or misuse of public funds or trust. Newsmen, often with the help of informants, traditionally have performed such a service.

Denied the privilege of protecting their sources, reporters either will face jail for remaining silent in governmental inquisitions, or will find their sources dried up if they talk.

Testifying before the House Judiciary Committee last week, Representative Dan Kuykendall (R-Tenn.) said, "We have the right to tell our doctors and lawyers anything, in absolute confidence, and indeed we must, to receive proper treatment or counsel. And I submit that this same right should and ought to be granted to the men and women whose daily task it is to present us with a priceless and precious commodity — truth."

Mr. Kuykendall has introduced one of the almost 20 bills to "shield" newsmen and their sources which are now before the House. The Senate has four such bills in front of it.

THE HIGH COURT ruling has made it apparent that such shield legislation is now necessary. The Tennessee legislature had before it last year a model "Newsmen's Privilege Act," but did nothing. We hope to see it brought up early in the 1973 session, and passed.

A similar act of Congress to protect the newsman at the federal level ought to be approved this year. But since that is unlikely at this late date, let us hope it receives early attention next year.

No privilege would apply where a life was in danger, or espionage or foreign aggression were involved.

The purpose is simply to guarantee that the news may be gathered freely, and then published so that the people may know.

Los Angeles Times

Los Angeles, Calif., November 29, 1972

William Farr went to jail Monday. He was imprisoned by order of Superior Judge Charles H. Older of Los Angeles, who convicted the newspaper reporter of contempt of court for refusing to identify the source of a news story about the Charles Manson murder trial.

Farr's imprisonment has less connection with his refusal to betray the confidence of his news source than with two other elements: first, an ugly streak of authoritarianism that is pervading some of the courts and, second, the false free press-fair trial issue that masks an attack on First Amendment protections of press and speech.

The Sixth Amendment, which guarantees a fair and public trial, and the First Amendment are not antithetical. They are allies in freedom, but the First Amendment is the basis of all our liberties. Without a free press and free speech—which mean freedom of thought and, more important, the right to express thought—the administration of justice becomes shrouded in secrecy, which breeds the germs of injustice. The sunlight of disclosure is the best and only disinfectant. All history, and events in present-day totalitarian regimes, bear witness to this truth.

Americans, with our strong tradition of liberty dating from the birth of this nation, can be counted on to repel frontal assaults on freedom. Oblique attacks, advanced in the name of freedom itself, are more difficult to recognize and harder to resist.

The current assaults on press and speech come dressed in noble robes. Restrictions on information about court proceedings have been imposed in the name of a cherished right—a fair trial. Thus, three years ago, the American Bar Assn. suggested compromising the First Amendment in the name of justice. The ABA recommended stringent controls on the release of information in criminal trials, not only by prosecution and defense attorneys and judicial employes but by law enforcement officers as well. In doing so, the ABA gave assurance that its proposals were not aimed at newsmen, but that assurance—since proved false—made the proposal no less repugnant.

The impulse toward censorship by those in authority is always strong. The courts have recognized this by repeatedly rejecting restrictions attempted by other government agencies, but some judges—not all by any means—have now decided that censorship is the basis of a fair trial. They welcomed the ABA proposals that shielded some stages of judicial proceedings from public scrutiny. The flow of restrictive orders increased, and judges often went far beyond the ABA recommendations:

—A Monterey County judge not only restricted the release of information to the media but removed the press and public from the courtroom while the censorship order was argued. Furthermore, he forbade public complaints about the order. A New York justice barred the public from a criminal trial.

—The secret proceedings ordered in a court in Ventura County were so bizarre that an appellate court commented: "In the present case, it is startling to see the evils of secret proceedings so proliferating in seven short weeks that the court could reach the astonishing result of committing a citizen to jail in secret proceedings, could contemplate inquisitorial proceedings against the newspaper reporter for reporting this commitment, and could adopt the position that the district attorney, the chief law enforcement officer in the county, was prohibited on pain of contempt from advising the public that someone had been sent secretly to jail . . ."

—A Superior Court judge in Los Angeles County attempted last August to enforce direct censorship. He ordered the media (an order that was appealed) not to print or broadcast anything relating to a murder case except proceedings in court, over which, of course, he exercises direct control.

—A Superior Court judge in Los Angeles prohibited any comment on a pending case by the county, its sheriff and district attorney, the city of Los Angeles, its chief of police and Board of Police Commissioners. His assertion of power was so broad that a writer on legal affairs stated, "Thus a single judge in a single community felt it appropriate to . . . assume the role of the Legislature, the Supreme Court, the executive head of local government, the promulgator of rules of professional conduct and, most importantly, a censor of speech."

—Another judge, in a flight of imagination, named the district attorney, the sheriff, the chief of police and the police commissioners of Los Angeles as "Ministers of Justice," and declared, as such, that their "speech is peculiarly subject to judicial control."

—A Baton Rouge, La., judge ordered newspapers not to publish news about the trial of a civil rights case.

—An Arkansas judge ordered a newspaper not to publish the news on the verdict of a rape trial.

Such decisions are not aberrations by the few judges; a pattern is emerging—a pattern that reflects a no-more-extreme view of judicial power than the State Court of Appeal did in the Farr case. That three-member court waived aside a California law that protects the confidentiality of news sources and said it regarded such laws as "an unconstitutional interference by the legislative branch with an inherent and vital power of the court to control its own proceedings and officers." This was a naked claim to power that mocked the Constitution it invoked.

We have reached this juncture step by step:

First, the assertion, supported by the ABA, that the courts have the right to gag attorneys.

Second, the extension of this power to law enforcement officers and to elected executives of government.

Then, an attempt at direct censorship of the media by telling them what they can and cannot print or broadcast.

And, finally, the assertion that the courts are not a coordinate branch of government, but supreme and answerable only to themselves.

All this on the mere presumption, barren of evidence, that pretrial news is always and without question prejudicial to a fair trial.

Judge Harold R. Medina, U.S. senior circuit judge for the 2nd Circuit, foresaw these consequences several years ago. A report prepared under his supervision for the Bar of the City of New York said, "The prospect . . . of judges of various criminal courts of high and low degree sitting as petty tyrants, handing down sentences of fine and imprisonment for contempt of court against lawyers, policemen, reporters and editors is not attractive. Such an innovation might well cut prejudicial publicity to a minimum. But at what a price . . . With respect to the police and the press in the entire pretrial period, we think it unwise and detrimental to the public interest to give such contempt powers to the courts and the judges."

Judicial censorship that smothers the public's right to know how law enforcement agencies and the courts are functioning will not assure fair trials, but will guarantee the opposite. Censorship will lead to secret investigations, secret arrests and secret trials.

Today, as a portent of things to come, William Farr is in jail. His cellmate is the First Amendment. Judge Charles H. Older of the Superior Court of Los Angeles put them both there.

Detroit Free Press

Detroit, Mich., November 25, 1972

FOR THE FIRST TIME in American history, a scholar has been jailed for protecting sources of information. Already well on the way to curtailing the First Amendment guarantee of freedom of the press, the government has now apparently begun an assault on academic freedom. This should deeply concern all citizens, for it is another sign that this country is drifting toward a state in which the people are servants of the state, rather than the other way around.

His wrists bound with handcuffs, Prof. Samuel L. Popkin of Harvard University was taken to a Massachusetts jail this week for declining to answer certain questions posed by a federal grand jury investigating the distribution of the Pentagon papers. Prof. Popkin, who is certainly no radical, had already testified under oath that he had no knowledge of the unauthorized release of the secret Pentagon study, and since he was in Hong Kong at the time engaged in research, this testimony is certainly believable.

The only question that he refused to answer concerned confidential research

Popkin

sources which, Prof. Popkin argued, had no bearing on the stated purpose of the grand jury. The Justice Department pursued him anyway.

In a dramatic display of the university's concern about the threat to academic freedom posed by the Popkin case, Harvard's young president, Derek Bok, a lawyer who was former dean of the Harvard Law School, got permission from the court to argue final motions for Prof. Popkin.

Popkin himself, in a statement read by his wife after he was led away in shackles, best summed up the threat to the scholarly community posed by his contempt conviction:

"For me to answer these questions would betray my personal and scholarly ethics. Beyond that, for me to answer these questions would create a dangerous precedent. If scholars are to be questioned without restriction about their sources, grand juries will become the government's instrument to limit the free flow of informa-

tion about the government to the public. This is intolerable in a democracy, and I could not justify any part I might take in setting this precedent."

The danger is real and clear. Many academics, especially those who study foreign affairs and government, write penetrating books which are often based on interviews with government officials who, usually for fear of getting in trouble with their bosses, wish to remain anonymous. If scholars can be forced to come before a grand jury and reveal these sources, the flow of information to the public is seriously impaired. Such grand juries could become, and for that matter apparently are now, almost like inquisitions.

We do not believe that any high administration officials actually sent an order singling out Prof. Popkin for persecution. But the entire thrust and atmosphere created in the Justice Department under John Mitchell and Richard Kleindienst, with the obvious approval of President Nixon, has been one which would encourage suppression of individual rights, especially the right of the citizen to have access to information.

If the government can succeed in stifling the press and the academic community, then democracy in America will be effectively ended.

San Jose Mercury

San Jose, Calif., November 20, 1972

The natural adversary relationship between the press and government in a free society is never easy to sustain, and it is sometimes painfully expensive for the individual newsman.

Peter Bridge of Newark, N.J. and William Farr of Los Angeles could, and very well may, write books about the subject. Both are free at the moment, but each remains in jeopardy because he refuses to divulge the identity of confidential news sources. These reporters could be back in jail at any time.

Ironically, they have no effective protection under the law as it is now written, and interpreted by the United States Supreme Court. Their only hope is that the American people, who are the ultimate beneficiaries of this stubborn — and expensive — dedication to principle, will demand that their elected representatives write an all-inclusive "shield law."

California grants limited immunity to newsmen, but not enough to keep Farr, now a reporter for the Los Angeles Times, from being jailed indefinitely for contempt of court. He refused, while a reporter for the Los Angeles Herald-Express, to identify the sources of a news story regarding the trial of the so-called Manson Family.

Farr was ordered to jail last week by Superior Judge

Charles H. Older after the United States Supreme Court refused to review Farr's contempt of court case. The reporter was released hours later by the Second District Court of Appeal until it is determined whether Judge Older has jurisdiction.

If the finding is that Judge Older is acting within the scope of the law, Reporter Farr will be back behind bars, and he could theoretically stay there the rest of his life — or until he reveals his news sources, whichever comes first.

In New Jersey, the case of Reporter Peter Bridge is roughly similar. Bridge, while working for the now defunct Newark Evening News, refused to identify a confidential news source to a grand jury. He was jailed until the grand jury's term expired. If the succeeding grand jury calls him again and asks him the same questions, he could be back in jail again — and on and on and on.

All of which greatly hampers a free people's ability to govern themselves intelligently.

A news source who demands — and gets — anonymity does so because he fears reprisal. Obviously, if he cannot be protected against reprisal he will not talk, and the people will not learn what he has to tell — whether it concerns corruption

in public life, the malfeasance of a superior or, for that matter, the inner functionings of the criminal justice system.

If the people cannot learn what is going on they have little hope of correcting the deficiencies in their society. This is why an inclusive federal "shield law" should be enacted by Congress. Simply stated, such a law is in the best interests of the people.

If it is in the public interest to protect the confidential relationship of doctor and patient, attorney and client, clergyman and parishioner, why is it not in the public interest to give legal sanction to the same relationship between newsman and news source? Each of the professionals now protected enjoys immunity because of this society's belief in the primacy of the individual. There are, in other words, some things the state has no business knowing if the individual doesn't want to divulge them. Society is strongest when its individual members are freest.

This is as it should be, of course, but the rationale should apply as well to the press in all its forms. Let the media be responsible for what they publish, but let there be no prior restraint on publication and no harassment of newsmen in the discharge of their professional duties and obligations.

The New York Times

New York, N.Y., November 23, 1972

In sending a Harvard specialist in Asian affairs to jail for contempt of court, a Federal judge in Boston has all but wiped out the right of either newsmen or scholars to protect confidential sources of information before grand juries. He has also taken a long step toward legitimizing misuse of grand juries as instruments of political intimidation.

The all-embracing compass given by District Judge W. Arthur Garrity to the Supreme Court's recent decision on press subpoenas confirms the gloomiest fears of those who felt that the Supreme Court was thereby acquiescing in serious infringement of First Amendment guarantees of a free press. The limitations on the sweep of the Supreme Court ruling, which Justice Powell had noted in a separate concurring opinion, were brushed aside by the Boston judge as of little significance. The Powell opinion had specifically rejected the notion that state or Federal authorities were free to annex the press as "an investigative arm of government."

* * *

Judge Garrity's interpretation of the law was given as he overrode last-minute objections to the jailing of Prof. Samuel L. Popkin for refusing to answer certain questions put to him early last year by a Federal grand jury investigating the distribution of the Pentagon Papers.

In the end, Professor Popkin's refusal came down solely to an unwillingness to reveal the names of governmental officials who had aided him in his research on aspects of the Vietnam war. He had already testified that he had no direct knowledge about the distribution or publication of the papers themselves and he had made clear his readiness to answer questions pertaining to other scholars, including Dr. Daniel Ellsberg, who is under Federal indictment in California in connection with release of the documents. The Government itself hinted that it did not believe Professor Popkin had any information that would help the grand jury in its mission.

* * *

Unquestionably, there is room for argument on the extent to which the First Amendment provides the same immunities to scholars that it does to the press—if, indeed, those immunities remain in place even for the press.

The Supreme Court has made the point in the recent subpoena cases that validation of a reporter's claim to use the First Amendment as a shield might open the way for similar claims by lecturers, opinion pollsters, dramatists, novelists and others wrapping themselves in the mantle of public information. Without pretending that the line would be easy to draw, we believe that a valid distinction is possible for experts with bona fide academic credentials. The Kinsey Report, for example, relied on the accounts of 5,000 people who told of committing adultery—a crime in virtually all states. Certainly, no one would have expected its authors to have given a grand jury their names.

There can be no argument about the chilling effect of the Popkin jailing on freedom of research in controversial areas of current public policy. Continuation of the present trend in judicial decisions, prompted by far-reaching Federal prosecutions, will make it increasingly difficult for reporters or scholars to penetrate the wall of official secrecy behind which public officials can hide their errors and transgressions.

The Salt Lake Tribune

Salt Lake City, Utah, November 30, 1972

Whether Los Angeles reporter William T. Farr is a martyr or not is immaterial. The important thing to determine is truth.

After Tuesday's hearing before Superior Court Judge Charles Older, during which Farr was ordered to jail on contempt charges, some very sharp discrepancies developed in the testimony presented.

Six attorneys denied under oath they had provided Farr with a potential witness's statement on which he based a 1970 story in the Los angeles Herald-Examiner. After Farr again refused to divulge the source of his information, the reporter told Judge Older:

"The two attorneys involved have implored and beseeched me not to disclose their identities regardless of what they said in court today."

The implication is clear. Someone is not telling the truth. Six attorneys say they did not tell Farr the contents of a probable witness's potential statement. Farr says two attorneys have "implored and beseeched" him not to reveal their roles in the issue, implying that two of the six attorneys gave him the contested material.

Each of the six lawyers, under questioning by Los Angeles County prosecutor William Stewart, said they would release Farr from any ethical, moral or legal obligation to disclose his source. This would tend to support their testimony that they did not reveal the witness's future statement.

The burden of proof has suddenly fallen on Farr because he has effectively accused two of the six attorneys of perjury, a felony.

While Farr is standing on what is now a legally shaky principle of American press freedom, a reporter's right to conceal his sources, he has introduced another element — the possiblity of perjury.

While the attorneys are liable for contempt of court punishments if, in fact, they did reveal the witness's statements to Farr, their conviction of perjury would in all likelihood carry the greater penalty. A contempt penalty could be limited to a fine, but conviction of perjury demands a prison sentence and in the case of lawyers, disbarment.

As the situation now rests, Farr in his militant effort to safeguard one tenet of a free press seems in danger of sullying an even greater principle of press liberty — the ultimate obligation to seek out and expose the truth. Until further facts are divulged no one can possibly determine the truth in the case.

THE WALL STREET JOURNAL

New York, N.Y., November 23, 1972

We're happy to see Harvard Professor Samuel L. Popkin released from jail, where he had been confined on a contempt charge for refusing certain testimony to a grand jury investigating the leaking of the Pentagon Papers. The sudden dismissal of the grand jury certainly suggests that Mr. Popkin was not sent to jail over anything very important.

There is one aspect of the affair that has escaped attention, though, that we think is worth some comment before it all slips into instant history. This concerns the rather easy analogy between secret sources in journalism, which the press has been trying to find ways to protect, and secret sources in scholarship, which Professor Popkin asserted.

Confidential sources are certainly necessary in journalism, especially given the government's present system of overclassification and selected leaks. Such sources also may very well be necessary in whatever it was Mr. Popkin was doing, but it is quite another issue whether they are necessary to or even admissible in anything we can call scholarship.

There are serious doubts about this part of Professor Popkin's argument within the academic community. During a Harvard Government Department meeting last year on Professor Popkin's troubles, the late Merle Fainsod, then the department chairman, made a point worth repeating. Professor Fainsod, a Sovietologist, is famous for his study of Smolensk under Soviet rule, which was made possible by the fact that the archives of that Russian city, captured by the German invaders, had subsequently fallen into the hands of the U.S. Army. Professor Fainsod stated at this meeting that he had refused to undertake this study until these archives had been declassified.

In other words, scholarship depends on open sources, available to other scholars who want to do some independent checking. As another of Professor Popkin's colleagues puts it, "I believe in footnotes, that is, in identifying sources. I admire his courage, but I don't agree with his principle and I don't agree with this application of it."

There is little comfort here for policy analysts or others trained as scholars but applying their skills to current public issues. We have little doubt that activities such as Mr. Popkin was engaged in are worthwhile ones, just as we believe it's worthwhile for the government to sponsor research in areas that need to be classified. But classified research has been refused academic standing at Harvard and many other universities precisely on the grounds that true scholarship should be done openly. So it comes as something of a shock to hear someone from Harvard argue for a "scholar's" right to confidential sources.

None of this means Mr. Popkin ought to have gone to jail. The striking thing in both his case and that of New Jersey reporter Peter Bridge is that the final disposition of the grand jury made it clear that the information sought was insignificant, not vital and irreplaceable, as some of the correspondents alongside insist on assuming. Even without the weight of the First Amendment, both cases would share the elemental consideration that in free societies, people ought not to be sent to jail over trifles.

We also think, though, that the traditional concept of scholarship is something worth protecting. It will do no one any good if the result of the Popkin case is to rob that word of some of its meaning—or worse, to give it one meaning in some cases and another in others, depending on what political sentiments prevail on university campuses.

The Charlotte Observer

Charlotte, N.C., November 30, 1972

The academic world has been even more sleepy-headed than the press in failing to recognize that the Nixon Administration is serious about controlling embarrassing information. But it has been partially awakened by the case of Samuel L. Popkin.

The Popkin case, actually, does not squarely present the problem. Mr. Popkin was manacled and sent off to jail because he refused to tell a grand jury the names of persons he had interviewed in doing research on the Pentagon Papers. Although his civil contempt sentence might have lasted 18 months, he was released after a week because the grand jury and the federal court in Massachusetts pressed the matter no further.

Mr. Popkin has been implicated in no way in obtaining or disclosing the Pentagon Papers. Nor has anyone suggested any act of disloyalty or violation of the Espionage Act — or any other statute, for that matter. Nor did he have information bearing upon a particular criminal act. He was simply doing research, and the grand jury wanted to pump him for whatever information might turn up. As he noted, grand juries are becoming "the government's tool for gathering intelligence." His is a case of abuse of authority by a grand jury.

It will, at least, make more scholars think about the dangers inherent in the administration's contention that it has the right to control information and that courts and grand juries can force researchers and journalists to divulge their sources of information. A lot of academic research is rooted in maintaining confidentiality. With no assurance that what they say will be confidential, many sources of information will simply refuse to help an academic researcher. As Mr. Popkin said, the grand jury's questions "have nothing to do with catching criminals" but "have everything to do with silencing officials."

It may be that scholars should be protected in interviewing for publication for the same reasons that journalists should be protected, under the First Amendment free-press guarantees. Mr. Popkin's case did not squarely rest upon that question. It is, however, closely related to the Nixon Administration's efforts to make it a crime to disclose anything the government does not want disclosed. Has the administration proposed anything so outrageous? Yes, but the public is generally unaware of it.

The government is contending in the cases of Daniel Ellsberg and Anthony Russo that they should be imprisoned for communicating the Pentagon Papers "to persons not entitled to receive them." It does not contend that those persons were foreign agents. There are other charges, too, but this is the one that should most concern the press and public because it embodies a contention that the government can conceal whatever information it wants to conceal.

Congress has never tried to give the government such a right, even if it could constitutionally do so. The administration is trying to establish the right through the Ellsberg-Russo trial. If it succeeds, it then can prosecute anyone for conveying information which it, with or without any reason related to national security, has chosen to deny the public. As extraordinary as that proposition may seem, it is the nut of the government's argument in the Ellsberg-Russo case, which will be tried in December.

The government already has succeeded in denying journalists the right to keep their sources confidential. It did so by arguing for this in the Earl Caldwell case. The four Nixon appointees to the court agreed with the government and, joined by one other member of the court, thus prevailed in the momentous Caldwell decision last June.

The court earlier had seemed to open the way for the administration to engage further in "prior restraint" of the press; that is, in actually stopping a newspaper from printing the news. The government did that in the case of the Pentagon Papers. No other administration has engaged in "prior restraint" of the press, which has always been regarded as unconstitutional under the First Amendment.

Thus the administration continues with what can only be regarded as a very determined effort to control information about the government, and to do so by a variety of methods, some of them based upon the idea that only the government can determine what people should know.

In the meantime, the administration sends out open-faced agents like Herb Klein, a former newspaperman, to innocently maintain that it is not doing this at all. Such protestations should be treated with contempt. They are a part of an extremely ominous effort to shroud big government in secrecy — not from enemies abroad, but from the American people.

Oakland Tribune

Oakland, Calif., November 29, 1972

The continued judicial assaults on newsmen who refuse to disclose confidential news sources make it imperative that legislation be adopted to give newsmen the legal immunity they need to carry out the functions of a truly free press.

Unless legislation is passed, the nation's courts can continue to cite reporters for contempt of court and sentence them to jail as they have in the celebrated William Farr case in Los Angeles and others in recent months.

Farr was found in contempt for withholding the name of a source of a story he wrote concerning the Charles Manson murder trial. He has been jailed until he names the source

The right to protect sources is vital if the public is to be adequately informed about the events around them, whatever they may be. Many important stories may have gone unpublished had their sources believed their names would have been revealed.

Farr and others in the newspaper fraternity stand firmly behind the First Amendment which they believe gives them a free hand in serving the broad public purpose of gathering and disseminating information on public affairs.

The courts have not seen it that way, and, from all indications, unless a newsman's rights are definitively spelled out reporters may continue to be jailed.

U.S. Sen. Alan Cranston, D-Calif., has introduced a bill in Congress which would give reporters immunity from probing grand juries and courts on the federal level. Assemblyman William Bagley, R-San Rafael, says he plans to introduce a bill in the state legislature that would extend the same privileges to reporters on the state level.

This type of proposed legislation must become law. Newsmen should be granted the same sort of immunity now afforded attorneys, physicians, clergymen and other select individuals in their professional dealings with clients, patients and parishioners.

As Bagley said, "The government's sporadic need for evidence must not be allowed to override the freedom of the press to function within our society."

If the constitutional rights of a free press cannot be adequately upheld in the courts, then the press' interests must be protected through the legislative branch of government.

The Cincinnati Post

TIMES ☆ STAR

Cincinnati, Ohio, November 30, 1972

Legal atrocities like the jailing of a Los Angeles newsman this week for refusing to reveal his confidential sources are an insult to the integrity of the press and to the intelligence of the American people.

If judges can send reporter Peter J. Bridge to jail for 21 days in New Jersey, and sentence William T. Farr to an indefinite jail term in California, then the public's right to know isn't worth a penny any more.

THE "CRIME" these men committed was to protect their confidential sources against public disclosure. If sources can't be protected, newsmen (and their readers) might as well kiss good-by stories of corruption and bungling in high places.

For no tipster or informant in his right mind will confide in a reporter who later can be grilled by a judge, a grand jury or legislative committee.

The Los Angeles case is particularly shocking because Judge Charles H. Older has been badgering Farr to divulge the source of a story he wrote during the Manson murder trial two years ago. The jury never saw the story, but the judge seems determined to make an example of Farr, or anyone else who dares to print leaked information.

THE ONLY WAY to deal with such harassment is to guarantee newsmen an absolute or near-absolute right to protect their confidential sources.

This means passing state and federal shield laws so tight that no newsman can be required to break confidences except in rare and extreme cases—cases, for example, that involve threat to human life or national security. Ohio has such a law.

Both the American Society of Newspaper Editors and Sigma Delta Chi, the professional journalistic society, now say they favor broad rather than limited protection for newsmen and their sources.

In truth, it's time reporters and editors stop purring like kittens and start defending their right to report the news without judicial or governmental interference.

Federal Judge Harold R. Medina of New York offers some advice that bears repeating.

"I say it is their duty to fight like tigers," he says of newsmen. "This is the way our freedoms have been preserved in the past, and it is the way they will be preserved in the future."

THE KANSAS CITY STAR
Kansas City, Mo., November 19, 1972

None of the bills to relieve reporters from forced testimony before grand juries made it through the recent Congress. Thus the matter remains urgent business for the 93rd Congress Only the legislative branch can undo the damage done to freedom of the press by recent Supreme Court decisions as long as the court retains the narrow views of the present majority.

Reporters and editors should not be required to testify before grand juries because they will lose their worth as reporters and editors, once they do. It is not a matter of extending special privileges to them because they occupy an exalted position in society as individual men and women. The obvious fact is that any reporter who must reveal his sources to a prosecutor or to law enforcement officials will not have those sources again.

The court decision was in this tone:

"This case involves no intrusions upon speech or assembly, no prior restraint or restrictions on what the press may publish and no express or implied command that the press publish what it prefers to withhold . . . The use of confidential sources by the press is not forbidden; reporters remain free to seek news from any source by means within the law. No attempt is made to require the press to publish its sources . . . or disclose them . . .

"The sole issue . . . is the obligation of reporters to respond to grand jury subpoenas as other citizens do and to answer questions relevant to an investigation into the commission of crime. Citizens generally are not constitutionally immune from grand jury subpoenas; and neither the First Amendment nor other constitutional provision protects the average citizen from disclosing to a grand jury information he has received in confidence . . ."

This is the sort of legalistic logic that in the last few years has accompanied bar attempts to severely restrict pretrial information. It was said that guidelines would not restrict reporters from gathering and disseminating information, but merely forbid the prosecutors, defense lawyers and police from giving any information to the press. Thus the Supreme Court would not prevent the media from putting out news, or let anyone act as a censor, or force any publication or broadcast. It would, however, severely curtail the effectiveness of the media as news-gathering agencies. The court is going through the back door to accomplish indirectly what the Constitution directly forbids Congress to do. It is like promising a community unlimited access to water and then draining all the lakes, wells, ponds and rivers in the area.

The courts, and too many of their officers, continue to act as if the law exists in a vacuum, unaffected by people and events and circumstances. In theory, of course, the law must remain pure. But we have noticed that lawyers are able to take a practical view of it when it affects the legal profession. Freedom of the press and speech are necessities that make representative government work. Such freedom cannot be assured in an atmosphere of intimidation through the judicial branch which, after all, remains a product of the representative process.

The Detroit News
Detroit, Mich., November 26, 1972

Do college professors deserve special immunity from questions asked by grand juries? If so, where does society draw the line in creating privileged classes of citizens who stand beyond the laws that govern ordinary mortals?

These questions are posed by the refusal of Harvard Prof. Samuel L. Popkin to tell a grand jury how he knew the identity of a person who had helped write a secret government study — the Pentagon papers — before the study was released.

Popkin argues that answering the grand jury's questions would force him to violate sensitive sources vital to his scholarly research.

In the first place, his refusal to answer violates a cardinal rule of scholarship, which is that the scholar shall reveal his sources of information so that they may be weighed to determine the soundness and validity of his work.

In the second place, how does society determine the difference between scholars deserving of immunity and mere pretenders? One of Popkin's colleagues at Harvard, Prof. Martin M. Shapiro, an expert on constitutional law, observes: "I am very loathe to see a special class of citizens carved out, particularly when I can't see any neat boundaries. Who is the scholar? Once you establish this rule, then nearly everybody can claim it."

The ordinary citizen must, of course, fulfill his obligations under the law. How can he be expected to maintain his respect for law when he sees other citizens claim special privilege as an excuse for backing away from their obligations? Incidentally, how could he have any respect for the scholarly profession if it evaded duties of citizenship?

Prof. Popkin deserves and, we suspect, will get little sympathy for his point of view. The thrust of American society is away from, not toward, elite and privileged classes.

The Boston Globe
Boston, Mass., November 29, 1972

Samuel L. Popkin, a Harvard assistant professor and research fellow, who last week became probably the first American scholar to be sent to jail for protecting his sources of information, yesterday became the first to be released from jail because the government did not want to call him to the witness stand anyway.

This leaves Prof. Popkin free, but where it leaves the Justice Department is quite another matter. Popkin spent a week of the Thanksgiving season behind the bars for contempt in refusing to answer two questions concerning talks with participants in the Pentagon Papers study.

He was released because a Federal grand jury that was supposed to hear Popkin's testimony was discharged after 16 months at the request of the Justice Department, which told the Federal court it had decided not to present any more evidence in the Pentagon Papers case until the pending trial of Daniel Ellsberg is over in Los Angeles.

But that, in essence, is what president Derek Bok of Harvard had told US District Court Judge W. Arthur Garrity Jr. eight days ago in arguing on Popkin's behalf that the contempt finding was then moot. Bok said the government had no intention "at this time" of recalling Popkin as a witness. The Justice Department had said then that Bok was the victim of a misunderstanding.

To be sure, Popkin may still be called when the Ellsberg case is finished. The Justice Department, through US Atty. James M. Gabriel, now says the "national publicity" given Popkin might hinder Ellsberg's chances of a fair trial, and to avoid this the grand jury was discharged.

But the Justice Department might have thought of this possibility in the first place. As it now stands, any such damage has already been done. Mr. Popkin has served eight days in jail in what someone in the Justice Department had to be aware would be bound to have a chilling effect on all scholars. The latter can take what cold comfort there is from the fact that the administration of Harvard worked hard, first to prevent Popkin's imprisonment, and then to effect his release.

As for the Justice Department, it had already won its point, even eight days ago, as to a scholar's not having a privilege under the First Amendment not to reveal his confidential sources. The US Supreme Court earlier this month had refused to hear Popkin's appeal, though no reason was given.

The question for the Justice Department then became one of the wise restraint of the government's power. We can be grateful that it finally used such restraint — but it came eight days too late, and therein lies the injustice. In the land of the free, freedom suffered a little.

THE ATLANTA CONSTITUTION
Atlanta, Ga., November 28, 1972

Let it be clear first that we have absolutely no sympathy for the legal proceedings against Professor Samuel L. Popkin, the Harvard professor who has chosen to go to jail rather than reveal his sources. Popkin has argued that he is a scholar, and therefore is not required to divulge the source of his information about the Pentagon Papers prior to their publication. The jail sentence against him seems less than worthwhile.

But we have no feeling that Popkin has a right to withhold his information from a grand jury simply because he claims to be a scholar. Since when did professors in colleges become immune to the citizenship requirements that must be met by the people living next door? And who qualifies as a scholar, anyway? Is a doctor a scholar? As much so as a professor. Is a lawyer a scholar? As much so as a law professor.

Popkin and his kind are asking for protection through the First Amendment to the Constitution. And we think they are wrong. They are about to do damage to teachers and scholars as a group by claiming that privilege. By setting themselves up as a special category, they prepare themselves for special rules.

That is true even though the court in Boston which made the harsh ruling seems to be pushing a technical point too far. The judge ordered the jailing of Popkin for refusing to answer questions put to him by a federal grand jury which doesn't even plan to meet again. In fact, he has said he has no direct knowledge on the point which the grand jury wanted him to testify — on the distribution of the Pentagon Papers.

This simply is a case of two wrongs, one on the part of a federal court, the other on the part of a professor. The nation would be better served if the professor stopped claiming the special category and the court stopped pushing a technical point beyond its logical conclusion.

The Des Moines Register

Des Moines, Iowa
December 25, 1972

A Los Angeles Times newsman went to jail last week for refusing to disclose information, given to reporters in confidence, about the Watergate bugging case. The newsman escaped a prolonged stay in jail only because the news source released the Times from its pledge not to reveal the information.

The U.S. Supreme Court ruled last June that the First Amendment does not prevent reporters from being forced to reveal information disclosed to them in confidence. The Watergate case illustrates the regrettable nature of the high court ruling.

The public had an overriding interest in learning about the circumstances surrounding the planting of listening devices in Democratic National Headquarters. The silence maintained by the persons responsible for the bugging made it necessary for investigative reporters to dig out the story. The public would have been totally in the dark if those with knowledge of the episode were unwilling to reveal it to newsmen.

The public learned what it did about the Watergate case only because news sources expected pledges of confidentiality to be kept. News sources usually are interested in keeping secret their identities or portions of their statements.

The expectation of confidentiality is sharply reduced when newsmen are threatened with jail. Though most newsmen rather would be jailed than break a confidence, a news source cannot be certain of this in every case. The upsurge in the number of subpoenaed newsmen, coupled with the increased willingness of judges to send newsmen to jail, is bound to shake the confidence of news sources in pledges of secrecy.

The purpose of the First Amendment is to assure Americans unfettered access to information. The practice of jailing newsmen, who seek to encourage the flow of information by protecting their news sources, is counter to the spirit and purpose of the free press guarantee. No one should be required to spend a minute in jail for seeking a better informed public.

★ ★ ★

Legislatures have recognized the importance of encouraging parishioners to speak frankly to their ministers, clients to confide in their lawyers, and patients to seek help from their doctors, by assuring that statements made in confidence to ministers, lawyers and doctors cannot be required to be divulged. These laws protect the parishioner, client and patient, rather than the minister, lawyer and doctor, and serve the interests of society as a whole.

A number of states have given journalists similar immunity from enforced disclosure. The Supreme Court ruling, and the rash of threats to jail newsmen, have prompted interest in federal legislation and additional state laws. Laws against forced disclosure are intended to protect news sources rather than newsmen, and in the larger sense, the public's First Amendment right to information.

Enactment of such laws will be necessary unless the courts show a better appreciation of the function of the press in a free society and quit putting newsmen in jail.

St. Louis Globe-Democrat

St. Louis, Mo., December 22, 1972

Still another newsman has been jailed for refusing to divulge confidential information. This time it was John Lawrence, Washington Bureau Chief of the Los Angeles Times, who was the victim.

A federal judge held Lawrence in contempt for refusing to turn over recordings of an interview with a principal witness in the Watergate bugging trial.

Even though the newsman now has been released on bond and the witness has released the Times from its promise to keep the information confidential, the issue remains.

The judge cited a Supreme Court decision that said reporters could be compelled to divulge confidential information in criminal cases as the basis for his citation.

This again illustrates the need for a federal law to give newsmen the same kind of protection for their confidential sources that now is given to lawyers, doctors and clergymen.

Unless the trend of jailing one reporter after another is stopped, it could seriously undermine the ability of newsmen to investigate suspected criminal behavior by public officials and others.

Those who might otherwise talk to reporters may decide to remain silent rather than risk the danger of public exposure and reprisal. Reporters also might be less eager to seek out such information if they know they can no longer hold it in confidence.

The result could be not only bad for the press but for the nation. Corrupt public officials could use the threat of jail to try to silence newsmen and muzzle the press.

The practice of jailing reporters must be stopped. It smacks of oppression, the kind found in countries where there is no free press.

The Washington Post

Washington, D.C., December 24, 1972

It would be comforting to be able to believe that all is truly well that ends well, but unfortunately, that is not always the case. This lesson was brought forcefully home the other day by the resolution of the dispute between the Los Angeles Times and Judge John J. Sirica in the preliminaries to the Watergate burglary trial. Although the Times' bureau chief won't have to spend Christmas in jail, Judge Sirica's orders before the issue was resolved give dark intimations of the mischief wrought by the Supreme Court's decision in the Earl Caldwell case last term.

First, it will be useful to run lightly over the circumstances of the Times' problems with Judge Sirica. Two of the newspaper's reporters had obtained an interview with Alfred C. Baldwin III, a prospective government witness in the burglary trial, with an understanding that they would would make no disclosures other than those approved by Mr. Baldwin. After conducting the interview and permitting him to review the story, the paper printed it.

Subsequently, lawyers for the defendants asked Judge Sirica to subpoena the tapes and other material from the interview in hopes they would contain material which could be used to discredit Mr. Baldwin's testimony at the trial. The judge issued the subpoena although the Times had argued that its confidential agreement with Mr. Baldwin was protected by the First Amendment guarantee of press freedom. When the Times refused to honor the subpoena, its Washington bureau chief was immediately jailed for contempt of court. He was subsequently released pending appeal. Then, pursuant to a suggestion by a Court of Appeals judge, Mr. Baldwin agreed to release the Times from its pledge and the materials were turned over to Judge Sirica. The contempt proceedings then became moot.

After it was all over, Ronald Ostrow, one of the Times' reporters said, "I don't think it's any bell ringing day for the First Amendment." We think Ostrow is just right. Judge Sirica's orders are troubling from a number of points of view. First of all, in overriding the Times' First Amendment arguments, the judge relied on the Caldwell decision. In Caldwell, the Supreme Court leaned heavily on the fact that the government was seeking information about alleged criminal conduct. In the Times episode there was no search by public authorities for evidence of criminal activity; rather, what was involved was a defense counsel's preparation to discredit a government witness. Despite the great differences in the two cases and despite the Supreme Court's comforting language in Caldwell to the effect that the courts would not fail to protect the rights of the news media when appropriate, Judge Sirica seemed to have little trouble in sweeping past the First Amendment and summarily dispatching a newsman to a jail cell. The Caldwell effect, if you will, had taken hold, at least in Judge Sirica's courtroom, and had severely lessened the force of the First Amendment.

We recognize that the defendant's motion to obtain information required the judge to balance First Amendment freedoms against fairness required for the defendants by the Sixth Amendment. One way of approaching that delicate balance is to consider what the defense would have lost if the judge had ruled against it and what the public lost by the enshrinement of Judge Sirica's ruling. At the trial, the defense will have the opportunity to cross examine Mr. Baldwin and, even without the benefit of the supoenaed material, it will have the first person story he gave to the Times to set against the testimony he gives. It will also have the information the defendants themselves have about their own activities and about Mr. Baldwin and it will have the fruits of whatever investigations the defense has conducted. Whatever the Times materials would add in these circumstances would seem to us to be marginal.

On the other hand, Judge Sirica's ruling, going far beyond Caldwell, promises great losses to the public's right to information. Few have put it more succinctly than James C. Hagerty, press secretary to President Eisenhower, who said, in an affidavit filed in support of the Times reporters, that confidential agreements are "crucial to the newsgathering function of the media in the United States." If the people generally draw the conclusion from Judge Sirica's actions that any party to a litigation—or even just a party to a criminal proceeding—has a license to rummage through a reporter's notes, the cost to the public will, as we said after the Caldwell decision, be "the stories that will never be written about the hopes and plans of political dissenters, the corruption and political deals made inside the government and the activities of organized crime." And that is a high cost indeed—one which in our view outweighs the defendant's Sixth Amendment rights in this case.

One other observation may sharpen the focus just a bit more. Under federal statute, a defendant has a right to review a statement or report made by a government witness which is in the government's possession, but only *after* that witness has testified. If that standard is fair for a defendant when the document is in government hands, it would seem to be fair—even absent any First Amendment considerations—when the document or tape is in a reporter's hands. But, when First Amendment considerations and the federal statutory standard form the background for Judge Sirica's summary jailing of a newsman weeks before the beginning of the trial, neither an enterprising newsman nor an informed member of the public can avoid feeling chilled. If judges conclude, as Judge Sirica apparently did, that the Caldwell decision gives them the keys to a newsman's files in situations not even remotely similar to Caldwell, then the First Amendment is in real trouble and so are we all.

THE WALL STREET JOURNAL.

New York, N.Y., December 26, 1972

We've tended to be a bit more relaxed than some of our colleagues about disputes between the press and government, figuring that the press too can and does sin. But our composure has frazzled the last few months as we've watched a parade of newsmen to jail. The reasons for the sentences have been anything but sins by the press.

These columns have already recounted the details that led to the jailing of New Jersey reporter Peter Bridge: In a nasty fight over an appointment, an official on one side said she had been offered a bribe by the other side. A grand jury had already heard some five different versions of her story, and subpoenaed Mr. Bridge to gather a sixth. Net result: The story-spreader goes unindicted for perjury and Mr. Bridge goes to jail for contempt.

Los Angeles Times reporter William T. Farr is still in jail for refusing to reveal the source of a story he wrote about the Charles Manson murder trial. Looking back on the episode it's impossible to believe his story ultimately affected the course of justice, though it did help to satisfy a need for public information about so threatening a case. The dispute continues today because the judge had ordered the attorneys involved not to talk to the press, and obviously one or more of them did talk to Mr. Farr, though before the court they all deny doing so. The judge's order to silence the attorneys was in the spirit of the rules the American Bar Association suggested a few years ago to prevent possibly prejudicial publicity in cases like the Manson one. When the rules were being debated, we were solemnly assured that this was not an attack on the press; that the bar was putting its own house in order. Shortly thereafter New Orleans District Attorney Jim Garrison came forth with some of the most blatant prejudicial publicity ever; the bar did nothing, only the press complained. Now it seems that the real result of the bar's efforts to put its own house in order will be to send newspaper reporters to jail.

John F. Lawrence, the Los Angeles Times bureau chief in Washington, was jailed briefly last week for refusing to supply tape recordings of an interview members of that bureau held with Alfred C. Baldwin III, who is expected to be a key witness in the trial of those indicted in the Watergate bugging episode. Though the paper's story identified Mr. Baldwin as its source, the reporters had allowed him to make some remarks on a confidential basis during the interview. He has now released the Times from the pledge of confidentiality, and delivery of the tapes to court has ended the legal issue.

In this case the dispute arose because defense attorneys wanted to see if they could find something in the tapes that might impeach the witness' courtroom testimony. His willingness to release the tapes certainly suggests that in fact they contain no such material. The defense attorneys offered no particular reason to believe they did. In other words, not only grand juries but defense attorneys will be allowed to rummage through a newspaper's files on a routine basis. Contestants in civil suits cannot be far behind.

Some of the likely effects of this are apparent in the Watergate case. Mr. Baldwin has his own copies of the interview tapes, and had destroyed them on the advice of counsel. The Times' legal position would have been far better if it had not identified its source, though its story would have been far poorer. In other words, if the number of reporters hauled into court continues to increase, such canons of good journalism as identifying sources whenever possible and keeping your notes in important matters may have to give way to the quite opposite exigencies of the courtroom.

The case also illustrates something even more important. Certainly nearly anyone looking at the larger interests involved would conclude that the public was served by knowing as much as possible about the Watergate incident before the presidential election. Yet Mr. Baldwin has said that he never would have granted the interview if he had not been allowed to make some remarks confidentially.

Any working reporter knows how typical this is. Sources are willing to talk on an informal basis, but they do not want to feel as if they are in a court proceeding or something. Yet once they are relaxed and start to talk the essential information comes out. If some remarks are confidential, or if some sources need anonymity before they can talk at all, the information provided allows the reporter to insure the accuracy of what he prints. If anyone talking to a newspaper reporter is in effect thrust into the middle of a court proceeding, this informality will be lost and the essential information will never reach the public.

We are happy to learn that, at least so far as confidential sources are concerned, there is far broader understanding of the press's needs than the court cases would suggest. The Gallup Poll recently reported that only 34% of the public thought newsmen should be forced in court to identify confidential sources, while 57% supported the press's position. Support for the press increased with education. Apparently the public recognizes that what is at stake is its own access to information on current affairs.

This public access to information is the reason freedom of the press is mentioned in the First Amendment. And if newsmen continue to be jailed over the kind of trivia they have been in the past few months it will inevitably cripple the practice of journalism and stifle the free flow of information the First Amendment was intended to promote.

The Boston Globe

Boston, Mass., December 26, 1972

John F. Lawrence, the Los Angeles Times's Washington bureau chief, has become the fifth newsman in printed or electronic journalism — and the fourth this year — to go to jail for contempt of court in refusing to divulge confidential sources or material. Released after three hours, he can enjoy Christmas with his wife and four children only because his case is being appealed.

The case is a direct outgrowth of the US Supreme Court's 5-to-4 ruling in the Caldwell case last June 30 that newsmen's notes and tape recordings could be subpoenaed by grand juries and government bodies. Since then there have been 12 reported cases of such subpoenas.

The tapes in the L.A. Times case are recordings of an interview with Alfred C. Baldwin 3d, a former FBI agent who said he had witnessed parts of the break-in at the Democratic National Committee offices at the Watergate complex June 17, for which seven men, two of them former White House aides, face trial Jan. 8. Baldwin's account was printed Oct. 5.

The defense in this case says it wants the tapes solely to try to impeach the testimony of Baldwin, the key prosecution witness. The Justice Department, from which precious little information about the bugging was available during the campaign, has told the court it has no objection to the subpoena.

The L.A. Times had publicly identified its source (Mr. Baldwin) when the story was printed. But it had obtained the interview on the promise that parts of it not used in the published story would be held confidential. We believe most strongly that the promise must be and should be kept if the press is to remain free.

In our view the subpoenaed tapes, to use the words of Mr. Justice Powell in Caldwell when he said harassment of newsmen would not be tolerated, "implicate confidential source relationships without a legitimate need of law enforcement."

Moreover, a precedent is being set here which could prevent future Watergate buggings and other such crimes from ever being revealed to the public. Sources simply won't talk if confidences cannot be kept.

Back in the days of Sen. Joseph McCarthy's committee hearings, the nation's courts finally called a halt to fishing expeditions. Today, since Caldwell, they are authorizing them by subpoena, penalizing journalists whose only transgression has been to inform their fellow citizens.

There is another aspect to confidential sources. Sometimes their information is unreliable, and responsible newspapers, subject always to the libel laws, will not risk printing it. Is it now to be opened up by court order for all to see?

That part of it which is reliable, on the other hand, will no longer even be offered to a newspaper if the source knows that disclosure is possible. Here again it is not merely the press but the public's right to know that suffers irreparable damage.

Involved here basically is government censorship of the press, as Sen. Vance Hartke (D-Ind) has said, and Congress should make the passage of an absolute shield law its first order of business.

Newsday

Long Island, N.Y., December 16, 1972

Yet another serious confrontation appears to be developing between the courts and the press, this time involving the Watergate scandals.

A federal judge has ordered three newsmen of the Los Angeles Times to hand over all tapes and notes of an interview with Alfred C. Baldwin 3rd, who claims he participated in the bugging of Democratic National Committee headquarters. Defense attorneys for the seven men indicted in the incident say they need the material to prepare their challenges to Baldwin's expected testimony.

That's absurd on at least two counts. In the first place, complete stories based on the interview have been in the public domain for weeks. And if the lawyers have further questions, Baldwin will be available to them—under oath—when the trial begins. Secondly, reporter's notes and tapes are unevaluated raw material, sometimes a sort of shorthand comprehensible only to the writer himself, sometimes full of items that require further checking—but in any case a private part of the reporter's thought process. The public part is his story, and that's readily available to all.

With these points in mind it's hard to avoid the suspicion that the Watergate defense has a different motive than the one it gave the judge: namely, to discourage further investigative reporting.

For it was the investigative reporters—from the Washington Post, Time magazine, the AP, the Los Angeles Times and others —who brought the full picture of the scandal to public attention and, finally, to trial. Not the FBI. Not the Justice Department. The reporters.

What we have here is a vivid illustration of exactly why the First Amendment protections are so vital to the functioning of orderly, lawful government—and of the peril in which these protections find themselves today.

The Hartford Courant

Hartford, Conn., December 24, 1972

With the release by the principal witness concerned of a pledge of confidentiality by the Washington Bureau Chief of the Los Angeles Times, the Times has turned the recordings over to the court. The contempt proceedings against the news man, John F. Lawrence, have been dropped—although not until after Mr. Lawrence had been briefly jailed. The outcome is a happy one for Mr. Lawrence—who, as the New York Times ironically pointed out, is the only individual to have been jailed as an aftermath of the Watergate case in which political espionage is charged.

But while the voluntary release by the witness of Mr. Lawrence's pledge to hold the recordings confidential removes him from the shadow of the jail to which the judge had threatened to recommit him, the fact is that, as the Reporters Committee for the Freedom of the Press said in a formal statement, "a further serious erosion of the First Amendment" had taken place. As the committee put it, "Two Federal judges did order the Los Angeles Times bureau chief to jail, and the only reason he escaped further imprisonment was, not by the protection of the First Amendment, but because a news source backed down on the confidentiality privilege."

At issue is the right of newsmen to hold in confidence names and materials they have received from any source, without being given the permission of the source to release it. The newsmen know all too well that if they do not respect the confidences they accept, their news sources will dry up and the public will be denied news to which they are entitled and which they will get only through a confidential leak. A Courant reporter last summer faced a situation similar to that in which Mr. Lawrence was involved when he was ordered on penalty of contempt to release the source of an important story. Like Mr. Lawrence, his source voluntarily released him from the confidence, and he testified.

Perhaps less important than the potential drying up of news sources when attempts are made to force the revelation of news sources—but nonetheless a clear violation of the freedom of the press—is the practice of some prosecutors and defense lawyers of trying to force reporters to reveal confidential material—not to supply otherwise unavailable information but to attempt to force the reporters to do the lawyers' work for them. Too often in the past, lazy lawyers have tried to force reporters to do their leg work for them. Happily, attempts to force reporters to serve the prosecutors have been largely and generally effectively resisted.

Since the Supreme Court's five-to-four decision last June that the First Amendment does not give reporters the right to withhold the names of confidential sources, four newsmen have gone to jail for contempt charges, and one is nearing the end of his first month of incarceration. It is becoming increasingly clear, that it is to the legislatures and the Congress that the public and the press must turn if the freedom of the press is to be established in that respect. In that connection, we are happy to see that Connecticut's Senator Weicker is planning to press a "shield law" when the next session of Congress reassembles.

The New York Times

New York, N.Y., December 21, 1972

A number of persons, some with close connections to the White House, were arrested and charged with a variety of criminal acts in the Watergate case of political espionage. But a newspaper editor who participated not in the crime, but in its exposure, is the first actually sent to jail in the aftermath of the incident.

This is the grim irony in the contempt citation and brief jailing this week of John F. Lawrence, Washington bureau chief of The Los Angeles Times. Mr. Lawrence had refused to turn over to the court taped interviews with Alfred C. Baldwin 3d, a key Government witness in the Watergate affair.

When Chief Judge John J. Sirica ordered Mr. Lawrence jailed—the United States Court of Appeals released him two hours later pending the appeal—he added the latest serious infringement on the First Amendment guarantee of a free press.

* * *

What is clearly at issue in the case is a newspaper's right to conduct interviews and discussions on a confidential basis. As the courts wield the subpoena power like a club over reporters' heads, the investigative capacity of the press shrinks. Informants will no longer be willing to provide vital facts in off-the-record interviews if they cannot expect their confidence to be protected. Yet, such confidential information is often the essential link in a newspaper's attempt to fit together the pieces of a controversial story.

The Supreme Court ruled in a five-to-four decision last June that the First Amendment did not give reporters the right to withhold the names of confidential sources or to refuse to testify about criminal acts they had been apprised of under a pledge of secrecy. At that time, Justice Powell tried to minimize the decision's potential effect by promising that "no harassment of newspapers will be tolerated." Yet, just such harassment has since escalated. Mr. Lawrence was the fourth newsman since that ruling actually to have gone to jail for refusal to disclose information, and William Farr, another Los Angeles Times reporter, is currently in his 25th day of incarceration in solitary confinement. Eleven other newsmen are under court pressure to disclose confidential information.

* * *

When a lawyer for the newspaper warned that the subpoena power would ultimately stop the flow of news, Judge Sirica replied: "I think you're getting alarmed about something that probably won't happen. Every judge doesn't have to agree with my opinion."

For the sake of this country's freedoms, one must hope that Judge Sirica is right about the majority of his peers —particularly about those hearing the appeal. But it would be dangerous indeed to entrust the freedom of the press to one judge's opinion that serious inroads on that freedom "probably won't happen."

If Judge Sirica has proved anything, it is that the Supreme Court's refusal to uphold the shield implicit in the First Amendment to protect freedom of the press has already eroded that freedom. When governmental vindictiveness is coupled with a mood of public frustration, the risk is particularly great that erosion may turn into collapse. To avert such a disaster—now that the courts have left the issue in limbo—swift enactment of specific legislation is needed to uphold the rights which seem so urgently implied by the First Amendment.

CHICAGO DAILY NEWS

Chicago, Ill., December 21, 1972

As Congress prepares to open its new session, the need for a stern new law shielding a reporter's rights to protect the confidentiality of his news sources becomes more urgent day by day.

For with increasing frequency that aspect of the freedom of the press is being trampled by lawyers (who would righteously and rightly defend their own confidential relationship with their clients) and by courts with narrow or distorted views of the meaning of the Constitution's First Amendment.

In four recent instances reporters have been sent to jail for refusing to divulge their sources. The latest involves the Washington bureau chief of the Los Angeles Times, John Lawrence. Lawrence refused an order by Chief Judge John J. Sirica of the U.S. District Court in Washington to submit tapes and other material relating to an interview with a witness in the Watergate bugging case. Judge Sirica ordered Lawrence jailed and held until he produced the documents.

The Times, which has taken possession of the documents, appealed on the ground that the tapes contain confidential information protected by the First Amendment. Lawrence said that parts of the information in the withheld documents was obtained on the promise that it would be held confidential unless released by the witness who provided it.

Circumstances of the various cases have differed, but the principle involved is the same in each instance.

That is the principle that violation of the confidential relationship shuts off the reporter's sources of information and directly interferes with the public's right to know.

No responsible newspaper denies its obligation to help in every valid and legitimate way to preserve a defendant's right to a fair trial. But the instances where that right is involved in this issue are negligible; the necessary information can virtually always be obtained by other means than to force the reporter to betray his trust and become — as is too often the case — an unwilling agent for the government.

The plain fact is that press freedom has come under formidable and systematic attack. The Times put the matter admirably in its argument in Lawrence's behalf:

"Freedom of the press belongs not to the press but to the public. By protecting the press, the First Amendment protects the people's right to know. Without that right, the people become not the masters of their government but its servants. The First Amendment became the First Amendment because the founders of this republic wanted to protect the nation from that fate."

What is needed at this point is the clearest kind of mandate from Congress protecting that basic right at the fundamental level of the reporter who seeks, often against great resistance, to discover and print the news.

The confidentiality of the lawyer-client, doctor-patient and priest-confessor relationships have long since been recognized as inviolate. The need to protect the reporter-source relationship is no less urgent and valid, and no less in the public interest.

The Pittsburgh Press

Pittsburgh, Pa., December 23, 1972

Some non-newspaper people are starting to believe that newspapermen are getting a bit paranoid about this freedom-of-the-press thing.

They say the newsmen are screaming before they get bit, peering suspiciously over their shoulders at Washington and seeing threats to free expression where none exist.

Well, maybe the outsiders are right and the insiders shouldn't be so sensitive when, say, Spiro Agnew and the White House speech-writing crew belabor some newsmen as elitist snobs.

Or when George Wallace goes around telling people newsmen don't even know how to park a bicycle.

Or when the Vietnam War goes badly and part of the public blames the press for telling them about it instead of the military and diplomatic geniuses in charge of that enterprise.

Or when President Nixon takes to spending long sojourns at Camp David and Ronald Ziegler makes reporters lurk in a duck blind where they can't see what's going on.

Or when the White House's broadcasting czar draws up legislation that seems aimed at getting local TV stations to censor network news broadcasts he disapproves of.

(Can you imagine? He wants to leave under-arm commercials alone and clean up news shows.)

★ ★ ★

As if all this wasn't enough to make newsmen nervous, consider the Watergate caper.

Everybody remembers that smelly case of last June, when a bunch of spy types, a couple of them with close White House ties, broke into the Democratic National Committee headquarters, bugging devices in hand.

Since the Watergate break-in involves felonies like burglary and wire-tapping, obviously somebody should be punished, and the defendants will be tried.

But who is the first villain thrown into jail? The Washington bureau chief of the Los Angeles Times, who knows a couple of fellows who wrote something about the case.

And the non-newspaper people tell the newsmen not to worry, that they're merely imagining things!

St. Petersburg Times

St. Petersburg, Fla., December 31, 1972

Once again, First Amendment liberties have been challenged by court action in the case against John F. Lawrence, the scholarly Washington bureau chief of the Los Angeles Times.

Lawrence was thrown into jail, then let out on appeal, for refusing to release tape recordings of a confidential interview subpoenaed by defense attorneys for two former White House staffers and five others charged with burglary of the Democratic National Headquarters. Lawrence has tapes of an interview with Alfred C. Baldwin III, a former FBI agent who said he witnessed parts of the break-in. The newspaper obtained the interview, part of a broader investigation, with the promise not to release information except with Baldwin's permission.

Defense attorneys say they need the tapes to prepare their cases, including trying to impeach Baldwin's testimony.

SO WHY doesn't the newspaper give the tapes to the defense lawyers?

The reason is fundamental to the workings of a free press. Who would give confidential information to a newsman if he could be forced to reveal it? For the courts to force newsmen to yield information obtained in confidence is certain to restrict the people's right to know.

In this case, the defense attorneys are attempting to use Lawrence as a short cut in the hard work of case preparation. If the defense in this case requires information from Baldwin, the law provides better, more direct ways to get it without violating the First Amendment. The attorneys can (1) request a voluntary interview or, if Baldwin refuses, (2) get a court order requiring him to give a deposition under oath.

Meanwhile, the newspaper won't give the tapes to the prosecution either, so their contents can't be used against the defendant. So why jail Lawrence?

IN THE Lawrence case, a newsman is refusing to violate the First Amendment or do the work of the defense. A recent incident in St. Petersburg illustrated the other side of the coin.

To inform readers about housing discrimination in the city, the Evening Independent published a series — without names and addresses — relating the experience of a black couple looking for an apartment. Last week, the FBI requested the names and addresses of the apartment owners interviewed. The newspaper had to refuse. It can't do its job of informing the public if its reporters are legmen for the FBI. They went out to report the news, not to put white landlords in jail.

Again, the law provides the prosecution side better, more direct ways to obtain evidence without violating the First Amendment. The FBI agents can do the same thing the Independent did — send a black couple to rent an apartment.

The First Amendment is under broad attack in the United States today. More reporters will be going to jail to defend it. But the press can't defend it alone, because the First Amendment doesn't belong to the press. It belongs to the people.

The Evening Gazette

Worcester, Mass., December 21, 1972

The dilemma of John F. Lawrence, chief of the Washington bureau of the Los Angeles Times, is another chapter in the tortuous story of the free press in our free society. Lawrence was ordered jailed because he refused to surrender tape recordings of the Watergate bugging affair to a federal court judge. He remains free pending his appeal.

Lawrence and his paper maintain that the court's order is a violation of the First Amendment, which says that "Congress shall make no law . . . abridging the freedom of speech, or of the press." But the judge disagrees. He apparently bases his decision on the Supreme Court's 5-4 decision in the Caldwell case last June that the First Amendment does not give newsmen the right to conceal the identity of their sources from a grand jury. Whether a district court is the same in this regard as a grand jury is the subject of an appeal by The Los Angeles Times.

The problem is complex, and newspapers have a special interest in it. But so does the public. For all its admitted faults, the press in this country is the people's last bulwark against the tendency of officialdom to cover up the truth when it is embarrassing. An informed people is the linchpin of democracy.

In order to inform the public accurately and fully, newsmen have developed certain techniques. One of the most effective is the promise of confidentiality to informants.

It is hard to exaggerate the importance of this. For generations, newsmen have been getting stories that were printed only because they were able to promise they would not reveal their sources.

This privilege can be abused.

In our opinion, it was abused by William T. Farr of Los Angeles and his editors in covering a case connected with the Manson murders.

In that instance, the presiding judge — in an effort to guarantee the defendant a fair trial — warned the lawyers, defendants, witnesses, police and court officials against passing unauthorized and prejudicial information to the press. Despite that, Farr's paper published a lurid account by a cellmate of the young woman on trial. It was titillating and sensational, but hardly essential information. On the day the story was published, the defense lawyers moved for a mistrial.

In an effort to find out whether the defense had leaked the information to Farr in order to justify a mistrial, the judge jailed Farr. Farr is still in jail. The punishment seems excessive. But is he a martyr to "investigative reporting"? We do not think so.

However, in the long run, abuses like that one are not nearly as dangerous as a stifled press would be. Fortunately, many people outside of the media are becoming concerned about the situation. Various "shield law" proposals, to protect newsmen in the proper pursuit of their investigative reporting, are being considered in the states and at the federal level.

We do not pretend there is any easy answer. The press should not be granted any right withheld from other citizens unless an overriding principle is involved. We believe that is the case. We also believe such laws can be written to protect the interests of society, both in the proper administration of justice and from the standpoint of full information.

The Honolulu Advertiser

Honolulu, Hawaii, December 21, 1972

For a while it appeared that the Los Angeles Times' bureau chief in Washington, John F. Lawrence, was headed for jail for failing to reveal a confidential news source on a judge's demand.

But now the source, a witness in the Watergate bugging case, has released Lawrence from the confidentiality of parts of a taped interview he'd given Lawrence—and the tapes have been given to the court. Contempt charges against Lawrence will be dropped.

But with another Los Angeles Times reporter, William Farr, things are unchanged. He remains in "solitary" in the L.A. County Jail for failing to reveal a confidential source for a story during the Manson murder trial.

The increasing regularity of such cases is cause for the greatest alarm on the part of the public, the real victim. The press is an agent for the people, and when it digs into possible government corruption or into other newsworthy areas it is doing so on behalf of its readers.

It would be easy for the press to take it easy, to not take on the hard work involved in investigative reporting, to serve up a lot of pabulum and be popular with everyone. But that is not the function of the media in a democracy, and it is not what the Founding Fathers intended when they built press protection into the First Amendment.

That protection has now been increasingly eroded by the courts, and unless the situation is remedied by Congress and legislatures the public's access to information will be more and more choked off. On this subject, the editorial below is a worthy commentary.

The Salt Lake Tribune

Salt Lake City, Utah, December 24, 1972

For the fourth time in recent months a newsman has been jailed for refusing to disclose confidential information to a court or grand jury. And if the reasoning of Federal Judge John J. Sirica is accepted by judges in the future, John F. Lawrence, Washington bureau chief for the Los Angeles Times, will be but one of many reporters sent to jail for contempt of court.

The Lawrence case is somewhat different from the other three. For one thing it seems to confirm an emerging pattern of judicial harassment of the media. What else can explain Judge Sirica's ordering Lawrence to jail on the spot before an appeal could be heard?

A more disturbing thing about Judge Sirica's line of thought is that it will, if adopted by others, open the floodgates for attorneys, both prosecution and defense, to subpoena, on the slightest whim, any reporter's notes, tapes or any other confidential information.

Lawrence was held in contempt for refusing to turn over tapes of an interview conducted by two other Times reporters. The interview was with Alfred C. Baldwin III, a former FBI agent who says he witnessed part of the break-in at Democratic National

headquarters in the Watergate complex in Washington. Attorneys for one of the defendants in the Watergate break-in wanted the tapes in order to discredit Baldwin as a prosecution witness.

The Times said the tapes contained certain unpublished information which it withheld at Baldwin's request. Baldwin later released the paper from its pledge of confidence. The disputed tapes were handed over to the judge and contempt charges against Lawrence were dropped. But the basic question posed and the threat it raises remain unresolved and will rise again.

In asking Judge Sirica to quash the subpoena for the tapes, Times attorney Timothy Dyk observed that, "It is difficult to see why similar subpoenas would not be available in hundreds of other civil and criminal cases in which a potential witness has been interviewed by a newspaper. In criminal cases in particular a defense attorney has nothing to lose from subpoenaing a reporter or publisher who might possibly possess material . . . which the attorney hopes will weaken the government's case. . ."

If Judge Sirica's ruling sets a precedent then any attorney on a mere fishing expedi-

tion for possible favorable information could force any newsman to break a confidence made in good faith and in the higher interest of the public's right to know.

Judge Sirica and others of like mind justify their stand on the assumption that a reporter has the same responsibility to give all available evidence as any other citizen, promises to news sources notwithstanding, and that the demands of an open trial override the First Amendment guarantee of a free press. Newsmen respond that if they are forced to reveal their sources and confidential information, the sources will "dry up" and the public will be deprived of its right to know vital facts. They hold that in such instances the fair trial claim (but not a fair trial) must give way to the higher benefit of a well informed public.

Actually, a fair trial is not the real issue here. If the ruling in the Lawrence case prevails, the power to subpoena confidential information can, and surely will, be used in countless instances where the fair trial issue has no bearing whatever. Therein lies the greater danger, not only to a free press, but to a free people.

LEDGER-STAR

Norfolk, Va., March 15, 1973

The warning by a Justice Department official the other day as to the boomeranging danger which "shield" legislation may pose for the press w a s eminently well founded and touches a point we have also raised in opposition to this type of statute.

The argument of Assistant Attorney General Roger C. Cramton, before a House Judiciary subcommittee, was to this effect: A law specifically immunizing n e w s m e n from disclosure of their sources would bring government into the field of news-gathering in a most threatening way. It would raise the possibility of still further legislative action in a field now covered by the broad, unspecific wordage of the First Amendment—"and so, step by step you go down the road and what started out as being a privilege or a favor to the news media ends up as a species of regulation."

An examination of a subcommittee staff report prepared prior to the hearings provides at least one good intimation of the hazard Mr. Cramton refers to. For in that report the questions which the hearings are attempting to answer are enumerated and among them is this one: "Who should be entitled to claim the privilege?"

In other words, who is to be considered a newsman? What is to be the definition of the "press" under the supposedly protective coverage of a "shield" law? Obviously, the law would have to have some kind of answer. And this would put the government itself in the position of saying who is and who isn't a newsman. The law would be l a y i n g down rules for what is and what isn't "the p r e s s." Patently, this would be an intolerable authority for any branch of the government or any agent to be wielding. And this is just one type of regulation to which the door would be opened.

So entirely aside from the dubious proposition of trying to treat news people as some kind of special creatures who are not required to give evidence and perform other legal duties incumbent upon most American citizens, the "shield" approach must almost inevitably turn into a very serious undermining of press freedom itself.

San Jose Mercury

San Jose, Calif., March 16, 1973

The N i x o n administration this week reaffirmed its opposition to a comprehensive "shield l a w" protecting the confidentiality of news sources. The position is both unwise and untenable.

Assistant Atty. Gen. Robert Dixon Jr. contended in Senate hearings that, "the press is asking for a greater shield against disclosure of p u b l i c l y needed information than our system of justice has accorded even to a person who properly pleads the privilege a g a i n s t compulsory self-incrimination . . ."

That is at best a d u b i o u s proposition, but its chief shortcoming is that it begs the issue. The press is not asking for a self-serving privilege; it is seeking legislation that will implement the intent of the First Amendment to the C o n s t i t u t i o n.

The g u a r a n t e e of a free press is rendered meaningless if those who gather the news are effectively blocked from doing so by the fear of reprisal on the part of news sources. This fear has been n u r t u r e d in recent years by the abuse of the subpoena.

No reporter should be forced to choose between jail or revealing the identity of a confidential news source because a judge or a grand jury or a legislative committee has s u b p o e n a e d him. N e w s m e n should not be forced to become unwilling and u n p a i d police investigators, which all too often is what the subpoena seeks to make them.

This is bad for the p r e s s, bad for the police, and worst of all, bad for society as a whole.

Reports of corruption, malfeasance in office and similar illegal a c t i v i t i e s frequently come to light through the confidential news source, the individual who would be fired, or worse, if those on whom he has i n f o r m e d could -manage to identify him. Obviously, these individuals will not risk talking to reporters if they fear their trust will be abused.

Compelling reporters to violate a news source's trust is not only wrong it is self-defeating in the l o n g run. In such circumstances, t h e s e individuals would s i m p l y refuse to talk. The press would suffer initially, and so would the police, who wanted free investigators; the reporters w o u l d have nothing to tell.

But the people would suffer most grievously b e c a u s e they would have been d e n i e d one very real, very effective check on the men to whom they have delegated power.

At bottom, shield laws protect the public, and this is why they are needed. It is also why the arguments a g a i n s t them tend to lack substance.

Anchorage Daily Times

Anchorage, Alaska, March 17, 1973

FORTUNATELY, not a whole lot of progress is being made in Juneau with a bill that is designed to give reporters a special privilege not allowed ordinary citizens.

The idea behind the bill sounds impressive and is somewhat in tune with various tides rippling across the land in the wake of the jailing of some reporters and editors who have declined to give testimony when demanded by the courts.

Furthermore, the concept of the measure is one generally embraced by the newspaper profession as a whole — standing on constitutional guarantees of a free press and extending those provisions to cover all sorts of problems being encountered in today's troubled times.

AS WE HAVE SAID before on this subject, however, our feelings are mixed.

We don't necessarily hold that reporters are some special breed of citizens. In our view, they are citizens like everyone else — with certain and specific obligations that also are based on constitutional doctrines.

The bill now before the legislature at Juneau would make a reporter something above the ordinary man.

Not only that, it is so broad in its scope as to be almost repugnant.

It would define "privilege" as an unconditional right "granted to reporters to refuse to testify and to refuse to produce notes, recordings, photographs or other materials regarding a source of information."

And it would define a "reporter" as a person "regularly engaged in the business of collecting or writing news or articles for publication," which would mean just about anybody from a free-lance magazine writer to a professional newsman to any unqualified and inexperienced person with a vendetta, writing in any sort of publication, without restriction.

THE PRESS doesn't need this kind of shield to be effective and responsible.

Those professionals in the field of journalism rightly bear a burden and challenge to represent the public in covering — and uncovering — the events of the day. But in the course of doing that work, the reporter and the editor must likewise be. responsible members of society as a whole, answerable to the courts and the law in the same fashion as any other member of society.

Rather than be impressed by the bill introduced at Juneau in the Alaska House, we are more persuaded by the arguments presented against this sort of thing by a National Observer reporter, writing in that newspaper on Jan. 20:

"I understand the need for protecting the identity of some news sources, especially in government affairs. But I don't like it. For example: How do you, as a reader of newspapers, know that a charge made by an anonymous individual but spread across the front pages by a scoop-happy reporter is true, half-true, or totally untrue? How can the reporter himself be sure? How do we know, in fact, whether the reporter himself invented all or part of the story?

"Newsmen are forever lamenting the public's suspicion of what they see in print. I suggest that stories hung on anonymous sources do little to increase the incredibility of the press."

CERTAINLY there are problems in the area of protecting the public's right to know.

Perhaps these problems are greater today than they have ever been — and thus the challenge given to the press, and to individual reporters, is greater than ever before.

But this is not to say that in the process of protecting the right of people to know what is happening those who report it need to be placed on a pedestal above the law that applies to others.

And in the defense of the public's right to know, the press should move very cautiously and study very closely proposed laws of special privilege and special shields — and be wary of too often crying of oppressions and harassments by people in power.

Said Mr. Roberts in the National Observer:

"Freedom of the press requires vigilance, of course. But if we journalists send up the red flares too often, the public may decide those flares are a permanent part of the firmament. And then if we ever need the people on our side, we may not be able to get their attention."

THE MIAMI NEWS

Miami, Fla., March 3, 1973

Even as Sen. Sam J. Ervin Jr.'s Constitutional Rights subcommittee was hearing testimony this week on the need for a newsman's "shield law," about a dozen reporters in New York and Washington received supenas issued in behalf of the Committee to Re-elect the President.

The Committee to Re-elect the President wants to use newsmen's notes and film in civil cases growing out of the Watergate bugging affair, with which its name has been linked repeatedly.

The reader may ask, so what? If the reporters notes and tapes can help speed justice in the Watergate matter, why not make them available? The answer is that the notes and tapes may yield the names of persons who provided newsmen with information under a promise of anonymity. Their cooperation aided the newsmen, of course, but more important it provided the public with information on Watergate which might not otherwise been available, information which did far more to speed justice than anything that may emerge in the civil suits now pending.

Should the identity of those anonymous informants now be revealed, they may face serious recrimination from the administration, which was well represented on the Committee to Re-elect the President.

That's a textbook example of the problem being addressed by Sen. Ervin's subcommittee. The senators are trying to determine what kind of protection newsmen need to keep press freedom alive in the face of what The New York Times Thursday called the ". . . well-calculated effort to intimidate, discredit and legally curb the press."

There are now a half dozen bills in Congress and many more in state legislatures which would "shield" newsmen from having to reveal confidential sources of information. Apparently many legislators and congressmen, including Sen. Ervin, agree that some sort of shield legislation is necessary. But there is wide disagreement over whether or not it should be "absolute." That is, should it apply in all circumstances, or should exceptions be made in cases where the confidential information might help solve a crime or catch a traitor or so on?

The Miami News agrees with the newsmen and other interested persons who dislike shield legislation of any kind. We join the school which holds that absolute protection is implied in the First Amendment to the Constitution. It has been made clear at the Ervin hearings that this nation cannot enjoy freedom of the press while reporters are threatened, harassed and jailed by the courts and government for not revealing their news sources. Reporter after reporter has testified that information sources are drying up rather than face threats to their jobs or possibly their lives. As a consequence the public is being denied information which it may well need to perform its critical role in this democratic government.

Unfortunately the U.S. Supreme Court decided last June that this right of confidentiality does not extend to newsmen and their sources under the First Amendment.

Reluctantly therefore, we conclude that a shield law should be adopted, and that it should be as inclusive as possible. It ought to protect not only the embattled New York Times but the guy with the mimeograph machine on his kitchen table and the underground press as well, because that's what press freedom is all about.

Although Sen. Ervin seems to feel that a bill needs to be replete with limitations and definitions, we would hope they keep it simple and absolute.

A shield law that could be set aside by government or judicial fiat in cases deemed to have special importance would be self defeating. Breathes there a general, for example, who would not regard every news leak in the Pentagon as a threat to national security?

We should explain that in seeking this legislation, newsmen do not request some sort of super status in which they would be immune from the ordinary obligations of citizenship, or from the responsibilities of their job. A newsman who witnessed a crime in the ordinary conduct of his affairs would be obliged to respond to a court summons, as would any other citizen. The law of libel would still apply when people were damaged by the written word.

A proper shield law would merely spell out a right which many of us had assumed for years was implicit in the First Amendment of the Constitution.

The Evening Star and The Washington Daily News

Washington, D.C., March 6, 1973

Senator Sam Ervin of North Carolina has been converted by his own subcommittee hearings, which is something out of the ordinary on Capitol Hill. Not that he needed any conversion to the idea of protecting the confidentiality of press news sources, against a growing threat to that privilege. As always, when First Amendment rights are in jeopardy, Ervin has taken the lead in defending them. But in this case he had difficulty deciding on the proper means, and at first he tended toward a narrow remedial approach.

In fact, the bill he offered last month, as his Constitutional Rights subcommittee began hearings on the subject, was worse than nothing at all. So limited was the immunity it proposed for newsmen, against forced testimony, that its effect in some cases might have been antithetical to its purpose. And Ervin wouldn't extend its application to state and local courts, along with the federal courts. He questioned Congress' constitutional power to go beyond the federal limits with this kind of law.

Well, a remarkable transformation has taken place during the hearings. "I have changed my mind about the scope of the newsman privilege law," he said during the Tuesday session. "I certainly agree it has got to cover the whole nation." So he's whipping up a new bill that will apply to all kinds of courts and grand juries, regardless of jurisdiction. Newsmen could, under its provisions, refuse to name their sources of information who had been promised anonymity. Nor could they be compelled to produce unpublished information such as notes, tapes or photographs. They could be subpoenaed only to testify about crimes they had actually seen being committed.

This is a great improvement over his previous bill. Especially important is the fading of his doubt about the constitutionality of bringing state and local courts under a "press shield" law. No doubt the broad range of expert testimony his panel has heard was the deciding factor. Governor Nelson Rockefeller of New York got to the point of local applicability, telling how prosecutors depend heavily on the press for information about crime. The problem is that more and more prosecutors are hauling reporters before grand juries to "fish" for unpublished information, for the identities of press informants who have been promised anonymity in return for their revelations. Earlier, Rockefeller aptly stated the ultimate result of this: "I'm convinced that if reporters should ever lose the right to protect the confidentiality of their sources, serious investigative reporting will simply dry up."

We still think that a proper construction of the Constitution would afford newsmen absolute immunity from forced testimony before juries, judges, legislative committees or government agencies. This conviction is held because of the centrality of a free flow of information to the whole process of popular government. But unfortunately the Supreme Court, in a 5-4 decision last year, has construed otherwise. And Ervin doesn't believe that legislation setting up an absolute shield has the slightest chance of passage. We hope he's proved wrong as the session progresses.

But in any case, the public's right to know has been placed in serious peril by the Supreme Court decision. Congress must remove this cloud, in the largest degree possible, and the Ervin bill (still to emerge in its final form) may offer the most acceptable deviation from total immunity. Even this would run contrary to the First Amendment, but we suppose that limited protection — if not too limited — would be better than none at all. At least until the Supreme Court changes its mind.

Los Angeles Times
Los Angeles, Calif., March 4, 1973

Three central facts emerged from the testimony heard by the Senate subcommittee on constitutional rights, which held hearings last week on legislation to protect confidential news sources from compulsory disclosure:

—It is the public, not the news media, that is the victim when the flow of information is restricted by the forced revelation of confidential news sources.

—It is the public, not the news media, that would primarily benefit from legislation to protect news sources.

—Such protection should be absolute, and should apply to the states as well as to the federal government.

Immunity from compelled disclosure should be absolute for two reasons: Any law providing less than full immunity would be subject to judicial interpretations that would render it ineffective. The privilege should be absolute because the public's right to be informed about the operations of government is an absolute precondition of self-government.

Two misapprehensions should be cleared away. First, complete immunity would not create a favored class of newsmen or remove them from the obligations of citizenship that they share with all other citizens; the purpose would be to protect their function as a conduit of information on which the life and vigor of our society depend. Second, the request for complete protection of this function is neither unprecedented nor extreme. To the contrary, the extreme position is taken by those who assert that the First Amendment can be abridged and the public can be denied information at the caprice of any agency of government. Until the recent, authoritarian trend developed in the courts on this issue, it had always been accepted that the First Amendment provided the protection now sought by statute.

The First Amendment became the first because the liberties it enumerates, like freedom of speech and of the press, are basic to all other constitutional rights. No judge, no prosecutor nor any other public official would directly attack the First Amendment, but its guarantees are under a powerful assault just the same.

Some courts, including the Supreme Court, have sanctioned evasions of the First Amendment that are more dangerous than a frontal assault on freedom because they are thrust forward in the name of justice.

The Supreme Court last June, ruling that grand juries can compel newsmen to reveal their sources, encouraged a steadily rising number of similar decisions in lower courts. Such decisions, in effect, convert the news media into an investigative arm of the government. Not only the government but defense lawyers have been inspired to look on the investigative and reporting functions of the press as their own preserve. Subpoenas fly from every direction.

The malign effect of forced disclosure was spread on the record by many witnesses before the Senate subcommittee. William F. Thomas, the editor of this newspaper, told the subcommittee, "In the past few years, The Times has been served with more than 30 subpoenas and threatened with more than 50 others. So far we have successfully resisted all of them, but the cost has been high." The cost, he said, would be ruinous to smaller newspapers. "So what happens? They stop printing stories that could cause them legal problems, and sources—

clearly perceiving that all this means their confidentiality rests upon an increasingly frail reed—stop giving information to all of us."

Without the aid of confidential news sources, this newspaper would have been unable to gather and reveal information that disclosed corrupt practices in city and county government in recent years. Today such sources are dwindling because of the subpoena threat that the courts hold over the press. "If our known sources are refusing to talk to us for admitted fear of disclosure," Thomas told the subcommittee, "we wonder how many unknown sources just stay away, or how many others plead ignorance when the honest explanation is fear."

The fear is justified. When confidential sources are revealed, the source, not the wrongdoer, is often punished. An exposé of brutality against mentally retarded children in a Tennessee state hospital led to the dismissal of a hospital secretary when angry officials learned that she was the origin of part of the information.

Forced disclosure is invoked in the name of justice, but was justice served by the discharge of the hospital secretary? Is justice served when an honest public official, in fear of losing his job, fails to reveal corruption in government? Is justice served when an honest businessman, vulnerable to retaliation, decides not to disclose his knowledge of corrupt practices?

It is a fallacious view, and historically inaccurate, that the administration of justice requires testimony under any circumstances. The doctor-patient and the attorney-client relationships are protected, and illegally obtained evidence is excluded in the long-range interest of justice. Compelled testimony by newsmen will have two certain consequences: The public will be deprived of information, and reporters, with their sources blocked by fear of disclosure, will soon have nothing to testify about. These attacks on the First Amendment can be thwarted only by complete immunity from compelled revelation of news sources. One qualification, the exclusion of the protection in defamation cases, appears reasonable, but the exception would destroy the purpose of the law. Most investigative reporting involves the publication of defamatory matter, and the qualification would provide an easily available means of identification of the news source and subject the source to retribution. In a libel action, failure of a newspaper to reveal its sources would impair its defense. That is a sufficient check against irresponsible publication.

The need for Congress to enact a press shield law is underscored by the particular nature of the present crisis between the media and the courts. The judiciary has been a bulwark against encroachments on the First Amendment by the legislative and executive branches. But, as Robert S. Warren, an attorney for The Times, said to the subcommittee, the courts have been unwilling to restrain their own power when that power collides with freedom of speech and of the press. The legislative branch, restrained by the courts from eroding constitutional freedoms, must in turn restrain judges who are unwilling to concede that their authority must also be exercised within those same constitutional limits.

The battle is not primarily between the courts or any other government body and the press. It is between the people and their government. The stakes are high. They are no less than the right of Americans to govern themselves. A people deprived of information become the subjects, not the rulers, of their government.

The Greenville News
Greenville, S.C.
March 4, 1973

The proposition that Congress should pass a news media "shield" law permitting reporters to withhold sources of information from grand juries poses a constitutional conflict which may be unsolvable.

An absolute privilege law would comply with the First Amendment ban on laws abridging freedom of the press. But it would run into the legitimate functions of the grand jury, which also is required by the Bill of Rights.

A qualified shield law, granting immunity only in some instances would have the reverse effect. It would automatically violate the expressed words of the Constitution that Congress shall pass "no law" abridging the freedom of the press.

In addition, any shield law, qualified or unqualified, applying only to news personnel would run up against the "equal protection" clause of the Constitution, because it would give reporters legal privileges denied to other citizens of the United States.

All things considered the best way for the news media to safeguard the First Amendment is to keep Congress completely out of the picture. "No law" means "no law," and the press should rely on that.

Better for the press to fight this thing on a case by case basis than to risk erosion of the First Amendment under the guise of congressional protection. The free press has many weapons and can protect itself more effectively than any branch of government.

AKRON BEACON JOURNAL

Akron, Ohio, February 27, 1973

The public's right to know may be better served by dropping the current efforts toward some Federal law defending and defining a newsman's right to refuse to tell a court where he got his information, or what he was told or saw or judged that he didn't print or air.

The problem is the limits of what is practically possible.

★

This "confidentiality right" is of real value to the public. It helps bring to public exposure misbehavior in public office, improper court and law enforcement procedure, victimization of consumers and many other kinds of crime and abuse of public trust.

Often the first step toward their exposure has been a confidential tip to a reporter.

Somebody has been moved by indignation or anger or spite to spill what he knows or suspects — but at the same time has been so afraid of reprisal that he would talk only if he felt sure the reporter would never reveal his source.

Knowledge that the reporter may later face choice between jail and breaking his promise of confidentiality could add enough to the calculated risks in a potential tipster's mind to cause him to hold his tongue.

What is thus denied the press is also denied to police and courts. The whole public loses.

★

Last year the Supreme Court refused to overturn New York Times reporter Earl Caldwell's contempt citation and punishment for refusal to break confidentiality in answering grand jury questions about his knowledge of Black Panther activities in California.

The reasoning, in brief, was that a newspaper reporter has no special right or privilege beyond that of any other citizen to refuse to testify.

Since then several other reporters and one historian have been jailed for contempt in cases where the central issue has been the same thing.

★

In the Caldwell ruling, the Supreme Court invited Congress to reconsider "shield" legislation establishing a statutory area of privilege for newsmen — spelling out a clearly specified kind of immunity from any questioning that might too greatly invade proper confidentiality.

In a heartening display of concern for the public's right to know, more than 25 bills variously defining newsmen's confidentiality privilege have been framed for congressional consideration.

It is in the discussion and debate on the relative merits and shortcomings of these that the problem of what is practically possible has become apparent. A sober look at this suggests that newsmen and public alike may be better off with no new law than with the most that is likely of passage and if surviving court testing.

★

Sen. Sam Ervin of North Carolina, viewed by many as Congress' foremost constitutional scholar and most jealous and astute defender of constitutional rights, has pared the problem to its core.

The chance that Congress will pass an "absolute privilege" bill of the ironclad type favored by the American Newspaper Publishers Association is nearly zero, says Ervin. Doubts about the news media run high enough among lawmakers, he says, to make it virtually certain that even if such a bill squeaked through the Senate it would fail in the House.

If somehow it overcame these obstacles and survived the probable presidential veto, it would still face a strong chance of being overturned the first time it reached a test in the Supreme Court.

★

To hope for such a law is to dream. What, then, asks Ervin, of the "qualified privilege" bills that are real and practical possibilities? Are they better or worse than nothing?

Each defines press freedom more narrowly than it has been defined by the courts in the absence of statutory law.

Further, by the very act of setting up specified definition in what they say, such projected laws would lay the whole field open to almost unlimited restrictive court interpretation in the things they **don't** say. It would become legitimate to assume that what is not legislatively said was not legislative intended.

★

It may be, then, that the best answer is not new national law at all.

It may instead be simply for the news media to go on, without new law, doing their job as vigorously and as aggressively as they are able — and fighting it out on constitutional grounds when one of their people comes a cropper with a judge or even a Supreme Court with reservations a b o u t "too much privilege for the press."

The Honolulu Advertiser

Honolulu, Hawaii, March 5, 1973

There are legitimate fears that many in the media will go to jail unless Congress and state legislatures pass laws against requiring newsmen to disclose sources of confidential information.

Some already have been put behind bars for refusing to reveal who gave them information on such a private basis for use in developing news reports. More will go in the interest of not breaking faith with sources who for various reasons can't be revealed.

STILL, THE PUBLIC should be even more concerned because a number in the media will choose not to put themselves in a position where they might have to go to jail.

Under present conditions, the best way for newsmen to stay out of trouble and jail is to not accept confidential information.

That involves taking the handouts of government and others and skipping entire stories or important bits of information which, because they are adverse, are often provided newsmen on a private basis by persons who have reason to fear retaliation in some form.

THE CONTROVERSIAL 5-4 U.S. Supreme Court ruling of last June to the effect newsmen have no inherent constitutional right to protect confidential news sources has already led some sources to stop providing important information.

There has also been an element of economic intimidation. The editor of the Los Angeles Times last week testified that his newspaper has spent over $200,000, most of it in the past year, to resist more than 30 subpoenas seeking to force its reporters to reveal news sources.

While the Times is affluent, he noted that the threat of costly court action can lead other papers to simply stop printing stories that might cause them legal problems over confidential sources.

THIS IS THE kind of a problem that is not apparent to the public at once. After all, newspapers can fill up their pages and the broadcast media their programs with plenty of less controversial "n e w s." Advertising revenue will continue.

There will, however, be a deterioration in the quality of the news and in information the public has a right to know in making its judgment on public affairs.

The Supreme Court provided a way out by saying Congress and the state legislatures could pass laws giving newsmen the right to protect the confidence of their news sources. That is all that is being sought now in Hawaii and around the nation.

THE KANSAS CITY STAR
Kansas City, Mo., January 5, 1974

A group of reporters and editors has objected to the American Telephone & Telegraph Co.'s practice of disclosing to government investigators the records of their telephone calls. A.T.&T. replied that it was required by statute to reveal the information "upon a valid subpoena or on demand pursuant to lawful processes." This practice is an example of how easily the privacy of journalists can be invaded.

The phrase "demand pursuant to lawful processes" is the danger. This really means that records can be divulged on written request by prosecutors or police of command rank. As a practical matter it could lead to identification of news sources.

A.T.&T.'s position raises the question of the protection that individuals are entitled to under the Constitution. The Fourth Amendment prohibits unreasonable searches and seizures. The Bank Secrecy Act brings up similar issues. A federal court has ruled that the law is unconstitutional because it allows the government access of information that should be a private matter. The case has been appealed to the U.S. Supreme Court. Legislation is now before Congress that would require advance notification of bank customers when the government wants to check records.

The protesting newsmen have threatened court action if A.T.&T. continues to reveal records of journalists' calls.

Admittedly the work of governmental probers could be made far easier if they could tap into the investigative talents of the journalism profession. But sometimes investigations by government can be more beneficial to politicians than to the public. The point is, of course, that government, and the politicians who run it, can have a stake of its own in investigations. That could be detrimental to the public.

The press should be free to investigate on its own without this force looking over its shoulder. The disclosure of such records is a short cut that threatens not only the press but the public's right to a free flow of information unfettered by governmental interference.

Arkansas Gazette.
Little Rock, Ark., January 7, 1974

The wire service advises that a "majority" of news media organizations are in general agreement with a House subcommittee on a bill to protect newsmen in protecting the sources of their information. In actuality, we have doubts that majority sentiment in the newspaper, radio and television businesses does favor the so-called "shield" bill, but, in any case, no one speaks for the news media as a class because under the free press concept every newspaper or radio or television station speaks for itself.

As for the Arkansas Gazette, we take specific exception to the so-called "shield" law. Not because its purpose is not worthy but because, in our view, the newspaperman's right to withhold the identities of his sources is a constitutional right which is not subject to congressional purview, anyway. What the Congress might give — and the legislation "agreed upon" is not absolute — the Congress might take away. It is our own view that each attempt to force disclosure should be fought in each case in the courts, on constitutional grounds, and that Congress should stay out of the fray.

San Jose Mercury
San Jose, Calif., January 4, 1974

The protection of confidential news sources is essential if a free flow of information to the public is to continue, particularly about the inner workings of government.

Last month, 10 news organizations and the Reporters Committee for Freedom of the Press asked American Telephone & Telegraph to halt the practice of disclosing records of reporters' telephone calls.

AT&T argues that it is required by law "to submit such records to government agencies upon valid subpoena or on demand pursuant to lawful processes."

Lawful processes turn out to be nothing more than a written request from prosecutors or police officers of command rank for a record of telephone calls.

AT&T says it does not care to place itself into "controversies between government authorities and private citizens." But in supplying such records it does precisely that.

This is one more example of the snooper gone berserk. In an effort to determine just how berserk, the news organizations have asked the telephone company to disclose all instances in which records of calls were requested in the last five years. This is a reasonable request.

Let's air the activities of the probers, and correct this undue intrusion into the gathering of news.

The Des Moines Register
Des Moines, Iowa, January 2, 1974

The American Telephone and Telegraph Co. (AT&T) has rejected a request from news organizations that it stop telling the government about telephone calls by reporters. AT&T claims it is required by law to honor such requests.

The phone company said it wanted to stay out of disputes between government and private groups and therefore wouldn't even give news organizations notice when their phone records are being disclosed.

The use of phone records provides a back-door method of breaking down the confidential relationship between a reporter and his news source. When a journalist interviews a news source, and the source requests that his identity be kept secret, the pledge of confidentiality ordinarily suffices to encourage the source to provide information.

Most reporters would rather go to jail than break a confidentiality pledge. An examination of the reporter's phone records, however, can make the pledge meaningless by revealing his contacts and pointing the finger at the likely source.

The only sure way to safeguard news sources under a system in which the government can secretly obtain phone records of reporters is for newsmen to avoid use of the telephone or never to use their home or office phones when speaking to someone who may want to remain unnamed.

Such protective measures are appropriate for police states, not for a country that values a free press and the free flow of information to the public.

Fortunately, most news sources are willing to be identified, and reporters have little occasion to use information from unnamed sources. But every now and then it becomes necessary to protect the name of an informant. This happens most often in cases of official wrongdoing — such as the Watergate cover-up — and it is these cases in which the public has the greatest stake in being informed.

It is unthinkable for the government to seek — and the phone company to provide — records showing phone calls between a psychiatrist and his patients. Such records would breach both the privacy of the individuals and the confidential relationship between patient and therapist.

It ought to be just as unthinkable for the phone records of news organizations to be subject to government snooping.

Los Angeles Times

Los Angeles, Calif., January 13, 1974

With the best of intentions, some defenders of the freedom of the press have proposed a newspapermen's shield law that we must oppose.

It was no accident that the First Amendment to the Constitution dealt with the great freedoms—freedom of religion, the right to petition government, freedom of speech and freedom of the press. Without the latter, the others would be sharply limited. Their full exercise depends upon unfettered communication beyond the church, beyond the meeting hall, beyond the office of a government official receiving a petition. Freedom of effective communications—which means communication with the public—is the freedom we must have to protect and support all our liberties.

Yet this freedom, which sets the United States apart from most other nations, has always been under attack. It is often an affront to those in authority, from the village school board member to the occupants of the White House going back to George Washington. It is often an affront to private institutions, which, nurtured in freedom, see no contradiction in the denial of freedom to others.

Among the staunchest defenders of a free press have been the courts. They have thwarted attacks on the press by the other branches of government and their agencies. They have defended the press from assaults by private groups. Great judges like Oliver Wendell Holmes, Charles Evans Hughes and Hugo Black have left an eloquent legacy to the press.

But now an anomaly has arisen. In recent years, the sharpest assaults on this First Amendment freedom and its instrument, the press, have come from the courts. The attack is not direct, but its consequences have been substantial and are potentially lethal. It is difficult to repel because it is advanced in the name of preserving another vital constitutional protection: the right of every man to a fair trial.

The conflict over this issue has developed between the courts and the press because many judges have interpreted this right—and the power of courts, grand juries and other public bodies to compel testimony—in a way that has undercut the First Amendment.

The attacks have come from several directions. One is the unprecedented assertion of authority by some judges to impose censorship on proceedings in open court. Another is the proliferation of gag orders imposed by judges against defense and prosecution attorneys, court personnel and law enforcement officers.

And two years ago the U.S. Supreme Court struck a hard blow at a vital element in news gathering by ruling that a reporter has no constitutional right to protect his confidential relationship with news sources. Dissenting Associate Justice Potter Stewart correctly emphasized that the decision would have the effect of converting the press into something it was never intended to be: an arm of the government.

The court held that reporters can be compelled to reveal confidential information and disclose its source to grand juries, but the thrust to subvert the independence of the press is not limited to that area. The news media in recent years have been showered with subpoenas from both prosecutors and defense lawyers in both civil and criminal cases. In the past few years, this newspaper alone has been served or threatened with some 80 subpoenas related to litigation.

An independent press—independent of judicial censorship, secure from the power of courts to compel testimony that breaks down the confidentiality of news sources—is indispensable to democratic government. Associate Justice Byron R. White said in the 1972 decision that newsmen should not have an immunity from compelled testimony that other citizens do not have. That is a malign interpretation of the issue. Newsmen seek no protection for themselves but protection for their function. A wiser Supreme Court said nearly 40 years ago that the purpose of the First Amendment "is to preserve an untrammeled press . . . and the suppression or abridgment of the publicity afforded by a free press cannot be regarded otherwise than with grave concern."

Since the 1972 ruling, many bills have been proposed in Congress offering newsmen qualified degrees of protection against forced disclosure. Among the leading bills is one approved by a House judiciary subcommittee. Under this legislation, no newsman could be required to disclose confidential information or its source to a federal or state grand jury or in any pretrial hearing. But a trial judge could require disclosure under certain conditions. The party seeking the information would have to show that it was indispensable to the prosecution or defense, that it could not be obtained from any other source and, finally, that it served a compelling public need.

The Times and other newspapers have contended with these "certain conditions" before, and rarely have they protected us against attempts by courts, defendants or prosecutors to enlist us in their causes.

The bill is supported by Rep. Robert W. Kastenmeier (D-Wis.), chairman of the subcommittee, and by others whose devotion to freedom of the press is unquestioned. A majority of news media organizations favor it on the basis that it offers newsmen protection they do not have now under court rulings.

The Times, however, opposes the bill. It protects —up to a point—the confidential relationship that must exist between the press and its news sources, but in the end simply gives the game away. It does this by conceding to the courts the authority to compel a newsman to betray his news source. Such a concession will give, for the first time, statutory sanction to the authoritarian trend to annex the press as an agent of the court, the prosecution and defense in civil as well as criminal cases. Confidential sources will not fail to understand the implications of this.

If reporters can be forced to testify for or against one side or the other in court, the ability of the press to continue its function as an independent gatherer of news will be gravely diminished. One example of many should suffice. During the street demonstrations of recent years, reporters and photographers witnessed crimes by both demonstrators and police. Had newsmen been forced to testify against one side or the other, they would thenceforth have been denied access to either, and the independent status of the press would have been undermined. And for what gain? It is a rare case that depends solely on the testimony of a newsman. Even in that rare circumstance, what would be the price? The price would be impairment and eventually destruction of the basic duty of the press to inform the public.

In the absence of legislation providing absolute protection for the press against compelled testimony, the issue must be fought case by case under the First Amendment's guarantee. The short-range chances of success may not be good, but the effort must be unremitting and it can be won.

The sanctions imposed on the press are penalties imposed on this nation against a tradition of two centuries of freedom under an unwritten, absolute privilege that was commonly thought to be essential to an effective press.

The battle can be lost before it hardly has begun, if the press accepts a solution that reduces the First Amendment to a simple admonition that judges can ignore at will.

FORT WORTH STAR-TELEGRAM
Fort Worth, Tex., January 8, 1974

The majority of news media organizations are reported to be satisfied with a new bill, being put together in a House judiciary subcommittee, to protect newsmen from being forced to disclose confidential information or its sources.

If so, the news media are making a mistake.

The bill looks like an acceptable "shield" for press freedom on paper. It provides that no newsman could be forced to reveal information and sources to a federal or state grand jury or any pretrial proceeding. In an actual trial, such disclosures could be required only if the court could be persuaded that the information was indispensable to the prosecution or defense of the case, that it could not be obtained from any other source, and that there was a compelling public interest in disclosure.

Under close scrutiny, holes appear in this shield even as it stands. For in the skillful maneuverings that take place in the courtroom, it might be possible in almost any case to convince a judge that the desired information did meet the three-fold requirement for inclusion in the non-shielded category.

Further, it must be recognized that the bill stands little chance of retaining its present form until it becomes law, and that it would be subject to repeated amendment after enactment.

The Texas Legislature provided a perfect illustration of this danger during the last session. A state bill that originally seemed to offer reasonable protection for news sources acquired so many exclusions and exceptions during the legislative process that not even the enemies of the so-called "newsmen's privilege" wanted it passed.

The Star-Telegram said then, and affirms now, that the news media would be better off without a "shield law," since any such shield would be subject to being shot so full of holes that it would provide only a false illusion of protection.

Newsmen would be wise to go on insisting that the First Amendment to the Constitution does offer the protection they must have in order to assure a free flow of truthful information to the public. Perhaps eventually a future Supreme Court will reverse the high court ruling denying that such protection now exists in the Constitution. Meanwhile, the media can hopefully rely on most judges to recognize the danger that forcing newsmen to disclose confidential information and sources could pose to freedom of the press, whether the Supreme Court does or not.

The Charleston Gazette
Charleston, S.C., January 4, 1974

A three-judge federal court in Mobile correctly has struck down a new Alabama law that would have trampled on First Amendment freedoms. The law, tacked onto a sweeping ethics bill, would have required reporters to disclose all sources of income before they could file stories on state politics or cover the workings of the Alabama legislature.

Objection to the law should have been obvious, even to the Alabama legislature and to Gov. George C. Wallace, who signed it. It would have set up the state in the business of saying who could and who could not be reporters. One of the many roles played by the press in a free country is to maintain a watch over governmental affairs. If the press were to become enslaved to governmental licensing it could not perform that vital function.

THE MILWAUKEE JOURNAL
Milwaukee, Wis., March 10, 1974

Polls show that a sizable majority of citizens frown on forcing a reporter — under power of subpena and pain of jail — to reveal his confidential sources. Instinctively, people grasp that confidentiality of this kind is essential to investigative reporting, exposure of corruption, the free flow of information.

The US Supreme Court, in holding that a reporter has no constitutional right to conceal the identity of sources, pointedly declared that Congress and state legislatures had the power to give newsmen statutory shields "as narrow or as broad as deemed necessary." But the debate has bogged down over the type of shield.

While some lawmakers want none at all, some advocate absolute immunity for the press. Many others, trying to balance the needs of the press and those of grand juries, courts and other bodies, favor some kind of limited shield. The press itself has been less than unified. Although most journalists agree that unqualified protection is the best answer, some argue that no legislation is better than a partial shield. The latter view reflects a hope that the Supreme Court might someday reverse itself.

Now, a tolerable compromise is emerging from a House subcommittee headed by Rep. Kastenmeier (D-Wis.). The bill rests on the realistic assumptions that the high court is unlikely to change its mind and Congress is unlikely to pass an absolute shield. Thus the aim is to provide substantial protection without destroying chance of legislative survival.

The bill offers two levels of safeguard. Before grand juries, legislative committees and other nontrial bodies, a reporter would have an absolute shield against compelled testimony about confidential information or its sources. But in an actual courtroom trial the protection would lessen. Disclosure could be required if the information was shown to be "indispensable" to the prosecution or defense, could not be obtained by "alternate means" and, finally, if "an overriding public interest" was served.

For a newsman, this is far from perfect. Source revelation would still be a problem under some circumstances — and this could make all sources more hesitant. But presently reporters are virtually without any protection. The Kastenmeier bill is much better than other limited shield proposals. It at least allows a reporter to resist grand jury fishing expeditions, a major trouble today, and confines forced disclosure to the narrow area of an actual trial.

Given the realities confronting newsmen, the bill is worthy of support. It would be an umbrella against a shower of subpenas at both the federal and state level. It would make it far more difficult to convert the press into an investigatory arm of government. It would be a gain both for journalists and for the public they serve.

The Fairness & Equal Time Doctrines

Limited monopolies licensed by the federal government were inevitable with the growth of commercial broadcasting. The alternative to official allocation of the air waves is chaos. The Federal Communications Commission (FCC) was created by Congress in 1934 to license broadcasting stations to the exclusive use of certain wavelengths and channels within limited areas. In return for this exclusive license, the station promises to assume certain responsibilities in the public interest. Stations are required to provide equal time for spokesmen representing conflicting opinions on public issues and to apply a "fairness doctrine" that grants free air time for responsible persons to reply to programs broadcast on controversial issues, if the station or network fails to adequately represent the conflicting points of view. The interpretation of these two doctrines has produced a great deal of controversy. The equal-time doctrine has developed into a particularly thorny issue in recent years as Presidents have commandeered the broadcasting media to speak directly to the nation.

Access to the airwaves during election campaigns is determined largely by the ability to buy time. The evident power of the broadcast media to reach mass audiences and the controlled safety of paid advertising has led many candidates to use paid television commercials as the key element in their campaigns. The high price of air time has rapidly inflated the cost of running for major public office. This, in turn, has led to abuses in political fund raising and to attempts to limit the amounts candidates for national office could spend on paid advertising.

'Fairness doctrine' upheld. In a 7–0 decision (Justice William O. Douglas was absent), the Supreme Court June 9, 1969 upheld the constitutionality of the Federal Communications Commission's "fairness doctrine." The court said the doctrine, which required broadcasters to air both sides of important issues, "enhances rather than abridges the freedoms of speech and press protected by the First Amendment." Justice White, who wrote the majority opinion, said: "It is the right of the viewers and listeners, not the right

of the broadcasters, which is paramount." The broadcast industry had argued that the doctrine prevented broadcasters from speaking out strongly on issues.

Two rules of the doctrine had come under fire: one requiring stations to give free time to any person or group whose character, honesty or integrity had been attacked over the station's facilities (the "personal attack" rule); and another stipulating that a station which endorsed a political candidate had to give his opponent the opportunity to reply (the "political editorial" rule). The court upheld the FCC order to station WGCB in Red Lion, Pa. to give free time to Fred J. Cook, a liberal writer, to reply to attacks made by the Rev. Billy James Hargis, a right-wing radio preacher. The court also reversed a decision of the 7th U.S. Circuit Court of Appeals in Chicago, which had upheld the assertion of the Radio and Television New Directors Association and 10 broadcasting companies that the "fairness doctrine" made broadcasters afraid to express their views.

FCC Rejects Complaint vs. TV. The Federal Communications Commission (FCC) Nov. 20 unanimously adjudged as fair television commentary following President Nixon's Nov. 3 Vietnam address. Mrs. J. R. Paul of Houston, Tex. had written to the agency to complain that "the newsmen were very one-sided in their post-talk analysis of the speech." In a letter of reply, signed by Chairman Dean Burch and endorsed by the entire commission, the FCC held that the TV commentaries in question had met its "fairness" standard and were constitutionally protected and that, therefore, no action was warranted on the complaints of bias.

Free time provided for Democratic rebuttal. The three major television networks provided free time Feb. 8, 1970 to 23 Congressional Democrats for an hour-long national TV program to rebut President Nixon's State of the Union address. The program was cast in the format of interviews with citizens in Los

Angeles, Detroit, Houston and Washington, D.C.

(Sen. Edmund S. Muskie (Me.), who participated in the program had expressed concern Feb. 1 that President Nixon's increasing and "skillful" use of TV could "build momentum on an issue or on a confrontation with the Congress ... that's very difficult to offset" and could lead to "an imbalance of forces in the political system.")

TV campaign spending curb. The Senate, by a 58–27 vote April 14, approved a bill to limit campaign spending on political broadcasts by candidates for federal office. The legislation also would reduce the cost of such broadcasts and repeal the Federal Communications Act provision requiring the allotment of "equal time" to all candidates, minor as well as major party candidates.

The spending limit would restrict TV and radio promotion spending to no more than 7¢ for every vote cast for the office in the previous election. It was adopted by a partisan 50–35 vote with the Republicans in opposition. Under the amendment, each presidential ticket in 1972 could spend $5.1 million for broadcast advertising, based on the 73 million-vote 1968 election. In 1968, the Republicans spent $12.6 million for these purposes, the Democrats $7.1 million.

To lower the cost of such broadcasts, the legislation would limit charges to the lowest rates given large commercial advertisers. Reductions of 35%–50% would be anticipated from such a provision.

Repeal of the "equal time" requirement would permit the offer of free network broadcast time to presidential and vice presidential candidates.

Democrats ask access to TV. The Democratic Party asked the Federal Communications Commission (FCC) May 19 for a ruling that broadcasters cannot refuse to sell time to "responsible entities such as the Democratic National Committee" for fund solicitation. The action, a request for a declaratory ruling by the FCC, arose from a denial earlier in the year of network advertising time to the Democratic committee even when it offered to pay commercial rates.

Joseph A. Califano Jr., the committee's general counsel, asked in a brief filed with the FCC: "Are the public airwaves—the most powerful communications media in our democracy—to be used to solicit funds for soap, brassieres, deodorants and mouthwashes and not to solicit funds to enhance the exchange of ideas?" In support of its request, the committee cited a 1969 Supreme Court ruling on the public's right of access to the airways when the court, under the FCC "fairness doctrine," upheld the right of response to personal attack. Although the court ruling did not involve the sale of commercial time, the Democratic petition quoted the court's opinion that a broadcaster had no right to "monopolize a radio frequency to the exclusion of his fellow citizens."

The issue arose when the committee's request for commercial time to raise funds was denied in January by the Columbia Broadcasting System (CBS). The National Broadcasting Co. (NBC) initially agreed to sell time for the Democrats' proposed half-hour program, but the network and committee could not agree on a choice of evenings. The committee did not press negotiations with the third major network, the American Broadcasting Co. (ABC). A CBS spokesman said March 21 that the refusal was based on network policies that "do not permit the sale of time for presenting currently controversial points of view except during electoral campaigns." In response to the Democrats' petition to the FCC, CBS said in a statement May 20 that a broadcaster's ability to conform to the "fairness doctrine" would be frustrated "if there were imposed upon him an obligation . . . to sell time to partisans."

The Democratic committee also had run up against network policy when it requested free time to reply to President Nixon's televised addresses to the nation. Democratic National Chairman Lawrence F. O'Brien had requested national television coverage of his own May 9 reply to the President's Cambodian policy, but the request was denied by NBC and CBS. ABC carried O'Brien's speech in its "news" coverage, but the network said it had no obligation to do so under the FCC "fairness doctrine." The committee's May 19 petition to the FCC made no request for access to free broadcast time and dealt only with paid commercial time.

The issue of President Nixon's use of the airwaves was raised, however, in a petition to the FCC made public May 25. The action—filed by a group of Yale University (New Haven, Conn.) students and professors and leaders of the Black Coalition in New Haven—argued that Nixon's access to the television networks violated the commission's "fairness doctrine" since opponents of the President's policies in Southeast Asia "do not have access to the same wide audience during a substantial bloc of uninterrupted time." The group, the Committee for Fair Broadcasting of Controversial Issues, contended that the President used free network time to politically justify his Vietnam policies.

In a related development, Sen. J. William Fulbright (D, Ark.), chairman of the Senate Foreign Relations Committee, said June 2 that if the constitutional balance of power were to survive among the branches of government, Congress must have the same access to television network time as President Nixon and President Johnson. Declaring that "communication is power," Fulbright said, "television has done as much to expand the powers of the president . . . as would a constitutional amendment formally abolishing the co-equality of the three branches of government." He asked for legislation that would require the networks to make time available to the President or Congress whenever it was requested.

FCC backs campaign broadcast reform. FCC Chairman Dean Burch, in testimony before a House Commerce Committee subcommittee June 2, endorsed the broad outline of legislation that would cut the cost of television advertising for political candidates and repeal the "equal time" requirement for presidential and vice presidential contests. In a statement substantially supported by the seven-man commission, Burch said the provision in the Senate version of the bill that would limit the amounts spent by candidates for radio and TV advertisement was "appropriate," and that Congress should set the specific limits.

Burch backed the Senate bill's provision to require broadcasters to sell reduced-rate time to candidates for federal offices, but he said the commission believed such reduced rates should apply to ad time sold to local and state candidates as well. Burch recommended that the "equal time" requirement be lifted only for major party candidates or for the nominees of significant minor parties in order to "promote the widest and most penetrating airing possible of views and issues in an election." The Senate version of the bill would repeal the "equal time" requirement for all presidential or vice presidential candidates.

CBS offers Democrats free time. The Columbia Broadcasting System (CBS) said June 22 that it would offer free television and radio time on a regular basis to the principal political party in opposition.

On the same day, the Democrats petitioned the Federal Communications Commission (FCC) to guarantee "responsible persons or entities" who opposed a president's policies free television network time to answer a televised presidential presentation. In another development, in response to an earlier Democratic Party petition to the FCC, the American Broadcasting Co. (ABC) offered in a letter released June 15 to relax its rules against selling time for political fund solicitation.

CBS position—CBS's free time offer to the Democrats came in a telegram by Frank Stanton, the company's president, to Lawrence F. O'Brien, chairman of the Democratic National Committee. Stanton said CBS wanted to "maintain fairness and balance in the treatment of public issues, including the disparity between presidential appearances and the opportunities available to the principal opposition party."

Stanton also offered to let the party buy radio and TV time to raise funds outside the normal campaign months after the national nominating conventions. However, he said CBS rejected O'Brien's proposal in his May 19 FCC petition that the networks be compelled to sell time to the opposition party. Stanton also said CBS recognized that the president had "certain constitutional duties whose performance is enhanced by his ability to communicate directly with the people."

Acting on a June 18 request by Senate Majority Leader Mike Mansfield (D, Mont.), Stanton said the Democrats could have 25 minutes of free TV time to respond to President Nixon's June 17 economic message. Also on June 22, ABC offered the Democrats free response time. Julian Goodman, president of the National Broadcasting Co. (NBC), had been the first to grant Mansfield's request. Goodman had said June 18 that the Democrats could have from 12:30 to 12:55 p.m. June 24 at no charge. He had said NBC believed "it is in the national interest to provide an opportunity for Congressional spokesmen to discuss these issues."

Democrats' June 22 petition—In its petition for guaranteed free TV time to answer the President's policies, the Democratic National Committee asked the FCC to add a provision to a rule under consideration that would require broadcasters to give opponents opportunity to comment after presenting one side of a controversial issue.

Taking the position that presidential pronouncements almost by definition covered "controversial issues," the Democrats asked the commission to add the following: "When a network or a licensee broadcasts a presentation by the president of the United States of a viewpoint on a controversial issue of public importance, that network or licensee has an affirmative obligation to seek out responsible persons or entities with significant contrasting viewpoints on the controversial issue and afford them equal opportunites to present their views."

Echoing an earlier statement by Sen. J. William Fulbright (D, Ark.), the Democrats said in a brief to the FCC that "the combination of the president of the United States, the most powerful individual in the free world, and television, undoubtedly the most effective communications medium ever devised by man, has an impact on public opinion that is difficult to exaggerate."

ABC on sale of ad time—ABC offered to let major political parties buy broadcast time to solicit funds or to take positions on controversial issues. The company, in a June 10 letter to the FCC released June 15, said, however, that except for special public interest considerations, "we proposed to continue our general policy against the sale of time for controversial issue programs and announcements and solicitations for funds." In answer to an FCC request for a position on the Democrat's May 19 petition, Everett H. Erlick, ABC general counsel, said "because the strength and viability of the major political parties are vitally important, ABC would be prepared, consistent with its other obligations, to accept such orders for time from major political parties as can be accommodated on a reasonable basis."

FCC revokes radio licenses. The Federal Communications Commission voted 6-0 July 2 to take away the licenses of two radio stations in Media, Pa., both operated by Brandywine-Main Line Radio Inc., owned by Faith Theological Seminary. The commission said the licensee of WXUR and WXUR-FM had "simply ignored its plain duty to the public" under the "fairness doctrine" to give time for "opposing viewpoints on controversial issues."

Commissioner Robert E. Lee said it was the first time the FCC refused to renew licenses because of "fairness doctrine" violations. He said it was a "landmark case" which he expected eventually to be settled by the Supreme Court.

The Rev. Carl McIntyre, a fundamentalist preacher, was board chairman of the seminary that owned the licensee. The FCC said it had received complaints from "a number of civic and religious groups" in the Philadelphia area about WXUR programs featuring conservative spokesmen. It said the station management had no regular procedure for reviewing its presentations on controversial issues.

TV campaign spending curb. A bill to curb political campaign spending on television advertising was passed by the House Aug. 11 by a 272–97 vote.

The House version, which was sent to conference with the previously-passed Senate bill, extended the spending curb to primaries and state races for governor and lieutenant governor as well as Presidential and Congressional elections, as in the Senate bill. Like the Senate version, the House measure repealed the equal-time provision pertaining to presidential campaign broadcasts and required broadcasters to charge candidates the lowest time rate available to bulk commercial buyers. The spending curb provided that broadcast budgets could not exceed 7¢ for every vote cast in the last previous election for that office.

FCC orders TV time for war critics. The Federal Communications Commission (FCC), in a series of 5-2 rulings Aug. 14, said opponents of the President's conduct of the war in Indochina must be given an opportunity to present critical replies in prime television time. The commission based its decisions, all relating to media access, on the "fairness doctrine," a rule governing broadcast treatment of controversial issues. The FCC said none of the cases fell under the "equal time" requirement relating to broadcast coverage of political candidates.

In its ruling on war critics, the FCC said it was not creating an automatic right of response to any Presidential broadcast but based its ruling on "the unusual facts of this case"—that President Nixon used prime evening TV time for five speeches on his conduct of the war between November 1969 (when he explained his policy of Vietnamization) and June 1970 (when he defended the use of troops in Cambodia).

The commission rejected the argument that broadcasters could give fair coverage to war critics by normal use of the media—regular news broadcasts and discussion programs. It said opponents of Nixon's Indochina policies must be given access to uninterrupted prime time but left to the networks "the selection of some suitable spokesman or spokesmen ... to broadcast an address giving the contrasting viewpoint."

United in the majority on the rulings were FCC Chairman Dean Burch, a Republican, and Nicholas Johnson, a Democrat and frequent dissenter to the commission's previous "fairness doctrine" decisions. Also voting with the majority were Republican Commissioners Robert E. Lee and Robert Wells and Democratic Commissioner Kenneth A. Cox. The dissenters were Robert T. Bartley and H. Rex Lee, both Democrats.

The rulings dealt with the following related cases:

■The FCC said a coalition of 14 senators co-sponsoring the [Mark O.] Hatfield-[George S.] McGovern "amendment to end the war" had no special claim to be recognized by TV networks as spokesmen for the war opposition The 14 war critics had petitioned the FCC July 8 to obtain either free or paid time to oppose the President's Indochina policies. On May 12, five antiwar senators had opposed the President's policies on a paid TV program broadcast by the National Broadcasting Co. (NBC), but the coalition had been unable to obtain any more time, either paid or free, from the three major networks.

(National Educational Television [NET], an affiliate of the Corporation for Public Broadcasting, announced Aug. 10 that the 14 senators had accepted an offer of 40 minutes free time to oppose the President's war policies. The senators were to pay for production of a tape, to be broadcast over prime evening time, and NET was to pay the costs of relaying

the program and preparing a 20-minute analysis of the senators' position.)

■The FCC said Sen. Robert J. Dole (R, Kan.) and other Republican supporters of the President's Vietnam policy had no right to free reply time in which to answer the paid May 12 broadcast by the panel of antiwar senators. The commission was responding to a complaint filed by Dole July 10.

■The commission said the Columbia Broadcasting System (CBS), which had presented July 7 the first of a proposed series of programs to allow the Democratic National Committee free time to oppose the President's policies, must give the Republican National Committee time to reply to the Democrats. In a brief filed with the FCC July 13, the Republicans had demanded equal reply time. The brief charged that Democratic National Chairman Lawrence F. O'Brien had used the broadcast for "mere partisan advocacy and party propaganda." Rep. Rogers C. B. Morton, Republican national chairman, had accused O'Brien July 8 of a "personal attack" on the President. He renewed his charges against O'Brien and CBS July 16, a day after the network had denied the GOP request for equal time. O'Brien denied July 18 he had attacked Nixon personally and, in a letter to Morton, asked the Republicans to join in a plea to the FCC for an expanded "fairness doctrine" ruling.

Congress access to TV debated—The Senate Commerce Subcommittee on Communications held three days of hearings Aug. 4-6 on a resolution introduced June 11 by Sen. J. W. Fulbright (D, Ark.) to require broadcasters to supply time, as a public service, to authorized representatives of Congress. In testimony Aug. 4, Fulbright said his bill was based on an "institutional, not partisan" concern—that he feared for the balance among the three branches of government more than for the balance between the Republican and Democratic parties.

Sen. John O. Pastore (D, R.I.), chairman of the subcommittee, and several other members argued Aug. 4 that it would be impossible to decide on Congressional spokesmen for various issues. Fulbright suggested that the allotted TV time should be divided evenly between the House and Senate and that spokesmen for different issues would emerge naturally.

The presidents of the three major networks, testifying Aug. 5, opposed the Fulbright bill and argued that their freedom as journalists would be impinged upon if Congress, rather than the broadcaster, were given the right to choose representative spokesmen.

Leonard H. Goldenson, president of the American Broadcasting Co. (ABC), said the "freedom and flexibility" afforded a broadcaster under the "fairness doctrine" was the best way to insure public exposure to "all significant points of view on important public issues." (Fulbright's measure would fall under the "equal time" provision of the 1934 Communications Act. The FCC had promulgated the more general "fairness doctrine" in 1949.) Goldenson also said: "It is the public's right to be informed which is paramount ... rather than the right of a particular senator, representative, political party or group to broadcast its views on a given subject."

As an alternative to the Fulbright proposal, W. Theodore Pierson, counsel to the Republican National Committee, Aug. 5 called for the houses of Congress to schedule debates during prime time and allow TV coverage rather than "barring the doors as you now do."

Earlier FCC rulings—In two 6–1 rulings Aug. 6, the FCC upheld the right of broadcasters to determine "the manner in which the public is to be informed" and denied that political parties and other groups had the right to purchase time to speak out on issues. Commissioner Nicholas Johnson dissented in both cases.

In the first ruling, the commission upheld the right of WTOP-AM, a radio station in Washington, D.C. owned by the Washington Post Co., to reject antiwar spot ads by Business Executives Move for Vietnam Peace. The station had refused to sell time for ads on controversial issues, arguing that the Vietnam war issue had received ample and fair coverage in regular news broadcasts.

In the second ruling, the FCC said broadcasters must accept fund-raising commercials from the Democratic National Committee but could refuse to allow the time to be used for commentary on public issues. The ruling was in answer to a Democratic petition filed May 19.

In his dissents, Johnson said the Constitutional guarantee of free speech demanded wide access to television, which he said had become the principal medium of political communication. He said judicial precedent, though not specifically relating to broadcasting, "guarantees to individuals a right of access to forums generally open to the public for expression of views." He argued that the First Amendment "was not enacted to sanctify the views of the corporate owners of the mass media."

Democrats use free time to reply to Nixon. Democratic Sens. J. W. Fulbright (Ark.) and George S. McGovern (S.D.) made a televised rebuttal to President Nixon's Indochina policy Aug. 31. The telecast was the first broadcast by a major network (NBC) in compliance with a recent Federal Communications Commission (FCC) ruling requiring networks to give prime-time exposure to critics of the Administration's policy because of five presidential speeches on Vietnam since November 1969. NBC rejected a request from Sen. Robert J. Dole (R, Kan.) Aug. 28 to speak in opposition to the "end the war amendment" on the same program.

In a "clarification" of the FCC ruling, FCC Chairman Dean Burch stressed Aug. 18 that it was not a call for "equal time" to match presidential appearances. Objecting to press accounts of the ruling, Burch insisted that "we have expressly rejected any principle embodying right of reply or rebuttal to the president" and that the ruling "was not intended to discourage in any way the networks' presentation of presidential reports to the nation."

Establishment of the principle of right of rebuttal to the president was advocated by FCC Commissioner Nicholas Johnson in a statement Aug. 30. Every time a president spoke, he contended, it involved a controversial issue of public importance —"If it wasn't such an issue before he expresses his views, it is after he speaks." Johnson said it was "imperative that leaders of opposing parties and opposing viewpoints in Congress be given the opportunity to rebut ... [a president's] unilateral statements."

Campaign TV curb enacted. A bill limiting spending on political broadcast advertising was passed by a 247–112 House vote Sept. 16 and a 60–19 Senate vote Sept. 23. The measure was sent to President Nixon, whose dissatisfaction with it had been indicated by Senate Republican leaders.

The bill provided for repeal of the federal requirements that networks give minority party candidates equal time with major party candidates for presentation of their views. The provision served to hinder presentation of TV debates between two major party candidates.

The bill also imposed spending limits on political broadcasting for presidential, Congressional and gubernatorial elections. Such spending would be limited to the equivalent of 7¢ for each vote cast in the previous election for the office being contested, or $20,000, whichever was higher. Spending in primaries would be limited to half that permitted for general elections.

Another provision stipulated that broadcast time be sold to political candidates at the lowest price charged commercial advertisers. This was expected to be 25%–50% less than normally charged for political advertising.

The spending curb provision would limit, based on the 1968 vote, spending in the 1972 presidency campaign to less than $6 million per major party, contrasted to the more than $12 million spent by the Republicans in 1968 and $7.1 million spent by the Democrats.

Campaign spending curb vetoed. President Nixon acted Oct. 12 to veto the bill limiting radio and television campaign spending by presidential, Congressional and gubernatorial candidates (S3637). The bill, which had been passed by the House Sept. 16 and by the Senate Sept. 23, would also have repealed the Federal Communications Act's "equal time" provisions for presidential elections.

Explaining his veto, President Nixon said the bill had "highly laudable and widely supported goals" but that it was "worse than no answer to the problem— it is a wrong answer." He complained that the bill limited only radio and television spending and thus raised the prospect of more campaign spending in other media, thus allowing an overall increase in the total amount spent in political campaigns. In addition, the spending formula did not take into account differences in the cost of broadcasting in different geographical areas.

Among other reasons for Nixon's veto:

■ The bill, in requiring broadcasters to charge the candidates a minimum rate, would virtually mean "rate-setting by statute and ... [thus] a radical departure for the Congress which has traditionally abhorred any attempt to establish rates by legislation."

■ The legislation did not deal with expenditures by individuals and organizations "not directly connected with the candidate."

■ Enforcement would, in most cases take place after the election, raising "the possibility of confusion and chaos as elections come to be challenged for violation of ... [the bill] and the cases are still unresolved when the day arrives on which the winning candidate should take office."

■ The incumbent, with free media coverage of his official activities, would have an "immeasurable advantage" over the challenger, whose spending would be limited.

Reacting to the President's veto Oct. 12, Democratic National Chairman Lawrence F. O'Brien charged that Nixon was afraid the bill would have "stopped the Republican party's campaign to saturate the public airways with paid spot commercials."

Russel D. Hemenway, director of the National Committee for an Effective Congress which had sponsored the legislation, called the veto "a presidential effort to avoid the possibility of meeting his 1972 opponent in open debate."

Sen. Edmund S. Muskie (D, Maine) charged Oct. 13 that the President had vetoed the "first major election reform bill in 45 years," while Rep. Torbet Macdonald (D, Mass.), manager of the bill in the House, called the action a "partisan political maneuver of the first magnitude."

Joseph A. Califano Jr., general counsel for the Democratic National Committee, asserted Oct. 13 that Nixon had "served notice that he intends to buy the presidency from the American people at whatever cost in 1972."

TV spending veto upheld. The Senate Nov. 23 upheld President Nixon's veto of the bill to limit campaign television spending. The vote was 58–34 in favor of overriding the veto, four votes less than the required two-thirds majority. Five

Southern Democrats and Sen. Thomas J. Dodd (D, Conn.) joined 28 Republicans in supporting the President's position. On the other side, 49 Democrats were joined by nine Republicans.

A key Administration move to sidetrack an override was made by Senate Republican Leader Hugh Scott (Pa.), who announced Nov. 21 he would offer comprehensive campaign reform legislation in 1971. The move was endorsed publicly by President Nixon Nov. 22 and stressed in the debate Nov. 23 by Scott, who read a letter from Nixon expressing his desire to "work closely with you" toward a bill that would "deal with all problems of political campaigns, including spending limitations."

Other Administration supporters spoke against the bill Nov. 23 as discriminatory in curbing broadcast spending but not press, billboard or direct-mail campaign spending.

The chief Democratic sponsor of the bill, John O. Pastore (R.I.), urged passage as a first step in campaign reform and called the GOP promise of future legislation a move designed primarily to defeat the current bill. Senate Democratic Whip Edward M. Kennedy (Mass.) urged an override of the veto in view of television's undue influence on campaigns. "Like a colossus of the ancient world," he said, "television stands astride our political system demanding tribute from every candidate for major public office. . . . Survival is not of the fittest but of the wealthiest."

Democratic National Chairman Lawrence F. O'Brien deplored the vote later Nov. 23 as a reflection of the purpose of the veto "to protect the traditional Republican advantage in campaign finances and to protect Mr. Nixon from the possibility of having to debate the issues with his Democratic opponent in 1972."

The Senate vote was hailed Nov. 23 by the president of the National Association of Broadcasters.

Prior to the vote, the American Association of Political Consultants and the liberal Americans for Democratic Action called on Congress Nov. 14 to override the veto.

Radio licenses denied. The Federal Communications Commission (FCC), in a ruling Dec. 3, refused to renew licenses of five Star Stations Inc. radio stations. The commission ordered a hearing on 18 charges against the stations, including political favoritism, news slanting and trying to influence an audience rating company.

The stations involved were WIFE and WIFE-FM in Indianapolis; KOIL and KOIL-FM in Omaha, Neb.; and KISN in Portland, Ore. The FCC, in a separate action, held up renewal of the license of radio station WPDQ in Jacksonville, Fla. The commission ordered hearings on whether control of the station had been turned over to Don W. Burden, who owned 76% of Star Stations.

Democrats renounce infighting. Democratic national chairman Lawrence F. O'Brien said Feb. 10, 1971 that major Democratic presidential contenders had agreed at a meeting the night before to seek greater access to free broadcast time "to alleviate," as O'Brien put it, "the severe imbalance that now exists between the free use of electronic media by the Republican administration and the very limited amount of time given to the Democratic opposition."

Democrats rebut Nixon's Vietnam speech. A Democratic party rebuttal to President Nixon's April 7 television address on Vietnam troop withdrawals was broadcast by the American Broadcasting Co. April 22.

The national television and radio network made available for the program by ABC was in response to a request from Democratic National Chairman Lawrence F. O'Brien. He asked for time to rebut the President's attempt to blame the "tragic conflict solely on the Democratic party" and to present the "clear difference" between the party and the Administration "on the critical issue of troop withdrawal." ABC demurred on the rebuttal aspect, considering it had complied with the "fairness doctrine" by "balanced coverage" of the Vietnam problem, but it granted "additional coverage" in the public interest because of the national importance of the war issue.

Similar requests from the Democrats for rebuttal time were rejected by the National Broadcasting Co. and the Columbia Broadcasting System.

The Democrats also applied to the Federal Communications Commission April 13 for free time to respond to Nixon's two-hour NBC interview March 15 and to the President's one-hour ABC interview March 22. In addition, the party threatened court action on an 11-month-old request before the FCC for a rule requiring networks to make time available for responses to presidential addresses raising controversial issues.

Senate passes campaign bill. A campaign spending reform bill, passed by the Senate Aug. 5 by an 88–2 vote, was sent to the House. The Senate bill would limit the campaign spending on radio, TV, newspaper and magazine advertising to a total of 10¢ for each potential voter, 6¢ of that amount to be the limit on radio and TV ads. It also required sale of the broadcast ads at the lowest unit rates.

The equal-broadcast-time requirement would be repealed for federal elections. Reporting of spending and sources would fall under stricter rules administered by a new elections commission.

FCC rejects 'equal time' pleas. The Federal Communications Commission (FCC) Aug. 20 rejected bids from both

major political parties for "equal time" to rebut broadcasts by the other. The Democrats had sought to reply to four TV broadcasts by President Nixon in the spring, the Republicans to respond to a previous Democratic rebuttal. The agency declined to step into the "wholly impractical quagmire of deciding the partisan" content of individual appearances, and it did not consider the networks deficient in presenting contrasting views with regard to broad issues, such as the war in Indochina, covered in the President's broadcasts.

Court rules on political broadcasts. A three-judge panel of the U.S. court of appeals in Washington Nov. 15 rejected a Republican party request to reply to a televised Democratic speech, which was itself a reply to a Republican broadcast.

The decision reversed one by the Federal Communications Commission to grant the GOP request for a reply to a broadcast by Democratic National Chairman Lawrence O'Brien in rebuttal to televised speeches by President Nixon.

The court held the FCC had misapplied the "fairness doctrine" authorizing rebuttal by "providing the President's party with 'two bites of the apple.'"

The court also upheld the right of reply to televised presidential press conferences and to statements by Administration spokesmen.

House passes campaign spending bill. The House, by a 372–23 vote Nov. 30, passed a bill to limit campaign spending by presidential and Congressional candidates. The bill, similar in its major provisions to the Senate bill, was sent to conference.

Under the House bill, general election campaign spending by each presidential candidate would be limited to $13.9 million for radio, television, newspaper, magazine and billboard advertising and postage and telephone costs. The limit for radio and television spending would be $8.4 million.

According to the formula, communications and advertising spending could not exceed 10¢ per constituent in the Congressional district, state or nation, and no more than 6¢ of the 10¢ could be spent on one medium, such as television.

In addition, newspapers would be required to sell equal space to candidates, and newspaper and broadcast space and time would have to be sold at rates not exceeding those charged others for "comparable use."

A proposal to repeal the equal time provision of current law to permit television debates between major party candidates was dropped from the bill by the House so as not to jeopardize enactment of the bill. President Nixon was expected to veto any campaign spending bill that repealed the equal time provision only for his office, and many members of Congress opposed repealing the provision for Congressional campaigns because of concern that hostile local station owners would give only their opponents time.

Curb on campaign ad spending passed. The House Jan. 19, 1972 approved a bill to limit the amount presidential and Congressional candidates could spend in election campaigns on advertising in the media.

The measure had been passed by the Senate Dec. 17, 1971 at the close of the first session of the 92nd Congress.

Following passage in the House by a 334–19 vote, the legislation was sent to President Nixon. He had vetoed a similar bill in October 1970, but Deputy White House Press Secretary Gerald R. Warren said Jan. 19 that the new measure "meets the President's objectives" for political reform.

Under the bill, campaign spending by candidates for federal offices would be limited to 10¢ per constituent, with not more than 60% of the total to be spent in any one media. The media covered by the spending limit were radio, television, newspapers, magazines, billboards and mass telephone campaigns.

The bill's formula also limited spending by presidential candidates and their running mates to no more than $8.4 million on radio and television during the post-convention campaign. In 1968 the Republican national ticket spent $12.8 million in their television campaign, the Democratic ticket $6.1 million.

The legislation did not call for repeal of the equal-time provision for broadcasts.

Court denies equal-time bids. The U.S. Court of Appeals for the District of Columbia Feb. 3 rejected appeals by both the Democratic and Republican parties for "equal time" on television to rebut broadcasts made by the other.

In both instances, the court sustained rulings by the Federal Communications Commission (FCC) in August 1971 barring additional equal-time airtime for the two major parties.

The three-judge appellate court rejected the Democratic National Committee's contention that it should be given free television time after President Nixon was interviewed by television newsmen. The Democrats' case grew out of a broadcast by Nixon in April 1971 about the war in Vietnam.

In the Republicans' case, the appellate court ruled that they were not entitled to equal time to rebut a Democratic telecast that itself had been granted as equal time in replay to Nixon's April 1971 broadcast.

Campaign spending law signed. President Nixon signed into law Feb. 7 the Federal Election Campaign Act and hailed it as "an important step forward in an area which has been of great public concern." The new law, which the Presi-

dent said was "realistic and enforceable," would go into effect April 7.

Applying to all primary, general and special elections for federal office, it contained provisions for reporting campaign contributions received and spent and for limiting campaign spending for media advertising and from the personal funds of the candidate. The media fund curb would limit the candidate to expenditures of no more than 10¢ per person of voting age in his constituency, of which no more than 6¢ per person could be spent for broadcast media.

Equal time denied Democrats. The Federal Communications Commission rejected Feb. 17, in a 4–1 ruling, a request by the Democratic National Committee for free broadcast time to respond to seven broadcast discussions of the nation's economic situation—four by President Nixon and three by Treasury Secretary John B. Connally Jr. The commission held that its so-called fairness doctrine did not require equal time unless there was a personal attack. Commissioner Nicholas Johnson dissented.

Senate acts on equal-time law. The Senate voted 67–13 March 23 to repeal a provision of the communications law requiring the availability of equal broadcast time to all presidential and vice presidential candidates. Repeal of the provision would permit television debates between the major party candidates without the networks required to provide equal time to the minor party candidates.

The Senate rejected 41–39 on a straight party-line vote a Republican amendment to drop the equal-time provision also for Congressional candidates.

Station to pay for challenge. A three-judge panel of the U.S. Court of Appeals for Washington ruled March 28 that a Texarkana, Tex. television station had to pay legal expenses incurred by the United Church of Christ and community groups in challenging the station's license renewal.

The 1969 license challenge had been filed on grounds that the station had ignored the needs of local blacks in programming. An agreement was reached between the parties, and the challenge was dropped, but the FCC ruled in 1970 that no repayment would be permitted in such cases. The appeals court overruled that decision.

Pressmen delay anti-Nixon ad. Pressmen at the New York Times delayed publication of the newspaper's May 31 edition for 15 minutes to protest a two-page advertisement calling for impeachment of President Nixon on the grounds his Indochina war policy was unconstitutional.

The pressmen, calling the ad "traitorous" and "detrimental to the boys in

Vietnam and prisoners of war," demanded that the ad be withdrawn or that they be allowed to print their views along with it. The Times rejected the demands.

The pressmen were praised June 1 by Nixon's campaign manager John N. Mitchell, who sent a telegram to the pressmen lauding their "patriotism and responsibility" and accusing the Times of "irresponsibility."

Complaint on 'impeach Nixon' ad. The citizens lobby Common Cause filed a formal complaint June 19 against the New York Times and a committee that placed an ad in the Times calling for impeachment of President Nixon.

The complaint, filed with the clerk of the House and the Controller General, cited as violations of campaign-fund disclosure legislation the Times' failure to identify those financing such ads and the committee's failure to register as a supporter of Congressional candidates although the ad pledged support to House candidates who would vote for impeachment.

FCC permits racist political ads. The Federal Communications Commission (FCC) Aug. 3 upheld the right of a candidate to broadcast paid political appeals that contained racist remarks if no danger of violence or incitement to violence were involved.

Atlanta, Ga. lawyer J. B. Stoner had used radio and television ads in his Senate primary campaign asking the people to "vote white" and back "white racist J. B. Stoner." He said in the ads "the main reason why niggers want integration is because the niggers want our white women" and "you cannot have law and order and niggers, too."

The FCC said there was no "clear and present danger of imminent violence which might warrant interfering with speech which does not contain any direct incitement to violence." Federal law prohibited a broadcaster from censoring political ads of legally qualified candidates.

The ad protest was put before the FCC by the Atlanta chapter of the National Association for the Advancement of Colored People (NAACP), the Anti-Defamation League and a civic coalition.

(Stoner polled 5.2% of the primary vote Aug. 8. He was fifth behind Hosea Williams, a black, who received 6.4%.)

Impeachment committee sued. The Justice Department filed a civil suit Aug. 17 against the National Committee for Impeachment and two of its officers, Randolph Phillips and Elizabeth A. Most, charging them with election law violations.

The suit, the first filed under the Federal Campaign Election Act of 1971, charged that the committee which called for the impeachment of President Nixon, had failed to file a report of its campaign contributions with the U.S. comp-

A

B

C

D

E

F

G

troller general or the clerk of the House in connection with a two-page advertisement placed in the New York Times May 31.

In another violation of the new election law, no notice of where the financial reports could be obtained by the public was included in the ad.

The suit also alleged that the ad did not state that the candidates mentioned in it had not authorized the use of their names.

The ad featured a reprint of a resolution introduced in the House May 10 by Rep. John J. Conyers Jr. (D, Mich.). Seven other Democrats who had endorsed the House resolution were listed in the committee's "honor roll." Rep. Paul N. McCloskey Jr, (R, Calif.), who had not endorsed the Conyers' resolution, was also included in the "honor roll" listing.

Impeachment committee cleared. A federal appeals court ruled Oct. 30 that the National Committee for Impeachment was not a "political committee ... soliciting contributions or making expenditures, the major purpose of which is the nomination or election of candidates" and therefore was not liable under provisions of the Federal Elections Campaign Act which required each committee to register and make disclosures of donors and financial activities.

The impeachment committee had been enjoined from further political actions Sept. 5 as a result of an advertisement placed in the New York Times May 31 which had called for the impeachment of the President. No contributors to the sponsoring committee were reported at that time.

The appeals court concluded that, given the basis of the government's interpretation of the new election law, "every position on any issue, major or minor, taken by anyone would be a campaign issue, and any comment upon it in, say, a newspaper editorial or an advertisement would be subject to proscription—unless the registration and disclosure regulations of the act in question were complied with."

The suit, filed in federal district court in New York, sought permanent and preliminary injunctions against the committee to prevent its collection and disbursement of funds.

The Justice Department acted after the Office of Federal Elections received three complaints about the ad from the Committee to Re-elect the President, Common Cause and a public interest law group.

The Office of Federal Elections June 15 had asked the Justice Department to take action on an "apparent violation" committed by the Times for failing to obtain certificates of nonauthorization from the political candidates mentioned in the ad and for neglecting to publish a statement saying no candidate for federal office had approved the expenditure for the ad. The Times later published the requested disclaimer.

Times won't aid media council. The New York Times announced Jan. 15, 1973 that it would not cooperate with a media review council proposed by the Twentieth Century Fund to investigate public complaints of unfair or inaccurate news stories.

The Times said the council would only divert attention "from people who are attempting to intimidate or to use the press for their own ends," and would, despite the "good intentions" of the participating journalists, "encourage an atmosphere of regulation in which government intervention might gain public acceptance.

Plans for the council had been announced by the fund's director, M. J. Rossant, Nov. 30, 1972. It would be headed by Roger Traynor, former California Supreme Court chief justice, and include 14 representatives of the press and the public. An annual budget of $400,000 would be provided.

The panel's main function, the fund noted, would be to investigate public complaints against national print and electronic media—the national wire services, the largest supplemental wire services, the national news chains, national weekly news magazines, broadcast networks and public television and radio.

A 14-member task force, nine of whose members were newspapermen, drafted the proposal.

Black Caucus plea rejected. The FCC ruled 5-2 that the Congressional Black Caucus had no inherent right to free television time to respond to a Presidential address, it was reported Feb. 8. The case arose from President Nixon's January, 1973 State of the Union message.

The commission said it had "consistently rejected the claims of groups and individuals requesting a specific right of access to broadcast facilities," since Supreme Court rulings had "stressed the right of the public to be informed" rather than a broadcaster's or individual's right to be heard over the air.

Benjamin L. Hooks, one of the dissenters and the first black to sit on the commission, said the caucus, "as the major elected voice of the black community is the obvious entity to proffer positions on important racial issues and their proper resolution in contradistinction to those views and solutions held by the executive," just as one political party had the right of response to another under the fairness doctrine. Hooks said the networks had effectively deprived the public of minority viewpoints.

Regarding the caucus' contention that its First Amendment rights had been violated, the FCC noted that its earlier ruling, that a broadcaster could adequately give the public access to a group's views without granting the group air time, was before the Supreme Court after being overturned by a federal appeals court. The FCC said it was currently studying another plea raised by the caucus, that the network's policy of excluding broadcasts on controversial issues by nonmedia people be overturned.

TV, radio spending. According to the Federal Communications Commission (FCC) May 9, there was only a $700,000 increase over the 1968 elections in the amount spent on television and radio advertisements during the 1972 campaign. The FCC linked the small gain to the new federal expenditure law which required broadcasters to charge their lowest advertising rates for political statements. No candidate for office in 1972 approached the limits set by Congress—a total of $59.6 million was spent.

Among the findings: Democrats spent $6.2 million in the post convention period, Republicans $4.3 million; Democrats spent $3.4 million in the nomination fight, Republicans spent less than $100,000, a discrepancy attributed to Nixon's lack of major opponents in a primary race; Senate candidates spent $6.4 million (down 38% from 1968) gubernatorial candidates spent $9.7 million (up $3.5 million from 1968); 37.5% of all disbursements for media advertisements went to radio (up from 35.5% in 1968); 62.4% of broadcast advertising was spent in television (down from 64.5% in 1968).

Right to bar political ads upheld. In a complex decision marked by six separate majority opinions, the Supreme Court May 29 held 7-2 that radio and television stations had the right to reject controversial, paid political advertisements.

The court majority reasoned that broadcasters had the right to exercise journalistic discretion in not accepting certain paid political announcements, as long as the "fairness doctrine" of the Federal Communications Commission (FCC) was observed.

Chief Justice Warren E. Burger, who delivered the majority opinion, said that to force stations to accept such ads would be contrary to the intent of the laws that regulated broadcasters and would only lead to closer scrutiny by the FCC.

Justice William O. Douglas argued in a separate majority opinion that the broadcasting industry as a part of the press should be free of all regulation.

The ruling reversed an appellate court decision.

Plaintiffs in the case were the Democratic National Committee and Business Executives' Move for Vietnam Peace. They had charged their freedom of speech had been abridged, a contention rejected by the court majority.

Defendants in the case were the American Broadcasting Co., the Columbia Broadcasting System, the National Broadcasting Co., the Washington

Post-Newsweek Stations and the FCC. They maintained that compliance of broadcasters with FCC fairness rules was all that could be expected of them.

Dissenting were Justices William J. Brennan Jr. and Thurgood Marshall.

Court declines review of FCC ruling. The Supreme Court May 29 declined to review a decision denying renewal of broadcast licenses to two Pennsylvania radio stations on the grounds of violation of the "fairness doctrine" of the FCC. The president of the company owning the stations was evangelist Carl McIntire. Justice William O. Douglas voted to hear the case.

GAO cites Wisconsin papers. The General Accounting Office (GAO) announced May 31 that it had referred to the Justice Department for possible prosecution its report of "apparent violations" in the Federal Campaign Spending Act by four Wisconsin newspapers—the Eau Claire Leader-Telegram, the Janesville Gazette, the Kenosha Evening News and the Racine Journal-Times.

The papers were faulted for accepting campaign advertisements, which jointly supported President Nixon and several Congressional candidates, without obtaining a statement from Nixon reelection committee officials that their share of the ads' costs would not cause the Nixon campaign to exceed the statutory limit on media spending for the 1972 elections.

Such certification was required to enforce the spending ceiling voted by Congress.

Equal time newspaper law upheld. The Florida Supreme Court July 18 upheld a law that required newspapers to print replies from political candidates whom they criticized during election campaigns.

Pat L. Tornillo Jr. had sued the Miami Herald for refusing to print his rebuttal of an editorial critical of him during his unsuccessful race for the state legislature in 1972.

In a 6–1 ruling the court dismissed the Herald's argument that the law violated 1st Amendment guarantees of a free press. The court reasoned: "What some segments of the press seem to have lost sight of is that the 1st Amendment guarantee is not for the benefit of the press so much as for the benefit of us all. The right of the public to know all sides of a controversy and, from such information, to be able to make an enlightened choice is being jeopardized by the growing concen-tration of ownership of the mass media into fewer and fewer hands, resulting ultimately in a form of private censorship."

Senate votes repeal of equal time law. The Senate July 30 by an 82–8 vote passed a campaign reform bill that included a repeal of the current law's provision requiring equal broadcast time for all candidates for president and Congress. The other provisions of the bill would impose strict controls on campaign funding and expenses.

Section of campaign law struck down. Federal district court in Washington Nov. 14 struck down as unconstitutional a section of the 1971 Federal Election Campaign Act that had the effect of limiting political advertisements placed in newspapers and magazines and on television.

The court ruled that the section had a "chilling effect" on First Amendment rights of press freedom because implementation of the advertising restrictions imposed "impermissible prior restraint" on the media.

The case had been brought by the American Civil Liberties Union (ACLU) and the New York Civil Liberties Union, which were joined by the New York Times as a friend of the court. The Times had been forced to reject an ad placed by the ACLU in September 1972 criticizing President Nixon's support of antibusing legislation because the government contended that the ad was a partisan political advertisement.

The ad could have been run free of charge but in order to be paid for it, the Times would have been required, by the section ruled unconstitutional, to collect authorizations from each of the 102 congressmen listed in the ad allowing use of their names.

Newspapers were responsible for gathering these certificates of sponsorships and compliance with spending limits from parties involved in placing ads. The Times said it was unwilling to act as "policeman" for the campaign law and rejected the ad.

Powell enjoins equal space law case. Supreme Court Justice Lewis F. Powell Jr. issued an order Nov. 20 indefinitely staying execution of a Florida Supreme Court ruling that upheld a Florida law requiring newspapers to print replies by political candidates to published criticism.

Powell acted after the Miami Herald, a party to the litigation, asked the court to determine whether government could "command" the private press to print certain information and ideas.

FCC finds NBC 'fairness' violation. The Federal Communications Commission (FCC) ruled Dec. 3 that the National Broadcasting Co. (NBC) had violated the agency's fairness doctrine in its September 1972 broadcast of the documentary "Pensions: the Broken Promise."

The decision upheld a complaint by Accuracy in Media, Inc., a conservative watchdog group, which had said the program conveyed the "distorted and propagandistic" impression that "failure and fraud are the rule in the management of private pension funds," while "ignoring the great achievement of American private enterprise in developing a pension system that is overwhelmingly successful."

Under the ruling, NBC could have complied with the FCC judgment by programming "positive" testimony on pensions on network newscasts. Instead, NBC notified the FCC Dec. 21 that an appeal would be filed with the U.S. Court of Appeals because of the decision's potential impact on television's ability to broadcast investigative reporting.

NBC had argued before the FCC that the commission staff erred in extending the application of the fairness doctrine into news judgment. The program, NBC had said, was not a pro and con survey of the pension system but an investigative documentation of problems. Even so, the network added, portions of the program had pointed out positive aspects of pension plans.

Supreme Court accepts Florida case. The Supreme Court Jan. 15, 1974 accepted for review the appeal of a state court decision upholding a Florida law requiring newspapers to print replies by political candidates criticized in their columns.

Burch joins White House staff. The White House announced Feb. 15 that Dean Burch would leave his post as chairman of the Federal Communications Commission (FCC) to become counselor to the President with cabinet rank. Burch had been with the FCC since November 1969.

Press Secretary Ronald Ziegler said Burch would engage in special projects. He specified that the appointment was not a replacement for Melvin R. Laird, who left the White House Feb. 1 as counselor to the President to become a Reader's Digest executive.

Editorial
Comment

Arkansas Gazette.

Little Rock, Ark., October 14, 1970

THE NEW Richard Nixon is more than incidentally a creation of the electronics media. Even so, the old Nixon has been lurking off-cameras as big as life and it was that Nixon who on Monday vetoed the bill setting spending limits on radio and television commercials in election campaigns.

More than on most major pieces of legislation, the proponents and opponents of the spending bill voted along partisan lines, and for understandable reason. President Nixon's veto, however, raises strong doubts that any kind of bill limiting campaign spending can be enacted within the foreseeable future.

It was Hubert Humphrey, we believe, who was quoted a few months back in a contemplative moment as wondering what would have been the outcome in 1968 had he had access in the closing days of the campaign to the kind of money that Mr. Nixon seemed to have so plentifully for television appearances. Mr. Humphrey closed fast and we are willing to believe, at least, that with

equal television exposure he might have gained that extra momentum needed to win.

The spending bill would not have affected the current fall campaign, but would have been in effect for the 1972 presidential election year for all federal offices and those for governor and lieutenant governor in state elections. It would have limited broadcast spending in general elections to seven cents for each vote for the office involved in the last general election, or $20,000 whichever were higher. For primary elections spending would have been half those figures.

Mr. Nixon cites familiar reasons for his veto, but that does not hide the fact that radio and television have proven valuable tools for campaigning and that he has better access to the sources that can supply the tools. He has a built-in advantage without any limitation on broadcast spending and clearly is not going to relinquish it.

A man who understands the packag-

ing and selling genius of Madison Avenue better than many of us is Nicholas Johnson, a member of the Federal Communications Commission, and a Democrat, and he had this to say about the veto:

"The big money people of corporate America who are paying the skyrocketing costs of television politics, defense contractors and consumer manipulators, are not complaining. They're getting their money's worth from a government that makes better deals with business than it does with people. But it's a sad and tragic day for those who had hoped for some limitation on the power of money to dominate our politics and our government."

Evidence lies all about us that the historical ties of the Republican Party nationally to the interests of big money and big business are still as close as they have been for generations. Its resources for campaigning are enormous and the real Richard Nixon is not about to throw away the advantage this gives him in radio and television exposure over his Democratic opponent in 1972.

The Morning Star

Rockford, Ill., October 14, 1970

President Nixon quite properly has vetoed a bill that would limit the amount of money political candidates could spend on radio and television commercials.

As President Nixon himself said, the measure was "a good aim, gone amiss." He branded the bill as "worse than no answer to the problem — it is the wrong answer."

There is an outside possibility that the President's veto could be overturned in the Senate, but there appears to be little chance that the House would vote to override the veto.

In his veto message, the President enumerated all of the serious wrongs of the bill.

"It unfairly endangers freedom of discussion, discriminates against the broadcasters, favors the incumbent office holder over the office seeker and gives an unfair advantage to the famous," Mr. Nixon said.

Taken individually, any one of these points would be sufficient to call for a presidential veto.

In addition, the measure would not necessarily be effective in curtailing campaign spending.

Candidates could merely switch their advertising from radio and television into other channels—newspapers, magazines, billboards, pamphlets and direct mailings to voters.

It might be asked why a newspaper would object to a bill which could work to its financial advantage.

The bill patently discriminates against the broadcasters. Further, it would require that broadcasters must offer candidates their lowest unit rate for the time period in which the broadcast is made, thus establishing price fixing by government.

It is not the business of Congress to seek to control spending on political advertising nor to

discriminate against one segment of the media.

If the spending control bill became law and it was found that candidates merely shifted their advertising to other media, the proponents of limited campaign spending would try to hamstring the rest of the media, too.

It already is too late to do anything regarding political spending this year. Any law would not apply to campaigns for the Nov. 3 elections, since it would not take effect until 30 days after becoming law.

The President, in exercising his veto, called upon Congress to "analyze and consider" ways to solve the problem more equitably.

As it stood, the bill represented an unwarranted intrusion into the political process and discrimination against the broadcast media. It was the wrong approach to the problem — if, indeed, it is a problem that demands congressional attention.

St. Petersburg Times

St. Petersburg, Fla., October 14, 1970

Well-heeled politicians got a campaign boost Monday when President Nixon vetoed the bill to limit political spending for radio and television commercials, beginning with the 1972 election.

Mr. Nixon was right in saying the measure "plugs only one hole in a sieve" of spending issues; however, he was wrong to veto it for that reason. It was a start at reducing the impact of the dollar on political races.

AND BY waiting until yesterday instead of objecting when the bill was being drafted, Mr. Nixon cast doubt on the sincerity of his interest in campaign spending reform.

Congress should override the veto.

Unfortunately, Florida's congressional delegation is unlikely to help much. Only five Florida Congressmen voted for the bill when it passed the House 273 to 98.

Florida's U.S. Sen. Edward Gurney is not expected to buck the President on this issue. He joined 34 other opponents when the Senate passed the measure 50 to 35, according to the Congressional Quarterly.

Sen. Spessard Holland, however, voted in favor of candidates and programs over dollars.

The time has come to start curbing the dominance of money on American government.

The Boston Globe

Boston, Mass., October 21, 1970

President Nixon's message accompanying his veto of the bill limiting political campaign expenditures is one of the most plausible communications that will be awaiting Congress when it reconvenes after the election. A vote to override the veto will be high on the docket at that time. If Congress reads the President's message carefully, it will find that his stated reasons for vetoing the bill are the very reasons which most persuasively argue for overriding the veto.

Mr. Nixon concedes that the bill he has vetoed "is aimed at highly laudable and widely supported goals of limiting political campaign expenditures and preventing one candidate from having an unfair advantage over another."

This is indeed the bill's aim. It would limit the sums that candidates for major elective office may spend on radio and television to seven cents per vote cast for the office in question in the last election or $20,000, whichever is greater. Contrast this with some expenditures of candidates in next month's election, and the need for legal limitation cannot be lightly passed off.

Rep. Richard Ottinger (D-N.Y.) spent $1.8 million on radio and TV in his primary campaign for the United States Senate and is spending an estimated equal sum in the current campaign. Sen. Ralph Smith (R-Ill.) will spend an estimated $1 to $2 million on radio and TV in his campaign for reelection. New York's Gov. Rockefeller (R) had a TV and radio budget of somewhere between $2 and $5 million in 1966 and will spend at least that much in the current campaign. In Texas, where it is virtually impossible to get figures on spending, both the Republican and Democratic candidates have what the Committee for An Effective Congress calls 'multi-million budgets." Sen. George Murphy (R-Calif.) is another of several who is spending well over a million in his campaign for reelection.

The Republicans spent $12 to $13 million on television to elect Mr. Nixon in 1968, and the Democrats spent $6.1 million on TV in the Humphrey campaign. It is fair to wonder whether the difference in TV funds contributed to Mr. Nixon's win. The Congress seems to believe this is possible, for its bill would limit TV spending to $5.1 billion per party in 1972.

The need for a limitation is demonstrated by the fact that total radio and TV expenditures by all candidates in 1968 was $59.4 million, up 70 percent over the previous figure. A large part of it was for so-called spot plugs which usually serve no purpose except to denigrate the opposition through innuendo. The suggestion that candidates thus are buying public office may be unfair. But even if the suggestion is as wide of the mark as may be, it nevertheless does demonstrate that an unfair advantage accrues to the candidates who either are very wealthy themselves or have access to lush contributions.

"Nearly everyone who is active in the political process wants to find some way to limit the crushing and growing cost of political campaigning," Mr. Nixon has conceded.

This being so, his argument that the bill he has vetoed does not put a limit on all avenues of expenditure is not compelling. The answer to his objection is not to throw away the limitation that has passed the Senate by a vote of 60 to 19 and the House by 247 to 112. The answer is to save what the Congress has done and improve upon it as time goes by. Mr. Nixon, in vetoing the bill, has scored what might be called debater's points. But a reading of his message suggests that it must have been written with tongue in cheek.

Los Angeles Times

Los Angeles, Calif.
October 14, 1970

It is unfortunate that President Nixon saw fit to veto legislation which would have imposed limits on how much candidates for major political office can spend for radio and TV campaign commercials. Overriding the veto should be an early order of business when Congress returns next month for a post-election wrapup session.

The President's explanation of his veto made good sense up to a point—but only up to a point.

As he said, the bill would deal with only one aspect of the fundamental problem—which is the unfair and unhealthy advantage enjoyed by wealthy candidates in this era of enormously expensive campaigns.

There is nothing in the bill to prevent the rich candidate from spending his money on billboards or newspaper ads, or using his enormous personal resources for pre-campaign image-building.

It is also true, as Mr. Nixon said, that limitations on TV campaign spending tend to favor the incumbent officeholder over the challenging officeseeker. This is because the incumbent has a built-in ability to generate free publicity through the conduct of his office, and is therefore less dependent on campaign advertising.

Partial solutions are better than none, however. The bill deserves enactment because, while not perfect, it constitutes a step in the right direction.

A future Congress, of course, can and should deal with other aspects of the problem—including one, the evils of the 30-second TV spot, which the President did not mention in his veto message.

The professional image-makers use these brief campaign commercials to sell the candidate very much as though he were a cake of soap. The object is not so much to discuss the issues as to avoid or distort them, not so much to display the candidate's real personality as to project a more robust and appealing facsimile.

As one practitioner told Times political writer Bill Boyarsky, "Nobody can be straightforward. You don't have time to be. You have to get in there with the most compelling, provocative statement for your client."

Even some political professionals worry privately about the corrosive effect of such campaign techniques on the democratic process. The suggestion has in fact been made that the 30-second campaign commercial be outlawed.

That may or may not be the best solution. But the problem, along with the whole business of political contributions and campaign spending, deserves continuing attention both from Congress and a concerned citizenry.

The Charlotte Observer

Charlotte, N.C., October 14, 1970

President Nixon's veto apparently dooms the first major reform of political campaign financing to clear Congress in 45 years.

The campaign broadcast reform act cleared both houses of the Congress with strong bipartisan support. Now that the President has made it a partisan issue, it will lose Republican votes needed to override the veto.

This act was an attempt to bring down soaring campaign costs by limiting the amount of money spent for radio-television time by major candidates.

The President's veto message called the measure a "wrong answer" to the problem. But it was a product of several years of research, plus decades of trying to find other answers.

If the administration had its own plan to curb increasing campaign costs, the veto message would be more credible. The President has made no suggestions. There are no serious alternatives pending in Congress. "Control" of campaign spending is left to the loophole-riddled Corrupt Practices Act of 1925.

The campaign broadcast reform act was a novel approach. But given the experience of recent years, it was and is a logical approach to holding campaign costs down.

Increased outlays for radio-television time have been the largest single contributor to the soaring cost of campaigning. From 1956 to 1968, the total spent on radio-television in national campaigns increased 312 per cent from $9.8 million to $40.4 million. The total jumped by 64 per cent from 1964 to 1968. The sky is now the limit.

A cash limit on spending for air time isn't unworkable nor would it preclude a political candidate from getting his name known as the veto message suggests.

Senate candidates in Ohio and in Michigan are voluntarily using the reform act's limits. Each candidate pledged to spend no more for air time than the equivalent of seven cents multiplied by the total vote in the last general election.

In Ohio each candidate (one of them a relative unknown) will thus limit his outlay for air time to $262,000 while in Michigan the limit will be $171,000.

Some cash unspent for air time might be diverted to other projects. But given the modern emphasis on electronic image-making, a ceiling on radio-television spending would reduce total campaign costs.

More important, it would make the cost of campaigning less awesome to would-be candidates for major offices. Everyone entering the race could figure in advance how much cash he would have to raise to match his opponent's potential paid radio-television coverage.

This means of discouraging the escalation of campaign costs isn't attractive at the moment to the well-heeled national Republican Party.

What's more, President Nixon may be less than happy with the feature of the act that would make it more awkward for him to avoid a "televised debate" with a Democratic challenger for the presidency.

In the long run a campaign broadcast reform act promised benefits to all contributing to a healthier political climate. If the veto stands, as expected, it will contribute to the cynical belief that major campaign spending reform is impossible except in the aftermath of a campaign scandal.

The Courier-Journal

Louisville, Ky., October 14, 1970

PRESIDENT NIXON'S veto of a bill that would have reduced the costs of political campaigning is a disappointment. His reasons for the veto are unconvincing. To say, as he did, that he rejected the measure because it doesn't solve all of the problems of campaign financing, won't wash. Of course it wouldn't. No one said it would.

The measure he has probably killed, however, would have reduced the costs of campaigning on television and radio, and it is these media that get the lion's share of campaign budgets now.

If, as the President said in his veto message, the limitation of campaign spending on radio and television is the "wrong answer" to the problem, then what is the right one? What does he suggest as an alternative? Nothing.

A variety of proposals have been advanced to help correct the existing imbalance that makes it all but impossible for a poorly financed candidate to mount an effective campaign for public office. They include cash subsidies to parties and candidates by federal and state governments, tax incentives to encourage political donations, government subsidies of campaign communications. Mr. Nixon was silent on which if any of these approaches he would prefer to the bill he vetoed.

The cost of buying radio and TV time is an increasingly important part of the whole problem of political financing in a democracy, and Congress was finally willing to do something to stem this inflationary trend, only to have the President say no.

The bill also would have repealed the equal-time provision of the Communications Act to allow broadcasters to present debates and other appearances by major-party nominees without giving the same amount of time to fringe candidates. Broadcasters have favored repeal of this provision—but many of them would rather be stuck with it than see political spending on radio and television limited.

Mr. Nixon's argument that the limitation discriminates "against the broadcast media" sounds reasonable. It would have been better to limit all forms of spending in political campaigns. However, the bill Congress approved did get at the most expensive form of political exposure, and one the politicians obviously consider the most effective.

Television and radio spots also lend themselves to great oversimplification of issues and empty sloganeering.

There is another consideration. Radio and television are subject to government control that no other media are subjected to; the airwaves belong to the people but are assigned by the government to broadcasters. If Congress is to limit campaign spending in any of the media, radio and television would be the logical place to start.

President Nixon knew what he was doing when he vetoed the bill. He was pre eminently the radio and television candidate in 1968 and spent twice as much on these media as the opposition; of course, he had twice as much to spend, as the Republicans usually do.

The National Committee for an Effective Congress worked hard for passage of the bill the President has vetoed. Russell D. Hemenway, its director, called the veto "the most flagrant example of partisan interest we have witnessed in NCEC's 22-year history." He said the real reasons for the veto were a Republican interest "in preserving the current GOP financial advantage" and a presidential effort "to avoid the possibility of meeting his 1972 opponent in open debate."

The latter was a reference to the section of the bill repealing the equal-time clause, the clause which Mr. Nixon used to his advantage to avoid a television debate with Hubert Humphrey in 1968.

It will be difficult for Congress to muster the two-thirds majority necessary to override a veto, but the effort ought to be made.

PORTLAND EVENING EXPRESS
Portland, Me., October 17, 1970

We think President Nixon has made a grave error in vetoing the bill that would have curbed the spending of political candidates for radio and television time, while it suspends the "equal time" provision that has been a great problem for the electronic media.

Since the measure puts a limit of seven cents per vote cast in the previous election on TV-radio spending, or $7,000 per 100,000 votes, the ceiling in the 1972 presidential election would be $5.1 millions for each party's national ticket. In contrast the Democrats are estimated to have spent just over $6 millions two years ago, with the GOP more than doubling that figure.

There are some valid objections to the bill, but House and Senate felt it was a start in the right direction. It's true that since TV costs are higher in large cities, urban candidates would be discriminated against, and it is probably true that the spending limit, in some cases, tends to benefit incumbents, who have the advantage of being better known.

But it is significant that this measure had broadly-based support in Congress on both sides of the aisle, and in the four votes taken in House and Senate more than two-thirds of those voting each time backed the bill.

If Mr. Nixon's veto is overcome, which is possible in the Senate, and the measure becomes law, it can be refined by the next Congress, and improved even more on the basis of the 1972 outcome. There has to be a limit on political spending in U.S. elections, and currently the man with meagre resources runs at a disadvantage, in both primary and general elections.

The Washington Post

Washington, D.C., October 14, 1970

President Nixon's veto of the bill to limit television and radio campaign spending is a flimsy excuse for having undone the most significant reform in this sphere for half a century. While ignoring the virtues of the bill, the President grossly exaggerated its weaknesses and distorted the probable consequences. So eager was he to avoid the charge that he acted to perpetuate a Republican advantage in excessive campaign spending that he even pretended that the bill might increase the outlays of candidates to get elected.

It is utterly misleading to say, as the President did, that the bill "plugs one hole in a sieve." Everyone with any information about the costs of campaigning these days knows that a large part of the money is being spent for television and radio broadcasting. Congress decided, in the absence of any effective device for limitation of campaign expenses in general, to strike at this one source of excessive use of money for political purposes. But the President fell back on the lame pretense that half a loaf is worse than nothing at all.

His complaint that the bill would "favor the famed over the worthy but little-known" is an especially transparent smoke-screen. The implication is that an obscure challenger should be allowed to spend more to offset the incumbent's natural advantage of being well known. But only a few wealthy individuals can spend millions to get themselves elected to public office. The vast majority of candidates must rely upon campaign contributions, and in raising money for campaign purposes the well-known, famous or incumbent candidate usually has a substantial advantage over an obscure challenger. The veto, if it should be sustained, will tend to magnify this advantage instead of reducing it.

In expounding upon all the imaginary inequities associated with the bill, the President completely ignored the very real inequity which it would help to correct. The use of broadcast commercials has reached a point where it can be accurately said that some candidates are buying their way into office. The first purpose of the bill was to put a reasonable ceiling on this kind of spending. But the President ripped off the ceiling at a time when his own party has millions to spend for commercials and the Democratic opposition is in financial straits.

While the President refrained from condemning the "equal-time" repealer, which was also in the bill, it is widely assumed that his veto was also intended to discourage television debates between the presidential candidates in 1972. If broadcasters have to give equal time to all the fringe candidates, they will not offer free time to the chief contenders for debates or other means of getting the issues before the public. Here again the President has knocked down a provision that could have substantially reduced the cost of at least some campaigns. The other significant provision that went down was a requirement that broadcasters charge candidates no more than the lowest unit fee of the station for comparable time.

Since the bill does have substantial merit, despite its shortcomings, and since the veto appears to reflect at least 90 per cent political motivation, we think Congress should override it.

Portland Press Herald

Portland, Me.
October 16, 1970

Although the timing of his words may have given them the ring of campaign oratory, there is a barrel full of truth in the statement by Sen. Edmund Muskie that political candidates of modest means will not be able to run for major office if the spiraling costs of a campaign are not halted.

In this case, the Senator's target was President Nixon who has vetoed a bill that would have limited broadcast campaign spending by candidates for top offices.

We can't agree with his conclusion that Nixon's act was an effort to "make the winning of elections a product of . . . the capacity to dominate the communications media." Legislation limiting campaign spending in only one of the media is not, of course, a real solution for the problem to which Senator Muskie refers. And we certainly could never agree that saturation of broadcasting would even come close to domination of the entire communications media.

However, Senator Muskie is in the process of deciding whether he will be a candidate for the Presidential nomination in 1972, and the tremendous cost of the campaigns undoubtedly will be a major factor in his decision.

An idea of campaign costs may be gained from a report of expenditures by Nelson A. Rockefeller in his current bid for reelection as governor of New York. Rockefeller people estimate they will spend $6 million. A ranking Republican familiar with the campaign estimates $10 million. Rockefeller's opponent, Arthur J. Goldberg, says he believes the Governor may be spending as high as $20 million.

The Governor's campaign staff has 370 full time employes, and if those were the only paid workers the total campaign payroll alone would be over $1 million. Add to this the cost of using printed media, poll data, computerized information, direct mail, miscellaneous campaign materials—and autographed copies of the Governor's $5.95 book, "Our Environment Can Be Saved."

Much of the money is being contributed by Rockefeller's family, one of America's wealthiest, and this may be called an extreme case of campaign spending for governor of a single state. But it is an indication of the problem confronting a candidate of modest means.

Election reform legislation is needed. But a more equitable solution must be found than the bill vetoed by the President.

BOSTON HERALD TRAVELER

Boston, Mass., October 24, 1970

President Nixon vetoed the bill limiting campaign expenditures because, his critics say, he wanted to give Republican "fatcats" a chance to win elections.

"The votes of the American people are not for sale," fumed one Democratic spokesman, "not even at the price the Republicans are willing to pay." The vetoed bill, he continued, would have "stopped the Republican party's campaign to saturate the public airways with paid soft commercials."

To use a word borrowed from the Dutch language, that's a lot of poppycock. Congressional Quarterly, a reliable periodical, recently listed eight "rich" candidates who spent a lot of money in this year's primaries. Seven of them are Democrats: Rep. James H. Scheuer of New York, Richard L. Ottinger, New York senatorial candidate, Milton J. Shapp, gubernatorial candidate in Pennsylvania, Howard M. Metzenbaum, Ohio senatorial candidate, Lloyd M. Bentsen, senatorial candidate from Texas, Charles Woods, gubernatorial candidate in Alabama, and Howard J. Samuels, gubernatorial candidate in New York.

The lone Republican on this list, California millionaire Norton Simon, lost a primary contest in spite of a $1.9 million campaign — which brings us back to the important point about the "elections for sale" canard. Of the eight candidates on the list, three lost the primaries. Other candidates not included in this list also spent a lot of money and lost. For example the defeat of Tennessee multi-millionaire Maxey Jarman and Florida multi-millionaire Jack M. Eckerd in Republican primaries certainly do not prove that, given the money, voters can be bought.

The presidential veto was not based on opposition to limiting campaign expenditures. "The legislation is aimed at the highly laudable and widely supported goals of controlling political campaign expenditures and preventing one candidate from having an unfair advantage over another," said Mr. Nixon in a veto message. "Its fatal deficiency is that it not only falls far short of achieving these goals but also threatens to make matters worse."

The bill, contrary to widespread belief, would not have imposed a monetary limit on all campaign expenses, but only on expenses related to radio and television. The huge sums could be diverted to other forms of campaigning. By setting a dollar limit rather than a time limit on broadcast campaigning, the bill would have discriminated against urban candidates who must pay much higher rates for air time. It also would have discriminated against candidates who do not have the incumbent's built-in advantage of free media coverage.

There were other faults in the bill and it would have been unwise for the President to approve it with the hope that future amendments might straighten out the problems. The veto, in fact, will serve as a useful blueprint the next time Congress gets down to the business of formulating a bill on campaign expenses.

The New York Times

New York, N.Y., October 14, 1970

President Nixon's veto of the bill to curb radio and television spending in political campaigns is a transparent and deplorable act of partisanship.

Everyone, including the President, now gives lip-service to the concept that limits should be set on the advantages that money can buy in the election process. Yet the first significant attempt in a quarter of a century to curb the inequities of campaign finance—a measure passed overwhelmingly by both houses of Congress—is vetoed by the President himself.

The reasons given are both glib and contradictory: The bill "plugs one hole in a sieve." Of course, but it is by so much the greatest hole that the others are minor leaks Congress can patch up in another session. It "unfairly endangers freedom of discussion." By preventing one candidate from buying up ten times the volume of broadcasting that his opponent can afford?

The law, Mr. Nixon goes on, would "favor the incumbent over the officeseeker." Arthur Goldberg, running against incumbent Governor Rockefeller, will be glad to know what he has escaped. The moral may be less clear to incumbent Senator Goodell running against monied challenger Richard Ottinger. And the bill would "severely limit the ability of many candidates to get their message to the greatest number of the electorate." Unlike the present arrangement, presumably, which limits some candidates fatally and others not at all.

Behind the veto, it seems clear, are none of these high-sounding considerations at all, but only the overriding fact that Republicans all too often can afford adequate television time and Democrats can not. The Republican National Committee started this fall's campaign with a cash surplus of $1.5 million; the Democrats, with a party debt of $9 million.

When Congress reconvenes, the 1970 elections will be over. By then perhaps tensions will have abated sufficiently for the veto to be overridden in a triumph of principle over party.

THE COMMERCIAL APPEAL

Memphis, Tenn., October 14, 1970

PRESIDENT NIXON'S veto of the bill which would have limited television and radio spending in political campaigns has brought sharp criticism and talk of a move to override in the post-election session of Congress which will begin Nov. 16.

Before such action is taken the members should take another look at the President's veto message.

He gave seven specific reasons for opposing the bill.

One of these was highly speculative. It was the one in which he said the electronic limitations simply would mean greater campaign efforts through newspaper ads, billboards, pamphlets and direct mail which might mean even larger campaign budgets. Another point seemed to be a peripheral issue —whether Congress could require broadcasters to charge a minimum rate for political broadcasts.

But in the other five points there were some solid objections.

Setting a dollar limit on such spending, he pointed out, rather than a time span limit for campaigning by such media would discriminate against urban candidates who must pay a higher rate for air time. The President seems to have slipped in a suggestion for rephrasing this point in the bill by mentioning in passing the possibility of a time limit. Some countries do set such time limits on the campaigns. Canada, for example, allows only 60 days. The length of United States political campaigns has been a subject of objection from both some candidates and many voters.

Also, the President notes that the bill did not cover broadcast spending by committees or individuals other than candidates. This would be a serious weakness. In some campaigns the spending by such committees and friends far exceeds the amount spent by the candidate personally. This provision, if allowed to stand, would facilitate subterfuge on behalf of the candidates.

The bill also seems to fall short on the question of offsetting the advantage an incumbent has in a campaign. If the challenger is limited in his spending, the advantage to the incumbent could be increased measurably.

Congress should look at the President's objections again for the possibilities of writing perhaps an even tighter bill in some respects and a more specific bill in any event. It is something that needs doing.

ARKANSAS DEMOCRAT
Little Rock, Ark., January 21, 1974

In July the Florida Supreme Court sent shivers through all of journalism by upholding a 60-year-old statute that guaranteed the right of reply to any person attacked by a newspaper. Last week the U.S. Supreme Court agreed to consider the case, itself an indication of its importance since the high court tries not to take cases from state supreme courts whenever it can avoid it.

A controversial school teacher, Pat Tornillo Jr., a candidate for the Florida legislature, was opposed by the Miami Herald, which is five times the size of its only competitor and a member of a national newspaper chain. It called Tornillo irresponsible and accused him of illegal conduct in two editorials. The Herald refused to print his reply verbatim, and Tornillo resurrected this old statute and sued. A lower court decided against Tornillo, but he persisted and suddenly came the thunderbolt from the state supreme court. The decision, which was 6 to 1 against the newspaper, quickly drew such predictable reactions as this one from the editor of the Wall Street Journal: "The government is now our new managing editor."

While we do not endorse the decision, we must say that it is neither nutty nor insignificant. At the beginning, we should say that the conventional interpretation of the first amendment demands the overturning of this or any other law that seeks to regulate the press. After all, government telling a newspaper what it has to print is just as obnoxious as telling it what it cannot print.

But the Florida Supreme Court has made a new and arresting interpretation. The first amendment, it says, did not create a privileged class for just newspaper editors. What it means is that everyone should enjoy freedom of expression, not just journalists. Obviously, when a newspaper has a monopoly — or a near-monopoly — it is absurd to say that a person enjoys freedom of expression when he is denied the opportunity to respond to an attack — and to the same audience addressed by his attackers. This is no longer the day of the pamphleteer, when everyone's publication had about the same circulation, which was determined largely by how far the publisher-editor-printer wanted to carry his broadsides.

As a matter of fact, this is not even 1904, when there were 17,000 different newspapers in America. Today, there are only 11,000, with the Miami Herald being one of the very largest. The man shouting from the roof of his house, buying a billboard or even speaking on the radio to defend himself is not quite the same thing as having it printed in the Miami Herald.

So maybe this old statute is not as ridiculous as it first appears to be. In fact, just last year, Jerome Barron, a scholar who has written a great deal about access to the media, wrote a book, "Freedom of the Press for Whom?", that suggested that the right of reply was so important that a national law should be drawn very similar to the Florida statute. This is more important now because of libel decisions that virtually give public figures no chance to recover damages unless they can prove malice. After all, they argue, the broadcast media have been able to live and to profit with the fairness doctrine — a guarantee of the right of reply — so why not the newspapers?

Well, without getting into that thicket, we can only say that the question is not one that is going to be solved by hysterical outbursts or by counting on the first amendment as a complete shield. It is marvelously broad but in this day of disappearing newspapers — more precisely, their acquisition by a few owners — there is reason to question whether it is broad enough to protect us from the luxury that we have enjoyed until now, which is every publisher doing as he damned well pleased.

While we think and hope that the Miami Herald will win its case at the Supreme Court, the question is not certain and will by no means be settled finally. The case should certainly cause newspaper owners to look to their ethics and to think about the wisdom of having some voluntary self-policing. The alternative is to one day have government decide that, like so many other things, the first amendment needs a modern interpretation.

The Pittsburgh Press
Pittsburgh, Pa., January 19, 1974

Judges and politicians are no more competent to edit newspapers than editors are to pass laws and preside in court.

For that reason, telling newspapers what they must or must not print is an assault on the integrity of the press.

The Florida Supreme Court didn't see it that way last September when it upheld a 1913 state law requiring newspapers to print replies from political candidates criticized in editorials.

Fortunately, the U. S. Supreme Court has agreed to rule on the constitutionality of the Florida law—a law that could spread to other states where thin-skinned politicians hold sway.

The issue is whether the Miami Herald should have published replies (it didn't) to two 1972 editorials criticizing a candidate for the state legislature.

The Florida Supreme Court, citing the 1913 law, said such replies must be published "upon request."

As a matter of policy, some newspapers print self-serving letters from politicians. Some don't. Most try to present all points of view in one form or another.

But if the Florida ruling stands, editors may shy away from election commentary rather than open their columns to every peeved candidate who demands space.

It seems logical that if a state has no right to restrict publication, it has no right to require publication either.

The alternative—to have judges upstage editors and decide what should be printed—is not exactly what the founding fathers had in mind.

St. Petersburg Times
St. Petersburg, Fla., January 30, 1974

Newspaper readers, we hear, tend to skip reports of court cases involving newspapers. Legal stuff, and self-serving besides, they probably figure, and sometimes they are right. But here is a case affecting readers far more than newspapers.

It involves an old Florida law that was dug up in 1972 and invoked against the Miami Herald. The law says newspapers that criticize politicians must print their replies.

IN THIS CASE, the Herald elected not to print one, and was haled into court, where a judge said the law was unconstitutional. But on appeal the Florida Supreme Court last July said 6 to 1 that it wasn't. The issue now awaits hearing by the Supreme Court of the United States.

On its face, the law sounds reasonable. Most newspapers in fact, on their own, go out of their way to print replies from aggrieved politicians, in an attempt to be fair. The Times invites replies to its political recommendations.

But the law doesn't leave a decision on this to the editor's judgment. It says he will print, free of cost, "any reply" the politician may make, in a place as conspicuous and a type as large as the matter complained of.

Suppose the reply is libelous of another candidate or some other innocent third party? Is the editor then compelled to abdicate his judgment and print it? It could be obscene, or vicious, or in bad taste. Must the paper abrogate its own ethical standards?

AND CONSIDER the ultimate test. Suppose the editor is arbitrary and capricious and simply refuses to print it. Maybe he hasn't even tried to be fair.

That's bad. But even in this worst of all possible theoretical cases, is it as bad as letting the government — any government — dictate what papers shall print?

It isn't surprising that the First Amendment to the U.S. Constitution dealt with just such government meddling. The Founding Fathers had seen plenty of that. The First Amendment says "no law" shall be passed restricting freedom of speech, religion or press.

That is pretty plain language. The Supreme Court shouldn't have much trouble determining that "no law" means what it says, including Florida's 1913 law granting political candidates the right to reply.

Sure, the press has a special interest in cases like this. (A similar case against The Times has been held in abeyance pending a ruling on the law's constitutionality.) But whatever the outcome, the press can survive it. It is the readers who are most likely to suffer should the law be upheld.

In that event the tendency of many papers would be to play safe. How much easier not to report wrong-doing by public officials than risk frequent suits under such a burdensome law. In many cases that would mean don't cover the news.

Certainly, there have been, there are, and there will be abuses by the press. Weigh them, though, against the sterility and dishonesty of a press subject to government rule. Under the latter arrangement — prevalent in much of the world — Watergate today would be no more than a fancy address.

LEDGER-STAR
Norfolk, Va., January 24, 1974

Censorship rears its head just as surely in a command to print something as when the publication of something is prohibited.

This is one of the central points made in the column by The New York Times' Tom Wicker, appearing elsewhere on this page today. And he is absolutely correct in thus attacking the logic of the Florida law which requires the publication of answers from those who may be criticized in the press. A decision is now being awaited from the Supreme Court on a Miami Herald case involving this law.

It is plainly an infringement on the Constitution's guarantee of a freedom of expression for the government to undertake to overrule the editorial judgment of a newspaper and to require display of material the paper has chosen not to use.

But the argument against enforced publication can be stated another way, too. And this goes to the heart of the "fairness" concept which lay behind the Florida law and which was reiterated by the Florida Supreme Court.

Ideally, all members of the press would strive to be totally fair and responsible. But the judgments to that end, or to whatever purpose they commit themselves, must be theirs alone except, obviously, in the areas of libel, obscenity and incitement to violence or rebellion.

The point is that true freedom of expression, including that of the press, must embrace the freedom to be wrong, the freedom to be unfair, yes, even the freedom to be irresponsible. The First Amendment does not say that freedom of speech and press shall not be abridged as long as the utterances meet certain ethical standards.

For if it did, there would be no guarantee of freedom at all. Every published word would have to be judged for its possible unrighteousness, unfairness or irresponsibility by some official or agency according to such official's or agency's view of things. The press would have to dance to whatever the current line on proper press conduct happened to be.

This is precisely the governmental despotism at which the First Amendment was aimed.

THE MIAMI NEWS
Miami, Fla., January 19, 1974

We are encouraged that the U.S. Supreme Court has agreed to hear arguments on the validity of Florida's right-to-reply law, a 60-year-old statute that never should have been adopted.

The court left itself an out by retaining the option to decide after the arguments whether it has jurisdiction. The case has reached the highest court only because the Florida Supreme Court lost sight of the real reason for the suit, filed by school union official Pat Tornillo against The Miami Herald.

Tornillo wanted equal space to respond to editorial criticism levied against his political candidacy. The state court, in a weak decision last July, reasoned that right-of-reply would add to the flow of information under the First Amendment. It ignored the resulting intrusion upon the newspapers' constitutionally protected right to decide its own content, an independence that has sustained the American press for two hundred years.

Newspapers have always published contrary opinions from persons who feel they have been abused. More often than not the complaint follows from a simple difference of political positions.

Society's interest in the free flow of ideas far outweighs the interest of the occasionally wronged, in our opinion. A decision to the contrary by the Supreme Court will both invite government interference and weaken the freedom of expression.

OREGON Journal
AN INDEPENDENT NEWSPAPER
Portland, Ore., January 24, 1974

Decision of the U. S. Supreme Court to review a Florida case which compels newspapers to give free reply space to politicians the newspapers have criticized again focuses attention on the freedom of press and speech amendment to the Constitution.

The case comes from the Florida Supreme Court and involves a candidate for the state Legislature whose candidacy had been criticized in an editorial in the Miami Herald.

He demanded free space in which to reply; the newspaper refused, and he sued under an old and seldom used Florida statute, giving such free space for reply. The Florida Supreme Court upheld the statute.

The Florida court based its opinion on two grounds. First, that the public's right to know all sides of a controversy is being jeopardized by growing concentration of the ownership of the media, which results ultimately in a form of private censorship.

Second, that such a requirement is similar to the "fairness doctrine" for television and radio which requires "equal time" for candidates.

As to the first justification, there is a tendency to regard the "freedom of the press" battle as one between newspapers and various opponents.

A rereading of the 1st Amendment to the U. S. Constitution should dispel this idea. The amendment says, "Congress shall make no law respecting an establishment of religion, or prohibiting the free exercise thereof; or abridging the freedom of the press; or the right of the people peaceably to assemble, and to petition the government for a redress of grievances."

In short, the amendment concerns rights of people as individuals. The rights of a free press are no more a defense of the newspapers than the right of free exercise of religion is a defense of a particular church or churches.

Thus an attempt to tell newspapers what they must print is basically an attempt to tell the individual what he must write.

The second justification — comparing the Florida statute to the "equal time" rule for television and radio is equally invalid.

On the basis that the broadcast media use public airwaves, the courts and Congress have specifically held that they are not covered by the 1st Amendment guarantees of a free press, and are subject to licensing regulations that stipulate how they may use the airwaves.

The press field is wide open to anyone who wants to start a magazine or newspaper or print a pamphlet.

A citizen may print and distribute an "open letter" to his congressman. Under the Florida court's reasoning, this citizen could be required to print and distribute, at the citizen's cost, a reply from the congressman.

It is true that there has been a growing concentration of the mass media, and with this growth comes greater responsibility.

Thus it is that any newspaper worthy of the name will normally print, in its letters to the editor column, a reply to a critical editorial.

Also the newspaper normally opens its news columns to speeches and statements of all candidates. But it does reserve the right to express its opinions in the editorial columns.

Granted that the mass media are quantitatively different from the individual, a policy which allows one government to tell a newspaper what it must publish is just one narrow step away from the government telling the individual what he may or may not say or what he must say. This is what Russia is doing to its authors.

The Houston Post
Houston, Tex., January 18, 1974

The main thrust of the challenged Florida law requiring newspapers to grant free space for replies by political candidates they have criticized is repressive enough, but it raises an important side issue.

The 61-year-old law, never used until recently, was upheld by the Florida Supreme Court and is now before the U.S. Supreme Court. Strong arguments against the constitutionality of the state law have been presented in and outside of Florida.

Even the Florida attorney general claimed the statute violates press freedoms guaranteed by the U.S. Constitution. If the nation's highest court now finds it unconstitutional, this will erase an example that encourages those who would impose controls on the press and regulate the free flow of information. Mississippi is the only other state to have a similar law. But since the Florida issue arose in 1972, efforts have been made in other states, including Texas, to pass newspaper reply legislation.

If the Supreme Court should uphold the Florida law, it could open a Pandora's Box of legal questions. The Florida law, for instance, provides jail terms and fines for refusing free space to reply in a publication which "assails" or "attacks" him. When is a person editorially attacked or assailed? Some candidates are more thin-skinned than others.

Statements of fact can be construed as criticism for no other reason than that they were brought up. Failure to mention some facts a candidate deems important has been taken as a personal affront. And could the reply rule be applied to the published quotations of an opponent? Such questions could keep the courts busy for years while the dissemination of news and the public's right to know suffer.

Broadcast Programming & Ownership

In recent years, government policies have influenced almost every aspect of broadcasting. Programming, ownership, advertising, cable transmission and employment practices have all come under federal scrutiny or regulation. The government has even organized and financed a Corporation for Public Broadcasting to compensate for the lack of educational programming by commercial broadcasters. This chapter surveys the major governmental actions in these areas during recent years.

Program Contents

FCC votes fine for 'indecency.' In a test ruling reported April 6, 1970, the Federal Communications Commission (FCC) voted to fine Eastern Education Radio, a licensee of WUHY-FM in Philadelphia, $100 for allegedly "indecent" programming in violation of FCC regulations. The commission invited courts to review the ruling "in order that the scope of the agency's authority to act in this sensitive area may be definitely established." In its first such action, the FCC charged that the station had broadcast "patently offensive words" Jan. 4 in an interview with Jerry Garcia, leader of a California rock music group called "The Grateful Dead."

FCC limits network shows. The Federal Communications Commission (FCC), in a 5–2 ruling May 7, said that local television stations in the 50 top market areas would have to fill at least one of the four nightly prime-time hours (7–11 p.m.) with independently produced material rather than network programs, network reruns or previously broadcast movies. The FCC said the rule, which would become effective in the fall of 1971, was designed to promote "competitive development of alternate sources of television programs."

FCC Chairman Dean Burch, who with Commissioner Robert Wells dissented from the ruling, said that the programming picked by the stations was likely to be "more of the same—more games, more light entertainment along proven formulas, more 'emcee' talk shows." Rather than providing diversity, Burch said, the ruling would only benefit independent production companies. He said the ruling was sound if its object was to make money for "the syndicator of 'Son of Lassie' or 'Daughter of I Love Lucy.'" Burch also indicated that he hoped the rule could be modified or canceled before it went into effect, as the composition of the commission changed.

Burch reprimands Johnson. Nicholas Johnson, a commissioner of the FCC, was publicly reprimanded Oct. 23 by FCC Chairman Dean Burch for having used an "unnecessarily offensive or grandiose phrase" during the taping of a television program. Johnson had used the phrase "get laid" during a taping Oct. 10 of the "Georgetown University Forum" on WRC-TV in Washington. The program's editors had deleted the phrase and Johnson had called the station's action the "height of arrogant irony."

FCC cites song selection. The Federal Communications Commission (FCC) warned the nation's commercial broadcasters March 6, 1971 that they faced punitive action if they failed to keep off the air song lyrics "tending to promote or glorify the use of illegal drugs."

The FCC, which controlled broadcasting licenses, said the agency had voted Feb. 24 to issue the directive. It was passed 5–1, with Nicholas Johnson dissenting. In an opinion accompanying the order, Johnson called it "an unsuccessfully disguised effort to censor song lyrics" and said he considered it an unconstitutional action.

In the order, the FCC said complaints had been received about broadcasting of lyrics that "promote or glorify" the use of marijuana, LSD and other illegal drugs. The FCC said it expected broadcasters "to ascertain before broadcast, the words or lyrics of recorded musical or spoken selections" to be broadcast on their stations.

Study of TV violence. A report by the surgeon general's Scientific Advisory Committee on Television and Social Behavior released Jan. 17, 1972 said that "viewing violence on television is conducive to an increase in aggressive behavior" in at least some children. Critics later charged that the report had deferred to the broadcast industry by diluting and qualifying the evidence.

The report concluded that "violence depicted on television can immediately or shortly thereafter induce mimicking or copying by children," and that "under certain circumstances television can instigate an increase in aggressive acts." However, the evidence "does not warrant the conclusion" that television violence "has an adverse effect on the majority of children."

Among the factors that might predispose a child to a harmful reaction were "pre-existing levels of aggression," "parental control of television viewing, parental affection, parental punishment," "parental emphasis on nonaggression," or socio-economic status.

The report documented the prevalence of violence on television, caused by a belief that "action is among the best, fastest, and easiest ways of attracting and keeping large audiences, and 'action' is considered as almost synonymous with violence."

While a 1971 study, included in the report, showed that 71% of all Saturday morning dramatic segments "involved at least one instance of human violence," another study showed that comedies, and in particular cartoons, had the most violent content. The latter study found that while the general level of violence on all programs remained constant between 1967 and 1969, "fatalities declined and the proportion of leading characters engaged in violence or killing declined."

The studies found no support for the thesis that televised violence may have a cathartic effect on aggressive tendencies, according to Dr. Ithiel de Sola Pool, a member of the advisory committee, Jan. 17.

Surgeon General Jesse L. Steinfeld, in releasing the report, called it "a strong, positive report" which would have a "significant impact," although the report itself included criticism of the selection process for the 12-member advisory committee. Steinfeld admitted that seven potential members had been vetoed by the National Broadcasting Co. and the American Broadcasting Co., which participated in the 1969 committee selection, but he said "we didn't want to be accused of picking a committee slanted against the television industry."

Some of those rejected by the networks had been associated with previous research in the field. Of the 12 members finally selected, two were broadcast executives, two were network consultants, and one was a former consultant.

Several scientists who had participated in the research studies on which the report was based were among its critics. They charged, according to a Feb. 19 New York Times report, that the report's use of ·qualifying language like "tentative" findings and "modest" links might have confused newspapers and the public.

Dr. John Murray of the National Institutes of Health said the final report gives the impression "that the findings are trivial," adding "there is no question in my mind that normal children watching a large amount of TV violence will become more aggressive."

Other critics said the report should have noted that, while other causes contributed to aggressive behavior, violence on television would be the easiest to remedy. In addition, the report should have emphasized that even if only some children were affected, some reform was needed.

Sen. John O. Pastore (D, R.I.), who had requested the study in 1969, scheduled March 21 hearings of the Communications Subcommittee on the matter. In the House, Rep. John M. Murphy (D, N.Y.), a strong critic of the report, introduced a bill asking the Federal Communications Commission to undertake a new study.

U.S. trust suit vs. TV networks. The Justice Department filed civil antitrust suits April 14 in federal district court in Los Angeles against the three major commercial television networks and a television program distributor formerly owned by one of the networks. The suits sought to prevent the networks "from carrying network-produced entertainment programs, including feature films, and from obtaining financial interests in independently produced entertainment programs," with the exception of first-run exhibition rights. The defendants claimed that the suit was superfluous in light of recent Federal Communications Commission (FCC) rulings that already, they claimed, had sharply reduced their control of entertainment programming.

Columbia Broadcasting System (CBS), National Broadcasting Co. (NBC) and American Broadcasting Co. (ABC) were charged with violating Sec-

tions 1 and 2 of the Sherman Antitrust Act. Viacom International, Inc., a former CBS subsidiary which controls some CBS program syndication rights, was also named as a defendant.

According to the Justice Department, the networks "have used their control of access to air time to monopolize prime time television entertainment programming and to obtain valuable interests in such programming," depriving "the viewing public, independent program suppliers, and advertisers" of "the benefits of free competition."

In particular, the suit alleged that the networks' entry into motion picture production threatened free competition in that industry as well.

The Department said the networks had spent $840 million for programs in 1969 and received $1.5 billion in revenues. In 1967, the suit charged, ABC had ownership interest in 86% of the entertainment programs it broadcast during prime time (which the suit defined as 6–11 p.m., and the networks considered 7–11 p.m.), NBC had interests in 68% and CBS in 73%.

Network officials, reacting to reports of the suits published the day before they were filed, claimed that the situation had changed drastically since 1967. In the last quarter of 1971, a CBS spokesman said April 13, the network had financial interests in only two of its prime time entertainment programs, and its own production accounted for only 8.2% of its prime time schedule. NBC and ABC spokesmen said over 90% of their prime time programs in the last quarter of 1971 were bought from outsiders.

An April 13 ABC statement cited a 1970 ruling by the FCC requiring every station to buy at least one hour of prime time entertainment from non-network sources. Other FCC rulings had barred network equity ownership in all shows produced or televised in 1971 or thereafter, and curbed network control over syndication, the sale of programs to individual stations. The latter decision had caused the separation of Viacom from CBS. A Justice Department spokesman noted April 14, however, that FCC chairman Dean Burch had opposed the 1970 ruling, and changes in Commission membership could bring about its reversal.

ABC vice president Eugene S. Cowen disputed the Justice Department's income figures April 13. He said about $500 million of total network revenues were distributed to affiliates as station compensation, and about $60 million more was paid to the American Telephone & Telegraph Co. for line charges.

The Justice Department, in a statement April 14, said its suits had resulted from an investigation dating back to the 1950's, but suspended during an 11-year FCC inquiry. The New York Times said April 15 that the suits had been approved by former Assistant Attorney General Richard W. McLaren more than a year and a half before they were filed. They were said to have been revived after re-

peated complaints by Antitrust Division staff lawyers about delays in antitrust enforcement, and after the controversy surrounding the out-of-court settlement of antitrust suits against the International Telephone & Telegraph Corp.

Some network executives, however, were reported to feel the suits reflected continued Administration hostility toward the networks, which in the past had led to charges of intimidation of the media.

The suits generated speculation that the networks would lose control over programs to a handful of large advertisers, and lose revenues needed to subsidize news and public affairs programming. But some industry critics· saw a new opportunity for program diversity.

One provision in the Justice Department's brief asked for the networks to be enjoined from "tying programs to time." CBS president Robert D. Wood warned affiliated stations in a telegram April 13 that this "would reduce stations and networks to mere conduits," by forcing the networks to sell time to advertisers or independent producers who would provide their own programs, rather than the networks buying programs first and then selling advertising time, as at present.

Paul C. Harper, chairman of Needham, Harper and Steers, Inc., a large advertising agency, said April 13 "advertising agencies are equipped neither financially nor professionally to fill the gap," and "do not want the risk" of production. Other industry executives, according to the Wall Street Journal April 14, argued that high production costs would limit the market to a small number of the largest advertisers. Still others recalled that in the 1950's advertisers and film producers had exercised more power over broadcasting, and reformers had demanded greater network control to improve the quality of programming.

But the Justice Department's April 14 statement said that "networks would continue to exercise responsibility for programs they accept for broadcast," and a spokesman explained that the network still would make the final choice in buying programs.

Beverly C. Moore, an antitrust expert and a member of consumer activist Ralph Nader's Corporate Accountability Research Group, was reported to have praised the Department's initiative April 14, as leading, if successful, to more program diversity. He said that "the perception of audience desires of a large number of television advertisers, who will be sponsoring the programs directly, is more varied than the perceptions of the networks."

FCC curbs TV network role. The FCC lifted a stay June 8 on rules proposed in 1970 limiting network control of television programming.

Beginning Aug. 1, the networks would be barred from acquiring any financial or proprietary rights in any program they did not exclusively produce, and beginning June 1, 1973, they would be barred from distributing any programs to independent stations.

The commission explained that "fair competition" was "unlikely when the heavy dependence of program suppliers on their network patrons renders them vulnerable to demands for syndication rights or share of profits."

The rules had been stayed pending court tests, which were resolved in favor of the commission.

Curb on reruns sought. In a letter to the AFL-CIO Screen Actors Guild in Hollywood Sept. 14, President Nixon informed the union he supported its position that the increasing use of reruns constituted a threat to jobs and domestic sources of new programming. "I am convinced that in cutting the amount of original programming the television networks are failing to serve their own best interests, as well as those of the public," the President said.

Nixon said he had instructed White House director of telecommunications, Clay T. Whitehead, "to thoroughly investigate this problem" and was hopeful that Whitehead, "working with the networks, will find a voluntary solution, otherwise we will explore whatever regulatory recommendations are in order."

The guild, along with other unions in Hollywood, had petitioned the FCC to limit network reruns to no more than 25% of prime evening time (8–11 p.m.). According to the networks, reruns constituted an estimated 45% of prime time during the current year, much of it in the summer.

Bill planned to curb TV news bias. Nixon Administration plans to introduce legislation to make local stations responsible for the objectivity of network news programs were disclosed in a speech Dec. 18 by Clay T. Whitehead, director of the White House Office of Telecommunications Policy. Addressing the Indianapolis chapter of Sigma Delta Chi, a professional journalism society, Whitehead said the Administration had drafted legislation to revise the TV station license renewal procedure.

Under it, Whitehead said, each TV station would be required to meet two criteria for renewal of license by the Federal Communications Commission (FCC). The broadcaster "must demonstrate," Whitehead said, "he has been substantially attuned to the needs and interests of the community he serves . . . irrespective of where the programs were obtained, . . . and the broadcaster must show that he has afforded reasonable, realistic and practical opportunities for the presentation and discussion of conflicting views on controversial issues."

The planned legislation also would extend the license renewal period from every three years to five and would require community groups to prove complaints against local broadcasters before a

hearing was held.

Among other remarks by Whitehead:

■ "When there are only a few sources of national news on television, as we now have, editorial responsibility must be exercised more effectively by local broadcasters and by network management. Station managers and network officials who fail to act to correct imbalance or consistent bias in the networks—or who acquiesce by silence—can only be considered willing participants, to be held fully accountable . . . at license renewal time."

■ "When a reporter or disc jockey slips in or passes over information in order to line his pocket, that's 'plugola' and management would take quick corrective action.

"But men also stress or supress information in accordance with their beliefs. Will station licensees or network executives also take action against this ideological 'plugola'? . . . Station licensees have final responsibility for news balance. . . ."

■ Local broadcasters "can no longer accept network standards of taste, violence and decency in programming. If the programs or commercials glorify the use of drugs; if the programs are violent or sadistic; if the commercials are false or misleading, or simply intrusive and obnoxious; the stations must jump on the networks rather than wince as the Congress and the FCC are forced to do so."

■ If a station "can't demonstrate meaningful service to all elements of its community, the license should be taken away by the FCC. The standard should be applied with particular force to the large TV stations in our major cities."

■ "The First Amendment's guarantee of a free press was not supposed to create a privileged class of men called journalists who are immune from criticism by government or restraint by publishers and editors."

■ "Who else but management can or should correct so-called professionals who confuse sensationalism with sense and who dispense elitist gossip in the guise of news analysis?"

A spokesman for the National Broadcasting Co. commented later Dec. 18 that the proposed legislation seemed "to be another attempt to drive a wedge between television stations and the networks," which would be "regrettable because the ability of our broadcasting system to expand its service to the public depends on continuation of a close and cooperative association of networks and stations, particularly in the area of news and information, without government interference."

An American Broadcasting Co. spokesman expressed concern that Whitehead's "remarks may represent an obstacle to the continued good relationship between the networks and local stations."

Among other comments Dec. 18:

Lawrence H. Rogers 2nd, president of Taft Broadcasting Co.—"I happen to believe the networks leave a great deal to be desired in terms of taste and balance," but current legislation made "it abundantly clear that licensees are the sole statutory censors of what they put on the air. When the networks do something I don't agree with, my response is to take it off the air or raise hell until they change it."

Tom Chauncey, president of TV station KOOL in Phoenix, Ariz.—"I'm just plain apoplectic. If Whitehead really means this, we might as well be living in the Soviet Union. This would mean censorship of news and entertainment, the government telling us what to broadcast and telling the people what they should see or hear."

End to football blackout sought. President Nixon Dec. 20 personally entered the controversy over the National Football League's (NFL) policy of blacking out television coverage of local games.

At the President's direction, Attorney General Richard G. Kleindienst asked NFL Commissioner Pete Rozelle to lift the television ban on the upcoming playoff games if they were sold out 48 hours before game time. But Rozelle rejected the request, maintaining that the blackout policy was necessary to protect the live gates for the games.

Under present policy, no NFL game could be televised within a 75-mile radius of the game site.

Shortly after Rozelle denied the President's request, Kleindienst indicated that the Administration would seek Congressional re-examination of pro football's antitrust exemption. In a statement which he said had the support of the President, Kleindienst said the Administration would "urge the new Congress to re-examine the entire exemption statute and seek legislation that is more in keeping with the public interest."

Chief Justice Warren E. Burger refused Dec. 24 to order a Supreme Court review of lower court rulings, which had permitted a television blackout of the Washington-Green Bay playoff game that day. A three-judge panel of the U.S. Court of Appeals in Washington said the blackout was constitutional, and could be lifted only by an act of Congress.

Administration asks rerun study. Clay T. Whitehead, director of the White House Office of Telecommunications Policy, asked the FCC to study ways to require networks to use fewer reruns, or repeat programs, during prime time, it was reported March 23, 1973.

Whitehead said the use of reruns had risen sharply in recent years, allowing "networks to maintain profit levels in the face of rising program costs," but causing reduced employment in Hollywood. Whitehead also asked the FCC to reduce the amount of non-network programs that stations must broadcast during prime time, 7–11, from one hour to one half hour.

FCC to probe obscenity. The Federal Communications Commission (FCC) said March 27 it had voted 5-1 March 22 to investigate alleged obscenity on radio and television stations to determine possible law violations.

The FCC had received 3,000 complaints since December 1972 about alleged obscenity, mostly concerning late night radio call-in shows, during which some women allegedly discussed their sex life in graphic detail, a few cases of pornographic movie showings on cable or commercial stations and obscene language and displays of sexual organs on public access programs in two major cities.

The commission had been questioned about the complaints during Congressional hearings by Sen. John O. Pastore (D, R.I.), and by Rep. Torbert H. MacDonald (D, Mass.) March 14. MacDonald said March 27 he was "delighted that [FCC Chairman Dean] Burch and a majority of his fellow commissioners have acted with such dispatch."

Nicholas Johnson, the only commissioner to dissent, said the "FCC has no business listening to subject matter of programs," except in determining the percentage of program categories on a station or in application of the fairness doctrine. He said the FCC action, coming during a Washington convention of the National Association of Broadcasters (NAB), constituted "intimidation," and a step toward "censorship."

The FCC said an administrative law judge, with subpoena powers, would conduct the probe. Stations could be charged under federal law banning the broadcast of "obscene, indecent or profane material," or could be subject to early hearings on license renewal.

Burch told the NAB convention March 28 that if broadcasters allowed themselves to "cop out" of their "responsibilities" to remove obscene programming, they would "end up paying the price for a handful" of broadcasters.

Pastore bill reported out. The Senate Commerce Committee July 18 reported out a bill sponsored by Sen. John O. Pastore (D, R.I.) that would lift television blackouts on home games that were sold out 48 hours in advance. That day, Rep. Stanford E. Parris (R, Va.) introduced an identical bill in the House.

The NFL remained opposed to laws lifting local television blackouts. An NFL "yellow paper" issued Feb. 16 and reaffirmed May 16 argued that when games were televised locally, fans holding tickets would not appear, especially late in the season during cold weather. Subsequent ticket sales would suffer, the NFL argued.

Football TV blackouts barred. President Nixon Sept. 14 signed into law a bill, passed the day before by Congress, that ended for a three-year period television blackouts of National Football League (NFL) and other pro sports home games if they were sold out 72 hours in advance.

The House passed the bill by a roll call vote of 366–37 and the Senate, minutes later, approved the same bill by a voice vote.

On the first day the ban was lifted—Sept. 16—there were 49,551 no-shows among the more than 530,000 fans holding tickets to nine NFL contests that had been sold out 72 hours in advance. The Miami-San Francisco and Kansas City-Los Angeles games, both played in stadiums that seated about 80,000, had no-shows totaling 27,806.

High Court upholds song censorship. The Supreme Court Oct. 15 announced it would not disturb a lower court ruling that upheld a Federal Communications Commission (FCC) regulation requiring broadcasters to censor songs whose lyrics promoted or glorified the illegal use of drugs.

Prime time access rule eased. The FCC voted Nov. 29 to ease restrictions which had limited network-originated television programming to three of the four prime-time viewing hours (7–11 p.m.) in the 50 top market areas.

Under the new rules, the three networks would be barred from local stations only between 7:30 and 8 p.m., Monday through Saturday, although one such period a week could be used for children's specials, documentaries or public-affairs programs produced by networks.

The FCC also directed the affected local stations to use "some portion" of the daily half-hour for independently-produced minority affairs programs, community coverage or children's shows.

CBS charges reprisal in suits. In a brief filed in response to federal antitrust suits against the three television networks, CBS charged Dec. 21 that the government had embarked on "an unlawful plan" to "restrain, intimidate and inhibit criticism of the President of the United States and his appointees."

CBS, along with NBC and the American Broadcasting Co. (ABC), responded in federal district court in Los Angeles to antitrust suits filed in April 1972 which sought to prevent the networks from producing their own serials and feature films and from obtaining financial interests in independent production operations.

Both NBC and ABC asserted defenses based on First Amendment rights, but—according to network sources—neither was as explicit as CBS.

The CBS brief argued that "as early as October 1969" the Nixon Administration had prepared plans to "use the power and machinery of the federal government" to stifle television news coverage. The purpose of the suits, CBS contended, was not to enforce antitrust law, but to threaten or punish news organizations.

Cable & Pay Television

Court upholds state CATV control. The Supreme Court Feb. 2, 1970 upheld a lower court decision affirming the power of states to control community antenna television (CATV) operations by licensing and rate regulations. TV Pix Inc. and Wells TV Inc. had challenged Nevada CATV regulations on the ground that the Federal Communications Commission (FCC) had asserted jurisdiction over the regulation of CATV systems. The justices affirmed the lower court ruling that the federal and state controls did not overlap.

Pay-TV authorized. Over the dissent of Justice Douglas, the Supreme Court Feb. 24 upheld a 1968 Federal Communications Commission (FCC) ruling to permit the government to license subscription TV systems. The court rejected an appeal by the National Association of Theater Owners and the Joint Committee Against Toll TV, which contended that the FCC had acted without Congressional authority and that pay-TV constituted "a direct and unconstitutional discrimination against low income groups." The justices let stand an appeals court decision that pay-TV would encourage "diversity of expression" and might "spur the free broadcasting networks and stations to make substantial improvements in their services."

The FCC had first authorized trial subscription TV operations in 1957 and the Zenith Radio Corp. had patented a Phonevision pay-TV system and had sponsored a trial system in Hartford, Conn. The FCC issued rules in 1968 limiting pay-TV transmissions in an effort to preserve free television.

FCC votes CATV expansion. In a preliminary vote May 15, the Federal Communications Commission (FCC) approved a plan to remove restrictions on cable television, or CATV, systems by permitting importation of out-of-town programming. Under current rules CATV (Community Antenna Television) systems could import signals only within 35 miles of a community. The new plan, announced May 17 and backed 4–3 by the commissioners, was subject to an FCC staff study and formal vote before it would go into effect.

Cable television systems, using large master antennas to pick up signals to be distributed by wire to subscribers' homes, currently served four million U.S. households. Most of the subscribers were in remote communities where normal TV reception was poor, and development of CATV systems in larger communities was restricted because of limited programming allowed under the current rules.

The new plan, sponsored by FCC Chairman Dean Burch and endorsed by Commissioners Robert E. Lee, Nicholas Johnson and H. Rex Lee, while permitting out-of-town programming, would require substitution of locally-sold advertising for commercial breaks on the imported signal. To compensate for expected incursion into the market of local ultra high frequency (UHF) stations, revenues from the locally-sold CATV advertising would go to UHF stations. In addition, 5% of a cable system's income would be diverted into a fund to subsidize non-commercial public television.

Cable TV agreement. Three broadcasting and cable television organizations approved an agreement Nov. 11, 1971 on the future extension of cable television. Under the agreement, cable operators were permitted to import two out-of-town signals without negotiating rights and fees for specific shows. Some compensation, such as a percentage of the cable industry's gross income, was to be negotiated for owners of film copyrights.

In the 50 largest markets (from New York City, the largest, to Wilkes-Barre-Scranton, Pa., the 50th largest), cable companies would be permitted to import only programs for which local broadcasters had not purchased exclusive rights. In the next 50 largest markets (Little Rock, Ark., the 51st, to Columbia, S.C., the 100th), exclusive film rights were limited to two years, after which such films would be available to cable companies.

The plan, part of which emerged from the White House Office of Telecommunications Policy, was designed to slow cable television's growth in the largest markets while extending it from remote rural areas where it began into small cities.

The plan was accepted Nov. 11 by the National Cable Television Association meeting in Washington, and two broadcasting organizations—the Association of Maximum Service Telecasters, meeting in Atlanta, and the National Association of Broadcasters, meeting in Las Vegas.

Cable company guilty of bribery—Irving B. Kahn, former head of Teleprompter Corp., the largest cable TV firm in the country, was sentenced in federal court in New York Nov. 30 to five years in prison on charges that he had obtained an exclusive cable TV franchise by bribing Johnstown, Pa. officials.

A jury Oct. 20 had found Tele-prompter and Kahn guilty on chargers of paying $15,000 in bribes to three town officials, two of them had pleaded guilty. The trial of the third official, who pleaded not guilty, was pending. Kahn, who conceded payments but said they were paid to protect his company, resigned as chairman of the firm after his conviction.

New cable TV rules set. The Federal Communications Commission (FCC) announced Feb. 3, 1972 a series of new rules designed to regulate the future extension of cable television.

The new policy would promote the growth of cable television from rural areas into the nation's smaller cities, while restricting its encroachment into big-city viewing markets.

The decision to check the spread of cable television into the major metropolitan areas was deemed necessary to win approval of the overall policy by television broadcasters, who had fought it for five years. One of the new rules permitted the existing broadcast stations to retain control over program material in the 50 largest TV markets, effectively checking the spread of cable TV into those areas.

The new rules were approved by the FCC, 4-2. One of the dissenters, Commissioner Nicholas Johnson, charged that "secret bargaining" among Administration officials, broadcast industry leaders and FCC Chairman Dean Burch had led to the decision to block the expansion of cable TV into the cities where Johnson said it was needed most.

The new rules, which were scheduled to go into effect March 31, could be stopped by court action.

Under the new rules, almost every aspect of cable TV's growth would be regulated, although the question of how fast it was to expand was left unresolved. Presently, about 9% of the nation's 60 million homes with TV sets were equipped with the cable setup. Most of them were in rural areas.

Cable television, also known as CATV, brought programs into homes through coaxial cable rather than by regular broadcast transmissions. CATV subscribers usually paid a monthly fee of about $5 for the service.

Specifically, the new regulations would require all CATV systems to:

■ Carry a minimum of 20 channels, some of which would have to carry all local television stations while they were broadcasting.

■ Make available for five years without charge two channels for the use of local government and educational broadcasts.

■ Designate one channel as a free "public access" station. Air time for the channel would be determined on a "first-come, first-served basis," without censorship except that "advertising, including political spots, lotteries, obscene or indecent matter will be prohibited."

■ Provide for a system that would enable viewers to transmit signals back to a central office.

But the key to the consensus policy, however, was the decision to restrict CATV's growth into the big-city markets. Accordingly, in the top 50 viewing markets (from New York City, the largest, to Wilkes Barre-Scranton, Pa., the 50th largest) cable companies would be permitted to import only programs for which local broadcasters had not purchased exclusive rights. In the next 50 largest markets (Little Rock, Ark., to Columbia, S.C.), exclusive film rights were limited to one year. In still smaller viewing markets, there would be no exclusive film rights.

Cable TV merger called off. Columbia Cable System's planned merger with Viacom International was called off April 21 because of an antitrust suit filed in federal district court in Los Angeles April 14 by the Justice Department.

The suit charged that Viacom and the three major television networks "monopolized and restrained trade" in prime time television entertainment programs. Viacom, an independent cable television operator, was spun off from the Columbia Broadcasting System in 1971.

Supreme Court upholds FCC. The Supreme Court June 7 ruled 5-4 that the Federal Communications Commission (FCC) did not exceed its authority when it ordered cable television operators to originate some of their own programming.

The decision overturned a ruling by the U.S. circuit court in St. Louis that the FCC had overstepped its authority in 1969 when it ordered cable systems with more than 3,500 subscribers to present programs other than automated services.

Viacom settlement proposed. The Justice Department announced a proposed consent judgment Dec. 14 to settle the Viacom International Inc. antitrust suit.

The agreement would require that Viacom seek Justice Department approval for disposition of program syndication rights obtained in 1970 from Columbia Broadcasting System Inc. (CBS) until the government suit against CBS was settled. Viacom had been spun off from CBS in 1970, and under terms of the settlement, would be required to furnish the government with data needed in the television network suit.

Court lets stand Kahn conviction. The Supreme Court May 14, 1973 left standing the conspiracy convictions of Tele-PrompTer Corp. and its former chairman and president, Irving B. Kahn, in a case involving a cable television franchise in Johnstown, Pa.

Eased cable TV rules urged. A White House report, released Jan. 16, 1974 by the Office of Telecommunications Policy, called for division of the cable television industry into cable system operators and independent programming organizations, and eventual removal of most government regulation.

The report, prepared by a Cabinet committee, recommended that cable TV be given the same freedom-of-the-press status as the print media: subject to the strictures of copyright, antitrust, libel and obscenity laws, but exempt from the fairness and equal time rules applied to broadcast media.

The need for the current broadcast restrictions would be removed, the report said, by making cable system operators "essentially neutral" distribution systems and requiring them to lease their channels to others who would provide programs. Operators would be prohibited from using the channels themselves, with such minor exceptions as the use of a channel for listing a system's programs.

The report also recommended that TV networks, local broadcasters and newspapers be permitted to enter the cable industry either as system owners or programmers. (Current Federal Communications Commission [FCC] regulations prevented network ownership of cable operations and ownership by local stations of cable systems within their broadcast area.)

Among the report's other proposals:

■ Local governments should have the sole right to franchise cable systems but would be prohibited from granting exclusive franchises.

■ "Pay-TV," involving a charge per program on top of subscription fees, should be unregulated except for a current FCC rule preventing cable TV from taking live sports events from broadcasters and transmitting them on Pay-TV.

■ Safeguards to protect individual privacy and assure access to cable systems by minorities, the poor and rural populations.

The report urged that most of its proposals take effect when about 50% of "TV households" were wired to cable systems, with gradual deregulation in the interim. The report estimated a transition period of about five years, but cable industry spokesmen suggested 10 years was more realistic.

Cable TV wins copyright ruling. The Supreme Court ruled 6–3 March 4 that cable television systems were not subject to U.S. copyright laws when they imported distant TV signals and broadcast them to paid subscribers. In 1968, the court had exempted cable TV from payment of royalties for copyrighted programs originating locally.

As in 1968, the court majority determined that reception and retransmission of signals was "essentially a viewer function, irrespective of the distance between the broadcasting station and the ultimate viewer." Moreover, the court majority reasoned, cable TV merely

enhanced a signal, making a program easier to view. Justice Potter Stewart, author of the majority opinions in the 1968 case as well as the present one, said broadcasters of the original signals would be compensated because the size of their markets would be calculated "on the basis of the size of the direct broadcast market augmented by the size of the CATV market."

Justices William O. Douglas and Harry A. Blackmun and Chief Justice Warren E. Burger dissented.

The cable television industry also won another ruling March 4 when the court ordered the Federal Communications Commission (FCC) to reconsider the annual fee system it imposed on the industry to pay the cost of regulating it. The court majority suggested that charges be calculated on the basis of specific services rendered to a company and for services rendered at large. Justices William J. Brennan Jr. and Thurgood Marshall dissented. Justices Lewis F. Powell Jr. and Blackmun did not participate.

Public Broadcasting

FCC rules on service to CPB. In a declaratory ruling requested by the Corporation for Public Broadcasting, the Federal Communications Commission (FCC) said Nov. 10, 1969 that interconnection service provided at a reduced rate by carriers to noncommercial stations should be comparable "in all material respects" to service furnished to commercial users. The commission said that preemption of noncommercial hookups for commercial customers or classification of noncommercial programs as "lower priority" violated the intent of authorizations under the 1967 Public Broadcasting Act. A commission spokesman said the ruling was offered "to remove some misconceptions" about service offered noncommercial stations by carriers.

TV program ban voted. Mississippi's State Commission for Educational Television voted May 2, 1970 to ban the broadcasting of "Sesame Street," regarded by some educators as the leading television show for preschool-aged children, on the state's educational network because of racial considerations.

TV program ban revoked. Mississippi's State Commission for Educational Television May 24 reversed an earlier decision and announced that it had approved for statewide telecasts the showing of the educational series "Sesame Street." The commission had said May 2 it would not allow the program, regarded by some educators as the leading TV show for preschool-age children, to be shown because of its integrated cast.

One member of the commission said the panel opposed the screening of the program "because it uses a highly integrated cast of children." "Mainly," he said, "the commission members felt that Mississippi was not yet ready for it."

The commission was created by the Mississippi legislature after it had appropriated more than $5,000 for operation and expansion of the state's educational television network. Some legislators contended that the commission was necessary to screen programs that should not be shown in Mississippi.

Nixon names CPB officers. President Nixon May 18 nominated three new members to the Corporation for Public Broadcasting: Frank E. Schooley, 64, for reappointment to a six-year term; John Hay Whitney, 65, president of the John Hay Whitney Foundation, to succeed Saul Haas; John D. Wrather Jr., 51, owner of radio and TV stations in San Diego, Tulsa and New York City, to succeed Erich Leinsdorf. The Senate confirmed the three nominees Aug. 28.

Delaware drops ETV. Delaware's state-wide educational television network—the first in the nation—became the first to be scrapped June 30 when the General Assembly adjourned without appropriating any funds for program telecasts. The abandonment of the five-year-old network left $1 million worth of equipment unused and the staff unemployed. Critics had attacked the networks' emphasis on programs of a non-academic nature and charged that many classrooms lacked television receivers.

Congress divided on CPB budget. Different versions of a bill authorizing appropriations for the Corporation for Public Broadcasting were approved by the Senate May 18 and House Sept. 10. The Senate version called for open-ended authorizations through fiscal 1973. The House, after being advised of a committee decision to exert pressure on the Administration to devise a permanent financing plan, adopted a one-year authorization for fiscal 1971 of $30 million and an additional appropriation of up to $5 million for matching grants. The Corporation received a $15 million appropriation from Congress for fiscal 1970 plus an additional $2.4 million from non-federal sources.

Two-year funding approved. A two-year funding plan for the Corporation for Public Broadcasting was given final Congressional authorization Sept. 29. Voice votes in the House Sept. 28 and Senate Sept. 29 approved $30 million annually for fiscal 1971–72 and an additional $5 million annually to match funds from non-federal sources for the Corporation.

TV report stirs debate. A report prepared by National Education Television (NET), charging that FBI agents had hired "provocateurs" to encourage and participate in radical violence, was deleted by the Public Broadcasting System (PBS) shortly before its scheduled showing Oct. 6, 1971 as part of the "Great American Dream Machine" program. It was broadcast two days later amid charges of censorship and reports of FBI displeasure.

The report, put together by Paul Jacobs, a California radical political activist, presented interviews with three youths, two in Seattle and one at the University of Alabama in Tuscaloosa, who said they had been paid by the FBI to infiltrate radical groups and encourage illegal acts that could lead to prosecutions. The program included denials by the FBI agents named by the alleged infiltrators.

FBI Director J. Edgar Hoover, in a letter sent after press screenings of the show, called the charges "totally and absolutely false." He added that the Bureau had "referred this matter to the Department of Justice."

After New York's Channel 13 announced it would broadcast the deleted report Oct. 8, PBS officials offered it for broadcast to all its stations. According to the New York Times Oct. 9, the program was broadcast in most major areas.

Responding to charges by NET officials that PBS had exercised "censorship" in its cancellation decision, Hartford N. Gunn Jr., PBS president, said the report had lacked on-screen "documentation" and that PBS had wanted the subject presented in greater depth as a separate program.

Public television bill vetoed. President Nixon June 30, 1972 vetoed a bill authorizing funds for the Corporation for Public Broadcasting for two more years on the grounds the corporation was becoming too powerful and the bill's funding procedure was faulty. The President indicated he had been influenced by the "public and legislative debate" over the bill during which program content and the corporation's trend to focus on public affairs had drawn much criticism.

Conservatives had complained in the House debate June 1 that the corporation had concentrated on public affairs and cultural programs at the expense of educational programs and that news programs and personnel were biased toward the liberal side.

The House had passed the bill June 1 by a 254–69 vote.

In the Senate debate, Sen. Howard H. Baker Jr. (R, Tenn.) complained June 22 that a nude ballet shown on public television was "not the sort of thing our federal Treasury should be involved in." He also objected to an anti-war program telecast by the same station. In the 82–1 vote June 22 approving the bill, the opposition vote was cast by Conservative-Republican James L. Buckley (N.Y.), who opposed a federal role in the communications business.

Nixon said in his veto message there were "many fundamental disagreements concerning the direction which public broadcasting has taken and should pursue" and "perhaps the most important one is the serious and widespread concern expressed in Congress and within public broadcasting itself—that an organization originally intended to serve only local stations, is becoming instead the center of power and the focal point of control for the entire public broadcasting system."

Of the $65 million which would have been authorized for the corporation for fiscal 1973 under the bill, 70% was for operations and programming at the national level, 30% for local stations. The bill also authorized $90 million in fiscal 1974 and an additional $10 million over the two years for improvement of station facilities. The President had requested a one-year $45 million authorization, which was $10 million more than its current funding.

Reflecting the Congressional debate, the bill also would have prohibited the corporation from conducting public opinion surveys on governmental elections and from paying salaries of more than $42,500 a year.

Nixon signs appropriations bill. President Nixon Aug. 30 signed a 1973 appropriations bill for the Corporation for Public Broadcasting which totaled $45 million.

Macy quits. John W. Macy Jr., 55, resigned Aug. 10 as president of the Corporation for Public Broadcasting, effective Oct. 15. Macy resigned after a dispute with the Nixon Administration on the future direction of public television and radio.

President Nixon nominated Henry W. Loomis, 53, deputy director of the U.S. Information Agency to replace Macy as president of the corporation.

Public TV chairman resigns. Thomas B. Curtis, board chairman of the Corporation for Public Broadcasting (CPB), resigned April 14 in the midst of a bitter controversy over the control of public, non-commercial television. Curtis, 62, a Republican and former Missouri congressman, had been trying to mediate a dispute between CPB, which channeled federal funds to public television, and the Public Broadcasting Service (PBS), which was set up by CPB to operate the interconnection among the system's more than 200 stations.

The immediate cause of his resignation was an April 13 vote by the CPB board, allegedly in response to White House pressure, to defer action on a compromise plan backed by Curtis to create a CPB-PBS "partnership" to control the network in defiance of Administration demands that CPB keep control in its hands. The plan would have left control of federal funding with the CPB, but responsibility for network programming would have been shared by CPB and PBS and the individual PBS stations would have been allowed to schedule programs on the interconnection even when the content displeased CPB.

The conflict dated back to June 1972, when President Nixon vetoed a CPB fund bill, expressing concern over centralization of the PBS system. The Administration was also reportedly displeased with the political content of PBS public affairs programs, including William F. Buckley Jr.'s "Firing Line," "Black Journal" and "Washington Week in Review," all of which were scheduled to continue in fiscal 1974, possibly with private backing, despite a CPB move to end federal funding of them. The CPB leadership—most of whom, including Curtis and CPB President Henry Loomis, were appointed by Nixon—had been trying since January to take over all responsibility for programs distributed to local stations.

According to the Wall Street Journal April 2, a partial compromise had been reached in late March, with a concession to localism in the formation of a new PBS leadership, which included community leaders, educators, businessmen drawn from local public television boards, as well as station heads. Factions within the ranks of station managers merged to deal jointly with CPB. The result was the compromise favorable to local licensees on the control of scheduling.

An additional factor in the negotiations was the position of the Ford Foundation, which had long been a major contributor to public television. According to the New York Times April 14, the foundation would not continue funding national programs unless the station licensees retained the "integrity of the interconnection system."

Interviewed in Chicago April 23 by the New York Times, Curtis charged that the White House had "tampered with" the CPB board in an attempt to influence the vote on the compromise. He alleged that calls had been made to at least four of the members on the eve of the meeting, an act which he considered a threat to the Congressionally-mandated independence of CPB. He said that when he was appointed it was with "the clear understanding that the President wanted us to so set up the Corporation for Public Broadcasting that public broadcasting could not be made a propaganda arm for the Nixon Administration or for any succeeding administration." Curtis said he had resigned when it became clear that the White House no longer respected CPB's integrity.

Ralph B. Rogers, a leader of the PBS licensees, suggested April 19 that Clay T. Whitehead, director of the White House Office of Telecommunications Policy, had been primarily responsible for the political pressure on the board; Rogers, however, conceded this was only a "suspicion."

Three CPB board members were quoted by the New York Times April 26

A as calling the charges of political interference inaccurate and a "phony issue." Irving Kristol, a Republican appointee, said the board—without political influence—was unwilling to allow PBS complete control of scheduling. He asserted that the board simply agreed with the law governing PBS operations and the Administration's ideology on public broadcasting: "decentralization and diversity."

B **Public TV accord reached.** The two administrative units of public, noncommercial television—the Corporation for Public Broadcasting (CPB) and the Public Broadcasting Service (PBS)—approved an agreement May 31 on programming control and financial relationships, ending a dispute which had led to the resignation of CPB Board Chairman Thomas B. Curtis April 14.

C The CPB directors, a majority of whom were appointed by President Nixon, elected James R. Killian Jr. to replace Curtis May 9. Killian, former president and chairman of the corporation of the Massachusetts Institute of Technology and vice chairman of CPB, was considered the director least committed to total CPB control of programming, a major issue in the dispute with PBS. PBS, which was set up by CPB to operate the interconnection among the system's stations, had charged that CPB was vulnerable to political pressure on the content of programs carried on the interconnection.

D After his election to the chairmanship, Killian offered PBS a plan under which responsibility for scheduling on the interconnection network would be shared equally by the two groups, with the assistance of an outside arbitrator. Ralph B. Rogers of Dallas, leader of the PBS licensees, countered May 17 with a proposal to give Killian final authority on scheduling disputes but to leave the decision on "emergency scheduling," such as coverage of the Senate Watergate hearings, to PBS.

E Rogers also urged May 22 complete freedom from political interference. Without such independence, CPB "should not exist," Rogers argued, since it was responsible for channeling federal funds to the system. He said one way of assuring freedom from political pressure was long-term federal financing, rather than the annual grants advocated by the Administration.

F The Senate had moved in that direction May 7 by approving, 66–6, and sending to the House a two-year funding bill for CPB which provided $55 million for fiscal 1974 and $65 million for 1975 and up to $5 million each year to match private donations. CPB had been given $35 million in 1973.

G The two-year funding was backed by some Senate Republican leaders, who placed partial blame for the dispute between CPB and PBS on the interference of Clay T. Whitehead, director of the White House Office of Telecommunications Policy.

The final agreement, adopted unanimously by the boards of both groups, provided:

■ CPB would clear all federally-funded programs after consultation with PBS and the public; disputes would be settled by the chairmen of the two groups.

■ PBS would retain the right to transmit privately-funded programs on the interconnection, with timing disputes to be resolved by a third party.

■ Conflicts over balance or objectivity of programs, regardless of the source of funds, would be sent to a committee of three representatives from each of the two groups, with four votes needed to block a program from the interconnection.

The accord reflected the wishes of CPB and the Administration by allocating additional funds to local stations. Under the formula, 30% of a $45 million annual federal grant would go, unrestricted, to local stations; the proportion would increase to 50% at an $80 million annual funding level.

The agreement reaffirmed that public affairs programs were an "essential responsibility" of public broadcasting. Fred W. Friendly of the Ford Foundation, a major source of funds for such programs, said May 31 that the foundation would act to clear funds which had been withheld pending an agreement between CPB and PBS. Public affairs and commentary programs had been a target of Administration criticism.

Killian said the new CPB-PBS partnership would "strengthen the independence" of public television. He emphasized that the system should "never become an instrument of propaganda or be politicized."

Suit filed on program control—The American Civil Liberties Union and Network Project, a public interest group, filed a suit May 31 seeking to prevent any form of centralized control of programming on public television.

The suit, filed in U.S. District Court for the District of Columbia, charged CPB, PBS, Whitehead and presidential aide Patrick J. Buchanan with illegally "censoring" or interfering with program content. President Nixon's former domestic affairs adviser John D. Ehrlichman was also accused of improper interference but was not named as a defendant because he had resigned.

Gregory Knox, a spokesman for Network Project, said the suit was aimed at forcing the use of an automatic formula for the distribution of funds to the stations and program preparation centers of the system, regardless of the type of programs involved.

The complaint alleged that actions by the defendants had been designed to eliminate controversial material, minimize objective news coverage and deny public access to programs which might contain "commentary critical of the present Administration and any officers or employes of the United States."

The suit also alleged that the CPB board was not broadly representative, as required by law. The court was asked to enjoin CPB from putting into effect the funding planned for fiscal 1974 because funding decisions had "been tainted by government interference."

CPB gets 2-year authorization. A bill authorizing funds for two years for the Corporation for Public Broadcasting was cleared by a 363–14 House vote July 20 and Senate voice vote July 24. The Senate action approved House changes in the Senate's original bill.

The bill authorized $55 million for public broadcasting for fiscal 1974 and $65 million for fiscal 1975. The CPB would be required to raise $10 million in matching grants from non-federal sources. Public broadcasting stations receiving federal funds would be required to keep logs of their programs on which public issues were aired.

The legislation also authorized $25 million in fiscal 1974 and $30 million in fiscal 1975 for construction of public broadcasting facilities.

During the House debate, members of the Congressional Black Caucus mounted an effort to insure equitable minority hiring and programming policies in the public broadcasting structure. One proposal, to bar grants for facilities unless compliance could be demonstrated with civil rights legislation, was narrowly defeated by a 190–189 vote. Another proposal, to limit the authorization to one year, was withdrawn after assurance the issue of minority programming would be considered later.

Ford Foundation to end public TV aid. The Ford Foundation, one of the major supporters of public, noncommercial television, decided to end its financial aid, it was reported Jan. 24, 1974.

A foundation spokesman said an "orderly withdrawal" over the next four or five years had been decided upon because public television was becoming increasingly able to stand on its own as government appropriations and viewer donations grew.

The foundation decision had prompted a meeting of station operators to adopt a "marketplace cooperative" plan for programming under which individual stations would pay for production of nationally-distributed programs and determine which programs would be produced. Local stations would have such options as paying prorated amounts to receive national programs, keeping extra funds to produce local shows, or joining with other stations to invest in regional programs.

Licensing & Antitrust Policy

FCC Splits on Licensing Policy. In individual statements presented before Sen. John O. Pastore's communications subcommittee Dec. 1, 1969, the Federal Communications Commission (FCC) divided along partisan lines over radio and TV licensing policy. The Senate committee resumed hearings Dec. 1 on a bill sponsored by Pastore (D, R.I.) that would bar competing license applications against stations that met minimal broadcasting standards.

Three Republicans on the commission—Chairman Dean Burch, Robert E. Lee and Robert Wells—argued that the industry's financial position must be protected against license challenges. The four Democratic commissioners—Robert T. Bartley, Kenneth A. Cox, Nicholas Johnson and H. Rex Lee—said license challenges provided a valuable "spur" to uphold performance standards.

Among licensing actions by the commission:

■ The commission agreed Dec. 5 to consider challenges against licenses held by WLBT-TV in Jackson, Miss., owned by the Lamar Life Broadcasting Co., and WNAC-TV in Boston, an RKO General Inc. station. With the two new challenges, the commission and the courts were considering threats to at least nine stations seeking to renew licenses.

■ The FCC said Nov. 28 that it had refused a request by Milton J. Shapp that WFIL-TV in Philadelphia be denied license renewal on the ground that the owner, Triangle Publications Inc., had a "near news monopoly" in the Philadelphia area. Walter Annenberg, ambassador to London, was principal stockholder of Triangle Publications.

■ The commission agreed Nov. 28 to renew the licenses of WTOP-TV and WTOP-AM and FM owned by the Washington Post Co. The FCC dismissed complaints that the Post's editorial views were imposed on the stations and that the company's ownership constituted undue media control in the area.

■ Pacifica Foundation, owner of educational stations KPFA-FM and KPFB in Berkeley, Calif., KPFK-FM in Los Angeles and WBAI-FM in New York, Oct. 31 was granted FCC permission to operate a new FM station in Houston.

FCC to reject license challenges. The Federal Communications Commission (FCC) announced Jan. 15, 1970 that it would not consider license challenges against radio and television stations that had "substantially" met the programming needs of their communities. The FCC said the action was not a new ruling but rather a clarification of past decisions on license challenges. The FCC statement said that when a broadcast license holder came up for renewal every three years, other parties could file petitions to deny the application on grounds that service criteria had not been met. However, if the broadcaster's past performance was adequate, the commission would not consider a new applicant even if he were "willing to provide superior services." The FCC said the procedures were designed to preserve "stability and predictability" in the broadcasting industry.

Dissenting Commissioner Johnson said the "American people have been deprived of substantial rights by our action today." He argued that a broadcaster whose performance was merely satisfactory would be protected from competition from a superior challenger. Sen. John O. Pastore (D, R. I.) hailed the ruling Jan. 16 and said that action on his broadcast bill might be postponed because of the FCC decision. Pastore's bill would require the FCC to ignore license challenges unless it had already denied a broadcaster's renewal application.

The commission Feb. 19 proposed to increase by 500% the fees broadcasters pay for licenses, applications and other FCC services. The proposed increase would raise the commission's total revenues from $4.5 million annually, received under present schedules, to $24.9 million annually. The commission said the proposal was the result of recommendations by the Budget Bureau and the House Appropriations Subcommittee for Broadcasting, which had suggested adjusting fees so that the agency could become "more nearly self-sustaining."

FCC announces media merger curbs. The Federal Communications Commission, following a two-year study, announced March 26 that it would prohibit any new combinations of radio and television ownership in the same city. The commission said that in granting future broadcast licenses, it would follow a "single market" rule, "designed to prevent undue influence on local public opinion by relatively few persons or groups."

The commission also proposed new regulations that would give media combinations five years to divest themselves of ownership of more than one mass medium in a single community—an AM-FM radio combination, a television station or a daily newspaper. These proposals, which would be subject to hearings before adoption, applied only to media concentration on a local level, not on a state or national level.

The FCC actions were endorsed unanimously by the commission's four Democratic members—Robert T. Bartley, Kenneth A. Cox, H. Rex Lee and Nicholas Johnson, the principal advocate of media diversification. FCC Chairman Dean Burch and Commissioner Robert E. Lee, both Republicans, endorsed some of the actions but dissented in part. Among exceptions permitted under the new rules on future media combinations were owners of limited-power AM radio stations in communities of 10,000 residents or less who would be able to acquire FM radio outlets, holders of daytime-only AM outlets who would be allowed to buy FM stations in the same market, and owners of AM-FM radio combinations who would be allowed to sell their holdings to a single buyer if it could be shown that they could not be sold separately for economic or technical reasons.

According to an FCC report released the week of March 22, 256 daily newspapers in the U.S. were owned jointly by broadcast license holders in the same city; in 68 relatively small communities the only commercial radio station and the only daily paper were jointly owned; and in 11 cities the only TV station and the only newspaper were jointly held.

Boston TV franchise shifted. After a three-year legal battle, the Federal Communications Commission (FCC) Jan. 21, 1972 ordered television channel 5 in Boston shifted March 19 from the Boston Herald-Traveler Corp. to Boston Broadcasters, Inc.

The FCC's 1969 refusal to renew the Herald-Traveler license had been the first refusal in FCC TV history. It was motivated by the company's concentration of communications media ownership in the Boston area.

FCC clears Time Inc. TV sale. The Federal Communications Commission (FCC) March 9 approved the sale of five television stations by Time-Life Broadcast Inc. to McGraw-Hill Inc. for $69.3 million.

The TV stations were WFBM, Indianapolis; WOOD, Grand Rapids, Mich.; KLZ, Denver; KOGO, San Diego; and KERO, Bakersfield, Calif.

FCC approval was conditional on a pending ruling by the commission concerning a proposal to raise the limits from 1% to 3% on bank ownership of stock in broadcasting stations. Eight banks each held at least 1% of McGraw-Hill's voting stock, although only four of the banks were empowered to vote 1% of the stock and they had indicated they would not try to "control or influence" McGraw-Hill's management policies.

Time-Life was forced to sell the stations because of FCC rules, adopted in June 1970, barring common ownership of cable TV operations and over-the-air TV stations within the same community.

Publishers' license renewals opposed. The Justice Department asked the Federal Communications Commission Jan. 2, 1974 not to renew the broadcast licenses of radio and television stations owned by newspaper publishers in Des Moines, Iowa and St. Louis, charging that renewal "would perpetuate the high degree of concentration in the dissemination of local news and advertising."

One of Texas's largest privately owned publishing and communications organizations, Carter Publications, Inc., announced Jan. 5 an agreement to sell its newspaper, television and radio interests to two New York firms. Capital Cities Broadcasting Corp. would acquire the Fort Worth Star Telegram and WBAP AM and FM radio stations for $80 million. LIN Broadcasting Corp. would acquire WBAP-TV, the NBC affiliate for Dallas-Fort Worth, for $35 million.

Burch joins White House staff. The White House announced Feb. 15, 1974 that Dean Burch would leave his post as chairman of the Federal Communica-

A
tions Commission (FCC) to become counselor to the President with cabinet rank. Burch had been with the FCC since November 1969.

Hartford station sale approved. The Wall Street Journal reported March 16 that Travelers Corp. had reached a preliminary agreement to dispose of its two Hartford, Conn. radio stations. The move paved the way for the Washington Post Co.'s planned acquisition of the financial holding company's television station, announced in January. Under Federal Communications Commission rulings, the firm was barred from purchasing both VHF television and radio stations in the same market.

In St. Louis, the licenses up for renewal were KSD radio and TV, owned by the Pulitzer Publishing Co. (publisher of the Post-Dispatch); and KTVI-TV, owned by Newhouse Broadcasting Corp. (publisher of the Globe-Democrat).

In Des Moines, the department said, Cowles Communications Inc. (owner of KRNT radio and TV) and the Register and Tribune (morning and afternoon newspapers), were controlled by the Cowles family.

Racial & Sexual Bias

Negroes win radio-TV accord. A black citizens' group in Atlanta announced March 30, 1970 that it had successfully negotiated agreements with 22 of the city's 28 TV and radio stations calling for increased black involvement in programming and employment. Details of the agreements varied with the size of the 22 stations.

The accord was reached after the Federal Communications Commission (FCC) had granted the bargainers for both sides an additional 30 days to settle their disputes over minority hiring and increased programming aimed at Atlanta's black community. The citizens' group, the Community Coalition on Broadcasting, had asked the FCC to grant the 30-day extension in February after protracted negotiations had been stalemated.

The coalition announced March 30 that it would actively oppose the re-licensing of the four stations that failed to ratify the accord. Two other stations had been granted a two-week extension by the FCC for further negotiations.

The agreements included more coverage of black community news, more black employes in both the technical and broadcasting fields and the placement of blacks in decision-making posts at the stations.

Judge bars sex designation in ads. Judge Edwin J. Martin, of Allegheny County (Pa.) Common Pleas Court, ruled March 24, 1971 that Pittsburgh's

two daily newspapers must run employment advertisements under a single category rather than classifying jobs according to male help wanted and female help wanted.

Martin noted two federal court precedents in his ruling, but he said it was the first time a state court had been required to rule on the issue. A spokesman for the Pittsburgh chapter of National Organization for Women (NOW), which had filed the original complaint, said it was a "landmark case." She noted that some cities had local ordinances requiring that help wanted ads not be segregated.

U.S. moves to end housing bias. The government announced federal guidelines May 21 to prevent the use of racial and religious designations in newspaper advertisements for housing. The Department of Housing and Urban Development (HUD), which issued the policy, said the guidelines were intended to reduce discrimination in housing.

HUD published the new guidelines in the Federal Register, a daily publication of government legal notices. Under the policy, HUD would consider the placement in advertisements of certain words, signs and symbols as clear evidence of intent to discriminate. The evidence would be used in complaints filed under the Civil Rights Act of 1968.

The guidelines would apply to designations that implied that the sale or rental of dwelling units was for the benefit of any race or religion. The restrictions would also regulate the use of human models in real estate ads.

Hearings on the guidelines were scheduled June 17–18. After 30 days the restrictions could be altered, but would go into effect after the next entry in the Register.

The guidelines would ban the use of such phrases as "Jewish home, colored home" and "white private home." It would also bar the use of racial, religious and national-origin designations such as Negro, Hebrew, black, white and European. Words such as "ghetto, disadvantaged" and "restricted" would also be banned.

News bias charged. The Congressional Black Caucus March 8, 1972 called on President Nixon to nominate a black to the upcoming vacancy on the Federal Communications Commission (FCC) and planned a national task force of black political leaders and journalists to fight discrimination in employment and coverage of blacks in the news media.

The plans emerged after two days of hearings March 6–7 by the Caucus, at which blacks in the media charged employment bias, insensitivity by white-owned and edited newspapers, magazines and broadcast stations, and inadequate attention to the needs of black readers and viewers.

Charging that the FCC ignored "service to the community" when renewing

broadcast licenses, the Caucus called for local "media watchdog committees" to study hiring, promotion and coverage, and to file bias lawsuits and challenge license renewals.

Newspapers sue re job ads. Thirty-five Connecticut newspapers, including all 25 dailies in the state, sought a court order to allow them to continue classifying employment advertisements by sex, it was reported July 14.

The newspapers were appealing a July 3 ruling by the State Commission on Human Rights and Opportunities barring such classification. The newspapers said the state ruling would constitute prior restraint on publication in violation of the 1st and 14th Amendments. The papers denied responsibility for "policing" discriminatory practices of advertisers.

Minority cable channels set. Two major cable television franchisers and a coalition of 16 minority group organizations announced an agreement in San Francisco Nov. 29 that would give the groups control of several cable channels and train minority group members in broadcast skills.

The companies, Cox Communications, Inc. and American Television Communication, Inc., said the plan would be effective upon completion of pending merger plans. The new company would provide, over a five-year period, up to three full-time channels in each of their eight California franchise areas at a token fee of $1 a year to nonprofit minority organizations, provide all necessary video equipment in four of the areas, and begin training minority individuals in technical and program skills.

The 16 minority groups in the agreement included the Black Panther Party, the western office of the National Association for the Advancement of Colored People and the Mexican-American Political Alliance.

EEOC sees NBC bias. The Equal Employment Opportunity Commission found that WRC-TV and WRC AM-FM, the National Broadcasting Company (NBC)-owned broadcast stations in Washington, had discriminated against women in hiring and promotion, it was reported Jan. 31, 1973.

EEOC upheld 27 women employes in their charge that before 1971, NBC's "word of mouth method of recruiting and/or announcing vacancies was inadequate" in informing all potential employes about new jobs as required by the 1964 Civil Rights Act. In addition, the commission ruled, the company's maternity leave and training policies discriminated against women. EEOC said it also found reasonable cause to believe the stations discriminated against blacks.

The ruling left the way open for a court

enforcement suit by the EEOC or by the plaintiffs.

In reply, NBC claimed it employed larger proportions of women and blacks in important positions than most broadcast stations in the country. The company said the EEOC had held no hearings, heard no witnesses and allowed no cross-examination.

NOW to increase anti-bias effort. Meeting in Washington Feb. 18–20, the National Organization for Women (NOW) approved a broad program including efforts directed at improving the position of women in broadcasting. Whitney Adams, head of a NOW task force on the broadcast media, said the group would step up its efforts to force radio and television stations to hire more women, and to change programs "which make women look stupid." The organization had filed actions concerning license renewal applications of stations in New York, Washington, Columbia, S.C., Pittsburgh and Charlotte, N.C.

Court refuses to bar sex classification. The Supreme Court Feb. 20 let stand a lower court ruling barring an injunction against two San Francisco newspapers which put their employment advertising under separate headings of men and women. Justice William O. Douglas dissented.

Pittsburgh bar on sex classification upheld. The Supreme Court June 21 upheld a Pittsburgh ordinance barring newspapers from listing help wanted advertising according to sex.

FCC reports on broadcast jobs. The Federal Communications Commission said June 26 that in 1972 about 10% of broadcast employes were members of four key minority groups—black, 6.6%; Spanish-surnamed, 3%; Oriental, .5%; and American Indian, .4%. The study was compiled from mandatory reports filed by stations with five or more full-time employes.

The study also showed women making up 23% of the 130,656 employes covered.

Black network starts—The National Black Network, the nation's first black-owned and operated radio news network, began operations July 2 with hourly news feeds to 40 affiliated stations. The network, based in New York City, was scheduled to provide news reports of interest to black listeners daily.

Commercial Advertising

Senate passes cigarette ad ban. The Senate March 10, 1970 approved, 75–9, a bill that would outlaw cigarette advertising on radio and TV after Jan. 1, 1971. The bill also included a provision that would strengthen the health warning now required on all cigarette packages.

(The Senate had passed a similar ban Dec. 12, 1969 asking for a Dec. 31, 1970 cutoff date, but the measure was held up in a Senate-House conference committee after the House June 18 passed a pro-industry version of the bill. The conference committee unanimously reported the bill out March 3 and sent it to the House and Senate for approval. In a final concession to the broadcasting industry, which had expressed fears of a sharp slump in advertising revenue if cigarette commercials were banned, the conference committee extended the cutoff date to Jan. 1 to permit cigarette advertisements on the widely viewed telecasts of college football bowl games on New Year's Day.)

The bill passed by the Senate March 10 would ban regulation of cigarette advertising by state governments but would free the Federal Trade Commission, effective July 1, 1971, from the prohibition against federal regulation of cigarette advertising.

Cigarette ad ban signed. President Nixon signed a bill April 1 that would outlaw cigarette commercials on radio and on television starting Jan. 2, 1971. The date was selected to permit cigarette companies to broadcast their commercials during the widely viewed telecasts of collegiate football's bowl games on New Year's Day.

(An earlier version of the bill had set Dec. 31, 1970 as the cutoff date, but the House had voted down that provision. The Jan. 2 date was approved by the Senate March 10.)

The bill signed by Nixon would also strengthen the warning on cigarette packages to read: "Warning: The Surgeon General has determined that cigarette smoking is dangerous to your health." The bill also authorized the Federal Trade Commission to require warnings in other cigarette advertising after July 1, 1971, if it voted to do so.

FCC dismisses anti-pollution plea. The FCC Aug. 7 dismissed a complaint by the Friends of the Earth, a conservationist group that had asked that a New York City TV station be required to provide free time to anti-pollution groups to reply to automobile advertisements. The group had based its complaint on the 1967 FCC ruling ordering broadcasters to supply free time to anti-smoking groups to counter-balance cigarette advertising. Commissioner Johnson again dissented, arguing that the FCC's distinction between pollution and cigarette smoking was invalid. The commission majority said cigarettes represented a "unique" case because the surgeon general had officially found them "hazardous" to health. The majority argued that many products, besides automobiles, had "negative aspects."

Cigarette ad ban challenged. Six radio stations filed a suit in federal court Dec. 5 challenging the government's authority to enact a law that would ban cigarette advertising over the nation's radio and television airwaves. The ban, which was signed into law by President Nixon April 1, was to go into effect Jan. 2, 1971.

The suit charged that to impose such a law without including other forms of "informational media" was unlawful discrimination against radio and television. The lawsuit, which was filed in the U.S. district court in Washington, named as defendants Attorney General John Mitchell and U.S. Attorney Thomas A. Flannery.

The complaint was filed by radio stations in Columbus, Ohio; LaGrange, Ga.; Ft. Dodge, Iowa; Dover, Del.; Annapolis, Md.; and Charleston, S.C. The six stations asked the court to convene a three-judge panel to rule on the constitutionality of the measure.

The suit also asserted that Congress could not lawfully forbid advertisement of a product which may legally be sold.

FTC accepts cigarette ad plan. The Federal Trade Commission (FTC), setting aside its own mandatory regulation, accepted a proposal Dec. 23 to let eight of the country's nine cigarette manufacturers try a voluntary program for listing tar and nicotine ratings in their advertisements. An FTC spokesman said the program was to begin Feb. 4, 1971.

The FTC acceptance of the tobacco industry's plan superseded the agency's regulation which was announced in August. The FTC had temporarily suspended its rule Oct. 1 to give the industry a chance to draw up its own plan.

Under the terms of the plan, advertising materials prepared after Feb. 1, 1971 would include figures on tar and nicotine content as determined by laboratory tests conducted by FTC-sponsored researchers.

Cigarette ad ban to be obeyed. Dean Burch, chairman of the Federal Communications Commission (FCC), reported Jan. 8, 1971 that broadcasting and tobacco industry representatives had assured him the government's ban on radio and television cigarette advertising would be obeyed. Birch had called for the meeting Jan. 3 amid reports that the nation's cigarette producers were developing ad campaigns to circumvent the law. The ban had gone into effect Jan. 2.

Burch met with Horace Kornegay, president of the Tobacco Institute, and Vincent T. Wasilewski, president of the National Association of Broadcasters (NAB). Following the meeting, Burch said both men had assured him that their respective organizations "are committed to adhering to the spirit as well as the letter of the law."

A

B

C

D

E

F

G

A

Kornegay denied newspaper reports that some of the tobacco companies planned to advertise their pipe tobacco on television in packages resembling those used for cigarettes. Pipe tobacco and cigar advertising were not subject to the ban.

B

Broadcasters contest cigarette ad ban. The National Association of Broadcasters (NAB) asked the U.S. district court in Washington Feb. 9 to permit it to intervene as a plaintiff in a court case testing the constitutionality of the government's ban on radio and television cigarette advertising. The original suit was filed Dec. 5, 1970 by six radio stations.

At the same time, the NAB filed with the court a complaint charging that the ban discriminated against broadcasters and infringed on the freedom of speech guarantees of the First Amendment. The complaint asked for a permanent injunction against the ban, which took effect Jan. 2.

C

A spokesman for the NAB said the association wanted to affirm the right of broadcasters to air advertisements of any legal product, especially if such advertising was permitted in other forms of the media.

D

Regulation of children's food ads urged. In testimony Feb. 16 before the Citizens Board of Inquiry into Hunger and Malnutrition in a public meeting in Washington, Robert B. Choate, a critic of the cereal industry, urged regulation of child-directed food advertising on television. He said "a moderate watcher of children's television programs . . . receives over 5,000 messages per year, primarily advising him to eat snacks, sweets and soda pop."

E

Cigarette ad warning considered. In a letter made public March 14, Miles W. Kirkpatrick, chairman of the Federal Trade Commission (FTC) raised the possibility that the agency might soon revive a regulation requiring all cigarette advertising to carry a strong health warning.

F

Kirkpatrick's letter was made public by Sen. Frank E. Moss (D, Utah), to whom it was sent. Kirkpatrick told Moss that the agency would receive recommendations from its staff "in the near future."

Kirkpatrick also told Moss that the commission was gathering information to determine if there had been a shift of cigarette advertising to newspapers, magazines and other nonbroadcast media since Jan. 2, when cigarette ads were banned from radio and television.

G

Kirkpatrick pointed out that the FTC "has taken no formal position on the question of whether an increase in advertising expenditures in nonbroadcasting media would by itself amount to an unfair or deceptive act or practice in commerce in violation of the Federal Trade Commission Act."

Moss had accused cigarette manufac-turers of "unconscionable huckstering."

Enforcement of the regulation was set aside under a provision of the 1970 ban on broadcast cigarette advertising. The provision barred the FTC from taking action on it before July 1.

If enacted, the proposed warning would say: "Warning: Cigarette smoking is dangerous to health and may cause death from cancer, coronary heart disease, chronic bronchitis, pulmonary emphysema and other diseases."

FTC for free replies to TV ads. The FTC petitioned the Federal Communications Commission (FCC) Jan. 6, 1972 to require broadcasters to give free time for counter-advertising to commercials raising controversial issues of public importance. The FTC filed its recommendation as part of the FCC's review, begun June 1971, of the fairness doctrine and other policies governing public access to TV and radio air time.

The FTC said it was taking the unusual step of making recommendations to another regulatory agency because its proposals either exceeded its own authority to regulate false and deceptive advertising or offered less cumbersome methods to protect the public.

The FTC petition noted that advertising was possibly the only form of public discussion that did not provide for debate, giving advertisers "enormous power to affect consumer welfare."

In addition to issues of public importance, the FTC proposed that mandatory counter-advertising be required in cases where advertising (1) drew upon or relied upon "scientific premises which are currently subject to controversy within the scientific community," and (2) was "silent about the negative aspects of the advertised product."

Broadcasters challenge ad ban. Six broadcast companies asked the Supreme Court Jan. 10 for a hearing on the 1970 law that banned radio and television cigarette advertising.

News of the appeal was reported Jan. 27 by the Associated Press.

In their appeal for a hearing, the firms, which operated radio stations in the East, South and Midwest, argued that the law was unconstitutional because it restrained freedom of speech and discriminated in favor of the print media.

In October 1971, a three-judge U.S. district court in Washington had upheld the law in a 2–1 ruling. The majority said broadcast advertising was protected by the First Amendment only to a "limited extent."

Cigarette ad spending tripled. The Tobacco Institute announced Jan. 18 that six major cigarette advertisers in 1971 shifted more than $132 million to newspaper, magazine and outdoor advertising after a law banning cigarette advertising on television and radio went

into effect Jan. 2, 1971.

Although advertising was tripled in publications and outdoor advertising, total outlays of $200 million represented a 28% decline from 1970 expenditures.

The figures were obtained from American Brands Inc., Brown & Williamson Tobacco Inc., Liggett & Myers Inc., the Lorillard Corp., Philip Morris Inc. and R. J. Reynolds Industries Inc.

Cigarette ad ban review denied. In a summary disposition, the court March 27 upheld a decision by the U.S. District Court for the District of Columbia that the 1970 law banning cigarette advertising on television was not unconstitutional.

The court's summary disposition meant that it would not hear arguments on the case and would not change the lower court's decision.

The district court had ruled in October 1971 that the ban did not violate the First Amendment.

The original suit and the subsequent appeal to the Supreme Court had been made by the National Association of Broadcasters. The association had asked the courts to review the ban on the grounds that it restrained freedom of speech and discriminated in favor of the print media.

Children's vitamin ads withdrawn. Three major drug manufacturers separately informed Action for Children's Television (ACT), a Boston public interest group, that they would cease advertising vitamins on children's television programs, it was reported July 21.

Miles Laboratories, Bristol-Myers and Hoffmann-LaRoche reported that they had either removed their ads or would do so by Oct. 1. Peggy Charren, ACT president, said the group would continue to petition the Federal Trade Commission to ban all advertising aimed at children.

Cigarette sales up. For the first time in five years cigarette sales among U.S. smokers rose in 1971, the Federal Trade Commission (FTC) reported July 26. The total sales figure was a record 547.2 billion cigarettes, surpassing the old mark of 540.3 billion sold in 1968.

Releasing the statistics, the FTC urged Congress to require stronger health hazard warnings and to provide for dissemination of anti-smoking messages in newspapers and on radio and television.

Since 1970, federal law had required that all cigarette packages carry the statement: "Warning: The Surgeon General has determined that cigarette smoking is dangerous to your health."

Six months after it became law, the bill would require the warning on all cigarette packages: "Warning: The Surgeon General has determined that cigarette smoking is dangerous to your health."

Sen. Frank E. Moss (D, Utah), sponsor of the bill, said "thanks to this bill, Marlboro country will fade into television history, as of next January." Sen. Warren G. Magnuson (D, Wash.) hailed the passage as "landmark legislation in the health field."

Little cigar ads withdrawn. Faced with a Congressional threat to ban television advertisements of little cigars, Lorillard and Reynolds Feb. 15 and Feb. 16, 1973 announced that they were voluntarily withdrawing the broadcast ads "at the request" of Sens. Warren G. Magnuson (D, Wash.) and Marlow Cook (R, Ky.).

Sen. Frank E. Moss (D, Utah) had introduced a bill in January which would place little cigars under the same advertising restrictions faced by cigarette makers, according to the Wall Street Journal Feb. 20. Magnuson and Cook were the ranking members of the Senate Commerce Committee, which had scheduled hearings on the Moss proposal.

TV to curb drug ads. The nine-member National Association of Broadcasters (NAB) code review board voted unanimously Feb. 22 to impose limitations on nonprescription drug commercials beginning Sept. 1, in a move apparently designed to ward off consumer and Congressional criticism.

The rules would be obligatory, although not legally enforceable, for all stations subscribing to the NAB code, including the networks. The rules would bar on-camera pill-taking, advertising during or adjacent to children's programs, the use of children in commercials for adult drugs, personal endorsements by "authority figures or celebrities" and commercials which presented drugs as everyday or casual products.

Little cigar ads banned. President Nixon signed into law Sept. 21 legislation banning advertisement of little cigars on radio and television.

The law defined a little cigar as any roll of tobacco other than a cigarette, 1,000 of which weighed less than three pounds.

In reporting the bill to the House floor, the House Commerce Committee had stated that to allow advertising of little cigars to continue "would promote the impression that it is safer to smoke little cigars than cigarettes."

Editorial
Comment

WORCESTER TELEGRAM.
Worcester, Mass., April 16, 1972

The fight over who shall control television programming in the United States still goes on.

The Justice Department's decision to file antitrust suits against the major networks is the most direct challenge yet mounted by the government against the television broadcasting industry.

In the last two years, the Federal Communications Commission has been steadily chipping away at the powers of the networks to program shows as they see fit. Last year, for example, the networks were forced to release some prime time in the hope that local stations would produce shows of community interest. The results have been mixed, at best.

Also, the broadcast media have had to cope with a variety of hobbling "equal time" provisions, applying to everything from political statements to cigarette advertisements. The cigarette commercials were finally banned altogether.

The new Justice Department plan seems to go further than any previous move to weaken the networks. The charge is that the companies "have monopolized and restrained trade" in prime time entertainment. The Justice Department apparently wants TV advertisers to produce their own shows, and then buy time from the networks. This, television officials claim, would reduce stations and networks to "mere conduits."

No one would pretend that prime-time TV is beyond improvement. It still displays aspects of the "wasteland" that Newton Minow once complained about.

But it is beyond us why the Justice Department thinks that the advertisers would come up with any better — or even any different programs. Is Proctor & Gamble better qualified than CBS to judge what is best for the American people?

As far as the monopoly charge goes, this seems far-fetched. It is doubtful that anything in American life is more competitive than the three main networks for prime-time exposure. Their profits depend on it. And they are competing with a growing number of educational, sports and special features being aired by local and CATV stations as well as public broadcasting outlets.

Despite Vice President Agnew's repeated charges about the enormous power of the networks, the broadcast media in the country are vulnerable to government pressures. Every television station, like every radio station, is licensed by the government and must have its license renewed periodically.

It is this implied threat by the government over a private enterprise that makes this new antitrust suit seem slightly sinister. Television has become such a predominant communications medium that any government attempt to bring it to heel suggests Big Brother and 1984.

Miami, Fla., April 17, 1972

Sen. Sam Ervin, in opening a recent Congressional hearing on freedom of information, said:

"Whatever the dangers to freedom of expression that result from concentrated ownership of the broadcast media, it is nowhere as dangerous as leaving to a few government officials the power to decide what can be seen and what cannot . . . With broadcasting, much as with the printed press, government power to protect the public from excess and foolishness is governmental power to censor . . ."

We are reminded of the senator's concern in the latest threat by the Justice Department to haul the major television networks into federal court on antitrust charges. The networks, Justice will say, have monopolized and restrained trade in prime time entertainment programs and control of such programming should be transferred to advertising agencies and motion picture producers.

The industry finds it strange that Justice would enter an area where another agency charged with control of broadcasting, the Federal Communications Commission, already has rejected the concept that networks be prohibited from owning productions going out on the air waves.

More logically, the antitrust suit appears to be another attempt by the Nixon Administration to intrude upon the freedom of the nation's communications. There has been much smoldering resentment in Washington over network coverage of the war in Vietnam and charges of biased presentation have been heard before several Congressional Committees.

If one has any doubt about the Administration's feelings, he only has to listen to the oft-voiced opinions of Spiro Agnew. The vice president constantly berates the press and TV, challenging their right to print or broadcast without prior restraint, their right of access to public-owned information and their right to criticize the performance of public officials.

There is far greater significance to the Justice Department's threatened action than a mere decision on who's going to produce the next chapter of "All In The Family."

The Detroit News

Detroit, Mich., April 16, 1972

We admit TV network programing may leave something to be desired but we are confounded by the Justice Department's apparent belief that advertising agencies can do a better job.

The Justice Department has announced anti-trust suits against NBC, CBS, ABC and Viacom International, an independent company once part of CBS. The nub of the suits seems to be that the networks, as sellers of prime time, should not also be producing or controlling the shows that are presented in prime time. However, the facts of the TV industry today do not support the image of the networks as a ball and chain around our TV sets.

In the last quarter of 1971, CBS produced only 8.2 percent of its prime-time programs. And network prime-time programing has been cut to three hours per night under an order of the Federal Communication Commission. The FTC has also barred network ownership interest in programs produced by others. NBC has only one prime-time production, "Bonanza;" and produces none of its own movies. ABC has only one production, "Mod Squad," and produces about 40 percent of its movies.

It is true independent movie and program producers would prefer to have a clear shot at all network production but, with the network ratings battles as pitched as they are, we can't imagine the networks preferring to run their own inferior shows if the independents can offer something better. With CBS and NBC the leaders of the industry and relying so heavily on independent production now, we assume they only program their own shows when they are believed to be a superior product.

However, even if 100 percent independent production were the right answer, we still shake our head in wonderment over the Justice Department idea of having advertising agencies in charge of programing and production.

The agencies have never sought the reputation of cerebral creativity. Regardless of what their talents might be capable of producing their output is typically associated with the lowest common denominator, a maximum commercialism and a minimum of controversy. All this makes better sense in selling than in program content.

What, then, could possess the Justice Department to look to the agencies as a remedy for network programing? Certainly, not their record. Is the Justice Department impressed with the line that "today's commercials are better than the programs"? If so, we point out that Alka-Seltzer commercials are the exception, not the rule.

Detroit Free Press

Detroit, Mich., April 20, 1972

IT IS possible that the recent anti-trust suit filed by the Justice Department against the three major television networks is a laudable act of pure legal obligation untainted with political motives. Possible, but not very likely.

The government has charged that, because the networks are the only large buyers of programs of independent producers, they can and do force them to sell percentages of the profits. And the Justice Department maintains that the networks refuse to sell air time to producers with whom they are not financially involved.

According to the suit, this constitutes an illegal degree of control over program production in violation of the first two sections of the Sherman Anti-Trust Act.

Despite the Justice Department's lazy use of 1967 statistics and despite recent Federal Communications Commission rulings limiting to three hours the amount of network prime-time programming that any station can accept and prohibiting networks from gaining ownership interests in programs produced by others, the charges in the suit are serious, and should probably be heard in court.

In fact, a long-time Justice Department critic and Ralph Nader affiliate, Beverly C. Moore Jr., praised the Justice Department for filing the suit, saying, "I didn't imagine they'd ever have the guts to do it."

But the question deserving attention is why the Justice Department chose the present time to file the suit, which was approved more than a year and a half ago by Richard W. McLaren, then chief of the Anti-Trust Division.

But like similar suits prepared in the late 1950s and in 1964, the present suit got no further than the desk of the attorney general, in this case, John Mitchell.

Now, suddenly, the suit has been filed. There are several possible explanations. First, because of the ITT affair, the White House might well be anxious to offset the image that it is less than vigorous in the anti-trust field. Second, it is known that serious complaints have been made within the Justice Department about how slowly anti-trust cases were being pursued. The filing could have been in partial response to this internal discontent.

The long history of overt hostility that the Nixon administration has displayed toward the networks leads us, however, to suspect that the government has decided to exhume the long-buried suit to haunt the networks in an election year.

It is true that news, sports, public affairs programs and documentaries are specifically excluded from the action. But the very fact that a suit with such drastic implications for the networks is pending is bound to stifle to a certain extent the freedom to comment and criticize.

Whatever the actual merits of the suit, it is severely tainted by the suspicion that the administration is again tampering with the news media's independence. It is particularly galling that the suit comes during a presidential election year — a time when the people's right to know is more vital than ever.

Los Angeles Times

Los Angeles, Calif., April 26, 1972

The Justice Department has gone to court in an antitrust action against the three television networks of the United States, seeking to force them out of the business of producing entertainment programs. The action raises many questions, the most basic of which are: (1) Is this action necessary? and (2) will it help improve what we see on the tube?

For 15 years the Justice Department had postponed action against the networks, awaiting outcome of hearings by the Federal Communications Commission. Those hearings resulted in the 1970 regulations that reduced network programming in prime time, ordered the networks out of program syndication and banned network interests in independently produced programs.

The Justice Department wants to go beyond syndication and outside ownership limitations. It wants to ban all network production of entertainment programs as well as feature film production.

To support its charges of restraint of trade, the Justice Department asserts that the networks virtually doubled their financial interest in prime-time entertainment shows between 1957 and 1967, with the result that they had an interest in as much as 86% of these shows in 1967. The networks, it is asserted, excluded programs in which they had no ownership and forced outside producers to grant them a financial interest in shows selected for network time.

It's enough to make Lassie hide her head in shame. Except that the Justice Department has not explained its reliance on statistics outdated by new FCC regulations which now prohibit a network interest in the 90% or more of prime-time entertainment programming provided by independent producers.

A point worth remembering is that nothing in the new FCC regulations and nothing in the antitrust suit will limit or affect the absolute discretion of the networks as to the programs they choose. The pending action and the existing regulations do not touch the question of quality, including the controversial practice of the networks in excluding from the air a number of prestigious drama and classical music programs simply because they might put a dent in prime-time ratings.

The sweep of the Justice Department action has stirred another kind of controversy over program content. The suit leaves the networks free to do as they like with news, public affairs and sports programs. Some industry sources have argued that restrictions on entertainment program interests could affect network earnings in a way to impair the ability of networks to do effective public affairs programming. Other network and FCC experts argue that this fear is without foundation. It would be a more impressive argument if the networks did more. At last count, covering the 1970-71 season, only 2% of half-hour units in prime time were devoted to information and news.

There is also concern in the networks that a prohibition against all network interests in entertainment program production could lead to a deterioration by denying producers funds that have helped cover the high cost of developing new program ideas. In this area, of course, the Justice Department goes no further than the FCC.

Obviously, television is best regulated by the agency established for that purpose. The FCC has not inspired confidence by the fact that its new regulations are still not fully implemented almost a year after their court test. But the Justice Department has yet to prove that these failings justify the intrusion of another government agency. So there is doubt that the suits are necessary or will really help improve television programming.

PORTLAND EVENING EXPRESS

Portland, Me., April 18, 1972

The big television networks are stunned, and a good many other people close to the industry, and the federal government, are surprised by the decision of the Justice Department to sue NBC, CBS, ABC, and Viacom for monopolizing and restraining trade in prime-time entertainment programs.

In the first place, the government is using figures five years old in citing network financial equity in programs the networks either produce or program on their facilities. In the second place, only last year the Federal Communications Commission laid down an access rule that barred the networks from owning any equity in their programs. Additionally, the TV industry claims, CBS has only two programs, Gunsmoke and My Three Sons, in which it has a financial interest, while so far as NBC and ABC are concerned, it is Bonanza and Mod Squad. The suit is rendered even more inexplicable by reason of what President Nixon said last week to the National Association of Broadcasters, that broadcasters here have more freedom than anywhere else, and his administration is dedicated to "preserving that heritage."

Obviously, the industry's and the administration's definition of "freedom" do not agree.

What will happen, if the Justice Department wins, is that the networks will return to the role they played 20 years ago, when big advertising agencies produced the shows that they then sold to the networks. The business of filling the airwaves with a great variety of entertainment — news and sports are excluded from this suit — is now so complex that chaos would probably result. Further, there is not the slightest evidence to show that the quality of television entertainment would improve, and if anything is to be done about the medium, it should be a campaign to eliminate as much of the pablum as possible.

Minneapolis Tribune

Minneapolis, Minn., April 25, 1972

The Justice Department's stated aim in filing antitrust suits against the nation's three major television networks is a laudable one — to open the networks' schedules to a greater variety of programs. Whether the suits will further that aim, however, is open to question.

The suits would force the networks out of the business of producing the entertainment programs they present. The government points out that not only do the networks produce their own programs now, but they also acquire interests in those produced by independent companies. The result, the government contends, is that the networks have a financial stake in buying and presenting certain programs — with the obvious corollary that they're likely to reject programs in which they have no financial stake.

Good point. But if the networks don't produce the programs or put up at least part of the money for someone else to do so, who will? In the days when radio was the dominant entertainment medium, and in the early days of television, it was advertising agencies that produced programs— to order, for sponsors. Since then, however, production costs have gone so high that the agencies, as they were quick to say after the Justice Department's suits were filed, want no part of program development today.

The networks have another argument. Even if the agencies were willing to get involved in program production again, the networks contend, the quality and variety of programing wouldn't improve because the sponsors, who'd be paying the bills, would be interested mainly in getting their messages across at the lowest cost. And the cheapest and safest way of getting a message across is to utilize a proven formula. The result, according to the networks, would be bland, safe programs that wouldn't offend anyone and wouldn't have the slightest touch of innovation.

Well, the public wouldn't want anything like that, of course. But is it getting anything different from that from the networks now? No less than any ad agency, the networks have kept in mind their need to sell their programs to sponsors. As a result, they have little in the way of quality, innovative programing to cite to their credit. The best shows on television recently — and this year's Emmy Award nominations bear this out — were developed by the British Broadcasting Corp. (or, as is true of two popular American shows, were derived from earlier BBC series).

Will programing improve if the government wins its case, then? We doubt it. The best Americans can hope for, perhaps, is that the suits will help focus attention on the questions of who develops programs and why they make the decisions they do. If the public, which eventually pays the bills, maintains enough interest in those questions long enough, there may be better programs, no matter who produces them.

The Courier-Journal

Louisville, Ky., April 18, 1972

LAST WEEK the Justice Department filed an antitrust suit against the three major television networks, ABC, CBS and NBC, which would force them out of the programming business during prime evening hours. The networks will certainly resist the suit and it may be years before a final decision comes from the U.S. Supreme Court.

In the meantime, we can't help wondering if this move is intended to improve the quality of television programming or merely to harass the networks.

All of us learned during the quiz show scandals of the 1950s what could happen when programming got away from the control of the networks. "The $64,000 Question" and many other game shows were "packaged" by advertising agencies or outside producers, and the networks exercised little or no control over production techniques. The result was rigging and a scandal which rocked the television industry to its foundations.

In the ensuing efforts to see that this could not happen again, the networks vowed to exert closer supervision over their programming. Even shows purchased from independent producers were subject to network scrutiny. And that is as it should be.

Recently the presidents of the three networks have been in Washington to testify about violence in television entertainment programs, a legitimate subject of interest and concern to the American public. But how can these men be held accountable if they're forced to fill their evening schedules with outside, "packaged" programs?

Although the three networks produce only a small fraction of the prime-time entertainment programming they now air, the Justice Department alleges that they own an interest in about three-quarters of the evening programs scheduled. Ironically, this whole question was studied for approximately 11 years by the Federal Communications Commission (FCC), which issued the "prime time access" and "financial interest" rules over a year ago. The Justice Department concurred in those rulings.

Now, apparently, the Justice Department wants to go farther. In so doing, its action parallels a lawsuit brought against CBS and ABC in 1970 by the movie industry, which also contends that the networks monopolize too much prime time programming.

It seems to us that the prime issues are quality and responsibility. No one has attempted to demonstrate that the independent programmers can produce shows of better quality than the networks—in fact, the networks' financial resources would tend to indicate the reverse. On the issue of responsibility and accountability the Justice Department's suit is nonsense. Even though the networks are not licensed, they own stations which are, and they feed a chain of affiliates which are subject to FCC licensing and regulation. These stations need and deserve the assurance that the networks will be accountable for the programming they distribute.

This newspaper has long held that broadcasters should enjoy the same First Amendment rights as the printed press. While this Justice Department suit does not affect the vital areas of news, documentary and sports programming, it would chip away at the networks' control of the product they distribute. How this could improve the quality of American television or make the industry more responsive to the desires and needs of the viewing public is a mystery that only the Justice Department—perhaps influenced by other antitrust news in this presidential election year—seems to fathom.

The Des Moines Register

Des Moines, Iowa, April 19, 1972

The Justice Department has filed suit against the three commercial television networks, trying to break their hold on entertainment programs in the prime evening viewing hours.

The networks are charged with monopolizing and restraining trade in prime-time entertainment. The suit's objective is to restore what the government described as "a competitive programming industry." This would be done by barring the networks from carrying programs, series or films which they produced and from acquiring financial interests in independently produced programs.

A successful suit by the government presumably would open evening hours to independent producers, film companies and advertising agencies wishing to buy time for entertainment programs. The networks then would resemble the noncommercial Public Broadcasting Service, which simply transmits programs produced by independent firms or local and regional stations.

Under the present system, a network produces or buys a situation comedy series which it tries to sell to an advertiser. The network retains control of the series, rescheduling it for another season or killing it, depending on how well it does on audience rating systems.

Network executives contended that the government suit "would set the clock back 20 years or more" to the time when advertisers and advertising agencies selected and controlled radio and TV programming. They pointed out that the Federal Communications Commission (FCC), which regulates TV operations, previously rejected the kind of network non-involvement the Justice Department apparently wants.

The government suit is directed solely at entertainment programs, not at news broadcasts, documentaries or sports events. The government's motives are unclear. The suit could well be an indirect attack meant to intimidate the networks' news departments.

Greater flexibility in TV programming would be desirable. The networks ought to consider opening up some prime-time slots to independently produced shows, as they have been asked to do with public affairs programs. No broadcaster should have to run every program a sponsor wants to air, but neither should he live by rigid rules that block all programs done by non-network sources.

The government has not demonstrated how it intends to improve TV entertainment or network responsibility by stripping the executives of their authority. The FCC has been charged with overseeing TV, and it has not found the grievous faults discerned by the Justice Department. If the FCC is falling down on its job, Congress better look into it. If the Justice Department is trying to skirt the FCC, that deserves an explanation, too.

The Evening News

Newark, N.J., April 19, 1972

Undaunted by the ITT contretemps, or perhaps because of it, the Justice Department has filed suit against the TV networks, alleging they have "monopolized and restrained trade" during the prime evening hours. Not one, but several questions arise, among them:

Why the Justice Department? Why the networks? Why now?

It has been generally assumed that when Vice President Agnew is otherwise occupied, it is the Federal Communications Commission's duty to police the airwaves and the networks' use thereof. Therefore, with some justification, the networks are able to say that, under prior FCC advisement, some 10 per cent of prime time between 8 and 11 p.m. is devoted to network programming as against 90 per cent filled by independent producers.

Why us? the networks ask, contending that easy identity victimizes them at the hands of Justice Department monitors who haven't done sufficient spadework.

All of which adds interest to the matter of timing. Similar suits have surfaced and failed to materialize since the early '50s. It also is a matter of record that similar charges arose a year and a half ago and were not deemed worthy of pursuit.

Could, then, there be an element of spite in presently taking off against a medium which the Administration chooses to regard as generally unfriendly, except when following the directorial talents of White House Communications Director Herb Klein?

Or is there an effort to demonstrate vigor and vitality in a Justice Department now laboring under aspersions arising from handling of ITT?

Vigorous, impartial enforcement of the antitrust laws is undeniably necessary where monopoly and restraint of trade exists. But the pursuit of justice itself must be legally-based and not derived from partisan considerations or face-saving exigency.

In the matter of stifling of competition by conglomeration, or price-fixing through illegal agreements, the evils are readily identifiable. In the matter of entertainment, the lines — at least in this case — are not so clearly drawn. Obviously, Justice owes the public a fuller explanation.

Until then, about the only conclusion that can be drawn by anyone who has watched prime time TV recently is that the Justice Department might be assuming the role of critic or censor.

THE ROANOKE TIMES

Roanoke, Va., April 20, 1972

About 20 years ago the chief complaint against television stations and networks was that somebody else— the advertisers and their agencies— "owned" the time. The n e t w o r k s were pictured as run by automatons who passed out the time for shows the advertisers produced. In reaction to this, networks began to assume the responsibility for producing their own shows. Now it appears that if it is heads they lose, tails they lose; the Department of Justice is charging "monopoly."

The only monopoly the networks are visibly guilty of is a monopoly of technique. Each, for instance, tries to build a large audience for the 8 p.m. show, so it will stay with the channel for the 8:30 p.m. show, etc. The competition is for audience ratings which determine revenue, which determines the money available to put into shows and, of course, profit. Strange as it seems, or as bad as it may seem to the h i g h b r o w, the networks are trying to please people.

How the anti-trust laws can be s t r e t c h e d to cover programming practices is baffling. Is the Department of Justice, which doesn't look too good after the ITT case, trying to make noises to prove how brave it is? Is somebody trying to scare the daylights out of TV networks so they will be docile during the political campaign? These q u e s t i o n s are harsh; they may very well be unfair. They are asked only because no good explanation is at hand for the suit.

Listing all the ailments of TV would take a book. Anybody who would argue that TV stations and networks are all they should be would deserve to be laughed off the stage. But unless government is willing to go back 25 years (50 years in the case of radio) and unravel the whole method of broadcast operations, c o n c l u s i o n s more moderate than an anti-trust suit are in order.

The major hope for more public service, for more attention to cultural and other minorities, on television lies in expanded public service television, pay television and cable television. So far as the commercial station and network are concerned, the major goal should be to encourage responsible operation. Constant harassment from the Federal Communications Commission, and now the Department of Justice, is no way to encourage responsible operation. It is a way to drive the responsible operator to distraction and despair.

ST. LOUIS POST-DISPATCH

St. Louis, Mo., December 19, 1972

The Nixon Administration has just provided new evidence that it wants only the blandest kind of news coverage of its activities—or else news treatment so favorable that it borders on sycophancy. The unspoken but clearly implied desire of the Administration for a servile media is signaled in comments by Clay T. Whitehead, the director of the White House Office of Telecommunications. Mr. Whitehead said his office has drafted legislation to hold local television stations accountable at license renewal time for the balance and taste of all network news and entertainment programs.

Since the networks themselves are not subject to licensing, this demand that local stations censor network programs, or run the risk of losing their licenses, is an obvious device to intimidate the networks and their outlets into being even more cautious than they already are. Except for occasional brief forays into issues, such as CBS reports on the Watergate and Soviet grain scandals, network coverage of the recent presidential campaign was exasperatingly zealous in its pursuit of a vacuous balance. With candidate Nixon hiding in the White House, the networks repeatedly paired issue-pleading candidate George McGovern against the platitudes of minor surrogates.

Yet even this deferential treatment of the non-news representatives of the virtually silent Republican candidate was not enough to stem the gush of gibes against the networks by White House spokesmen after the election. Mr. Whitehead has now taken aim with charges of what he calls bias, "ideological plugola" and "elitist gossip in the guise of news analysis," which he proposes to stop by means of stricter licensing legislation.

The threat of legislation is enough to frighten already timorous broadcasters. If Congress takes this proposal seriously, it will be laying the groundwork for transforming the broadcast news media into what the White House seems to want—a gigantic public relations agency for the Nixon Administration, through which it would dispense approved propaganda, not news.

HERALD EXAMINER

Los Angeles, Calif., December 24, 1972

This is the part of the newspaper where we dispense "ideological plugolas." (If you want the news, turn to another page.) The following is a "plugola" for free expression and against censorship.

"Plugola" is not our choice of word. It is that of the Nixon Administration's director of the Office of Telecommunications Policy, Clay T. Whitehead. He announced, the other day, the Administration's intent to introduce legislation requiring TV stations to demonstrate that they serve the "needs and interests" of the public when applying for license renewals.

Whitehead was not clear about how the proposed law would be enforced, or what criteria would be used, or who would enforce the law.

Would the Federal Communications Commission, empowered by Congress to license and oversee stations, be bypassed? Would regulation of TV and radio stations fall under the jurisdiction of some executive branch office, such as Whitehead's? He didn't say.

But he made it obvious that the Administration is not satisfied with TV newcasting and that the Administration intends to do something about that.

If the executive branch, with its concentration of power, steps into this area of congressional authority, then the urge to please the White House — no matter who is in it — will be greater than the need of TV stations to serve their communities in order to keep their broadcast licenses.

This would be a subtle censorship that defeats the concept of a free press.

Whitehead did speak specifically to some points. He condemned "ideological plugola." He urged that TV newsmen be closely supervised by management. He charged that broadcasters deliberately "insulate" news departments from management. He said this leads to irresponsible newscasting.

News staffs and managements are, as much as possible, "insulated" from each other. It is true for TV stations, for newspapers, for radio stations and magazines. And it is true for good reason.

Newsmen serve the public with information. Management supervises newsmen; no station could operate without supervision. But management also supervises the sales department — which serves the needs and interests of advertisers.

The "insulation" protects the integrity of newsmen and management. The "insulation" is a pledge that a station's news reporting function will not be twisted, censored, in order to benefit the station's profit-making function.

Now here's the heart of this "plugola." If any administration can rule hat the public, in the thousands of diverse communities across America is best served when the federal government in Washington is served, then "ideological plugola" is guaranteed.

And how long will it be until it becomes "only right" to extend that guarantee to newspapers, to magazines and even to books?

The Miami Herald

Miami, Fla., December 20, 1972

CENSORSHIP in peacetime seems to be catching on for the first time in 174 years of American history. If the Nixon Administration has its way, Congress will enact legislation to punish television stations that "fail to act to correct imbalance or consistent bias in the networks — or who acquiesce by silence . . . "

These are the words of Clay T. Whitehead, director of the powerful Office of Telecommunications Policy. The title itself is almost as Big Brother-ish as Mr. Whitehead's words.

What kind of "imbalance"? Whose "bias"? Are the answers to be that some kind of super censor in the government structure will decide what is out of balance and who is biased? The decision could not possibly be objective because the record of the Administration is wholly subjective: Who ever heard Spiro Agnew scald a newspaper (and there are many) 100 per cent in tune with Administration policy and abusive of its opponents?

This is the most dangerous ground staked out by powerful politicians since the agony of the Alien and Sedition Acts in 1798 which forbade any criticism of government. In those days the penalty was a fine and time in prison. In these days the penalty would be loss of license, which is economic death.

We cannot believe that Congress would enact or the courts would sustain this statutory rape of the Constitution. It would leave no man safe under the First Amendment. We trust there will not be continued indifference of print journalism to the plight of broadcasters. As Bill Moyers, both newsman and bureaucrat by turns, has observed: "Here the domino theory becomes suddenly valid — let one man's jot fall from the First Amendment and your own little tittle may not be far behind."

OREGON JOURNAL
Portland, Ore., December 21, 1972

The President of the United States and the members of Congress all have taken a firm oath to support and defend the Constitution of the United States.

With that in mind, a very brief reading assignment should be undertaken by Congress before it acts on a piece of legislation to be submitted by the White House, and by President Nixon before he submits it.

"Congress shall make no law respecting an establishment of religion, or prohibiting the free exercise thereof; or abridging the freedom of speech or of the press; or the right of the people peaceably to assemble and to petition the Government for a redress of grievances."

The President and the Congress should recognize these words as the First Amendment of the Constitution they have sworn to uphold—a fundamental precondition to the union of the states as it has operated ever since and is still applicable.

But an administration spokesman now says the White House will ask Congress to make a law that at the least defies the spirit of the amendment.

Clay T. Whitehead, director of telecommunications, disclosed a scheme to require broadcast stations to "prove" that their news programs are fair and unbiased—a legal requirement that would apply to network news programs carried by the stations as well as the work of their own staffs.

It is true that the First Amendment says nothing about "abridging the freedom of broadcast stations," but that is true only because there weren't any when the Constitution was written. The press was the closest to it as a means of expressing information and ideas for the scrutiny of a wide audience and that freedom was deemed necessary for a free people trying to govern themselves through democratic processes. The intent of that guarantee should apply with equal force to the communication opportunities of modern technology.

With the development of broadcasting, it became apparent that the "public airwaves" could accommodate only a limited number of stations. A government agency was set up to see to it that the airwaves were not overloaded; but the Federal Communications Commission and its laws have ranged far afield from that role of traffic cop, all in the name of the "public."

Now the Nixon administration wants to go another step, and a dangerous step it is. Who is to determine what is fair and unbiased in the news programs? The government? That seems to be the intent; and if it is, it is safe to assume that "fair and unbiased news" will degenerate into propaganda.

There is no way to have free expression if that expression is under government control.

We are not defenders of vapid programing on television, or of opinion that may be offered under the guise of unbiased reporting, although we suspect that government regulations intimidate stations or give them an excuse to duck their responsibility.

But we do think that Congress should make no law imposing government regulation over news content on radio and TV. Nor should the President propose it.

Criticize, yes. Put the pressure on for fairness and accuracy, yes. But legislate, no.

The New York Times
New York, N.Y., December 20, 1972

The Federal Communications Commission is the agency responsible for regulating radio and TV stations under the law, but the White House is elbowing it aside in a crude effort to call the signals on what can reach the American people.

After an election campaign cease-fire, the White House czar for broadcasting, Clay T. Whitehead, head of the Office of Telecommunications Policy, has returned to the attack. In a speech to a journalism society, he has accused unnamed reporters of something called "ideological plugola" and announced the Administration's intent to sponsor legislation which would in effect permit the White House to discipline broadcasters who stray from the White House party line. Who is to decide when a journalist is delivering what the White House TV arbiter brands "élitist gossip in the guise of news analysis"?—who, but the head of the Office of Telecommunications Policy, acting for the President himself.

Mr. Whitehead's speech was wrapped inside an Administration plan to make the stations and their owners directly responsible for the network programs they carry and to insure a variety of conflicting views on controversial issues. The requirement of balance, fairness and access already exists within F.C.C. regulations; they are already a factor for assessment when stations come up for license renewal.

But Mr. Whitehead is delivering a different message. He is telling the affiliated stations of the commercial networks to censor major news programs and documentaries that offend the Administration. And he is doing so under the guise of interpreting the First Amendment as it applies to broadcasting news. That is the road to censorship and suppression through abuse of the power to license. It is a road Congress cannot let the Administration travel.

THE KNICKERBOCKER NEWS
••• UNION-STAR •••
Albany, N.Y., December 20, 1972

With imperious arrogance, the White House has sent out word to local television stations: "Think right, or else . . ." To think right, in the White House lexicon, is to think as the White House thinks.

Spokesman for the White House in this message to broadcasters is Clay T. Whitehead, director of Telecommunications Policy, who in previous pronouncements has made it clear that he equates any news program that happens to reflect on the administration with less than adulation as unfair if not traitorous. It would be naive to think he would say anything that did not have President Nixon's blessing. He carries a dangerous club supplied him by his boss.

In a speech in Indianapolis, Mr. Whitehead revealed that the White House has drafted legislation that threatens the licenses of local television stations if they fail to bear responsibility for network material they broadcast, including network news. For "bear responsibility" you may, if you choose, substitute the word "censor."

Mr. Whitehead indicated the legislation would be introduced in the next session of Congress, saying:

"Station managers and network officials who fail to act to correct imbalance or consistent bias in the networks—or who acquiesce by silence—can only be considered willing participants, to be fully accountable . . . at license time."

With these words Mr. Whitehead convicted the networks without trial of "imbalance" and "consistent bias." He presented as a fact what has consistently been a Nixon Administration assumption: "Either you are with us or you are biased."

To make matters even worse, Mr. Whitehead would not have the proposed regulation applied equally, but emphasized that it "should be applied with particular force to the large TV stations in our major cities, including the 15 stations owned by the TV networks."

What we see in all this is a continuation of the attack on press freedom that has become a hallmark of the Nixon administration. It is a new phase of the attack, aiming at network news through the individual stations. The ultimate victims of such attacks are the people, not the stations.

George Orwell foresaw such attacks on hard-won freedoms in his satirical novel "1984." It might be said that 1984 grows nearer every day.

Or, rather than looking ahead, one could look back 300 years and draw a parallel between the Nixonian dictates and that of Louis XIV of France who chose to say "I am the state."

But perhaps it would be most prudent to look neither forward nor back, but to look directly at this threat to press freedom of this very day, remembering as we do so those words from the Constitution:

"Congress shall make no law respecting an establishment of religion, or prohibiting the free exercise thereof; or abridging the freedom of speech, or the press; or the right of the people peaceably to assemble and to petition the Government for a redress of grievances."

CHICAGO Sun-Times

Chicago, Ill., December 20, 1972

In disclosing Nixon administration plans to draft legislation holding local television stations accountable for what they broadcast, Clay T. Whitehead, director of the White House Office of Telecommunications Policy, began with the obvious and ended with the outrageous.

Whitehead said that television executives should be thoughtful, that they should be aware of their power and their responsibilities. Nobody can challenge that. But this simple piece of advice takes on a different connotation when it comes from the government directed at those that the government may regulate. It carries the implication of a threat.

Whitehead also said that when TV stations seek to have their licenses renewed with the Federal Communications Commission, they will be required to demonstrate that they have been "substantially attuned to the needs and interests" of the communities they serve. He also assailed newsmen "who dispense elitist gossip in the guise of news analysis."

What does Whitehead mean by "elitist gossip?" Is he referring to the stories about the Watergate bugging incident, which involved White House staffers in a scheme to wiretap Democratic Party headquarters? Even if such a term could be defined, it is not the government's job to do so, or to hold anyone accountable for what he writes, says or thinks.

In threatening any medium, Whitehead is really threatening the people, since the people cannot operate a free society without freedom of communication. Over the door of many an American newspaper are the words: "Here shall the press, the people's right maintain." In a free society, the right of a reporter to report the truth, the right of a commentator to comment on events, even if it displeases the government, indeed, the right to be wrong (subject only to libel laws) is inalienable. Now the administration, which has so often assailed the networks because it disagreed with some of their news analyses, is threatening their local stations, which must be licensed.

George Orwell, who knew a great deal about the dangers of distorting the truth, put it well in a 1945 introduction to his novel, *Animal Farm:* "If liberty means anything at all, it means the right to tell people what they do not want to hear." And the right to tell public officials what they do not want to hear.

Rocky Mountain News

Denver, Colo., December 22, 1972

SOME OF THE NIXON administration's resentment toward network news coverage seeped out again the other day in a speech in Indianapolis by the President's chief TV adviser, Clay T. Whitehead.

Whitehead said the administration has drafted a bill which, among other things, would hold local television stations directly responsible for the content of network news shows.

"Who else but management," Whitehead asked, "can or should correct so-called professionals who confuse sensationalsim with sense and who dispense elitist gossip in the guise of news analysis?"

Whitehead said there is too much "ideological plugola" being broadcast by biased network news reporters.

The implication is that unless local stations do a better job of censoring the material they receive from the networks, their licenses may be revoked by the federal government.

It must be said first of all that every TV station already is—or should be—responsible for its program content, just as every newspaper is responsible for the stories and editorials it prints, no matter where they were written or who did the writing.

The disturbing thing about Whitehead's statement is that it assumes some agency in Washington might have better news judgment than the misguided blokes at ABC, NBC or CBS.

Who's to say, for example, whether TV commentary by John Chancellor is "elitist gossip?" or whether Eric Sevareid is indulging in "ideological plugola" when he points out that President Nixon may have made a mistake or two?

Much of the President's proposed TV legislation has merit—simplifying the criteria by which license renewals will be judged; extending the renewal period from three years to five; eliminating the "equal time" doctrine that discourages TV stations from airing political debates.

But to suggest, even remotely, that a local TV station might get into trouble if it uses network material the administration doesn't like is pretty heavy-handed stuff.

Never holler before you're hurt, grandmother used to say, but she was not much in favor of rolling over and playing dead either.

The Charlotte Observer

Charlotte, N.C., December 22, 1972

An ominous piece of legislation being drafted in the White House could give the government new tools to keep American broadcasters politically in line. The bill would make local stations accountable to the government, at the risk of losing their licenses, for the network material they broadcast.

Not all the details of the measure have been revealed. But apparently the administration is making no secret of its intentions. As outlined recently to a group of Indiana journalists by Clay T. Whitehead of the White House staff, the bill would almost certainly limit what the American public may see and hear on the evening news and special documentaries.

Mr. Whitehead said the bill would force local stations to monitor network presentations of news, entertainment and advertising (all of which account for about 60 per cent of television broadcasting). The main intent of those drafting the bill probably was revealed in Mr. Whitehead's comment that it is designed to "correct imbalance or consistent bias in the networks." We can guess fairly well at what the government, once empowered to look over the shoulders of local stations' news directors, would consider "imbalanced" news. The world is full of examples of such government control of news.

Mr. Whitehead indicated that the administration plans to introduce the bill, without substantial change in Congress early in the new year.

Assuming network journalists would continue to perform their professional duties of reporting and interpreting the day's events, what can we expect if this bill passes? Ultimately, perhaps local stations will be left with two choices. They can chop up network news shows according to the management's tastes and fears or they can refuse to run them. In either case, the public will be the victim. Are we ready to substitute "My Mother The Car" for news programs put together by news people? Maybe so. But, despite many people's complaints about television in general and television news in particular, we doubt that the public wants that.

On the surface one would expect television stations to be up in arms over such a plan. Right now, they are. But the draft legislation is dangling a pair of carrots in front of broadcasters.

The measure would give the broadcast industry at least two long-sought concessions. First, it would cut down the red-tape required at license renewal time; second, it would lengthen the term of a license from three to five years. Moreover, it would severely limit challenges to a local license by not accepting new applications until actual revocation of an existing license. In other words, the licensing body — now the Federal Communications Commission — would not be simultaneously looking at competing applications but only, initially, at the question of renewal for the license holder.

This proposal will have great appeal to many broadcast ownerships, some of which currently feel threatened by the possibility of losing their licenses at renewal time to groups attempting to show the FCC they are more representative of their communities.

Thus the proposal, as outlined by Mr. Whitehead, is rather ingenious. It threatens broadcast news people and at the same time, by appealing to the financial interest of the stations' owners, probably would undermine much of the support the news people might ordinarily expect under such duress. Which would most station owners put first — the integrity of the news operations or the prospect of greater security in holding their licenses? We offer no answer to that question, but it seems to us the proposed legislation is insidious just by virtue of forcing such a question.

We have often been critical of the FCC, believing it does not act as forthrightly on behalf of the public interest as we would like. Too often, for instance, it merely rubber-stamps license renewal requests for stations that get rich by skimping on "public service" broadcasts and news operations. As a result, much of what is broadcast over the airwaves today is pap. The FCC needs to be strengthened in this direction—and it needs to be kept away from control of the contents of news programs. The bill being drafted in the White House would strengthen station owners in offering the pap and at the same time would put the government in the center of the news rooms. We find that prospect exceedingly dangerous to a free society.

Index

This index includes references both to the news and the editorial sections. Those index entries printed in a roman typeface refer to the news digest. They: (1) Describe the event; (2) Note the date of the event, e.g. 1-15-73; (3) Indicate the page, the marginal letter parallel to the item on the page, and the column in which the item appears in that order, e.g. 11E3. Index entries referring to editorials are printed in *italic type* after the news entries under the **boldface alphabetical headings**. Editorial entries refer only to the page number.

BALK, Alfred W.
Court upholds 5-7-73, 120F2
BALTIMORE Sun
Ct rejects Md case 4-23-73, 120E2
O'Neill on list 6-27-73, 96C3
BANCROFT, Harding
Media freedom hearings held 9-28-71, 14E3
BARRON, Jerome A.
Media freedom hearings held 9-30-71, 15B1
BARTLEY, Robert T.
FCC orders TV time for war critics 8-14-70, 160E2
BATON Rouge Advocate
Ct lets fines stand 10-23-73, 121D1
BATON Rouge State Times
Ct lets fines stand 10-23-73, 121D1
BEALL, George
Agnew denounces leaks 8-21-73, 97B2
BEECHER, William
1969 taps rptd 5-11-73, 95F1
Nixon authorized wiretaps 5-16-73, 56E3
Nixon authorized taps 5-17-73, 95D2
BERNSTEIN, Carl
Awarded Polk award 1-31-73, 95A1
Nixon lauds press on Watergate 4-30-73, 94F3
Admin plot rptd 5-17-73, 95G2
BICKEL, Alexander M.
Pentagon news curb debated 6-15-71, 47E2
BINGHAM, Rep. Jonathan B.
Protests 'harassment' of Times 6-16-71, 47F3
BIRMINGHAM Times
Lewis opposes law 9-14-73, 120F3
BISHOP, Jim
On 'enemies' list 6-27-73, 96G2
BLACK, Justice Hugo L.
Sup Ct upholds Times, Post 6-30-71, 50E1
Opinion in Pentagon Papers case—78
BLACKMUN, Justice Harry A.
Sup Ct upholds Times, Post 6-30-71, 50E2
Opinion in Pentagon Papers case—83
BLACK Panthers
Gov't to get CBS film 1-26-70, 115G1
Caldwell subpoenaed to testify 2-2-70, 115E3
Data sought 2-23-70, 115E2
News disclosures limited 4-9-70, 116A1
Caldwell found guilty 6-5-70, 116A2
Press subpoenas limited 11-17-70, 116B3
Court limits newsmens' right to silence 6-29-72, 117E2
Immunity law hearings begin 2-5-73, 119G1
CBS film subpoenaed—122-124, 126
Caldwell case—123-125, 128, 130-140, 146
BLASI, Vincent A.
Immunity law hearings begin 2-8-73, 119E2
BLEWETT, Judge Howard
Contempt citation quashed 3-2-73, 119D3
BLOCK, Herbert
Criticizes attacks 5-22-70, 11D3
BOK, Derek C.
Popkin case dismissed 11-28-72, 55G3
BOSTON Globe
Barred from publishing Pentagon Papers 6-22-71, 48F1

Grand jury probing charges 7-12-71, 53E1
Suit dropped 9-8-71, 53F3
La. convictions appealed 1-15-73, 119E1
Frazier on list 6-27-73, 96A3
Charges vs Oliphant dropped 7-5-73, 121A1
Richardson to widen press protection 10-4-73, 120G3
BOSTON Herald-Traveler Corp.
TV franchise shifted 1-21-72, 181B3
BRADEN, Thomas
On 'enemies' list 6-27-73, 96G2
BRADLEE, Benjamin C.
Defends Post's Watergate coverage 10-16-72, 93G1
BRANDON, Henry
Phone tapped 5-11-73, 56F2
1969 taps rptd 5-11-73, 95F1
BRANZBURG, Paul M.
Appeals court upholds confidentiality 1-22-71, 116G3
Court limits newsmens' right to silence 6-29-72, 117F2
BRENNAN Jr., Justice William J.
Sup Ct upholds Times, Post 6-30-71, 50F1
BRIDGE, Peter J.
Loses plea; jailed 10-3-72, 117G2
Freed 10-24-72, 117C3
Immunity law hearings begin 2-7-73, 119C2
Supreme Court rejects case 3-19-73, 120G1
Jailed—137-140, 142-144, 147
BRINKLEY, David
Media freedom hearings held 10-19-71, 15A1
BRISTOL-Myers
Children's vitamin ads withdrawn 7-21-72, 184D3
BRITISH Broadcasting Corp. (BBC)
USIA facilities barred 6-26-73, 97B1
BROADCASTING—see CABLE & Pay Television, CAMPAIGN Advertising, COMMERCIAL Advertising, EQUAL Time Provision, FAIRNESS Doctrine, LICENSING & Anti-Trust Policy, PROGRAM Contents, PUBLIC Broadcasting, RACIAL & Sexual Bias
BROOKINGS Institution
Dean on press 'enemies' 6-25-73, 96G1
BRUCKNER, D.J.R.
On 'enemies' list 6-27-73, 96G2
BUCHANAN, Patrick J.
Scores media 4-28-72, 15D2
Suit filed on program control 5-31-73, 180E2
Attack on media pressed 10-29-73, 100B3
BUCKLEY, Sen. James L.
Public TV bill vetoed 6-30-72, 179G1
BUCKLEY Jr., William F.
Admits papers' hoax 7-21-71, 53C2
On Nixon resignation 11-2-73, 100F3
BUNDY, William P.
Attacks Agnew speech 11-15-69, 10G2
BURCH, Dean
Lauds Agnew network views 11-14-69, 9G3
FCC rejects complaint vs TV 11-20-69, 158F2
FCC limits network shows 5-7-70, 173F1
FCC votes CATV expansion 5-15-70, 177A1
FCC backs campaign broadcast reform 6-2-70, 159D2
FCC orders TV time for war critics 8-14-70, 160D2

Clarifies FCC ruling 8-18-70, 161A2
Reprimands Johnson 10-23-70, 173D2
Cigarette ad ban to be obeyed 1-8-71, 183F3
Media freedom hearings held 10-20-71, 14G3
New cable TV rules set 2-3-72, 177C2
FCC to probe obscenity 3-27-73, 176C1
Joins White House staff 2-15-74, 181G3
BURDEN, Don W.
Radio licenses denied 12-3-70, 162F1
BUREAU of Indian Affairs
Whitten freed 2-15-73, 119G2
BURGER, Chief Justice Warren E.
Urges 'civility' 5-18-71, 117E1
Sup Ct upholds Times, Post 6-30-71, 50F2
Comments on Pentagon Papers 7-5-71, 52A3
End to football blackout sought 12-20-72, 175F3
Ct upholds right to bar political ads 5-29-73, 164E3
Opinion in Pentagon Papers case—83
BUSINESS Executives' Move for Vietnam Peace
FCC rules on case 8-6-70, 161D1
Ct upholds rights to bar political ads 5-29-73, 164G3
BUTZ, Earl L.
Attacks urban press 2-20-73, 94C1
BYRNE Jr., Judge William M.
Ellsberg mistrial declared 12-8-72, 56C1
Charges dismissed 5-11-73, 56D2
Ellsberg tap revealed 6-14-73, 57E1

C

CABLE & Pay Television
Sup Ct upholds state CATV control 2-2-70, 176B3
FCC votes CATV expansion 5-15-70, 176F3
Pay-TV authorized 2-24-70, 176C3
Cable TV agreement approved 11-11-71, 177C1
Cable co. guilty of bribery 11-30-71, 177G1
New cable TV rules set 2-3-72, 177A2
Cable TV merger called off 4-21-72, 177B3
Supreme Court upholds FCC 6-7-72, 177D3
Minority cable channels set 11-27-72, 182D3
Viacom settlement proposed 12-14-72, 177E3
Court lets stand Kahn conviction 5-14-73, 177F3
Eased cable TV rules urged 1-16-74, 177D2
Cable TV wins copyright ruling 3-4-74, 178G1
Sup Ct orders to reconsider fee system 4-4-74, 178B2
CAHN, William
Committees consider immunity laws 2-27-73, 120D1
CALDWELL, Earl
Subpoenaed to testify 2-2-70, 115E3
News disclosures limited 4-9-70, 116A1
Found guilty 6-5-70, 116A2
Press subpoenas limited 11-17-70, 116B3
Court limits newsmens' right to silence 6-29-72, 117E2

IPI scores decision 12-31-72, 15C3
Immunity law hearings begin 2-5-73, 119G1
Not guilty of contempt—123-125, 128, 130, 131
Sup Ct rules—132-140, 146
CALIFANO Jr., Joseph A.
Dems ask TV access 5-19-70, 159A1
Nixon vetoes campaign spending curb 10-12-70, 161G3
CALIFORNIA
Reagan signs newsmen law 12-30-72, 119C1
CAMPAIGN Advertising
Senate votes TV curb 4-14-70, 158D3
FCC backs campaign broadcast reform 6-2-70, 159D2
ABC offers to relax rules 6-15-70, 159G2, 160B1
FCC rulings 8-6-70, 161C1
House passes TV spending curb 8-11-70, 160F1
TV curb enacted 9-23-70, 161C2
Nixon vetoes cmpgn spending curb 10-12-70, 161G2
Veto upheld 11-23-70, 161G3
Senate passes campaign bill 8-5-71, 162F2
House passes spending curb 11-30-71, 162D3
House passes bill 1-19-72, 163A1
Campaign law signed 2-7-72, 163G1
Impeachment committee sued 8-17-72, 163G3
Impeachment committee cleared 10-30-72, 164C1
FCC rpts on spending 5-9-73, 164B3
Nixon vetoes TV spending limit—166-170
CANADA
Police seize U.S. magazine 12-12-70, 12G2
CANHAM, Erwin D.
Informed Travers re material 6-29-71, 51F1
CARMICHAEL, Stokely
Agnew attacks networks 11-13-69, 9C3
CARTER Publications Inc
Announces sales agreement 1-5-74, 181G3
CAULFIELD, John
Dean on press 'enemies' 6-25-73, 96E1
CAVETT, Dick
Show accused of SST bias 3-22-71, 12G3
CENTRAL Intelligence Agency (CIA
Cooper introduces bill 7-7-71, 52C3
Rptdly uses journalists 11-30-73, 101C3
CHARREN, Peggy
Children's vitamin ads withdrawn 7-21-72, 184D3
CHAUNCEY, Tom
Bill planned to curb TV news bias 12-17-72, 175B3
CHESAPEAKE & Potomac Telephone Co. (C&P)
IRS returns Times phone rcds 2-13-74, 121F2
CHICAGO Daily News
Eaton on list 6-27-73, 96G2
CHICAGO Sun-Times
Publishes Pentagon Papers 6-23-71, 48G1
Hines on list 6-27-73, 96A3
CHILDS, Marquis
On 'enemies' list 6-27-73, 96G2
CHILES, Sen. Lawton
Proposes end to secrecy 8-4-72, 55G1
CHOATE, Robert B.
Regulation of children's food ads urged 2-16-71, 184D1

TV program ban revoked 5-24-70, 178G2

Delaware drops ETV 6-30-70, 178D3

2-year CPB funding approved 9-28, 29-70, 178G3

TV report stirs debate 10-6-71, 179A1

Public TV bill vetoed 6-30-72, 179E1

Macy quits CPB 8-10-72, 179E2

Nixon signs appropriations bill 8-30-72, 179D2

Curtis resigns 4-14-73, 179F2

Suit filed on program control 5-31-73, 180E2

Accord reached 5-31-73, 180B1

Macy on list 6-27-73, 96E3

CPB gets 2-year allocation 7-20, 24-73, 180B3

Ford Foundation to end public TV aid 1-24-74, 180E3

PUBLISHERS Hall
Evans on list 6-27-73, 96G2

PULITZER Prize
Times, Anderson awarded 5-1-72, 54D3

Post awarded 5-7-73, 95A1

PURSLEY, Lt. Gen. Robert E.
Rptd wiretapped 8-31-73, 57E3

R

RACIAL & Sexual Bias
Negroes win radio-TV accord 3-30, 70, 182E1

Judge bars sex designation in ads 3-24-71, 182G1

U.S. moves to end housing bias 5-21-71, 182C2

News bias charged 3-8-72, 182F2

Newspapers sue re job ads 7-14-72, 182B3

Minority cable channels set 11-27-72, 182D3

EEOC sees NBC bias 1-31-73, 182F3

NOW to increase anti-bias effort 2-18-73, 183B1

Court refuses to bar sex classification 6-20-73, 183D1

Court upholds Pitt bar on sex classification 6-21-73, 183E1

FCC rpts on broadcast jobs 6-26-73, 183E1

Black network starts 7-2-73, 183F1

RADIO & Television News Directors Assn.
Ct upholds 'fairness doctrine' 6-9-69, 158E2

Johnson rebuts Nixon 10-30-73, 100E2

RAND Corporation
Security tightened 7-1-71, 52B2

RATHER, Dan
Anti-media plans revealed 10-31-73, 101C1

REAGAN, Gov. Ronald
Signs newsmens' sources bill 12-30-74, 119C1

Blasts media over tax story—40

REBOZO, Charles
Dean on press 'enemies' 6-26-73, 96D2

Nixon duels with press 10-26-73, 100C1

REEDY, George
Secrecy hearings held 3-6-72, 54B3

REID, Rep. Ogden R.
To press suit 6-23-71, 49C2

REPORTERS' Committee on Freedom of the Press
La. convictions appealed 1-15-73, 119C1

Immunity law hearings begin 2-8-73, 119E2

AT&T cites law on call disclosures 12-24-73, 121C2

To seek injunction 2-11-74, 121E3

AT&T promises notice of subpoenas 2-15-74, 121E3

Formation announced—17

ATT disclosed newsmens' records to U.S.—155

REPUBLICAN Party—see also DEMOCRATIC Party
FCC orders TV time for war critics 8-14-70, 160C3

Broadcast request rejected 11-15-71, 162B3

Court denies equal time bids 2-3-72, 163F1

RESTON, James
Agnew attacks 5-22-70, 11D3

Addresses ASNE 4-21-72, 15D2

On 'enemies' list 6-27-73, 96D3

RICHARDSON, Elliot L.
On Agnew leaks 8-18-73, 97C2

Agnew denounces leaks 8-21-73, 97G1

Kissinger wiretap role investigated—9-7-73, 57D3

Agnew attacks prosecution 9-29-73, 98G2

To widen press protection 10-4-73, 120F3

RICHEY, Judge Charles R.
Quashes subpoenas 3-21-73, 94G1, 120B2

RICOTTA, Joseph J.
Judge: public gets only 1 Attica view 10-1-71, 117A2

RIGHT of Reply—see EQUAL Time Provision, FAIRNESS Doctrine

ROCKEFELLER, Nelson A.
Agnew praises re Attica 9-27-71, 14G2

Nixon vetoes TV political spending limit—169

ROCKWELL, George Lincoln
Agnew attacks networks 11-13-69, 9C3

ROGERS 2nd, Lawrence H.
Bill planned to curb TV news bias 12-18-72, 175A3

ROGERS, Ralph B.
Curtis resigns from CPB 4-14-73, 179G3

Public TV accord reached 5-31-73, 180E1

ROGERS, William P.
Pentagon news curb debated 6-15-71, 47B2

On Pentagon Papers 7-1-71, 52G1

Olsen withdraws 8-31-70, 12G1

On FBI probe 9-3-71, 53G2

Document series speedup ordered 3-8-72, 54G2

ROMNEY, George W.
Lauds Agnew's speech 11-14-69, 10G1

ROSENBAUM, David E.
IRS returns Times phone rcds 2-13-74, 121A3

ROSENTHAL, A.M.
Committees consider immunity laws 3-1-73, 119G3

ROSSANT, M.J.
Times won't aid media council 1-15-73, 164C2

ROSTOW, Eugene
Attacks Agnew speech 11-15-69, 10G2

ROSTOW, Walt W.
Defends U.S. role 7-11-71, 53B1

ROVERE, Richard
On 'enemies' list 6-27-73, 96D3

ROWAN, Carl T.
Agnew attacks 5-22-70, 11D3

On 'enemies' list 6-27-73, 96D3

ROZELLE, Pete
End to football blackout sought 12-20-72, 175C3

RUCKELSHAUS, William
Halperin's phone tapped 5-9-73, 56G2

1969 taps rptd 5-11-73, 95B2

Agnew attacks prosecution 10-1-73, 98C3

RUSSO, Anthony J.
Subpoenaed to testify 6-23-71, 49F3

Anderson discloses documents 6-26-72, 55C1

Trial delayed 8-5-72, 55B2

Appeal rejected 11-13-72, 55F2

Popkin case dismissed 11-28-72, 55E3

Mistrial declared 12-8-72, 56C1

Defense begins case 2-27-73, 56D1

Charges dismissed 5-11-73, 56D2

S

SAFIRE, William
Rptd wiretapped 8-31-73, 57E3

ST. CLAIR, James
Attacks Post story 2-17-74, 102B3

ST. LOUIS Post-Dispatch
Ellsberg named as source 6-17-71, 49D3

Publishes material, restrained 6-25-71, 51D1

La. convictions appealed 1-15-73, 119E1

Childs on list 6-27-73, 96G2

Reporters' panel to seek injunction 2-11-74, 121D3

SALANT, Richard
Defends CBS documentary 3-23-71, 13C2

Rebuts documentary criticism 12-25-71, 12E3

Rebuts Nixon attack 10-27-73, 100D2

Defends 'Selling of the Pentagon'—27-29, 38

Responds to Post editorial—30-31

SAMUELSON, Paul
On 'enemies' list 6-27-73, 96E3

SARRO, Ronald
Subpoena served 10-5-73, 99D1

SCANLAN'S (magazine)
Canadians seize 12-12-70, 12G2

SCHOOLEY, Frank E.
Named to CPB 5-18-70, 178C3

SCHORR, Daniel
Probe disputed 11-11-72, 15B2

Ervin probes case 2-1-72, 15C1

Admin plot rptd 5-17-73, 95B3

Dean on press 'enemies' 6-26-73, 96C2

FBI investigated—44, 45

SCIENTIFIC Advisory Committee on Television and Social Behavior
TV violence study released 1-17-72, 173C3

SCOTT Jr., Sen. Hugh D.
Lauds Agnew speech 11-14-69, 10G1

Campaign spending curb veto upheld 11-23-70, 162B1

On release of Pentagon Papers 6-14-71, 47B3

Meets w Mansfield 6-30-71, 51D3

SCRIPPS Howard Newspapers
Levey on list 6-27-73, 96B3

SEARS, John P.
Rptd wiretapped 8-31-73, 57E3

SEATTLE Times
Prochneau on list 6-27-73, 96C3

SEEBOHM, Han Christian
Olsen withdraws 8-31-70, 12A2

SEGRETTI, Donald
Nixon aides deny Post story 10-16-72, 93G1

Testifies bfr Watergate panel 10-3-73, 99D2

'SELLING of the Pentagon, The'
Dispute continues 3-18-71, 13D1

Documentary subpoenaed 4-18-71, 13D2

Subpoenaed again 5-26-71, 13F2

Stanton bars data 6-24-71, 14A1

Contempt citation killed 7-13-71, 14B2

Attacked 12-25-71, 12C3

Agnew, others blast—23-32

Staggers subpoenas film; Stanton defies—32-39

Relation to Pentagon Papers case—72

SESAME Street
Miss. bans program 5-2-70, 178F2

Program ban revoked 5-24-70, 178G2

SEYMOUR Jr., Whitney N.
Restraining order extended 6-19-71, 48B3

SHEEHAN, Neil
Grand jury probing charges 7-12-71, 53F1

New grand jury empaneled 7-20-71, 53B2

Rptd tapped 6-14-73, 57E3

SHERIDAN, Walter J.
Subpoenas issued 2-26-73, 94F1, 119C3

Court quashes subpoenas 3-21-73, 94C2, 130D2

SHERMAN, William
Subpoena served 10-5-73, 99D1

SHERRILL, Robert
On 'enemies' list 6-27-73, 96E3

SIDEY, Hugh
Agnew attacks 5-22-70, 11D3

SIGMA Delta Chi
Attacks Agnew speech 11-15-69, 10F2

SIMONS, Howard
Subpoenas issued 2-26-73, 94F1, 119B3

SINAY, Lynda R.
Copied documents for Ellsberg 6-24-71, 52C1

SIRICA, Judge John J.
Lawrence jailed 12-19-72, 93G2

Anderson stops publishing grand jury leaks 4-25-73, 94B3

Nixon lauds press on Watergate 4-30-73, 94D3

Lawrence jailed—146-150

'SIXTY Minutes'
Gov't to get film 1-26-70, 115G1

SMITH, Hendrick
Phone tapped 5-11-73, 56F2

SMITH, Howard K.
Urges Nixon resignation 11-2-73, 100E3

On network news bias—17, 18

SONNENFELDT, Helmet
Nixon authorized taps 5-16-73, 56E3 95E2

SPECIAL Commission on Campus Tensions
Linowitz on Agnew attacks 5-31-70, 11E3

STAGGERS, Rep. Harley O.
CBS documentary subpoenaed 4-8-71, 13D2

CBS refused subpoena 4-30-71, 13B3

Stanton bars dt 6-24-71, 14A1

CBS contempt citation killed 7-13-71, 14D2

Subpoenas CBS for film; Stanton defies—32-39

STANTON, Dr. Frank
Defends CBS vs Agnew attack 11-13-69, 9D2

Attacks Agnew, Nixon 11-25-69, 11C1

CBS offers Dems free time 6-22-70, 159B3

Press coverage criticized 6-13-73, 95G3

Dean testifies on press 'enemies' 6-25-73, 96E1

USIA facilities barred 6-26-73, 96G3

Press shield law stalled 7-1-73, 120B3

Nixon holds news conf 8-22-73, 97F2

Polls rpt press support 9-8-73, 98E1

Memos on press campaign released 9-26-73, 98G1

Segretti testifies 10-3-73, 99D2

Nixon duels with press 10-26-73, 99E3

Anti-media plans revealed 10-31-73, 100G3

Nixon aide blasts media 11-24-73, 101F3

Ziegler: more Nixon briefings 1-22-74, 102F1

Ziegler denounces comment on Post rpt 2-1-74, 102C2

Nixon recalls attacks on Lincoln 2-12-74, 102F2

St. Clair attacks Post story 2-17-74, 102B3

Nixon holds news conference 2-25-74, 103B3

Media coverage viewed—104, 105, 107, 108

Anderson leaks probed—105, 106

White House deception campaign revealed—106

TV broadcasting of hearings at issue—107

Enemies list viewed—108

Nixon Aug. 22 news conf viewed—109

Nixon Oct. 26 news conf. veiwed—114

Lawrence jailed—146-150

WECHSLER, James
On 'enemies' list 6-27-73, 96D3

WEICKER, Sen. Lowell P.
Dean on press 'enemies' 6-26-73, 96C2

Anti-media plans revealed 10-31-73, 100G3

WELLS, Robert
FCC limits network shows 5-7-70, 173F1

FCC orders TV time for war critics 8-14-70, 160E2

WHALEN, Rep. Charles W.
Backs news shield law 9-28-71, 15A2

Backs news shield 9-28-72, 15D3

WHITE, Justice Byron
Ct upholds 'fairness doctrine' 6-9-69, 158G1

Sup Ct upholds Times, Post 6-30-71, 50F1

Authors Ct decision limiting newsmens' right to silence 6-29-72, 117C2

Opinion in confidentiality case—135, 136

WHITEHEAD, Clay T.
Curb on TV reruns sought 9-14-72, 175C1

Rerun study asked 3-23-73, 175F3

Public TV accord reached 5-31-73, 180G1

Bill planned to curb TV news bias 12-18-72, 175E1

Curtis resigns from CPB 4-14-73, 179G3

Suit filed on program control 5-31-73, 180E2

Admin vs TV bias—190-192

WHITNEY, John Hay
Named to CPB 5-18-70, 178C3

WHITTEN, Leslie H.
Freed 2-15-73, 119G2

Richardson to widen press protection 10-4-73, 120G3

Reporters' panel to seek injunction 2-11-74, 121D3

WICKER, Tom
Agnew attacks 5-22-70, 11D3

On 'enemies' list 6-27-73, 96D3

Supreme Court to rule on Fla. press reply law—172

WILLIAMS, William A. H.
Held in Murphy kidnapping 2-20-74, 103B2

WILLS, Gary
On 'enemies' list 6-27-73, 96D3

WIN (magazine)
Stolen FBI papers printed 3-72, 54F1

WITZE, Claude
Views on 'Selling of the Pentagon'—24

WOERHEIDE, Victor C.
Caldwell convicted 6-5-70, 116B2

WOOD, Robert W.
U.S. trust suit vs TV networks 4-14-72, 174C3

WOODWARD, Bob
Polk prize awarded 1-31-73, 95A1

Nixon lauds press on Watergate 4-30-73, 94F3

Admin plot rptd 5-17-73, 95G2

WOUNDED Knee
CBS crew arrested 5-8-73, 120G2

WRATHER Jr., John D.
Named to CPB 5-18-70, 178C3

WRIGHT, Judge J. Skelly
Dissents on reversal of ruling 6-19-71, 48G3

Y

YOUNG Jr., David R.
Ellsberg tap revealed 6-14-73, 57C2

Z

ZENITH Radio Corp.
Pay-TV authorized 2-24-70, 176C3

ZIEGLER, Ronald L.
On Agnew's anti-network speech 11-15-69, 10D1

Federal censor identified 10-25-70, 12E2

Admin reacts to publication of Pentagon documents 6-14-71, 47A1

Nixon to release documents to Congress 6-23-71, 49F1

Schorr probe disputed 11-11-72, 15E3

Action on security leaks taken 1-17-72, 54D1

Nixon Watergate statements 'inoperative' 4-17-73, 94E2

Denies Post charges 10-16-72, 93E1

Denies charge vs Haldeman 10-25-72, 93C2

Nixon lauds press on Watergate 5-1-73, 94F3

Dean on press 'enemies' 6-25-73, 96A2

Nixon displays anger at press 8-20-73, 97C1

Nixon on brush 8-20-73, 97C3

News Council unable to get data 11-24-73, 101E3

Denounces comment on Post rpt 2-1-74, 102C2

Says press too sensitive to criticism—43

ZION, Sidney
Canadians seize magazine 12-12-70, 12A3

Names Ellsberg Times' source 6-16-71, 49C3

ZIRPOLI, Judge Alfonzo J.
News disclosures limited 4-9-70, 116A1

Caldwell found guilty 6-5-70, 116A2

10 Interim History Paperbacks

Books that bridge the gap between the daily perspective of journalism and the retrospective view of history.

Agnew: The Coining of a Household Word
The transformation of a Maryland politician into a controversial world figure. How an almost unknown man became a focal point of dispute over TV, the press, Vietnam and other major issues. "A balanced view of the vice president, including the texts of some. of his most controversial speeches" —*The Sunday Oregonian.* Indexed. 181 Pages. **$3.95.**

Berlin in the East-West Struggle: 1958–61
A study of Berlin's role in the "cold war" during the troubled period beginning with the 1958 crisis and culminating in the Communist wall separating East Berlin from West Berlin. Edited by Glen D. Camp, Jr., associate professor of political science, Fordham University. Indexed. 252 Pages. **$4.45.**

Biafra
Tragic case history of Ibo efforts to win independence from Nigeria. The background of the dispute, the creation of the state of Biafra, the suffering of the civilian population, the international repercussions and the destruction of the secessionist state. Edited by Peter Schwab, assistant professor of political science, State University of New York. Indexed. 142 Pages. **$3.45.**

Cambodia and the Vietnam War
The geography of Indochina made it inevitable that Cambodia would become involved in the war in Vietnam. This book explains the background of the events that brought U.S. and South Vietnamese troops into Cambodia in 1970. The complete 1970 campaign and aftermath are recorded in detail. Indexed. 222 Pages. **$3.95.**

Cyprus: 1946–68
A case study of a country kept in almost perpetual turmoil by the rivalry of its two antagonistic ethnic communities—the Greek and Turkish Cypriots. This book records events from the successful campaign for independence to a U.N. intervention that ended a threat of war between Greece and Turkey. Indexed. 138 Pages. **$2.45.**

Dominican Crisis: 1965
A case study of U.S. and Organization of American States action during a Caribbean crisis. This book records the turmoil that followed the assassination of Rafael Trujillo, the political situation that brought U.S. Marines to the country, the international controversy and the aftermath. Edited by Richard W. Mansbach, Political Science Department, Rutgers University. Indexed. 133 Pages. **$2.45.**

Ethiopia and Haile Selassie
A study of an ancient African country and its modern emperor. The book details Ethiopia's recent history, Haile Selassie's efforts to modernize his country, the traditionalist opposition," ... a handy reference work on Ethiopia since 1930.... Recommended for undergraduate libraries"—*Choice.* Edited by Peter Schwab, assistant professor of political science, State University of New York. Indexed. 151 Pages. **$3.95.**

France Under de Gaulle
The record of Charles de Gaulle's 11 years as head of France. The book's three parts cover (1) the Algerian war years of 1958–62, during which de Gaulle found a solution to the Algerian problem, (2) the foreign policy years of 1963–67, involving problems of Western defense, Asia, the Middle East and international finance, and (3) the domestic crisis of 1968–69. Indexed. 319 Pages. **$3.95.**

Indonesia: The Sukarno Years
Progress of a former colonial nation, under the leader who led it to freedom, during the first two decades of independence. The successful struggle against colonialism, the new state's problems with local revolt and domestic and international policy, and the overthrow of the original leader. Indexed. 140 Pages. **$2.45.**

Presidential Election, 1968
An examination of the political campaign and election that brought Richard M. Nixon to the White House. The book records the disputes over Vietnam, race and violence in American life. It details the positions and actions of the major candidates, the turbulent national conventions and the assassinations of Martin Luther King, Jr. and Robert F. Kennedy. Indexed. 328 Pages. **$3.95.**